12/19

The

History

of Philosophy

The

History

of Philosophy

A. C. GRAYLING

PENGUIN PRESS | *New York* | 2019

PENGUIN PRESS

An imprint of Penguin Random House LLC
penguinrandomhouse.com

First published in Great Britain by Viking, part of the Penguin Random House Group of
Companies, 2019

ISBN 9781984878748 (hardcover)
ISBN 9781984878755 (ebook)

Printed in the United States of America
1   3   5   7   9   10   8   6   4   2

Contents

Preface   xi

Acknowledgements   xiii

Introduction   xv

PART I

Ancient Philosophy

Philosophy before Plato   3

The Presocratic Philosophers   9

    Thales   11

    Anaximander   14

    Anaximenes   16

    Pythagoras   18

    Xenophanes   24

    Heraclitus   27

    Parmenides   31

    Zeno of Elea   35

    Empedocles   39

    Anaxagoras   43

    Leucippus and Democritus   47

    The Sophists   51

Socrates   58

Plato   65

Aristotle   80

Greek and Roman Philosophy after Aristotle   98

    Cynicism   100

    Epicureanism   103

    Stoicism   108

    Scepticism   115

    Neoplatonism   123

PART II

Medieval and Renaissance Philosophy

Philosophy in Medieval Times   137
   Augustine   137
   Boethius   142
   Anselm   145
   Abelard   148
   Aquinas   150
   Roger Bacon   158
   Duns Scotus   161
   William of Ockham   164

Philosophy in the Renaissance   168
   Renaissance Platonism   171
   Renaissance Humanism   175
   Renaissance Political Thought   185

PART III

Modern Philosophy

The Rise of Modern Thought   195
   Francis Bacon   197
   Descartes   200
   Hobbes   207
   Spinoza   211
   Locke   217
   Berkeley   226
   Leibniz   232
   Hume   240
   Rousseau   250
   Kant   256
   The Eighteenth-Century Enlightenment   268

Philosophy in the Nineteenth Century   279
   Bentham   280
   Hegel   287
   Schopenhauer   297
   Positivism   302
   Mill   303

Marx   307
Nietzsche   314
Idealism   320
Pragmatism   328

PART IV
Philosophy in the Twentieth Century

Analytic Philosophy   339
  Russell   344
  Frege   357
  Moore   365
  Wittgenstein: The Early Philosophy   370
  Logical Positivism   377
  Carnap   386
  Quine   388
  Popper   395
  Wittgenstein: The Later Philosophy   400
  Ordinary Language Philosophy   405
    Ryle
    Austin
    Strawson
  Philosophy of Language   417
    Davidson
    Dummett
    Kripke
  Philosophy of Mind   433
  Ethics   444
    Stevenson
    Hare
    Mackie
    Virtue Ethics
  Political Philosophy   457
    Rawls
    Nozick
  Feminist Philosophy   466

Continental Philosophy   471
  Husserl   473
  Heidegger   476

Merleau-Ponty   482
Sartre   485
Gadamer   492
Ricoeur   497
Deleuze   500
Derrida   503
Continental Thought: *Un Salon des Refusés*   506

PART V
Indian, Chinese, Arabic–Persian and African Philosophy

Indian Philosophy   519
   Vedas and Upanishads
   Samkhya
   Nyaya–Vaisheshika
   Buddhism
   Jainism
   Carvaka–Lokayata

Chinese Philosophy   534
   Confucianism
      Confucius
      Mencius
      Xunzi
   Mohism
   Daoism
      Daodejing
      Zhuangzi
   Legalism
      Han Feizi
      Yijing

Arabic–Persian Philosophy   554
   Falsafa and *Kalam*
   Al-Kindi
   Al-Farabi
   Ibn Sina (Avicenna)
   Al-Ghazali
   Ibn Rushd (Averroes)

African Philosophy   575

Concluding Remarks   583

Appendix: A Sketch of Logic   585
    Fallacies of Informal Logic   593
Timeline of Philosophers   596
Bibliography   599
Index   611

Preface

This survey of philosophy's history is intended for the general interested reader and for those embarking on the study of philosophy. There are fine scholarly treatments of particular periods in the history of philosophy for those who wish to take their enquiries further, and I hope that some readers will be motivated by the following pages to turn to them, and above all to the primary literature of philosophy itself. Not all the classics of philosophy have an impenetrable veil of technicality and jargon draped over them, as is the case with too much contemporary philosophical writing, the result of the relatively recent professionalization of the subject. It was once taken for granted that educated people would be interested in philosophical ideas; the likes of Descartes, David Hume and John Stuart Mill accordingly wrote for everyone and not just for trained votaries of a profession.

To tell the story of philosophy is to offer an invitation and an entrance, much as Bertrand Russell did in his *History of Western Philosophy*, a book that achieved near-classic status for the sparkling clarity of its prose and its wit – though not always for its accuracy, adequacy or impartiality. Nevertheless that was a book I relished as a schoolboy, along with its nineteenth-century predecessor, G. H. Lewes' *A Biographical History of Philosophy*. It is a testament to both that, after the long intervals that have elapsed since they were written, one can enjoy them still, despite knowing that the explosion in more recent scholarship has added much to our understanding of philosophy's history, and that philosophy's history itself has grown longer and richer since their time. The ambition in what follows is to iterate their achievement for our own day, and to supplement the endeavour by looking not only (though mainly) at the Western tradition but beyond it to the other

great traditions of thought – the Indian, Chinese and Arabic–Persian –
even if only in outline, to indicate comparisons.

An historical overview obviously does not pretend to offer a complete treatment of the thinkers and themes it discusses; for this one must go to primary sources and scholarly examinations of them. But not all readers intend to carry the study of philosophy further, and for their purposes it is important that they should be given a reliable account of the thinkers and debates constituting philosophy's great story. That aim is fully in view here.

My method, accordingly, is to give as clear and concise an account as I can of philosophy's main figures and ideas. Notes are kept to a minimum, and almost all are asides or amplifications, not textual references; there are bibliographies citing the main texts referred to, and works which will take readers further.

It is an almost irresistible temptation to discuss and debate, criticize and defend, when writing of philosophical ideas, for that is the very essence of philosophy. But in this kind of book that temptation has to be restrained to a considerable degree, not just because yielding to it would quadruple the book's length, but because doing so is not the main point. At times, though, it is necessary to show *why* what followed from a given philosopher's ideas was influential or prompted disagreement, so an evaluative element is not wholly absent.

Acknowledgements

My thanks go to my colleagues at the New College of the Humanities, especially to Dr Naomi Goulder and Dr David Mitchell, and friends and colleagues in philosophy there who have made the experience so rewarding: Simon Blackburn, Daniel Dennett, Peter Singer, Christopher Peacocke, Ken Gemes, Steven Pinker, Rebecca Goldstein and the late Ronald Dworkin. My thanks go also to Daniel Crewe of Viking Penguin, to Bill Swainson who first commissioned this book, to Catherine Clarke, to Mollie Charge and to the many students over the years who have taught me much about the thinkers and ideas surveyed in the following pages, proving the deep truth of the tag *docendo disco*.

Introduction

Philosophy's history, as today's students and teachers of philosophy see it, is a retrospective construct. It is chosen from the wider stream of the history of ideas in order to provide today's philosophical concerns with their antecedents. This fact has to be noted if only to avoid confusion about the words 'philosophy' and 'philosopher' themselves. For almost all of its history 'philosophy' had the general meaning of 'rational enquiry', though from the beginning of modern times in the Renaissance until the nineteenth century it more particularly meant what we now call 'science', though a 'philosopher' was still someone who investigated anything and everything. Thus it is that King Lear says to Edgar, 'First let me talk with this philosopher: What is the cause of thunder?' On William Hazlitt's tombstone, engraved in 1830, the famous essayist is described as 'the first (unanswered) Metaphysician of the age', because at that time what we now call 'philosophy' was called 'metaphysics' to distinguish it from what we now call 'science'. This distinction was often marked by the labels 'moral philosophy' to mean what we now call 'philosophy', and 'natural philosophy' to mean what we now call 'science'.

The word 'scientist' was coined as recently as 1833, giving the related word 'science' the sense it now familiarly has. After that date the words 'philosophy' and 'science' took on their current meanings, as the sciences diverged more and more from general enquiry by their increasing specialism and technicality.

In contemporary philosophy the principal areas of enquiry are epistemology, metaphysics, logic, ethics, aesthetics, the philosophy of mind, the philosophy of language, political philosophy, the history of debates in these areas of enquiry, and philosophical examination of the assumptions, methods and claims of other fields of enquiry in science and social science. Most of this is, and certainly the first three are, the staple of a study of philosophy at universities in the Anglophone world and in Europe today.

And correlatively, these are the fields of enquiry that determine which strands in the general history of ideas are selected as today's 'history of philosophy', thus leaving aside the history of technology, astronomy, biology and medicine from antiquity onwards, the history of physics and chemistry since the seventeenth century, and the rise of the social sciences as defined disciplines since the eighteenth century.

To see what determines which strands in the history of ideas to fillet out as 'the history of philosophy' we therefore need to look backwards through the lens of the various branches of contemporary philosophy as listed above, and this requires a preliminary understanding of what these branches are.

Epistemology or 'theory of knowledge' is enquiry into the nature of knowledge and how it is acquired. It investigates the distinctions between knowledge, belief and opinion, seeks to ascertain the conditions under which a claim to know something is justified, and examines and offers responses to sceptical challenges to knowledge.

Metaphysics is enquiry into the nature of reality and existence. What exists, and what is its nature? What is existence? What are the most fundamental kinds of being? Are there different kinds of existence or existing thing? Do abstract entities outside space and time, such as numbers and universals, exist in addition to concrete things in space and time such as trees and stones? Do supernatural entities such as gods exist in addition to the natural realm? Is reality one thing or many things? If humans are wholly part of the natural causal order of the universe, can there be such a thing as free will?

Metaphysics and epistemology are central to philosophy as a whole; they are, as it were, the physics and chemistry of philosophy; understanding the problems and questions in these two enquiries is basic to discussion in all other areas of philosophy.

Logic – the science of valid and sound reasoning – is the general instrument of philosophy, as mathematics is in science. In the Appendix I give a sketch of the basic ideas of logic and explain its key terms.

Ethics, as a subject in the philosophy curriculum, is enquiry into the concepts and theories of what is good, of right and wrong, of moral choice and action. The phrase 'as a subject in the philosophy curriculum' is employed here because the word 'ethics' has multiple applications. Even when used as the label of an area of philosophy it serves to denote two separable matters: examination of ethical concepts and reasoning – this is more precisely described as 'metaethics' – and examination of 'normative' moralities which seek to tell us how to live and act. Normative morality is distinguished from the more theoretical metaethical enquiry by describing normative morality as a 'first order' endeavour and metaethics as a 'second order' endeavour. By its nature philosophy is a second-order enquiry, so 'ethics' in the context of philosophical study standardly means metaethics.

But the word 'ethics' also, though relatedly, denotes the outlook and attitudes of individuals or organizations regarding their values, how they act and how they see themselves. This is a familiar and good use of the term; and – interestingly – reflection on this use shows that the words 'ethics' and 'morals' do not mean the same. This is easier to grasp when we note the etymologies of the terms: 'ethics' comes from the Greek *ethos* meaning 'character', whereas 'morals' derives from a coining by Cicero from the Latin *mos, moris* (plural *mores*) which means 'custom' and even 'etiquette'. Morality, accordingly, is about our actions, duties and obligations, whereas ethics is about 'what sort of person one is', and although the two are obviously connected, they are equally obviously distinct.

This distinction naturally appears in the arenas of metaethical and normative discussion too. In their identification of the locus of value, some metaethical theories focus on the character of the agent, others on the consequences of actions, others again on whether an action conforms to a duty. When it is the character of an agent that matters, we are discussing ethics in the sense of *ethos* just described; when it is the consequence of actions or conformity with duty that matters, it is the narrower focus of morality which is in view.

Aesthetics is enquiry into art and beauty. What is art? Is beauty an objective property of things natural or man-made, or is it subjective, existing in the eye of the beholder only? Can something be aesthetically valuable whether or not it is beautiful and whether or not it is a work of art? Are the aesthetic values of natural things (a landscape, a sunset, a face) different from those we attribute to artefacts (a painting, a poem, a piece of music)?

Philosophy of mind is the enquiry into the nature of mental phenomena and consciousness. It was once an integral part of metaphysics because the latter, in enquiring into the nature of reality, has to consider whether reality is only material, or in addition has non-material aspects such as mind, or perhaps is only mental as the 'idealist' philosophers argue. But as consensus has grown around the view that reality is fundamentally and exclusively material, and that mental phenomena are the products of the material activity of the brain, understanding those phenomena and in particular the nature of consciousness has become a topic of intense interest.

Philosophy of language is enquiry into how we attach meaning to sounds and marks in a way that enables communication and embodies thought, indeed perhaps makes thought above a certain rudimentary level possible in the first place. What is the unit of semantic meaning – a word, a sentence, a discourse? What is 'meaning' itself? What do we know – or know how to do – when we 'know the meaning' of expressions in a language? Is there such a thing as *a language* such as English, or are there as many idiolects of English as there are speakers of those idiolects, thus making *a language* in fact a collection of not completely overlapping idiolects? How do we interpret and understand the language-use of others? What are the epistemological and metaphysical implications of our understanding of language, meaning and language-use?

For good reasons the philosophies of mind and language have become conjoined into a single overall enquiry in more recent academic philosophy, as the titles of books and university courses ubiquitously attest.

Political philosophy is enquiry into the principles of social and political organization and their justification. It asks, What is the best way to organize and run a society? What legitimates forms of government? On what grounds do claims to authority in the state or a society rest? What are the advantages and disadvantages of democracy, communism, monarchy and other forms of political arrangement?

The *history of philosophy* as it is viewed backwards through the lens of the above enquiries is an essential part of philosophy itself, because all these enquiries have evolved over time as – so to speak – a great conversation among thinkers living in different centuries in different circumstances but nevertheless absorbed in the same fundamental questions; and therefore knowing the 'case law' of these debates is crucial to understanding them. This prevents us from unnecessarily reinventing the wheel over and over again, helps us to avoid mistakes and to recognize pitfalls, allows us to profit from our predecessors' endeavours and insights, and gives us materials to use in trying to understand the subject matter at issue, and to frame the right questions to ask about them.*

Philosophical examination of the assumptions, methods and claims of other fields of enquiry is what is meant by such labels as 'philosophy of science', 'philosophy of history', 'philosophy of psychology' and the like. Every enquiry rests on assumptions and employs methodologies, and self-awareness about these is necessary. Philosophical questions about science, for example, are asked by scientists themselves and not only by philosophers; philosophical questions about the study of history likewise are raised by historians in discussing their methods and aims. Consider each in turn more particularly, as follows.

Should science be understood in realist or in instrumentalist terms – that is, are the entities referred to by technical terms in science really existing things, or are they useful constructs that help to organize understanding of the phenomena being studied? Is scientific reasoning deductive or inductive? Is there such a thing as scientific *knowledge* or, on the understanding that all science is open to refutation by further evidence, should it be understood as a system of powerfully evidenced theories which are nevertheless intrinsically defeasible?

As regards history: if there is no evidence one way or the other for a claim about something that happened in the past, is the claim nevertheless definitely either true or false, or is it neither? History is written in the present on the basis of evidence – diaries, letters, archaeological remains – that has survived into the present (or so we judge): it is partial and fragmentary, and many of the past's traces are lost; is there therefore such a thing as *knowledge* of the past at all, or is there only interpretative reconstruction at best – and perhaps, too often, just surmise?

Reflection on the kinds of enquiries, and kinds of questions those enquiries prompt, shows that philosophy is the attempt to make sense of things, to achieve understanding and perspective, in relation to those many areas of life and thought where doubt, difficulty, obscurity and ignorance prevail – which is to say: on the frontiers of all our endeavours.

---

* Everything in philosophy and the history of philosophy is up for debate. The claim that the whole philosophical tradition is one long conversation would be contested by those who think that we cannot understand the thought of a philosopher of the past without putting him firmly in the context of his times. This is true: but it does not preclude seeing the continuity of his ideas and concerns with our own. Our own very often arose either from them, or from the same things that prompted them.

I describe the role of philosophy to my students as follows: we humans occupy a patch of light in a great darkness of ignorance. Each of the special disciplines has its station on an arc the circumference of that patch of light, straining to see outwards into the shadows to descry shapes, and thereby to push the horizon of light a little further outwards. Philosophy patrols the whole circumference, making special efforts on those arcs where there is as yet no special discipline, trying to formulate the right questions to ask in order that there might be a chance of formulating answers.

This task – asking the right questions – is indeed crucial. Until the sixteenth and seventeenth centuries, philosophers did not often enough ask the right questions in the right way about nature; when they did, the natural sciences were thereby born, developing into magnificent and powerful fields of enquiry which brought the modern world into existence. Philosophy thus gave birth to science in those centuries; in the eighteenth century it gave birth to psychology, in the nineteenth century to sociology and empirical linguistics, in the twentieth century it played important roles in the development of artificial intelligence and cognitive science. Its contributions to aspects of neuroscience and neuropsychology continue.

But the core of questions in epistemology, metaphysics, ethics, political philosophy, the 'philosophy of' pursuits, and the rest, remain; they are perennial and perennially urgent questions, because efforts to answer them are part of the great adventure of humanity's effort to understand itself and its place in the universe. Some of those questions seem unanswerable – though to act on the thought that they are so is to give up far too soon. Moreover, as Paul Valéry said, *Une difficulté est une lumière. Une difficulté insurmontable est un soleil*: 'A difficulty is a light. An insurmountable difficulty is a sun.' Wonderful saying! for it teaches us that the effort to solve even the seemingly unsolvable teaches us an enormous amount – as the history of philosophy attests.

What follows, then, is the history of philosophy in today's meaning of the word 'philosophy', showing how the subject matter of today's philosophical enquiries began and evolved. It is mainly the history of Western philosophy that I describe in these pages, but I give overviews of Indian, Chinese and Arabic–Persian philosophy (and a consideration of philosophy in Africa) to note some connections and differences among the great traditions of thought: see the opening pages of Part V. In all cases I have of necessity focused on the main figures and ideas, and in the case of the non-Western traditions I write as a spectator observing from the other side of a linguistic barrier, having extremely little access to Sanskrit, Pali and ancient Chinese, and none to Arabic.

A difference between this and other histories of philosophy is that this one does not detour into what most others give, namely, accounts of the *theologies* of Augustine, some of the Church Fathers of early Christianity and the 'Schoolmen' of later medieval times such as Aquinas and Duns Scotus. This is a history of philosophy, not of theology and religion. An oddity of histories of philosophy which include theologians among the philosophers is that there is no better reason to include Christian theologians while excluding Jewish or Islamic ones; and no better reason to include theology in a history of philosophy than to include a history of science (indeed, there is rather more reason to include this latter). A fundamental difference between philosophy and theology is that philosophy is the enterprise of trying to make sense of ourselves and our world in a way which asks what we should think and why, whereas theology is the enterprise of exploring and expounding ideas about a certain kind of thing or things taken to exist actually or possibly, namely, a god or gods – a being or beings supposed to be different in significant and consequential ways from ourselves. As I write in dealing with this point in connection with Arabic–Persian philosophy in Part V, 'if the starting point for reflection is acceptance of a religious doctrine, then the reflection that follows is theology, or theodicy, or exegesis, or casuistry, or apologetics, or hermeneutics, but it is not philosophy': and that is the principle of demarcation I apply throughout.

A way of dramatizing the point more polemically is to say that philosophy is to theology what agriculture is to gardening: it is a very much bigger, broader and more varied enterprise than the particular, localized and focused one of 'talking or theorizing about a god' (which is what *theo-logos* means). Of course in philosophy the question whether supernatural entities or agencies exist, and what difference would follow for our picture of the world and ourselves if one or more did so, from time to time arises; and there are philosophers who, drawing on a conception of deity from 'natural theology' (that is, some general considerations about a supernatural mind or agency), use it to guarantee the possibility of knowledge (as Descartes did) or as a basis for existence (as Berkeley and not a few others did). These views are discussed in the appropriate places in the following pages. But the tangled efforts to make sense of something like deity as traditional religions wish to have it understood – omnipotent, eternal, omniscient being or beings, and so forth – is not except tangentially a fruitful part of the story of philosophy, and is left to its own historians therefore.

PART I

Ancient Philosophy

Philosophy before Plato

There is a wall standing between us and the world of antiquity: the period of the decline and fall of the Roman Empire and the rise to dominance of Christianity. Edward Gibbon connected the two phenomena, blaming the former on the latter. He is in significant part right. Remember that in 313 CE the Emperor Constantine gave Christianity legal status and protection by the Edict of Milan, and not long afterwards, in 380 CE, the Emperor Theodosius I decreed by the Edict of Thessalonica that Christianity was to be the official religion of the Empire, outlawing others. The change brought rapid results. From the fourth century of the Common Era (CE, formerly cited as AD) onwards a vast amount of the literature and material culture of antiquity was lost, a great deal of it purposefully destroyed. Christian zealots smashed statues and temples, defaced paintings and burned 'pagan' books, in an orgy of effacement of previous culture that lasted for several centuries. It has been estimated that as much as 90 per cent of the literature of antiquity perished in the onslaught. The Christians took the fallen stones of temples to build their churches, and over-wrote the manuscripts of the philosophers and poets with their scripture texts. It is hard to comprehend, still less to forgive, the immense loss of literature, philosophy, history and general culture this represented. Moreover, at the time Christianity existed in a number of mutually hostile and competing versions, and the effort – eventually successful – to achieve a degree of consensus on a 'right' version required treating the others as heresies and aberrations requiring suppression, including violent suppression.

In its assault on the past Christianity had help from others with a similar lack of interest in high classical civilization: Huns, Goths, Visigoths and others – the 'barbarians' – whose migrations and invasions into the ever-weakening Roman Empire hastened its collapse.* The shrinking of mental and cultural life was both a cause and an effect of diminishing education; fewer books were written and published, prohibitions were imposed on what could be read and discussed, and the predictable consequences of such circumstances followed in the form of increasing ignorance and narrowness. Christianity congratulates itself on the fact that the preservation of fragments of classical literature which managed to scrape through this period of appalling destruction was the achievement of monks, in later centuries, copying some of the manuscripts that survived; and although this was a merely partial, belated and inadequate response to the wanton zealotry of the earlier faithful, one must be grateful even for that.

As one would expect, only those texts regarded as most significant and outstanding, by individuals themselves thus regarded, managed to survive – and even so, much of the work of some of the greatest figures perished. Only think: Aristophanes was one of a large number of playwrights in fifth- and fourth-century BCE ('Before the Common Era') Athens. From quotations and allusions we know the names of about 170 other comic playwrights and 1,483 titles of their plays. All are lost; just eleven out of more than forty of Aristophanes' own works survive. We have only seven plays by the tragedian Aeschylus out of seventy whose titles we know. Imagine if, of the thirty-six plays printed in the First Folio of Shakespeare's works (we know of at least one lost play, *Cardenio*, said to have been co-written with John Fletcher), only four were still extant. If we knew the titles of the other thirty-two, what a mighty speculation they would prompt. Imagine if our remoter descendants had just four of Shakespeare's plays, no Cervantes or Goethe but only their names and reputations, a fragment or two of Schiller, no Jane Austen or George Eliot but again just admiring mention of them, a few quotations in others' works from Marx, one leg from Michelangelo's *David*, one copy of a copy of a Poussin painting, a single poem by Baudelaire, just a few lines of Keats, and so on – scraps and remnants, and not always from the best of their time; this is how things in fact stand with regard to classical and Hellenic antiquity. (And consider: by the accidents and ravages of history the future might indeed

---

* We mean of course the Empire of the West; Byzantium preserved enough to enable the invading Muslims of later centuries to benefit from the remnants of classical thought: see pp. 171–2 below.

have little more to offer its inhabitants than this.) It is an irony perhaps that it was people associated with another oriental religion – Islam – which, a couple of centuries later, also irrupted into the classical world (or rather, into what was by then the carcass of the classical world), who saved some of that carcass's legacy from oblivion.*

As these thoughts tell us, what we know of Plato's predecessors in philosophy – they are conventionally known as 'Presocratic philosophers' even though some of them were contemporaries of Socrates – has come to us in shreds and patches. There are two kinds of sources for our knowledge of them: *fragments*, which are quotations from them in the writings of later commentators, and *testimonia*, which are reports, paraphrases or summaries given by later writers. The scholarly task of identifying and collating this evidence is known as 'doxography'. The term 'doxographer' is also applied to those individuals in ancient times who preserved scraps of the Presocratics' writings or views by quoting or reporting them.

Plato and Aristotle both summarized and quoted Presocratic thinkers – sometimes inaccurately, which well illustrates how careful doxography has to be, given that even these giants could get it wrong. Aristotle is indeed a major source of our knowledge of the Presocratics, because he discussed them often and had three of his students, Eudemus, Meno and Theophrastus, write treatises on various of them. Meno concentrated on their medical writings, while Eudemus wrote about their mathematics and astronomy. Only a few traces of the resulting books survive, as quotations and summaries in the work of yet later writers. Theophrastus discussed the Presocratics' theories of perception in his *On Sensation* and their science in his *Tenets of Natural Philosophy*. A few sections of the first book survive; only the title of the latter remains.

Aristotle and his students were writing about thinkers some of whom lived two hundred years before their time. The next important source is Cicero, writing two hundred years after Aristotle's time, in the first century BCE. Thus already the thread was growing longer and thinner – the thread of memory and transmission of sources (manuscript copies following earlier manuscript copies, with mistakes

* Remember that by this time the Roman Empire of the East had been transformed into fully Christian Byzantium, no more interested in a careful and full preservation of pre-Christian culture than any other part of Christendom.

creeping in). Cicero was a serious student of philosophy who sought to inform his Roman contemporaries about Greek thought. But by his time the first age of philosophical genius had passed, and in the centuries that followed other causes of inaccuracy entered the picture, not least polemics – as in the writings of Clement of Alexandria in the second century CE, whose comparisons between Christian thought and Greek philosophy were not designed to favour the latter. Nevertheless he quotes some of the Presocratics, adding to the doxographical store.

The second century CE in fact offers a fairly rich harvest for doxography. The sceptic philosopher Sextus Empiricus quoted extensively from the Presocratics on knowledge and perception, while Plutarch's *Moralia* quotes them on a wider range of topics. An anonymous work of the same period called the *Placita* ('Opinions') does the same. This book was originally thought to be by Plutarch, so for convenience its unknown author is called 'pseudo-Plutarch'. Later that century Alexander of Aphrodisias quoted a number of Presocratics in his commentary on Aristotle.

In the early third century CE Bishop Hippolytus of Rome wrote a *Refutation of All Heresies* arguing that Christian heresies arose from Greek philosophy, in the process quoting extensively from the Greek philosophical tradition in order to refute it, thus paradoxically preserving the views he sought to demolish.

One of the most useful sources for the history of Greek philosophy is *The Lives of the Philosophers* by Diogenes Laertius, written in the third century CE. It is an informative and entertaining work, though again not always accurate. It also sometimes, perhaps indeed too often, relies on legend and hearsay, which tempers its value; but nevertheless its value is great. In addition to summaries of biographies and views it gives a bibliography of philosophical works, demonstrating yet again how much has been lost.

There was an earlier text, of course lost, on which the *Placita* drew, which later served as a source for the 'Selections on Natural Philosophy' of John Stobaeus in the fifth century CE. That earlier text is attributed to Aetius, who lived around 100 CE, and who is thought to have himself used Theophrastus' book. Another important fifth-century source is Proclus, one of the last heads of the academy Plato had founded nine centuries before. Plato's Academy (the 'School of Athens') was closed by the Emperor Justinian in 529 CE, along with a general ban on the teaching of philosophy because it conflicted with Christianity.

A very important doxographical source, for all that it dates from a thousand years after the beginning of Presocratic philosophy, is the writings of Simplicius in the sixth century CE. In his commentary on Aristotle's *Physics* Book I he quotes a number of the more important Presocratics, in some cases thus serving as the only source of information we have about their views. Significantly, he says that his reason for quoting so extensively from one of them, namely Parmenides, giving more of the text than was necessary for his argument, was that copies of Parmenides' work were extremely rare and difficult to find, so he felt the need to preserve some of it.

These are the major sources, but not the only ones. Scattered here and there in other writings are mentions, anecdotes and tidbits which the fine net of doxographic scholarship has trawled up. They come, for some examples, from what remains of the writings of Agathemerus the geographer of the third century BCE, the *Chronicles* of Apollodorus of Athens, written in the second century BCE, the book *On Birthdays* by the Roman grammarian Censorinus in the third century CE, and others.

As already noted, neither the fragments nor – perhaps even more so – the *testimonia* can be regarded as completely reliable. Apart from their brief and scanty nature, they were quoted or reported by writers with their own agendas in mind, sometimes hostile to the views of the philosopher being quoted or paraphrased. Questions of language, interpretation, context and relationship to other fragments pose difficulties for understanding what was really meant by the fragment or reported view. This caveat has to be borne in mind.

As a result of the great scholarly achievements of the nineteenth century, when the study of the doxographical sources benefited from advances in philology (the study of language in historical texts), a story of early philosophy emerged which quickly assumed the status of orthodoxy. More recent scholarship, including the discovery of texts like the Strasbourg Papyrus with previously unknown lines by Empedocles, and the Derveni Papyrus containing philosophical quotations among Orphic hymns, complicates the neat picture that the orthodoxy gives, and throws some of it into question.* However in its broad outlines the

---

* The Strasbourg and Derveni papyri are celebrated cases in point. The latter is the earliest Greek original text ever discovered, dating from about 330 BCE. It was found at a gravesite north of Thessalonica in 1962, and has taken many years of scholarly effort to

orthodox story is a good starting guide; the detailed refinements and criticism of recent scholarship make better sense if one knows what it is adjusting.

That orthodox story goes as follows.

read and interpret – a task still incomplete. The scroll was preserved because it was partially charred in a funeral pyre. It contains quotations from Anaxagoras, Parmenides and Heraclitus among material from an Orphic creation hymn attended by a commentary saying that the hymn is allegorical. The Strasbourg Papyrus contains a poem by Empedocles, and it has played a major part in debates about the interpretation of his thought.

The Presocratic Philosophers

The Presocratics were given this name by the aforementioned nineteenth-century scholars not because all of them predated Socrates – some were his contemporaries – but because the scholars recognized a significant difference of interest between them and Socrates. This is that the Presocratics were concerned with questions about the nature and origins of the world, whereas Socrates focused his attention on ethics. Accordingly the scholars, following Aristotle's name for them, described the Presocratics as *phusikoi* – physicists.

Before giving an account of each of the major figures individually, it is useful to see where they fit in the first millennium of philosophy.

The first of the *phusikoi* came not from Athens but from Ionia, a flourishing group of cities originally founded by Athenians on the eastern shores of the Aegean Sea. One of the cities, Miletus, was home to Thales, regarded by the Greeks themselves, and by all historians of philosophy since, as 'the Father of Philosophy'. Of course he was no such thing; it cannot be the case that in the scores of thousands of years of human history before the sixth century BCE no one had speculated about the nature and origins of the universe. Indeed, for several millennia before Thales lived, great civilizations were flourishing in Mesopotamia and along the Nile, possessed of astronomy, architecture, bureaucracy and writing, and based on great cities and organized economies; there must have been many thousands of citizens of these elaborate cultures who pondered philosophical questions. But Thales is the first person we definitely know of who wondered about the nature and origins of the universe, and not only wondered, but put forward ideas about them which are distinctively philosophical rather than religious or mythological in character. More on this shortly, because it is indeed a significant matter.

We do not know Thales' dates of birth and death but we do know that he was said to have predicted an eclipse that took place in 585 BCE, so this date is taken as roughly the midpoint of his life – his *floruit* ('he flourished'). The traditional way of viewing the history of early philosophy is to connect the members of a geographical 'school' of thought as if they were members of a real school, with pupil following teacher. This might be right, and I think probably was, even if sometimes a figure identified as someone's pupil might more accurately be described as a follower or as a younger colleague. In any event, history gives Thales a pupil, Anaximander, who likewise had a pupil, Anaximenes, and these three are bracketed together as the first Ionian philosophers.

Whereas Thales and his Ionian successors lived on the eastern margin of the Greek world, the next significant steps in the story were taken on its western margin, in the Greek colonies of southern Italy. Pythagoras – he of the theorem about the square on the hypotenuse – in fact came from Ionia originally, but transplanted himself to Croton on the heel of Italy. The city of Elea, not far from Croton, was the birthplace of a towering figure in early philosophy, Parmenides; the adjective 'Eleatic' is therefore applied to him and to the school of philosophy he founded, his principal followers being Zeno and Melissus. Contemporary with Zeno was Empedocles, from Acragas in Sicily.

Parmenides is one of the two greatest of Presocratic philosophers; the other is Heraclitus, whose birthplace was back across the Greek world in Ionia. Towards the end of their lives – Heraclitus was slightly the older of the two; Parmenides was still alive when Socrates was born in 470 BCE – the seat of philosophy became, and for several centuries thereafter almost exclusively remained, Athens. Athens saw, apart from Socrates himself, the flourishing of Protagoras, the sophists, the atomists Leucippus and Democritus, and then Plato and Aristotle; and after the latter the schools of Epicurus, the Cynics and the Stoics.

In the final century of the first millennium BCE the centres of philosophy began to multiply again, including Rome and Alexandria as increasingly important homes of debate and enquiry. The last great philosophical movement of antiquity, Neoplatonism, which began with Plotinus in the third century CE and flourished until the seventh century CE, included thinkers associated with those two cities as well as Athens and elsewhere.

Such is an overview of ancient philosophy, a thousand years of it, stretching from the beginnings with Thales in Ionia through Plato, Aristotle, Epicureanism, Stoicism (which provided the outlook of many educated Hellenes and Romans until the advent of the Christian era) and finally Neoplatonism. We now look at the leading figures in this story in more detail.

THALES

Thales was traditionally regarded as one of the Seven Sages of Greece. His *floruit* of 585 BCE suggested to later commentators that he was born in 625 BCE, on the assumption that men reach the midpoint of their lives about the age of forty. His birthplace of Miletus on the eastern shores of the Aegean was a wealthy and flourishing city. He was an astronomer, a mathematician and – despite a reputation for unworldly philosophizing – an engineer of note.

The imputation of unworldliness comes from a story recounted by Plato in the *Theaetetus*, that Thales fell into a well because he was gazing up at the stars so intently that he did not look where he was going.* It is reinforced by a story Aristotle tells in his *Politics* that Thales' neglect of worldly ambition meant that he was poor, and was reproached for being so by his contemporaries.

The story of the well might have its roots in the fact that if you descend to the bottom of a well you can see the stars even in daylight. The possibility that Thales was doing just that is suggested by other evidence of his practicality. When he was criticized for his poverty he said nothing, but studied the weather carefully until, one year, he was able to predict that there would be a glut of olives. Before this became obvious to anyone else he rented all the olive presses in Miletus, and rented them back at a premium to their anxious owners when the latter came begging for them. Aristotle says, 'In this way he proved that philosophers can easily be wealthy if they wish, but that is not what they are interested in.'

A clincher regarding Thales' practicality is the story that he was hired by the ruler of neighbouring Lydia, King Croesus, to find a way for his army to cross the River Halys without building a bridge. He did it by having the army camp on the bank, then digging a ditch round it and diverting

---

* He was, said Plato, laughed at by a 'witty and charming Thracian serving-girl' for this.

part of the river's flow to make it pass on both sides of the camp, so shallowly that it could easily be forded in either direction.

These credentials help us to evaluate the views Thales held and his reasons for holding them. Obviously he had a serious mind, and there was a good reason why his successors in the tale of philosophy regarded him as the first of their name.

Recall that one of the chief interests of the Presocratics was the question of the nature and source of the world (in the sense of 'universe': the term they used was *kosmos*): hence the label given to them of *phusikoi*, 'physicists'. Their distinctive mark is their rejection of traditional mythological accounts of the cosmos. One such account is offered by Hesiod in his *Theogony*, written about 700 BCE, a work of great and even powerful poetic charm, but scarcely satisfying to an intelligent and genuinely interested enquirer into the nature of the world. Hesiod tells us that 'First of all Chaos came into being . . . From Chaos were born Erebos and black Night; From Night, again, were born Aether and Day, whom she conceived and bore after mingling with Erebos . . .'

In desiring a more intellectually compelling account, Thales sought to identify the cosmos's *arche*, a word which can be translated as 'principle' and which in the context denotes what the cosmos consists of, or from which it comes into existence, or both. As Aristotle put it in talking of the Presocratics and indeed of Thales specifically, the *arche* is 'that of which all existing things are composed and that from which they originally come to be and that into which they finally perish . . . this they state is the element and principle of the things that are . . .' Thales' candidate for this principle was: *water*.

Why did Thales nominate water? One might reconstruct his thinking as follows. Water is ubiquitous – it is in the sea, it falls from the sky, it runs in your veins, if you cut a plant you see that it has liquid inside, if you rub a clod of earth in your hands it is damp, we and all animals and plants die without it and therefore it is essential for life. Moreover water could be said to produce the earth itself, for you need only look at the vast quantities of soil produced by the Nile as it floods every year (a reference to the silt thus washed down). And moreover again, as a kind of clincher, water is the only substance Thales knew that can occupy all three material states: solid (when it freezes), liquid (in its basic state) and gas (when it boils away into steam). You might indeed say that water – ubiquitous, essential, productive, metamorphic – is a rather brilliant choice of *arche*, if you lived in sixth-century BCE Ionia.

But it is not so much *what* Thales chose to identify as the *arche* as *how and why* he did so. He did not rely on legends, myths, ancient scriptures, teachings or traditions. He relied instead on *observation and reason*. That is why he is the first philosopher. The contrast with accounts of the cosmos of the kind given by Hesiod is sharp. Hesiod himself no doubt regarded his account as figurative or symbolic, but there is a large difference between being content with figurative accounts and trying to offer a theory that can be supported by observation and reason.

Aristotle also tells us that he interpreted Thales as having held that 'soul' (*anima*) is what causes motion, for he is reported to have said that a magnet has a soul because it moves iron; and further, that 'soul is mixed in with the whole universe, and perhaps this is why Thales supposed that all things are full of gods.' Here one must recall that at the very beginning of philosophy, which is also the very beginning of science, the conceptual resources for explaining motion and change were few. The one thing available for an explanation of how things can move or change was an analogy with one's own human experience of agency: I pick up a stone and throw it into a pool, making a splash; I made this sequence of events happen; so by analogy there must be some similar active principle that accounts for motion and change in the world.* Indeed we speak of something *animating* something else, harking back to the idea that things other than animals (this word itself betokening 'animated things') have a power of agency, can move, change or act on other things. What Thales was therefore groping for was an account that would allow a generalization from such phenomena as my experience of agency and the magnet's power to move iron, to an inclusive explanation for alterations of place and state. How else, without a vocabulary yet sufficient for the purpose, to talk of this than to say a magnet has a 'soul', thereby meaning an animating principle, a power of causation or of interaction with other things?

Thales is credited with the injunction 'Know thyself.' He is said to have died when old 'of heat and thirst' while watching a gymnastic contest on a hot day – in short, from dehydration. For one who held

---

* The English words 'agent', 'actor', 'agency', 'activity', 'action' all have the same root in the Latin verb *ago agere egi actum*. This verb is a complicated one with a number of different meanings in Latin, but among them are 'do' and 'drive' (as in 'drive a horse') and in combination with other expressions can have the sense of bringing something about.

that water is the *arche* of the cosmos, this is an ironic end. Diogenes Laertius records a different account of his death, quoting a letter said to have been written by Anaximenes (whom we meet shortly) to Pythagoras. Here the story is that Thales went out one night with his serving woman to look at the stars, 'and, forgetting where he was, stepped over the edge of a steep slope and fell'. Anaximenes then adds, in testament to Thales' position at the fountainhead of philosophy, 'Let us, who were his students, remember the man, and . . . continue to regale one another with his words. Let all our discussions begin with Thales.'

ANAXIMANDER

Thales' pupil Anaximander rather startlingly fast-forwards the concept of the *arche*, saying that it is the *apeiron*, 'the unbounded' or 'indefinite' or 'infinite'. This is a remarkable leap from the idea that the *arche* must consist of some form of matter. Unlike his teacher, he wrote a book, 'On Nature', *Peri Phuseos*, and a quotation from it by Simplicius counts as the very first recorded words of philosophy.

Like all the early philosophers, Anaximander was a man of many abilities. He is credited with being the first person to draw a map of the entire world, as the world was then thought to be; and he is said to have predicted an earthquake. The ability to foresee awesome natural phenomena (Thales had his eclipse) seems to have been a mark of genius attributed by later writers, for whereas eclipses might – with difficulty – have been predictable in those days, the ability to predict earthquakes is still, so far, largely beyond science.

Anaximander was said by Eusebius to have developed gnomons for identifying 'solstices, timespans, hours [*horai*] and equinoxes'. Modern scholarship suggests that what he made was a sundial for marking the seasons – not the hours of the day; apparently no sundial for telling the time of day has been recorded as existing before 350 BCE, and *horai* anyway meant both hours and seasons. Diogenes Laertius reports that Anaximander erected a gnomon in Sparta. As this suggests, he travelled; he is said among other things to have been involved in establishing a Milesian colony on the shores of the Black Sea.

Anaximander thought that humans came originally from fish, which looks like an anticipation of evolutionary theory but to think so would be to 'read in' present ideas to what superficially sounds suggestive in ancient ideas. In any case he said we should not eat fish, on the grounds that they are our kin.* He said that the sun is pure fire and is not, as most people appear to have then believed, smaller than the earth. He said that the moon shines by reflecting light from the sun, and that rain comes from vapours that rise and condense into clouds. He attempted calculations of the relative sizes of the sun, moon and earth, and said that the earth is cylindrical; it is a short fat cylinder, and the upper flat end is where we live, surrounded by an ocean. Diogenes Laertius, however, says that he thought the earth is spherical. In either case the earth hangs motionless in the midst of the infinite, having no more reason to fall than to rise, or indeed to move in any direction at all.

Anaximander's most distinctive thesis, however, concerns the *arche*. He said that the *apeiron*, 'the infinite' or 'indefinite', is that from which everything comes into being and into which everything finally reverts, by a process which is like reciprocity or compensation. Those famous first-ever words of philosophy, as quoted by Simplicius, express this idea: 'where things have their origin there too their passing away occurs according to necessity; they pay justice and reparation to one another for their injustice in conformity with the ordinance of time.' The concept at work is that nature operates according to laws, and when they are disturbed 'reparation' sets in to restore their proper operation. When 'justice' is interpreted as 'balance' the point becomes yet clearer. His view is reported at more length by Plutarch thus: 'the infinite is the universal cause of the generation and destruction of the universe. From it the heavens were separated off and in general all the worlds, infinite in number. He asserted that destruction, and, much earlier, generation occur from time immemorial, all the same things being renewed.'

The reasoning behind Anaximander's view is suggested by Aristotle in the *Physics*, where he discusses why it might be held that the infinite is the principle of things. First he notes that the infinite can have no other purpose than to be a principle, and can itself have no principle – that is, cannot derive from anything more fundamental than itself, for if it did it would not be a principle. The idea of the infinite is attractive, Aristotle remarks, when we think of the nature of time, and also of mathematics. Moreover if it is held that 'the region outside the heavens is infinite, then body and worlds also seem to be infinite, for why should

* Evolution tells us that all living things are kin; humans share a quarter of their genes with rice, so on Anaximander's view we should not eat anything.

there be "here" rather than "there" in the void? If body is anywhere, then it is everywhere. Again, if void and space are infinite, body too must be infinite – for with eternal things there is no difference between being possible and being actual.' And Aristotle then identifies a consideration that might relate more closely to Anaximander's view: that 'generation and destruction will come to an end unless there is something infinite from which what comes into being is subtracted.'

The range of Anaximander's interests is impressive, as is the nature of his thinking. His ideas are imaginative and striking – from drawing a map of the world to measuring time and the seasons and the relative sizes of the sun and moon, to conceiving of nature's laws and their balance, of a plurality of worlds, and finally of the cosmos itself as emerging from the infinite – all this indicates a gifted and ingenious mind. Among the early Ionian philosophers he is the most imaginative.*

ANAXIMENES

As one might expect from a pupil or younger colleague of Anaximander, Anaximenes learned from both his predecessors. He agreed with Anaximander that the *arche* is *apeiron*, infinite; but he did not agree that it was indeterminate. Rather, he agreed with Thales in thinking that it was material, but he identified a different material candidate, with what he took to be greater metamorphic capacities than water and therefore better able to be the source of the variety of things in the world. His candidate was *aer*, somewhat loosely translated as 'air', but meaning a sort of dense moist air or vapour.

His view is given in epitome by Simplicius, quoting Theophrastus: 'Anaximenes . . . like Anaximander declares that the underlying nature is one and unlimited but not indeterminate, as Anaximander held, but definite, saying that it is air. It differs in rarity and density according to the substances it becomes. Becoming finer, it turns to fire; when condensed, it comes to be wind, then cloud; and when further condensed, it becomes water, then earth, then stones, and the rest come to be from these. He makes motion eternal, and says that change also comes to be

---

* Martin Heidegger lectured and wrote on the Anaximander fragment in Simplicius: 'The Anaximander Fragment' (1946).

through the eternal motion of the air.' Note that this last point provides a basis for motion and change without the need to suppose that things have little souls in them.

Anaximenes held that the earth is flat and sits on the air like a lid (thus did Aristotle describe his view). His theory allowed him to say that cloud is 'thickened' moist air, that when it is squeezed rain falls from it, which becomes hail when the water freezes, or snow when there is an admixture of wind in the moisture. Earthquakes occur when the earth is either too dry or too wet, for when too dry it cracks, when too wet it falls apart.

The sun, moon and stars are air refined into fire; they too are flat and 'ride upon the air'. The stars are too distant for us to feel their heat. The sun does not circle underneath the earth to reappear at dawn, but instead rides round the circumference of the flat earth rather as one can make one's hat revolve on one's head. It is hidden from us by distance and mountains as it makes its passage back to the starting point, which is why the night is dark.

A significant point of interest is Anaximenes' concept of condensation and rarefaction as the mechanism of the transformations *aer* undergoes. Thales had not offered a suggestion about how his *arche* could change from liquid to solid and gas, but Anaximenes does. Moreover Anaximenes regarded heat and cold as properties of air, not as substances in their own right; Plutarch writes,

> As Anaximenes of old believed, let us leave neither the cold nor the hot in the category of substance, but as common attributes of matter, which come as the results of its changes. For he declares that the contracted state of matter and the condensed state is cold, whereas what is fine and 'loose' (calling it this way with this very word) is hot. As a result he claimed that it is not said unreasonably that a person releases both hot and cold from his mouth. For the breath becomes cold when compressed and condensed by the lips, and when the mouth is relaxed, the escaping breath becomes warm because of rareness.

The observation that air blown through pressed-together lips is cool, but warm when exhaled from an open mouth, is verifiable: one can do the simple experiment and feel the proof on the back of one's hand. This shows that Anaximenes' views were attempts to make sense of observation, and – this is the significant point – doing so in a systematic, inclusive theory that brought all phenomena together into a single explanatory framework constrained by those observable facts. That the resources both conceptual and practical for devising such a framework were primitive – these thinkers were starting from scratch – only makes one admire them more.

PYTHAGORAS

Next in historical order is Pythagoras, but he is personally something of a mystery. There was certainly a Pythagorean school or cult, perhaps a religious order, that had something to do with a charismatic individual called Pythagoras, and the contribution of this order to mathematics and related subjects is very considerable. Its teachings influenced Plato, who however mentions the individual Pythagoras only once by name, saying that his followers were profoundly devoted to him. The remark occurs in Book x of Plato's *Republic*: 'his disciples loved him for his teaching . . . even now his latter-day followers stand out for their manner of life.' Aristotle mentions him only twice in his extant works, but wrote a book on his school which has been lost. Quotations from it in later sources suggest that Aristotle wrote chiefly about the religious aspects of Pythagoreanism. Indeed the stories associated with the individual Pythagoras tend mainly to appear in the later doxographical tradition, by that time relying on legends and mystical traditions of a dubious kind.

The earliest reference to Pythagoras occurs in verses by Xenophanes, which relate that Pythagoras stopped a man from beating a dog because he heard the voice of a deceased friend in the dog's howling. This conforms with the Pythagorean doctrine of metempsychosis, that is, the transmigration and reincarnation of souls. Pythagoras is said to have forbidden his followers to eat beans because they contain the souls of the dead.

Another early reference to Pythagoras is found in a fragment of Heraclitus' work. Heraclitus, who lived just a generation after Pythagoras, praised the advances he had made in science, but said that he had misused them for charlatanry. This lends credence to the idea that the Pythagorean group was more than a philosophical school, being dedicated to a religious way of life also.

By origin Pythagoras was an Ionian. His *floruit* is given as 532 BCE, suggesting a birth year of about 570 BCE. He was born at Samos, an island close to the Ionian coast between Ephesus and Miletus, during the reign of Polycrates, and is said to have left Ionia for the city of Croton in Italy in order to escape Polycrates' tyrannical rule. This detail is implausible; other sources say that he undertook diplomatic missions at Polycrates' behest, and in any case the court of Polycrates has been regarded as an enlightened one, at which the poet Anacreon and the famous engineer Eupalinos of Megara lived. Whatever prompted Pythagoras to leave Samos, legend has it that he first travelled widely in Egypt and the East before settling in Croton, and hagiographers credit some of the doctrines associated with him to his studies there. It is something of a reflex among doxographers to credit several of the early Greek thinkers with acquisition of wisdom 'from the East'. The belief that the East is a source of especially deep wisdom persists into our own day.

It seems that the religious aspect of Pythagoreanism was focused on worship of Apollo. For a time the order wielded considerable political influence in the Greek cities of south-eastern Italy, but lost its influence in an uprising that followed Croton's destruction of the city of Sybaris in 510 BCE. A follower of Pythagoras, a famous champion wrestler called Milo who led the Crotonites in their victory over the Sybarites, was burned to death with other Pythagoreans in their lodge when the citizens of Croton rose against them, thinking that Milo intended to impose a dictatorship on them. Only two members escaped. In Diogenes Laertius' account, Pythagoras himself was present in the house when it was attacked, and attempted to flee; but he was captured when he found himself at the edge of a beanfield, which he would not cross because of his scruples. 'And so', says Diogenes, 'his pursuers cut his throat.' Other lodges in other cities were burned down also, the cohesion of the order being thus destroyed and its survivors dispersed.

Neither Plato nor Aristotle quotes any sayings of Pythagoras, and much of what is claimed to be reports of his teachings has turned out to be forgery. What is at least certain is that the Pythagoreans believed in metempsychosis, and were vegetarians (though, as we have seen, they avoided beans) on the basis that animals and humans are kin and to eat flesh is a kind of cannibalism. Indeed some of the teachings ascribed to Pythagoreans, especially the *akousmata* ('things heard'), that is, the symbolic rules of the order, suggest a survival from concepts of taboo. They include proscriptions against breaking bread, stepping over crossbars, touching white cockerels, walking on highways, letting swallows live in the roof of your house, and looking at yourself in a mirror next to a light. Pythagoreans were instructed to roll up their bedclothes when they got up in the morning, and to smooth out the impress of their bodies on the mattress.

It is unfortunate for our understanding of the philosophy of Pythagoras that the legends which grew around him centuries after his time obscure how much influence he had on Plato and others. In the texts of the Neoplatonist philosophers Porphyry and Iamblichus, writing much later in the third and fourth centuries CE, he is represented as a prophet-like holy man who had received divine revelations. Iamblichus calls him 'the divine Pythagoras' in his treatise *On the Pythagorean Life*, and Porphyry says, 'No one else has had greater or more extraordinary things believed about them' (*Life of Pythagoras*). Some of these views led to the theory that much of Plato's own thought is borrowed from Pythagoras.

It would be easy to think that Pythagoreanism is just another of many cults and movements predicated on primitive beliefs. But the school's contribution to mathematics and science make it unignorable. Indeed even among the more cult-like aspects there are points of interest: Pythagoreans believed that music purifies the soul, important for a belief-system seeking to help the soul escape from 'the wheel of rebirth' as was the aim also of Orphism and other mystical cults. Moreover Pythagoreans divided people into three kinds, on analogy with people who attend the Games: some come to compete, some to buy and sell under the stands, and some to spectate – for which the Greek verb is *theorein*, from which we get 'theory'. The philosophers are those who spectate or look upon the world to study it. These latter are the best kind of people therefore, said the Pythagoreans, and closest to purification and consequently to escaping from the cycle of rebirth.

The mathematician Aristoxenos said that Pythagoras was the first to take the study of arithmetic beyond the practical needs of commerce. The Pythagoreans introduced a way of representing numbers by arrangements of dots in triangles, squares and rectangles, and demonstrated a number of arithmetical properties through the geometries of these arrangements. The number-shapes had religious significance too: the one by which Pythagoreans swore their oaths was the 'tetractys of the decad', that is, a triangle of dots with a row of four along the bottom, three above that, then two, and then one, adding up to ten. Pythagoreans thought that ten is the natural basis of counting, and gave it a mystical significance. There is of course an infinity of 'triangular numbers' – three is represented as the triangle of two dots with one dot above it; six is represented as a triangle of dots arranged '3–2–1'; ten we have seen, fifteen is '5–4–3–2–1',

and so on. Rows and columns of the same number of dots as each other give 'square numbers', while 'oblong numbers' are those in which the columns have one less dot than the rows:

We now use numerals ultimately derived from India (though now called 'arabic numerals' because the Arabs transmitted them to the world at large), but we still often call numbers 'figures'.

If there is one thing almost everyone knows about the Pythagoreans, it is 'Pythagoras' theorem', stating that the square of an hypotenuse (this being the longest side of a right-angled triangle, opposite the right angle itself) is equal to the sum of the squares on the other two sides: where a is the hypotenuse, $a^2 = b^2 + c^2$. This was in fact known to Thales, to Egyptians in their geometry of land-mensuration and to Babylonians and Indians long beforehand; but it is possible that Pythagoras or a follower discovered a proof.

A major achievement of the Pythagorean school was its discovery that the pitch of a musical note depends on the length of a string whose vibrations produce the note, and that simple numerical ratios explain the consonant intervals of the scale: 2:1 octave, 3:2 perfect fifth, 4:3 perfect fourth, and so on. To understand this, think of two guitar strings of equal length, tension and thickness. If they are both plucked together they sound the same. If different lengths of each are plucked, they sometimes sound dissonant and sometimes consonant. This latter observation underlies measurement of consonant intervals – an interval being the distance between two notes, and a consonant interval being one in which the two notes sound good together. Experiment will show that if you have two lengths of string of equal length, tension and thickness, plucking one while simultaneously plucking exactly half the length of the other will yield a consonance – this is the octave. If the second string is plucked at two-fifths the length of the first, the resulting consonant is a perfect fifth (go to a piano and play the notes middle C and G above middle C together: that is a perfect fifth).

This discovery, even more than the theorem about the square on the hypotenuse, has been hailed as the first step of true science, because it provides a quantified description of an observable phenomenon. And in its extension to the idea of the 'harmony of the spheres' it generalizes the idea to all nature. The Pythagoreans thought of the heavenly bodies as emitting a hum as they flew through space, the distances between them being such as to form a scale: earth and moon are a tone apart, moon to Mercury a semi-tone, Venus to the sun a minor third; Mars to Jupiter and Jupiter to Saturn are each a semi-tone, and Saturn to the sphere of the fixed stars is a minor third.

For the Pythagoreans as for others – including Plato – the idea of harmony came to have more than just the mathematical significance of ratios producing consonances; it became a key metaphor in thinking about matters ethical and psychological also. Just by itself, however, without further philosophical applications, it represents a notable step.

The insights and discoveries of Pythagorean mathematics led not just to ethical ideas but to a metaphysics in which reality itself is regarded as constituted by number. Allegedly the motto above the entrance to a Pythagorean lodge was 'All is number'. Think of the dots as atoms; that is not how the Pythagoreans put it, but the connection is a natural one to make, the more so as the structure of material objects – think of a crystal – is informatively describable in terms of geometries. This might not have been what the Pythagoreans meant, for Aristotle reports that they assigned numerical values to certain abstractions such as justice and marriage: justice is four, marriage three, 'the right time' is seven. Odd numbers were said to be male, even numbers female. The meaning of such views is unclear. But it is also likely that they thought of the world as consisting structurally of whole numbers and their ratios, as their reaction – their horrified reaction – to the discovery of *irrational numbers* suggests. This is explained as follows.

Consider the relationship between the length of a side of a square and the length of the diagonal drawn from one corner of the square to the opposite corner. There is no way of expressing the ratio of the length of the diagonal to the length of a side in integers (whole numbers). Pythagoreans regarded this incommensurability as a ghastly, indeed an evil, phenomenon.

To see what is at stake, consider a square of which each side is one metre in length. To determine the length of the diagonal seems easy, for it is the hypotenuse of the right-angled triangle it forms with two sides of the square. We know that the square of the diagonal's length is the sum of the squares on the other two sides: it is two metres square, for $(1 \times 1) + (1 \times 1) = 2$. But what is the square root of 2? Well, obviously, it is the number which, when multiplied by itself, makes 2. What is that number? It cannot be 1, because $1 \times 1 = 1$. It cannot be 2, because $2 \times 2 = 4$. It is therefore something in between 1 and 2. But whatever it is, it cannot be expressed as a ratio of two integers; it is not a simple fraction. This is best understood in decimal terms: an irrational number is one whose decimal expansion never either terminates or becomes periodic (repeats regularly). How can nature consist of numbers that misbehave in this way?

The discovery of irrational numbers was so traumatic for the Pythagoreans, legend has it, that the man who made the discovery (or, some of the legends say, the man who revealed it after the order's members had been sworn to secrecy about it), namely Hippasos of Metapontum, was punished by being drowned.

The discoveries and views of the Pythagoreans seem so different from those of their Ionian predecessors that it is a relief to find oneself on more familiar ground with their cosmology. Here indeed they seem to have borrowed from both Anaximander and Anaximenes. Aristotle relates that the Pythagoreans thought that beyond the heavens there exists a 'boundless breath' which the world inhales, thereby acquiring cohesion and order. This is a little reminiscent of Anaximenes, as is an extension of his concept that the *arche* is *aer* into the idea that darkness is very condensed air. Anaximenes' *aer* is unlimited, like Anaximander's *apeiron*, and the Pythagoreans make Darkness 'the Unlimited' and Light 'the Limit'.

Pythagoras is credited with thinking that the earth is a sphere, and later writers also claimed that he thought the cosmos is heliocentric, which is why the Copernican heliocentric model of the universe was described as 'Pythagorean'. The idea that the heavens beyond the system of the planets, however arranged, are wheels of burning air which we see through apertures in the underside of the sky – these apertures therefore being the stars – is a conception that the Pythagoreans might have taken from Anaximander. The latter thought there were three such wheels, and the Pythagoreans very likely identified the gaps between them with the three musical intervals they had discovered, namely, the octave, fifth and fourth: the 'music of the spheres'.

It was the musical discovery that the consonant intervals can be expressed as simple numerical ratios that is the great legacy of Pythagoreanism. The idea of *harmonia*, harmony, opened a set of conceptual possibilities which proved to be very influential. It suggested that opposites can be brought into harmony, or can produce harmonies in their interactions, not least by blending – as when wet and dry, hot and cold balance each other or temper each other's excesses. Indeed the idea of temperament in early medical science – the harmonious balancing of the choleric, phlegmatic, melancholic and sanguine 'humours' – was held to be constitutive of good health; the concept of temperature as a relation between hot and cold, and the ethical 'Doctrine of the Mean' as the virtuous middle path between vicious extremes (thus, courage is the middle path between cowardice and rashness), all owe themselves in one or another way to the idea of *harmonia*. 'It is not too much to say', wrote the historian of ancient philosophy John Burnet, 'that Greek philosophy was henceforward to be dominated by the notion of the perfectly tuned string.'

XENOPHANES

Xenophanes' *floruit* lies somewhere after the middle of the sixth century BCE, making him a contemporary of Pythagoras. But he lived a long time, dying in his nineties after a life of wanderings. We have a quotation from him which says, 'By this time sixty-seven years have tossed my careworn soul up and down the lands of Hellas; and [these wanderings] began twenty-five years after my birth,' thus making him ninety-two at the time he wrote these words.

We can imagine these words as a reply to a question he asks in one of his poems: 'This is the kind of thing we should say by the fireside in winter, as we lie on soft couches after a fine dinner, drinking sweet wine and crunching chickpeas: "What country do you hail from, good sir, and how old are you? And how old were you when the Mede came?"' The reference to 'the Mede' is to the conquest of Ionia by Harpagos, a Mede who served as a general in the army of the Persian King Cyrus. The Ionian cities had formerly been under the sway of King Croesus of Lydia, and when Cyrus attacked Lydia he asked the Ionians to revolt in his support. They refused, so after his victory in 540 BCE Cyrus sent an expedition to punish them. Rather than submit to Persian rule many of the Greeks sailed away from their cities; the entire population of Phocaea did so, resettling in Sicily. Xenophanes' poignant question, 'How old were you when the Mede came?' doubtless resonated with the diaspora of refugee Ionians who could still remember their homes on the eastern shore of the Aegean.

His dates, though uncertain, are bracketed by several facts. One is that he is said to have heard Anaximander lecture. Another is that he referred to his contemporary Pythagoras in the past tense, which indicates that Pythagoras died before he did. An unreliable tradition says that he was a tutor to Parmenides, which would place him in southern Italy some time in the last two decades of the sixth century BCE. In his own turn Heraclitus refers to Xenophanes in the past tense, suggesting that he was dead by the time of Heraclitus' maturity in the early fifth century BCE.

Xenophanes' birthplace was Colophon, an Ionian city between Miletus and Ephesus and therefore close to Pythagoras' birthplace of Samos. Assuming the references in his fragments mean what they seem to mean, he left Colophon when it fell to Harpagos' army, aged twenty-five, and thereafter wandered until his death. He wrote in verse on a wide range of subjects, some of them philosophical, though it is a matter of controversy whether he wrote a philosophical poem as such. Quotations of a philosophical bent mainly come from his satirical attacks on Homer and Hesiod, whose anthropomorphic account of the gods he despised.

This latter is indeed one of the most distinctive facts about Xenophanes: his emphatic rejection of traditional religion and its anthropomorphic Olympian deities. He argued that there is no such thing as divination; such natural phenomena as earthquakes and rainbows are not messages from the gods, he said, but should be naturalistically investigated and understood.

He was critical also of the Greeks' obsession with athletics and athletes, and the expenditure of public money on both, saying, 'Far better is our art [i.e. poetry] than the strength of men and horses! These are but thoughtless judgments, nor is it fitting to set strength before goodly art.' He points out that even if there arises a boxer mightier, a runner swifter, a wrestler more skilful, than others, 'the city would be none the better governed for that. It is little joy to a city if a man conquer at the Games; that does not fill its store-houses.'

In line with his attitude to enquiry he took a keen interest in the natural world, noting the presence of fossils of fish and seaweed on mountain tops, and speculating about meteorological phenomena and the extent of the world in both breadth and depth. Regarding this latter, he thought that the earth extended indefinitely downwards, and that therefore the sun could not circle beneath it at night. Instead there is a new sun every day, gathered together out of 'many small fires'.

It is in Xenophanes that we read the anecdote about Pythagoras hearing a dead friend's voice in a dog's howls. This was satire on Xenophanes' part; he thought the doctrine of metempsychosis silly. He was scathing about Homer and Hesiod because they 'ascribed to the gods all things that are a shame and a disgrace among mortals, stealings and adulteries and deceivings'. He said that 'if oxen and horses or lions had hands, and could paint with their hands, and produce works of art as men do, horses would paint the forms of the gods like horses, and oxen like oxen.' He thought instead that there is a god which is nothing like anything we know, and which (see below) might in fact be the same thing as the world itself.

In the passages where he addresses topics central to the thought of his Ionian predecessors he shows that he knew their ideas well, and had been influenced by them. 'All things come from the earth, and all things end in earth . . . All things are earth and water that come into being and grow.' He seems to have thought that the earth is being progressively dissolved into the sea: 'All human beings are destroyed when the earth has been carried down into the sea and turned to mud. This change takes place for all the worlds.'

That last sentence has caused a debate among scholars. It suggests, under the influence of Anaximander, that there is a plurality of worlds; but elsewhere in the commentaries on Xenophanes, and in Aristotle's remarks about him, he appears to have held that 'the World is One,' a doctrine which, as we shall see, was held by Parmenides, who was influenced by Xenophanes even if he was not actually taught by him. But the unclarities and apparent inconsistencies in Xenophanes' views are not all to be blamed on him. A later member of the school founded by Aristotle – the Peripatetic school – wrote a treatise on Xenophanes and two other thinkers, in which he said that Xenophanes claimed that the world is neither finite nor infinite, and neither in motion nor at rest. Simplicius, writing much later, was frankly baffled by such claims.

But, whatever Xenophanes actually meant, there are suggestive hints in these views that relate him to Parmenides. Aristotle says in the *Metaphysics* that Xenophanes was the first to argue that reality is 'One', and Plato called Xenophanes 'the first of the Eleatics', these being the philosophers of Parmenides' school who subscribed to the doctrine that reality is a single unchanging eternal thing. Aristotle went further to suggest that Xenophanes thought that the world and god are the same thing; in one fragment indeed he says that the world and god are 'equal every way'.

As the commentators remind us, it would be a mistake to interpret talk of 'god' in this context as if it has the same sense as in far later views about deity, such as those familiar from Judaism and Christianity; for in effect Xenophanes' denial of the existence of the traditional gods, and his assertion that god and the world are one and the same thing, are jointly intended to imply 'there is no god but the world.' Apart from the connection with Parmenides' views, these notions – if indeed this is what Xenophanes meant – also anticipate the philosophy of Spinoza, who lived more than two thousand years later.*

Something that anyone reading these pages might cherish in Xenophanes is his account of a dinner of philosophers, in which he writes, 'The floor is clean, so are our hands, and so are the cups . . . a mixing bowl stands by, and another bowl of gentle flower-scented wine . . . there is cold sweet pure water, golden loaves of bread, and a magnificent table laden with cheese and rich honey . . .' The 'cheerful men' (always only *men*, alas) pour a libation pledging always 'to do acts of justice'; the drinking is continent, just enough to allow everyone to get home afterwards unaided; and the talk is not of myths and wars, but of 'excellence' (*arete*).

HERACLITUS

One sure way to live in philosophical memory is to issue striking remarks that are obscure or ambiguous – or better still a mixture of both. Heraclitus is an example. Known as 'the Obscure', 'the Dark' and 'the Riddler', he sauced his obscurities with arrogance and misanthropy. He was an aristocrat, born in Ephesus about 540 BCE or soon afterwards, whose family were part of the city's ruling elite. He gave his hereditary political office of 'Basileus' to a brother, and later in life went to live a rustic hermit's life, though he returned to the city when he fell ill, and died at about the age of sixty.

* See pp. 211–17 below.

He wrote a book, a copy of which was given to Socrates by the playwright Euripides (so says Diogenes Laertius, reporting what is probably a mere legend). Euripides asked him what he thought of it. Socrates replied, 'What I understand of it is splendid, what I don't understand of it is probably splendid too; but it would take a Delian diver to get to the bottom of it.'

A major problem with understanding Heraclitus' philosophy is that the surviving fragments of his book are obscure in themselves, and it is not clear how to arrange them in order, which is a problem because different orders support different interpretations. Aristotle in the *Rhetoric* complained that it was hard to know how to punctuate Heraclitus' sentences to clarify their sense, and gives as an example the only sentence whose position in the work we know, namely, its opening sentence: 'Of this account [*logos*] which holds forever men prove uncomprehending.' Is it the *logos* that holds forever, or are men forever uncomprehending?

We do not even know the title of his book, which would be some guide to what it is about; later doxographers said that it had three parts, one on nature, one on politics and one on theology. This is a break with the philosophical tradition to that point, in ranging more widely than cosmology. But which of these subjects contained the main point of what he wished to say? Given that it appears to have been written in a consciously oracular style – one imagines that comparisons with Nietzsche's *Thus Spake Zarathustra* might be suggestive (and perhaps with its author too) – one can see how difficulties increase.

The account Heraclitus gives of the nature of the world is accompanied by remarks on perception, knowledge and enquiry: 'Nature loves to hide . . . the eyes are more exact witnesses than the ears' (does he mean: To observe for oneself is better than to listen to what others say?). Even those who, like Pythagoras, engage in scientific enquiry do not get things right: 'The learning of many things does not teach understanding, otherwise it would have taught Hesiod and Pythagoras, and again Xenophanes and Hecataeos.' In any event Heraclitus thought that he had grasped the correct *logos* – a word used by Greek philosophers in such a variety of ways that it can be taken to mean any and more of 'account', 'theory', 'framework', 'word', 'reason', 'significance', 'principle' and as we might say 'the underlying logic (of something)'. One reasonable reconstruction of Heraclitus' account is as follows.

Everything is in flux; as Plato puts it in the *Cratylus*, 'Heraclitus says that all things pass and nothing stays, and comparing existing things to the flow of a river, he says that you could not step into the same river twice.' Heraclitus' disciple Cratylus, who was so convinced that everything is constantly changing, would not reply when spoken to but would only waggle his finger to indicate that he had heard, because by the time he was ready to answer, the world had changed.

Some commentators disagree that Heraclitus meant what Plato says he meant. Rather, they say, he meant that things stay the same only by changing – as is the case with a river; its flux does not destroy its continuity as the same river, but in fact constitutes it.

This latter reading is more consistent with another of Heraclitus' doctrines, that of the 'unity of opposites'. One interpretation of this is that a thing can combine opposite qualities: 'sea is simultaneously the purest and the foulest water: for fish it is drinkable and healthy, for men it is undrinkable and harmful.' Likewise youth and age, waking and sleeping, life and death are 'the same thing in us . . . for having changed round they are these, but when changed round again they are those', though in these cases not simultaneously. But others of his fragments seem to say that opposites are in fact identicals: 'the straight and the crooked path of the fuller's comb is one and the same . . . the way up and the way down is one and the same.' These remarks are true: a staircase is both up and down simultaneously, differentiated only by whether you are ascending or descending. 'Men do not know how what is at variance agrees with itself. It is an attunement of opposite tensions, like the bow and the lyre.'

Another identification of opposites requires, however, a more studied interpretation: one fragment says, 'good and ill are one.' Does this imply a version of Hamlet's 'there is nothing either good or bad, but thinking makes it so'? Most likely the explanation is deeper, for Heraclitus seems to have held that it is by the conflict or tension that holds opposites together that existence itself is made possible: 'Homer was wrong to say, "Would that strife might perish from among gods and men!" He did not see that he was praying for the destruction of the universe, for if his prayer were heard all things would pass away . . . all things come into being and pass away through strife . . . strife is justice, all things happen according to strife and necessity.'

Following Aristotle, many commentators see Heraclitus as conforming to the tradition of the earlier Ionians in being a material monist, that is, as holding the view that there is a single underlying material *arche*. As we saw, his predecessors had successively nominated water, the infinite and air; he nominated fire. 'The cosmos, which is the same for all, was not made by gods or men, but it was ever, is now, and ever shall be, an ever-living fire, parts of it kindling, and parts of it going out . . . fire is lack and abundance . . . All things are an exchange for fire, and fire for all things.' Fire turns into water, and half of water turns into earth and half into a fiery wind, and both can turn back into water and water back into fire. These changes are the result of the strife that is an application of justice which reverses the domination of one thing by another.

It might seem that the fact of eternal flux and change makes knowledge impossible, and Plato thought that Heraclitus meant this. But his remarks about the value of learning, and his criticism of others for not achieving understanding even though they study and enquire, suggest otherwise. Indeed it appears that he attached great ethical significance to knowledge: 'Sound thinking is the greatest virtue and wisdom; [it is] to speak the truth and act on a proper understanding of the nature of things.' This is why he says of himself that his preference is for 'seeing, and hearing, and learning'.

Pythagoras had taught a way of life; Heraclitus offers wisdom teachings of his own. Like many others he counselled moderation and self-control in such activities as drinking and eating, but unlike many others he frankly extolled the pursuit of fame: 'The best choose one thing above all else, everlasting fame.' Since he also thought that the best deaths occur in battle, it is not clear that he meant philosophical fame. He said 'character is fate,' and that it is not good always to get what one wants.

In politics he advocated the rule of law – 'The people must fight for [the city's] laws as for its walls' – and a wise choice of rulers. Both pieces of advice are consistent with the idea that there is a cosmic *logos* (which can be interpreted as saying: the cosmos is governed by universal laws) and that rationality – the rational apprehension of these universal laws – applies as much to ethics and politics as in cosmology. But he was not a proto-democrat; he had no time for 'fools' and 'the many . . . the mob'. 'Most men's teacher is Hesiod; they are convinced he knew most things – he, a man who could not recognize that day and night are one.'

It cannot be denied that other and later philosophers were struck by Heraclitus' views – how can one say 'influenced' by them given that neither they nor we are quite clear what they were? Of course his contemporaries and successors had their interpretations of what he meant, and were doubtless influenced by those; but one could extrapolate quite different results for later thinking from this. Some think Parmenides developed his philosophy in opposition to Heraclitus, others see Democritus echoing Heraclitus in his ethical pronouncements; Plato is often read as employing an interpretation of Heraclitus in arguing for the transience and instability of the material world, and from Parmenides in arguing for the eternity and immutability of the intelligible world. Some saw Heraclitus as squarely in the Ionian tradition of physics, others as a sceptic. Such is the fate, and the usefulness, of being a 'Riddler'.

PARMENIDES

Parmenides was born to a wealthy family at Elea either around the year 515 BCE, as Diogenes Laertius says, or a decade or two later, so that Plato's claim that the young Socrates met him around 450 BCE can be regarded as plausible. Diogenes follows Aristotle in saying that he was a pupil of Xenophanes, but that he did not agree with Xenophanes' views. However, like his teacher he wrote his philosophy in verse, using Homeric hexameters embellished with Homeric images, especially from the *Odyssey*. Diogenes says that it was also claimed that Parmenides studied with Anaximander, and that at one point in his life he associated closely with a Pythagorean called Ameinias, of whom he was very fond, as evidenced by the fact that when the latter died he built a shrine to him 'as to a hero'. One reason suggested for this devotion was that Ameinias had persuaded Parmenides to dedicate his life to philosophy. Some in the doxographic tradition described Parmenides as a Pythagorean, and there is no reason to think he might not have been one in his earlier days, though by the time he wrote his poem he no longer was.

Parmenides' poem tells of a young man who is taken up in a chariot to meet a goddess, who promises him that he will learn all things from her.* But, she says, even though everything she tells him will be true, he must test what she says for himself: 'judge by argument', she says,

---

* This was a literary device; in Islam a comparable device is taken to be literally true. This is one of many differences between philosophy and religion.

'the much disputed proof uttered by me.' After a lengthy introduction, the Proem, the poem itself begins with the first of two sections, entitled 'Truth'. We have about 150 lines of the poem, over two-thirds of it from this section. The second section is entitled 'Opinion', and the goddess warns that it concerns a view of the world that is deceptive; it is about our ordinary, sense-based view of the world, and the senses are misleading. By contrast, the first section, 'Truth', tells us that knowledge properly so called is possible only in relation to 'What Is', to *reality*, because 'What Is Not' literally cannot be thought or said. Only reason can get us to the truth about What Is.

This truth is that What Is must be a single unchanging and complete thing, perfect, whole and eternal. The views of other philosophers, premised on the transformation of an *arche* into a plurality of things based on motion and change, on interaction, flux, reparation, mingling or whatever the thinkers in question have suggested, are false in the light of reason, for only an eternal, immutable and comprehensive One is thinkable.

At the beginning of the section entitled 'Opinion' the goddess says, 'Here shall I close my trustworthy speech and thought about the truth. Henceforward learn the beliefs of mortals, giving ear to the deceptive ordering of my words.' She then sets out a cosmology in which fire is of the heavens and is opposed to 'dark night, a compact and heavy body . . . everything is full at once of light and dark night, both equal, since neither has anything to do with the other.' In the heavens 'Necessity' binds the stars; the sun, moon, Milky Way and other phenomena are either 'unmixed fire' or have their portion of night, this explaining the variation among them; and 'in the midst of these is the divinity that directs the course of all things; for she is the beginner of all painful birth and all begetting, driving the female to the embrace of the male, and the male to that of the female.'

But this 'way of opinion' or 'way of seeming' is, to repeat, deceptive; it is the path 'wandered by know-nothing two-headed mortals' who think they live in a world of contingency, plurality and change. On the deceptive evidence of their senses they believe that things can both be and not be – because, for example, a thing can have a certain property at one time and lack it at another. 'Do not follow this path out of habit, relying on your senses,' the goddess again warns the young man; 'judge by reason.' But it is important to know this 'way of seeming' so that one can contrast it properly with the way of truth. 'You must find out everything,' she tells him, 'both the steadfast heart of well-rounded truth and the opinions of mortals. In these opinions there is no truth, but you must learn them anyway.'

The central point in Parmenides' system turns on what he meant by 'What Is'. He has the goddess say that What Is is 'unborn and unperishing ... a unique whole ... unmoved ... perfect, complete'. And she adds, 'Nor Was It once, nor Will It be, for It Is Now, One, Continuous.' The questions this raises are: is the What Is physical, or is it a non-physical thing, an abstraction like 'the infinite' or perhaps a god? If it is physical how do we make sense of the fact that, on almost all views, spatio-temporal properties are distinctive, indeed defining, of the physical, whereas Parmenides' What Is is both all there is (all space) and does not change (at very least complicating what can be understood by time, if time exists at all)?

Obviously this interpretative question is controversial, but the larger consensus is that Parmenides viewed the What Is as physical. One fragment describes it as a sphere, and Aristotle stated that Parmenides did not believe in any sort of non-physical reality. Nor does he speak of a 'god' or 'gods' in connection with reality (the goddess of the poem is a literary device merely), but appears to regard What Is as the universe itself, as everything viewed in totality as one thing – a plenum or complete fullness of physical reality.

This raises the question whether the sphere is infinite, for if not then space has to be finite so that the sphere can fill it completely. Either way, if the sphere is physical it has to comprehend all space because it is unmoving and unmovable; and because it is unchanging we have to think either that there is no such thing as time, or What Is comprehends all time in one changeless present. This seems to be the meaning of the fragment stating 'Neither is there, nor will there be, time apart from being, because fate has bound it down to the whole and unmoved.' That at least is consistent with the central thesis that reality is an unchanging One; on the view that time exists only where there is change, in the envisaged plenum of What Is there can be no change and hence no time, or only an eternal present.

Indeed as there can be nothing beyond or outside What Is, the particular concepts of change and motion are empty. There could only be change and motion if beyond What Is there is also What Is Not, in this sense: if you think with Anaximenes that the *arche* rarefies and condenses, then the change of one state (more rarefied) into the other state (more condensed) and vice versa presupposes that the state into which the *arche* changes its aspect was, as it were, not there – there was no 'being more condensed' for the 'less condensed' to become more of, for if there were no such not-then-existent state, there would not be something for a different state to change into. Likewise, the Pythagoreans' talk of the air outside the cosmos which enters to separate the cosmos into distinct units also assumes the existence of 'what is not', as the thing that motion and change act upon to turn it into 'what is'.

The key point for Parmenides is that one cannot think about *what is not*, whereas anything that can be thought must *be*. 'It is the same thing that can be thought and that can be . . . It needs must be that what can be spoken and thought *is*; for it is possible for it to be and it is not possible for what is nothing to be.' Another way of putting this is to say: if you think, you must be thinking of something; therefore there cannot be *nothing*. 'Only that can exist which can be thought . . . thought exists for the sake of what is.'

Note that Parmenides does not offer mere assertions in the section on Truth; he offers arguments. The striking contrast between the two sections of the poem lies in the fact that in the first we are asked to consider that What Is has to be comprehensive – it has the character of tautology to say 'whatever is, is' – and that one cannot think or say What Is Not because What Is Not is by definition nothing. It appears paradoxical to think that one might have Nothing as the object of one's thought. One might reasonably have much to say about how in fact we talk about what is not the case (but which is possible, or was the case, or will be the case but is not so yet, and so on), and one might question the claim that the realm of the real and the realm of the conceivable are necessarily the same and exclusive. But at least these are deep challenges, and philosophy has grappled with them throughout its history. This is very different from saying 'there is fire and dark night, and the mixture of the two, and in the midst of things the divinity that directs their courses . . .' We see from earlier Presocratics that not all such theorizing – 'the *arche* is water . . . is air' – is mere assertion, but rests on some sort of observational and inferential support; but the 'way of seeming' in Parmenides' poem does not have quite that character, even if it borrows from what was undoubtedly an observational base in asserting that fire is of the heavens, because where could the light of the heavenly bodies come from if they were not themselves fires or emanations of fire? And as it happens, they are indeed fires – or, for the more local of them, reflections of fire.

Parmenides was not quite as obscure a writer as Heraclitus, but the hexameter verse in which his system is expounded nevertheless creates difficulties for a clear interpretation. Despite that, he marks a highly significant moment in the history of philosophy; he is a turning point, for the influence he exerted on those who came after him was enormous, whether they accepted his views or disagreed with him. His followers Zeno and Melissus defended his theory of the One, Zeno with his famous paradoxes – Achilles and the tortoise and the rest: see below – aimed at demonstrating the impossibility of time and change, while any thinker who accepted the reality of change and plurality had to address Parmenides' arguments and find ways of overcoming them.

Parmenides' greatest influence, from the point of view of impact on the entire subsequent history of philosophy, was on Plato and the Platonists. Plato admired Parmenides greatly; he has him worsting Socrates in a late dialogue, and he derives from him the view that the senses and what they tell us about the world of appearances – the familiar world around us, which seems plural and subject to time and change – deceive us as to the true nature of reality. That is a theme which has underwritten an enormous amount of what philosophy and, later, science has achieved.

ZENO OF ELEA

Plato's *Parmenides* and Diogenes Laertius' *Lives of Eminent Philosophers* are almost the only sources of information we have about Zeno's life. If Plato's account is correct, Zeno was born in 490 BCE, and accompanied Parmenides to Athens in about 450 BCE where the young Socrates met them.

Zeno was said to be not just Parmenides' pupil but his adopted son and his lover. He was a tall and handsome man, Plato says; and Diogenes says that his books 'are brimful of intellect'. Aristotle said that Zeno invented 'dialectic', the form of philosophical argument aimed at arriving at truth (as opposed to 'eristic', argument conducted merely for the sake of argument or for point-scoring), in part by starting from the views of an opponent and demonstrating that they lead to unacceptable conclusions.

Diogenes says Zeno was a man of 'noble character, both as a philosopher and as a politician', for when his attempt to overthrow the tyrant Nearchus failed he was arrested and tortured before being killed, but did not betray his friends.* His death produced a multiplicity of legends. Saying to Nearchus that he had something private to whisper in his ear, Zeno 'laid hold of it [the ear] with his teeth, and did not let go until stabbed to death'. Another version says it was the tyrant's nose, not his ear, that he bit off. A third says that he bit off his own tongue and spat it at the tyrant rather than reveal any secrets, and this so roused the citizens that they stoned the tyrant to death. When Nearchus told him to reveal who was behind the coup attempt, Zeno said, 'You, the curse of the city!' whereupon Nearchus had him thrown into a giant mortar and pounded to death.

One might think these picturesquely gory details are intended to enliven what anyone would think is the otherwise staid tale of people whose greatest excitement consists in thinking; but in fact philosophers have had a lively time, as their biographical details often show – for ideas can be dangerous things, demanding courage to express them or live by them. Diogenes wrote a tribute to Zeno as follows: 'You wished, Zeno, and noble was your wish, to slay the tyrant and set Elea free from bondage. But you were crushed; for, as all know, the tyrant caught you and beat you in a mortar. But what is this that I say? It was your body that he beat, not you.'

In Plato's *Parmenides* Zeno is reported as saying that his arguments about the impossibility of motion and plurality are offered as a defence of the Parmenidean thesis that reality is One and unchanging: '[my arguments are] a defence of Parmenides' argument against those who try to make fun of it, saying that if What Is is One, the argument has many ridiculous consequences which contradict it. Now my treatise opposes the advocates of plurality and pays them back the same and more, aiming to prove that their hypothesis "that there are many things" suffers still more ridiculous consequences than the hypothesis that there is One.' In other words, Zeno's arguments have the form of a *reductio ad absurdum* of an initial hypothesis, by showing that contradictions can be deduced from it.

Zeno created about forty paradoxes, of which ten are known. Aristotle's *Physics* is the chief source for Zeno's arguments against motion. They can be described as follows. Suppose you are walking from one end of a stadium to the other. To do this you must get to the halfway

* Nearchus was the tyrant of Elea where Parmenides and Zeno lived.

point. But to get there, you have to get to the place halfway to the half-way point. Indeed to get to any point you have to get halfway to it, but first you have to get halfway to that halfway, and before that halfway – and so on ad infinitum. But one cannot traverse an infinite number of points in a finite time; therefore motion is an illusion.

Again, consider Achilles racing a tortoise. If the tortoise is given a head start, however small, Achilles can never overtake it. For to do so he must reach the point from which the tortoise started; but by the time he does so, the tortoise will have moved on, and Achilles must therefore reach that next point. But by the time he does so . . . and so on.

A third argument is this. Consider an arrow fired at a target. At any point in its flight the arrow occupies exactly the space that is its length. It is therefore motionless in that space, for (says Zeno) all things are at rest when occupying a space equal to their own size. But then because the arrow occupies its own exact space at every point on its flight, it is motionless at every point in its flight.

Some answers are suggested by Aristotle himself. Zeno's argument assumes that it is impossible to traverse an infinite number of points in a finite time. But this is to fail to distinguish infinite divisibility and infinite extension. One cannot traverse an infinite extension in a finite time, but one can an infinitely divisible space, for time itself is infinitely divisible; so one is traversing an infinitely divisible space in an infinitely divisible time.

As to the arrow argument: Aristotle says that it depends on the assumption 'that time is composed of "nows" [that is, discrete inter-vals]. If this is not conceded, the deduction will not go through.'

Zeno's arguments are so framed as to suggest that he principally had the Pythagoreans in mind. In arguing that number is the basis of real-ity they correlatively held that things are sums of units. Zeno is reported to have said, 'If anyone can explain to me what a unit is, I can say what things are.' He here offers a classic case of deducing a contradiction from the premise 'that there are many things', as follows: 'If things are a many [a plurality], they must be just as many as they are, and neither more nor less. Now, if they are as many as they are, they will be finite in number. But: if things are a many, they will be infinite in number, for there will always be other things between them, and others again between those. And so things are infinite in number.'

Another argument against plurality turns on the supposition that things can be divided into parts. You have to assume that the parts themselves have to be something, because if the divisions of things finally reach nothing, how can something be composed out of nothing? Suppose you argue that the parts are not nothing, but have no size; how then can the thing they compose have size, given that no number of things without size can constitute a thing with size? So you are left with the assumption that the elements of things have to be something, and with a size. But then they are not the elements of things, because they can be further divided, and if their parts in turn have size they are therefore divisible, and their parts likewise – and so on; so the dividings can never stop.

The Pythagoreans also appear to be the target in Zeno's argument against space, given their doctrine about air coming into the cosmos from outside the cosmos. 'If there is space, it will be in something, for all that is, is in something, and what is in something is in space. So space will be in space, and this goes on ad infinitum; therefore there is no space.' Leaving aside the assumption that space is regarded as a container in something like Newton's sense of absolute space, rather than (say) a set of relationships between objects, and whether there are fallacies of equivocation (that is, multiple senses in the same word) in the words 'something' and 'in', there is the question why the concept of infinite space should be intrinsically incoherent, as Zeno assumes.

This raises the question of Zeno's deployment of the concept of infinity. What has come to be called 'the standard solution' to Zeno's paradoxes of motion invokes calculus, invented independently by Newton and Leibniz in the seventeenth century, and his talk of infinity prompts discussions about actual and potential infinities, the concept of the former only receiving a full formal defence in the work of the mathematicians Richard Dedekind and Georg Cantor at the turn of the twentieth century. Ideas variously to the effect that the elements of physical reality cannot be infinitely divisible, that the notion of space, or of perceived reality as a whole, is contradictory, that there is a need to construct paraconsistent logics in which both arms of contradictions can be held to be true, are just some of the outcomes that reflection on Zeno's paradoxes has prompted.

One relevant consideration for paradoxes such as the 'Stadium' and 'Achilles' is that if you sum $\frac{1}{2} + \frac{1}{4} + \frac{1}{8} \ldots$ you get 1 for intervals of both space and time. So if you sum the distances that one must traverse to get to each halfway point (halfway across the stadium, halfway to that halfway point, and so on) you get the finite distance between the two ends of the stadium. The same applies to the time that elapses for each successive act of getting to a given point, then to a next given point, and so on. Once again, the conclusion is that one can traverse an infinitely divisible space in a finite time.

A suggestive result of reflection on the paradoxes is that they arise from conflicts between the conceptual conveniences we put to work to organize our experience. For example: when we are thinking of motion as a continuous event that occurs over an interval of time, we are thinking of an object travelling from one position to another against a background of fixed reference points, and from this perspective we do not, and arguably cannot, think of the object as being successively and determinately at given points in space different from immediately neighbouring points at discrete instants of time. But when we think of the object from this second and different perspective, namely the perspective of it being at a given point in its journey, we do not and arguably cannot think of it in the way we think of it from the first perspective, that is, as passing through that point in a way unspecifiable as 'a place at a time', given that this is exactly what we are doing from the second perspective. The problem therefore lies in us; sometimes our ways of describing the same things for different purposes from different perspectives are inconsistent with each other. This does not entail that motion itself is illusory.

Whatever the merits of Zeno's arguments individually, and however well the counterarguments to them fare, the fact is that they further provoke reflection on the Parmenidean idea that so influenced Plato and a great deal of subsequent philosophy: the idea, namely, that appearance is not reality.

EMPEDOCLES

Like Parmenides, Empedocles was born to a wealthy and influential family, and played a part in the politics of the city of his birth, Acragas in Sicily. Although he was an aristocrat he favoured the democratic party, but apparently kept his aristocratic ways, dressing flamboyantly, claiming to have superior talents and disdaining modesty about them: 'I go among you, an immortal god, no longer mortal, honoured by you all, wreathed in garlands and crowns.' He might have earned some at least of this reputation because, as a physician, he had performed some notable medical feats, saving another Sicilian city, Selinus, from the plague, and allegedly engaging in sorcery and magical acts. Among his powers he claimed to be able to control the winds and storms, to reverse old age and to avert evil. 'To whatever famous town I go,' he wrote, 'I am praised by men and women, and accompanied by thousands, who thirst for deliverance, some asking for prophecies, and some to be cured from all kinds of diseases.'

His reputation as a medical man seems to have been based on more than pretensions to magic. Galen describes him as the founder of the Italian school of medicine, equal in importance to other medical traditions of the time. His school taught that illness results from imbalance of heat, cold, dampness and dryness, these properties in different combinations being associated with the four elements he identified as the basis of all things: fire, air, water and earth. Some of the school's doctrines seem perceptive, as for example that respiration occurs through all the body's pores and not just the lungs, and is connected with the movement of the blood. In other respects they bear the marks of more primitive thought, for example locating the seat of consciousness in the heart.

The proximity of his home city to both Croton and Elea makes it very plausible that, as he is said to have done, Empedocles studied with both Parmenides – indeed, as a fellow-student of Zeno's – and the Pythagoreans. One story has it that he was indeed a Pythagorean but was expelled by the order for stealing some discourses. The claim that he was for at least a time a Pythagorean, and certainly influenced by that school, is supported by his vegetarianism and belief in metempsychosis.

Empedocles wrote in verse, as Parmenides had done, and was the last of the Greek philosophers to do so. There was not another great philosophical poem until *De Rerum Natura* by Lucretius in the first century BCE. Far more of Empedocles' writings survive than those of any other Presocratic; on one estimate about a fifth of the lines from his poem *On Nature* are known. Among his other poems was one called *Purifications*, and he is said to have written an account of the invasion of Greece by Xerxes, a hymn to Apollo, a treatise on medicine, and plays. What is understood about his views has been influenced by the twentieth-century discovery of a papyrus – the Strasbourg Papyrus – containing lines by him, suggesting an alternative arrangement of their order which hints at different ways of interpreting his views.

Empedocles' cosmology is premised on the idea that there are four eternal and indestructible elements, or 'roots' as he called them, from the combinations of which all things arise. He was the first to introduce this fourfold *arche*. He said that things are mixtures of the four roots in different proportions, and change is the process of the four roots combining and separating when acted upon by one or other of two motive powers which he called 'Love' and 'Strife' respectively. These powers fluctuate in strength relative to one another, which explains how first one then the other can result in the aggregation and then segregation of things.

The cosmos is eternal, and passes through cycles determined by whether it is Love or Strife that has the overall upper hand. In its best state the cosmos is inert, the two powers at rest and the four roots in unmixed separate equilibrium. It is a sphere, held together by Love, with Strife guarding the outer periphery. The notion of a still, inert sphere is Parmenidean in inspiration, but Empedocles' sphere does not long remain in stasis, for Strife begins to wax in power, pulling at the bonds forged by Love and thus initiating a tug of war between them from which arises the plurality of things. As Strife's power grows ever greater the struggle eventually plunges the cosmos into chaos. No life can exist in this part of its cycle. But then Love's power starts to wax in its turn, and the cosmos passes through another phase of tug of war in which things arise out of the mixtures of the elements. Finally Love's victory brings the cycle to another resting point of inertness; and the cycle begins again.

An intriguing aspect of Empedocles' theory is his view that the combinations of elements are random, producing a multiplicity of weird things such as animals' heads on human bodies, shoulders without arms, hermaphrodites and other such malformations, which disappear as quickly as they appear because only the well-adapted ones survive and reproduce themselves.

He thought that we see by emitting streams of light from our eyes that illuminate the objects we look at, and that the whole surface of our skin is a sensory organ receptive to the effluences given off by things around us, with the combinations of elements constituting us responding to the combinations of elements in things outside us, so that we know them because of our similarity to them.

He had learned from Parmenides to think of the senses as delusive, and therefore argued that we must apply reason in order to grasp the nature of things from all perspectives. From the Pythagoreans he took the doctrine of metempsychosis, and thought with them that the acquisition of knowledge so purifies the soul that it can escape the cycle of rebirth.

Empedocles' death is surrounded by anecdote, the best known of which is that he leaped into Etna in order to disappear completely, so that people might think he had been assumed into heaven without dying, thus confirming his divine status; but that his ploy was found out because the boiling lava ejected one his famous golden sandals on to the lip of the crater. Variations of this story exist, jointly prompting the couplet, 'Great Empedocles, that ardent soul, / Leapt into Etna, and was roasted whole.' A more sober alternative, also recounted by Diogenes Laertius, is that he broke a thigh when old, died soon afterwards and was buried in Megara where his tomb was known in antiquity.

Reflection on Empedocles' views, as with those of other Presocratics, shows in what ways they are not as fanciful as they at first seem. The four 'roots' identified by Empedocles – earth, air, fire and water – can be seen as embodying or representing the forms in which physical things exist, as solids, liquids or gases and as combinations of these. Aristotle says that Empedocles intended us to understand that fire stands in a particular relation to the other three, as acting upon them in the course of their Love- and Strife-driven interactions. His inclusion of air, which he called *aither* rather than *aer* in order to distinguish his own from Anaximenes' view, was based on the discovery that air is an actual physical substance. It is said that he showed this experimentally by means of a clepsydra or water clock, by putting his thumb over the spout, inverting it and submerging it in water, then removing his thumb so that the trapped air bubbled out, thus demonstrating its real existence to those who had been waving their hands in front of their faces to support their claim that there was nothing there. Some, rather hyperbolically, have claimed that this is the first scientific experiment on record.

Consider also Empedocles' account of the forces that impel change in the form of aggregation and disaggregation of the elements: 'Love' (*philotes*; some translators prefer 'Friendship') and 'Strife' (*neikos*). In humans these are emotions that govern a great many of the interactions between people, and as in other Presocratics the need for an explanation of how the related phenomena of change and motion arise is attractively offered by generalization from our experience of agency, and in particular how emotions

of attraction and repulsion in general explain connections and discon-
nections with others. In the absence of other candidates for a motive
force or forces, projection from the one clear and familiar example of
such a thing is understandable.

Aristotle had nominated Zeno as the originator of dialectic; to
Empedocles he gave the credit for being the originator of rhetoric. This
was no doubt because of his reputation as a great orator, and for the
eloquence of his poems.

ANAXAGORAS

In 467 BCE the Greek world was stirred by a dramatic event: a large
meteorite – 'as large as a wagon-load' – fell from the sky into the Aigos-
potamos in the Dardanelles. From around the same time observations
were reported of a comet, now thought to have been Halley's comet. In
the usual way that legends accrete around individuals of note, Anaxagoras was said to have predicted the arrival of the fallen meteorite; an
impossibility, and more illustrative of his reputation in his own and
succeeding times than of his powers as a scientist. In addition to his
intellectual reputation he acquired another, as the stereotypical absent-
minded thinker who forgoes worldly things to devote himself to a life
of enquiry and reflection.

Anaxagoras was born in Clazomenae in Ionia about 500 BCE or perhaps a little earlier, making him an older contemporary of Empedocles.
The doxographers say that he was a pupil of Anaximenes, but this is
extremely unlikely given that the best dates we have for both tell us
that Anaximenes died before Anaxagoras was born. However, what
could be meant is that he began his philosophical career under the
influence of Anaximenes' views, a probability supported by Theophrastus' remark that Anaxagoras was 'an associate of the philosophy
of Anaximenes'.

An interesting aspect of Anaxagoras' story is that he is the first of
the notable philosophers to make his career in Athens, and moreover
that he arrived in Athens in 480 BCE, the year of the naval battle of
Salamis, in which the Greek allies under Themistocles decisively beat
Xerxes' Persians, thus ending the threat posed by the latter's invasion
of the Greek world. The Persians had long been in control of the Greek
cities on the eastern side of the Aegean, however, including of course

those in Ionia, which meant that Anaxagoras was technically a Persian subject. This in turn suggests that he might have come to Athens in the Persian army.

Whether or not this is so, he was already a philosopher, and of sufficient note as to become, so Plato tells us in the *Phaedrus*, tutor to the young Pericles, later the greatest statesman of the age. Anaxagoras taught him 'the theory of things on high', says Plato, and 'knowledge of the true nature of mind and intellect'. A less secure tradition says that Anaxagoras was also the tutor of the playwright Euripides.

The association with Pericles was a fateful one, for it probably played its part in Anaxagoras being brought to trial in 450 BCE on charges of impiety. The charges were brought by Cleon, a general of the Athenian army in the First Peloponnesian War. Cleon was a political opponent of Pericles, and is described by both Thucydides and Aristophanes as an unscrupulous man. The allegation in the charge against Anaxagoras related to his theory about the nature of the sun and moon – namely, that the former is a red-hot stone and the latter is the same in substance as the earth. Pericles is said to have spoken in Anaxagoras' defence at the trial, and afterwards to have arranged for him to be released (or perhaps to escape) from prison and to leave Athens. He went back to Ionia, and at length settled in a colony of Miletus in the Troad, at Lampsacus. When he died the Lampsacenes dedicated an altar to Truth and Mind in his memory, and the date of his death was thereafter an annual school holiday for children. Apparently he had requested that this should be so.

Diogenes Laertius says that Anaxagoras wrote a book in an eloquent and pleasing style. What remains of it now are some quotations from its first part, preserved by Simplicius.

Like Empedocles, Anaxagoras had to grapple with the challenge posed by Parmenides: how to account for the world of plurality and change presented to us by our senses, in the light of Parmenidean arguments against both, and the metaphysical problem of what ultimately exists. He accepted Parmenides' view that what ultimately exists must be unchangeable and eternal, to which nothing can be added and from which nothing can be taken away. He either agreed with Empedocles – assuming he knew his work, which is quite likely – or he arrived independently at the same conclusion, that 'coming to be' and 'passing away' are not creation and destruction but in fact rearrangements – mixings and separations of eternally existing elements.

But he added the idea that the fundamental elements or 'seeds', *panspermia*, of things are always all present together in everything, individual things being differentiated from one another only by the preponderance of one over the others, not by the absence of the others. It follows that the elements are never separated from one another into their pure forms, as Empedocles thought must happen in what he had described as the resting state of the universal cycle.

What originally exists before the worlds come into existence, said Anaxagoras, is an undifferentiated and unlimited mass of stuff, consisting of an indiscriminate mixture of the seeds of things, each of them itself composed of infinitely small parts. In addition there is *nous*, 'mind' or 'reason', which acts upon this mass, puts it in motion and thereby produces individual things by aggregation of seeds, and their demise by separation of the seeds. Every individual thing has every kind of seed in it, but as mentioned they will have the character of whichever one is present in the largest quantity. There is no void, no 'nothingness'; the universe is everything there is; and in support of this he gave, as did Empedocles before him, experimental demonstrations of the real corporeal existence of air to show that it is not the 'nothing' that the senses seem to suggest.

The idea of *nous* as the external cause acting on the mass of seeds was required in response to Parmenides' argument that body has no motive force of itself. Anaxagoras' predecessors in the Ionian tradition appear simply to have assumed that the *arche* is self-moving or inherently causal, but the views of Empedocles and Heraclitus had introduced the idea of causal agency separate from and additional to the elements: Love and Strife, the operation of *logos* or *nous*. But it would be a mistake to think that Anaxagoras' *nous* is an immaterial thing, as 'mind' came to be viewed; he says it is the 'thinnest of all things', can penetrate everywhere among the other seeds and is itself 'pure' or unmixed, which gives it causal efficacy with respect to everything else, or as he puts it 'power over' the rest. Yet puzzlingly he also says that *nous* 'knows all things', as an infinite mind would do; unless he means that it is 'acquainted' in the sense of 'in contact with' all things.

Aristotle's criticism of Anaxagoras' conception of *nous* is that it is merely an expedient filler of explanatory gaps: 'Whenever he is at a loss to explain why anything necessarily is, he drags it in.' The concept works rather like 'the god of the gaps' argument, invoking a deity at any opportunity to explain what seems inexplicable. It is certainly hard to find a justification in the fragments for how *nous* imparts a 'rotary motion' to the initial mixture of things, thereby causing separation of cold from hot, rare from dense, dry from wet, and so on – though never completely; the dry always has a little wet in it, the hot always a little cold, and vice versa. Eventually the swirl of separation produces two separate masses, one with a preponderance of the hot, light, dry and rare elements, the other with a preponderance of the cold, dark, wet and dense elements. The first is *aether* or fire, the second is air.

Because it has a preponderance of rare over dense, aether constitutes the 'outside' and air, being more dense, constitutes the 'inside' of the world. Air then aggregates into clouds, water and earth, and earth into stones. There are many worlds, one fragment suggests; and if this is what Anaxagoras meant he is in conformity with the Ionian tradition before him on this point. He thought the earth is flat, and rides on air; earthquakes result from turbulence in the air under the earth. He said that rivers get their water from rain and the oceans get their water from rivers, though the Nile gets its water from snows melting in Ethiopia. The stars are stones that were torn from earth and made red-hot by the speed of their flight, but we do not feel their heat because they are too far away. They, along with the sun and moon which are also hot stones, are carried by the rotary motion of the aether. The sun is – more accurately, feels – hotter than the stars because it is not so far up. It is bigger than the Peloponnese, and its light is reflected from the moon as moonlight. Lunar eclipses occur when the moon passes into the shadow cast by the earth when it is between the sun and moon.

Much of this is very astute. Anaxagoras must have had exceptionally clear eyesight, for he said that the moon, which is the same as the earth in physical composition, has plains and valleys in it. But he was perceptive in other ways too; he said that plants are living creatures, and they and animals of course come from the same original *panspermia* or seeds of things, differing only by the admixtures within them. His theory of perception is that we sense things 'by opposites', as when I sense that the same bowl of water is cool if my hand is hot, but warm if my hand is cool. The image on the pupil of the eye has to be a different colour from the pupil in order to be seen. We see less well at night because things then have colours closer to the colour of the eye's pupil.

Anaxagoras is an interesting case-study in the Presocratic moment of philosophy, because in his theory the combination of *a priori* reasoning and inductions from observation, typical enough not just of philosophy's beginnings but of its entire history, manifests itself in clear outline. What he says about the source of river water, eclipses of the moon and some of the phenomena of sensory perception interestingly anticipates not just later views but the possibility of empirical verification of them. What he accepts from Parmenides about how reality has to be – namely, eternal and unchanging in its fundamental nature – and how he solves the problem this raises – how therefore can there be change, growth and decay? – is a paradigm of philosophy's early grappling with the question of appearance and reality – the perennial problem. His approach to these questions is a paradigm in another way too: of reason operating on observation, when these are the only available instruments of enquiry.

LEUCIPPUS AND DEMOCRITUS

It is not clear whether the idea of 'seeds' in Anaxagoras' theory had any influence on the atomism of Democritus and Leucippus, but there is at least a superficial similarity in the basic conception.

Atomism is the theory that everything is composed of tiny imperceptible objects each of which is 'uncuttable' (*atomos* means 'uncuttable' or 'indivisible'). It was the chief competitor to the systems, different in other respects but alike in not being mechanistic, put forward by Plato and Aristotle. The atomism of Leucippus and Democritus appears to deal so well with the problems bequeathed by Parmenides and addressed by the other post-Parmenidean Presocratics that Aristotle, impressed even though he disagreed, felt obliged to study atomism in great detail. He therefore wrote a work in several volumes on Democritus – alas, lost save for a few fragments quoted by Simplicius.*

Hardly anything is known about Leucippus, and it is even possible that he did not exist – indeed Epicurus, whom we meet later, denied that he did. Other doxographers variously say that he was born at Miletus in Ionia or Elea in Italy – that is, on one or other extremity of the Greek world, which suggests that this is evidence not so much about where he was born as about the combination of Ionian and Eleatic

---

* The geographical propinquities of the philosophers often suggest reasons for influence and interest among them. Aristotle's birthplace, Stagira, was not far from Abdera, where Democritus and perhaps also Leucippus came from.

elements in the philosophy attributed to him. Yet other traditions say that he was born in Abdera in Thrace, on the northern extremity of the Greek world; this is where his pupil Democritus hailed from.

Assuming that Leucippus existed, and he probably did, the books attributed to him, *On Mind* and *The Great World System* ('Macrocosmos'), were written some time about 440–430 BCE. He was therefore a contemporary of Empedocles and Anaxagoras, and like theirs his thinking was shaped in response to Parmenides. Democritus was born about 460 BCE, and he was reputed to have lived until he was a hundred years old. That means he was not only a contemporary of Socrates and Plato, but was still alive when Aristotle was studying with Plato. He was a great traveller, leaving among his many books accounts of his journeys around the ancient world, even to India according to some doxographers. Indeed he was a very prolific author, for in addition to his philosophical works, which ranged over metaphysics, ethics, mathematics and natural science, he also wrote on farming, art, medicine, grammar, literature and military matters. Some more recent commentators think that many of these books might have been written by his pupils in Abdera; rather as with the treatises attributed to Hippocrates, they would thus be the productions of a school, not of an individual. In any case one of the philosophical works more securely attributed to him was entitled *The Little World System* ('Microcosmos'), a tribute to his teacher Leucippus.

The works of Democritus are among the lost treasures of the ancient world, surviving only as quotations and *testimonia* as in the case of so many others. But there is an added consideration here, which is that most of the quotations and reports are from Aristotle and the commentators on Aristotle, which means that we see atomism through the eyes of its opponents.

The nub of the atomic theory is that there is an infinite number of uncuttable, indivisible, fundamental entities which are eternal and unchangeable in every respect but position. Their eternal and immutable nature makes them satisfy the Parmenidean requirement for reality. In addition to them there is 'the void', nothingness – but nothingness is real, contrary to Parmenides' claim that there cannot be nothingness. The void is like space in that it separates the atoms, which are therefore able to move in the void, and to bump into one another; the idea is that their various shapes make it possible for them to link together into larger agglomerations, and for the agglomerations to break apart again later, thus giving rise to all the phenomena of things and their changes in the sensible world. This captures the idea, found also in Empedocles and Anaxagoras, that 'coming-to-be' and 'passing-away' are just changes, not actual creations and destructions of what exists.

The atomists called atoms 'What Is' and the void 'What Is Not'. Aristotle in the *Metaphysics* describes the atomists' account of how atoms constitute things as follows: 'They declare that the differences [between atoms, 'What Is'] are three: shape, arrangement and position. They say that What Is differs only in "rhythm", "touching" and "turn-ing" – "rhythm" is shape, "touching" is arrangement, and "turning" is position. Thus A differs from N in shape, AN from NA in arrange-ment, and Z from N in position.' And he then adds, 'Concerning the origin and manner of motion in existing things, these men also, like all the others, lazily neglect to give an explanation.'

The most authoritative account of the atomic theory occurs in a long quotation Simplicius gives from Aristotle's book on Democritus, where he writes:

> Democritus believes that the nature of the eternal things is small sub-stances which are infinite in number. As a place for these he hypothesizes something else which is infinite in size, and he calls it 'the void', 'nothing', 'the unlimited'. The substances he calls 'thing' and 'the compact' and 'What Is'. They have all kinds of forms and shapes and differences in size. Out of these elements he generates perceptible bodies. They are at odds with one another and move in the void because of their dissimilarity and other differences, and as they move they strike against one another and become entangled . . . the bodies fit together and hold each other fast. For some of them are rough, some are hooked, others concave, and others convex, while yet others have innumerable other differences. So he thinks that they cling to each other and stay together until some stronger necessity comes along from the environment and shakes them and scat-ters them.

Note that in this account Aristotle reports an explanation offered by the atomists for motion: that the atoms 'move in the void because of their dissimilarity and other differences'. Theophrastus reports that Leucippus had said that one could infer, from the unceasing change and motion of the things we experience, that their parts must be in unceas-ing activity too. So they were not so lazy on that point, as Aristotle had complained, but instead offered a naturalistic theory which dispensed with appeals to metaphors of 'Love' and 'Strife' and 'Justice' as putative explanations of motion and change.

As regards an 'explanation of the origin . . . of existing things' two comments might be offered. Atomism certainly offers an explanation of sensible phenomena, this being the combinings and separations of the atoms. In this sense the atomists do what the Ionian Presocratics previously did, which is to say how the *arche* gives rise to, or constitutes, the world we experience. By contrast, it is hard to find in Parmenides an account of why the world *seems* to us as it does, as a plural and changing realm, other than by just saying our senses are 'deceitful'. Aristotle of course meant that the atomists did not offer an account of how atoms and the void come into being in the first place; but then neither does anyone else say how reality, or whatever *arche* they nominate, comes to be.

But what is interesting about the atomists' response to the Parmenidean challenge – namely, that anything real must be eternal and unchanging – is that it both accepts it and defends pluralism. The Parmenidean argument was that, if there were many things, each must have the same character as the One; and the atomists in effect said, 'Fine; but why can't there be infinitely many things with the metaphysical properties of what the Eleatics call the One?' On the question of infinite divisibility they rebutted Zeno's argument in effect by accepting it; Zeno had said that it is incoherent to assume infinite divisibility, and the atomists said, 'We agree, which is why we argue that the atoms are, as the name implies, not divisible infinitely or otherwise.'

As with their predecessors the atomists offered views about the heavenly bodies, perception, and the contrast between what Democritus called 'true-born' and 'bastard' knowledge. Whereas the cosmologies of the ancients can illuminate the metaphysical and epistemological views that underwrite them, they otherwise have, in the main, historical interest only, and this might be said also of the atomists' account of the sun, moon and stars, and of the 'vortex' in which (oddly, given that in centrifugal systems the heaviest objects are flung the furthest) heavier bodies lie at the centre of the cosmos. Theophrastus is the chief source for what the atomists say on these matters.

Along with the philosophies of Plato and Aristotle, atomism is the most influential of the ancient philosophies. It was the inspiration for Epicurus later, and through him of the Latin metaphysical poem *De*

Rerum Natura by Lucretius, and eventually of the science of the modern world in the ideas of Gassendi and the seventeenth-century 'corpuscularians' ('corpuscle' is in effect another word for 'atom' though it means 'little body' rather than 'uncuttable thing'). These views have been praised as a high point in Presocratic philosophy by such scholars as Jonathan Barnes, who describes atomism as 'the culmination of early Greek thought', and Theodor Gomperz, who said it was 'The ripe fruit on the tree of the old Ionic doctrine of matter'. As just noted, however, this Ionic fruit was served by the atomists in an Eleatic dish; hence its greatly enhanced intellectual piquancy.

THE SOPHISTS

In the original meaning of the word, a 'sophist' was an educated person with expertise in one or more fields of learning (*sophos* means 'clever', 'skilful', 'wise'). By the fifth century BCE 'sophist' had come to designate something more specific than this: a person who made a profession – and earned a living thereby – out of offering to teach the techniques of rhetoric and oratory. Being good at public speaking was a highly prized skill in the cities of classical Greece, still largely an oral culture and certainly one where the reputations and status of individuals turned in significant part on the showing they made in public debates – in advocacy, by eloquence, persuasiveness and power of command over an audience. Because this was such a desirable skill, sophists made a good living teaching it. It was at a particular premium in the Athenian democracy of the fifth century, where political and legal debate lay at the centre of the city's life.

Socrates and Plato disliked the sophists on the grounds that they offered to teach, in exchange for money, the ability to persuade others to any point of view, which meant that they taught people how to win arguments, not how to discover truth. In the *Euthydemus* Plato gives examples of the tricks that sophists offered to teach anyone wishing to beat opponents in debate. No doubt this was indeed what many sophists did, and because Socrates and Plato were critical of them the word 'sophist' now has a pejorative connotation. We talk of a tricksy argument as 'sophistical', the act of bamboozling others is called 'sophistry', and the word 'sophisticated' – though now used to describe a refined taste, superlative elegance, and the like – in its original meaning implies anything deliberately made complicated and bewildering in order to mislead others.

This denigratory view of the sophists is, although no doubt more justified than not, at the same time not entirely fair. In addition to teaching rhetoric and oratory the sophists also taught what was required to accompany an ability to be a good public speaker, for there is no use in being eloquent if you have nothing to be eloquent about – if you know no history or literature, if you know nothing about ideas, if you have never reflected on right and wrong, the state of society and how to live a successful life. Greek society had in general become more literate, wealthy and advanced in the fifth century BCE, and the desire for an education beyond the traditional basics of arithmetic, literacy and gymnastics had greatly increased. The theories of philosophers, and an interest in geography, history and other societies and cultures, fuelled the appetite for rational discussion and intelligent debate. The sophists accordingly were educators in more than just rhetoric, and part of what they offered to teach was a 'philosophy of life' or ethic. This aspect of what they did drew the particular attention of Socrates, whose own primary interest was the question of what constitutes a genuinely good life, and he therefore engaged with and challenged others, not least the sophists, to explain and justify their views on this matter.

Although they are bracketed together, the sophists were not a school and did not have a joint outlook or doctrine. They were individual teachers, travelling professors, even performers in that they gave displays of rhetoric also. They were not inclined to hide their lights under bushels, it seems, as we learn from Plato's account of the most famous of them: Protagoras, a native of Abdera where Democritus hailed from.

Protagoras lived between 490 and 420 BCE, and was one of Pericles' associates while the great statesman was alive. Plato gives a compelling portrait of him, having him say, 'My boy, if you associate with me, the result will be that the very day you begin you will return home a better person and the same will happen the next day too. Each day you will make progress.' Moreover, Protagoras claimed, the pupil will become stocked with good counsel, so that he can effectively manage both his household affairs and the affairs of the city; and he will be 'powerful in acting and in speaking'.

Other quotations from Protagoras, reported by Stobaeus, pseudo-Plutarch and others, suggest that he was no mere blusterer. He said that learning must begin early, that it must sink deep roots to be effective and that it requires much practice and dedication: 'Art without practice and practice without art are nothing.' But he also gave reason for Plato's antipathy towards him: he disliked mathematics – 'the subject matter is unknowable and the terminology distasteful' – and he is credited with being the first to state the view that 'there are two mutually opposed arguments on any subject,' one of the reasons invoked by later sceptics to deny the possibility of knowledge. It was on this basis that he also said that one could successfully argue either side of the same case: as one doxographer put it, 'Protagoras made the weaker the stronger argument and taught his students to blame and praise the same person.'

Plato puts a speech into Protagoras' mouth in which, after agreeing with Socrates that what should be taught is how to run a city and make good citizens, he sets out his view that good citizenship consists in the practice of justice and self-restraint. He says that these are natural propensities which education can and should foster in people, because they conduce to the preservation of good order in society, and therefore to the survival of its members. These views are unexceptionable.

But in the *Theaetetus* Plato reports another and more controversial of Protagoras' views, that 'man is the measure of all things, of things that are, that they are, and of things that are not that they are not,' which is said to be the opening sentence of his lost book *Truth*. This seems to be a statement of relativism, implying that there is no objective truth, but that what is true for one person might not be true for another, truth being relative to the different experiences or circumstances of different people. Before refuting this view Socrates explores ways in which it might be the case that different points of view have validity although appearing to contradict each other; for example, one city might have a law against something which in another city is permitted. Then a citizen of the first can say, 'such-and-such is wrong' while the citizen of the second can say, 'such-and-such is not wrong,' and they can both be right. But this is not what Protagoras' contemporaries and successors took him to be saying; they saw him as asserting subjective relativism, which has two people holding with equal personal justification opposite views on the same question, no adjudication between them being possible.

This view does not look consistent with the idea that justice and continence must be universally accepted in order for society – indeed, for the human species itself – to survive, as Plato reported Protagoras as arguing. The point is a significant one, for one of the great debates of the fifth century BCE concerned the question of convention or law, as invented by humans, versus nature: *nomos* (law) versus *phusis* (nature). Are moral norms the result of human agreement and custom, or are they rooted in the nature of reality? There was widespread agreement that for morality to be genuinely authoritative, the latter must be the case. This allowed critics of conventional morality to argue that as it was merely the product of human preference it should be rejected. Defenders of conventional morality replied that it did indeed have its roots in nature.

The debate was a vigorous one. In his dialogue *Gorgias*, named for another famous sophist, Plato has Gorgias' pupil Callicles argue thus: conventional morality was invented by the weak to protect themselves against the strong, inhibiting the latter from doing what by nature they have a right to do, which is to use their inferiors for their convenience. The genuine norms are those exemplified by beasts, which behave wholly in accord with what nature dictates. A somewhat milder version of this view is held by Thrasymachus in the first book of Plato's *Republic*, where he praises the tyrant who overcomes the restraints of conventional morality in order to assert himself.* Where Callicles and Thrasymachus agree is in holding that a life of self-assertion is a supremely happy life, because it is lived in accordance with nature.

In his speech in the *Protagoras*, Protagoras is on the side of those who hold that moral conventions arise from nature. The inconsistency of this with his famous 'man is the measure' view therefore raises the question of what exactly he meant. The fragmentary nature of the evidence leaves it open that there could be an interpretation which eliminates the inconsistency; this much is suggested by a fragment in which the word *chremata*, 'things used', occurs, suggesting that differences of subjective attitude apply to things produced by human choice and thought – especially beliefs, attitudes and judgments – rather than to things determined by nature. Since the basis of morality lies in nature, as Protagoras otherwise held, there would not be two opposed but equally supportable truths about it as there would be in the kind of

---

* If these views appear to anticipate Nietzsche, they do so only in part; Nietzsche certainly described 'slave morality' as the weak's promotion of their sufferings and vulnerabilities into virtues, and argued that the 'Superman' should assert himself positively instead; but not as I read him at the expense of anyone less robust.

case where one person feels cold while another feels hot in the same place on the same day.

That way of reconciling the conflict in Protagoras' views runs into the difficulty, however, that his celebrated dictum 'man is the measure of all things' reminds one of Aristotle's definition of truth and falsity, and its contrast with Protagoras' view: 'To say of what is that it is not, or of what is not that it is, is false; while to say of what is that it is, and of what is not that it is not, is true.' Protagoras seems to be asserting that what we say *makes things be* as we say they are; Aristotle's definition tells us that what we say must *correspond to how things are* in order to be true. Hamlet says, 'there is nothing either good or bad, but thinking makes it so'; Protagoras appears to be saying that *everything* is what people say it is, as opposed to being objectively the way it is, independently of our interests. This would indeed conflict with the view ascribed to him in the *Protagoras* that there are natural propensities in people to manifest restraint and a sense of justice.

Among other leading sophists mentioned by Plato in his writings we have seen one name, Gorgias, already; others that merit mention are Prodicus, Hippias, Antiphon and Critias.

Gorgias, a contemporary of Protagoras, was born in Leontini in Sicily. He lived until he was a hundred years of age, and became celebrated for his elaborate rhetorical style in both speech and writing. He is said to have taken Athens by storm when visiting there on a diplomatic mission in 427 BCE, because he gave public displays of his oratorical and rhetorical skills, demonstrating the power of persuasion in a defence of Helen of Troy. To do this he chose the most indefensible of the reasons for her going to Troy with Paris, namely that he persuaded her to do so (the other reasons were that fate, necessity or the spell cast by Aphrodite made her helpless in the case, and therefore unblameable). This is an example of making the weaker case the stronger.

Prodicus was a native of Ceos, an island in the Aegean near the coast of Attica. His date of birth is estimated at 460 BCE, making him a contemporary of Socrates, and indeed it is said that he was an associate, and perhaps even a teacher, of Socrates. A passing remark by one Didymus the Blind says that Prodicus denied that contradictions are possible, on the grounds that if two people appear to be contradicting one another in conversation, they cannot be speaking about the same thing. He is also said to have denied the existence of the gods; this puts him in the same boat as Protagoras, who was also either an agnostic or an atheist, if certain quotations from him bear that interpretation. Perhaps this is another reason that Plato disliked the sophists.

As a result of his fame as a teacher and speaker Prodicus grew wealthy, and so did Hippias, the fourth of this group of famous sophists. Hippias was born at Elis in the Peloponnese; his dates are unclear, but he was known to be still alive when Socrates died in 399 BCE. He was a man of wide interests, who in addition to teaching rhetoric and mnemonics (the art of memory) contributed to mathematics and made a collection of poetic and philosophical texts. He was celebrated for his speeches, which included improvised discourses on any subject proposed by members of his audience. The breadth of his interests and talents prompted Plato to poke fun at him, saying that he was such a polymath that he could even cobble his own shoes. A remark attributed to him by Xenophon is 'How can anyone take laws seriously, given that it often happens that the same people who make them later repeal them and put others in their place?'

Antiphon, an Athenian, was born about 480 BCE. He was a contributor to the debate about nature and convention in morality. He said that when in society one should obey the conventional laws, but when alone one should obey the laws of nature. He thought that conventional laws often contradict natural laws, making 'people suffer more pain when less is possible, have less pleasure when more is possible, and receive injury when it is not necessary.' Nevertheless he took the view that the power of rhetoric can make the worse seem the better in an argument, which presumably means that one could defend conventional morality against the claim of nature even when this makes people suffer more. 'However convincing the accusation is on behalf of the accuser,' he said, 'the defence can be just as convincing; for victory comes through speech.'

Critias was another Athenian, and an associate of Socrates. He was also an older relative of Plato's and therefore, like him, an aristocrat. He took the opposite view in the convention–nature debate, defending convention: 'Human life was once without order, on the level of the beasts, subject to force; there was no reward for the good or punishment for the bad. Then people established laws as punishers, so that justice could be the mighty ruler of all equally, and make violence its slave.' For him, as for Hobbes many centuries later, the state of nature was the source not of good but of ill, and it took the application of reason to bring justice into the world.

From the viewpoint of subsequent history, the antipathy felt by Plato for the sophists is highly consequential. The key point for Socrates and Plato is that philosophy is the pursuit of truth, and it cannot be constrained by the necessity of winning a case or earning a fee. In our own day we are rightly sceptical of expressions of opinion that have been paid for – 'sponsored editorials' in newspapers, pharmaceutical companies paying doctors to prescribe certain drugs, politicians acting on behalf of donors, and the like. The point that Socrates and Plato insisted on holds: that truth should not be for sale.

Socrates

'Socrates' is a character in Plato's dialogues, portrayed as the paradigm of the philosopher, disinterestedly pursuing truth, keen to promote clear thought, deep understanding and knowledge of virtue. He is portrayed as loved and admired by his friends and the young, as kindly and witty, and as ferociously clever.

But 'Socrates' is also the name of a real human being, and the great question – the 'Socratic question' – is how far Plato's dialogues actually represent the historical Socrates. There can be little doubt that the 'Socratic method' – the method of questioning, dialogue and cross-examination – was indeed Socrates' way, and there is no doubt that his chief, indeed almost exclusive, interest was ethics. But how much of the philosophy in Plato's dialogues is Socrates' philosophy, and how much is Plato's? The probable answer is that Plato's early dialogues are, to a fairly large extent, representative of the historical Socrates, but by the middle dialogues 'Socrates' has become a literary device for the exposition of Plato's own views.

Socrates was born in Athens around 470 BCE, and died there, in prison, in 399 BCE, having been condemned to death for 'impiety and corrupting the youth of Athens'. Although given every opportunity to escape, he chose to obey the law; he had been found guilty and condemned to death, so he dutifully drank the hemlock, and died as his fellow-citizens said he should.

The chief sources of our knowledge of Socrates are Plato's writings and to a lesser extent those of another of his pupils, Xenophon, though their accounts of him differ somewhat. For example, Plato (an urbanite) says that Socrates liked the town and disliked the country, whereas Xenophon (who loved the country) says the reverse. There are also reports of him in Antisthenes, Aristippus and Aeschines. He figures as the butt of jokes in Aristophanes' comedy *The Clouds* and in half a dozen other satirical plays.

He was consistent in his principles, showing courage in battle and dedication to his mission to persuade his fellows to think seriously about the nature of the good and worthwhile life. The famous or infamous Alcibiades, a handsome statesman and general who was at last the downfall of his own city of Athens, claimed to be in love with Socrates and to have tried unsuccessfully to seduce him. Although Socrates was married – to Xantippe, unkindly alleged to be a 'shrew' – he was not without an interest in beautiful boys, an acceptable proclivity in his day; in the *Charmides* he confesses to being flustered by the charms of the handsome boy of that name, but wished to talk to him to find out if he had that thing which is greater than physical beauty, namely, a noble soul.

A famous story has it that when a man called Chaerephon asked the oracle at Delphi who was the wisest man living, the oracle said 'Socrates'; and that Socrates was astonished to learn of this, until he realized that it was doubtless because he knew that he knew nothing. He did however see himself as a 'gadfly' stinging his fellows into reflection on questions about virtue and the best kind of life.

There are no reports of Socrates having written anything, though he is said to have co-authored or anyway contributed to some of the plays of his friend Euripides. As noted, it is plausible to think that the early dialogues of Plato give a fairly accurate picture of the real Socrates in both manner and opinions, but that by the middle and later dialogues Plato's own philosophy comes to the fore and the 'Socrates' who appears in them is his mouthpiece – and in some cases not a leader of the discussion but merely a participant; and indeed occasionally a defeated one, as in the *Parmenides*.

Perhaps the most accurate portrait of Socrates occurs in the *Apology*, which is the speech given by Socrates in his own defence at his trial. That this work accurately reports his speech in all main respects is very likely, given that its contents would have been public knowledge, and still in the memories of many when Plato published it. Moreover Plato says that he was present at Socrates' trial, a claim that could easily have been challenged by contemporaries were it untrue. If Plato had been prone to invent significant things he would almost certainly have claimed to be at Socrates' deathbed, but he reports that he was not there that day, because he was ill, and that he only learned at second-hand about the conversation between Socrates and other friends on that fatal day.* I think this further suggests that Plato was not in the close circle of Socrates' acquaintances – he would have been at Socrates' side on the day of his death had he been so, however ill. Socrates was a man in his seventies when he died, Plato in his twenties; the dramatic dates (so to speak) of many of Plato's dialogues predate his own birth; he never places himself among those present at those conversations. In short, the personal connection between them was likely the same as between a professor and the majority of university students who attend her classes. He was, however, an exceptionally gifted such student.

Taking it that the various accounts and caricatures of Socrates indicate something about the man Socrates, and that Plato's early dialogues give us some insight into the views and methods of Socrates the philosopher, one can venture an account of him as follows.†

Remember that the Athens of Socrates' lifetime was the Athens which had been triumphant as a leader of the Greek world in the war against Persia, and had become wealthy and powerful as a result. It was the Athens of Pericles, who had used the tribute from the states in Athens' new empire to adorn the city with beautiful temples and statuary and to sponsor the arts. In this high point of classical antiquity the great ideal was beauty, not least of the male form and face, and the social and political skills acquired by an education at the hands of leading sophists, skills that would lead to fame, honour, riches, influence and a high position in public service. Socrates was, in his person and manner of life, in effect a rejection of all this. He was famously ugly, with bulging eyes, a big snub nose and thick lips, a burly frame, an indifference to dress and personal cleanliness; and he had strange habits such as standing in a trance for entire days, lost in thought. He did not seek public honours or position, though he fought with notable courage alongside his fellows in the wars. He therefore stood out, an anomaly, an eccentric, all the more so for incessantly asking questions

---

* The works by Plato which relate to the trial and death of Socrates are *Euthyphro*, *Crito*, *Phaedo* and *Apology*. Near the *agora* of Plato's time as one visits it in today's Athens, one can see the outlines of the prison where Socrates was kept and died. He had a bath on the day that he drank the hemlock; only one of the cells in the prison had a bathroom attached, also visible in the outlines of the foundations; one can therefore stand on the likely spot where these signal events took place. For those who are moved by such things, the place is a considerable prompt to thought.

† The relevant early dialogues are *Laches*, *Charmides*, *Euthyphro*, *Crito*, *Apology*, *Protagoras*, *Meno*, *Gorgias*.

and confusing his interlocutors when they tried to answer them. One such, Meno in the dialogue named for him, after his several attempts at a definition of virtue have been refuted by Socrates, says to him, 'You are like a stingray, you have numbed my lips and tongue; I don't know what to say!' To which Socrates replies, 'Good! Now that you know that you don't know what you're talking about, we can begin to make progress!'

It was the Socrates of poverty and indifference to worldly things who was imitated by the Cynics later; it was the Socrates of dedication to thought and fidelity to principle who inspired the Stoics later; it was Socrates' preaching of the 'considered life' which inspired Aristotle to see reason as the distinguishing characteristic of humanity, and practical wisdom (*phronesis*) as the basis of ethics. And of course it was Socrates whom Plato took as his point of departure for a philosophical achievement of enormous range and influence.

The first thing to note about Socrates as a philosopher is his method, the 'Socratic method', known as *elenchus* or 'refutation'. It proceeds thus: Socrates asks his interlocutor for a definition of an important ethical concept such as justice, continence or courage. He wants to be told what is the essence of (say) courage, that single fundamental thing that defines all courageous actions and people. He does not want examples, or lists of characteristics that some courageous acts or people might exemplify and that timid or cowardly acts or people do not exemplify. Then, when a definition is offered, Socrates demonstrates that other things held by the interlocutor to be true are inconsistent with that definition.

A good example of the method is to be found in the *Laches*. Laches was a general in the Athenian army who knew of Socrates' courage in battle (Socrates fought as a hoplite – a heavily armed infantryman – in the battle of Potidaea, and was in the army with Laches on the retreat from Delium). In a discussion between them about how to train young men as hoplites, the question of the nature of courage arose, and Socrates asked Laches to define it. Laches said, 'Courage is endurance of the soul,' by which he meant steadfastness. But Socrates soon shows him that not all forms of steadfastness are good – for example, when it is merely stubbornness, or foolish bravado, or when it is displayed by a doctor refusing a sick patient's request for water when water would be harmful. So 'steadfastness' cannot be the essence of courage.

Another participant in the discussion is Nicias, an associate of the sophist Prodicus, whose technique of 'pulling words apart' – that is, drawing fine semantic distinctions and logic-chopping with them – is criticized by Socrates in this dialogue. Nicias offers a different definition; that courage is a form of knowledge, namely, knowledge of the grounds of hope and fear. Laches objects to Nicias' definition on the grounds that it entails that we cannot call lions and other such animals courageous; to which Nicias in effect replies, 'No, indeed you can't call them courageous, though you can call them fearless: these are not the same thing. You cannot call them courageous any more than you would call a human baby courageous who put its hand in the fire; for it is not courage when you are ignorant of the possibilities.' This is a good point, and although Socrates says, 'He has got this . . . from Prodicus, who of all sophists is considered the best puller-to-pieces of words,' he does not disagree with him about it. But he does disagree that 'knowledge of the grounds of hope and fear' is an adequate definition of courage, because (I paraphrase) 'hope and fear pertain to what lies in the future, but virtue applies to all times, and as courage is a virtue, it too must apply to all times, and not just to future possibilities. So, Nicias has given only a partial definition.'

And there, like all the early dialogues, the conversation ends: in *aporia*, inconclusiveness, no definition having been found. But at least the wrong or inadequate definitions have been exposed, and something has been learned along the way; namely, that one is ignorant about the true nature of X, whatever this happens to be, and that therefore one needs to think about it more.

Clarification, and awareness of one's ignorance, are good things. But if the method of *elenchus* is meant to lead to knowledge, it is not entirely satisfactory if it only ever produces knowledge of one's limitations. The central problem seems to be the Socratic quest for *essential* definitions. Does everything have an essence which can be captured in a definition? Is it not the case that some concepts apply when this or that subset of a larger group of characteristics applies, the subsets overlapping but not jointly and exhaustively constituting the 'essence' of the thing? Consider: courage on the battlefield, in the dental chair, in taking an examination for the fifth time, in living cheerfully among the creaks and pains of old age, in getting up every morning despite grief or despair – is there one essence of all these manifestations of courage?

In any case, on what grounds is it right to say that one cannot know what courage is unless one can give a definition of its supposed essence? The 'I know it when I see it' response is a good one in many cases, and it might be that unless one in some sense had knowledge of a thing, one would not be able to acquire further knowledge of it – suggesting that knowledge in some degree precedes being able to grasp the essence of a thing, if it has an essence. Another version of this thought is to ask, Do we not ascend to knowledge in general of something – say, knowledge of dogs – by first knowing individual or particular instances of that thing: this individual dog and that individual dog?

As it happens, Aristotle said that this was indeed Socrates' method, an inductive method of moving from the particular to the general, or of inference by analogy from examples to the whole. If so, matters are less satisfactory still, given the intrinsic insecurity of inductive arguments.* But there is also the sense one has, especially in the earlier dialogues, that Socrates himself is not entirely unsophistical. Take for example Laches' attempted definition: when he nominated 'steadfastness' he of course intended that to mean 'in the face of challenge, difficulty, threat or danger'. Socrates 'refuted' him by taking cases of steadfastness where these are not at issue. The fallacy seems to be his, not Laches'; a form of fallacy of equivocation made possible by refusing to consider the qualifications that nail down a general concept to a set of specific applications.

Socrates said that when he was young he heard philosophers lecture about the nature of reality and the cosmos, yet (like the poet in the *Rubáiyát of Omar Khayyám* who 'evermore came out by the same door as in I went') was none the wiser for it because the different theories went round and round fruitlessly, and – worse still – ignored the truly great question, as he saw it: the question of how to live. His focus was *arete*, a word that means 'virtue' and 'excellence', and which he construed as 'moral excellence'. He saw the chief virtues as courage, justice, temperance and wisdom. Virtue itself, he said, is knowledge. He thought that if one knew the right thing to do or be, one could not do or be otherwise; vice is ignorance, and ignorance makes vice possible. This means that the good life is the life examined and chosen; the 'considered life'. Indeed he said, 'the unconsidered life is not worth living.' A considered life is a life based on knowledge of right and wrong. This is why, Socrates claimed, nobody ever does a bad thing knowingly or deliberately; to do

* See the Appendix on logic.

a bad thing is harmful to oneself, and no one ever harms himself knowingly, by choice.

Noble as they are, these views do not bear much scrutiny, for they are not psychologically realistic. For one thing, they take no account of the possibility of *akrasia*, 'weakness of will', which is something most of us experience quite a lot of the time – think of the difficulties involved in dieting, giving up smoking, refusing temptation. Socrates in fact denies outright that there is such a thing as *akrasia*; he asks in Plato's *Protagoras*, 'How is it possible for someone to do something knowing it to be wrong?' The answer is – alas! – that it happens all the time. The proof is *ab esse ad posse*, 'from what is the case to what is possible'.

Socrates also believed in the unity of the virtues – that if a person has one of the virtues he has them all. But this too contradicts experience. An unjust person might be courageous, a just person timid. It is true that it seems improbable that an unwise person might be temperate – but then this raises the problem that wisdom and temperance are themselves not single universals; for a person might be wise as a father but unwise in business, temperate as to alcoholic drinks but intemperate as to chocolate. And so on.

Whether or not one agrees with everything Socrates appears to have said, there is no question that he serves well as an example of a philosopher seriously and sincerely engaged in trying to know, to understand, to work out the best kind of life, and to do it by thinking, discussing, finding out, challenging, reflecting – in short, a thinker committed to achieving clarity and to discovering the truth if possible.

Plato

In the standard but somewhat simplified picture of the great period of philosophy in classical antiquity, the figures of Socrates, Plato and Aristotle make a kind of trinity by lineage, Plato being the pupil of Socrates and the teacher of Aristotle. This is true, but stated thus baldly it might mislead. Plato was one of Socrates' devoted acolytes, and is named as one of the young men whom Socrates allegedly 'corrupted' by his teaching. But remember that Socrates' method was not conventionally didactic; he did not lecture and instruct, but enquired and discussed. He did not have a school, and did not offer himself as anyone's teacher. Plato, by contrast, founded an academic institution, and it had a curriculum (a condition of entry was knowledge of mathematics), and Plato himself had a wide-ranging, deep and interconnected set of views which he taught and which his most notable pupil, Aristotle, engaged with when, in his own turn, he founded a school and lectured to pupils in it.

Plato (c.425–347 BCE) came from a wealthy and aristocratic family. Because of his celebrity his biography soon became encrusted with legends; it was said that he was descended from early kings of Athens and from one of the Seven Sages, and that when he was an infant bees settled on his lips as an augury of the honeyed words that would later flow from them. It is certainly the case that he was well connected: many of the characters who appear in his dialogues are relatives, and many of these held leading positions in the political life of Athens. But he says little about himself, and even his name might be a pseudonym; it is thought that he might have been named Aristocles by his family, and that 'Plato', from *platon*, 'broad', was a nickname bestowed either by his wrestling-master because of his sturdy frame or by admirers for the breadth of his teaching.

Partly no doubt because of his aristocratic heritage, Plato was an opponent of the Athenian democracy whose failings resulted in the city's defeat by Sparta in the Peloponnesian War. He was also a vigorous opponent of the concept of democracy itself. Socrates' trial and execution were most probably the result of political turmoil in the years after Athens' defeat in 404 BCE. Socrates was executed in 399, and Plato's belief that political chaos must inevitably result in tyranny – because a tyrant would step in to restore order, only making matters worse thereby – underlay his view that the state should be run by 'philosopher-kings' living in monk-like freedom from the corrupting influences of wealth-seeking and family ties that could warp their judgment.

It has been suggested that Plato's early writings were contributions not to philosophy but to literature.* Not only athletics but dialogue competitions were held at the Games that were major periodic events in Greek cultural life – the Panathenaic Games, the Olympic Games, and others. The suggestion is that Plato's early *aporetic* dialogues did not aim at philosophical conclusions because that was not their point. His writings are admired as much for their aesthetic qualities as for their intellectual content, and it is their style rather than the conclusions they reach which most distinguishes his earliest works. On this view, it was only after the death of Socrates that Plato became more seriously interested in the philosophical ideas he had hitherto been using as vehicles for his literary ambitions.

Although some of the philosophers of antiquity were pure theoreticians – ivory-tower academics, as might be said today – many were engaged in the practical and political lives of their city states. Plato did not take an active part in Athenian politics after Socrates' death, but he had a long-standing interest in the Greek city of Syracuse in Sicily, to which he was three times invited by its rulers to advise on its government. He accepted the invitations because he was friendly with Dion, who became ruler of Syracuse following a rebellion; Dion was a disciple and admirer of Plato, and he offered the philosopher a chance to put his ideas about government into practice. In the event Dion proved a poor ruler, and his period in office, during which he sought to establish a Platonic aristocracy, bequeathed a legacy of turmoil and failure that lasted for decades afterwards. To say that the fault lay with Plato's ideas and the advice he gave would only be partly true;

---

* This is a suggestion advanced by Gilbert Ryle in his *Plato's Progress* (1966).

the intractable materials of human nature and economic reality, and Dion's own failings, doubtless had parts to play that were as large or larger.

Plato's philosophy is a system, or at least it aspired to be one (he was too self-critical for the aspiration to be fully realizable). Its different components were meant to fit together to provide answers to the fundamental questions that he, more clearly and more comprehensively than his predecessors, saw had to be answered so that all the answers together make sense. Those questions are, What is the right kind of life, and the best kind of society? What is knowledge and how do we get it? What is the fundamental nature of reality? You might note that these questions have an order: to answer the first you need an answer to the second, and to answer the second you need an answer to the third.

Many philosophers after Plato likewise recognized that to answer the great questions of ethics one has to answer questions about the nature of the world and humanity in it, and therefore of how we can acquire knowledge about both. And that means we have to find answers to a number of sub-questions; for example, to understand knowledge and how to get it we have to have views about truth and reason, about the powers and therefore the nature of the mind, and about its relationship to the rest of reality.

Almost the whole of philosophy consists in approaches to the related set of questions addressed by Plato. It is because Plato identified them and the way they connect with each other that Alfred North Whitehead, a mathematician and philosopher who collaborated with Bertrand Russell on the *Principia Mathematica*, said that 'Philosophy is footnotes to Plato.' That is an exaggeration, but not too much of one, for indeed almost all the major questions of philosophy are addressed or at very least touched upon by Plato. In comparison not just to what went before in the history of philosophy, but to all that followed, Plato's achievement is vast – a mountain towering over foothills.

One way to enter Plato's philosophy is by noting the import of an analogy he uses to describe how things are for human beings, so far as their understanding of the world and life is concerned. This is the Allegory of the Cave in Book VII of the *Republic*. We are like prisoners held in a cave, chained so that we face the cave's back wall. Behind us, and between us and the tunnel that leads out of the cave, is a fire. Our captors walk up and down between our backs and the fire, casting shadows on the rear wall of the cave. We see the shadows. If we were released from our chains we would see the fire and the perambulating captors, and would therefore understand the source of the shadows. But if we were allowed out of the cave and saw the daylight, and above all the sun, we would know things as they truly are.

Most people, says Plato, are like the prisoners watching shadows. Some attain to the level of understanding possible for a prisoner free enough to move about the cave. But the goal is to step into the sunlight, and to see the truth in its full glory.

How is it possible to do that? We get the first indications in the *Meno*, an important dialogue in that it marks the move away from Socratic *aporia* – inconclusiveness – with at best negative answers to the questions being addressed, and on towards Plato's provision of positive answers. Remember that Socrates had identified virtue with knowledge, and that therefore the question 'What is knowledge and how do we get it?' becomes crucial for understanding what the best life should be. So, how do we acquire knowledge? Plato had been persuaded by his philosophical predecessors, not least by Parmenides, that the senses are delusive and do not reveal to us the true nature of reality. Therefore to have knowledge we must have a means of acquiring it which is not dependent on the senses. At most and at best the senses can only give us *opinions* about the world they reveal to us – a world consisting of a plurality of transitory and imperfect things. Whatever else the objects of genuine knowledge must be, they cannot be like this; they must be eternal, perfect and unchanging, thus possessed of at least some of the essential characteristics Parmenides specified as essential to what truly exists.

To deal with this Plato put forward the following thesis. There are, he argued, two realms, the Realm of Being inhabited by perfect and unchanging things, and the Realm of Becoming, which is the world offered to us by our senses, the world of imperfect and temporary things, always changing (always becoming something else: hence the name). Things in the Realm of Becoming are imperfect copies of the things in the Realm of Being; these latter things are the Forms (also called Ideas) which are the exemplars and paradigms for the many imperfect and temporary copies of them in the Realm of Becoming. The Forms are eternal, perfect and unchanging; they are the 'real reality' of which the world of sense-experience is merely a shadow.

We are not capable of inferring the existence of the Forms from their imperfect copies, given our delusive powers of perception and our finite intellects; therefore there must be another way we know them. This is that we have immortal souls which, while in their disembodied state before we are born, occupy the Realm of Being and are in direct contact with the Forms – and therefore, while in that state, we know everything. But when our souls enter our bodies they forget everything. The process of education is the process of being (partially) reminded of what we knew in our disembodied state – literally, of 'unforgetting' what we knew when disembodied ('unforgetting' is literally what the word *anamnesis* means). This view is known in English as the 'theory of recollection'.

The theory of recollection is demonstrated in the *Meno* by the example of an ignorant slave boy from whom Socrates elicits a geometrical proof by 'reminding' him of what his immortal soul once knew. Critics point out that Socrates' questions are rather artfully phrased, and that any clever boy might have been able to construct the proof with their help. But the example is intended to show how knowledge of virtue can be gained – more accurately: regained – by such prompting. In the *Symposium* we are given an account of how this works: love of another's beauty can be a royal road to love of beauty itself and thence to intellectual love of the highest beauty of all, which is 'the Good'. In the Allegory of the Cave, the Good is represented by the sun.

In the *Meno* discussion several important ideas emerge. One concerns the difference between knowledge and true belief. Suppose someone believes that one can get to a certain town by a certain route, and is right about it. Suppose he just happens to be right; he has never been there himself, but thinks he remembers someone saying that this is the route. So, he has a true belief about the route. But you cannot say he *knows* it, because his reason for believing it is not a good one. If he had been there himself, or had consulted an authoritative map, he could claim to know the route. Plato distinguishes between knowledge and a correct belief by saying that the latter becomes knowledge when it is 'tied down', that is, has a satisfactory justification.

Plato's theory requires acceptance of the view that we have souls, and that they are immortal. Arguments to this effect are presented in the *Phaedo*, a dialogue appropriately set in Socrates' prison cell shortly before he is due to drink the hemlock. Here the logical order of dependence between knowledge, the doctrine of the Forms and the doctrine of

ANCIENT PHILOSOPHY

recollection is rearranged to make the fact that we know some things
count as a reason for taking the soul to be immortal, given that we
could not know those things otherwise.

There are two other arguments in the *Phaedo* for the soul's immortality. One is that the soul is like the Forms, that is, it is not a physical,
empirical, structured thing, but an immaterial, single or unitary thing;
and therefore like the Forms it must be eternal and indestructible. And
of course it thereby satisfies, like them, the Parmenidean requirements
for being *real*.

The 'Final Argument' is that the concept of the soul is incompatible with the concept of death. The soul is a thing of life; when
death approaches it escapes, for otherwise its very nature would be
negated.

These are not satisfactory arguments, and one notes that they turn
in the first place on the assumption that there is such a thing as a soul.
What, then, is a 'soul'? The *Phaedo* does not give a clear answer beyond
assuming that it is distinct from the body and survives the body's death.
At one point Plato lists many things that the body does, and says that
by contrast the soul has just one activity, namely, reasoning. That seems
odd, because if there were such things as souls it would seem plausible
to ascribe the rest of mental life to them too, such as remembering,
hoping, intending, desiring, and more. At another point, however,
Plato appears to identify the soul with the personhood of its possessor;
when Socrates is asked how he wants to be buried he says, in effect, 'I
am not my body; it is not *me* who will be buried.'

In Book IV of the *Republic* a somewhat more elaborate theory of the
soul is advanced. Here Plato says that the soul has three parts: reason,
spirit and appetite. With the first we learn, and pursue truth by rational
enquiry; with the second we feel emotions such as anger or determination, and this is the part of us that seeks honour; while the third
focuses upon such bodily desires as food, wine and sex.

In the *Phaedrus* Plato offers an account of the way we can sometimes
be conflicted within ourselves because the different parts of the soul
pull in different directions. He likens us to a flying chariot with a driver
and two horses; the driver is reason, one of the horses is spirit, the other
is appetite. Appetite tries to pull the chariot down to earth, while spirit
seeks to obey reason's aim of taking it to the heavens. The charioteer
has to struggle with the opposing forces thus represented. Plato gives
more practical examples of this in the *Republic*, one of which is of a

man who desires to fulfil a certain appetite but is angry with himself for having that appetite.

These are the main outlines of Plato's system. They are fully present in the best known of his works, the *Republic*. This is a dialogue about justice, and it uses the analogies that can be drawn between a person and a *polis* – a state – to illustrate the virtue of justice in each, justice being achieved when balance or harmony between the aspects of the state is achieved, analogously with balance or harmony among the aspects of the soul.

Book I of the *Republic* is thought by some scholars to be an early Socratic dialogue of the familiar *elenchus–aporia* type, and the later books to be additions and expansions made by Plato as he developed a positive theory. This is because in the first book Socrates' interlocutors offer definitions of justice – one says 'it is the art of doing good to friends and harm to enemies,' and the other, Thrasymachus, says it is whatever the strong wish to do – and Socrates shows that they are each unsatisfactory. But then in Book II others take up consideration of Thrasymachus' point, variously arguing that justice arises from the social contracts put in place to protect the weak against the strong, and that unjust men will not be punished because they can use their injustices to grow rich enough to make pleasing sacrifices to the gods, who will therefore forgive them. This prompts Socrates to suggest that instead of seeking to define the just individual, they should see what is meant by justice in the state. In later books the ideas worked out for what would make an ideal state are applied to what would make a just person.

The main thesis of the *Republic* is that the ideal society would be one that is ruled by guardians or 'philosopher-kings', chosen when children for their intelligence and carefully and thoroughly raised so that, on reaching adulthood, they can fulfil the role of incorruptibly virtuous, dispassionate and wise rulers. This allows Socrates to take a detour into discussion of an ideal education. The chief idea is that children should be brought up by the state in ignorance of who their biological parents are. The state will decide which men and women should mate, on grounds of suitability; a form of eugenics. As the children grow up in state nurseries they will be separated into three groups: those suitable for training as guardians, those suitable for training as warriors (the 'auxiliary guardians'), and the rest. Both males and females can be guardians, and should receive the same training. They should be educated in the virtues of wisdom, temperance, justice and courage. They should be physically well trained in gymnastics to ensure good health. They should have no private property, so that there are no temptations to accumulate more, and wives should be shared to prevent partiality. They should live and eat with moderation.

Plato's ideal state is an aristocracy, a state ruled by 'the best'. The term 'aristocrat' did not then mean an hereditary social caste, but in fact is better understood as 'meritocrat', denoting the best of the citizens in respect of intellect and virtue. If the virtues are expressed by all degrees of citizens in the appropriate way, the state will be happy. The guardians will be wise, the auxiliaries courageous, everyone will be temperate and the government will be just. Harmony will prevail; and this is the key for the analogy between the state and the individual – for if harmony prevails likewise within the individual, he will be virtuous likewise.

In Book VIII Plato describes a set of political systems in order of merit, beginning with the kind he advocates and descending to the worst kind, namely tyranny. He regarded tyranny as the worst form of government, because, as Lord Acton long afterwards noted, 'Power tends to corrupt, and absolute power corrupts absolutely.' If power lies in the hands of a single individual, its arbitrary exercise can do great harm.

Between aristocracy as the ideal arrangement and tyranny as the worst, there are several intermediate forms. In the ideal arrangement the state is governed by the most knowledgeable, virtuous and wise of the citizens, whose rule is disinterested because, as noted, they have no vested interests in anything but the welfare of the state. The next best form is *epistocracy*, rule by those who know, in other words by experts. The difference between aristocracy and epistocracy is that in the ideal state the rulers are not merely experts, they are *virtuous* experts; they have expertise in the nature of the Good as well as in government and other practical matters.

Plato wished his rulers to be virtuous and disinterested, with no ambitions other than to rule wisely, in order to prevent the state from degenerating into a *timocracy*. In modern parlance timocracy is rule by those who have a certain minimum of property, but in Plato's usage it denotes rule by those who seek honour, status and military glory. Ambition for these things reveals a mistaken confusion of the Good with its outer shows – wealth and reputation being erroneously regarded as the greatest goods worth having. Whereas aristocracy would ensure stable government because no inner divisions threaten it, with timocracy and the other less satisfactory forms of the state, rivalry enters the picture, and with rivalry comes instability.

Timocracy can easily become *oligarchy*, by which Plato meant rule by the rich over the more numerous poor (this form of oligarchy – rule by a few – is nowadays called *plutocracy*). Timocracy degenerates into oligarchy because timocrats are permitted to accumulate wealth, from which follow the vices encouraged by wealth: pursuit of pleasure and luxury, and belief that the accumulation of wealth is more important than virtue. Timocrats might care about honour, said Plato, but oligarchs care only about money.

And the inevitable result will be – *democracy*, for Plato a term of malediction. The rich enjoy freedom because their wealth buys it for them. Envy of that freedom causes oligarchy to be overcome by democracy. The populace, the *demos*, rises against the oligarchs in order to dispossess them, often with violence and turmoil. But when in democracy everyone claims the freedom and the right to make and break laws, what soon follows, said Plato, is anarchy, for such freedom is not freedom but merely licence.

Implicit in the idea of a declension from the ideal form of government is Plato's claim that the *demos* lacks the knowledge and virtue that philosopher-kings would have, and which is what makes them fit to govern. He thinks that the collapse of the democratic state into anarchy is inevitable given the supposed characteristics of the *polloi* or general public: ignorance, self-interest, prejudice, envy and rivalry. Anarchy very soon invites the intervention of a strongman to restore order; given the insupportable nature of anarchy, he will be welcomed at first with open arms. Once he is in power, removing him can be difficult, and the people will be in the worst situation of all: they will live under tyranny.

Just as the best state is ruled by wisdom and virtue, so the best kind of life is lived by the person who rules himself or herself by wisdom and virtue likewise. Plato's idea of justice is *balance* or harmony: balance between the three orders of people in the state, balance between the three parts of the soul in an individual. The different kinds of state have their analogies in different kinds of people – those ruled by wisdom and virtue, those driven by desire for honour, those driven by desire for wealth, those ruled by ignorance and unruly passions.

The *Republic* is something of a high point in Plato's philosophy, bringing together his metaphysics of the Forms, his epistemology of 'recollection' and his ethical conception of virtue as knowledge, into a system that provides a view of both the good individual and the good state. Other thinkers might have felt justifiably pleased with themselves for having worked out such an interlocking system and its comprehensive application to key questions. But Plato did not rest content. His thinking continued to develop after the *Republic*, and he came to challenge his own most significant ideas, both the theory of the Forms and his theory of knowledge. In doing so he took the philosophical examination of these matters to new levels.

In Plato's philosophy the Forms in the Realm of Being are real things; they are not mental objects only. They are Beauty, Truth, Goodness; but they are also Man, Tree, Horse, Mountain, and everything else – although Plato was somewhat conflicted over whether there are Forms of such things as Hair and Dirt. Faces that are beautiful are beautiful because the beauty in them 'participates in' or is an imperfect copy of the Form of Beauty. A mountain is a mountain because it likewise 'participates in' or is a copy of the Form of Mountain.

To begin to see that there is much that is problematic here, note first that 'participate in' and 'copy' are two quite different notions. Which did Plato mean? To understand why this question takes the lid off a major philosophical problem, consider the important distinction between *things* like tables, apples, aircraft and rabbits, and the *properties* that things might have, such as being white, red, flat or round. We speak naturally about many things having the same property: this tablecloth is red, that apple is red, that person's nose is red. This seems to suggest that there is something, *redness*, that all these particular things share or have in common.

Tablecloths and apples are called *particulars* and properties such as redness and flatness are called *universals* because many particulars can exemplify them. In philosophy long after Plato's time, during the late medieval period, the 'Schoolmen' (as the philosophers of that period were collectively known: see the section on medieval philosophy below) were deeply divided over the question of whether universals *really* exist, or whether words like 'redness' and 'flatness' are just *names* that we give to similarities we see between different particulars. Some of the Schoolmen said that universals are real things – there really is Redness in the universe, existing apart from individual red things, and that it would exist even if there were no red things. They are accordingly called *realists*. Others denied that universals really exist, and regarded 'redness' as merely a name that we use for our descriptive convenience – hence, from 'name', they are called *nominalists*. The realism–nominalism debate was one of the most hotly contested questions in medieval philosophy.

Plato, as we see, was a realist about the Forms, but he was a realist also about the difficulties that the concept of the Forms raises. He addresses these difficulties in the *Parmenides*, where he has the elderly Parmenides challenging a young Socrates to defend the theory, and Socrates finding considerable difficulty in doing so. Both the idea of particular things 'participating in' the Forms, and the quite different notion that particulars 'resemble' or are copies of the Forms, come under Parmenides' scrutiny.

First, Parmenides asks Socrates what kinds of things have Forms. Beauty and Goodness, yes; relations like Equality and Plurality, yes; Man and Fire and Water; yes; Mud, Hair, Dirt – no. In fact Socrates gives an answer to the question whether Man and Fire have Forms that is different from the answer he gives about Beauty and Equality. And his negative answer about mud and dirt is puzzling, given that according to the metaphysics behind the theory of Forms the fact that a particular gobbet of mud is mud is (or should be) because it has (participates in, copies) 'mudness' or – if one were not metaphysically too snobbish to allow this – the Form of Mud. For if this boot is muddy and that boot is muddy, they both have the property of being muddy, so is there not a respect in which they both therefore share, have or exemplify, muddiness?

This matter is left in an unsatisfactory state. Then Parmenides tackles 'participates in'; Plato sometimes says 'shares in' or 'shares'. If a particular apple is red because it 'shares in' the Form of Redness, does it have a little bit of the Form in it, or is the Form fully in it? Is the Form divided into as many bits as there are things to share it, or is it in some other way 'participated in' or 'shared by' many things while still itself being one? Socrates suggests in reply that one should think of a Form as one thinks of a day: the same day is present in many places, but it is still one thing. This leaves unspecified the nature of the relation of 'participating in'; how is *redness* something separate from this particular apple and that particular apple, and not of the same kind or nature as physical particulars like apples (given that it is not something in space and time), nevertheless 'in' each of the apples?

It might seem more plausible to opt for the 'resembles' or 'copies' option, because at least that is a more intelligible notion. But here the 'Third Man' problem arises, so called because in Aristotle's discussion of the argument he uses the example of an individual man's relation to the Form of Man. The problem is as follows. A man is a man because he resembles the Form of Man. Both he and the Form share 'Manness'. Now, there are two possibilities. One is that the man and the Form of Man – call this latter 'Man Form 1' – are similar in virtue of something that makes them similar, which would be their each resembling another, more comprehensive Form of Man, call it 'Man Form 2'. But if they each resemble that Form, there would have to be a yet more comprehensive Form – 'Man Form 3' – in virtue of which the resemblance between the man and Man Form 1 resembles Man Form 2 – and so on ad infinitum.

The alternative is to argue that there has to be one Form for each particular to be a copy of, requiring therefore an infinite or at least indefinitely large number of individual Forms. But this not only is implausible in unnecessarily duplicating each individual thing – why is each individual not its own Form, dispensing with a parallel universe of individual Forms? – but fails to solve the problem that the theory is offered to solve: how different particulars can have (share) the same property.

The first alternative assumes that the Forms 'self-predicate', that is, apply to themselves: the Form of Beauty is itself beautiful, the Form of Largeness is itself large, the Form of Man is itself a man. The result, as we see, is regress. The second alternative offers an even less compelling solution. Yet Plato did not give up the theory, even though he could not find a satisfactory response to these challenges. In a very late dialogue, the *Timaeus*, the theory is still alive; he uses it in his account of how the creator of the universe (the 'Demiurge' or 'divine craftsman') uses the Forms to make the plurality of individual copies of them which constitute the world.

Plato also questioned his own theory of knowledge. This occurs in one of the most challenging of his dialogues, the *Theaetetus*. Note first that there are three ways one can think of knowledge: as knowledge *that* something is the case, knowledge *how* to do something, and knowledge in the sense of 'knowing X, being acquainted with X', as when one says 'I know New York' or 'I know Fred.' Plato often speaks as if his basic notion of knowledge is the last of these three, which would make sense in light of the theory of Forms, because what the *Meno* and the *Republic* tell us is that knowledge pertains exclusively to the Forms – we only have opinions and beliefs regarding everything else – and accordingly knowledge is 'acquaintance with the Forms'. On this view, just as we say 'I know New York' we would say 'I know Beauty' or 'I know Truth.'

But in the *Theaetetus* the Forms do not appear. Instead the discussion focuses on three theories: that knowledge is acquired through sense-perception, that it is 'true belief', and that it is 'true belief with a justification'. The first theory is rejected on the grounds that knowledge involves judging, which is an activity of mind, not of the senses. This prepares the way for the next two theories, both based on the idea that knowledge is judgment or belief under certain conditions (the word *doxa* translates as both 'belief' and 'judgment'). The second theory is that knowledge is true belief. As we saw in the argument of the *Meno*, Plato rejects this, but here adds a detour into the question of how false belief is possible. In the *Meno* Plato makes the point that one can have beliefs which are true but which we cannot claim as knowledge because our reasons for holding the belief are not the right ones to count as knowledge. This point recurs in the *Theaetetus*, and leads to the third theory, which is that knowledge is true judgment with a justification or account, a *logos*.

The effort to specify what kind of *logos* turns a belief into knowledge is inconclusive; Socrates ends by saying to the young Theaetetus, 'And so, Theaetetus, knowledge is neither sensation nor true opinion, nor yet definition and explanation accompanying and added to true opinion?' – a recurrence of *aporia*. But in exploring what the required *logos* might be, Plato initiates a long and detailed philosophical debate about the nature of knowledge which has lasted to our own day. For in our own day the definition of knowledge as 'justified true belief' – Plato's third option – still bedevils us with questions about the nature of that justification (to say nothing of questions about what 'truth' is).

There is a mystery attached to Plato in one respect, relating to the idea that he taught an 'unwritten doctrine', *agrapha dogmata*, that is, views that he did not commit to writing but kept privately within the circle of his pupils. Aristotle alludes to the existence of such views in his *Physics*, and many centuries later Plotinus, the founder of Neoplatonism, seems to have known them, or about them, or had surmises about what they were. Recent scholars of the Tübingen School of Platonic studies have attempted a reconstruction of them, saying that Plato 'reserved' his views (for his pupils) about the ultimate principles of things, of which there are two: that reality is One, and that it manifests itself through the action upon it of something called 'the Indefinite Dyad' which is variously the *large and the small*, the *lack and the excess*, the *ambiguous and the definite*, and so on – that is, opposites which act on the One and produce all reality from it as a result.

It is further suggested that the One is the Good – Aristotle reported that Plato lectured on 'the Good', and in the written doctrines the Form of the Good is nominated as the highest Form, so the identification would be plausible. But this, and indeed the entire speculation about an 'unwritten doctrine', is controversial. Aristotle speaks not of an 'unwritten doctrine' but of '*the so-called* unwritten doctrine'. Did he employ the phrase 'so-called' neutrally, or was he thereby casting cold water on the belief that there was such a thing? Yet in others of his writings, for example the *Metaphysics*, Aristotle refers to ideas of Plato that do not appear in the latter's texts. And one notes that Plato's immediate successors as heads of the Academy, first Speusippus and then Xenocrates, appear to have developed ideas about the One and a principle whose opposition to it generates reality; Speusippus talks of 'plurality' and Xenocrates of 'inequality'.

Was there an 'unwritten doctrine' and if so was it *esoteric* and kept within the circle of disciples because it was too precious to be made public? Some folk like that kind of suggestion; it gives a frisson, and a vague promise of deep dark secrets. Much more likely is the fact that what was discussed in Academy seminars ranged widely, and ideas were explored that did not happen to find their way into a written record, and that Plato advanced more thoughts than he found occasion to develop in a dialogue for publication. That would be wholly consistent with what has happened, and happens still, in philosophical discussions everywhere.

The school founded by Plato, the Academy, lasted nearly eight hundred years, until 529 CE. In that year the Roman emperor Justinian, a Christian, abolished it and banned the teaching of 'pagan' philosophy because it was inconsistent with Christian doctrine. But its long history before that saw a number of philosophically significant changes and developments. About eighty years after Plato's death the Academy fell under the influence of scepticism when Arcesilaus (316–241 BCE) became its head, prompting Cicero to rename it 'the New Academy'. Historians of philosophy accept this label, and treat the sceptical phase as lasting until 90 BCE when Antiochus of Ascalon rejected the sceptical teaching he had received from Philo of Larissa at the Academy. Thus commenced 'Middle Platonism', a stage in which Plato's doctrines were modified by the introduction of elements of Aristotelian and Stoic thought. Middle Platonism lasted until Plotinus in the third century CE developed the Platonic tradition into the powerful school of thought that historians call Neoplatonism.

The immediate consequence of Plato, and one of the greatest legacies he bequeathed, must however be accounted his star pupil, Aristotle, whose disagreements with his teacher, combined with his own genius, constituted the next major step in the history of philosophy.

Aristotle

If Aristotle were alive today he would be a scientist, and most likely a biologist; he would have a lively interest in scientific method and logic, perhaps to the extent that he would have sympathized, even if he did not agree, with the attempt by the twentieth-century biologist J. H. Woodger to apply the logic of Russell and Whitehead's *Principia Mathematica* to the foundations of biology. As this suggests, Aristotle's genius was universal and synoptic: he wished to bring all knowledge into a great system.

Some contemporary scholars of Aristotle would not agree with that last remark; they regard him not as a systematic philosopher, but as an 'aporetic' one – that is, after the manner of the inconclusive explorations of Socrates ending in *aporia*, that he was an examiner of opinions, problems and puzzles thrown up by our experience of the world, often without coming to a settled view. But Aristotle himself seems to think differently about this, as we see from his introductory remarks to his *Meteorology*: 'I have already dealt with the first causes of nature and with all natural motion [in his *Physics*] and with the heavenly bodies arranged in their upper paths [in his *On the Heavens*], and with the number and nature of the material elements, with their mutual transformations, and with generation and destruction in general [in his *On Generation and Corruption*]. The remaining part of this enquiry concerns what earlier thinkers called "meteorology" [he means the phenomena of the lower heavens] . . . then we shall see if we can give some account . . . of animals and plants . . .'

As this shows, Aristotle was systematic in his intention to achieve an encyclopaedic science. It ranged from the most fundamental questions about the nature of reality itself (in his *Metaphysics*) through his scientific enquiries as just noted, to his psychological studies of human beings (in his *On the Soul* and *Short Treatises on Nature*), to art and literature (included in his account of 'productive sciences' in his *Poetics* and *Rhetoric*), to matters of ethics and politics (in the *Nicomachean Ethics*, *Eudemian Ethics* and *Politics*). And alongside this great scheme lay his seminal studies of logic and reasoning; he created the science of logic almost from scratch, in the six books known as the *Categories*, *On Interpretation*, *Prior Analytics*, *Posterior Analytics*, *Topics* and *Sophistical Refutations*.

By any standard this is a hugely impressive corpus of work. What comes as a yet greater surprise in a first encounter with Aristotle is that all these works are texts of his lectures and his research notes – more accurately, those which have survived; and that the works he polished for publication have all been lost. The polished works were written in dialogue form, on Plato's model, and in contrast to the rough-hewn nature of the works we have, they were said to be of outstanding literary quality. Plato's Greek is a thing of beauty; yet so great a stylist in his own language as Cicero could say that whereas Plato's style was silver, Aristotle's was 'a river of gold'.

Most of Aristotle's lost dialogues were probably productions of his earlier years, when he was still a student and colleague of Plato in the Academy, and still under the influence of his teacher. This is surmised from such evidence as the fact that in fragments of his lost dialogue *Gryllos* on rhetoric he appears to put forward the same view as Plato had offered in his *Gorgias*, to the effect that rhetoric is not an art (a *techne*). The difficulty with lost works known only from fragments and *testimonia* is that they can seem to commit their author to a view which he might in fact be mentioning only so that he can criticize it. This reminds one to point out that Aristotle was a philosopher who kept thinking, developing and revising his views; the writings which are collected as the *Rhetoric* that we have today followed now lost works on the same subject known as the *Technon Sunagoge*, thought to be Aristotle's earlier thoughts on the matter. It is these rather than the *Rhetoric* that underlie Cicero's writings on rhetoric.

It is a lucky accident that we have as much of Aristotle's writings as we do, given the vulnerability to disappearance of the works of antiquity. Plato's dialogues survived because his school lasted for nearly a thousand years; Aristotle's nearly did not survive at all. They did so because – so we are told by Strabo – they were left to his successor in his own school, Theophrastus, who in turn left them to his disciple

Neleus. Neleus took them to his home at Scepsis in the Troad, and bequeathed them to his descendants, none of whom was in the slightest interested in Aristotle or philosophy. They stored the manuscripts in a cellar, where they were attacked by damp, mould, insects and mice. Fortunately they were bought by a wealthy Athenian bibliophile and collector called Apellicon who lived in the first century BCE. His great library was taken as booty by the Roman general Sulla the Dictator when, in 86 BCE, during the First Mithridatic War in which Rome conquered Greece, he captured Athens. The texts were taken to Rome, where Andronicus of Rhodes, one of the few survivors of Aristotle's school (which had all but died out in the third century BCE), set about editing the works. We owe to Andronicus the form and arrangement of what we have of Aristotle.

Aristotle was born in 384 BCE – fifteen years after the death of Socrates – in Stagira in Macedonia. He died at Chalcis sixty-two years later. His lifetime spanned an epoch: it stretched from the last days of an independent and truly classical Athens, where he went as a teenager to study in Plato's Academy, to the subsumption of all Greece in the Macedonian monarchy and the Empire of Alexander the Great.

Aristotle's father was the court physician to the King of Macedonia, Amyntas III, which meant that the family belonged by birthright to the medical guild of the Asclepiads, named for Asclepius the god of medicine. Aristotle's father died while he was still a minor, so he was left to the care of a guardian, Proxenus, who sent him at the age of eighteen to study in Athens with Plato. He remained a member of the Academy, first as a pupil then as a colleague, for twenty years, until Plato's death in 347 BCE. He and a fellow-student, Xenocrates, left Athens because, it is thought, they did not like the appointment of Plato's nephew Speusippus as next head of the Academy. Aristotle might have been a candidate for the headship and was not elected; or it could be that he disagreed with Speusippus' philosophical approach, which was markedly Pythagorean. Whatever the reason, he and Xenocrates went to teach at a branch of the Academy in the little Aeolian city of Assos.

The ruler of this city, Hermias, was a remarkable man who had started life as a slave and rose by his own great talents. He was an enlightened individual who encouraged the Academicians in his city. Aristotle had three contented years there, during which he married Hermias' niece Pythias, and then he moved to the nearby island of

Lesbos. This was almost certainly because he wished to pursue his empirical interests in marine biology.

In 343 BCE Aristotle went to Pella, the seat of King Philip of Macedon, where he was appointed tutor – in all likelihood, *one* of the tutors – to the heir to the throne, then a boy of thirteen. This was the youth known to history as Alexander the Great. Much speculation surrounds the fact that the great philosopher and the great conqueror bore this relation to one another, though the briefest reflection shows that Aristotle could not have had very much influence on the prince. Aristotle liked the idea of small republican polities; Alexander created a vast empire, all the way to the banks of the Jumna in India. Aristotle's ethics taught moderation in all things; Alexander drank himself to death at an early age. If indeed there was any influence it seems therefore to have been an entirely negative one. But legend was too tempted by the juxtaposition of these mighty names not to wrap itself around them: Plutarch exemplifies the point, uncritically quoting supposed letters between the philosopher and the king, letters which are almost certainly forgeries.

Philip was murdered in 336 BCE and Alexander succeeded him. Aristotle left Macedonia and went back to Athens, there founding his own school. It was located in the Lyceum, a gymnasium in the northern suburbs of Athens. His school came to be called the Peripatetic school because he lectured in the building's portico (the *peripatos*). The word 'peripatetic' means 'walking up and down'; it is unlikely that Aristotle read from those elaborate lectures of his on the move, with disciples scurrying behind him; the name of the school is architectural, not descriptive of classroom activity.

The school lasted for twelve years under Aristotle's direct leadership. But then his former pupil Alexander, by now ruler of a great slice of the known world, suddenly took an unwelcome interest in him. Alexander thought that Aristotle was part of a conspiracy to have him assassinated, and therefore instructed his viceroy at Athens, Antipater, to arrest him. The reason lay with a cousin of Aristotle's called Callisthenes, who was the historian at Alexander's court appointed to keep a record of the conqueror's campaigns. Alexander had begun to adopt the style of the oriental rulers he conquered, aping their pomp and circumstance, among other things requiring his subjects to prostrate themselves on the floor before him. This caused resentment among his Greek followers. Callisthenes criticized Alexander for this, thereby angering him (though shortly afterwards he gave up the 'oriental despot' pose for good). Callisthenes was accused of trying to incite Alexander's pages to assassinate him, and was hanged. Alexander thought that Aristotle lay behind the attempt.

The charge brought against Aristotle was the convenient one of 'impiety', just as with Socrates. The alleged impiety related to a poem he had written in praise of Hermias twenty years before. It was claimed that Aristotle's intention in the poem was to deify a mortal. Discretion being the better part of valour, and Aristotle being a man of common sense, he left Athens, saying – in allusion to its treatment of Socrates – that he was saving it from committing a second crime against philosophy. He went to Chalcis on Euboea with his pupils, and there died a year later.

In his *Physics* Aristotle describes the division of philosophy (or 'the sciences': they were the same thing) as he saw it. This was the general framework of the studies mentioned above in connection with Aristotle's systematic approach. The overarching division is between theoretical or 'speculative' philosophy and practical philosophy.

Theoretical philosophy has three components; the most general is 'first philosophy', afterwards known as 'metaphysics'; then mathematics; then physics. Physics deals with *phusis*, nature, and all it contains, from the heavenly bodies to plants and animals. The phenomena studied in physics are material, and have motion. This is the most specific of the theoretical sciences. Mathematics deals with measurement and quantity. It is less specific, more general, than physics. Metaphysics is the most general of all. It deals with 'being *qua* being', with the fundamental and universal characteristics of everything in reality.

Practical philosophy is one thing: it is politics, of which ethics is an integral part. 'Politics' means the study of the *polis* – the state – and since the state is the society of people who constitute it, ethics and politics are continuous with each other. You might say that Aristotle thought of politics as 'the theory of conduct' in general. In later thinking, practical philosophy tends to be arranged into three branches: ethics, economics and politics. But Aristotle saw these pursuits as too intimately related to subdivide them.

Some add a third division to Aristotle's scheme, to give a place to art in the Greek sense of *techne*, which includes craft and skill of all kinds. It would seem that the *Rhetoric* and the *Poetics* fit this bill, but in fact they differ from Aristotle's other works in being practical manuals rather than critical explorations of their subject matter.

And if one were in the business of expanding the catalogue of Aristotelian enquiries, one would add what he called 'Analytics', the science of logic. Because logic is required in all the sciences he himself saw it not as a separate department of enquiry, but as methodologically presupposed to the others, in the sense of laying down enquiry's rules and procedures.

What follows is an account of Aristotle's contributions in each of these domains, beginning with logic. It should be pointed out that as the extant works of Aristotle are edited versions of lectures and research notes, there is often considerable obscurity in what he wrote, much of it is extremely difficult, and scholarly debate rages around it. The following outline must be read in that light.

Aristotle's writings on logic are known as the *Organon*, which means 'instrument', indicating that they are treatises on the methods of enquiry and reasoning. His brilliant systematization of the science of logic itself is laid out in the *Categories*, *On Interpretation* and *Prior Analytics*. What might be thought of as an epistemology, in that it addresses the question of valid reasoning in science, is given in the *Posterior Analytics*. Discussions of tentative and probabilistic reasoning, and of fallacious reasoning, constitute the *Topics* and the *Sophistical Refutations* respectively.

It is helpful to know something about Aristotle's logic because important developments in later philosophy either turned upon it or were sparked by extensions and developments of it, especially in the work of Gottlob Frege, Bertrand Russell and others in twentieth-century 'Analytic philosophy'.

Aristotle took it that the fundamental unit of logical interest is the *proposition*, the 'what is said' by an utterance, this 'what is said' being either true or false. A proposition is not a sentence: the sentences 'snow is white,' 'Schnee ist weiss,' 'la neige est blanche,' 'xue shi baide,' respectively in English, German, French and Mandarin, all express the same proposition. So do the sentences 'snow is white,' 'whiteness is a property exemplified by snow,' 'precipitated ice crystals nucleated around atmospheric particles typically scatter all the visible wavelengths of light.' Likewise 'I have a headache' as said by me might be false but as said by you might be true; here therefore the same sentence expresses different propositions.

The structure of propositions is analysed by Aristotle into two chief components, the *subject* and the *predicate*. The subject is that about which something true or false is asserted; the predicate is what is asserted about the subject. So in 'snow is white' the *subject term* is 'snow' (and the subject is snow) and the *predicate term* is 'is white' (and whiteness is 'predicated of' – said about – the subject). These *terms* are the focus of his attention. His logical writings contain two slightly different accounts of how they are to be classified. One is the scheme of *categories* (sometimes known as the *predicaments*) and the other is what came to be known as the *five words* or *five predicables*.

The intention behind the notion of the categories is to reveal what we are saying when we make an assertion of the forms 'A is B,' 'A is a B,' 'As are Bs.' For example, if I say 'A is white,' the predicate is in the category of 'quality' – that is, it tells us what A is like. If I say 'A is a snowflake' the predicate falls into the category of 'substance', that is, it tells us what thing it is. If I say 'there are five snowflakes' the predicate falls into the category of 'quantity', how many there are. If I say 'one snowflake fell after another snowflake' the predicate is in the category of 'relation', how they were related to each other (in this case, in time. 'John is Peter's father' is another example of the category of relation, in this case, in genetics).

Substance, quality, quantity and relation are the four main categories. Aristotle adds six others: place, time, position, condition, activity, passivity. He does not claim that this list is complete or exhaustive, and because there are prefigurings of this classification in Plato it is likely that Aristotle took his starting point from there.

From noting that we often talk about all things, or some things (or at least one thing), of a certain group having a certain property, or that we deny that they have such a property, Aristotle distinguished between *universal* and *particular* propositions, and between *affirmative* and *negative* propositions. 'All As are B' is a universal affirmative proposition, while 'no As are B' is a universal negative proposition. 'Some As are B' and 'some As are not B' are respectively particular affirmative and particular negative propositions. Think of the terms in question as denoting classes of things, so that when we say 'all As are B' (or for this purpose better: 'all As are Bs') we can think of the things that are B as represented by a circle, and the things that are A as represented by a circle the same size or smaller, so that when we say all As are Bs we are saying that the circle of As lies wholly on or within the circle of Bs.* Likewise, when we say 'some As are Bs' we mean that the circle representing As partly overlaps with the circle representing Bs. And so on.

Aristotle's investigation of how such classes relate to each other as representable in these ways gave him the concept of a classification into *genus*, *species*, *difference*, *property* and *accident*. These are the 'five words' (*quinque voces*) as later logicians called them, and they list the ways in which a predicate can relate to a subject – or, alternatively put, the ways in which we can speak about something. You can speak about something specifically, or generally; that is *species* and *genus*. You can talk about the differences between species of things that separate them from each other; that is *difference*. You can talk about the characteristics of something that are found in all instances of the class of things it belongs to – these are *properties*. Or you can speak of a characteristic that something happens to have but which it could just as likely not have – which it has accidentally, so to speak; these are *accidents*, like the shape of a shoe or the colour of a shirt.

The 'species', or as Aristotle first called it the 'definition', of a thing relates to its essence, the 'what makes it what it is' factor. It is *specific* to the thing in question. The *genus* is that part of the thing's essence which is not unique to it, but is shared with other things of the same kind *in general*. So 'lion' is a species of the genus 'animal'. (Biological taxonomy differs from this classification, having a more detailed hierarchy – in descending order: domains, kingdoms; phyla, classes, orders, families, genera and species.) The *differentia* distinguish one species from another within a genus; they are what make circles different from squares though they are both instances of 'shape'. These concepts gave Aristotle his fundamental view about how we categorize or define anything: we do it 'by genus and difference'.

What Aristotle wished to achieve was *understanding* – that is, he wished to give explanations of things and ultimately of the universe itself. The Greek word for explanation, *aitia*, also means 'cause', and Aristotle framed the task of explaining things as ascertaining their causes: to know or understand something, he said, is to know its cause. Now, causes themselves have causes, and there is a risk that the chain of explanation by causes might run back for ever. This is where

---

* These relationships are well represented by Venn diagrams.

definition enters the picture. Suppose you explain A by saying it was caused by B, and that B was caused by C; you will reach a point, say D (or perhaps eventually Z), where the explanation stops because at that point we say 'because it is what it is'; we have reached the definition of the thing, an account of its nature, from which explanations of C and B and A follow.

Aristotle identified four 'causes': *material, efficient, formal* and *final*. Suppose you wish to explain what a table is. You cite the material cause (the wood from which it is made), the efficient cause (the carpenter's work that brought it into being), the formal cause (the form of the thing; the pattern or design that the carpenter followed in making the table) and the final cause (the end, aim or purpose for which the table was made). When you have given all four causes you have given an explanation. Of these the most important is the final cause, the purpose or aim – the *telos*. Explanations given in terms of final causes are called *teleological explanations*.

Aristotle's epistemology and metaphysics are sharply different from Plato's. Plato's theory requires transcendent Forms as the only appropriate objects of knowledge properly so called, and therefore they must exist in a realm accessible only to the mind. Aristotle described Plato's theory as merely a poetic metaphor. Its worst fault, in his view, is its inability to explain change and how new substances come into being. How can transcendent, eternal, unchanging Forms cause anything in the realm of Becoming, where everything is in constant motion, change and flux? Aristotle's view is that instead of thinking of individual things as copies of, or somehow 'participants in', a Form, we should see them as composites of both matter and form, the form being immanent in the matter. When we say 'snow is white' we are not attributing the presence of a really existing abstract universal, 'whiteness', to the snow, we are experiencing a concrete thing ('con' signifies 'with' or 'together'; 'con-crete' denotes the accretion or joining together of two or more things) constituting white snow.

Aristotle's account of change turns on the idea of potentiality (in Greek *dunamis*, from which we get the word 'dynamic'). Substances have a potentiality either to be changed by something acting on them, which is 'passive potential', or to cause change in other substances, which is what animate things can do because they possess 'active potential'. Change requires the realization of potentiality – the making of the potential actual – which he calls *energeia*.

This leads to Aristotle's thesis about the 'first cause' of all things. Given that everything is a concretion of matter and form which have been united by a cause, and given that the causal chain cannot regress to earlier and earlier causes for ever, there must be a first cause, which to break the regress must be self-caused. This self-causing 'first mover' of the universe must, said Aristotle, be a mind, the nature of which is pure thought. It thinks about the highest thing there is, which is thought; hence it is pure thought thinking about itself. To this he gives the name God.

His reason for thinking that the first cause must be a mind or soul is that the explanation for how animate beings can move themselves is that they have souls. (Yes: the account is circular.) All animate things have 'nutritive souls' which motivate them in their most basic functions of eating and reproducing. All animals and some plants also have a 'sensitive' aspect to their souls, which enables them to perceive the environment and respond to it. Human beings have both these and a third aspect to the soul: rationality, which enables them to think. For a living thing the soul is the efficient, formal and final cause of its being; only the material cause relates to its body.

Aristotle took the view that sensation is a passive quality of souls, allowing them to be changed by their bodies' contact with things in their external environment. We use the word 'informed' now as an echo of this theory: when one of our sense organs is acted upon by an external object the soul becomes 'potentially' what the external object is 'actually', by taking on the form (not of course the matter) of the object. Suppose I pick up a ball; the feeling of a round object consists in having the form of that object carried to my soul from my hands: I am thus in*formed* of (more accurately, *by*) the shape of the ball.

Thought is the soul focusing upon forms without necessarily, or even often, being prompted to do so by the action of an external thing. Of course there could not be such thought without preceding contact with things, Aristotle says, thereby giving rise to the principle 'nothing in mind that was not first in the senses', a principle of empiricism. But both thought and imagination consist in the soul presenting to itself forms and the relationships between forms independently of an actual stimulus to do so from outside.

Activity and motion are the result of desire, Aristotle said; all animate things, to a greater or lesser degree, are aware of their internal states and what in the external world might address those states – satisfy or remedy them – whether they are of hunger, pain, a wish for pleasure, and more.

The foregoing account summarizes the salient points in Aristotle's metaphysics and psychology. In regard to metaphysics Aristotle attached great significance to the question of 'being *qua* being', of '*What Is* purely in its character of *Being* and the properties which it has as such'. Metaphysics is accordingly the attempt to grasp the fundamental nature of existence. In this enquiry the category of primary importance is substance (*ousia*). As we see in the logic of the categories, substance-predicates are those invoked in answer to questions of the form 'What is x?' The answer to the question 'What is Socrates?' is appropriately 'He is a man,' where 'man' is the substance-predicate. But this is not yet to get to the bottom of things. For Aristotle the more fundamental point, both literally and logically, is that substances are 'ultimate subjects', and they are 'separable'. By 'ultimate subject' he means that they exist in their own right; by 'separable' he means that they can be separated from the accidents that characterize them. For example, a man is an individual substance. Suppose he has a limp; his limp cannot be separated from him and exist on its own, so 'limping-ness' is not a separable substance, but the man is; he can be conceived of apart from his limp.

This account of a difficult doctrine in Aristotle doubtless amplifies rather than clarifies the problems in it. If anything helps to clarify it somewhat, it is the etymology of the word 'substance' itself: 'sub-stance' or, as one might say, 'standing under (or underneath)' somewhat captures the idea of what exists or has being in its own right, as a fundamental category of thing, upon which other things supervene or are dependent; colours cannot exist without being colours *of* something, nor can there be limps unless there is something doing the limping; they are dependent things.

Aristotle's views in practical philosophy, ethics and politics, are much plainer sailing than his metaphysics and psychology. They turn on the idea that the best kind of society is one whose individual members live the best kind of lives. Later philosophy has found the ethical aspect of his views more enduringly important than the political aspect, because they are philosophically far richer. But to see how the different aspects of Aristotle's practical philosophy hang together, we can note the following.

A person who makes swords has the production of swords as the 'end', *telos* or goal, of his activity. But to the soldier the sword is merely an instrument to his own, different end, which is to kill or incapacitate his enemy. But this in turn is only part of the yet higher goal of the ruler, whose aim is to defend the state. The ruler directs the soldier whom and where to fight, and the soldier tells the sword-maker what length and sharpness he requires in a sword. The highest art lies with the ruler, for he has direction of the state; what the others do, each in achieving his own more particular end, serves this highest end. Therefore, says Aristotle, politics is the highest art; all other arts and crafts are subservient to it, for politics aims at the overall well-being of a society.

Among the various subordinate arts that help in the achievement of this highest end is *education*, because this is what forms character, the combination of intellectual and moral qualities that make the best kind of person. What is the best kind of character? That is the question to be answered by *ethics*.

There are two ethical treatises bearing Aristotle's name, the *Eudemian Ethics* and the *Nicomachean Ethics*. These are names given by later commentators; Aristotle himself refers in the *Politics* to what he had earlier said in a work he describes as *ta ethika*, on character. The names of the treatises allude to his friend Eudemus and his son Nicomachus who were said to have edited them. The *Nicomachean Ethics* is a fuller and doubtless later work than the *Eudemian Ethics*, and quite likely postdates the *Politics* itself.* Aristotle's writings on ethics are the first-ever treatises devoted wholly and systematically to the subject, and they are among the greatest.

Aristotle's technique was to look at commonly held views about things (the *endoxa*) and the disagreements that arise about them, and to find a resolution to the disagreements. In the *Nicomachean Ethics* he begins by noting that every pursuit aims at some good, which means that there are as many different kinds of good as there are pursuits. Such things as boat-building, military strategy and getting rich each requires subordinate goods to be attained – in carpentry, sword-making, starting a business – each of which has its own set of subordinate ends to be achieved first: and so on. Each 'good' is an end serving a higher end. But what is the supreme end, the highest good? It

---

* A text called *Magna Moralia* has also been attributed to Aristotle, but is more likely the work of a student or follower.

will be the end desired for its own sake, not as a means to anything beyond itself.

And what is that end which is desirable for its own sake? There is 'very general agreement' about this, Aristotle says; both 'the general run of men and people of superior refinement say that it is happiness' (*eudaimonia*). ('Happiness' is an inadequate translation of this term: 'well-being and well-doing', 'flourishing', would be better.) But then they disagree about what happiness is. Some say it consists in the possession of wealth, others say of honour, others again of pleasure. And their opinions differ according to the condition they happen to be in: the poor man says wealth is happiness, the sick man says it is health.

But a little thought shows that wealth, honour, pleasure, health, or any other such, are not ends in themselves; they are themselves instrumental to whatever is truly the highest good. Not only is the highest good not instrumental, because it is desired wholly for its own sake and is sufficient of itself, but it is the thing towards which all other instrumental goods strive, the 'single final end' of all activity. It is indeed happiness: but not as identified with any of the individual instrumental ends. Instead it will be what we attain when we live in accordance with 'the function of human beings'.

What is 'the function of human beings'? Aristotle approaches an answer to this question by analogies. What makes a good flute-player? Skill at playing the flute. A good carpenter? One good at making things from wood. Each is 'good' because he performs his particular function, his work (*ergon*), well. To do his work well is the virtue or excellence (*arete*) of a flute-player *qua* flute-player or carpenter *qua* carpenter. What is the *arete* of a human being *qua* human being? It is to do the 'work' of being human well. And what is the 'work' of a human being? It is to live up to that thing which is distinctive and defining of humanity, namely, the possession of reason. A good person is therefore a person who lives and acts rationally in accordance with virtue. 'The human good', says Aristotle, is 'activity of soul in accordance with virtue, and if there is more than one virtue, in accordance with the best and most complete'.

So now we must understand the nature of virtue. There are two kinds of virtue, says Aristotle: those of mind, and those of character. The virtues of mind further subdivide into 'practical wisdom' and 'theoretical wisdom'. Virtues of character include courage, temperance and justice. Everyone* is born with the capacity to develop the virtues, but they have to do so by acquiring good habits in childhood and eventually, as we attain maturity, practical wisdom (*phronesis*). By 'good habits' Aristotle means a settled disposition to feel and act appropriately, an important point for him because he disagrees with Socrates and Plato that virtue is knowledge, a doctrine that makes no sense of the phenomenon of weakness of will (*akrasia*); this latter exists, he says, and is caused by ungoverned emotions; therefore acquiring the habit of strength of will is important.

On the basis of these thoughts he offers a definition of *virtue* itself. A virtue is the middle path between opposing vices, one of deficiency and the other of excess. Thus courage is the middle path or 'mean' between cowardice (deficiency) and rashness (excess); generosity is the mean between meanness (deficiency) and profligacy (excess). The flute-player and the carpenter know how to steer a middle course between the excesses and deficiencies that spoil their work; so too a human being can acquire something analogous to a technical skill in knowing how to navigate between the vicious extremes between which the mean is the associated virtue.

Is there a general, invariant rule about the mean in all cases? No; the individual nature of a situation matters in determining what the mean is in that case. For example, one might think that the virtue of gentleness implies that one should never be angry, for remaining calm when faced with (say) an injustice is what lies between indifference and fury in reaction to it. But Aristotle says that the nature of the case might justify being angry; to be angry 'in the right way, to the right degree, for the right reason' is virtuous. But not to such a degree that it undermines reason.

'Virtue makes the goal right, practical wisdom teaches how to reach it,' Aristotle says, and habits formed in developing character will help to identify the right goals. If we do not have, or do not yet have, the practical wisdom to work out how to reach those goals, we must imitate those who do have such wisdom. And Aristotle concedes that 'moral luck' plays its part; those in fortunate circumstances find it easier to attain *eudaimonia* than those for whom life is a struggle.

It would be a mistake to regard the doctrine of the mean as implying

* Aristotle actually says 'all free males'.

that every goal should be a compromise. The doctrine is about how we act, not about always seeking halfway-house results. The critics who say that Aristotle's ethics of the middle way is by its nature 'middle class, middle aged and middle brow' are confusing intended action with intended outcome. Of course the idea of reflecting on the best course of action in a given situation, taking that situation's details into account, is intended to bring about the best outcome; but the best outcome is not therefore necessarily the outcome intermediate between what would happen if the actions implicit in either of the flanking extremes were taken. Suppose one decides to be generous to a person in need of money. The opposing vices are giving him nothing and giving him far more than he asks for, or even everything you have. The generous amount is what you can afford, not half what you have. (In some cases, his needs and what you can afford might prompt you to give him more than half of what you have! – it will depend entirely on the case.)

Aristotle defined human beings as 'political animals' – that is, beings alone capable of living together as citizens in a state. It would seem from this that his definition of the best life for people should therefore be that it is the life of cooperation, of achieving harmony, in the interests of a state. And that indeed is an end Aristotle identifies as a great desideratum, especially if the state is a *polis* of the kind he most approved – a small state, the ideal size being one where the voice of the town crier – the *stentor* – can be heard from one end to the other. This illustrates reasons why he disliked monarchy and empire, the very opposites of the kind of state he thought desirable. But in fact there is a higher 'best life for man' than life as a citizen, but which being a citizen enables. Being a citizen by its nature is a life of activity – activity as a citizen of the *polis* – but the yet higher life is a life of *contemplation*. Or in short: the life of a philosopher. For this, after all, is the life lived in greatest conformity with the distinguishing feature of a human being: the possession and exercise of reason.

In line with this view, Aristotle argues that the well-run state will be so if it provides an opportunity for leisure, for the opportunity to learn, discuss and contemplate, not depending for our happiness on externals of status and material goods, but on being our own masters, and enjoying the purest of pleasures: the exercise of our intellects. This ultimately is why we educate ourselves, he says: so that we can make 'a noble use of our leisure' – a view very different from today's belief that education is almost wholly about getting a job.

It might seem that Aristotle's subordination of ethics to politics has been reversed here, but this is not so, for in his *Politics* Aristotle argues that the state came into existence in the first place so that men might live, but then as the state matures its point develops into ensuring 'that men might live *well*'. Only in the settled and secure circumstances of a state can people have the leisure and opportunity to develop their intellectual interests, which provide them with what makes life supremely worthwhile.

It is necessary to end this account of Aristotle's views with a sketch of his cosmology. This is because his cosmology provided the dominant view of the universe for nearly two thousand years afterwards, and much of modern science and philosophy resulted from a rejection of his picture of the cosmos. This makes his book *On the Heavens* (*Peri Ouranou*, for most of history known as *De Caelo*) one of the most influential in human history.

Aristotle's universe is a sphere. The fixed stars are its outer circumference and the earth lies motionless at its centre. Within the circle of the fixed stars are layers of spheres, each carrying one of the planets, and the spheres of the sun and the moon. Whereas on earth everything is formed out of the four elements earth, air, fire and water, the spheres are formed of a wholly different fifth element, the aether, an invisible substance purer than fire. The apparently irregular motion of the planets – from *planetai*, 'wanderers', in Greek – results from the fact that each sphere rotates on its own axis, but is influenced by the rotation of the sphere above it; so the spheres of the planets do not move synchronously with the sphere of the fixed stars, but their rotations are affected by the outermost sphere's rotation. Ingenious mathematical descriptions of these irregularities were achieved, first by Hipparchus about 150 BCE, then most notably by the second-century CE Alexandrian astronomer Ptolemy, whose system remained the dominant one until Copernicus in the sixteenth century CE.

The sublunary sphere, the one below the sphere of the moon, which is the lowest of the heavenly spheres, is the region of earth, air, fire and water, the inferior elements ('inferior' does not automatically mean 'bad' or 'second rate' but simply 'below'; however, it comes to have the connotation we now attach to 'inferior' because it lacks the purity and other distinguishing properties of the aether, the 'superior' – 'above' – element constituting the spheres, known also as the 'quintessence' because it is the 'fifth essence' additional to the inferior four). Whereas the natural motion of the aether is circular – the most perfect path for anything heavenly is a circular one – the inferior elements move either upwards or downwards: earth and water move downwards, fire and air upwards; earth is the heaviest, fire the lightest. Things composed of inferior elements move in straight lines, unlike the superior heavenly things with their circular motion.

The doctrine of the four inferior elements came from Empedocles, along with their properties of being cool, moist, hot and dry. Things made out of them are corruptible and perishable. The heavenly bodies, made of quintessence, are incorruptible, imperishable and eternal – again satisfying the Parmenidean requirements.

Much of Aristotle's cosmology is suggested by Eudoxus, another of Plato's pupils, but the form in which it came to be adopted by the Christian Church was Aristotle's, and this is the reason for its longevity: as late as the seventeenth century CE the Roman Catholic Church was still putting people to death if they refused to picture the universe to themselves in Aristotle's way.* The temptation to regard theories such as this as merely quaint should be tempered by the fact that until the seventeenth century anyone looking up at the night sky would have seen the heavens rotating about the earth, and had no reason to think it was he or she who was rotating relative to them: that shift of perspective took a great intellectual revolution to make it possible, and at one point in the history of our species this shift must have been a vertiginous, and even terrible, surprise.

In the centuries immediately after Aristotle's own time his logical works were studied and in interesting respects developed by thinkers collectively known as the 'Megarian school', though they were not strictly a school. The name comes from Megara, birthplace of a follower of Socrates called Euclides, whose later followers devoted themselves to logic. In other respects, however, Aristotle's influence was, to begin with, to all intents and purposes null. Yet although his thought was almost completely lost for a time – the tenuousness of the survival of his works, as described above, makes one shudder – their rediscovery and survival have had an immense influence, directly and by

* As happened to Giordano Bruno in 1600 CE, Giulio Cesare Vanini in 1619 – and nearly to Galileo in 1632.

opposition, on the later history of philosophy and science. In fact he was twice rediscovered: once by Andronicus over two centuries after his death, and again in the twelfth century CE when works that had survived in lands conquered by Muslims became once more accessible in Europe. In the high medieval period, as a result of this second rediscovery, he was known simply and with justification as 'the Philosopher', a label bestowed by Thomas Aquinas.

Greek and Roman
Philosophy after Aristotle

Seven and a half centuries lie between the deaths of Alexander the Great and St Augustine of Hippo; Alexander died in 323 BCE, Augustine in 430 CE. Historians divide this long stretch of time into two main periods, the Hellenistic and the Imperial. Alexander's death marks the end of the classical and the beginning of the Hellenistic period, while the end of the latter is placed at the start of Augustus Caesar's principate in 27 BCE, which inaugurates the Imperial period. Four hundred years later, in the lifetime of St Augustine, Christianity became the official religion of the Roman Empire, and for more than the next thousand years philosophy was almost exclusively subordinated to the demands of Christian doctrine and Church authority.

The four most notable philosophical schools in the Hellenistic and Imperial period, apart from the already existing Academy of Plato and (briefly at the outset) Peripatetic school of Aristotle, were the Epicurean, Stoic, Cynic and Neoplatonist schools – though it would be wrong to call the Cynics a 'school' in any organized sense; here the word has its informal meaning of an outlook or tradition of thought. Aristotle's school – a formal one – dwindled away not long after his death because its main followers, like Aristotle himself, left Athens and settled in various parts of the Hellenic world, so that for a number of centuries the school's teachings ceased to be influential. In the third century BCE Plato's Academy fell under the influence of sceptical thinkers, though it survived as an institution until 529 CE when the Emperor Justinian abolished it and forbade the teaching of 'pagan philosophy'.

For most of this period the Epicurean and Stoic schools were dominant. Cynicism was a minority commitment in terms of adherents, but it influenced the formation of Stoicism, and in fact lasted considerably longer than Stoicism and Epicureanism, some people still claiming to be Cynics in the fifth century CE. This was chiefly because, after its founding by Antisthenes, Cynicism was an exclusively ethical outlook and way of life, with no logical, epistemic or cosmological theories involved. It therefore encapsulates in purest form an interesting major feature of philosophy in this period, which is its greater focus on achieving *ataraxia*, 'peace of mind'. One reason why this concern came to greater prominence alongside the philosophical aims, already well established, of *understanding the world* and *achieving the good life* is arguably the greater insecurity of Hellenic times, the loss of civic autonomy under the empires of Alexander and Rome, and the need felt by people to seek within themselves for a sense of security and stability that outer events could not guarantee. Whatever the prompt for it, philosophy increasingly came to target the question of how to strengthen the inner psychological resources of the individual so that he or she can achieve *ataraxia*.*

Although Cynicism, Epicureanism and Stoicism are the principal movements of thought in the Hellenic and Roman periods until the rise of Neoplatonism, their roots lie in the lifetime of Socrates. The founding figures of Cynicism – Antisthenes and Diogenes – were contemporaries of Plato, and Antisthenes was a pupil or, more accurately perhaps, companion of Socrates. Democritus the atomist, whose views provided an inspiration for Epicurus, was likewise a contemporary of Socrates and Plato. Although the founder of Stoicism, Zeno of Citium, lived nearly a century later – he was a child of eight when Aristotle died in 322 BCE – his school shared these Socratic roots; he was influenced by the Cynics who had taken their cue from the hardier and more convention-opposing aspects of Socrates' outlook and style of life. Accordingly Stoicism, which came to claim the adherence of almost all educated Romans for centuries, and had one of its most eloquent voices in the Emperor Marcus Aurelius in the second century CE, is also appropriately seen as an outcome of the Socratic moment.

---

* The writings of Seneca, Cicero and Marcus Aurelius, and the teachings of Epictetus, are classics of this trend.

CYNICISM

The Cynics sought to live 'according to nature' and in opposition to convention. The most famous of them, Diogenes of Sinope, known better as 'Diogenes the Cynic', took these commitments to their logical limit; he went about naked, slept in a barrel, masturbated in public, saying that he wished hunger was as easily appeased by rubbing the stomach, and carried a lantern in broad daylight, remarking, when asked why he did so, that he was 'looking for a man' and adding that he had 'once seen some boys in Sparta' – the point being that the way of life there was less effete than in Athens.

Diogenes was not however the founder of Cynicism, though he was its most dramatic exemplar. Diogenes Laertius ascribes the movement's origin to Antisthenes, and his views to the example set by one side of Socrates' outlook and style of life. Antisthenes was born in Athens and lived between 445 and 365 BCE. He had begun his education with Gorgias the sophist, becoming a highly accomplished speaker as a result, but switched his adherence to Socrates on being persuaded that virtue is the source of happiness, and that the route to virtue lies through asceticism.

Antisthenes believed that virtue can be taught, and requires nothing but the 'strength of a Socrates', that is, courage and self-command. Virtue is ennobling, he said; it expresses itself in deeds and requires few words. Anyone good deserves to be loved, and how one acts should be dictated by the laws of virtue whether or not they conform to the laws of the *polis*. These two latter views are such as an outsider would be well placed to form: Antisthenes was a *nothos*, or 'bastard-born', because his parents were not married (his mother was moreover a Thracian), so he did not have Athenian citizenship. His follower Diogenes undoubtedly acquired from Antisthenes a dislike for the aristocratic Plato; Antisthenes accused Plato of pride and conceit, once remarking to him, on seeing a spirited horse capering in a procession, 'If you were a steed you would be just such a proud, showy one.'

The list of Antisthenes' books is long, though very little remains of what he wrote. His influence on those who both followed and furthered his example – Diogenes the Cynic, Crates of Thebes and Zeno of Citium (who founded Stoicism) – is what justifies his nomination as founder of the school; Diogenes Laertius said that he 'gave the impulse to the indifference of Diogenes, the continence of Crates, and the hardihood of Zeno'. Indifference to convention and conventional ambitions, continence and hardihood are the essentials of the Cynical outlook. The Stoics shared the two latter characteristics, but what made them markedly different was that they cared about their duties to society.

Antisthenes embraced poverty and the ascetic life, and it was claimed that the symbols of adherence to Cynicism – a ragged cloak, a staff and a 'wallet' or small bag – originated with him (some say, with Diogenes). The idea that the only thing you need by way of a bed is a folded cloak is certainly attributed to him.

Diogenes the Cynic, as noted, took the idea of spurning convention and living 'according to nature' to its limit. Born in 412 BCE at Sinope on the Black Sea, he lived for nearly ninety years, dying in 323 BCE. It appears that life did not begin well for him, because he suffered banishment from Sinope for a crime: his father ran the mint in that city, and father and son were together convicted of debasing the coinage.

In Athens Diogenes attached himself to Antisthenes, persistently following him about though Antisthenes did not want him as a pupil. One source of the name 'Cynic', which means 'dog', is that Diogenes was said to follow Antisthenes around like a faithful hound. Other sources for the name came from the lifestyle of an ownerless cur adopted by Diogenes, and his curmudgeonly criticism of all things conventional. In Greek *kyon* is 'dog' and *kynikos* 'dog-like'.

According to Diogenes Laertius, Diogenes had a sparky adversarial relationship with Plato, whom he criticized for having carpets in his house and attending banquets. Treading on Plato's carpets one day he said, 'I trample on the pride of Plato,' to which Plato replied, 'Yes, Diogenes, with pride of another kind.'

One story says that Diogenes was later captured by pirates and sold into slavery at Corinth. He was purchased by one Xeniades who made him tutor to his sons. He became a much loved member of the family and remained with them until his death. Among many different accounts of the cause of his death is that he was bitten by a dog and died of blood-poisoning – an obvious punning tale for the death of a Cynic.

Although Diogenes is also said to have written books and plays, his views are chiefly expressed in the anecdotes of his life, many doubtless apocryphal. One such is that he was visited by Alexander the Great who offered him anything he wished, to which Diogenes replied, 'You can stand out of my sunlight.'

Diogenes' chief tenet was that one should live simply and naturally, indeed like a dog – and he accordingly urinated and defecated anywhere in public, ate whenever he happened to feel hungry and observed no taboos about what could be eaten, including food taken from temple sacrifices. He advocated living in complete independence of convention, and described himself as a 'citizen of the world', a *cosmopolitan*. He charged his contemporaries with living artificially, their minds befogged or 'smoky' because of the folly of desiring wealth, fame and honour. The goal of life should be *eudaimonia* (happiness) and *atuphia* (clarity of mind; literally, 'unsmokiness'), achieved through *askesis* (asceticism), which gives *autarkeia* (self-sufficiency), strength and peace of mind. This meant living and acting without shame – shamelessly – and spurning the laws of society and the state wherever they conflict with the simple, natural, truly virtuous life.

It is noteworthy that whereas others who have rejected society and its artificialities as barriers to virtue – for a later and more familiar example, the Christian 'desert fathers' and hermits – the Cynics did not take themselves into the wilderness in search of their simple life, but lived it in the midst of the city. The Christian hermits went to the desert to escape temptation; Diogenes challenged temptation right in its midst. The point was to encourage people to embrace simplicity and a natural way of living by confronting them with an example of it. And the confrontation was not just by example, but by criticizing, poking fun, embarrassing and even horrifying people to get them to think.

Diogenes might be thought to have had nothing to lose, as a criminal exile and perhaps, later, as a slave, in choosing and extolling a dog's existence. The opposite is true of the next in the succession of leading Cynics, Crates of Thebes, who was born to great wealth but gave it away, after he had heard and witnessed Diogenes. He said he was a 'fellow-citizen of Diogenes' – thus, a citizen of the world – and with him repudiated conventionality.

Crates and his wife Hipparchia of Maroneia, also from a wealthy family, accordingly chose to live as beggars on the streets of Athens. They came to be well known and respected for their good humour and principled stance, and were welcomed everywhere, not least in their role as conciliators, soothing family quarrels and settling arguments with kindness. Their version of the simple life was less confrontational than that of Diogenes, and their focus appears to have been more on the *ataraxia* achievable by freedom from the desires and aims of convention than on attacking people for their adherence to convention.

Diogenes Laertius said that Crates' philosophical letters were as beautifully written as Plato's dialogues, but none survive; there are thirty-six extant letters attributed to him, but they have been shown to be later forgeries. He enjoined the philosophical life because it liberates one from dissatisfactions and trouble; when you have money, he said, you can share it liberally, and when you have none, you will not be unhappy about it, but will be pleased with whatever you have. He encouraged people to live on a simple diet of lentils, saying that luxurious living eventually leads to strife because the reason that people compete for position and wealth is that these are necessary for making a luxurious life possible, and for maintaining it thereafter.

Crates and Hipparchia are attractive proponents of the claim that simplicity and naturalness are the route to happiness. It is not implausible to suppose that they succeeded in following this route because they had each other's company on the way.

EPICUREANISM

An entire book of Diogenes Laertius' *Lives* is dedicated to Epicurus, and it includes extensive quotations from three letters by Epicurus summarizing his views on physics, ethics and the heavens respectively. Collections of his sayings, documents in the library of the first-century BCE Epicurean philosopher Philodemus (found under the Vesuvian ashes at Herculaneum), and above all the fine poem *De Rerum Natura* ('On the Nature of Things'), written by Lucretius also in the first century BCE, give a comprehensive account of the Epicurean theories. Lucretius' poem is an adaptation in hexameter verse of Epicurus' book *Peri Phuseus* ('On Nature'). Cicero, writing at the same period as Philodemus and Lucretius, made a critical examination of the Epicurean philosophy in his *Tusculan Disputations*. The enduring reputation of Epicureanism in the Hellenic and Imperial periods is evidenced by the fact that its chief doctrines were inscribed for public benefit on the wall of a portico built in the Lycian city of Oenoanda by another Diogenes in the second century CE.

Epicurus was born in 341 BCE in the Athenian colony of Samos, and moved to Athens itself at the age of eighteen, in 323 BCE, when the colonists were expelled from Samos following the death of Alexander that year. His interest in philosophy was prompted at the age of fourteen when he found that his schoolmasters could not explain the meaning of 'chaos' in the writings of Hesiod. In Athens he studied with one Nausiphanes, a pupil of Democritus the atomist, before moving first to Mytilene and then Lampsacus, in both places starting a school and gathering pupils. Eventually he settled back in Athens, where he bought a garden as a site for his school, and lived there until his death at the age of seventy-one. His school was known as 'the Garden' accordingly.

One of the startling things about Diogenes Laertius' life of Epicurus is the lengthy report it contains of the calumny and hostility heaped on the philosopher by his enemies. He was accused of practising magic and casting spells for a fee, writing scandalous letters, consorting with courtesans, flattering influential people, plagiarizing other philosophers and devoting himself to luxury and sensual pleasures. It was said that he was bulimic (so that he could eat more) and was so physically feeble that he could hardly rise from his chair; and that he aspersed others including Aristotle and Heraclitus – he said Aristotle had wasted his patrimony and made money by selling drugs, and that Heraclitus was a 'muddler'. Diogenes Laertius says that those who spoke thus of Epicurus were 'mad', because everyone else testified to his kindness and good will, his generosity, gentleness, piety, consideration for others and humility, his restraint and frugality, and the famous moderation of the Garden's lifestyle. Part at least of the hostility felt by some for Epicurus and his school doubtlessly arose from misunderstanding of his view that happiness consists in 'the pursuit of pleasure and the avoidance of pain' – which as we shall see does not at all mean what it seems to mean – and his rejection of religion.

The starting point for Epicurus' philosophy is that the fundamental stuff of nature is matter in the form of atoms, which are individual solid material particles that cannot be divided further. They are too small to be perceived, and they move or 'fall' in the void (empty space), understood as 'where matter is not'. The theory is Democritean, but it incorporates solutions to problems that Aristotle and others had seen in Democritus' theory. For one thing, there was the problem of making sense of the idea of an 'infinite void' – no up or down, no direction; how can anything 'fall' or move in such a space? – and for another, as Aristotle argued in Book VI of his *Physics*, the idea of a 'minimum' particle of matter is incoherent, for consider: if two such minima cross paths, how could they ever be halfway past each other, given that if they were so, then they are not minima? An implication of Aristotle's view, interestingly, is that if there are minima of matter, then space and time themselves must be quantized. But if atoms are discrete minima, then they do not move continuously but must jump from point to point in space and time, and must all do so at the same speed.

Epicurus' response is ingenious. It is, first, that although atoms are (as their name implies) indivisible, they are not the same thing as the least conceivable amount of matter, that is, the minima; atoms are composed of minima but cannot be broken down into them. No minimum of matter can exist independently by itself. As indissoluble aggregates of material minima, atoms have shapes – hooks and indentations – which is why they can adhere to each other to form larger objects of the kind we perceive. He accepted the idea that time and space consist of discrete quanta, and that all atomic motion occurs at the same speed. These motions cancel out in the aggregations of atoms constituting familiar macroscopic objects, through their collisions, deflections and conjunctions.

Atoms are indefinitely various in their shapes, explaining the variety of things built out of them, and they are 'in continual motion throughout eternity'. The atomic theory is the result of noting the implication of two propositions taken together: that what we encounter in experience is complex, that is, consists of parts; and that nothing can come from nothing. Therefore there must be fundamental units of material reality. And for them to move, combine and decouple, there must be space, a void, for them to move in. The properties of things we perceive – their colours, tastes and the rest – are caused by the configurations of the atoms constituting them, and how these interact with the configurations of atoms that constitute our sense organs.

This latter point is central to Epicurus' theory of mind and perception. Our perceivings (seeing, hearing and the rest) are reliable, Epicurus held, and arise from the interaction between the world and our sense organs. The world is entirely physical; there are no non-physical things, which means in particular that there are no non-physical souls or minds (the word for 'soul' and 'mind' is the same: *anima*). Our bodies are moved by our minds, and our minds are affected by what happens to our bodies, but neither could occur if minds were not made of the same stuff as bodies. Our souls or minds are accordingly themselves made of material atoms, though they are especially fine ones, which are dispersed throughout our bodies, and we perceive and feel by the causal interactions between the body-constituting and mind-constituting atoms. When the body dies these soul atoms are dispersed, and the functions of sensation and thought thereby cease. There is no life after death. And therefore there is nothing to fear in regard to death, Epicurus says; 'death is nothing to us, for good and evil imply sentience, and death is the privation of all sentience.'

In Epicurus' celebrated view, the 'alpha and omega of a blessed life' is pleasure: 'Pleasure is our first and native good.' The whole of the Epicurean ethic can be summed up as 'the pursuit of pleasure and the avoidance of pain'. We get the modern meaning of 'Epicureanism' – indulgence in wine, feasting and partying, devotion to the pleasures of the senses – from a completely erroneous interpretation of what Epicurus meant by this remark. For he immediately goes on to say:

> We often pass over many pleasures when a greater annoyance arises from them ... and we often regard certain pains as preferable to pleasures when in consequence they bring a greater pleasure to us later ... We regard being independent of outward things as a great good, not in order always to make use of little, but so that we are not inconvenienced when we do not have much; for they most enjoy luxury who have no need of it, and we know that what is natural is easily procured, while only vain and worthless things are hard to get. Plain food gives as much pleasure as a costly diet, bread and water confer the highest pleasure when conveyed to hungry lips ... To habituate ourselves to a simple and inexpensive diet supplies all that is needful for health, and enables us to meet all life's necessities without shrinking.

And that is why he nominates pleasure as 'the end and aim': 'We do not mean the pleasures of the prodigal or of sensuality ... we mean the absence of pain in the body and trouble in the mind ... what produces a pleasant life is sober reasoning, searching out the grounds of every choice, and banishing those things that cause tumults in the mind.' Understanding the nature of the world is the ground of this rational view; when we know that the universe is a material realm we are no longer afraid, as Lucretius points out in his great poem, of 'our foe religion' and superstition, but instead base our view of the world on reason and a clear understanding of reality.

Among the difficulties with Epicurus' theory is the problem that its picture of a mechanistic universe raises for the question of free will – a problem that continues to bedevil philosophy today, all the more so because the discoveries of neuroscience place mental phenomena ever more securely in the physical realm. Epicurus tried to deal with this by saying that the atoms swerve slightly as they move through the void, giving rise to accident and randomness; but this is not a satisfactory solution, for if our choices are not connected causally to the actions that, as we take it, follow from them, but instead occur randomly or accidentally only, then 'free will' is neither will nor free.

One of the greatest pleasures, according to Epicurus, is that of friendship, *philia*. Friendship might begin with considerations of the usefulness that people have for each other, but soon develops into a bond of deep and abiding mutual altruism.* The process mirrors the evolution of society, as Epicurus saw it; human beings were solitary creatures in the beginning, who over the course of history began to form families and communities, acquiring language and sharing the development of skills such as agriculture and building. (There is something in this of the idea of society emerging from an idealized 'state of nature', as Locke and Rousseau conceived of it much later, when the utility of cooperation was recognized.) In course of time the increasing complexity of societies saw the appearance of kings and tyrants, of religion and of fear of punishment. But the true source of justice is the perception of mutual benefit in the keeping of compacts, and the belief that a prudent, honourable and just life is the most pleasant one. If everyone lived by this ideal, Epicurus said, there would never be tyranny, and no need of religion, because society itself would be good.

For Epicurus the chief purpose of philosophy is to help people see what the best kind of life is, and why it is so. Philosophy is an education of the mind and a therapy for the soul: 'if philosophy does not heal the soul it is as bad as a medicine that does not heal the body,' he said. The happy life is the life of *ataraxia*, and one achieves it through philosophical understanding of the true nature of things, and by living in conformity with that understanding.

---

* Following Aristotle's laudatory account of friendship in the *Nicomachean Ethics* the concept became a central trope for much practical philosophy, from Epicurus to Cicero and on through the tradition to G. E. Moore.

STOICISM

Crates the Cynic is reputed to have been the teacher of Zeno of Citium, founder of Stoicism, who as we shall see can be said to have taught the internalization of the Cynic virtues of continence and self-mastery, and to have applied the concept of 'indifference' – *apatheia* – not to society and the goal of an honourable life, but to the vicissitudes of fortune and the inescapabilities of ageing, illness and death. What recommended Stoicism to educated and patrician Romans later was its high ideal of a noble self-mastered life, a life of courage and fortitude, a robust and manly life which could, with equal dispassion, bear the hardships of the military frontier abroad and the demands of duty at home.

Zeno hailed from Citium on the island of Cyprus, where he was born in 334 BCE. He began adult life as a merchant, but after reading Xenophon's account of Socrates he decided to study philosophy. It is said that while on a visit to Athens he asked a bookseller for advice on whom to approach among the teachers of philosophy, and at that moment Crates passed by, so the bookseller pointed him out. Zeno acquired from Crates his dedication to the Cynic virtues of continence and simplicity, but his modesty prevented him from living with 'shamelessness' in the preferred Cynic manner; hence his idea of internalizing the virtues – of being a semi-Cynic in private, as it were. In addition to modesty he also had a strong sense of civic duty, which requires that one perform one's responsibilities as a citizen rather than rejecting society altogether. His convictions in this respect are illustrated by the fact that when he was offered Athenian citizenship he refused it in order to keep faith with his native Citium, where he had endowed the public baths and was held in great esteem.

Crates was not Zeno's only teacher; he listened to teachers of the Megarian school of logic and the philosophers of the Academy, and whereas Cynicism gave him inspiration for his ethical teaching it was from these other influences that he developed views in logic and physics. He set up his own school in the painted colonnade or Stoa (*stoa poikile*) of the Athenian *agora*, from which the name of the school derives. His pupil and then colleague Cleanthes (*c.*330–*c.*230 BCE) succeeded him as head of the school when he died in 262 BCE. The logical and physical teachings of Stoicism were developed by Cleanthes and his own successor as the school's head, Chrysippus (279–206 BCE). It is not known which of them is chiefly responsible for the doctrines of early Stoicism, but later Stoicism, as exemplified by Seneca, Epictetus and Marcus Aurelius, was almost exclusively devoted to the ethical question of how to live, though this aspect of Stoicism was present from the outset.

In their physics the Stoics were committed to the view that the signature of reality is the capacity to act or be acted upon, and they therefore said that the only things that exist are physical bodies. Matter, therefore, is a fundamental principle (*arche*) of the universe. But they pointed out that we also refer to many other things that are not bodies, for example places, times and imaginary objects such as mythical beasts. These things do not exist but 'subsist', that is, have a kind of courtesy semi-existence because they can be talked about. Unlike Plato who held that universals really exist (albeit in a Realm of Being accessible only to the intellect), they described these objects of reference as mental entities only, much as did the nominalists of later philosophy.

The *arche*, matter, is indestructible and eternal. But there is another fundamental principle of the universe alongside matter, also indestructible and eternal; this is *logos*, reason. It pervades and organizes the universe, making it go through a cycle of changes beginning with fire, passing through the formation of the elements – fire, air, water and earth, the first two active and the latter two passive – thence on to the emergence of the world as we know it, constituted by combinations of these elements, and thence back again to the universal fire, which begins the cycle over again, in eternal recurrence. This *logos* the Stoics also called 'fate' and 'god', and it is a material thing, like the physical universe which it orders through these endlessly repeating cycles.

The Stoics held that the universe is a plenum of matter, meaning that there is no empty space. This raises the question of how things can be individuated – told apart – externally, and how they can maintain themselves internally as individual things. The answer is that they are kept apart as different individuals, and kept together internally each as a single individual, by *pneuma* or breath, which is a combination of fire and air. Pneuma penetrates all things, and because it comes in different 'grades' it is the cause of things having different properties. It is what gives plants and animals their respective kinds of life, and it is what gives reason to humans. It is unclear whether this view committed the Stoics to thinking that, because pneuma is physical stuff, its role as the rational part of a human being cannot survive a bodily dissolution at death. Chrysippus said that the pneuma of the wise would survive the death of their associated bodies until the next fiery conflagration, perhaps because the pneuma of the wise has greater self-integrating power than that of the unwise; but the view smacks of compromise.

'Logic' was a broad topic for the Stoics, including not just reasoning and its science but also epistemology and philosophical grammar. Their contributions to logic strictly so called were significant; unlike Aristotle's logic of terms they explored the inferential relations between whole propositions, and identified three basic rules of inference (actually they thought there were five, but three of them are the same rule written three different ways), which are familiar and central in today's propositional calculus.* An interesting feature of their logic is that it is committed to strict bivalence, that is, the principle that there are two and only two 'truth-values', namely, *true* and *false*, and that every assertion must be one or the other. Aristotle had wrestled with the question whether this must be so, by contemplating a proposition about the future: 'there will be a sea battle tomorrow.' Is this *now* definitely either true or false? If it is either, there must *now* be a fact about the future. But the future does not exist, so how can there be a fact about it? Aristotle therefore decided that the proposition is neither true nor false – bivalence does not, he said, apply to future-tensed propositions about contingent matters.

Chrysippus however thought that all statements, even future-tensed ones, must be definitely either true or false, and this therefore committed him to strict determinism: if 'there will be a sea battle tomorrow' is now either true or false, it is now already settled that there will or will not be a sea battle tomorrow. In asserting the Stoic metaphysical principle that *logos* as 'fate' drives the universe through its repeating cycles of history, he is to be taken quite literally.

This view brought the Stoics into conflict with the Academy, Plato's school which had by this time been converted to scepticism (see below). The Stoics argued that the criterion of a belief's truth is whether or not the experience that gives rise to it is caused in one's mind by the thing itself; as they put it, truth consists in the *phantasia kataleptike* or

---

* The basic 'indemonstrables' or rules of inference they identified were: *modus ponens* (p → q; p; therefore q); *modus tollens* (p → q; ¬q; therefore ¬p); and the Disjunctive Syllogism in three different guises which they do not seem to have recognized as such: (p ∨ q; p; therefore ¬q); (p ∨ q; ¬p; therefore q); (¬(p & q); p; therefore ¬q). This last is equivalent by De Morgan's Theorems to (¬p ∨ ¬q); ¬p; therefore ¬q. See the Appendix on logic.

'cognitive impression' being 'stamped and impressed [on one's mind] in accordance with the very thing itself, and is such that it could not arise from what is not'. The sceptics pointed out that 'no impression arising from something true is such that an impression arising from something false could not be just like it.' This is a point that has made sceptical arguments a central concern in epistemology throughout its history. The Stoics did not think that merely having an impression amounted to knowledge, just by itself, nor did they think that having an impression and assenting to it or believing it is enough. The impression has to be supported by something further, something that 'nails it down' as Plato had said. What is that 'something further'?

This is the $64,000 question that all epistemology has tried to answer. The answers have included 'watertight justification of some kind', 'conformity with other known truths', 'a logical relationship to foundational or "self-evident" or "basic" propositions' – the candidates have been numerous. Zeno of Citium had himself given the following illustration: hold out your hand: that is *perceiving*. Fold the fingers back: that is *believing*. Clench your fist: that is *comprehending*. Grasp your fist very tightly and securely in your other fist, so that it is supported: that is *knowing*. Like these other suggestions this indicates the *form* of what a definition of knowledge should be like, but not the substance.

It was however the ethics of Stoicism that made it so influential for so long, especially in the Roman world. The fundamental Stoic idea in ethics is that happiness – which they agreed is the end or goal, *telos*, of life – consists in 'living in accordance with nature'. What is in accordance with nature is what is good. The good is what benefits us in all circumstances, unlike things which are only good in some circumstances and not in others, for example, wealth. Things that are sometimes good and sometimes bad the Stoics called 'indifferents'. The things that are always good are the virtues of prudence, courage, moderation and justice. Given that wealth can sometimes be good though it is not an unqualified good like prudence, we need to distinguish between 'what is good' *as such* and what can sometimes have value (*axia*). Things which have value can be preferred over their opposites – wealth, health and honour can be preferred to poverty, illness and dishonour – because they are usually of advantage to us, or 'appropriate', *oikeion*, for us; and as such we have a natural tendency to seek them. But if they interfere with the realization of what is wholly and unqualifiedly good, they are of course not to be preferred to it.

Living well consists in rationally choosing those things that are good, and those things that are appropriate when consistent with things that are good, and the choices will be governed by seeking to conform to nature. It may well be that we do not succeed in achieving certain of the 'indifferents' which we rationally and appropriately pursue, such as wealth; but if we have what is good – courage, prudence, moderation – we will still be happy. An important aspect of this is the idea that what lies within our own control, for example our appetites, desires and fears, we should seek to master; but as to what lies beyond our control, those things we can do nothing about such as ageing, or suffering because of an illness or earthquake, we must face them with courage. The difference is between action and passion: action is what we do, passion is what we undergo or suffer as recipients without a choice. To bear the passions, *pathe*, courageously means not letting them master us; we must be *ap-athetic* with regard to them. That is the original meaning of this term.

The ancients also thought that emotions we now regard as active ones, such as love and anger, and to which we give the name of passions, were indeed truly so in the sense of their being inflicted on us as passive recipients of them: the passion of erotic desire, lust, was thought to be an infliction, even a punishment, from the gods. Excessive versions of the passions are 'disobedient to reason' and it is necessary to school oneself to be ready for them, so that one can be – well, *stoical* about them.

Unlike the more technical and difficult philosophies of Plato and Aristotle, and unlike the practically unliveable if entertaining example provided by the Cynics, Stoicism was immediately applauded by the Athenian public. A statue was raised to Zeno and its inscription included the words 'Zeno of Citium ... [was] a man of worth ... exhorting the youth who were his pupils to virtue and temperance, affording by his own conduct a pattern in perfect accord with his teachings ...' It was a popular philosophy, and it received widespread recognition, including among its admirers the King of Macedon, Antigonus II Gonatas, who as a young man had attended Zeno's lectures in Athens, and who wished Zeno to come to Macedon to tutor his son. Cleomenes III of Sparta introduced reforms in line with Stoic teaching, and by the first century BCE it had become a significant part of patrician education in Rome; Octavian, who became the Emperor Augustus, had the Stoic Athenodorus Calvus as his tutor when he was young.

In the first two centuries CE the three leading Stoics were Marcus

Aurelius and Epictetus, who wrote in Greek, and Seneca, who wrote in Latin. Whereas Epictetus taught, and Seneca published, Aurelius did neither: his statement of a Stoic outlook in his *To Himself* (now known as the *Meditations*) was a private diary written while he was with his army on the troubled and dangerous Danube frontier in the years 170–80 CE. The desire for privacy was his reason for writing in Greek. The humanity and Stoic dedication to service exemplified in his book have been admired ever since.

Epictetus was born a slave in Phrygia; his name in effect means 'bought' or 'owned'. He was taken to Rome in early life, where his owner (himself a former slave who had served the Emperor Nero) allowed him to study philosophy with the Stoic Musonius Rufus. After he had gained his freedom Epictetus set up as a teacher. In 93 CE the Emperor Domitian proscribed philosophy in Rome and banished the philosophers, whereupon Epictetus moved to Nicopolis in Greece and established a school. He wrote nothing himself, but his teachings have been preserved in the *Discourses* and, for a more popular readership, in the *Encheiridion* ('Handbook') by his pupil Arrian.

Self-knowledge and self-mastery are the key ideas in Epictetus. He argued that the distinction between what is within our power and what lies outside our power shows where the good is to be found, namely, within ourselves. Our use of reason, and our freedom to choose, allow us to evaluate the experiences we have and to ask ourselves, 'Can I do something about this?' If the answer is Yes, then act; if the answer is No, then say, 'It is nothing to me'; this is the *apatheia* connoted in the idea of bearing with ('being stoical about') the unavoidable or inevitable. Everything turns on our attitudes, which lie under our own control, guided by reason. Acceptance of inevitabilities is freedom; it is 'the price paid for a quiet mind'.

There is something of fatalism in Epictetus' teaching. 'Ask not that events should happen as you will, but let your will be that events should happen as they do, and you shall be at peace . . . Behave in life as you would at a banquet. A dish is handed round and comes to you; put out your hand and take politely. It passes you; do not stop it. It has not reached you; do not be impatient to get it, but wait until your turn comes . . . Remember that foul words and blows are no outrage in themselves; it is your judgment that they are so that makes them so. When anyone makes you angry, it is your own thought that has angered you. Therefore make sure not to let your impressions carry you away.'

Seneca (the Younger) was born in Spain in 4 BCE and became a senator and adviser to the Emperor Nero in Rome. His efforts to mitigate the increasing cruelty of Nero's rule failed, so he twice tried to retire but the Emperor refused to let him go. Eventually he was implicated in the Pisonian plot to assassinate Nero, and his punishment was an order to commit suicide, which he did. This occurred in 65 CE. The historian Tacitus gives a graphic account of the occasion; because of his age and condition Seneca was unable to bleed to death effectively after cutting open several veins – the blood flowed too thinly and weakly – and so he took poison as well, eventually immersing himself in a hot bath to speed the blood loss. Tacitus says that he was 'suffocated by the steam'.

Seneca's works included essays, moral letters, dialogues and tragedies, almost all published in his lifetime, and they had a wide readership and great popularity. He knew the thought of his Stoic predecessors well, and applied it eclectically to the business of living a good, fortitudinous and reason-governed life. 'No doubt troubles will come; but they are not a present fact, and might not even happen after all – why run to meet them? . . . More things make us afraid than do us harm . . . Do not be unhappy before the crisis comes . . . Some things torment us more than they ought, some torment us before they even happen; some torment us which should not torment us at all. We exaggerate, or imagine, or anticipate sorrow, unnecessarily.' The theme is the central Stoic one that it is our own attitudes and beliefs that make life good or bad. Hamlet was epitomizing Stoicism in his remark that 'there is nothing either good or bad, but thinking makes it so.'

There is nothing theoretical about the adjurations of the Stoics, for whom philosophy was a practical matter, aimed at making a real difference to the felt quality of life. Understanding oneself and how things are in the world is liberating, they argued, precisely because it puts the key to happiness into our own hands: we can choose to be indifferent to what we cannot influence, while at the same time rationally governing our own feelings. It was a commentator on Stoicism, Cicero, who best found a way of summing up their ethical outlook: 'to learn to philosophize', he wrote, 'is to learn how to die,' meaning that a right understanding of death frees one from the fear of it, so that one can live with greater courage and autonomy. If you are not afraid of death you are ultimately and completely free, because you always have an escape from the intolerable. Freedom from the oppression of anxiety and fear, and from desiring what one cannot oneself achieve or gain, is happiness itself.

The idea that happiness is the aim is, as we shall see, shared by all in the ethical debate from Aristotle onwards. Ideas about how to achieve it have much in common too, for in Aristotle, Epicurus and the Stoics *reason* is the liberator. The differences between them, on this particular point, lie chiefly in what aspect of reason's application they emphasize.

SCEPTICISM

Reflection on the course of philosophy in the classical and Hellenistic periods suggests why it should be that, from the third century BCE until the second century CE, there was a school of thinkers who called into question the very possibility of knowledge. These were the sceptics. The Presocratics had focused attention on the distinction between appearance and reality, concentrating on the incontrovertible fact that how the world seems is not a straightforward guide to how it is, and proposing different accounts of what the underlying 'real reality' is, among them Parmenides' 'One', Heraclitus' flux, Democritus' atoms, Plato's Forms. Moreover the sophists had illustrated how one could reason with equal cogency on either side of the same question, prompting one to ask, 'Which side, therefore, is really right?' Socrates said that his turn from 'physics' to ethics as a young man was prompted by the indecisive, indeed fruitless, quest to know reality, a waste of energy when the far more important question of 'how one should live' goes unanswered; and even here, as the Socratic *aporia* shows, the answers are hard to find.

In Plato the question of what knowledge is and how we can acquire it is a recurrent theme, and one which in the end is not fully resolved: in the late dialogue *Timaeus* he reaffirms his view, set out in the *Meno*, *Republic* and elsewhere beforehand, that knowledge of the world around us can only ever at best be probabilistic. He had already acknowledged the problem of relativism in the *Theaetetus*, the idea that what is true for one person might be false for another, with no way of judging between them.

Reflecting on all this might make someone wonder whether knowledge is possible at all, and whether enquiry will ever get us anywhere. Scepticism seems a natural response to this apparent general *aporia*. Aristotle in several places addresses the question of enquiry, for example in the *Metaphysics* and *Posterior Analytics*, advocating a method that begins from experience or common knowledge, and then works to refine it. We have beliefs, and act on them; in his view there can be no question of 'suspending belief' or not believing, because then we would be no different from plants. So the question is, How can we arrive at the best beliefs, and how can we rationally select the point at which explanations and justifications stop? In making these points – in offering what can in effect be construed as rebuttals to scepticism – Aristotle shows that he was well aware of scepticism's intellectual temptations.

Those temptations were, however, great, and they produced a sceptical reaction in two forms: the scepticism of the Academy, and the even more uncompromising scepticism of the Pyrrhonian school. As this suggests, there are significant differences between these two sceptical schools, even though Sextus Empiricus, who in the second century CE wrote the most comprehensive account of scepticism, regarded the differences as superficial.

It was the sixth successor of Plato as head of the Academy, Arcesilaus (316–241 BCE), who turned it in a sceptical direction when he became its leader in 266 BCE. He left no writings, and his views have been inconsistently reported by later commentators, among them Cicero, Plutarch and Sextus Empiricus, so it is difficult to attribute a precise set of doctrines to him. But in reaffirming the Socratic conception of philosophy as enquiry which proceeds by way of dialectic, and accepting the aporetic – indecisive – outcome of such enquiry, he argued that we must withhold belief, not accepting either side of an argument, because there is no criterion of truth that can help us to choose between them. In denying that there is a criterion of truth he was directly rejecting both the Stoic and the Epicurean commitments to the existence of such a thing.

This last point reminds us that Zeno, Stoicism's founder, who was about twenty years older than Arcesilaus, had been a member of the Academy too, and also claimed Socrates as the inspiration for his outlook. In his case, however, he took the equation of virtue with knowledge, and the achievability of virtue through a Stoic life, to entail that knowledge must therefore be possible – even though it is as difficult to attain as it is to live the fully Stoic life itself.

The chief difficulty for Arcesilaus was, as just noted, the claim that truth is discoverable. His view was that it is not discoverable. A key point for Stoicism was the thought that suitably constrained perception gives rise to 'cognitive apprehensions', that is, accurate representations of what is perceived. In a distantly similar way Epicurus thought that it is possible to test claims about what is not evident, for example claims about the microstructure of matter, against what is evident, especially what appears in sense-perception; for, he said, the latter will place boundaries around what can be claimed about the former. But Arcesilaus rejected all such views on the grounds that there is no way to distinguish between perceptions that are misleading from those that are veridical. The Stoics responded by saying that 'cognitive apprehensions' are those that arise in such a way that it is not possible for them to be non-veridical. But then of course the question is: what way is that? And this, to repeat yet again, has been the nub of the sceptical challenge throughout philosophy's history.

Aristotle's point, that if you do not have beliefs you cannot act, was echoed more strongly by the Stoics who argued that action is based on assent to – acceptance of – a belief relevant to the matter in hand. This was an important point for them because it meant that they could escape the problem of determinism: perceptions are caused by external things, so if perception and belief are the same thing, and belief prompts action, then action is the outcome of the world acting causally on us. They argued therefore that *assent* to belief is required as the prompt for action; and assent is an act of mind and will. If there is no assent to a belief but there is action, then the action is merely a happening, no different from the behaviour of a mindless thing.

Given these considerations, how is Arcesilaus to explain action, or does 'suspension of belief' imply that one cannot act?

One reconstruction of Arcesilaus' reply is that just as the commitment to suspension of belief is the outcome of reasoning, so likewise would action be, in the following way: we receive many sense-impressions, often in conflict with each other. If they all triggered action the result would be confusion and even paralysis. So we just act 'in conformity with the reasonable' (*eulogon*), not by assenting to what seems reasonable (that is, holding it to be true), but simply by going along with it because it's the best of the options presented by experience. A Stoic might ask, What is the difference between, on the one hand, judging that it is more reasonable to act on *this* impression rather than *those* impressions, and, on the other hand, believing that *this* impression is more reliable or even true? To which Arcesilaus might answer, To think that it is more *eulogon* to act in accordance with *this* impression rather than *those* impressions does not require one to believe that what it conveys is the case (is true).

Arcesilaus is said by Cicero to have claimed that 'he knew nothing, not even his own ignorance.' That seems to leave open the possibility that he thought that such a thing as truth exists, but that we are not equipped to discover it. If so, this would be another way of distinguishing between the Academic sceptics and the Pyrrhonians. That this is possible is illustrated by Arcesilaus' successor as head of the Academy, Carneades (214–129 BCE).

Famously, Carneades was one of a group of philosophers invited to Rome in 155 BCE, where on one day he argued in favour of justice, and on the next against it, in what would seem classic sophistical style. His point was the sceptical one about the impossibility of knowledge (and, in particular, of knowing whether justice conforms to nature; he sought to argue that justice is an artificial construct, based on expediency). The Roman intelligentsia were disgusted by the display and it was another fifty years before Greek philosophy recovered from the stigma it thus acquired for them. Like his predecessor, Carneades did not write, and in Academic style employed the method of Socratic dialectic. What we know of his views comes in the first instance from his pupil and lover Clitomachus. Also like Arcesilaus he engaged with the Stoics on the questions that divided the Academy from them, but under the influence of their views he modified – one might say, softened – the sceptical stance, allowing a role to belief and to a kind of assent.

While emphasizing that there can be no criterion of truth, on the grounds that we have no way of judging the truth of sense-experience – which is the basis of our concepts and these in turn of our reasonings – Carneades nevertheless suggested that there is another, more modest, criterion which helps us choose how to act in practical life. This criterion is 'the persuasive' (*pithanon*). He did not mean that sense-experience might be causally persuasive, so to speak, by compelling us to assent to what it impresses on us, by (as the Stoics thought) some quality of the impressive relationship itself. Instead he meant something like 'plausibility' or 'rational convincingness'. In any matter of significance a sceptic will act on the most persuasive impressions. If it is a really important matter, the sceptic will act according to what is 'persuasive and undiverted', meaning by 'undiverted' that there are no competing impressions pulling in another direction. And in the great matter of what concerns happiness, the impressions on which sceptics will rely will be not only persuasive and undiverted, but those they have thoroughly explored. 'Thoroughly explored' impressions are those which remain persuasive after surrounding or related impressions have been examined fully.

The criterion of persuasiveness might itself be persuasive as it relates to action in practical affairs, but Sextus Empiricus claims that Carneades thought it was also intended to serve as a criterion of truth as such. Cicero understood *pithanon* to mean 'probable'. This therefore raises the question whether Carneades meant *belief* by 'persuasive impressions'. He spoke of 'approving' of persuasive impressions, which does not seem much different from the Stoics' 'assent', though he himself claimed it is not in fact the same. Clitomachus, who was closest to Carneades, said that he did not mean 'belief' by 'approved persuasive impression', though others of his pupils (Metrodorus of Stratonicea and Philo of Larissa) said that he did. Cicero accepts Clitomachus' understanding of the matter.

The dispute might seem to be largely a semantic one, but remember what was at stake for Academicians. The founder of their school, Plato, had sharply differentiated belief and knowledge, and regarded the former as insufficient, imperfect, a mere matter of opinion, unrelated to truth. It might even be 'shameful' to embrace mere beliefs, as Plato suggests in the *Republic*. If knowledge is impossible, as the sceptics argued, then belief is not merely a poor second-best but a shameful or even a dangerous thing. But this is so only if 'to believe' is taken to mean 'to believe *that it is true*'. Carneades suggests that if you know it is merely a belief you have before your mind, and do not fool yourself into thinking that it is or could be the truth, then it is acceptable to consider it and evaluate its plausibility in relation to action. In any case this is necessary, for as Plato himself had said in the *Meno*, one has to start from somewhere, and where else but with an hypothesis. An hypothesis – a suggestion, an idea, a proposal – is not a 'belief that something is true'; Carneades might have had some such idea in mind.

It seems that Carneades' successors in the Academy were as uncertain about what he said and meant as any good sceptic should be about anything. In 127 BCE he was followed as head by Clitomachus, who claimed that Carneades had argued for 'suspension of judgment' and had not believed in belief. Philo of Larissa, Clitomachus' fellow-student (or perhaps student?) and in 110 BCE his successor as head of the Academy, thought differently; he interpreted Carneades' notion of hypothetical belief as amounting to acceptance of tentative or defeasible belief.

After Philo the Academy had ceased to be sceptical; some

commentators saw it as returning under his leadership to a more orthodox Platonism in which, though there cannot be knowledge of the world accessed by our senses – about which there can only be opinion since all is transitory and imperfect – nevertheless there can be knowledge of eternal truths. This stance is known as 'dogmatic', in a non-pejorative sense to mean commitment to the view that truth is knowable and can be expressed.

True to its traditions as a school of philosophy, the Academy even in its sceptical phase was concerned with the topics of knowledge, belief, truth, reason, enquiry and action. The other sceptical movement, Pyrrhonism, was almost wholly concerned with one thing: attaining *ataraxia* (peace of mind, tranquillity). The man who gives Pyrrhonism its name, Pyrrho of Elis, was an unusual character, a stand-out figure like Diogenes the Cynic though with a very different persona. He too wrote nothing – it would not at all have fitted his chosen demeanour to do so – and his views come to us through his adherent Timon of Phlius, quoted by Diogenes Laertius, Aristocles, Eusebius and others.

Pyrrho (360–270 BCE) was said to have begun life as a painter, but on reading Democritus he decided to study philosophy, and went as a pupil to Stilpo, a teacher of the Megarian school. (The Megarians took their ethics from Socrates and devoted much attention to logic, making significant contributions to its development.) He travelled with the army of Alexander as far as India, where, so Diogenes Laertius tells us, he encountered the gymnosophists (the 'naked philosophers') of that region, having already met with the magi of Persia. This led him to adopt 'a most noble philosophy', consisting in 'agnosticism and suspension of judgment', saying that nothing is either just or unjust, nothing is honourable or dishonourable, indeed that nothing really exists; and only custom and habit guide human affairs.* Neither our experience nor our beliefs (our *doxai*) are true or false; there is no logical difference between them, and therefore they are undecidable. Accordingly we should have no views about anything, and should refuse to take sides on any matter.

Diogenes Laertius tells us that Pyrrho lived in perfect accordance with this doctrine. He was supremely relaxed and calm; he was indifferent

---

* Compare this view to the widely held view in schools of Indian philosophy – see below pp. 519–33 – that the world is an illusion, that reality is nothingness, that one's aim should be to escape existence. It is very plausible that Pyrrho should have acquired these views from the 'naked philosophers' of India, and lived accordingly.

to events – he did not even try to get out of the way of oncoming traffic and had constantly to be rescued by his friends from being knocked down. The combination of the assiduity of his friends and the relaxation of his attitude to life jointly explain the fact that he lived to the age of ninety. He had ardent followers who sought to imitate his lifestyle, and no doubt many philosophers would be delighted if their own countries followed the example of his country, Elis, which honoured him by freeing all philosophers from the obligation to pay tax. A less attractive aspect of his indifference appears in an anecdote telling us that he passed by a drowning man, for neither the man's plight, nor saving him or not saving him, mattered.

There are definite resonances between Pyrrho's views, as the legends about him present them, and what he might have learned from some Indian philosophers to the effect that the world is an illusion, and that believing and desiring are therefore pointless (they would have added, harmful). But from Timon and other sources we find that he had a definite theory: the points quoted earlier about the indistinguishability and undecidability of everything entail an outcome, which is that understanding these points will result 'first in speechlessness, then in freedom from worry'. But in themselves these points constitute claims of a substantial kind. The idea that everything is indistinguishable is the idea that reality is in itself formless, unstable and indeterminate. That is a metaphysical thesis. From it follows the epistemological thesis that mandates scepticism: our inability ever to determine whether anything is true or false rests on the indeterminacy of reality.

Pyrrhonian scepticism gets its major statement not from Pyrrho but from a later figure, Aenesidemus, a Cretan-born philosopher who lived in the first century BCE (his dates are uncertain) and who is said to have been a member of the Academy but left it when Philo of Larissa rejected scepticism. His book *Pyrrhoneoi Logoi* ('Pyrrhonian Discourses') argues that neither sense-experience nor thought provides a basis for knowledge, for arguments or evidence in favour of one side of an argument can always be opposed by evidence and argument on the other side. He begins his book by charging the Academy with dogmatism in confidently asserting some things and denying others, whereas Pyrrhonists are 'aporetic and free of doctrine', which is why they are at peace whereas other philosophers 'wear themselves out uselessly and expend themselves in ceaseless torments'.

Suspending judgment is called *epoche*. Aenesidemus set out ten *modes* or *tropes* which state the grounds for claiming that we must suspend judgment. They come down to saying that things appear differently to the same perceiver at different times or under different conditions, and differently to different perceivers, so that no appearance can be regarded as definitively representing how anything really is. People differ from one another, and therefore they experience and judge differently. Our different sensory modalities – vision, hearing, touch, taste, smell – and the complexity of the things we take ourselves to perceive, make it impossible to claim that we definitively know about anything. The variability in our moods, age, health and sickness render our perceivings and judgings variable: which are the ones that contain the truth? These arguments variously exploit considerations about perceptual variabilities, relativities and the conflict between how things appear and what we think about them.

Sextus Empiricus reports the views of someone (identified as Agrippa by Diogenes Laertius; very little is known about him other than that he lived late in the first century CE) who summarized the grounds for suspension of judgment in 'Five Tropes', which have come to be regarded as the most famous arguments of ancient scepticism. The first is that any subject of debate prompts conflicting views among both ordinary people and philosophers, making it impossible to accept or reject either side of the dispute. So we must suspend judgment. The second is that when one tries to justify a claim in an argument, one has to appeal to a prior claim. But this in turn must be justified – and so on in a regress that never ends. So we must suspend judgment. A third is that everything is relative: things appear as they do only depending on the conditions or circumstances of their being perceived or judged. So we must suspend judgment. The fourth is that all attempts at judgment rest on assumptions, but alternative assumptions could be invoked, making it impossible to decide. So we must suspend judgment. And finally, we often enough discover that in trying to confirm a judgment we find ourselves already invoking considerations implicit in that judgment; this is circular. So we must suspend judgment.

One of the chief sources of information about ancient scepticism is, as the foregoing shows, the writings of Sextus Empiricus (160–210 CE): his *Outlines of Pyrrhonism* and *Against the Mathematicians*. His name tells us that he belonged to the Empiric medical school founded several centuries before his time, in the third century BCE, by Serapion of Alexandria. The Empiric school came to accept Pyrrhonism gladly, because it gave them a philosophical foundation for their opposition to the Dogmatic school that followed the tradition of Hippocrates. The Dogmatics argued that it was necessary to understand the 'hidden causes' of illnesses, whereas the Empirics argued that the impenetrability of nature made it pointless to seek hidden causes, and instead a physician's focus should be on what is evident and observable, namely, the symptoms. The Empirics saw that different practitioners disagreed with each other, that different countries and medical traditions had different forms of treatment and understandings of disease – and that the only sure way to deal with a wound or an illness was to use tried and trusted techniques based on experience; or if a disease was new, to base one's effort to cure it on what one could see.

Sextus describes the sceptic as one who is committed to investigation, not as one who arrives at and advocates set doctrines. Accordingly sceptics do not offer teachings, but stick to their enquiries; they conform to the appearance of things in the sense that they act on what they perceive, they accept traditions and customs and live accordingly, they obey the promptings of nature in the matter of hunger and thirst, and they acquire practical skills – such as medicine – but they do not claim to know or strive to know, and they do not assert but merely report how things seem, like a chronicler or historian who simply records what happens.

Latin translations of Sextus' writings were published in the mid-sixteenth century CE and had a great influence on the rise of modern philosophy, not least on Montaigne, Descartes, Pascal, Bayle, Hume and other thinkers of the Enlightenment, and thence to more recent and contemporary philosophy where philosophical scepticism continues to motivate efforts at constructing epistemological theories which either answer or embrace sceptical considerations.

NEOPLATONISM

By the middle of the third century CE the dominance of the Epicurean and Stoic schools had begun to wane, and a new movement of philosophical ideas was emerging, thinking of itself as Platonist but in fact richly synthesizing itself from many of the strands of philosophy that had flourished in the six centuries since Plato's day. This new movement, which later scholars named 'Neoplatonism', provided a comprehensive view of the universe and humanity's relationship with it, which many people found satisfying and which in its later phases became in effect a religion. As a religion it was both an alternative to Christianity and a source of ideas for Christianity, which adopted and adapted a considerable amount from it. One reason for Neoplatonism's appeal, especially to educated people, in the period of its chief flourishing between the third and seventh centuries CE, is that it rejected the materialism of Epicureanism and Stoicism – that is, their view that reality is exclusively physical – and argued instead that *mind* is the ultimate basis of reality.

The label 'Neoplatonist' is somewhat misleading, for although the thinkers of this movement called themselves 'Platonists' and valued Plato's views more highly than those of other philosophers, they were engaged not simply in reviving and teaching his views but in making use of them as the basis for their large-scale novel synthesis drawing creatively on all but the materialist aspects of preceding debates.

The two principal doctrines of Neoplatonism are, first, that mind is more fundamental than matter – as the philosophical jargon has it: is 'ontologically prior' to matter, which means that it comes first in the order of existence – and second, that the ultimate cause of all things must be a single unitary principle. They held that the cause of anything must contain at least as much and typically more 'reality' than its effect, in order to have sufficient causal potency to bring the effect about; and therefore the cause of the universe must be as real or more real than the universe itself.

The conjunction of these theses constitutes the basis of Neoplatonism. Since mind is ontologically prior to matter, the ultimate cause of the universe is therefore mind or consciousness, and moreover is a single, unitary mind. They regarded this unitary mind as divine and variously called it 'the One', 'the First', 'the Good'. It is easy to see why Neoplatonism seemed so attractive to Christians of the period, which is why they were not slow to adopt congenial aspects of it into their metaphysical and moral theology.

The immediate metaphysical problem to be addressed by anyone who thinks as the Neoplatonists did about the universe is, How does the material reality that we are familiar with arise from a singular mental consciousness? Neoplatonism's most distinctive features arise from the elaborate and detailed answer it offered to this question.

The thinker who is nominated as the founder of Neoplatonism is

Plotinus, an Egyptian or Egyptian-born Greek or Roman. He was born in Lycopolis in Egypt's Nile delta in 205 CE, dying sixty-six years later in Campania in southern Italy. He studied philosophy under Ammonius of Alexandria, going at the age of forty to Rome where for a number of years he lectured on Ammonius' teachings. It is said that he began to work out and write down his own views in response to questions his students asked. One of these students, Porphyry, edited Plotinus' writings in six books each containing nine treatises, the result therefore named the *Enneads* (from Greek *ennea*, 'nine'). The fifty-four treatises contain much difficult technical material, and they progress thematically from things earthly to things heavenly and finally to discussion of 'the One' itself, starting with human goods (the first group of nine treatises), proceeding to an account of the physical world (groups II–III), then the soul (group IV), then knowledge and intelligible reality (V), and finally the One (VI).

As already mentioned, Plotinus regarded himself as a follower of Plato's philosophy, but to think that he was straightforwardly so would be misleading. This is, first, because a great deal had of course happened in philosophy since Plato, and Plotinus' Platonism is influenced by the debates, criticism and responses to Plato's views that had accumulated over the intervening six centuries. The main targets for his defence and development of Platonism were Aristotle and the Stoics. Secondly, Plotinus accepted the validity of the letters ascribed to Plato, and what he knew about the 'unwritten teachings' alluded to by Aristotle and which Plotinus seems to have known. Moreover, as one would expect from a major philosophical thinker of great powers and creativity, Plotinus' thinking develops Plato; he says things that are Platonic in spirit but have no source in Plato's own writings.

This latter fact is unsurprising, given that (for example) there is no single, unequivocal 'Theory of Forms' in Plato – his own self-criticisms leave it open as to what if anything he finally decided about the theory – so it is plausible to regard Plotinus' contributions as developments of the intention or spirit of the Platonic theories if not always their letter. Better still, one can identify what is distinctive about Plotinus' Platonism by saying that it consists in accepting the underlying logic of the Platonic outlook, and developing it. For example: the theory of Forms rests on the idea that there are eternal truths about perfect, immutable and eternal entities, and that these have an exemplary or foundational status in relation to what exists in the Realm of Becoming. They are fully accessible to mind only when mind is disembodied. We recall also that Plato was influenced by Parmenides, who argued that complexity and plurality cannot be ultimate. Did Plato's 'unwritten doctrine' address this point, and hint at or even terminate in a view that reality must ultimately therefore be 'One'? In any event Plotinus himself took it that Platonism entailed that there must be a first and absolutely simple principle that underlies the appearance of complexity and plurality, and is the embodiment of the eternal truth of things: and this in essence is Plotinus' doctrine of the 'One'.

Recall that Plato died in 347 BCE, and that the headship of the Academy went first to his nephew Speusippus, and after the latter's death in 339 BCE to Xenocrates. Both of them developed Plato's ideas in ways which, though comprehensibly arising out of them, prompt controversy, most especially in connection with the 'reduction' of the Forms to a 'One' and a 'Dyad' (this latter a principle of opposites or multiplicity, as noted earlier). If it is right that there was an 'unwritten teaching' expounded by Plato to his pupils, it is possible that these ideas were aspects of it, providing the seeds for Neoplatonist development centuries later.

Philosophical ideas were hot topics in Alexandria in the first three centuries of the Common Era, for the city was a lively scene of debate. The Jewish philosopher Philo Judaeus (20 BCE–50 CE) and Neopythagoreanism both contributed to metaphysical speculation there. Plotinus attended a school of philosophy founded by one Hermeias, which during Plotinus' eleven years as a student was headed by Hermeias' son Ammonius Saccas. This person has prompted some speculation among historians of philosophy. Little is known about his doctrines, but he is thought to have been a Christian, at least for a time; Porphyry says he had been brought up a Christian but converted to 'paganism' on becoming acquainted with Greek philosophy (a common direction of travel through the ages). Both Eusebius and Jerome deny this, saying that he remained a Christian throughout his life; but they are probably confusing him with someone else of the same name, because his great influence on Plotinus did not make the latter a Christian.*

Others, speculating on the name 'Saccas', which suggests that Ammonius had an Indian origin, say that he might have been a

---

* There was an 'Ammonius the Christian' who wrote on the Bible. The Christian writer Origen was a pupil of Ammonius of Alexandria also, and he was in turn Eusebius' teacher; which adds to the confusion of the story about Ammonius' relation to Christianity. In fact Ammonius had two pupils called Origen, the other one a pagan. He also taught Herennius and Cassius Longinus.

second-generation Indian immigrant to Alexandria, and had retained elements of the philosophical tradition of his forebears' homeland. This chimes with Porphyry's report that Plotinus had once desired to visit Persia and India in the hope of learning from their philosophers, but was unable to carry out his plan.

A fifth-century CE account of Ammonius says that his chief tenet was that Plato and Aristotle were in full agreement with each other. Given that his most famous pupils – Plotinus, Origen the Pagan (so called to distinguish him from the Christian Origen) and Longinus – thought of themselves as Platonists in their respective ways, it is plausible that Ammonius had succeeded in persuading them that Plato was right and that Aristotle had not diverged from him. Origen and Longinus were orthodox in their commitment to 'Middle Platonism' – that stage in Platonistic thought after the Academy abandoned the scepticism of the 'New Academy' and modified Plato's doctrines with elements of Aristotelianism and Stoicism (thus Middle Platonism occupies the period between the beginning of the first century BCE and Plotinus). But Plotinus did not accompany them along that path; he gave a highly original new direction to the Platonic tradition, and it is this that bears the name 'Neoplatonism'.

In noting that the occasion and a large part of the platform for Plotinus' views is Plato's thought as modified by Aristotelian and Stoic criticism and by a rejection of materialism, one should add – for a clearer understanding of the development especially of later Neoplatonism – the influence also of certain mystical ideas from cults such as Orphism, and from Judaism, which had come to be more widely known following the translation of a collection of Hebrew scriptures into demotic or *koine* Greek in the text known as the *Septuagint* (because it is said to have had seventy translators; *septuaginta* is Latin for 'seventy'). All these factors together contributed to a climate in which Neoplatonism found an increasingly receptive audience.

As so often happens with important developments in intellectual history, the founder of a tradition of ideas had gifted successors who added to, adapted or extended it in several directions. In the case of Neoplatonism the chief successors to Plotinus were Porphyry (233–305 CE), Iamblichus (245–325 CE) and Proclus (412–85 CE). Porphyry has already been mentioned as the compiler of Plotinus' *Enneads*; he wrote a commentary on Euclid and a number of other works. Whereas he shared with Plotinus the view that rational enquiry is the route to understanding the divine nature of reality, Iamblichus and Proclus are credited with taking Neoplatonism in mystical directions, making of it a religious philosophy in which theurgy – the practice of magical rituals to summon deities or to secure their aid – plays a key part. Given that Proclus was head of the Academy in the fifth century CE, one can see how far Plato's doctrines had been taken in the centuries since he lived.

The doctrines of Neoplatonism are elaborate. From the fundamental metaphysical principle of 'the One' or 'the First' the universe unfolds into existence in stages in an eternal flow, each stage the ground or principle of the next. Of the 'One' or 'First' nothing can be said other than it is a unity and it is absolutely fundamental, for it is 'beyond Being' or prior to it. The first activity of the One is consciousness or mind, *nous*. *Nous* is the second ultimate ground of being, after the One. The self-reflexive understanding that *nous* has of its source, the One, produces dualities such as change and rest, greater and smaller, identity and difference; and it produces number, ideas, the Forms and the soul.

The soul gazes upon the Forms and is affected by them – is 'in*formed*' by them – in such a way that in consequence it produces images of the Forms in time and space. These spatio-temporal images of the Forms are the physical things that furnish the world. Thus reality is the output of mind or consciousness; Neoplatonism is a species of idealism, the metaphysical view that the ultimate stuff of the universe is mental. For Neoplatonists, soul and the nature it produces are on two different levels of a hierarchy, soul on the higher plane and matter on the lower plane. But matter is still an emanation of *nous*, and therefore partakes of the divine. It is passive, it is the lowest level of reality, it is the terminus of the chain of activities flowing from the One, a penumbra or fringe on the outer limits of existence.

Matter is invoked by Plotinus as the explanation of evil. How can there be anything evil in a universe that flows entirely from the One, the Good? Yet evil manifestly and tragically exists; so, how does it arise? Matter cannot itself be the cause of evil because it is passive, inert, with no powers of its own. Plotinus' ingenious answer is to say that when beings further up the chain of existence, in particular human beings, concentrate on material things below them instead of the higher things above them, evil results. He regarded people as essentially good but corruptible, and that this is the means of their corruption. His view proved controversial among later Neoplatonists; Proclus devoted a whole treatise to refuting him on this point, arguing that human souls are capable of evil on their own account, a view consistent with the Christian doctrine that people are born sinful because of Adam's Fall. Christian moral theology invoked the idea that the deity gave humankind free will and that this is the source of evil; but the problem for believers in a good God is not quite made to go away by this, for it does not explain such 'natural evils' as the suffering produced by cancer, tsunamis, earthquakes, and the like. Indeed 'the problem of evil' is one of the most persuasive of the anti-theist arguments, answerable only by conceding that if there are any deities, they are not wholly good, or not wholly powerful, or both.

The ethics of Neoplatonism constitutes a major source of disagreement between its adherents and Christians. Because humans emanate from the One as the source of all being, Neoplatonism says, humans are themselves divine or partake of the divine, and the purpose of a life of virtue is to revert to unity with the One. The shortest route to reabsorption into the One is (as one would expect a philosopher to say) the philosophical life devoted to understanding the nature of reality and living in accordance with that understanding. This is par excellence the life of the mind, abjuring things of the body. So far, this rejection of things worldly is consistent with the strenuous version of early Christianity that saw so many of its votaries going to the desert to escape temptation, even in certain cases adopting the extremes of self-castration or living permanently atop a pillar. But the Christian claim that salvation had been achieved for humanity by a one-off self-sacrifice of God in human guise was rejected by Neoplatonists outright; in one version of the Christian view, all you need for salvation is to believe that claim, a very cut-price offer indeed in comparison to the Neoplatonistic view of the universe.

The later transformation of Neoplatonism into a religious practice involving theurgy was in large part a response to the nature of late antiquity – the period of the demise of the Roman Empire in the West, the rise of Christianity and its vigorous and prolonged assault on 'paganism' including destruction of the literature and art of the preceding thousand years, the existence of many other sects and movements, the hordes of holy men, mystics and magicians who swarmed that darkening world in competition with each other – which meant that, for the purposes of attracting followers, pledges of salvation and the aid of the gods had to be made.* Philosophical examination of ideas had a hard time competing with bald assertions, claims, miracles and promises, the more fanciful the better; a familiar story. For a time philosophy all but vanished in the swamps of religious claims and practices. Later Neoplatonism followed down that path.

Nevertheless Neoplatonic ideas proved extraordinarily influential even in this morass, not least perhaps because the morass was itself in part made by them, and most effectively by Proclus. Augustine in Western Christendom, and such figures as Basil and the two 'Fathers' named Gregory in Eastern Christendom, were influenced by Neoplatonist ideas, as was the theology developed in later medieval times by Aquinas and others. When the Arab conquest began in the seventh century CE, the regions of Eastern Christendom where Greek philosophy still survived, chiefly Syria and Mediterranean Egypt, immediately influenced thinking in the expanding Islamic world. In the Renaissance rediscovery of Greek philosophy, Neoplatonism was what Plato meant to the greatly influential Marsilio Ficino and through him to the culture of the day; and its later theurgic elements fed the flames of interest in magic, Hermeticism, the Cabala and other mystical movements in the sixteenth century CE in lands that the Reformation had made Protestant and where, therefore, religious authority was insufficiently strong to keep the explosion of such interest down.† In all forms of idealism in modern and contemporary philosophy, traces of Neoplatonism remain.

Neoplatonism is not the only example of a philosophy that was transformed over time into a religion – the same happened to Buddhism, Jainism and Confucianism, which are strictly not religions because they lack a god or gods, though more popular versions of Buddhism have become submerged beneath layers of supernaturalism of various kinds. Two elements in human nature, the propensity to superstition and the hunger for simple stories to provide a framework for some sort of understanding of the universe and one's place in it, are powerful in explaining how this happens.

* The 'Prosperity Gospel' movements of Christian revivalism in Africa and America are versions of this phenomenon.
† For more on this see Grayling, *The Age of Genius* (2016), Chapter 13, passim.

PART II

Medieval and Renaissance Philosophy

In line with what is said in the Introduction about this being a history of philosophy and not of theology, and in light of the fact that much of what was debated in medieval times was the latter rather than the former, this section concentrates on those aspects of medieval thought that are most philosophically significant in themselves and in their influence.

The chief reason for the almost wholesale subordination of philosophy to theology in the medieval period is that after the abolition of the School of Athens – the Platonic Academy – by the Emperor Justinian in 529 CE, and his proscription of the teaching of 'pagan' philosophy, intellectual activity fell under the authority of the Church, and as time went by it became increasingly risky to diverge from doctrinal orthodoxy. Doing so could and too often did attract the severest of sanctions: the death penalty.

Even when speculation devoted itself wholly and only to philosophical matters there was no guarantee of safety. If one's views had, or seemed to have, implications that cast doubt on matters of theology, or on what the currently winning side in doctrinal struggles considered orthodox, the risks were equally severe. As one would expect, this had a chilling effect on enquiry.

The problem is that the concept of deity – of a 'god' or 'gods' – is exceedingly ill-defined. Indeed a good deal of theology argues that it cannot be defined, or if defined (as, say, 'the sum of all perfections' or as the plenitude of some such state as 'goodness' or 'love') then it cannot be understood; it 'passes all comprehension'. To one kind of sceptical viewer this makes the vastness of the literature of theology incomprehensible: how can so much be said about what nothing can be said about? But to a different kind of sceptical viewer the intrinsic unclarities and perhaps ineffabilities of the concept, into which traditional religious notions of deity rapidly mutate on inspection, actually explain the vastness of that literature: from this single point of unclarity, attended with so much hope, anxiety, fervour and tradition – not a little of it literally of murderous importance to its votaries – you would expect volcanic amounts of debate and disagreement to erupt.

Participants in theological debates of course deployed philosophical ideas, and in their applications of them at times made significant philosophical (and not just theological) contributions. Moreover they had to address central philosophical problems – time, free will, the idea of what is good – from their theological perspective. How can there be evil in the world if it was created by a good god? How can there be time if god is eternal or even outside time? If god can foresee the future, being omniscient, can there be such a thing as free will in humanity? It is these aspects of the thought of medieval times – where philosophy arises from, or impinges upon, theological thought – that I now survey.

It is well to recall that later philosophers almost always knew the work, the ideas, the theories, of at least some of the philosophers who came before them. They built on predecessors' ideas, or rejected them, or enriched or circumvented them with new insights; but whichever of these they did, their work is related to a continuing conversation. It is also good to be conscious of the distances of time that elapsed between the figures discussed here and indeed everywhere in this book. Augustine lived seven hundred years after Aristotle; Anselm lived six hundred years after Augustine; Aquinas lived two hundred years after Anselm. So 1,500 years separated Aquinas from Aristotle whose work, a substantial part of it newly rediscovered shortly before Aquinas' time, was of such great importance to him. In those great gaps of time hundreds of other thinkers and writers, and thousands of teachers and students, discussed and interpreted the ideas of the major philosophers. So the outstanding names mentioned in these pages are literally that: outstanding – projecting like high mountain peaks above an extensive range of hills.

Two things help to make sense of the history of medieval philosophy: the respective influences of Plato and Aristotle, and the methods of philosophical and theological debate developed in the high medieval period of the twelfth and thirteenth centuries.

Augustine, like the various early Christian theologians known as the 'Church Fathers', was influenced by Plato, largely through the medium of Neoplatonism but also through the late dialogue *Timaeus* which

Christian commentators found congenial as offering a cosmology inter-
pretable in ways consistent with scripture. Aristotle was for centuries
little known except through translations of some of his writings on
logic, for example those made by Boethius. Or rather, it would be more
accurate to say that Aristotle was little known in European Christendom, but his works were still known among Syrian Christians, which
is why, in the course of the first three centuries after the Arab conquest
of the Middle East, an assimilation of his philosophy into Islamic intellectual culture was able to occur. A number of Aristotle's works were
translated into Arabic, and in due course two great commentators on
Aristotle appeared: Avicenna (Ibn Sina, 980–1037 CE) and Averroes
(Ibn Rushd, 1126–98 CE). One could add the Jewish thinker Moses
Maimonides (1135–1204 CE), like Averroes born in Cordoba in Spain,
as a commentator on Aristotle likewise, and therefore as a contributor
to the intellectual stir that prompted an upsurge of interest in Aristotle
in European Christendom in the twelfth century CE.

As a result of this interest translations into Latin of forgotten major
works of Aristotle began to appear in considerable numbers in the
twelfth century, especially during its second half: the *Ethics*, *Politics*,
Physics and *Metaphysics* among them. The commentaries of Avicenna
and Averroes were also translated, and those by the latter proved particularly influential in some quarters. This created a difficulty: Averroes'
reading of Aristotle was such that it conflicted with important aspects
of Christian doctrine, not least about the creation of the world and the
nature of the soul. Heated discussions arose on the question whether
Christians could and indeed should be heeding a pagan philosopher.
For much of the first half of the thirteenth century it was a question
whether study of Aristotle would be banned by the Church. In 1231 a
commission was appointed by Pope Gregory IX to examine the matter.
Under Siger of Brabant at the University of Paris there were enthusiastic
pro-Aristotelians and Averroists. On the other side were those who
agreed with Bonaventure, head of the Franciscans, who argued that
Aristotle's views were incompatible with Christianity and who therefore favoured Plato.

The dispute was resolved by Thomas Aquinas (1225–74 CE), who
saw a way to render his own enthusiasm for Aristotle consistent with
Church dogma. He argued that the Averroist interpretation of Aristotle
was wrong, and provided his own interpretation in its place. By his
magisterial writings he made Aristotelianism the official philosophy of

the Church. Known as 'Thomism' after Aquinas' name, it is still the official philosophy of the Roman Catholic Church.

The second point concerns method. In the first half of the twelfth century a bishop of Paris and professor at its university, Peter Lombard, edited a compilation of biblical and exegetical texts called *The Book of Sentences*. It instantly became a textbook for students of theology; attending lectures on it was a requirement for a bachelor's degree, and anyone wishing to progress to a master's degree in theology had to write a commentary on it. This remained the case until the fifteenth century, and both the compilation and its centrality to the curriculum shaped the nature of theological and philosophical debate throughout that time.

Alongside the *Sentences* there developed a tradition of learning by means of disputation, a question-and-answer dialectic which consti- tuted both a method of teaching and a method of examination. A version of it called *quodlibetical* disputation ('quodlibet' means, in effect, 'whatever pleases') involved a scholar accepting the challenge of answering any question posed to him in a public forum. Quodlibetical writings were those that addressed the widely debated standard questions – including controversial and problematic ones – that schol- ars and lay persons alike were interested in.

A final introductory point: for the sake of organization, and adher- ing rather closely to the usual historical classifications, I take the medieval period as starting at the turn of the fifth century CE and cul- minating in the early fourteenth century, and the modern period as commencing in the late sixteenth century CE, labelling the period in between – the early fourteenth to the late sixteenth century – the 'Renaissance'. Some historians of culture regard the Renaissance, under the label of the 'northern Renaissance', as persisting into the seventeenth century.

Although these labels are conveniences merely, and sometimes clumsy and misleading, they are indeed convenient, for they capture at least some important features of the periods they parcel out. It is hard to imagine Machiavelli living – surviving – in the Christendom of, say, the twelfth century; it is impossible to imagine the sixteenth-century explosion of interest in magic, alchemy and other occult sciences, lead- ing as it did in the seventeenth century to great advances in science, being possible before the Reformation, whose birth date is the moment in 1517 when Martin Luther attached his theses to the church door in

Wittenberg. But religious control of, or interference in, thought and enquiry was still sufficiently great in the early seventeenth century – recall that Galileo was put on trial by the Vatican in 1632 for espousing Copernicus' heliocentric view of the universe – for the period between Augustine and the late sixteenth century to be considered as a whole.

However, in the Renaissance period itself, as here denominated, there is only one thinker whose work persists in philosophy as an object of study, and that is Machiavelli. The others, responsible as they variously were for the Platonism, humanism and in some cases the occultism of the age, such as Leonardo Bruni, Nicholas of Cusa, Leon Battista Alberti, Marsilio Ficino, Giovanni Pico della Mirandola, Thomas More, Erasmus of Rotterdam, Francesco Guicciardini, Michel de Montaigne and Giordano Bruno, are not now read as philosophers. Accordingly, apart from Machiavelli, I shall discuss themes (humanism, Platonism) associated with these individuals rather than the individuals themselves.

Philosophy in Medieval Times

AUGUSTINE (354–430 CE)

St Augustine of Hippo, as he is known in ecclesiastical circles, was born in that part of the Roman province of Numidia which is now called Algeria. His mother Monica was a Christian and raised him as one, though as a student in his teens he become a Manichean. He reconverted to Christianity in his early thirties, after a life typical enough of educated young men; he had a long-term mistress by whom he had a son, and – as he tells us in his *Confessions* – he enjoyed his sins so much that when he first began to pray to become good he added 'but not yet'.

Once converted, Augustine devoted himself to the philosophical problems that his beliefs obliged him to address, not least among them the related problems of evil, free will and predestination. He had been attracted to philosophy long beforehand by reading Cicero's now lost dialogue *Hortensius, or On Philosophy*, so the difficulties posed by theology were quickly obvious to him.

In addition to offering solutions to philosophical problems that challenged the faith, Augustine served the Church well in other respects, not least in providing ways to make its teachings more acceptable to an empire in which Christianity competed with older traditions of thought that did not require acceptance of factual as opposed to symbolic miracles, and did not require quite as much ethical self-denial. Christianity had been given legal status by the Emperor Constantine in 313 CE in the Edict of Milan, and had then been proclaimed as the official and only permissible religion of the Roman Empire by the Emperor Theodosius I in the Edict of Thessalonica, 380 CE – a very rapid conquest. Constantine's protection of Christianity and ultimate conversion to it had helped make it fashionable among the wealthy bourgeois and patricians of the Empire, who however were more than somewhat concerned by certain aspects of the faith they now embraced. For one example, the scriptures said that it is harder for a camel to pass through the eye of a needle than for the rich to enter heaven. For another, the scriptures encouraged loving one's enemies, promoting peace and turning the other cheek – a pacificist-seeming outlook – whereas Rome was a mighty military empire. Augustine rode to the rescue on both counts; he said that giving alms would result in the souls of the poor conducting the souls of the rich into paradise, and that the parable of the centurion who asked Jesus to heal his son proved that Jesus was accepting of the military. To his credit, however, Augustine addressed the question of a 'just war', providing the basis for Aquinas' just war theory nine centuries later.

Manicheism, the doctrine espoused by Augustine before his conversion, was a movement founded by one Mani or Manes, who lived about a century before Augustine's own time. Mani – this was not his name, but a title approximately translatable as 'the Enlightened One' – was born in southern Babylonia but lived and preached mainly in Persia. His teaching was a combination of Zoroastrian dualism, Buddhist ethics and Babylonian folklore, with bits of Gnostic Christianity added. He taught that the universe is the theatre of a great struggle between two principles, Good and Evil, the former being the principle of light, the latter the principle of darkness. The Good Principle is 'the Father of Majesty', the Evil Principle is 'the King of Darkness'. This latter has the head of a lion and four feet, but is otherwise half fish and half bird. The two Principles would have coexisted peaceably had not the King of Darkness decided to invade the Realm of Light. In response to this invasion the Father of Majesty 'emanated' the Mother of Life, who in turn emanated the First Man, who in his turn emanated some sons and gathered an army. A complex and lengthy set of events, with numerous further emanations including a Messenger and assorted virgins, followed. The Manichean cosmology and universal history has the proportions of epic, and the surprising thing about it is that Mani claimed that it was all an embodiment of reason, untainted by fantasy and mysticism (he criticized Christianity for its miraculous and mystical elements).

It might accordingly seem odd that Augustine should be an adherent, given his intellectual powers, to which the elaborate Manichean structure must surely have seemed fanciful.* The Christian picture, by contrast, would have appeared relatively restrained. But the Christian picture was itself not, as already indicated, free of problems. There were major matters of doctrine at issue, not least in the opposition between the Roman, Donatist and Arian versions of Christianity. These doctrinal conflicts were roiling the faith with conflict, power struggles and accusations and counter-accusations of heresy and error; typical fare in these domains. But these are matters of theology and dogma; of interest here, by contrast, are the philosophical problems that Christianity raised.

One was the problem of evil. It is simply stated: if God is good and created the world, how can it contain evil? Augustine set out an answer in his *De Libero Arbitrio*. First he distinguishes between the evil that people do and the evil they suffer. The latter evil is caused by God, by way of punishment for sins; for if sins are not punished they would eventually overcome what is good. So the sufferings imposed by God make the world a better place, and they encourage sinners to repent.

This prompts the thought that a god who imposes suffering as punishment for sin is a just god, but not necessarily a good one. Would a good god not be merciful – mercy sometimes subverting justice? Moreover: what of the suffering of little children, for example those afflicted by disease? This is not a matter of justice, for it cannot be punishment for sin. Augustine replies (in *De Vera Religione*) that the suffering of little children is good for the rest of us in various ways, and anyway the infants will be compensated for their sufferings eventually.

But what of the evil people do? How can God allow that to happen? Some argue that God thinks a world in which people have free will, given that having free will results in people sinning, is a better world than one that has neither freedom nor sin in it. Others suggest that God is not powerful enough to stop people from sinning. Augustine's view is in effect a version of the first view, not for the comparative reason that

---

* The worlds of the King of Darkness have as attributes or 'aeons' Pestilent Breath, Scorching Wind, Gloom, Mist, Consuming Fire, Wells of Poison, Columns of Smoke, Abysmal Depths, Foetid Marshes and Pillars of Fire. A dramatic place. But it is interesting how the imagination of human beings is just a hyperbolic version of the familiar. Compare science, whose discoveries transcend imagination.

it makes the world 'better', but for the superlative reason that it makes the world *perfect*. 'As long as men who do not sin gain happiness,' he wrote, 'the universe is perfect. When sinners are unhappy, the universe is perfect.' As we all alas know, the world is not perfect; this must presumably be because it contains so many happy sinners.

Augustine's view of evil has to be made consistent with the idea that everyone is born sinful because of the Fall (this being Adam's and Eve's sin – the sin of disobedience – in the Garden of Eden). But that could be achieved by the liberation from original sin offered by baptism, and by subsequent periodic absolutions for sins thereafter committed. Augustine does not seem to rely on this option, instead talking of 'grace' as what enables a person to live sinlessly. But this raises the difficulty that anyone who has not received grace is therefore not *able* to live sinlessly – and therefore if such people suffer as punishment for their sins they are being treated unjustly.

In saying that the evil committed by people is the outcome of their having free will, Augustine has to provide an account of free will itself. In commenting on the evils people do, and on the rebellion of Lucifer, he exonerates God from being the ultimate cause of those evils – which his role as creator of the agents who enacted them would seem to make him: he created them with a propensity to sin, and his omniscience might have forewarned him that they would act accordingly – by saying that the cause of evils is the individual sinners themselves. This suggests that nothing outside the sinners causes them to sin: the sinful events begin within them. This gives human beings a special place in the causal chain as first or originating causes themselves. But this view is inconsistent with what Augustine has otherwise to accept: that the serpent persuaded Eve and Eve persuaded Adam to eat the forbidden fruit – which means the cause of their sin lay outside them. It is also inconsistent with what he elsewhere says, about God inclining or moving people's hearts to do good as instruments of his mercy, or to commit evil as instruments of punishment he wishes to administer. For contrary to Augustine's claims, this latter makes God the cause of the evils that people commit.

The difficult question of predestination and foreknowledge, which would seem to be attributes of omniscience, also therefore arises. Familiarly, it contradicts free will and human agency. It also presents Augustine with insuperable problems about time. In *The City of God* Augustine says, 'God comprehends in a steady and sempiternal gaze everything that happens in time, whether future, present or past ... His knowledge of the three times does not change as ours does, for in him there is no change.' This is inconsistent with his claim in the *Confessions* that the future does not exist; there he says that prediction is a matter of noting signs or symptoms available in the present which suggest how things will turn out, entailing that it is false to say that the future can be seen because 'the future is not here yet, and if it is not here yet, it does not exist.' This was an argument against seers and witches claiming to tell fortunes, but it serves as an argument against divine foreknowledge too. Augustine's other doctrine that the future is not future to God, but present to him along with the present and past because all times are one to him, still does not help; for from our perspective that would mean there *is* a future which, from the perspective of our present, already exists, contrary to Augustine's denial that it does.

An interesting point Augustine raises, however, is that although we speak of past, present and future what we mean is the past relative to the present, the present relative to the present, and the future relative to the present. What time itself is he says he does not know: if you ask me to meet you at a certain hour tomorrow I can do it, he says, but if you ask me what time itself is, I have no answer. It mattered to him, though, that he excuse God from existence in time, in order to answer those who ask, 'What was God doing before he created heaven and earth?' For those who ask this can then ask, 'Why did he not continue doing nothing? Or why might he not return to doing nothing, as he did before? Or is he in fact not eternal?' Augustine's answer is that God is 'exempt from the relation of time'.* And moreover, before God made 'the times' (past, present and future) there was no time.

In the course of his various writings in explication of Christian theology Augustine anticipated several philosophical ideas that came into prominence later. His thoughts on just war, as noted, provided Aquinas with materials for a development of just war theory; he anticipates Anselm's 'ontological argument' for the existence of God; and he is 1,200 years ahead of Descartes with a version of 'I think therefore I

---

* Augustine had a sense of humour; in dealing with the question 'What was God doing before he created the world?' he says he will not rely on the answer, 'Preparing hell for people who ask difficult questions.'

am' – he says, *fallor ergo sum*, 'If I am deceived, I exist,' although this idea also occurs in Plotinus before him, and before Plotinus in Aristotle. In fact Augustine was so much taken with this idea that he repeated it seven times in various works. Descartes almost certainly learned of it as a schoolboy at La Flèche, whose Jesuit teachers were admirers of Augustine.

And finally Augustine's remarks on how children learn language are quoted by Ludwig Wittgenstein at the beginning of the *Philosophical Investigations* – as a mistaken view. Of all Augustine's works, however, some are inclined to say that the charm of the purely autobiographical early parts of his *Confessions* is the greatest.

BOETHIUS (477–524)

Anicius Manlius Severinus Boethius was a Christian Roman aristocrat who was born at the very end of the Roman Empire in the West; the last Western Emperor, Romulus Augustulus, was deposed in the year before Boethius was born. The new ruler of Italy, the Ostrogothic conqueror Theodoric, was however a civilized man who had been educated at Constantinople, and he was content for the Roman way of life to continue much as before, so Boethius and his family lived in Rome as they would have done under the Empire.

Boethius was highly educated in the best Roman way; he knew Greek as well as Latin, and might have continued his leisurely life of scholarship, studying and translating philosophical classics, if he had not accepted a senior position in Theodoric's government, which had its seat at Ravenna. This was a mistake; centres of arbitrary power are dangerous. As he recounts in his *Consolation of Philosophy* Boethius was arrested and tried both for treason and for indulging in magic, quite likely trumped-up charges because of a court intrigue. He was presumably executed, but not before he had completed the *Consolation of Philosophy*, the book for which he is best known.

The ambitious task Boethius had set himself when young was to translate and provide commentaries on all the works of Plato and Aristotle. In the event he managed to complete his work on Aristotle's *Categories* and *De Interpretatione*, and he also wrote commentaries on Porphyry's *Isagoge* and Cicero's *Topics*. He was the author of textbooks on arithmetic and logic, and although he produced a work of theology entitled *Opuscula Sacra*, his chief passion was logic, in which he was a follower of Porphyry.

In the *Isagoge* Porphyry raises a set of questions about *universals* – the properties or qualities that many particular things can have in common, such as redness, roundness, being human – only to set aside discussion of them as too difficult for an introductory work. He does however state what questions about them need to be answered. Do universals exist separately from the particulars that instantiate them? Or are there only particular things, universals therefore being mere concepts, just names that we apply to a number of different particulars to draw attention to their similarities? If universals really exist apart from particulars, are they corporeal (physical) or incorporeal, and either way, how do particulars instantiate them? This is the same problem Plato faced regarding the relation of Forms to particulars, as discussed in his *Parmenides*.

Boethius argued that universals are not independently existing things, but that it would be wrong to think that the concepts of them are merely empty, as had been argued by those who thought that, if universals are not independently existing things, talk of them is therefore talk of nothing. Instead Boethius took the Aristotelian view that universals exist but always and only in the particulars that exemplify them. They are universal in thought, but particular in their actual existence: 'it is universal in one way, when it is thought, and singular in another way, when it is sensed in the things in which it has being'. This view is in line with that of the nominalists in subsequent medieval philosophy, for which the problem of universals was such a big issue that people came to blows over it.

Boethius adopted a stance similar to Augustine's on the problem of free will in the light of divine omniscience and foreknowledge. The argument for the incompatibility of free will with God's foreknowledge is that if God knows the future, the future must be fixed in advance, and therefore there can be no such thing as free will. But if everything mortals do is inevitable and they cannot do otherwise, then they cannot be praised or blamed for what they do. The solution, says Boethius, is to see that God is not in time but in eternity, and everything that we mortals think of in temporal terms – past, present and future – is all present to him.

To this it might be objected that mortals are not saved from unfreedom by this view of God's relationship to time, because if God can see what, from a mortal's perspective, lies in the future, the mortal cannot do otherwise than what happens in that future. Boethius answers that the inevitability of the future as God sees it is a necessity relative only to God, not to the mortal whose future it is. This requires a distinction between two kinds of necessity, one applying divinely and the other not. What this means, if anything, is unclear.

As noted in connection with Augustine, two alternatives to the contradiction between God's omniscient foreknowledge and the requirement that mortals have free will so that they can choose whether or not to sin are these: either deny foreknowledge (and therefore omniscience) to God, or deny free will to mortals. Neither is palatable to traditional theology. Boethius would have had another option had he elected to follow the classical Greek way of handling the subject of fate, which likewise implies that futures are fixed and inevitable. This is to take the unsettling view that whatever one's fate, and despite its being fixed and unavoidable, one would be punished or rewarded for it anyway. Think of Oedipus, whose fate was to kill his father and marry his mother, by whom he would then have children. He followed his fate, not knowing that he was doing so and anyway unable to avert it even if he had indeed known. And he was severely punished for it.

Boethius' *Consolation of Philosophy* is a work of great literary merit, taking the form of a dialogue, in a mixture of prose and verse, between Boethius awaiting death in prison and Philosophy in the figure of a woman. He is in despair at the sudden and terrible stroke of ill-fortune he has suffered; she offers him consolation – but not in the form of sympathy. Rather, she reminds him that his happiness lies elsewhere than in the chances and changes of worldly luck. Boethius complains that his fate shows that the good suffer while the wicked prosper, and Philosophy says that she will show him that this is not true.

She begins, as much of the philosophical tradition does, by distinguishing between worldly goods such as riches and status, and the true goods of virtue and love. These latter Boethius has not lost. So even though he has lost wealth and power, he has not lost what brings real happiness. She then argues that happiness and goodness are the same thing, so the wicked, in not being good, are of necessity unhappy. And finally she argues that everything that happens is the result of God's providence, and that apparent suffering and unhappiness in fact serve a higher purpose which might not be apparent at the time of suffering.

At this point Boethius thinks that he catches Philosophy out. Ah, he says; so if everything unfolds to the good through God's providence, it means that everything happens of necessity; so there is no free will. Philosophy gives much the same answer as above – that God is outside time and therefore the future and the past are all together present to him.

Commentators on Boethius remark on the fact that he has pagan Philosophy consoling a Christian: how, they ask, can a Christian accept this? Some answer that Boethius was demonstrating the insufficiency of Philosophy to provide a consolation as satisfying as Christianity does – which means that the *Consolation of Philosophy* is an elaborate work of irony. But to think this is rather a stretch; the views Philosophy offers chime well with views for which Boethius argues elsewhere.

Moreover Boethius' successors in medieval thought did not interpret him as an ironist. Along with Aristotle and Augustine he is a dominating figure in that tradition; for centuries his writings were a standard source for the study of logic, but the *Consolation* outstripped even those works in importance and influence. It was read, admired, translated and imitated right up to the eighteenth century.

ANSELM (1033–1109)

Archbishop Anselm of Canterbury was not an Englishman but the son of an aristocratic family at Aosta in Italy. As a teenager he tried to become a monk, but his father would not allow it. After his father's death he led an itinerant life, travelling through Italy and France, until at the age of twenty-seven he decided to give up his worldly inheritance and take the tonsure, choosing to join the Benedictine order at the Abbey of Bec in France.* He became its abbot, and in his time there made it one of the leading schools of Europe, attracting students from many countries.

After the Normans conquered England in 1066 the Abbey of Bec was endowed with lands in the new domains, so Anselm crossed the English Channel to visit them. He was nominated as successor to Archbishop Lanfranc of Canterbury, but at first was denied that position by William II (William Rufus), who wanted the revenues of Canterbury

---

* The tonsure, a shaved patch on the crown of the head, was the mark of slavery in pre-Christian times, and was used by the Christian monks to signify absolute obedience – enslavement – to God.

for himself. Only when Rufus thought he was on his deathbed and asked Anselm to give him the last rites was Anselm allowed to take up the archbishopric. This occurred during a period of turmoil in the Church, which at the time had two popes in competition with each other.

William survived both his illness and his satisfaction at having Anselm as Archbishop of Canterbury. The two men were in frequent conflict, and the quarrels continued between Anselm and Rufus's successor, Henry I. The victory – after two periods of exile and other controversies – in the end went to Anselm, who was able to secure the independence of the Church from the Crown, and the supremacy of Canterbury over York, the quarrel between the two archbishoprics having been a considerable source of angry dispute for much of his period in office.

Throughout his busy and tumultuous public life Anselm managed to find time to think and write. Most of his work was in intricately dense theology, but with much dense and intricate philosophy alongside. The reputation of Scholasticism – the 'philosophy of the Schools', a generic name for medieval philosophy – as consisting in logic-chopping and minute distinctions, is not undeserved, and finds exemplification in Anselm. For example: in connection with words that can function as either nouns or adjectives, he asks whether they refer to a substance or a quality. To solve the problem he distinguished between *signification* and *appellation* – something rather like 'denoting' and 'describing' respectively – and said a term like 'red' signifies one thing, namely *redness*, but applies to many things: red balls, red noses, red flags. Moreover – and this is a nice point – although 'red' signifies redness, it does not 'appellate' or exemplify redness; for 'redness' is not itself red, any more than 'being a man' is a man.

Another example is his argument that truth has always existed – an important point for theological purposes. It goes as follows. Suppose that truth has not always existed. Then before truth came into existence, it was true that there was no truth. But that means there was truth before there was truth, which is a contradiction. So the supposition 'that truth has not always existed' is false.

Anselm is best remembered now for his arguments concerning the existence of God, which one finds in the *Monologion* and the *De Veritate*, but chiefly in Chapter 2 of the *Proslogion*. The principal argument, which seeks to prove God's existence from the mere thought of God, goes as follows. The concept of God is the concept of the greatest thing there is, something which is so great that nothing greater than it can be conceived. The concept of this greatest thing is, obviously, in one's mind; one is conceiving of it. But if the greatest thing were only in one's mind, one could indeed conceive something greater than it, namely, a greatest thing that actually exists in reality. Therefore the greatest possible thing – God – must really exist.

This argument has been known as the 'ontological argument' since Immanuel Kant's criticism of it in the eighteenth century. Kant's objection is that the argument makes *existing* a property on a par with any other property, whereas it is not a property but a condition of something's being able to have properties. The argument says that 'really existing' is a property that makes something 'greater' than something that 'exists only in the mind'. But consider: suppose there is a table in my room whose surface is brown and which stands a metre high. (The phrase 'there is' is another way of saying 'there exists'.) Now, I can paint the table a different colour, or I can chop some centimetres off its legs, and the table would still exist; but could I change the existence of the table into non-existence, leaving the colour or height of the table unchanged? Obviously not: how can a non-existent table have any colour or height? Anselm assumed that for the greatest conceivable thing to be the greatest conceivable thing, it must have the property of existing as an essential greatness; but Kant's argument says that to have any of the properties that putatively make it great, it must – so to speak – 'already' exist, so existence is not a property, essential or otherwise.

In any case, to say that something does not exist might be – if the thing does exist – to speak falsely, but it is not to contradict oneself. The ontological argument seeks to treat a denial of the existence of God as a contradiction, on the grounds that existence is an essential part of his nature. But to claim this is wholly a matter of definition; Anselm relies on a traditional conception of God as having all positive attributes (and no negative ones) in superlative degree; but that is purely stipulative.

Anselm distinguishes between 'existing in thought' and 'existing in reality', but does not carry the distinction through to the difference between something's having a property in thought and having a property in reality. This by itself is fatal to the argument. Moreover a critic might ask: what motivates saying that existing in reality is 'greater' than existing in thought? What does 'greater' mean here – does it mean better? Why should one automatically assume that being real is 'better' than merely being thought of? Is murder, for example, better for happening in reality than only being thought of?

What is regarded by some as the most effective argument against Anselm was provided by his contemporary Gaunilo of Marmoutiers, another Benedictine monk. It is known as the 'Lost Island' argument. Instead of 'the greatest thing that can be conceived' Gaunilo suggested we think of 'the greatest island that can be thought of'. This is a perfectly meaningful phrase; we understand it; so the greatest conceivable island exists in our minds. But Anselm's argument tells us that the greatest conceivable island which exists in reality would be greater than one that exists only in the mind. Therefore there must be a greatest conceivable island. Gaunilo took this to reveal the absurdity of Anselm's argument.

Scholars still debate Anselm's argument, and there are some philosophers today, among them Alvin Plantinga, who try to formulate versions of it that will unequivocally work. Interestingly, arguments for the existence of a deity are never what lead people to theistic beliefs: at best they are *post facto* justifications or rationales for what almost always is a commitment that arises from other sources.

ABELARD (1079–1142)

Peter Abelard is known outside the history of philosophy for his famous and tragic love affair with Héloïse. He was a clever, handsome and charismatic man, and as a teacher at the University of Paris was a celebrity among its students, who had flocked to hear him from all parts of Europe, so far did his fame extend. It came to his attention that one of the secular canons of Notre-Dame, named Fulbert, had a remarkable young niece lodging with him, brilliant, learned and beautiful. This was Héloïse d'Argenteuil. Abelard arranged to take lodgings with Fulbert also, and offered himself as her tutor.

Inevitably the two began an affair; she fell pregnant, and gave birth to a son they named Astrolabe in honour of the scientific instrument. Although Abelard and Héloïse married secretly, the furious Fulbert was not placated; he hired men to attack Abelard and castrate him. When he recovered from this trauma, after a period as a monk in retirement, Abelard returned to teaching and writing at a monastic school associated with the Abbey of Saint-Denis. Héloïse was cloistered as a nun at Argenteuil, from where she wrote Abelard poignant love letters saying she would rather love him than God, and wishing that she was in bed with him. His replies, alas, are stuffy and pompous, telling her to behave herself as a good nun. They were reunited in the end; Héloïse founded a nunnery called the Paraclete and Abelard became its abbot.

Abelard is a philosophically significant figure for a number of reasons, but not least among them is that he had a founding role in the form and manner of high Scholasticism – the logical, systematic approach to philosophical and theological questions, and the intermingling of the two. This is illustrated by his book *Sic et Non*, 'Yes and No', in which he places contradictory texts of scripture side by side, and states rules for reconciling the texts, one principal rule being that of taking care to identify equivocations. The technique is designed to promote a logical approach to dealing with problematic questions. As the insistence on logic suggests, he was instrumental, with Albertus Magnus and others, in promoting the influence of the newly rediscovered Aristotle, whose works had not long since begun appearing in Latin in greater numbers, and some of which Abelard knew.

Abelard is regarded as a leading figure among nominalists, both because he rejected the realism about universals associated with Plato and because he offered an account of universals as names, not things – names we apply to things that are similar, such as this individual rose and that individual rose, both of which accordingly we call 'rose', or which have similar properties, such as the red of this rose and the red of that, which for convenience we refer to as 'redness'. But there is no redness in the world apart from the red in each individual red thing, so 'redness' is simply a name, *nomen*.

The basic idea underlying Abelard's nominalism is that everything that exists is individual and particular. Although he regarded individuals as composites of form and matter, he was Aristotelian in regarding the form as immanent to the matter, that is, as individual to it and inseparable from it. It follows that the form 'informing' a given quantum of matter cannot be in more than one lump of matter at a time. Such a view implies that relations – 'before', 'to the left of', 'father of' – exist only because the related individuals exist.

For Abelard, logic and semantics are the basis of philosophy. If we understand how words signify things, and how they combine in sentences which, when declarative, denote dicta or propositions (a 'proposition' is the 'what is said' by an assertion; he recognized that not all sentences assert propositions; other sentences constitute questions, or commands, or expressions of wishes, and so on), then we can better understand the logical structure of arguments. For example, he showed that a conditional sentence of the form 'if p then q', where p and q are dicta or propositions, is not about the truth or otherwise of 'p' or of 'q' taken independently, but about the relationship between 'p' and 'q'.

Although Abelard was influenced by Aristotle he did not know all of Aristotle's works, and therefore some of his independently developed views are very unAristotelian. For example, he did not think that perception consists in having an *eidolon*, image, of an object entering one's mind and 'forming' it into a replica of the object. Instead he had a view more similar to the 'naive realist's' belief that we look out of our eyes as if through windows, and thereby get an initial apprehension of the object which imagination supplies with details and clarifications, thus achieving an understanding of what it is.

In a partial and superficial way Abelard's theory of perception prefigures Kant's views, and so do his views about ethics; for he says, as Kant later did, that the question whether an act is right or wrong is wholly settled by reference to the intention of the actor. If an actor's intentions are shaped by his love of God and his desire to obey him, his acts are good; otherwise they are wrong. This makes the outcome of the act irrelevant to judging its moral worth, even if, contrary to the actor's aim, it causes harm or evil. It is an immediate corollary of this view that the will must be free, otherwise we cannot be praised or blamed for what we intend. In *A Dialogue between a Philosopher, a Jew and a Christian* the Philosopher, a Stoic, argues that happiness is attainable in this life by the successful pursuit of virtue; Abelard has the Christian claim that final happiness is attainable only in the afterlife.

AQUINAS (1225–1274)

By a considerable margin St Thomas Aquinas, as he is known in religious circles, is the greatest philosopher as well as theologian of the medieval period. His combination of theology and philosophy survives today as 'Thomism', still taught in Catholic universities and colleges as the official philosophy of the faith.

A scion of an aristocratic family of Aquino in the region of Italy now known as Lazio, Aquinas was educated at the Benedictine abbey school of Monte Cassino, and then at the University of Naples. His family wished him to join the grand, genteel and centuries-old Benedictine order, as befitted his birth; but while a student at Naples he fell under the influence of a recruiter for the recently formed Dominicans, a mendicant preaching order founded to oppose heresy and fiercely committed to forging the intellectual tools to do so (very like the Jesuits more than three centuries later, who were set up to fight the Protestant Reformation of the sixteenth century). The Dominicans' reputation as hunters of heresy and heretics earned them the threatening as well as punning nickname of 'the hounds of God': *Domini canes*.

Aquinas' family did everything they could to dissuade him from joining the new order, which from their point of view seemed to be a collection of hippies and street fighters with its poverty, lack of history, zealotry and engagement in struggles with Albigensians and Manicheans. They went so far as to kidnap Aquinas, holding him prisoner in their family castles; his brothers even smuggled a prostitute into his room to seduce him from his religious fervour. Legend has it that he drove her away with a red-hot fire-iron, and was rewarded that night by a visit from two angels, an event which strengthened his resolve.

He was finally allowed to leave, and made his way to Paris to study at its university. He enrolled as a pupil of Albertus Magnus, and became so attached to him that when, later, Albertus was sent to inaugurate a new *studium* at Cologne, he accompanied him and soon afterwards began his teaching career there. Among his fellow-students and colleagues Aquinas was known as 'the dumb ox', mainly because he was a man of few words, but also because he was big and burly. Albertus said to them, 'You name him "the dumb ox", but his teaching will one day be a bellow heard throughout the world.'

Aquinas might have been a man of few words in the spoken sense, but he made up for it in the very many volumes of his writings. At Cologne he wrote commentaries on books of the Old Testament and an enormously detailed study of Peter Lombard's *Sentences*. Recalled to Paris to serve as regent master in theology for the Dominicans he set to work to defend the mendicant orders, which as his family's attitude demonstrates were controversial; the other notable new such order was the Franciscan, founded by St Francis of Assisi. The Franciscan and Dominican orders quickly became rivals, often bitter ones.

In his first stint as regent master in Paris Aquinas wrote a book on truth, commentaries on Boethius and a collection of quodlibetical responses to questions in theology put to him by his students and others. By the end of his time there he was working on one of his most famous books, the *Summa Contra Gentiles*.

Literally translated, *Contra Gentiles* means 'Against the Gentiles', the implication being 'Against the Unbelievers' (*summa* means 'summary'). As indicated by the standard English translation of the title, 'On the Truth of the Catholic Faith', the word 'unbelievers' denotes anyone not a member of the Roman Church, which claimed then as it does now 'that there is no salvation outside the Church'. Members of the Orthodox communions of eastern Christianity therefore came under the same heading. Some scholars say that the *Summa Contra Gentiles* was written as a handbook for missionaries to help with evangelizing efforts among pagans and Muslims in north Africa. Whether or not that is so, the book is unusual among Aquinas' works in that its first three-quarters relies not on scripture and revelation, but on 'natural theology' only – that is, on philosophical arguments rather than Church authority. This was so that unbelievers could be converted by appeal to reason without first having to accept the claims made by the Church. Accordingly its account of the nature of God, the creation and the way to achieve happiness – these being the subjects of the first three books of the *Summa* respectively; he tells his readers that happiness is secured by believing in God – do not appeal to scripture. The last book introduces the tenets of Catholic Christianity.

In the decade between 1259 and 1269 Aquinas was once again in Italy and engaged in a variety of educational initiatives and as a papal theologian in Rome. Despite the calls on his time his prodigious output continued: he wrote several searching commentaries on Aristotle's *De Anima*, the *Physics* and other works, and also *The Golden Chain*, the *Errors of the Greeks* (meaning the Orthodox Christians), *The Powers of God* and above all the first parts of the vast *Summa Theologiae* ('Summary of Theology') which he wrote as a primer for beginners in theology, justifying the production of an introductory work by quoting St Paul's remark in the first epistle to the Corinthians, 'as to infants in Christ I gave you milk to drink, not meat.' This is his most famous work.

For sheer size the *Summa Theologiae* is rarely beaten; it is over two million words long* – and Aquinas did not finish what he had originally intended to cover. It takes the form of questions, proposed answers of competing kinds, and discussions of those answers. This is similar to the form of a university disputation in the Scholastic tradition. The size of the book meant that Aquinas' ideas developed as he worked on it; for example, the third part of the *Summa Theologiae*, corresponding to the third part of the *Summa Contra Gentiles* on how to attain happiness, was written at the same time that he made his commentary on Aristotle's *Nicomachean Ethics*, and the influence shows.

In 1269 Aquinas was sent back to the University of Paris by his Dominican superiors to combat the rise there of a version of Aristotelianism associated with Averroes (Ibn Rushd). Averroes' commentaries on Aristotle promoted a strong pro-Aristotelian line against the Neoplatonism of his predecessors al-Farabi and Avicenna, and had thereby initiated a considerable and growing Aristotelian influence. His view of Aristotle involved interpretations uncomfortable for Christian doctrine – for example, the claim that the world is eternal, which contradicts the Church's teaching that God created the world – so Aquinas, an Aristotelian but opposed to the Averroist interpretations, undertook to combat it.

His endeavour in this regard became entangled in a quarrel between the Dominicans and Franciscans in Paris, one of whom accused Aquinas of secretly being an Averroist. The Aristotelian question was a delicate one therefore, for Aquinas was keen to defend what he admired in 'the Philosopher'; he devoted a series of disputations in the years 1270–72 to a demonstration of the consistency of Christian and Aristotelian views.

In 1272, two years before his death, the Dominican order invited Aquinas to found a university anywhere he wished. He returned to Naples, and both taught there and preached to the public in the city. It was in the Dominican chapel of St Nicholas in Naples that he was seen to levitate – so it is claimed – while receiving a commendatory book review from heaven. What is described as a 'long ecstasy' – probably a stroke – occurred not long afterwards, in December 1273, and although he made a partial recovery he was unable to continue his writing. He died three months later, and was canonized half a century afterwards.

One result of the Aristotelian controversy during Aquinas' second

---

* Eight times the size of what you hold in your hands as you read this.

sojourn in Paris was that some of his teachings were condemned by the Bishop of Paris, and his reputation then and posthumously suffered in some quarters. It was not until his proclamation as a Doctor of the Church two centuries later – placing him alongside the 'Latin Fathers of the Church' Ambrose, Gregory, Jerome and Augustine – that his reputation resumed its upward rise. At the sixteenth-century Council of Trent his *Summa Theologiae* was placed on the altar beside the Bible, and in 1879 Pope Leo XIII, in the encyclical *Aeterni Patris*, decreed that his teachings constitute the definitive statement of Catholic doctrine.

What this sketch of Aquinas' life only hints at is the central and pivotal fact that the recovery of the works of Aristotle and their translation into Latin, especially during the second half of the twelfth century – the century before Aquinas' own time – along with studies of them by Averroes and Albertus Magnus among others, were creating tensions between philosophy and theology, which to some meant between reason and faith. Aquinas encountered Aristotle's philosophy as a student at Naples, and was profoundly influenced by it. Indeed a great deal of his own philosophy is straightforward adoption from Aristotle: on the material world, time, motion, cosmology, perception, ethics and aspects of the question of the relation of God to the world. Aristotle was not the only influence; Augustine and Boethius, and Plato through Neoplatonism, played their part in his thought too. But it is evident from the searching nature of his commentaries on Aristotle that 'the Philosopher' was the chief source of his views. That is the principal reason why he set himself the task of reconciling faith and reason, by attempting to show that Christian doctrines have, or can be given, philosophical underpinnings.

In earlier Christian doctrine there were conflicting and unsettled views about the nature of the soul, ranging from Tertullian's view that the soul is corporeal to versions of Plato's non-corporeal theory adopted by Origen and Gregory of Nyssa. The problem required a suitable philosophical understanding of the concept of substance, which in turn involved thinking about matter, change and form. As one would expect, Aquinas found resources in Aristotle for formulating his own view about these topics.

Aquinas defined a material substance as the compound of an essence and a set of accidents. The essence is itself a compound of matter and form, while the accidents are all the other properties that the individual substance might contingently have. In the case of a human individual, the compound of matter and form that constitutes the essence is the *soul*, which Aquinas defined as 'the principle of life'. It is a 'substantial form' because in relation with matter it constitutes the substance that is a given individual human being. The relationship between matter and form is a necessary one: the matter can change (a thin body can become a fat one) but the form is what makes that matter the specific substance it is.

The accidents are forms too, but in virtue of being merely accidental they do not contribute to making a given thing the thing that it is. For example, the colours on the surface of a leaf do not contribute to making the leaf the thing that it is, for when the colours change the leaf remains the same substance it was. By contrast, a change of substance is either a coming-to-be, a *generation*, or a ceasing-to-be, a *corruption*.

One can see the Aristotelian influence in these ideas. But then one sees a Platonic influence also, in the particular case of human beings: the fact that the rational part of the soul is not matter – that it is immaterial – is what makes it the same in its nature as universals, and that is why it can apprehend them. The soul's rational aspect continues to exist after separation from the body at death; does this make Aquinas a dualist? He claims that the soul is incorruptible – and that means not susceptible to change – and that its existential independence of the body and therefore separability from it is demonstrated by the fact that its activities are not those of any of the body's organs. He says the soul is a 'subsistent' thing, by which he means that it can operate on its own, either independently or in conjunction with other things. But it is not a substance; substances are more than subsistents because they are in addition 'complete'. One can understand the idea of completeness by noting how it applies to the question of resurrection: the soul can exist apart from the body, but it is incomplete until reunited with the body at the physical resurrection.

These ideas about substance, matter and form have general application for Aquinas. Change involves both something that stays the same and something that does not. When a leaf changes colour, something stays the same – the leaf, a substance – and something changes – its colour, an accident. One can talk of changes of quality, quantity and other accidental properties without attributing change to the substance of which these are accidents. When a substance changes, what remains the same is the matter, and what changes is the substantial form. This can readily be seen when we ask, in relation to accidental changes, 'What has changed?' and then refer to the underlying thing which is the 'what', namely, the substance. But when one talks of a substance changing, the concept of matter comes into play. Matter does not exist apart from substance, but substance is matter *formed*, that is, compounded with a substantial form; so a change of substance is a change in the compound of matter and form constituting it.

Aquinas says that God is the only 'absolute being' because he is 'unique and simple'; all other things have a restricted kind of existence because of how they are composed. Human souls are created by God and are incorruptible and immortal. The soul has an active power within it, the intellect, capable of attaining to knowledge of universals by abstracting from what our bodily senses tell us. All human knowledge starts in the senses – 'whatever is in the intellect was first in the senses' – and intellect operates on the information thus acquired. The will is free and necessarily desires what the soul sees as good – though the soul's desires change with the changeability of our judgment. We do not have immediate intuitive knowledge of God's existence, nor (here contradicting Anselm) can we prove it *a priori*. But we can prove it *a posteriori* from the nature of creation, which needs a first cause and a necessary ground for its contingent nature, and which in its design and purpose manifests the wisdom and power of the deity.*

Following Aristotle in the *Nicomachean Ethics*, Aquinas says that 'the good' is the target of all striving, namely, the fulfilment of what can variously be described as the function, final cause or distinguishing feature (that is, what distinctively makes it a thing of its kind) of the striver. In the case of human beings the distinguishing feature is reason. Since everything has a function or distinguishing feature, everything has a 'good'; so evil is definable as the absence or lack of good: a *privatio boni*. To the observation that there are people who desire evil Aquinas replies that they mistakenly think that the evil thing is good. However, people can neither hope to do good nor actually do it without divine grace, and that means that they cannot be happy without God.

---

* These are respectively the 'cosmological argument' and the 'teleological argument' (or 'argument from design'). Unlike the ontological argument of Anselm they seek to rely on empirical considerations. See Grayling, *The God Argument* (2013), Chapter 3, passim, for a discussion of these arguments.

This does not, as it might appear to, cause a difficulty about free will, says Aquinas, because although God ultimately is the cause of everything, he operates according to the nature of the thing when he 'moves their causes': so he 'moves the voluntary causes' in humans.

There is much technical philosophy like this in Aquinas. His teachings constitute a complete system, which is why, as 'Thomism', they provide the Roman Catholic Church with its philosophy, whose official status was further confirmed by Pope Pius x in *Doctoris Angelici* (June 1914): 'The capital theses in the philosophy of St Thomas are not to be placed in the category of opinions capable of being debated one way or another, but are to be considered as the foundations upon which the whole science of natural and divine things is based; if such principles are once removed or in any way impaired, it must necessarily follow that students of the sacred sciences will ultimately fail to perceive so much as the meaning of the words in which the dogmas of divine revelation are proposed by the magistracy of the Church.' This places Thomistic philosophy and theology above all debate, which – at least in the case of philosophy – is precisely contrary to what philosophy should be. But even within the confines of an officially sanctioned dogma there can be room for debate, as we see from the fact that there are several differing schools of Thomist philosophy: Scholastic Thomism, Cracow Thomism, Phenomenological Thomism, Existential Thomism, River Forest Thomism and even Analytical Thomism, though this is hardly a school but a glancing reference to the fact that a few significant figures in recent Anglophone Analytic philosophy have been practising Catholics (Elizabeth Anscombe, her husband Peter Geach and their friend Michael Dummett chief among them).

The association of Aquinas with Aristotle meant that when, in the sixteenth and seventeenth centuries, the influence of Aristotle was challenged by the rising generations of philosophers and scientists then at work, Aquinas' own authority diminished – even among some individual Catholics, such as Descartes, whose views about the unreliability of sense-experience and the difference between mind and body as separate substances are in direct conflict with Aquinas' views. It was for this reason that Descartes' philosophy was not accepted by the Church, and why his writings were placed on the Index of Forbidden Books.

In the Catholic Church Aquinas' reputation has remained strong, not least because of the work of the Dominicans and the fact that the Pontifical University of St Thomas Aquinas has produced so many ecclesiastically influential graduates. As with almost all theologians, in philosophy in general his influence is far less.

ROGER BACON (1214–1292)

Perhaps the least characteristic figure in the philosophy of the middle ages, and the least like his fellow Scholastics, is Roger Bacon. His primary interest was 'natural philosophy', which we now call 'science', and he was an empiricist: he argued that 'theories supplied by reason should be verified by sensory data, aided by instruments, and corroborated by trustworthy witnesses.' To some historians of ideas, therefore, he appears as an anomaly in his age, a modern before modern times, who would have been more at home with Galileo and Newton in the seventeenth century as a colleague in the rise of science. Others, however, argue that his interest in alchemy and astrology keep him firmly among the medievals, while others again point to the work of Robert Grosseteste and Albertus Magnus whose own scientific interests were in some respects similar to those of Bacon.

Born in Somerset, England, Bacon studied at Oxford and taught at Paris, having taken the tonsure as a Franciscan friar. Like others of his time he lectured on the *Sentences* of Peter Lombard, but he argued that greater attention should be paid to the Bible itself and to the biblical languages, in which he was expert. He argued also that the university curriculum should be expanded to include optics, astronomy and more mathematics. His *Opus Maius*, covering grammar, mathematics, astronomy, optics, alchemy, the relation of theology to science, and an account of methods of enquiry together with an examination of the 'General Causes of Human Ignorance' was intended as a prospectus for a new university curriculum. Pope Clement IV was sympathetic to Bacon's views, having encountered them before becoming Pope, but he died too soon after his election to be able to help. The question of what influence a science-focused new university might have had on its times is an interesting speculation.

Bacon's work on optics, the calendar and the composition of gunpowder underwrite his credentials as an empirical scientist. Reform of the calendar had become a necessity, because the Julian calendar then in use had become misaligned with the movement of the heavenly bodies and the seasons. Bacon calculated correctly that the date of

Easter had shifted forward nine days since the First Council of Nicaea in 325 CE, a thousand years before. Something close to the remedy he proposed was eventually adopted, but not until another four centuries had passed.* Calendar reform required a knowledge of mathematics, astronomy and geography, which is why he proposed them as part of his curriculum reform.

It can be said that Bacon anticipated Noam Chomsky's idea of 'deep grammar' as the underlying capacity for language found in all human beings, for he wrote that 'Grammar is one and the same in all languages, substantially, though it may vary, accidentally, in each of them.' His experiments in optics led him to describe the use of ground lenses as burning glasses, focusing the rays of the sun on dry matter to ignite it. He is also credited with being one of the first to make spectacles, although historians of technology regard this as unlikely, locating the development of spectacles in Italy, and probably in Venice, where the earliest explicit references to spectacles occur (in decrees containing references to 'reading lenses', *vitreos ab oculis ad legendum*).

Bacon's interest in astrology, alchemy and the possibility that mystical experience might also be a source of knowledge is evidence of his openness to all forms of exploration in an age when sharper distinctions between fruitful and fruitless forms of enquiry were yet to be drawn.† He was influenced by Aristotle – indeed his empiricism drew its inspiration from that source – and incorrectly believed that a work called *The Secret of Secrets*, an Arab treatise of advice for princes and rulers, had been written by Aristotle for Alexander the Great, so he published an edition of it with an introduction and an apparatus of notes.

The chief of Bacon's works, the *Opus Maius*, begins with his discussion of the causes of error. He identifies these as reliance on untrustworthy authorities, custom, credulous popular opinion and the disguising of ignorance by learned-seeming displays of wordy rhetoric and jargon. Wisdom and truth, by contrast, are to be found in God's general revelation throughout history to the Jews, Greeks, Romans, Muslims and his own age. This view, allied with his study of grammar and semiotics (the science of signs), prompted him to believe that the study of Hebrew,

---

* This was the calendar reform of Pope Gregory XIII in 1582 CE – the 'Gregorian calendar'.
† His later namesake Francis Bacon, together with René Descartes, devoted careful attention to questions of methodology in their work in the early seventeenth century, influentially so. See Grayling, *The Age of Genius* (2016), Chapter 16, passim.

Greek, Arabic and Chaldean was necessary for a complete education. But he nominated Latin as the best language for philosophy and indeed all learning. The importance of language prompted him to offer what is in effect a philosophy of language, of a rather straightforward sort; he treats language as a system of signs that present information to a listener or reader about something other than the sign itself, thus enabling the transmission of thoughts from utterer to recipient, and standing for 'external things [which they] represent to the intellect'.

Bacon's championing of the study of light and optics, or *perspectiva* as it was known, bore fruit in that it became part of the curriculum after his time, adding to the original *quadrivium* of arithmetic, geometry, astronomy and music. It is linked to his acceptance of astrological ideas based on a theory of 'radiation' of influences from heavenly bodies on to the earth, including therefore human minds. He thought that mathematics forms the basis of logic – in recent philosophy Gottlob Frege and Bertrand Russell made unsuccessful efforts to demonstrate the reverse of this, by reducing mathematics to logic – but its chief application was to the geometry of light rays and the direct, reflected and refracted paths they follow. This interest led Bacon to examine the anatomy of the eye also, and to generalize a study of vision to questions of perception and perceptual error, illusions, hallucinations and the distorting effects of distance, darkness and other factors. For an empiricist, who as such thinks that observation is a key source and test of knowledge, these points are obviously important.

A commitment to knowing languages, and knowing about scientific methods and instruments, was central to Bacon's outlook. The first showed him that some of the translations of Aristotle from Greek into Latin were erroneous; the second prompted him to use, and to encourage the use of, instruments such as the astrolabe.

The seventh part of the *Opus Maius* demonstrates how Bacon drew together all his interests. Its topic is morality, and it comprehends religion, an account of the virtues, astrology and the science of rhetoric. In this section the influence of Aristotle is strong, but that of the Stoics is stronger, and Bacon extolled the wisdom of Seneca in particular.

Bacon did not have much influence on his contemporaries, and in fact might have suffered some discrimination by them both because of the nature of his interests and because of his pugnacious advocacy of them. In addition to his revolutionary views about the curriculum he was believed to dabble in the black arts, and rumour had it that he had made a brass head that could answer questions – in some versions of the story, *any* questions. Like Doctor Dee and other devotees of the occult arts three centuries later, he was viewed as a Faust-like figure who had trespassed over the boundary between the acceptable and the diabolic. He is said to have spent time in prison; there were long periods when he did not have a teaching post at a university; he found it difficult to find a patron to sponsor his work. These facts would be consistent with such a reputation.

But historians of philosophy, with the benefit of hindsight, are attracted by themes in Bacon's interests and writings that prefigure later developments, so he survives the sixteenth-century occultists' interest in him as a magus, celebrated for his Faust-like entanglement with things demonic in Robert Greene's *Honorable Historie of Frier Bacon and Frier Bungay*. Instead he is seen either as a modern before modernity, or as a particularly noteworthy example of a thinker with an interest in nascent science.

DUNS SCOTUS (1266–1308)

Like Roger Bacon, though unlike him in every other respect, Duns Scotus was a Franciscan. As such he was not automatically inclined to agree with the views of Dominicans such as Albertus Magnus and Thomas Aquinas. And indeed his work in significant part is characterized by disagreement with their approach to the questions that most occupied the Scholastic mind.

Little is known about Scotus' biography beyond what is written on his tomb in Cologne: 'Scotland bore me, England fostered me, France taught me, Cologne keeps me.' That says it all, except that the English fostering was at Oxford and the Paris education was as a student, then as a regent master, of the Franciscan order at its university. The welcome he received at Paris was not unalloyed; he and his fellow Franciscans were expelled for a while for siding with the Pope in a quarrel between the Vatican and the French King, but the banishment did not last long.* In 1307 he was ordered by the Franciscans to go to Cologne to teach at their college there, and he died the following year.

---

* The power of the papacy in those times must have been a vexation, although sometimes also a help, to medieval kings, whose countries were infested by religious orders loyal to

Scotus is known as the 'subtle Doctor' and this is an allusion to the Scholastic sophistication of his views. His chief work is his commentary on the *Sentences* of Peter Lombard, together with the additional commentaries on the *Sentences* from his Paris lectures. The most notable feature of them is their marked difference from the metaphysics of Aquinas. Scotus does not mention Aquinas often; he takes as his main target another leading figure of the day, Henry of Ghent; but a distinguishing feature of his views is their contrast with those of Aquinas. Like others he wrote commentaries on Aristotle also, concentrating on certain of the logical works.

The principal difference between Scotus and Aquinas was that Scotus regarded 'being' and 'goodness' as univocal concepts, that is, as having the same meaning whatever they are applied to, whether God or his creatures. Aquinas had argued that the being of a human and the being of God are not the same, but merely analogous. Scotus took Aristotle's definition of metaphysics as the study of 'being *qua* being' to support his view that 'being' has a single, universally applicable sense, and argued that the term denotes everything there is, both what is infinite and what is finite. An immediate consequence of this view is that there is no distinction in reality between *existence* and *essence*, as Aquinas had argued there is. Scotus' reason was one that George Berkeley reprised four hundred years later and made central to his attack on 'abstraction' in metaphysics: that there is no way to think of something without thinking of it as existing.

In further opposition to Aquinas he argued that the nature of God can be known only through revelation, not by reason alone – the latter view was the premise on which Aquinas' *Summa Contra Gentiles* had been written. And he disagreed with Aristotle about the nature of space and time; whereas Aristotle had argued that space is defined by the presence in it of bodies, and that time does not exist unless it is a measure of motion and change, Scotus held that both space and time are absolute and exist in their own right independently of body or motion. This is a view that Isaac Newton held also.

Scotus rejected approaches to proofs of God's existence of the kind found in Anselm and Aquinas, and instead offered a 'metaphysical'

---

the Pope and therefore constantly spying for him and acting on his behalf openly and otherwise. One of Henry VIII's motivations – apart from expropriating their wealth – for abolishing the monastic orders in England had its source in this.

proof couched in terms of the relation of being *first*: the first in the chain of efficient causes, that is, the causes that make other things happen; the first in the order of final causes, that is, the purposes or reasons why things happen (recall Aristotle's 'four causes'); and the first in all perfection and greatness. The argument for the first 'first' – the first efficient cause – is that there has to be a cause that is uncaused, cannot be caused and is therefore independent of causation other than as the first cause of everything. And since everything is caused by something other than itself, and since the causal chain cannot extend back for ever, there has to be a first, uncaused cause. This argument is in content indistinguishable from the 'cosmological argument' as employed by Aquinas, but it differs in emphasis. Like others who employed versions of this argument, Scotus assumed that the identification of a first, uncaused cause and the deity of revealed religion is unproblematic. It is, however, a very big jump.

Recall that Aquinas argued that all created substances are compounds of matter and form. Scotus argued that there can be matter without form, which he called 'prime matter'; and that there can be creatures (created substances) that have no matter – namely, spiritual beings; and that substances can have more than one substantial form, as in the case of humans who have both a soul as form, and a bodily form. What makes an individual thing *individual*, that is, different from every other thing and uniquely itself, is its *haecceity* or 'thisness', from the Latin *haec*, 'this'. At the same time, however, Scotus was a realist about universals, holding that there are 'common natures' in the plurality of individuals we call by the same name.

Scotus died young and suddenly, leaving his writings in an unordered state, so that they came to be mixed with the writings of others. He had followers in the period after his death, who engaged in controversy with the followers of William of Ockham, who disagreed with much in Scotus' views and is regarded as Scotus' chief rival. But the nineteenth and twentieth centuries' recovery and editing of Scotus' highly technical and sophisticated arguments, and separately his theological views (for example about the 'immaculate conception' of the Virgin Mary), prompted a revival of interest in both theological and philosophical quarters – though it has to be said, as in the case of others among the Scholastic philosophers, a recondite and very specialized one.

WILLIAM OF OCKHAM (1285–1347)

Ockham was yet another Franciscan, born in Surrey, England, and educated at Oxford, whose career differed from that of his predecessors because his commentary on the *Sentences* of Peter Lombard was condemned by a synod for unorthodoxy, and he was ordered to appear before a papal court at Avignon. There he met the Minister General of the Franciscan order, Michael of Cesena, who had been charged with heresy because the Pope, John XXII, objected to the Franciscans' rule of poverty. Ockham fled from Avignon with Michael and some other Franciscans, and found asylum at the Bavarian court of Louis (alternatively, Ludwig) IV, the Holy Roman Emperor, who was also at odds with the Pope. The Pope excommunicated Ockham, and Ockham charged the Pope with heresy for denying the poverty of Jesus and the apostles, and for contradicting the endorsement of the Franciscan order by previous popes.

Because of these quarrels Ockham never served as a regent master in one of the great universities, but lived and died in Louis IV's home realm of Bavaria, as leader of a small group of Franciscan exiles. From there his writings came to exert a considerable influence in philosophy and theology, and attracted yet further adherents.

Ockham consciously saw himself as an innovator, and as leaving behind the old way (the *via antiqua*) of treating central problems in philosophy, logic and theology, in order to pursue a new way (the *via moderna*) in which nominalism is a central commitment. He is credited with stating the principle of 'Occam's Razor' – the spelling of his name is a variant – which in summary is the advice 'not to multiply entities unnecessarily'. Its meaning is that there is no need to invoke more things than are sufficient for an explanation of something. It is excellent advice, and Ockham's theories of knowledge and metaphysics illustrate its application, not least in connection with the debate between nominalists and realists.

In direct opposition to Aquinas, Ockham argued that theological truths can be grasped only through faith, not by reason. 'The ways of God are not open to reason, for He has created the world and set the way of salvation in it independently of any laws of logic or rationality that humans can discover.'* This has the immediate consequence that there cannot be

---

* The temptation to see irony in these words is strengthened by speculation as to what an application of Occam's Razor would do to theology as part of any account of the world;

proofs of God's existence. God's freedom and omnipotence mean that he could have incarnated himself not as the son of a carpenter in Palestine but as an ox or donkey, and even as both a donkey and a man simultaneously. This was a view that attracted much criticism from his peers.

He further argued that God is the only necessary being in the universe, and that everything else is contingent and must be discovered through enquiry. 'Nothing ought to be posited without a reason given for it, unless it is self-evident, known by experience, or based on the authority of Scripture.' He was a nominalist, holding that there are only individual things and that there are no separately existing universals or essences. This feature of his thought demonstrates an application of his 'Razor'. His view about universals might be considered a version of 'conceptualism', which holds that universals are concepts in the mind under which we group individuals according to perceived similarities. Accordingly a term like 'redness' denotes a representation in thought, not an entity in the world. This differs from forms of nominalism which variously hold that universals are literally only names.

Ockham agreed with those who held that we acquire all contingent knowledge by means of the senses, but he added that because animals also do this, what is distinctive about human knowledge is that our powers of mind enable us to grasp the existence and properties of the things perceived, and by means of memory and abstraction to classify and organize what we experience. Thus we advance from merely sensory to propositional knowledge.

As one would expect from a philosopher of empirical and nominalist temperament, Ockham was interested in Aristotle's *Physics* and wrote a commentary on it, arguing – again on the basis of his principle of ontological parsimony – that not all of Aristotle's categories are required. He was far in advance of his time in the study of logic, discovering a form of De Morgan's Theorems and investigating a three-valued logic (true, false and neither-true-nor-false).* He also improved on Aristotle's logic of the syllogism by showing how to treat empty terms (words that do not refer to anything).

---

the circumstances of the time and Ockham's life suggest that the temptation has to be resisted.

* See the Appendix on logic. Augustus De Morgan was a nineteenth-century mathematician and logician, who showed that the Law of Excluded Middle ('Everything is either A or not-A') and the Law of Non-Contradiction ('You cannot have both A and not-A at the same time') are versions of each other.

Because of the Emperor's quarrels with the Pope, Ockham advocated a strongly secularist line regarding the respective spheres of temporal and spiritual authority, influenced by Marsilius of Padua's *Defensor Pacis*, a book that attacked the papacy's meddling in secular affairs and advocated a form of democracy for establishing legitimate government. Marsilius had also taken refuge with Louis IV as a result of the Pope's hostility to him. In his own contribution to political theory Ockham advocated complete separation of Church and state, arguing that Emperor and Pope were equal but with different spheres of responsibility, and said, quoting the second epistle of Timothy 2:24, that the papacy and clergy should own no lands or other property. Consistently, this very Franciscan view placed the Pope's authority in the spiritual realm alone.

As to the perennially vexed question of free will, Ockham was a decided voluntarist; he thought that the will is independent both of the intellect and of our natural appetites, so independent that it can even choose what does not appear to be good. This places him in opposition to both Aristotle and Aquinas, for whom the will is subordinate to reason. A younger contemporary of Ockham, Jean Buridan, attempted to reconcile the conflicts that are generated by the difference between these views by saying that the will is capable of suspending itself – or better: can defer making a choice – if faced with undecidable alternatives. This gave rise to the trope of 'Buridan's Ass', probably a facetious *reductio* of Buridan's view: it envisages a donkey starving to death because it cannot choose which to eat of two bales of hay it has been placed between.

Ockham's views were hotly debated in the Schools during the century after his death, not least because his excommunication for heresy added a sharp edge to the questions at issue. So bitter did the disputes become that Ockhamists were expelled from the University of Paris – the Thomists could claim that they followed a canonized saint whereas their opponents followed a condemned heretic. The Ockhamists responded that Thomism and Scotism (the philosophy of Duns Scotus) had led some of their adherents into heresy, one such being the condemned John Wycliffe. In each of the two 'ways' into which philosophy and theology were diverging – the *via antiqua* following Aquinas, Duns Scotus and Albertus Magnus, the *via moderna* following Ockham, Buridan and others – what was chiefly at issue was not just the realism–nominalism debate but the whole question of how Aristotle is to be understood. For example: on the question of form and substance, can there be several substantial forms in the same subject? Followers of the *via antiqua* said yes, those of the *via moderna* said no. Philosophical differences of this kind had theological consequences, which is why they were such a burning (literally) issue: for, according to the *via antiqua* view, many souls could inhabit one human being, while Ockhamists and their successors rejected such ideas.

Philosophy in the Renaissance

Compare the art of the Renaissance to medieval art. The latter is dominated by religious themes: annunciations, flagellations, crucifixions, depositions, resurrections, numerous iterations of the Madonna and Child. Renaissance art includes a far wider palette of subjects: it also has landscapes, still lifes, depictions of picnics and festivals, portraits of individuals, nudes, battles and legendary and mythological scenes. The turning away from a relentless focus on the world as a dangerous vale of temptations and tears to a celebration of life itself and its more joyous possibilities is a mark of the revival and refreshment of which poets, thinkers and artists of the period were fully conscious.

The same is true of intellectual life in the Renaissance: it saw many of its thinkers and writers turning away from the narrow technicalities of Scholastic philosophy to a broader focus on life and society. There is a striking parallel between the highly specialized pursuit of philosophy in the medieval Schools and the academic philosophy of recent times, and correlatively the subsequent turn to a broader application of intellectual endeavour following the rapid increase in remoteness of philosophy from what matters to life. One might venture the thought that the turn from technical to more general philosophical interest is even more apparent in the tradition of recent and contemporary Continental thought, where the work of such writers as Jacques Derrida and Michel Foucault exemplifies the same kind of relation to Heidegger's philosophy as Marsilio Ficino's relation to that of Aquinas: influenced by, but venturing into wider fields than, their heavyweight predecessor, they exhibit a contemporary version of Ficino's expansion of interest. Ficino (1433–99), who learned much from Aquinas' *Summa Contra Gentiles*, nevertheless remarked that his century – the fifteenth century CE – had 'restored to light the liberal arts, which were almost extinct: grammar, poetry, rhetoric, painting, sculpture, architecture, music'; it was, he said, 'like a golden age'. Likewise Foucault acknowledged a significant indebtedness to Heidegger, but as a critical explorer of the intellectual history of modernity his targets of interest were both different and broader.

Ficino's reference to rhetoric signals an important aspect of the intellectual turn in the Renaissance. Because it was an age in which intellectual endeavour was assumed to have, as its chief interest, life as actually lived, the relationship between logic, ethics and rhetoric was regarded as an intimate one. The theory of rhetoric says that, to attain maximum effect in persuading or educating an audience, composing a speech or treatise has to go through several important stages. These were *inventio*, the gathering of material and information, *dispositio*, the arrangement of the material, and *elocutio*, its appropriate expression in language. If it were a speech that was being prepared, then *memoria*, learning it by heart, and *pronuntiatio*, practising emphases, pacing, pauses, gestures and general manner of delivery, would be essential too. The *dispositio* stage had its own structure: *exordium*, introduction, *narratio*, setting out the case, *divisio*, specifying the chief points of the argument, *confutatio*, refuting objections, *conclusio* or *peroratio*, summing up and conclusion. Forensic speech of all kinds, political and legal; exhortation and instruction; invocation of principles or historical examples in order to influence the choices, decisions and actions of both individuals and rulers; all these addressed actual practical concerns. Accordingly rhetoric was not an academic exercise merely.

At the heart of rhetoric lies language, and therefore a focus on the first subject of the *trivium*, the medieval school curriculum of grammar, rhetoric and logic, acquired renewed significance. Originally it just meant the study of Latin, but now it reasserted its relevance to ethics, because rhetoric is about persuading, influencing, advising and challenging, and therefore immediately applies to ethical debate. Renaissance intellectuals looked not to the medieval writers, who had on the whole neglected rhetoric in preference for a technical interest in logic, but to the treatises on rhetoric and poetics of Aristotle and Horace, and in their commentaries on them and on Cicero emphasized both ethical and psychological aspects. Petrarch led the way in this recalibration of interest, but hundreds of treatises on rhetoric followed, many of the leading thinkers of the Renaissance contributing to the debate that linked rhetoric to the idea of the *vita activa* so much extolled in that epoch.

It is natural for an historian of philosophy to question whether the Renaissance emphasis on rhetoric represented a genuine contribution to philosophy, or whether – as some in the Renaissance itself argued – rhetoric is in fact anti-philosophical. Plato made a comeback in the Renaissance, his works appearing in Latin and attaining considerable influence, and his strictures against the sophists and their rhetorical tricks in his *Gorgias* (translated into Latin by Leonardo Bruni) were known. To those sceptical about whether the Renaissance did more than opportunistically help itself to rhetorically useful smatterings of philosophy from one or another source, they could point to the paradoxes, inconsistencies and relativism that resulted. The response is to say that thinking about the complexities of real life, the hard choices people are often forced to make, the changes and variabilities of experience and circumstance, of course results in the appearance of inconsistency. The Renaissance rhetoricians could claim that philosophy, which seeks absolutes, has the luxury of ignoring realities, while rhetoric respects and addresses them. They could cite Aristotle's point in his *Rhetoric* that this art or *techne* is central to the practicalities of life and society, and quote Cicero's remark that 'to us orators belong the broad estates of wisdom and learning.' And they could observe with Cicero that Plato himself was a formidable exponent of rhetoric in his writings.

It is however undeniable that the concerns of many of the Renaissance thinkers were far removed from the technical debates of the Schoolmen and their successors, even those who claimed adherence to the revived Platonism of their time. The Platonist revival, and humanism, are interesting; interesting also but in a quite different way is the intellectual energy invested by Renaissance thinkers in magic, alchemy, astrology, Hermeticism and the Cabala. All of these 'occult sciences' saw a tremendous upsurge especially in those parts of Europe which had been removed from the sphere of the Roman Church by the Reformation, the chief reason being that the religious authorities in Protestant parts of Europe did not have the authority or, more to the point, the power to stop an ebullition of interest in them. The drivers of this interest were the desire for eternal youth, immortality and wealth gained by transforming base metals into gold (or by persuading others that one could by one's 'skill' provide any of these).* As we see in Part III below, 'Modern Philosophy', it was in reaction to this that the science and philosophy of the sixteenth and especially seventeenth centuries arose.

RENAISSANCE PLATONISM

As the discussion above has shown, the dominance of Aristotle in later Scholastic philosophy brought with it tensions resulting in charges and counter-charges of heresy because of the bearing of philosophical disputes on theological doctrines. The combination of Plato's views and Neoplatonist interpretations of them made him a far more congenial and irenic figure from a Christian point of view, especially for Christians not embroiled in the fierce metaphysical disputes of the Schools. Indeed Platonic views were regarded as positively inspirational from a Christian perspective, and mystical significance was attached to his writings. His reintroduction was therefore welcomed by many Renaissance intellectuals.

Platonism did not usurp Aristotelianism, not by a long way; but interest in it had the effect of weakening the latter's authority, giving later philosophers and scientists, especially those in the seventeenth century, a less difficult task in rejecting it.

The Platonist revival is datable to a specific event in a specific place: Florence in the year 1439. In the previous year an ecumenical conference had been moved to Florence from Ferrara because plague had broken out in the latter city. This conference, a highly controversial one, ostensibly had the aim of healing the breach between the Orthodox and Catholic communions, but it was entangled with a variety of other complex matters, not least the powers of the papacy and military tensions between the Holy Roman Empire and the Ottoman Empire. Cosimo de' Medici the Elder, Florence's de facto ruler and founder of the Medicean dynasty, was a man of great culture, and embraced the opportunity provided by the transfer of the conference to welcome Byzantine scholars who accompanied the ambassadors from Constantinople. One of them was George Gemistos (1355–1452), known as Plethon.

* See Grayling, *The Age of Genius* (2016), Part III, passim, esp. Chapters 13 and 14.

Plethon was the leading scholar in Byzantium in that era, and a Neo-platonist. In 1439 he lectured in Florence on Plato and the differences between Plato and Aristotle, to Plato's credit and Aristotle's discredit. The lectures were later published under that descriptive title, *De Differentiis Aristotelis et Platonis*. This book naturally enough sparked a controversy, in which defenders of Aristotle attempted to discredit Plato by claiming that Platonism was in fact a religion which sought to rival Christianity. That was the allegation levelled at Plethon by George of Trebizond, a vehement Aristotelian who served for a time as secretary to the equally enthusiastic Aristotelian Pope Nicholas v. George's *Comparatio Philosophorum Aristotelis et Platonis*, to which Cardinal Basilios Bessarion, a former student of Plethon, replied in *In Calumniatorem Platonis* ('Against the Calumniator of Plato'), is a mixture of enormous learning and intemperate, almost lunatic, polemic.*

But Plethon had achieved his desired effect: interest in Plato was vitally stimulated, as was an interest in learning Greek so that Plato could be read in the original. The fall of Constantinople to the Ottomans in 1453 drove its scholars into a diaspora, among them John Argyropoulos (1415–87), who had earlier in life studied at Padua and now returned to Italy as his chosen place of exile. He settled in Florence and lectured on both the Greek language and philosophy. One of his pupils was Marsilio Ficino, who went on to translate Plato's works into Latin and to head the Platonic Academy founded and funded by Cosimo de' Medici in Florence. Ficino also translated writings by Plotinus, Porphyry, Iamblichus – and less helpfully, perhaps, the Hermetic Corpus which played such a large part in the promotion of 'occult sciences' then and afterwards.

The Platonic Academy was more a club than a university, but it was the single most influential body for diffusing Platonic ideas in fifteenth-century Europe. Ficino's role was central. In addition to translating all the works of Plato into Latin he wrote a work entitled *Platonic Theology*, which was both an introduction to Neoplatonism and an argument for its consistency with Christianity. He said that human souls are, in their immortality, the link between the abstract world of ideas and the material world, and they are what confer on human beings

---

* Bessarion was the Latin Patriarch of Constantinople, and was twice considered for the papacy in Rome. It is intriguing to speculate what difference a Platonist pope would have made to the subsequent history of philosophy and science.

their special dignity. Inspired by Plato's idea of the ascent to love of the Good in the *Symposium* he coined the term 'Platonic love' to describe the soul's love for God when, after ascending through levels of knowledge, it achieves unmediated contact with him.

Ficino's desire to synthesize Platonic philosophy and Hermeticism with Christianity was shared by his student Giovanni Pico della Mirandola (1463–94), who managed in his short life to give both humanism and the occult sciences a boost.

Pico was an aristocrat, the youngest son in a family that ruled Concordia and Modena in Italy and was related to a number of other leading Italian houses – the Sforza, Este and Gonzaga. He was precociously brilliant, and his mother wished him to enter the Church, against his inclination. She died when he was studying canon law at Bologna, freeing him to turn his attention to philosophy, going first to Florence and then to Paris to do so. His studies were eclectic, and in addition to philosophy, Latin and Greek he acquired a knowledge of Hebrew and Arabic, and became acquainted with Chaldean and Zoroastrian ideas and the mysticism of the Cabala (otherwise spelt 'Kabbalah').

On his return from Paris to Florence Pico met and studied with Marsilio Ficino, who introduced him to Lorenzo de' Medici. The first encounter between Pico and Ficino occurred on a day which Ficino had determined, by astrological means, to be most propitious for the publication of his Plato translations. Pico was sceptical about astrology, but this difference of view did not stand in the way of their relationship, nor of Lorenzo de' Medici's admiration for him.

Indeed without Lorenzo's support it is unlikely that Pico would have survived the next steps in his career, the most immediate of which was an adulterous affair that nearly ended in his being killed by the irate husband in the case. More risky still, however, was his plan to issue a challenge in Rome to all the scholars of Europe to debate his 900 *Theses*, a work he had begun composing while in Paris and which had since been expanded by his studies of treatises on magic, the Cabala and Hermetic texts. This eclectic array of sources had a Platonist foundation, as demonstrated by the essay he wrote to accompany and explain the intent behind the theses, *The Oration on the Dignity of Man*.

The opening words of Pico's *Oration* are: 'Most esteemed Fathers, I have read in the ancient writings of the Arabians that Abdala the Saracen on being asked what, on this stage, so to say, of the world, seemed to him most evocative of wonder, replied that there was nothing to be seen more marvellous than man. And that celebrated exclamation of Hermes Trismegistus, "What a great miracle is man, Asclepius", confirms this opinion.' Although a large part of the intent of the *Oration* was to seek legitimization for a syncretistic inclusion of the Cabala and other mystical and supposedly ancient wisdoms into Christian thinking, its primary effect was a rousing celebration of the worth of humankind and everything associated with life in the world – a 90-degree shift of focus from anxiety about getting safely into the afterlife at all costs. This is the key to humanism in the Renaissance; Pico's *Oration* has been described as a key text in capturing its essence.

Among the enquiries to be fostered and celebrated, said Pico citing Plato, is mathematics. In the Renaissance there was a close association, in the minds of nervous people, between mathematics and the occult arts; the terms 'calculating' and 'conjuring' were often used interchangeably. Legitimizing mathematics meant legitimizing all the other suspect enquiries. Pico argued that to search for knowledge anywhere and everywhere raised humankind above the rest of creation and led to closeness to God, just as Plato had argued that knowledge of the Forms and especially the Form of the Good is the great aspiration of philosophical endeavour.

In extolling the philosophical virtues of mathematics Pico was in agreement with his older contemporary Nicholas of Cusa (1401–64), the German scholar and mystic who viewed mathematics as the highest knowledge because it alone is certain. This view placed Plato's scheme of knowledge above Aristotle's empiricist interest in the natural sciences. Preferring Plato to Aristotle did not stop Nicholas from reliance on empirical methodology in certain respects; to him is attributed the idea of measuring a patient's pulse rate by means of a water clock. But Pico's interest in numerology and mystical implications of the alphabet place him in the tradition of Platonism which takes licence from the *Timaeus*, and from Plato's use of the technique of stating his doctrines in the form of revelations by deities, for emphasizing the mystical and revelatory over the empirical.

It is perhaps a contradiction that Pico's valorizing of humanism is not his chief legacy, which instead is the strain of Christian Cabalism he helped to promote. Raymond Lull in thirteenth-century Spain had been the first to take an interest in the Christian possibilities of Cabala, but Pico gave the idea greater currency. He was followed in succeeding centuries by Johann Reuchlin, Paolo Riccio, Athanasius Kircher and others. For Pico himself and the Platonic Academy in Florence, the tumultuous political circumstances of the late fifteenth century brought the Florentine promotion of Platonism to an end. When Lorenzo de' Medici died in 1492 – a year of other major events: the expulsion of the Moors and Jews from Spain, Columbus' 'discovery' of the New World, the publication of Leoniceno's 'On the Errors of Pliny', threats of invasion of Italy by France (which followed in reality in 1494) – the Platonic Academy was closed, and within two years Pico (and his fellow-humanist Poliziano – Angelo Ambrogini, 1454–94, also known as Politian) had died in suspicious circumstances, quite likely murdered.

RENAISSANCE HUMANISM

Today the word 'humanist' denotes a person who has a non-religious ethical outlook. In the Renaissance context it denotes scholars and intellectuals who believed that the *studia humanitatis* of grammar, rhetoric, history, poetry and ethics would help to develop rounded and effective citizens dedicated to an intelligent *vita activa*. The source and inspiration for the material of these studies was explicitly classical antiquity, and explicitly not medieval Scholasticism. The rediscovery and valorization of the intellectual culture of classical times was expressly seen as a rebirth – *renaissance* – by the leaders of the new movement, and its central defining feature is humanism.

The fourteenth-century poet and diplomat Francesco Petrarca (1304–74), more familiarly known as Petrarch, is called 'the Father of Humanism' because his collecting of ancient manuscripts, advocacy of the value of classical thought and letters, and description of the period between classical antiquity and his own time's rediscovery of its values as the 'middle ages' make him the self-aware promoter of a new outlook. His great fame as a poet in his own lifetime helped to spread his influence and ignite in other breasts a similar passion for the classical past. This included enthusiasm for finding forgotten manuscripts in monasteries and dusty archives, and encouraging their translation and publication, an enthusiasm shared to great good effect by others such as Petrarch's friend Giovanni Boccaccio, the Ciceronian Coluccio Salutati and, later, Poggio Bracciolini.

Boccaccio (1313–75) is best known for the *Decameron*, a collection of witty, perceptive and sometimes ribald tales written in a naturalistic manner in vernacular Italian. He was appointed by the Florentine *signoria* (the city state's ruling council) to provide Petrarch with hospitality when the latter visited Florence in 1350, and they became fast friends. Petrarch encouraged Boccaccio to study classical literature; Boccaccio called him 'my teacher and master', and the fruit was his encyclopaedia of Greek and Roman mythology, the *Genealogia Deorum Gentilium*, a key text for Renaissance humanism and art.

Coluccio Salutati (1331–1406), the great Chancellor of Florence whose letters were described by his arch-rival Giangaleazzo Visconti, Duke of Milan, as each more dangerous than a thousand cavalrymen, modelled his beautiful writing style on Cicero, and spent a fortune on collecting ancient manuscripts, in the process rediscovering Cicero's *Epistulae ad Familiares* ('Letters to his Friends') which contain commentary and argument on the loss of Rome's republican liberties. Salutati's late work *De Tyranno* ('On the Tyrant') owed much to Cicero's views. He was a generous promoter of talented younger contemporaries, Poggio Bracciolini (1380–1459) among them.

One of the greatest finds made by burrowing into old monastic libraries and archives is owed to Bracciolini. He sent his scouts far afield in search of manuscripts, into Germany, Switzerland and France as well as across Italy, and recovered a large number of lost works, by far the most significant being the *De Rerum Natura* of Lucretius. His position as papal secretary was a help in this endeavour, and he became rich as a result; the sale of a manuscript of Livy funded the purchase of a handsome villa in the valley of the Arno which he filled with antiquities.

Bracciolini engaged in a celebrated dispute with the philologist Lorenzo Valla (1407–57), whose work on the elegances of Latin literature, defence of Epicurus on pleasure, and exposure of the fraudulent 'Donation of Constantine' by linguistic detective work had made him famous. Valla argued that biblical texts should be subjected to the same philological analysis as texts by the classical authors. Bracciolini countered that secular and divine literature should be treated differently. Their battle was conducted in a series of detailed publications, and ended – though Bracciolini at one point described Valla as 'insane' for thinking as he did – in the two becoming friends. It was not until the nineteenth century in Germany that Valla's views about the application of radical criticism to biblical texts were fully implemented.

The poet and scholar Poliziano, mentioned above in connection with

Pico della Mirandola, was an innovator in Latin style, like Salutati in the century before his own. He translated Homer, Epictetus, Galen and Plutarch into Latin, and published editions of Virgil and Catullus that sought to be accurate. He served as tutor to the children of Lorenzo de' Medici, and was invited by Ficino to lecture on classical literature at the Platonic Academy. There he influenced many visiting students from across Europe, promoting interest in Ovid and the younger Pliny among others, and encouraging greater precision in the translation and editing of classical texts.

As these vignettes of leading humanists show, Renaissance humanism was above all else an educational movement. Florence's Platonic Academy was just one expression of this. In Ferrara the brilliant teacher Guarino Veronese (1374–1460), also known as Guarino da Verona, taught Greek, translated Strabo and Plutarch and wrote commentaries on various classical authors including Aristotle and Cicero. He had studied in Constantinople to advance his knowledge of Greek, bringing back a valuable collection of manuscripts of classical texts. In Mantua, Vittorino Rambaldoni (1378–1446), known also as Vittorino da Feltre, developed new methods to teach the classical languages and their literatures. Like Guarino he frequently paid for poor students out of his own pocket. His fame as a teacher prompted many of Italy's leading personalities, including Bracciolini, to send their children to his school, which was in effect Europe's first secular boarding school. One of his most celebrated pupils was Federigo da Montefeltro, later Duke of Urbino, whose recognizable hooked nose is a prominent feature in Piero della Francesca's portrait of him. Federigo made money for his duchy by hiring himself out as a *condottiere*, a mercenary general at the head of his own army; but Vittorino's teaching evidently stuck, because Federigo was in the habit of having classical and especially philosophical texts read to him as he breakfasted in camp every morning.

The humanist educators believed that classical literature provided intellectual discipline, moral training and civilized tastes. It was regarded as especially formative of those destined to take leading positions in society and culture. It was an ideal that persisted for a long time, only recently being abandoned for more practical and banausic aims. As the examples of Guarino and Vittorino suggest, the *studia humanitatis* was mainly though not exclusively a feature of school rather than university education; many more people attended school than university, and in the universities the study of law, medicine and theology, and the disputes in metaphysics and logic that lay at the heart of philosophy, still dominated. But even in universities the study of Greek, classical rhetoric and poetry increasingly gained a footing, and a number of the humanist intellectuals were invited to lecture in, or became professors of, universities – Guarino, for example, became professor of Greek at the University of Ferrara.

It was however an advantage for society that those who received a humanistic education were more likely to become chancellors of city states or secretaries to popes than university professors, because they took the liberal outlook and wider horizons of their education into practical affairs. And not only chancellors and secretaries, but princes and popes themselves received such an education, not a few of them becoming patrons of humanistic education and culture in their own turn.

In the middle of the fifteenth century Johannes Gutenberg's invention of a movable-type printing press gave a tremendous impetus to the book trade; within decades every major town in Europe had one or more printing businesses, and by the end of the century an estimated twenty million volumes had poured from them, including hundreds of editions of classical texts translated and edited by humanists. But in fact the book industry had been flourishing even before this, demand for scribes and copyists rising quickly and new forms of script being introduced to make copying both faster and more legible. The elaborate Gothic script which had been enough for monastic libraries and wealthy private collectors gave way to a form of minuscule invented by Bracciolini (he thought the original minuscule was Roman but in fact it was Carolingian), and to a popular and widely used cursive italic script invented by Niccolò de' Niccoli (1364–1437), one of the humanists who flourished under the patronage of Cosimo de' Medici the Elder, and who added to his calligraphic innovations the successful technique of editing texts into paragraphs and chapters, with tables of contents at the head. When printing first became widespread Niccoli's italic was the most frequently chosen form of script. Bracciolini's minuscule is however the ancestor of the kinds of font now most familiar.

The relation of humanism to philosophy in the Renaissance is seen most clearly in ethics and political theory, which together with 'oeconomics' formed a whole. The source of this view was a set of Aristotelian texts: the *Nicomachean Ethics*, the *Politics* and a work called *Oeconomics* attributed to Aristotle though not by him (its unknown author is therefore called 'pseudo-Aristotle'). Aristotle himself had described ethics and politics as continuous, and his later commentators followed suit in recognizing the tripartite combination of enquiries as constituting 'practical philosophy'. In the Renaissance both Aristotelians and Platonists continued the tradition, and it persisted into the seventeenth century.

There was a naturalness to this view in that each of the branches related to the others in a logical way: the individual, the home and the state were the respective topics of ethics, economics and political theory. Albertus Magnus had described the connection between them in terms of an individual's relationships: the relationship of an individual to himself, of an individual in his domestic relations to his family, and of an individual in his civil relations to his society. Albertus' student Aquinas elaborated this view of the natural sociality of humankind in his commentary on Aristotle's *Nicomachean Ethics*, and this view remained dominant throughout the Renaissance.

What the Renaissance added was an intensification of interest in human nature itself, given that this was the basis of practical philosophy. Petrarch laid claim to being the first to turn away from bewailing the misery of man – the 'vale of tears' on which medieval Christianity focused – and to celebrate human dignity instead. He did this in his *De Remediis Utriusque Fortunae* (translated as 'Petrarch's View of Human Life' by Susannah Dobson in 1791), a wise and often witty series of 254 dialogues, through which runs a Stoic theme of modesty and fortitude.

The 'dignity of man' theme had been mooted some time beforehand by Pope Innocent III (1160–1216), who in the preface to one of his writings on the misery of the human lot said that he intended to balance his account of that matter with something more positive, but had not managed to get round to it. Petrarch and Pico della Mirandola were just two of those who took up the challenge: other treatises followed, and in their turn prompted contrary replies repeating the idea that life in the flesh is anything but dignified and happy. One such responder was Poggio Bracciolini in his *De Miseria Humanae Conditionis* ('On the Misery of the Human Condition').

Discussion of the nature of humanity involved comparisons between humans and other animals. The idea became commonplace that man is the 'stepchild of nature' because alone in creation he comes defenceless and naked into the world, without claws or sharp teeth, without swiftness or the protection of a shell, and so on – but with one gift: that of intelligence. Ficino argued that the possession of intelligence makes man godlike, for by its means he can exploit all the advantages that animals have – the ox's strength, the horse's swiftness, the wool of the sheep to keep himself warm – whereas animals can use only the one advantage that nature gave them.

Man's superiority in these respects did not go unchallenged. A Franciscan monk who converted to Islam, Anselm Turmeda, who as Abd-Allah at-Tarjuman became a vizier or secretary in Tunis, wrote a witty account of a dispute between himself and an ass over the question of which was more noble. Turmeda points out that men build palaces and cities; the ass responds that bees and ants do likewise. Turmeda says that humans eat the flesh of animals; the ass says that worms eat man's flesh in the grave. Matters proceed without advantage to man until Turmeda – still evidently in his unconverted Franciscan frame of mind – points out that God made himself man, thus forcing the ass to concede.

The incarnation of Christ was taken as the chief point in extolling the dignity of man: that God himself had glorified human nature by becoming a man in order to fulfil his universal plan. There were parallels to celebrate: like the Trinity, man's soul has three parts: intellect, memory and will. A Platonist could modify this slightly by citing Plato's reason, spirit and appetite as the soul's three divisions. Nicholas of Cusa claimed that man's powers of imagination and creativity were a reflection of the deity's power in creating the world; man was the deity of his own created mental world. The Book of Genesis in the Old Testament was cited as proving that God had made man himself a god in the sublunary world, giving him dominion over all things.

Perhaps the logical ultimate of these increasingly self-congratulatory ideas about the dignity of man as a near-divine creature was Pico's view that man can create himself, can be whatever he chooses to be and can occupy any position in the scheme of things from lowest to highest. This implies that there is no predestined place for man, but instead an almost supernatural standpoint from outside, above and beside all other things, a heroic standpoint as observer and mirror of the world. This is the view of Charles de Bovelles (1475–1566). The dedicatory epistle in his *Liber de Sapiente* ('Book of the Wise') begins, 'When the Pythian Apollo was asked what would be true and most excellent wisdom, he is said to have replied, "Man, know thyself."' He adds that since the Psalms say that the greatest stupidity of which humanity is capable is ignorance of self, one can see that for man to know himself is to know a high thing indeed.

The exalted view of human nature fostered by Renaissance humanism met its hubristic opposite in the sixteenth-century Reformation and the Protestants' bleak reassertion of humanity's fallen nature, the result of Adam's sin in Eden. It is a key teaching of Calvinism, for example, that the hopeless corruption and impotence of man can be salved only by the grace of God; the fine phrases of Pico and Bovelles are false, for man is born deathly sick, and can be rescued only through the sacrifice of Christ on the cross. In less apocalyptic terms the rational scepticism of Michel de Montaigne (1533–92) also contributed to deflating the presumptions of the 'dignity of man' tradition; he pointed out that those who claimed a unique excellence for humans because they stand upright and can look at the stars whereas the beasts hang their heads low and look at the ground only, had forgotten about camels and ostriches, whose upright stance and longer necks place them closer to the stars than man.

Renaissance humanists were Christians, at very least in profession and practice, whatever they privately thought, since there was no life outside the religion. But doubtless the great majority of them believed enough of the Christian teaching to think that the greatest good for humanity was attainment of heaven after death, or at least a not too onerous spell in purgatory to be cleansed of the sins they had acquired through the exigencies of human nature and the pressures of an unjust world. Aristotle had taught that the highest good, the *summum bonum*, was happiness, *eudaimonia*, and the Renaissance identified this with eternal life in the presence of God, as promised to the faithful and virtuous as their reward. But it was of a piece with humanistic optimism to think that although *true* felicity could only be the posthumous one just described, nevertheless a form of happiness is attainable in this world, a reflection or imitation, of course flawed and imperfect, of the supreme posthumous happiness. Officially, so to speak, this was held to be most available to wise and learned people whose relationship with God while in this world is exemplary; but Renaissance art tells a more generous story about the sources of pleasure and joy, not least in the contemplation of beauty.

It must be remembered that in the first centuries of their religion's history Christians expected the imminent return of the Messiah and the institution of the Kingdom of God. St Paul had promised that 'the saints shall not see corruption' – that is: any saints, such as the martyrs among them, who had died, would not decay in the grave – before the *Parousia* or Second Coming. This is why the scriptures teach that one should give away all one has, for possessions are not needed in the Kingdom; should make no plans ('take no thought for the morrow'), for there is no tomorrow; and not marry, since there is no time or point in raising a family. The anchorites and hesychasts who fled to the desert to escape temptation and to obey these injunctions were among the few who tried to live up to them. But when in the fourth century CE Christianity became the official religion of the Roman Empire and the bodies of saints, exhumed to be placed in churches where they were expected to be a source of miracles, were found to have rotted, a new theory was required: and the doctrine of the immortality of the soul was borrowed from Neoplatonism to provide it.

But that was not the only need. The scriptural teachings were unliveable; so ethical views more adapted to a normal human lifespan in the world had to be borrowed. The only place from which they could be borrowed was 'pagan' philosophy. St Basil the Great of Caesarea (330–79) showed how; in his *Address to Young Men on Greek Literature* he advised a selective use of pagan philosophical writings as an aid to reflection on virtue, saying that if they chose texts consistent with Christianity and viewed them as 'the reflection of the sun in water before seeing the sun itself' they would profit thereby. Other Church Fathers followed suit, in general preferring Stoicism and Platonism to Aristotelianism and Epicureanism as sources of inspiration. Aristotle's ethical views received rehabilitation in the hands of Aquinas; but in the high Renaissance both Cicero and Seneca came to be admired, Erasmus of Rotterdam (1466–1536) in particular arguing that Cicero put many Christians to shame and merited being renamed 'St Cicero'. Such views were widely held, prompting one commentator to argue that God had permitted the writings of the pagans to survive precisely so that they could be an admonishment to Christians for their failings in comparison.

But the debate was by no means one-sided. Reflecting on pagan moral philosophy, Salutati observed that the ancients had been concerned with outward action, whereas Christianity is concerned with inner conscience. Others took the point further, saying that for the pagans ethical choice depended on reason, but for Christians what counts is the far superior matter of the operation within them of the

Holy Spirit. This led some thinkers eventually to reject the idea that classical ethics and Christianity were in any way consistent and mutually useful. Matteo Bosso (1427–1502) argued that philosophy offers nothing on the question of ethics because it lacks the divine light of Christ's wisdom. Lorenzo Valla and others agreed. When the Reformation took hold in the middle decades of the sixteenth century, a number of Protestant theologians joined them in this view.

But the Protestants were as divided on the issue as their Roman opposites. The Lutheran Philipp Melanchthon (1497–1560) held that although the Fall and the need for redemption through faith in Christ were the central considerations in Christianity, nevertheless the use of reason to grasp and follow the law of nature while in the flesh was consistent with God's will, since God provided man with reason to do so. Luther himself had followed St Paul in distinguishing between what appertains to God and what appertains to Caesar, the implication being that in this life in the world it is necessary to obey the dictates of moral reason. The result was that, courtesy of Melanchthon, some Protestant preachers and educators felt that they had licence to make use of pagan philosophical ethics as a supplement to scripture – providing the two were consistent.

Luther was in general agreeable to this, though he felt it necessary to attack the use made by Scholastic philosophers of Aristotle's ethics, which he saw as a denial of the doctrine of grace. Because he was not alone in criticizing Aristotelians rather than Aristotle himself, a branch of comparative studies of Aristotle and scripture became a fixture in sixteenth-century philosophical-theological debate. For Platonists among the humanists, it was easier to reconcile their admiration for Plato with commitment to scripture, for his notion of the supreme good was easily identifiable with the Christian view. After all, Plato had taught repeatedly – in the *Phaedo, Republic, Symposium* – that it is only in its disembodied state that the soul can perfectly contemplate the supreme Good, and this was scarcely distinguishable from what Christian doctrine taught regarding the ultimate posthumous felicity of eternal life with God. Chief among the aspects of Plato's views that humanist Christians found attractive was his theory of love as expounded in the *Symposium*, for it chimed so well with the optimistic doctrine of their faith that God is love, and that one's soul climbs to the embrace of his love through love.

In the universities Aristotle was still the dominant figure in studies

183

of ethics, commentaries on his *Nicomachean Ethics* continued to be written, and moral treatises based on it were published in numbers. Some of the commentaries and treatises were written in the Scholastic style, others in the more accessible and agreeable humanistic style. An example of the latter is the *Moralis in Ethicen Introductio* by Jacques Lefèvre (of Etaples, 1455–1536), a gracefully readable work full of examples drawn from literature and the Bible to illustrate Aristotle's views. He was a scholar who among other things wrote introductions to Aristotle's scientific, ethical, political, logical and metaphysical works, edited Boethius' *De Arithmetica* and translated the Bible. He was one of the chief importers of humanism to France.

Stoicism and Epicureanism were not as influential in the Renaissance as Platonism or Aristotelianism, but they were known. Stoicism influenced some, but Epicureanism mainly received a bad press because its identification of pleasure as the greatest good, even when what was meant by 'pleasure' was understood, was condemned. Those who sought to defend Epicurus by arguing that he was too often criticized by those who had not read him were likely to find that their effort was added to other charges against them: two such, Giordano Bruno (1548–1600) and Giulio Cesare Vanini (1585–1619), were burned to death at the stake.

As these remarks show, the Renaissance was a period not of original ethical debate, but of efforts either to reconcile moral philosophy with Christian doctrine or to reject it. In the former endeavour the best that was attempted was the opening of a space within which the rich and mature precepts of the pagan philosophers could be applied to life in this world, leaving scripture to deal with what was required for the next world. At the same time it is hard to deny that the humane spirit breathed by the philosophy of pagan antiquity had a great deal to do with the humanistic spirit of the Renaissance; Erasmus affords a prime example of one who was able to acknowledge this conformably with his orthopractic Catholicism. And the focus on human nature, and refreshed ideas about the possibility of finding joy and satisfaction in the flesh in this world, gave an impetus to painting, sculpture and poetry that we would not be without. That is unarguably the greatest contribution of Renaissance humanistic and ethical thought.

RENAISSANCE POLITICAL THOUGHT

The Italian city states of the Renaissance had been evolving for centuries, certainly since the eleventh century, by which time many had begun to assume recognizable forms as independent communes with their own established systems of government. With them had grown a literature of advice both for communes and for their rulers and administrators on the aims and arts of government.

Nominally the city states were part of the Holy Roman Empire, and by the thirteenth century the study of Roman law in the medieval universities had reached such a point of sophistication that the suzerainty of the Emperor over his dominions was, in legal theory at least, unarguable. The paradox was that the city states were, by sharp contrast, de facto independent, and de facto republican. In the course of the Renaissance many of the rulers of city states came to acquire the titles of duke and prince, and instead of elections for the office of *podestà* or 'power-holder' the dukedoms and principalities became hereditary. Not all: the *dogi* (dukes) of Venice remained elected office-holders always, though only by their peers among the rich leading families of the city. But even at the height of the Renaissance, in fifteenth-century Florence for example, the de facto ruler – in this case Cosimo de' Medici the Elder – exercised his authority under cover of the *signoria*, and did not flaunt either his power or the wealth that underwrote it. His successors behaved very differently.

In addition to the problem of the legal authority of the Emperor – and of kings, queens or princes elsewhere in Europe – there had long been a correlative view, premised on St Paul's argument that rulers are appointed by God, that allegiance and obedience are owing to them because they are God's temporal regents on earth. For the Italian city states these were not congenial doctrines, so the rediscovery of Aristotle and in particular his *Politics*, available in Latin for the first time in the translation by William of Moerbeke in 1260, was especially welcome. His enthusiasm for the city-state model, his support for elective systems of government and his extolling of the virtues of what he called *polity* were agreeable to the sentiments of the Italians. In his view the best system for a practicable state is one in which there is a large middle class, intermediate between the state's richest and poorest, whose members will be more inclined to fairness, moderation and justice than either of the other classes because, he says, moderately well-off people find it 'easiest to obey the rule of reason' and are least inclined to political machination. They will accordingly constitute 'a body of people acting for the common good'.

Commentary on and adaptation of Aristotle on politics thereafter flourished as a new discipline of 'political science', starting with Aquinas and continuing unabated to the classics of Machiavelli and beyond. In conformity with scripture it was held that whereas a 'virtuous monarchy' has to be the best form of government because it imitates God's monarchical government of the world, in practical terms the desiderata of peace and economic flourishing were regarded as justifying the application of Aristotelian principles to the doctrine of the state. So argued Marsilius of Padua (1275–1342), who went even further than Aristotle in arguing that final political authority should lie in the hands of the people. His famous tract *Defensor Pacis*, written during the quarrel between Pope John XXII and the Holy Roman Emperor Louis IV of Bavaria, argued for separation of the papal and imperial powers – a secularist view – and further argued in favour of Aristotle's claim that the purpose of government is to satisfy the rational need of the populace for a 'sufficient life'. One of the main arguments he employed in favour of democracy was that if the people are the ultimate source of the laws, they will be more inclined to obey them.

Alack for Marsilius, the growing factionalism and turmoil in Italy's city states made his faith in democracy seem misplaced. City after city replaced forms of quasi-democracy with oligarchies, in many cases hereditary, so that Dante's complaint that Italy had fallen under the sway of tyrants seemed, by the beginning of the fourteenth century, to be true. But this development was supported by Petrarch and numerous others on the grounds that one of the chief aims of government must be the maintenance of peace and order, so that individual lives can flourish. Under the influence of classical models and humanistic ideals, an added element was that the state should seek not just peace but fame, honour and glory too. They did not mean by military activity; they meant by promotion of arts and learning, the beautification of the city and achievement of the elegances of life: by what was called *virtus* rather than *vis* (force).

Such a view was emphatically opposed to Aquinas' argument that seeking glory is harmful to the character of a prince, and indeed that it is 'the duty of a good man to show contempt for glory and all temporal goods'. In sharp contrast, Petrarch claimed in his letter on government to Francesco da Carrara that his advice is precisely intended to show the way to 'fame and future glory'.

Aquinas had assumed, in common with other Schoolmen, that peace might often have to be attained by the use of force, which is why he had written on 'just war' theory, employing ideas on the topic found in Augustine. The early Renaissance humanists disdained the idea of force, regarding war as bestial and unworthy of civilized humanity. *Virtus* as the desired characteristic in a ruler included justice and generosity, and freedom from avarice and pride; such a ruler would never stir dissatisfaction in his own people or animosity in the rulers and people of other states. Petrarch's characterization of the ruler with *virtus* closely follows the model given by Cicero in his *De Officiis*, where he argued that the just ruler will do nothing that harms his people, but will keep his promises to them, thus securing their love and trust. This was likewise the early humanist picture of what a good ruler should be.

Practicalities, however, again pressed. In his encomium on Florence's greatness in his *Laudatio Florentinae Urbis*, Leonardo Bruni (1370–1444) praised the art, architecture, wealth and influence of Florence, and claimed that it was all owing to Florence's liberty. He meant two things by this. One was that Florence was able to defend itself from conquest from without, and the other was that its institutions protected it from being seized by a faction from within. Rivalry with Visconti Milan had honed Florence as a military power, which explained its external defences. The internal security Bruni praised was – so he claimed – a function of its mixed republican constitution. Rome's historians and poets had insisted that Rome's glory began only once it had liberated itself from the tyranny of kings; this provided Bruni with his lesson, which he took to be that, as he put it, 'what concerns the people must be decided by the people,' and that the administration of justice must be scrupulous.

Bruni's views differed from those of Petrarch and the earlier humanists in two ways. One was that Petrarch saw the peace of the city as enabling a life of *otium*, of graceful leisure in which the arts and learning can be cultivated. Bruni was aligned with the more robust later humanists who followed Cicero in extolling the *vita activa*. Secondly, Petrarch had enjoined the cultivation of *virtus* in the ruler; Bruni said that everyone in the state should cultivate it, so that the ideal citizen is one in whom justice, prudence, courage and temperance combine. This too is pure Cicero.

Hope that city states could adopt or persist in the Florentine model lauded by Bruni was short-lived; increasingly their governments fell into the hands first of oligarchies and then of princes. The role of writers on government changed with the changing times, coming to focus on advising rulers about ways of preserving and extending their power. Whereas earlier treatises had as their subject matter the flourishing of a state, these later treatises were of the 'Mirror for Princes' genre. The rulers of Milan, Mantua, Siena and other cities received such tracts from resident humanist intellectuals, and eventually in Florence too. By the end of the fifteenth century Medici rule was no different from Visconti rule in Milan, and though the temporary exile of the Medicis – between the French invasion of Italy in 1494 and their restoration eighteen years later – enabled Girolamo Savonarola to restore something like republican government, a Medicean principate was inevitable upon their return. It was in this context that Machiavelli wrote.

Niccolò Machiavelli (1469–1527) held senior office in the Florentine government for twelve of the tumultuous republican years between 1494 when Piero de' Medici was overthrown and Savonarola was ascendant, and 1512 when Medici rule returned. He was, in succession and in effect, the republic's foreign minister and minister for war. Because his role involved frequent travel to the courts of kings, emperors, popes and generals on behalf of Florence, he had a marvellous opportunity to observe different personalities and systems; and because he was charged with the delicate task of negotiating with powers far more formidable than Florence itself, he was able to refine his analytic and diplomatic skills to consummate levels. In all the years he served Florence his reports and letters of advice were highly valued, praised for their astuteness and wisdom, and for their literary qualities.

The Medicis' return in 1512 ended Machiavelli's career. His life nearly went with it; he was thrown into the Bargello dungeon and tortured on suspicion of conspiracy. Happily the menace was brief, and he was allowed to withdraw to his farm in the Florentine countryside, where during his remaining years he relieved his immense frustration at being excluded from political life by writing about politics instead. There was minor consolation; towards the very end he was again used, in lesser capacities, as a representative of Florence, and took an active part in efforts to save the city during the destructive Italian wars of the 1520s.

But Machiavelli's main legacy is his writings, and chiefly his classic of frank and frankly shocking political advice, *Il Principe* ('The Prince', completed in 1513). Its message is that princely *virtus* is not, as other humanist writers maintained, the promotion of justice and peace, but the ability to maintain the state by employing the lion's ferocity and the fox's cunning. To try to rule only by virtue, he said, would be ruinous, because less scrupulous opponents will take advantage.

However, Machiavelli introduces a highly significant qualification: when he looks to the past for examples of good and bad rulers, he condemns those who were cold-bloodedly cruel, naming the usual suspects among Roman emperors, but singling out for particular mention the Syracusan tyrant Agathocles, saying, 'it cannot be called virtue to kill one's fellow-citizens, betray one's friends, be faithless and pitiless ... by such means one may win power, but not glory.' This shows that Machiavelli thought a prince's actions should aim at the security and benefit of the state, not of his own person; and that too is why he tirelessly urged Florence to raise and maintain its own army, instead of using mercenary forces, or trying to buy off invaders; 'why give them money to make them stronger, when you could use it to protect yourself?' he repeatedly asked.

By far the most important task of the prince, said Machiavelli, is *mantenere lo stato*, to keep hold of power. Not only will this stabilize the state and bring it peace, but with peace it will bring honour. To keep hold of power the prince must possess *virtù*, a word he derived from Latin *virtus* as used by other Renaissance writers, but differing from it in a significant way because in addition to courage, pride, determination and skill it included, Machiavelli said, *ruthlessness* when necessary. Machiavelli's *virtù* is thus *virtus* plus *vis*, in contrast to the earlier humanists' view that *vis* is no part of *virtus*. Indeed he saw a preparedness to use force as central to a prince's chances of success, and the lack of such preparedness as the explanation for the weakness of too many states.

The earlier humanists had wished a prince's *virtus* to include such high moral standards as continence and sobriety, chastity, generosity and clemency. Machiavelli said, on the contrary, that personal vices were irrelevant provided they did not put the state at risk. But most important, he said, is the need to grasp this harsh reality: that although it would be wonderful if a prince could invariably be generous, merciful and faithful to his word, thereby gaining his people's love, these traits have to give way before necessity when necessity dictates. And necessity will soon reveal itself in many circumstances in which generosity and mercy would be ruinous, and where promises cannot be kept; so the prince might as well accept that he is going to be called cruel, and that his safety is better served by being feared than by being loved.

He summed up his view by saying that a prince 'must know how to behave badly when required', that indeed it was a prince's duty 'to learn how not to be good'. Cicero had said that a wicked ruler is no better than a beast, in his *De Officiis* criticizing the use of fraud and force by saying, 'fraud seems to belong to the cunning fox, force to the lion.' Machiavelli frankly accepted that a ruler must be both lion and fox.

Machiavelli makes the interesting claim that because so many princes pretend to generosity and mercy when in fact these are merely disguises for rapacity, the citizens of a state whose ruler is frank about his methods might come to admire and trust him more than one who pretends to the conventional virtues. But in the end it is the demands of maintaining power that dictate how the prince must behave, trumping all other considerations: *mantenere lo stato* is the supreme principle, and like a weathervane a prince must be ready 'to turn and turn about as the winds and the variations of fortune dictate'.

Other Florentine political theorists, chief among them Machiavelli's friend Francesco Guicciardini (1483–1540), were in the habit of praising Venice's constitution as the most perfect and desirable. Guicciardini's argument was that Venice had achieved a balance between the social orders in the state, by combining the best features of all kinds of states – those ruled by one, those ruled by a few and those ruled by the many. In Venice's case the mixed constitution shared power between the Doge, the Senate and the people. In response Machiavelli changed his mind, writing another book very different in outlook from *The Prince*. This was his *Discourses*, ostensibly a study of the first ten books of Livy's history of Rome, *Ab Urbe Condita*. In it Machiavelli maintained his view that the aim of government is to achieve *grandezza*, glory – not for the prince, however, but for the state itself, as had happened with Rome. And to achieve glory a state must be free, able to determine its own affairs for the benefit of all in it. Since the interests of an individual prince might well not coincide with the interests of the state he rules, the best kind of state is a republic. 'Greatness comes to cities not through individual benefits but through pursuit of the common good,' Machiavelli now wrote, 'and there is no doubt that this ideal can only be achieved in republics.' And he goes further, adding that when the people are the guardians of their own liberty, their liberty will be preserved more effectively than under any other form of government.

In marked difference from his predecessors and contemporaries, however, Machiavelli urged that to protect its liberty a state should arm its citizens, and accept that this might occasionally result in instability and turmoil. But that, he said, is a price worth paying for the *grandezza* that could come from independence and a martial spirit, as had happened with Rome. By contrast a state such as Venice could never aspire to a similar degree of grandeur. As to the turmoil that might result from an armed and independent people: well, if the citizens achieve *virtù* then the state will be well ordered internally, and turmoil will be avoided.

A significant point of continuity with *The Prince* is Machiavelli's insistence that the overriding aim – although in this case it is the life, liberty and security of the community rather than, as it had been in *The Prince*, the prince's power – must be preserved at the expense of everything else: 'whenever what is at issue is the basic security of the community, no consideration should be given to questions of justice or injustice, clemency or cruelty, praiseworthiness or ignominy; rather, setting every other feature of the situation aside, you must be prepared to follow whatever course of action will in fact save the life and preserve the liberty of the community as a whole.' The ruthlessness recommended to the prince is thus recommended to the people, if necessity demands it; Machiavelli's espousal of a frank form of realism survives to the last.

Thomas More (1478–1535) takes to its full extent the idea that a republic will flourish optimally if all its citizens are devoted to virtue – virtue, not *virtus*. Unlike such earlier humanists as Petrarch for whom a good state is a means to *otium*, leisure, in the service of an Aristotelian life of contemplation, for the citizens of More's Utopia the end is the pursuit of virtue for its own sake. When everyone takes delight in individual and collective virtue the state is at peace externally and internally, it is free, it is not wracked by the 'conspiracy of the rich pursuing their own private interests under the name and title of the commonwealth'. Public service is the noblest of callings; and More recognizes the force of a Platonic view (expressed by the character Raphael Hythloday) that the abolition of private property and a 'complete equality of goods' would make possible the Utopia he described. The view is consciously a derivative of Plato's *Republic*. But – perhaps not surprisingly – More himself ends on a note of doubt about such a complete system of communism, which he perceives is the 'foundation' of the Utopia Hythloday describes, that is, 'their living in common, without the use of money, by which all nobility, magnificence, splendour, and majesty, which, according to the common opinion, are the true ornaments of a nation, would be quite taken away'. He does not end by endorsing this latter view outright; he says he would himself like to see in his own country many of the things Hythloday describes; but he leaves open which things he would not like to see.

PART III

Modern Philosophy

The Rise of Modern Thought

From the fourth to the fourteenth century CE the increasing dominance of religion over the mind of Europe meant that philosophy was largely the handmaiden of theology, and as noted at the beginning of Part II it became increasingly dangerous for philosophical speculation to stray from the neighbourhood of doctrinal orthodoxies imposed by the Church. This grip was broken by the Reformation of the sixteenth century. It was broken not because the Reformation introduced a new intellectual liberalism – rather the opposite, when you consider the inflexibilities of Calvinism, for example – but because religious authorities in most parts of Europe that became Protestant did not have the power to enforce theological orthodoxy or to control speculation and enquiry. One immediate result was, as mentioned, an outburst of interest in the occult: magic, astrology, the Cabala, Hermeticism, alchemy and mysticism – but in the midst of this, and arising partly out of it, there was also a liberation of philosophical and scientific enquiry.

The Reformation was, famously, triggered by Martin Luther when he posted his ninety-seven theses on the church door of Wittenberg in 1517. He was not the first to object to malpractices by the Church, but he lived in the dawn of a new and powerful technology: printing. In the half-century before Luther made his protest, Gutenberg's printing press had been copied in hundreds of towns and cities across Europe, and millions of printed books had already poured from them. It was a dramatic instance of how the rapid adoption of new technologies changes history.

Interest in magic, alchemy and the other 'occult sciences' constituted in their various ways efforts to find shortcuts to the control of nature, with a view to achieving one or all of several great desiderata: changing base metals into gold, preserving youth, attaining immortality and predicting the future. Much nonsense followed.* But it was clear to more perceptive minds that among these endeavours were possibilities for achieving greater understanding of the world. What was required to disentangle sense from nonsense was, they saw, a *method*. The two chief figures involved in advocating responsible methods of enquiry were Francis Bacon and René Descartes. These two thinkers are therefore regarded as the founders of modern philosophy, not least because in describing and applying the methods they advocated they thereby rejected the assumptions, the jargon and the theological restrictions that since the middle ages had increasingly weighed down and cluttered up the philosophical enterprise.

What Bacon and Descartes had in common was their rejection of Scholasticism and its Aristotelian foundations, but they differed in a respect that was important for the subsequent history of philosophy. Bacon was an empiricist, Descartes a rationalist (in the epistemological sense of this term). This difference has led to a conventional grouping of the philosophers who came after them in the seventeenth and eighteenth centuries into two camps: the empiricists – whose leading figures are John Locke, George Berkeley and David Hume – and the rationalists, whose leading figures after Descartes are Baruch Spinoza and Gottfried Leibniz.

Empiricism is the view that all genuine knowledge must either originate in or be testable by experience of the world – and this means sensory experience: seeing, hearing, touching, tasting and smelling, aided by the instruments (telescopes, microscopes, oscilloscopes: scientific instruments, in short) that extend the range and power of observation.

Rationalism, in the epistemological sense, is the view that genuine knowledge can be attained only by reason, by rational inference from first principles, logical foundations or self-evident truths.

Natural science is the paradigm of knowledge for empiricists; it involves observation and experiment. Mathematics and logic provide the paradigm for rationalists; the conclusions of mathematical and logical thinking are eternal, unchanging and certain, which is what the rationalists argued truth should be. Plato is a major influence in this way of thinking.

The history of philosophy in the seventeenth and eighteenth centuries is capped by the giant figure of Immanuel Kant, who rejected the

---

* See Grayling, *The Age of Genius* (2016), Chapters 15 and 16, passim.

opposition between empiricism and rationalism, instead arguing for a synthesis between them. As we shall see, he argued that both experience and thought of the world, and the world as we experience and think about it, arise from the combination of the inputs of experience and the action of the mind upon them – and that neither experience of the world, nor the world as we experience it, is possible otherwise.

FRANCIS BACON (1561–1626)

Bacon was a statesman, lawyer, essayist and philosopher. He had a spectacular career between his admission to Cambridge University at the age of twelve and his fall from high office, probably as a result of political machinations, at the age of sixty in 1621. Despite being a busy and ambitious man he managed to devote time to his great love: the study of philosophy and science. But with the leisure enforced by his fall he set himself to finish an encyclopaedic work encapsulating everything known, together with his theories about how more knowledge can be acquired. It was called the *Instauratio Magna* – implying a great beginning for a new age of firmly based knowledge. He died before he could finish the project, but one of its influential legacies was a book called *The New Atlantis*, published posthumously in 1627. In it is set out his concept of a 'Solomon's House', a research institute for collaborative scientific effort – the idea that directly inspired the founders, as they themselves acknowledged, of the Royal Society in London in 1662.

Bacon's commitment to the promotion of serious science had the practical aim of improving humanity's lot through increased understanding and control of nature. Contrary to the usual view that he was merely a theoretician of method rather than a practising scientist, he did indeed engage in hands-on science, constructing a physical system and attempting experiments. It was as the result of an experiment on refrigeration (stuffing a dead chicken with snow to see how long it would last) that he caught a chill and died. His system of physics, geocentric and still owing too much to Aristotle despite his rejection of Scholasticism, did not advance matters.

He did however make two major contributions. One was his advocacy of cooperation in science, as therefore requiring an institutional basis for shared experimentation and the exchange of ideas. The magicians and occultists of his day were secretive, keeping their knowledge to themselves because they did not want others to steal a march on them. Bacon saw that progress requires a collegial endeavour, and he advocated it strongly; science has proved him right.

His second contribution lay in the idea of scientific method itself. He had sketched these ideas in an earlier work, *The Advancement of Learning* of 1605, and developed them in work for the *Instauratio Magna*, one part of which, the *Novum Organum Scientiarum*, had been published in 1620, and was of particular significance.

As an empiricist Bacon argued that science must be based on observation of facts, which underpin the theories that organize and explain them. This view is often caricatured as saying that enquirers should gather observations at random, and then find a theory to explain them; but that is not what Bacon meant. The caricature was nevertheless widely believed – even Newton and Darwin subscribed to it, and indeed both approved of it. In the second edition of the *Principia* Newton wrote, 'hypotheses . . . have no place in experimental philosophy. In this philosophy particular propositions are inferred from the phenomena and afterwards rendered general by induction.' Likewise Darwin in his *Autobiography* wrote, 'it appeared to me that . . . by collecting all facts which bore in any way on the variation of animals and plants under domestication and nature, some light might be thrown on the whole subject. My first notebook was opened in July 1837. I worked on true Baconian principles, and without any theory collected facts on a wholesale scale.'

What Bacon himself meant by his method is much closer to the now standard view that observations are gathered to test an antecedently formulated hypothesis that specifies which of those observations would be relevant to refuting or supporting it. This is set out in the *Plan* of the *Instauratio Magna*:

> the greatest change I introduce is in the form itself of induction and the judgment made thereby. For the induction of which the logicians speak, which proceeds by simple enumeration, is a puerile thing; concludes at hazard; is always liable to be upset by a contradictory instance; takes into account only what is known and ordinary; and leads to no result. Now what the sciences stand in need of is a form of induction which shall analyse experience and take it to pieces, and by a due process of exclusion and rejection lead to an inevitable conclusion.

This method is explicitly empirical, with observation and experiment as the foundation. It somewhat anticipates what are now known as Mill's Methods, after John Stuart Mill's account of induction in his *System of Logic* (1843). Bacon was alert to sceptical challenges to reliance on sense-experience, but he had a reply: we are to 'receive as conclusive the immediate informations of the sense, when well disposed . . . the information of the sense itself I sift and examine in many ways. For certain it is that the senses deceive; but then at the same time they supply the means of discovering their own errors . . . by experiments. For the subtlety of experiments is far greater than that of the sense itself, even when assisted by exquisite instruments; such experiments, I mean, as are skilfully and artificially devised for the express purpose of determining the point in question.'

A striking feature of Bacon's thinking is that it should be guided by the practical knowledge acquired in crafts and trades, in the experience of builders, butchers, carpenters, farmers and sailors – of people who know their materials, who know nature itself; who have practical experience of how things work and what can be done with them. In this way, he said, we ensure that the foundation of enquiry is how things are, not how we imagine them to be:

> Of this reconstruction the foundation must be laid in natural history, and
> that of a new kind and gathered on a new principle . . . For first, the object
> of the natural history which I propose is . . . to give light to the discovery
> of causes and supply a suckling philosophy with its first food . . . I mean
> it to be a history not only of nature free and at large (when she is left to
> her own course and does her work her own way), – such as that of the
> heavenly bodies, meteors, earth and sea, minerals, plants, animals, – but
> much more of nature under constraint and vexed; that is to say, when by
> art and the hand of man she is forced out of her natural state, and squeezed
> and moulded.

In insisting on a collaborative empirical method Bacon was urging something revolutionary in contrast to the long dominance of religious doctrine and *a priori* reasoning that had governed thought for nearly a millennium before his time. But his approach was not new: it was a recovery of the attitude to enquiry that had inspired the first philosophers of antiquity, such as Thales, in relying on observation and reason instead of authority and tradition.

Bacon's writings accordingly promoted a change of attitude to the nature of knowledge that helped to bring the modern mind to birth.* The standard view had always been that the ancients were superior in wisdom to later generations, their time a Golden Age to which later people could only look back with wonder. Later people were right, for a time; much knowledge was lost in the 'Dark Ages' under the hegemony of the Church: witness how many centuries lay between the Byzantine engineers' knowledge of how to raise the dome of the Hagia Sophia in Constantinople (built 537 CE) and Brunelleschi's Duomo in Florence (built 1418–34), hailed as an engineering marvel. A symptom of this looking-back with admiration is that Copernicus' heliocentric model was dubbed 'the Pythagorean system', signifying that his theory was merely a restatement of something known in antiquity.

Bacon did not share the Golden Age view. His outlook typified that aspect of the Renaissance which saw itself not merely as rediscovery but as rebirth, in the real sense of starting afresh. It was of course essential, for new progress to be possible, that enquiry should be free. Because it was still not everywhere free from religious orthodoxy, Bacon found it necessary to argue that it should be, by seeking a way to disentangle philosophy from religion so that the latter would not hamper progress. Part of this task was to combat superstition, religion's natural corollary. Bacon wrote, 'it was a good answer that was made by one who, when they showed him hanging in a temple a picture of those who had paid their vows as having escaped shipwreck, and would have him say whether he did not now acknowledge the power of the gods – "Aye," asked he again, "but where are they painted that were drowned after their vows?"' Bacon described 'blind immoderate religious zeal' as 'a troublesome and intractable enemy' to enquiry.

DESCARTES (1596–1650)

The other great advocate of method was Bacon's contemporary René Descartes. In applying his method to what he saw as fundamental problems Descartes raised questions that shaped much philosophical

---

* Grayling, *The Age of Genius*, is an exposition of the thesis that the philosophical and scientific revolution of the seventeenth century was *literally* the beginning of the modern mind and the functional dominance of the scientific worldview.

debate in the centuries that followed: questions about scepticism and certainty, the nature of mind and its relation to matter, and the role of reason. In recognition of these achievements and their influence, historians of philosophy have labelled him 'the father of modern philosophy'.

Descartes was born at La Haye, since renamed Descartes in his honour, in Touraine in France. He trained as a lawyer first, then went to the Netherlands to join the Dutch army in order to study military engineering. This fostered his interest in mathematics, to which he made important contributions. His chief interest was physics; he wished to replace the Aristotelian view of the universe taught by the Church (to which he otherwise remained loyal throughout his life) with his own. To prepare the ground for his science he felt that he needed to settle the question of how we can acquire knowledge and attain the truth. His book on this topic, *Meditations on First Philosophy*, is the classic text that earned him the 'father of modern philosophy' title.

There are two parts to Descartes' view about how we can acquire knowledge. One is that enquiry should consist in small, cautious steps from one clear idea to the next, each step carefully reviewed until the chain of reasoning is complete. The other consists in ensuring that the starting point of the chain is unquestionably certain. To achieve this certainty Descartes famously employed a *method of doubt.*

The first principle of his method is 'never to accept anything for true which I did not clearly know to be such ... and to comprise nothing more in my judgement than what was presented to my mind so clearly and distinctly as to exclude all ground of doubt'. He applied this method to a related set of four basic questions. The first is: 'What can I know with certainty?' The next two are: 'What is the constitution of the universe? and, what are the relationships between its fundamental constituents?' The last question concerns the existence of a 'good god', because Descartes needed the concept of such a thing to help with the answer to the first question. As often happens in philosophy, the answer to the first question determined the answers to the others.

The 'method of doubt' proceeds as follows. Even if I doubt everything I normally take myself to know or believe, I cannot doubt that I exist. This is the starting point of certainty. This argument, seemingly so simple and direct, is Descartes' celebrated *cogito, ergo sum*: 'I think, therefore I am.' He then immediately asks, What is this thing that I know with certainty exists, this 'me' or 'I'? He replies that a little reflection shows that 'I' am a mind or thinking thing, even if 'I' do not have a body (because it is possible to doubt that one has a body).

But how can one get from knowledge, however certain, that I exist as a thinking thing to there being anything other than me – most importantly, an external world and other selves? Descartes needs something to carry certainty beyond the starting point of the *cogito*. He finds it in the idea that there is a *good* god: the qualification 'good' is important, because a good god would not wish us to be deceived if we correctly use the faculties he has given us. (A bad deity would doubtless take pleasure in deceiving us.) Descartes accordingly offers proofs of the existence of such a deity, and correlatively argues that the errors we are prone to fall into are to be blamed not on the deity but on our own post-Adam fallen natures.

Note that Descartes' 'method of doubt' turns crucially on setting aside any belief or claim to knowledge which admits of the least doubt, however improbable or absurd that doubt might be. The aim is to see what, if anything, is left behind once one has called into question everything it is possible to question. Whatever is left will be absolutely certain. It would take impossibly long to subject each individual belief to scrutiny one by one, so Descartes needed a wholly general method of setting aside what can be doubted. This he did by employing the arguments of the sceptic.

His use of sceptical arguments does not make him a sceptic; on the contrary, he used the arguments merely as heuristics, as aids in setting up his theory of knowledge. He therefore merits the label 'methodological sceptic' rather than 'problematic sceptic', by which latter term is meant anyone who thinks that scepticism poses a real threat to the acquisition of knowledge. Most philosophers since Descartes' time have felt that he did not provide an adequate answer to the sceptical doubts he raised, and that therefore scepticism really is a problem.

The first sceptical consideration Descartes uses is a reminder that our senses sometimes lead us astray; perceptual misjudgments, illusions and hallucinations can and not infrequently do give us false beliefs. This might prompt us at the very least to be cautious in placing confidence on sense-experience as a source of truth. But even so there would be many things I believe on the basis of my current experience – such as that I have hands and am holding a book in them, that I am sitting in an armchair, and the like. To doubt this would seem to be madness, even given the senses' frequent unreliability.

Would it really be mad to doubt such things? No, says Descartes – and here he brings his second argument into play – for I sometimes dream when I sleep, and if I am now dreaming that I am sitting in an armchair holding a book, my belief that I am so doing is false. To be certain that I am sitting thus, I have to be able to exclude the possibility that I am only dreaming that I am doing so. How is that to be done? It seems impossible to do it.

But even if one were asleep and dreaming, one could still know that (for example) one plus one equals two. Indeed there are many such beliefs that could be known to be true even in a dream. So Descartes introduces an even more swingeing consideration: suppose that instead of there being a good god who wishes us to know the truth, there is by contrast an evil demon whose whole purpose is to deceive us about everything, even about '1 + 1 = 2' and all other such apparently indubitable truths. If there were such a demon one would have a completely general reason for doubting everything that can be doubted. And now we can ask: suppose that there is such a demon; is there any belief left that I cannot doubt? Is there anything that the demon could not fool me about?

And the answer is, Yes, there is something that is absolutely secure against doubt or deception. It is the proposition *that I exist*. This is certain because if I think that I exist, or even if I ask whether or not I exist, or even if indeed I think anything at all, the mere fact of my doing so by itself proves that I exist. I could not be tricked by a demon into thinking I exist if I did not exist. 'I think, therefore I am'; *cogito, ergo sum*; that is the indubitable starting point Descartes sought.

Some critics of this method have argued that the sceptical arguments used by Descartes do not work. They are just not credible: how can I doubt that I am now awake? How can one take seriously the idea of an evil demon seeking to trick me about anything and everything? Surely we would not know what we meant by talk of dreams or being deceived unless we understood the contrast with waking or being right, which would seem to require that we sometimes know we are awake or not deceived. So Descartes' method of doubt cannot even get started.

But these criticisms are misplaced. There is no need for the sceptical arguments to be plausible. They are simply an heuristic which helps us see how saying 'I exist' cannot be doubted; it must always be true when one says it.

A vulnerability in Descartes' method is that it turns out not to be sufficient by itself because it requires a guarantee for the reliability of what we take to be clear ideas and careful steps. He claims that this required guarantee is, as already mentioned, the *goodness* of a *deity*. His two arguments in the *Meditations* for the existence of a god purport to establish that it is the required kind of god – indeed, the God of revealed religion: an omnipotent, omniscient and wholly good being.

The first of these arguments relies on an idea found in Neoplatonism, that the cause of anything must have at least as much and usually more reality than its effect. The argument is that I have the idea of a perfect and infinite being. Since I am imperfect and finite, I cannot be the cause of this idea. Therefore the idea must be caused in me by something that has at least as much reality as the 'objective' content of the idea, that is, the thing existing outside my mind represented by the idea. And that can only be the perfect and infinite being itself, namely, God.

The second argument is a version of the 'ontological argument' made famous by St Anselm. It runs as follows. There is a being which is the most perfect being there is. A most perfect being which exists is more perfect than one that does not exist. Therefore the most perfect being necessarily (that is, essentially: of its essence) exists.

Neither argument works. The point of interest, though, is Descartes' reliance on these arguments. His successors in the tradition of philosophy did not find themselves able to think as he did about this matter, and he is therefore alone in saying that we can get from the contents of our minds to a world outside our heads because our inferences from the former to the latter (if responsibly drawn; he grants that our fallen natures can lead us into error) can be relied upon with the help of divine goodness.

The second major talking point in Descartes' philosophy, the mind–body problem, is the source of an important debate in philosophy and more latterly also in psychology and the neurosciences. What is mind, and what is the relation of mind to the rest of nature? How should we best understand such mental phenomena as belief, desire, intention, emotion and memory? How does the grey matter of the brain give rise to conscious experience and to the vivid phenomenology of colour, sound, texture, taste and smell?

Descartes gave the mind–body problem an especially sharp focus by arguing that everything that exists in the world falls under the heading either of material substance or of mental substance, where 'substance' – as noted earlier in Aristotle's metaphysics – is a technical term meaning 'the (or a) most basic kind of existing stuff'. Descartes defined the essence of matter as *extension* (that is, occupancy of space), and the essence of mind as *thought*. Matter is thus extended substance, mind is thinking substance.

The idea that mind and matter are really distinct things is supported by another of Descartes' significant claims: 'the fact that I can clearly and distinctly understand one thing apart from another is enough to make me certain that the two things are distinct.' By making matter and mind essentially different he raised the seemingly insuperable problem of how they interact. How does a bodily event like pricking one's finger result in the mental event of feeling pain? How does the mental event of thinking 'it's time to get up' cause the bodily event of rising from bed?

Descartes at first proposed the unsatisfactory answer that mind and matter somehow interact in the pineal gland located in the mid-brain, but his successors saw through the ploy; it merely hid the problem in a then-mysterious object whose main claim to be the mind–matter interface was its convenient location in the brain. They therefore had to resort to their own heroic solutions to the problem. Their strategy was to accept dualism but to argue that mind and matter do not in fact interact, their appearance of doing so being the result of the hidden action of God; such were the views of Malebranche and Leibniz. Malebranche thought there was in fact no interaction, but that the deity provided correlates for mental and physical events whenever they were required. This doctrine is known as 'occasionalism'. Leibniz likewise thought that interaction does not occur, and that God had set the mental and physical realms going at the beginning of time in exact parallel with one another, so that it looks as though mind and matter interact. This therefore is known as 'parallelism', and it comes at the price of commitment to a rigidly strict determinism – for without it the parallels between the two realms break down.

Other philosophers since the time of Descartes and his immediate successors, indeed the majority of them, think that the only plausible alternative to dualism is a form of monism ('mono' meaning 'one'). All forms of monism consist in the view that there is only one substance. There are three main possibilities. One is that there is only matter. The second is that there is only mind. The third is that there is a neutral substance which gives rise to both mind and matter. Each of the three has had proponents, but it is the first option – the reduction of all mental phenomena to matter – which has been most influential.

In the end Descartes himself never arrived at a satisfactory way of dealing with the problem whose deep intractability he had exposed. When pressed by Princess Elisabeth of Bohemia to explain how mental and physical phenomena interact, he ended by frankly acknowledging that he had no answer.

It is worth mentioning in passing that the *cogito* argument was not invented by Descartes. St Augustine in the early fifth century CE wrote that we can doubt everything except that we doubt, and even he probably did not think he was saying anything novel. Neither presumably did Jean de Silhon, whose book *The Two Truths* was published in 1626 and contained the sentence, 'It is not possible for a man who has the ability, which many share, to look within himself and judge *that he exists*, to be deceived in this judgment, and *not exist*.'

Descartes knew Silhon's work, which predates his own version of the *cogito* by at least five years (he drafted his *Discourse on Method* in about 1630, though it was not published until 1637), for he writes approvingly of Silhon's book though he does not quote it. Indeed Descartes owes more than the *cogito* argument to Silhon; in the passage where the latter states a version of the argument, he also says that a proof of God's existence can be constructed from one's own existence – a vital step for Descartes' programme as we see.

Descartes' views shaped a great deal of the philosophy that followed. His starting point in the theory of knowledge – that we begin from the private data of consciousness from which a route to an external world has to be underpinned by a guarantee of certainty, lest it be an illusion created by perceptual or ratiocinative error – was accepted by all Western philosophy until the twentieth century, and it was the source of endless difficulty. So was his dualistic commitment to the 'real distinction' between mind and body. For although Descartes laboured – most notably in the *Meditations* – to provide a guarantee for the route from private experience to knowledge of a public world, few if any of his successors could accept what he offered as the solution to that problem.

HOBBES (1588–1679)

When Descartes published his *Meditations* he included with it a series of comments and objections invited from fellow-philosophers to whom he had sent the book in manuscript. With them he printed his replies. One of the participants in this exercise was Thomas Hobbes, whom Descartes later briefly met in Paris.

Hobbes lived, as his dates show, for ninety-one years; he sang songs every night believing that doing so cleared his lungs and kept him well. He was born in Wiltshire, England, and with Machiavelli before him and John Locke after him is one of the founders of modern political philosophy.

His major work, *Leviathan* (1651), has all but eclipsed other contributions he made in philosophy, history and science. These other views are interesting, and in many respects in advance of his time. He was a materialist and empiricist who thought that everything is physical and that physical phenomena can be explained in terms of motion. Sensation, which is the source of all our ideas, he took to be the result of chains of causal events starting with objects in the world and exerting pressure on sense organs, which in turn cause motions to pass to the heart and brain. He was a nominalist about universals, and defined reasoning as a form of computation: 'By reasoning I understand computation . . . to reason is to add and subtract.' His materialism was thoroughgoing; he thought that God is made of matter, and was dismissive of religion, regarding it as largely indistinguishable from superstition and filled with delusive ideas about an afterlife and heaven. 'Thus,' he said, 'philosophy excludes from itself theology,' because theology does not lend itself to the kinds of causal explanations that he took to be required for *scientia*, true knowledge.

For most of the decade between 1640 and 1650 Hobbes lived in self-imposed exile in France to keep out of the way of the civil war raging in England. He was a Royalist, a fact that lends some colour to the view that his political philosophy's defence of absolutism is a defence of absolute monarchy. But in fact his views are consistent with republicanism also; the key point for him is that, to prevent the evils of civil war and dissension, the central authority of government, whatever form it takes, must be absolute.

Hobbes regarded membership of political society as the only

guarantee of individual safety. Without insurance against the depredations of each on each in the unpredictable and violent conditions of a
'state of nature', life would be – as he memorably put it – 'solitary,
poor, nasty, brutish and short'. In the absence of an authority capable
of keeping everyone safe, there can be no security; not even self-defence
pacts formed by groups of individuals would be sufficient. The only
sure source of safety is a 'common power', a central authority which
Hobbes named 'Leviathan', a biblical term denoting a huge monster.
The Leviathan's authority derives from the consent of each member of
society to accept its unlimited power over them. The Leviathan could
be an individual person, such as a monarch, or a group, or indeed any
other entity, so long as it possesses plenary powers:

> For by this authority, given him by every particular man in the common-
> wealth, he hath the use of so much power and strength conferred on him,
> that by terror thereof, he is enabled to form the wills of them all, to peace
> at home, and mutual aid against their enemies abroad. And in him con-
> sisteth the essence of the commonwealth; which, to define it, is *one person,
> of whose acts a great multitude, by mutual covenants one with another,
> have made themselves every one the author, to the end he may use the
> strength and means of them all, as he shall think expedient, for their
> peace and common defence.*

This sovereign power, thus instituted by the agreement of those over
whom it has complete sway, is thereafter under no obligation to its subjects, beyond ensuring their safety. Hobbes said the sovereign must have
two inalienable and unlimitable 'rights' in order to fulfil its function
properly: it cannot have its power taken away or limited by its subjects,
and it can never be charged with treating its subjects unjustly. The justification for attributing these 'rights' is that the sovereign embodies the
will of the people, having been created by them for their own safety. To
seek to overthrow the sovereign or disobey it would therefore be self-
contradictory; the people would be challenging their own reason for
creating it in the first place: 'by this institution of a commonwealth,
every particular man is author of all the sovereign doth; and consequently he that complaineth of injury from his sovereign, complaineth
of that whereof he himself is author.'

The two 'rights' in question are what make the sovereign's power absolute. Only the sovereign can decide on matters of war and peace, on
relations with other states, on what can be done in the state, on property,

punishments, official appointments, the award of honours and all matters at law. Hobbes says that these powers are the 'essence of sovereignty'; they are 'the marks whereby a man may discern in what man, or assembly of men, the sovereign power is placed and resideth'.

There is however one great constraint on the sovereign, which arises from the very reason for its existence, which is to ensure the safety of its subjects. If the sovereign fails in this duty, the overriding concern of the subjects for their own self-preservation gives them the right to disobey it and even to rebel. Self-preservation is a need and a duty that is not cancelled when all other freedoms are yielded up. At first blush this concession seems to lodge a contradiction at the very centre of Hobbes' thesis: for if the people are entitled to overthrow the sovereign who fails to protect their safety, then they indeed have the ultimate say in the commonwealth.

It might seem surprising that in this conception of an absolutist state Hobbes nevertheless brings into focus a number of ideas that have been significant in subsequent liberal thought, including equality, individual rights, the location of ultimate political authority in the consent of the people (even though, in his theory, it is effectively a case of 'one man one vote one time') and a view of liberty as whatever is not forbidden by law. The ideas of liberty and natural rights in particular have prompted significant discussion.

Hobbes invokes the idea of a 'law of nature' which binds the sovereign to his duty of guaranteeing the people's safety. The concept of a 'law of nature' is ill defined, and as to what provides the place for a regress to end – the regress of what ultimate authority provides a ground for the authority of the sovereign itself – it is ad hoc. If there are natural laws providing an ultimate justification for claiming that the safety of individuals is paramount, why can they not be operative in the state of nature, perhaps by the light of something else equally supposed to be natural, viz. 'the light of reason'? Why can each individual not be 'obliged by the law of nature, and to render an account thereof to God, the author of that law, and to none but him', to ensure the safety of others as well as himself?

A compelling criticism of Hobbes is offered by Quentin Skinner, who says that Hobbes' account of liberty undermines a better notion he calls 'republican liberty', which is 'liberty as the absence of dependence'. Free people are those who do not live under any form of arbitrary power, whether or not it is exercised. The view that liberty is merely lack of interference or restraint – or, as Hobbes eventually put it, mere absence of impediment to motion – is insufficient for people to be genuinely free; however benign the existence of power, says Skinner, its mere existence changes free people into slaves. And free people can exist only in a free state.

Skinner traces the history of the idea of republican liberty from ancient Rome to the Renaissance, and argues that it was at work during the Civil War in England in the 1640s, as the Parliamentary side fought against the Crown's claim to hold discretionary prerogative rights – which means arbitrary rights – superior to those of Parliament or individuals. As examples of defenders of the republican view of liberty Skinner cites James Harrington, Algernon Sydney and John Milton.

Even in the earliest of his books, *The Elements of Law*, Hobbes was already arguing that the authority residing in an absolute sovereign is derived from the voluntary surrender to it of the power that individuals otherwise hold over themselves, and that individuals do this in the interests of their own welfare. In his next book, *De Cive*, Hobbes countered the idea that the mere fact of government, by its very existence, makes people slaves – this being the republican view – by arguing that liberty is 'absence of impediments to motion' and that this is consistent with there being an absolute sovereign. In *Leviathan* this definition of liberty was refined to say 'absence of *external* constraints' – and this is what Skinner focuses upon as a signal moment in the history of political thought, because it introduces a distinction between *liberty* and *power*. Skinner says that this makes Hobbes 'the first to answer the republican theorists by proffering an alternative definition in which the presence of freedom is construed entirely as absence of impediments rather than absence of dependence'. From this has stemmed all subsequent thinking about liberty, says Skinner, which as a result misses the point about the many ways in which true liberty is rendered unattainable.

Liberty as 'absence of restraint' is described as 'negative liberty', following Isaiah Berlin's distinction between negative and positive liberty. It is the idea of liberty which – whether or not as a result of Hobbes' influence – many understand as the basic kind. But it is inconsistent not just with the idea of liberty as 'absence of dependence', but with the idea that there are fundamental rights to kinds of liberty that demand protection against any form of authority; these include the civil liberties of freedom of expression, inviolate aspects of private life, assembly with others, freedom from oppression by arbitrary and cruel authority, and more. This debate vividly continues.

BARUCH SPINOZA (1632–1677)

Whereas Descartes had a great influence on philosophy and a considerable influence on mathematics, Baruch Spinoza arguably had a greater and more general influence: nothing less than an influence on world history. This is because of the impact of his ideas on the Enlightenment. There were of course many others who had great influence too, not least among them Isaac Newton and John Locke. Newton's contribution to science was transformative; Locke's influence on social and political ideas – consider the impact of his writings on the American and French revolutions – was transformative in another way. Both of them could be openly cited and quoted by their successors, but Spinoza's influence was largely covert, chiefly because he was regarded as an atheist, and atheism was viewed with hostility and opprobrium.*

This attitude to Spinoza began among his own community of Sephardic Jewish exiles living in Amsterdam in the Netherlands, where he was born Baruch Spinoza in 1632. When he was twenty-four years old the synagogue excommunicated him for 'abominable heresies' (and also 'monstrous deeds'; these were not made explicit), and he was never readmitted. The reason was undoubtedly that he had begun to give voice to his philosophical ideas. As these included denial of the existence of a transcendent deity personally interested in human destiny, denial of the existence of immortal souls and denial of the continued relevance of Judaism's Law as set out in scripture, the fact of his excommunication is unsurprising.

Expulsion from one's community is a hard thing. Spinoza left Amsterdam and made a living in provincial towns as a lens grinder, a fact that has been cited in explanation of his early death, aged forty-five, from lung disease; inhaling the fine dust from ground glass would, either by itself or in exacerbation of another lung disease, have been

---

* The atheists of the time described themselves as 'deists', deism being the idea that the universe must have been created by a god, since at that time few could imagine a plausible alternative to thinking so; but they regarded this god as having since then either ceased to exist or lost interest, and they accorded little importance, other than sociologically, to religious beliefs.

the culprit. But by that time he had made a major philosophical reputation through his correspondence with other savants, although he published only two books in his lifetime, an examination of Descartes' *Principles of Philosophy* and his *Tractatus Theologico-Politicus*. Because of the unpopularity of his views with authorities he chose to restrict himself to private contacts with fellow-philosophers, for this reason refusing the offer of a professorship at Heidelberg University.

Spinoza spent many years writing his great work, posthumously entitled *Ethics*, which he interrupted to write a book in response to a worsening climate of religious intolerance in the Netherlands: his famous – in its own day and for too long afterwards, infamous – *Tractatus Theologico-Politicus* ('Theological-Political Treatise'). It was published anonymously and caused a scandal, one outraged critic describing it as 'a book forged in hell by the devil himself'. His reputation suffered further when his essay *Tractatus Politicus*, unfinished at his death, was posthumously published.

The *Ethics* is a comprehensive philosophical treatise embracing metaphysics, epistemology, psychology and science as well as ethics. Spinoza had made an early attempt to set out these views in his (posthumously published) *Short Treatise on God, Man and his Well-being*, which – if one adjusted it to *God, the World, Man and his Well-Being* would sum up quite well the subject matter of the *Ethics* itself. His aim was to show that the best life is a life in which reason reveals the true nature of things, so that by understanding them we can be liberated from the bondage both of false beliefs and of misdirected, because inevitably futile, passions. The five books of the *Ethics* are successively entitled 'Of God', 'Of the Mind', 'Of the Emotions', 'Of Human Bondage', 'Of Human Freedom'. Thus one sees the progression of the argument. The full versions of the final two books' headings make this yet clearer: Book IV is entitled 'Of Human Bondage, or The Strength of the Emotions', and Book V 'Of Human Freedom, or The Power of the Understanding'.

In Latin the *Ethics'* title is *Ethica Ordine Geometrico Demonstrata*, which illustrates the method in which it is laid out – as a geometrical treatise, with definitions, axioms and propositions with their proofs and corollaries. It looks forbidding, and it requires that one knows Descartes' philosophical views at least; but it is a monument of clarity and lucidity once one has grasped the concepts at work.

A key to understanding Spinoza lies in his use of the phrase '*deus sive natura*', 'god or nature', to denote the totality of what exists. For him the universe is God or God is the universe, nature is God or God is nature; they are one and the same thing. All there is, is the world; call it God if you wish, on the grounds that it is everything that exists. This view is a far cry from the idea that there is a separate transcendent providential deity with intentions and plans for what it has created, which judges and rewards or punishes, and is and does what traditional religious conceptions of deity describe.

The reasons for Spinoza's view are these: the idea of what fundamentally exists in its own right, that is, *substance*, is the idea of what exists necessarily, because it is of the nature of substance to exist. There cannot be a 'non-existent substance'. He rules out the possibility that substances can share attributes – 'attributes' being the essential properties of a substance. Since 'God or nature' possesses all attributes, there cannot be another substance – there can only be one substance. Therefore everything that exists is an attribute (or 'mode' – which means a 'way of being or doing') of *deus sive natura*. So the world is all there is, and everything is an aspect of the world, including us humans.

Spinoza says that the world, *deus sive natura*, has 'infinite attributes'. He almost certainly means 'infinitely many' as well as 'infinite in character'. But we humans, with our finite minds, know only two of them – thought and extension (recall Descartes' two substances: mind, which is thinking stuff, and matter, which is extended or spatial stuff). Being spatial, extended or material is therefore an attribute of *deus sive natura* – of God: such a view is cause for excommunication by any religious community – and likewise it is an attribute of *deus sive natura* to be mind or thought. Human minds are 'modes' of the infinite mind.

It follows from the fact that *deus sive natura* is a necessary being – exists *necessarily*, cannot not exist – and that all the truths about it flow with logical necessity from the infinite attributes constituting its essence, that therefore everything that is or happens is itself necessary. Nothing can be other than it is. This is strict and total determinism. Spinoza claims that it is acceptance of this great truth – that everything that is and happens must be as it is and must happen as it does – that liberates us: human freedom results from accepting the inevitability of things. How this notion connects with the concept of 'free will' I discuss below.

In the course of setting out this view about *deus sive natura*, and because of it, Spinoza offers ingenious solutions to various philosophical problems. One is the question of the place of mind in nature: the 'mind–body' problem that proved so intractable to Descartes. It was intractable for Descartes because he conceived of mind and matter as essentially different substances, making it wholly mysterious how they can interact. For Spinoza mind and matter are two attributes of the same substance – the one and only substance, *deus sive natura*. 'Mind and body are one and the same thing, conceived now under the attribute of thought, now under the attribute of extension,' he wrote. Both mind and body are 'modes' – ways of being or acting – of the single all-encompassing substance. It is a corollary of this that having an idea of a body consists in the idea and what the idea is 'of' – its 'ideatum' – being the same thing under two different descriptions. If the idea is 'adequate' (think of the etymology of this word: 'equal to') to the ideatum, it is true; if it is 'inadequate' it is false.

This last comment about 'adequacy' should provoke a doubt about Spinoza's solution. If an idea and its ideatum are the same thing under different descriptions, how can an idea ever be false? He sought to give an account of error – indeed, the epistemological aspects of the *Ethics* are almost wholly devoted to an account of error, since it is a real problem for his view – by saying that 'falsity consists in privation of knowledge, resulting from inadequate or mutilated and confused ideas.' Sense-perception is a good illustration of this: the sun looks like a small burningly golden disc to me, but it is not small. If I confused my *idea* of the sun with the sun itself – with the ideatum of the idea – I would be making a mistake. With Plato therefore, Spinoza consigns sensory experience to the lowest epistemological level, that of opinion. It is here that falsehood enters, for the next two levels of cognition, science being the second and 'intuition', being the highest, are concerned only with truth. This highest level, 'intuition', consists in a completely adequate grasp of the 'formal essence' of the attributes of *deus sive natura*.

Another problem to which Spinoza proposes a solution concerns individuality. If the universe is a single comprehensive substance, how can there be or seem to be such a vast plurality of individual things? And in particular, how can human beings be different from each other if they are really all part of the one thing that exists? His answer is that individual things are finite modes of the infinite substance, and each has an impetus to self-preservation and perseverance. This is 'conatus', desire or will to resist anything that 'can take its existence away'. Everything has conatus, but some modes of the universe, such as animals and humans, have more self-awareness and more conatus than other things.

This takes us back to the question of determinism, for now it might appear that conatus, at least in humans, is a form of free will; but Spinoza's theory excludes free will. In the *Ethics* Spinoza says that people 'are mistaken in thinking themselves free, and this opinion consists in this alone, that they are conscious of their actions but ignorant of the causes which determine their actions'. Yet the very title of Book v of the *Ethics* tells us what the point of his theory is: to explain how we can achieve freedom. What is 'freedom' for a human being if not 'freedom of will'?

The explanation Spinoza gives lies in the distinction he draws between active and passive mental states. We do some things, and we 'suffer' (that is, are recipients or receivers of) certain things; we act, or we are acted upon. The more adequate our ideas, the more active we are; the less adequate, the more we are on the receiving end of events. Because the only cause of everything is *deus sive natura*, it is the only thing that acts without being acted upon, and accordingly is the only thing that is free in the metaphysical sense. But insofar as we humans can progress from a less to a more active state by having more adequate ideas, to that extent we participate more in the active freedom of *deus sive natura*. Spinoza calls this independence from causes outside ourselves 'virtue', and says, 'virtue and power are the same thing,' where 'power' is the ability to do and achieve things. Exercising power in this sense gives us pleasure, defined as the emotion we feel as we progress to more adequate ideas and therefore greater freedom.

Because a whole book is devoted to the emotions or, as translations of Spinoza standardly call them, the 'affects', it is important to note his view of them, because they are central to his theory. He defines emotion as 'a confused idea' which arises because of our embodied existence and the conatus to self-preservation, which prompts us to escape what is harmful and to seek what gives us joy or pleasure. Quoting the Stoics, he says that the things we desire, and which our passions drive us to get, lie outside our control, and the more therefore they influence us the less happy we are – and therefore the less free. 'I call "bondage" our lack of power to moderate and restrain the affects.' If we can control our desire for what we cannot control, we thus far liberate ourselves. We attain freedom when we understand the nature of things, and this weakens the power of our affects over us. When we feel an 'intellectual love' for reality as it really is – which is to say: when we live according to reason and understanding – we acquire the power that is virtue, and we are free.

Spinoza's *Tractatus Theologico-Politicus* is a radical book. Its aim is to warn its readers against the power of religion to control their lives by encouraging in them the emotions of superstition, fear and hope, which the clergy use to influence them in the direction that the Church, and the temporal powers who find it such a useful ally, wish to lead them. He was especially concerned to argue that religion and philosophy (in the latter term including science) occupy completely different spheres, one depending on faith and the other on reason, and that religion should leave philosophy free to pursue its enquiries without interference. He argued that such freedom would conduce to public peace, because it is sectarian disputes that give rise to civil disorder, not science. He demonstrated by an examination of scripture that the prophets were not very intelligent or knowledgeable, that the laws of religion do not conduce to human happiness, that miracles are impossible and that in general superstition is 'the bitter enemy of all true knowledge and true morality'.

The *Tractatus* is a plea for toleration and the freedom to think and enquire. Spinoza argued that the Bible comes down to one simple message, if one leaves aside all the rest of its talk of laws and miracles and all its superstitious elements: 'love your neighbour.'

This claim has immediate consequences for politics, in Spinoza's view; indeed a large part of the aim of the *Tractatus* was to urge a political view. This is that it is a mistake for a state to think that it can control what people inwardly think, although it is right that it should aim to encourage outward behaviour that ensures peace, safety and well-being in society. He described the 'ultimate purpose' of the state as being 'not to dominate or control people by fear or subject them to the authority of another. On the contrary, its aim is to free everyone from fear, so that they may live in security . . . that they may retain to the highest possible degree their natural right to live and to act without harm to themselves or to others . . . to allow their minds and bodies to develop in their own ways, in security, and enjoy the free use of reason, and not to participate in conflicts based on hatred, anger, or deceit, or in malicious disputes with each other. Therefore, the true purpose of the state is in fact freedom.'

What is private and personal to each individual in the way of his or her thoughts and beliefs cannot be a matter for law or a sovereign's commands. 'Everyone is by absolute natural right the master of his own thoughts,' he wrote, 'and utter failure will attend any attempt in a commonwealth to force men to speak only as prescribed by the sovereign despite their different and opposing opinions.' There will be disagreements and arguments, but good government will be tolerant and will recognize that worse vices arise from trying to control thought than by allowing it to be free. Moreover, freedom of thought 'is of the first importance in fostering the sciences and arts for only those whose judgment is free and unbiased can attain success in these fields'.

It is easy to see why Spinoza's extraordinary achievement would be such a beacon to the Enlightenment. It says: what exists is the universe, and humanity is a part of the universe, subject to the same laws. The life of reason is a life free from the trammels of fear, superstition and unreasonable hopes and desires; it is a life based instead on knowledge, on science and rational enquiry, on what really matters in practice to humankind. Freedom of thought is essential for progress, and for the flourishing of individuals and society.

Spinoza's view breathes the clear air of intellectual freedom, and directs the attention to what matters: life itself, here and now, in society, with others, requiring thought and understanding. The liberation his views not only urged but helped to bring about in the Enlightenment proved to be a heady and extremely consequential one.

LOCKE (1632–1704)

John Locke, like Hobbes, wrote both about general philosophy and about politics, but unlike Hobbes, who is now discussed exclusively in connection with his political theories, Locke's contributions in both spheres proved highly influential.

Locke was born in Somerset, England. He studied at Oxford, taking his Bachelor's and Master's degrees in the then standard Aristotelian-based Scholastic curriculum before also taking a degree in medicine. He served as physician and secretary to the statesman Earl of Shaftesbury, assisting the latter in his ministerial duties in government. In

1683 Shaftesbury fell under suspicion for a plot (the 'Rye House plot') to assassinate King Charles II and his brother and heir James, the aim being to block the latter's succession to the throne because he was a Catholic. He had to flee England; Locke, who was under suspicion by association with him, accompanied him into exile in the Netherlands. After the 'Glorious Revolution' of 1688, in which James II abdicated and the English Parliament invited William of Orange to be king, Locke returned to England – in the same ship that carried William of Orange's wife, the English Princess Mary. He then published his *Two Treatises of Government*, which provided a justification for the dramatic constitutional change that the revolution had effected.

It is possible that the *Treatises* were written before the revolution, perhaps circulating in private; if so they might have served as part of what inspired James II's opponents to assert Parliament's authority against the Crown. In any event, the *Treatises*, and especially the second of them, proved greatly significant for political thinking thereafter, being quoted verbatim and extensively in the documents of the American and French revolutions, and providing a major inspiration for political liberalism in general.

Locke's contributions to other mainstream areas of philosophy were equally consequential. His *Essay Concerning Human Understanding* is a classic of empiricism. He and Isaac Newton were together held in esteem by the philosophers of the eighteenth-century Enlightenment; Voltaire (whose lover Emilie du Châtelet was Newton's translator into French) described Locke as the 'Hercules of metaphysics'. One reason for this high praise is that the weight of philosophical tradition had hitherto rested on the side of rationalism in epistemology, but Locke had helped swing it in favour of empiricism. In Voltaire's France the Cartesians – Descartes' followers – were dominant; in Locke's England the rationalist flag was flown by the 'Cambridge Platonists', chief among them Ralph Cudworth. But Locke's case for empiricism, constituting a defence of the rationale that underlay developments in natural science, was on the right side of intellectual history. It prompted the brilliant rationalist-inclined Leibniz to write a critique of Locke in his *New Essays Concerning Human Understanding*, and it was the immediate background to the philosophical thinking of George Berkeley and David Hume, who with Locke form the triad of British empiricists so influential for much subsequent philosophy.

Locke was a Fellow of the Royal Society, whose members were among other things interested, as Bacon and Descartes had been, in the question of how knowledge is best acquired. They did not accept Descartes' solution, nor the rationalist approach in general, and they wished to see a theoretical justification for the empirical, experimental methods they employed in their scientific researches. Locke offered to write an essay on the topic, 'to examine our abilities, and see what objects our understandings are, or are not fitted to deal with'. This meant examining 'the origin, certainty and extent of human knowledge, together with the grounds and degrees of belief, opinion and assent'. In the event the task took him twenty years, partly because of his busy political life, but partly also because of the task's scope and difficulty.

The Cambridge Platonists' version of rationalism was based on a commitment to 'innate ideas', the doctrine that we are born knowing a significant number of things, among them the fundamental truths of logic, morality and theology. They thought this for Plato's reason, namely, that experience cannot lead us to ultimate truths, but only to opinion about what is imperfect and transitory. This view stands in obviously sharp contrast with the empiricists' commitment to the primacy of experience in the acquisition of knowledge. Locke's *Essay* accordingly begins with a refutation of the doctrine of innate ideas (Book i). It then proceeds (in the remaining Books ii–iv) to discuss experience itself and how knowledge arises from it.

The 'great argument' for there being such innate ideas as *everything is self-identical, nothing contradicts itself, a whole is greater than its parts*, is that everyone knows or at least assents to them. Locke points out that as a matter of fact this is not true; there are plenty of cases of people never having thought about such matters. The ideas of *impossibility* and *identity* are absent from the minds of children and many adults, even if, on being prompted, they would assent to the idea built upon them that *it is impossible for something to both be and not be at the same time*. This is even more so regarding supposedly innate ideas about moral principles and notions of God, where much disagreement between individuals and cultures can flourish.

Locke says that knowledge is concerned with three topics: 'physics' or the nature of things, 'practics' or morality, and 'semiotics' or the signs that 'the mind makes use of for understanding things, or conveying its knowledge to others'. The two central books of the *Essay*, Books ii and iii, are concerned with the two kinds of signs we use: respectively *ideas* and *words*. These are 'the great instruments of knowledge'.

By 'idea' Locke means 'whatever the mind can be employed about in thinking'. Ideas come to us from experience, which takes the form either of sensation or of reflection. Sensation is seeing, touching and the rest; reflection is experience of the internal operations of our minds in remembering, comparing, inferring and the rest. Ideas are either simple or, when combined together, complex. Simple ideas of colour and taste are passively received by the mind. Complex ideas of things in the world, their properties and their relations to other things, are the result of how we arrange our ideas in the course of experience.

Ideas are, remember, signs; they stand for something other than themselves. Ideas are in consciousness; they represent – *re-present* – other things. In the case of sensory ideas they represent things outside the mind. So when one looks at a tree the idea of it is in the mind, while outside in the world is the tree itself. Locke thought that this theory of perception gives us grounds for thinking that we can know how things actually are. He distinguished between the 'primary qualities' of things, which he said 'are in the things themselves', so that our perception of them tells us what they are like; while the 'secondary qualities' that things appear to have are the result of the way our sense organs interact with them.

The primary qualities are extension, shape, motion or rest, number and solidity. Physical objects always have them. If you chop up a piece of wood into smaller and smaller pieces, the pieces themselves will always have these properties.

This is not the case with the secondary qualities. These are colour, taste, sound, texture and smell. Whereas primary qualities are 'in the objects', the latter are only 'in the objects as powers to cause us to have secondary quality experiences'. If someone is not looking, the rose has no colour – not because looking at it causes it to have colour, but because colour is something perceived in the mind as a result of the way that light reflected from the rose interacts with our eyes, stimulating messages to pass via the optic nerves to the brain.

One can see that Locke's theory of perception is causal, exactly as we ordinarily take it to be; objects outside us cause us to have ideas in consciousness that represent them. But however much this might seem to be a common-sense view, it creates a difficulty; ideas stand between us and things, forming a 'veil of perception' which we cannot put aside to see whether the ideas accurately represent what we suppose them to represent – or even indeed whether there is anything out there 'behind them' at all (remember Descartes: we might have the idea of a tree when we dream, but that idea is not 're-presenting' to us an actual tree).

Locke did not try to deal with this sceptical problem. He sidesteps it, saying, 'The light that is set up in us shines bright enough for all our purposes,' by the 'light' meaning the mind and its operations. This was not regarded as good enough by many of his successors in philosophy (George Berkeley most immediately among them, as we shall see), who recognized that the sceptical problem still awaited solution.

Words are also signs; they stand for ideas. Moreover they stand not only for particular ideas of individual things, but for *general* ideas – for example, not just for a particular idea of some individual dog, but for the *kind* of thing to which the term *dog* generally applies. Indeed most of our words are general terms, and knowledge is 'conversance with [the] general ideas' they denote. This has to be so because we cannot have a different individual name for every single thing in the world; knowledge would be impossible if so.

Words are needed, Locke says, because ideas are private to each person's consciousness, so there has to be a way of making thoughts public, and of conveying to others what we are thinking or experiencing. Language serves this function.

There are serious problems with this theory. The main one is that if words denote ideas and ideas are private, how can I know that the same words raise the same ideas in others' minds as in mine? How can I even know that their experience is the same as mine when we both use the word 'red' – that what I see as red they do not see as what I call green, for example?

In the second edition of the *Essay* Locke introduced a topic which proved of significant interest in subsequent philosophy: the question of personal identity. What makes me the same person over time, despite all the differences made to my appearance and character by the passage of years? In Locke's day and for centuries beforehand it was assumed that we each have an immortal soul which remains invariant through the merely accidental and relatively unimportant changes that happen to our bodies and circumstances, and which (on the Christian view, and most other religious views) survives bodily death. Accordingly it was thought that it is the soul, not the body, that carries personhood. This implies that 'a person' and 'a human being' are not the same thing, a view Locke accepted. Indeed the concept of a person is a forensic concept; it is the concept of a rational being responsible for what he, she or it does in morality and law. As this suggests, babies are not yet persons, and an elderly individual suffering from dementia might have ceased to be one. Corporations are regarded as persons in law, having rights and responsibilities. Given this, what constitutes the identity of a *person* over time? This is harder to answer than the question, What constitutes the identity of a body (a stone, a tree, a human body) over time? – for here one can simply point to the spatio-temporal continuity of the physical organization of the thing, even from acorn to mighty oak.

Locke's answer was that personal identity consists in 'consciousness of being the same person over time'. This consciousness is constituted by self-awareness, memory and a special self-regarding interest in the future. (Locke introduced the word 'consciousness' into English by this theory.) This view outraged churchmen because it set aside reference to immortal souls – Locke had a long-running battle with a cleric called Bishop Stillingfleet on this question – and it was criticized by other philosophers because it seemed to get matters the wrong way round: it made memory the basis of identity, whereas in fact personal identity is the basis of memory. How can this memory be *my* memory if I am not the same person who had the experience that originated the memory? It also has the unintuitive result that personal identity is not continuous: an old major-general might remember being an heroic young officer in battle, and the young officer might remember stealing apples from an orchard when he was a little boy, but the major-general might not remember stealing apples. Is he therefore not the same person as the boy? On Locke's view the answer is that he is not the same person because he is not aware of being the same person. But think of matters this way: suppose I borrow some money from you, and later you come to ask for it back. If I said that I am not the same person who borrowed it because I cannot remember doing so, you would not be amused.

In the final book of the *Essay* Locke gives his account of the nature of knowledge. He says it consists in 'the perception of the connexion and agreement, or disagreement and repugnancy, of any of our ideas. In this alone it consists.' When the connection or disagreement among ideas is immediately obvious, Locke calls it 'intuitive knowledge'. When reasoning is required to see the connection or opposition, he calls it 'demonstrative knowledge'. A rationalist would not object to this definition, and it does not yet count as a defence of empirical knowledge.

Surprisingly, Locke here fudges; he writes, 'There is indeed another perception of the mind, employed about the particular existence of finite beings outside us, which going beyond bare probability and yet not reaching perfectly to either of the foregoing degrees of certainty, passes under the name of knowledge.' This is empirical knowledge. It is not certain – indeed he here passingly acknowledges the sceptical difficulty – but it 'goes beyond bare probability' because of its source in sense-perception. He calls it 'sensitive knowledge'.

Locke's theory is almost exactly what we commonly think about empirical knowledge. It arises in us because of the causal interactions between the world and our sense organs; it is defeasible – that is, we accept that we can be wrong at times, for we make perceptual mis-judgments and other kinds of errors; but generally perception is a mainly reliable source of information about a world beyond our heads. In science our perceptual capacities are extended and enhanced by instruments – microscopes, telescopes, oscilloscopes, Large Hadron Colliders – and our intellectual capacities are enhanced by mathemat-ical techniques and another kind of instrument, the computer. But together these are all part of the equipment of empirical enquiry. Locke is right to say that for all practical purposes this picture is a compelling one, and powerfully justified by the results of its application. But in philosophy the urge remains to see whether the obvious sceptical chal-lenges even to this compelling picture can be met. That urge is what prompts the efforts made in epistemology.

The political philosophy of Locke is arguably his greatest contribution not only because it represents a philosophical advance in itself but because of its practical impact on the world in the following centuries.

England's 'Glorious Revolution' of 1688 established two linked points: the sovereignty of Parliament and the rejection of the doctrine of the 'divine right of kings'. By putting a crown on the head of William of Orange on its own terms, Parliament had achieved a new and per-manent constitutional settlement. Control of national finances and the armed forces lay with Parliament, and with those two things lay every-thing. Only Parliament could vote money to the government. The settlement also and crucially secured the independence of the judiciary and a right of petition, two bulwarks of a free society.

Locke described his aim in his political writings as justifying Wil-liam of Orange's possession of the throne 'to make good his title in the consent of the people' – by 'people' meaning 'as represented by Parliament', thereby vaguely seeming to denote the whole nation, the vagueness doubtless being intentional given that the franchise for elections to Parliament was anything but democratic.

The text – it became an instant classic – in which Locke sets out the justification for the 'Glorious Revolution' is his *Second Treatise of Government*. (The *First Treatise* consists in an extensive refutation of Sir Robert Filmer's defence of the doctrine of divine right in his *Patriarcha*.) One of the significant aspects of Locke's theory is its disagreement with a more powerful theory than Filmer's, the view of sovereignty put forward by Hobbes. Locke did not write directly about Hobbes because the latter's name was off limits – he was believed to be an atheist, and atheism was regarded with suspicion, if not indeed horror, at that time. Moreover Hobbes' views were equally applicable to monarchical and republican regimes. If anyone tried to defend William's entitlement to the throne by citing Hobbes, William's opponents could just as easily cite Hobbes on the other side of the case.

Like Hobbes, Locke also employs the idea of a 'state of nature' as existing before the creation of civil society, but for him it was not an arena of endless strife between people, but instead a place where individuals enjoyed freedom. Most of that freedom has to be yielded up to get the benefits of living in society, but Locke held that certain of those rights, chief among them rights to life, liberty and property, cannot be given away by a social contract. This fact by itself makes it impossible that there should be such a thing as absolute sovereignty; by its very nature absolutism is inconsistent with the natural rights that people bring into society when they enter the mutual contract that brings society into existence.

The ideas of natural law and natural rights are closely connected. In Locke's view, natural rights rest on the fact that in the state of nature individuals can freely use whatever nature offers in the way of shelter, comfort and sustenance. Natural law says what is allowed and forbidden to people given how things stand in nature: 'all Men are naturally in . . . a *State of perfect Freedom* to order their Actions, and dispose of their Possessions, and Persons as they think fit, within the Bounds of the Law of Nature, without asking Leave, or depending upon the Will of any other Man.' (Locke's alternative way of describing this state of affairs is to say, 'In the Beginning all the World was *America*.') This is because everyone is equal in the state of nature; no one has greater status or more rights than anyone else, and no one is in a position to dictate to others how they should live. He thus rejects Filmer's claim that a hierarchy of higher and lower among men was introduced in Eden by God's grant of lordship to Adam, first over his companion Eve, then over his sons, and thence over all humankind.

The importance of Locke's argument on this point is that it asserts that each person has a right to self-preservation, and therefore a correlative obligation to each other person to respect his or her right to self-preservation – and indeed to be actively concerned for the welfare of others in this respect. The obligation thus entailed goes beyond refraining from doing harm to others, but requires acting to protect them from harm and punishing those who do harm.

Locke points out that in the state of nature it is difficult to ensure the proper protection of these rights and the exercise of these correlative obligations; he calls this the 'inconvenience' of the state of nature. But to set up an absolute sovereign to enforce both would, he says, be worse than this inconvenience, because nothing could stop such a sovereign from preying on its subjects and even making war on them. It is therefore wrong in principle for people to yield their rights to an absolute ruler; to do so not only forfeits the right to self-preservation but makes them unable to carry out their associated duties to others.

Locke's point about civil society is persuasive. It offers protection to individuals' lives, liberty and property. It is based on laws that everyone can know, with independent judges to apply them, and agreed structures to enforce them. An arrangement of this kind resolves difficulties about how such rights and obligations are to be exercised properly. 'Having in the State of Nature no arbitrary Power over the Life, Liberty, or Possession of another,' Locke wrote, 'but only so much as the Law of Nature gave him for the Preservation of himself, and the rest of Mankind; this is all he doth, or can give up to the Common-wealth, and by it to the *Legislative Power*, so that the Legislative can have no more than this. Their Power in the utmost Bounds of it, is *limited to the publick good* of the Society.' If a government behaves in ways that run contrary to the 'publick Good' of society it thereby 'dissolves' itself – Locke's term – because it makes itself illegitimate. This is what happened in the case of James II; his legitimacy 'dissolved' itself when he acted in ways contrary to the interests of his subjects. Indeed Locke's point is stronger yet: if an illegitimate government tries to stay in power, the people have not merely the right but the duty to overthrow it.

In these ideas Locke introduced the concept that power is a trusteeship, and is held by the consent of those on whose behalf the power is
exercised. 'Who shall be judge, whether the Prince or Legislative act
contrary to their Trust?' Locke asked, and he answered, in a passage
which has been key to the subsequent development of democratic ideas,
'The People shall be Judge; for who shall be Judge whether the Trustee
or Deputy acts well, and according to the Trust reposed in him, but he
who deputes him, and must, by having deputed him, have still a Power
to discard him, when he fails in his Trust?'

Locke's views are regarded as the starting point for political liberalism.* They seem distinctively modern. He was not the first to formulate
such ideas; the debate about constitutional matters during the Civil
War in England in the 1640s had advanced and canvassed similar ideas,
sometimes considerably more radical. Indeed his views incorporate
much older traces, such as the Renaissance view that things were vastly
better in olden times, with history being a long declension from more
perfect arrangements in antiquity. The very idea of a 'state of nature' in
which people had lived in 'perfect freedom' (to use Locke's phrase) is a
giveaway of this attitude. But the manner in which he encapsulates
them has given them their enduring status in political debate since, and
explains why they exerted such influence on the leaders of the American and French revolutions.

BERKELEY (1685–1753)

The immediate prompt for George Berkeley's philosophy is Locke.
Berkeley agreed with Locke's empiricism, but could not accept his
fudge over the scepticism that arises because of the 'veil of perception'
theory – the theory that our ideas are intermediaries between ourselves
and a world that lies otherwise inaccessibly behind them and causes
them.

Berkeley was born at his family's home, Dysart Castle, in County
Kilkenny in Ireland, and educated at Trinity College, Dublin. He took
orders in the Church of Ireland and later became Bishop of Cloyne. As
these facts show he was a member of the 'Protestant Ascendancy', the

---

* Not in the pejorative sense employed by the American political right wing, for whom
'liberal' is a surrogate for 'socialist', both terms of malediction in their lexicon.

English-descended ruling elite. His major philosophical works were written early in life; his *Principles of Human Knowledge* was published in 1710 and his *Three Dialogues between Hylas and Philonous*, written to address the incomprehension that had greeted the *Principles*, in 1713. He published treatises on vision, motion and medicine later, but these two works contain his enduring philosophical contribution.

The contemporary reaction to Berkeley's *Principles* was that his views were neither refutable nor believable. He is still either misunderstood or ignored by some philosophers, even though he is an influence on two twentieth-century schools of thought that will be met with later in these pages, positivism and phenomenalism.

Berkeley's philosophical view is often described as 'immaterialism', by which is meant a denial of the existence of matter (or, more precisely, *material substance*). But he also, famously, argued in support of three further theses. He argued for *idealism*, the thesis that mind constitutes the ultimate reality. He argued that the existence of things consists in their being perceived: *esse est percipi*. And he argued that the mind which is the substance of the world is a single infinite mind – in short, God. These are four different theses, but they are intimately connected, the arguments for the first three sharing most of their premises and steps.

Berkeley's aim in arguing for these theses was to refute two kinds of scepticism. One is epistemological scepticism, which says that we cannot know the true nature of things because of the perceptual and psychological contingencies that oblige us to distinguish appearance from reality in such a way that the latter lies hidden behind the former, so that knowledge of it is at least problematic and at worst impossible.

The other is theological scepticism, which Berkeley called 'atheism' and which in his view included not only denials of the existence of a deity, but also 'deism', the view that although the universe might have been created by a deity, it continues to exist without a deity's active presence.

In opposing the first scepticism Berkeley took himself to be defending common sense and eradicating 'causes of error and difficulty in the sciences'. In opposing the second he took himself to be defending religion.

Berkeley took the root of scepticism to be the opening of a gap between experience and the world, forced by theories of ideas like Locke's which involve 'supposing a twofold existence of the objects of sense, the one *intelligible*, or in the mind, the other real and without [i.e. outside] the mind'. Scepticism arises because 'for so long as men thought that *real* things subsisted without the mind, and that their knowledge was only so far forth *real* as it was conformable to *real things*, it follows, they could not be certain they had any real knowledge at all. For how can it be known, that the things which are perceived, are conformable to those which are not perceived, or exist outside the mind?' The nub of the problem is that if we are acquainted only with our own perceptions, and never with the things which are supposed to lie beyond them, how can we hope for knowledge of those things, or even be justified in asserting their existence?

Berkeley's predecessors talked, as Locke had done, of *qualities* inhering in *matter* and causing ideas in us which *represent* or even *resemble* those qualities. *Matter* or *material substance* is the technical metaphysical concept denoting a supposed corporeal basis underlying the qualities of things. Berkeley was especially troubled by the unempiricist character of this view. If we are to be consistent in our empiricist principles, he asked, how can we tolerate the concept of something which by definition is empirically undetectable, lying hidden behind the perceptible qualities of things as their supposed basis? If the claim (that matter is the *substance* underlying things) cannot be defended, we have to look elsewhere.

Berkeley's answer is provided by his answer to scepticism itself. This answer is to deny that there is a gap between experience and the world – in his and Locke's terminology: between ideas and things – by asserting that things *are* ideas. The argument is stated with admirable concision in the first six paragraphs of the *Principles*, its conclusion being the first sentence of paragraph 7: 'From what has been said, it follows, that there is not any other substance than *spirit*, or that which perceives' ('spirit' and 'mind' are the same thing for Berkeley). All the rest of the *Principles* and *Three Dialogues* consists in expansion, clarification and defence of this thesis. The argument is as follows.

Berkeley begins in Lockean fashion by offering an inventory of the 'objects of human knowledge'. They are 'either ideas actually imprinted on the senses, or such as are perceived by attending to the passions and operations of the mind, or lastly ideas formed by help of memory and imagination, either compounding, dividing, or barely representing those originally perceived in the aforesaid ways'. Ideas of sense – colours, shapes and the rest – are 'observed to accompany each other' in certain ways; 'collections' of them 'come to be marked by one name, and so to be reputed one thing', for example an apple or a tree.

Besides these ideas there is 'something which knows or perceives them'; this 'perceiving, active being is what I call *mind, spirit, soul* or *myself*', and it is 'entirely distinct' from the ideas it perceives.

Thoughts, feelings and imaginings exist only in the mind. But so also do the ideas of things – which, remember, are collections of ideas: the idea of an apple is a composite of ideas of the colours, shapes and tastes that constitute it. So it is no less evident that the various sensations or ideas imprinted on the sense, however blended or combined together (that is, whatever objects they compose), cannot exist otherwise than in a mind perceiving them.

From these claims it follows that the gap between things and ideas vanishes; for if things are collections of qualities, and qualities are sensible ideas, and sensible ideas exist only in the mind, then what it is for a thing to exist is for it to be perceived – in Berkeley's phrase: to be is to be perceived: *esse est percipi*. 'For as to what is said of the absolute [i.e. mind-independent] existence of unthinking things [i.e. ideas or collections of ideas] without any relation to their being perceived, that seems perfectly unintelligible. Their *esse* is *percipi*, nor is it possible that they should have any existence, out of the minds or thinking things which perceive them.'

Berkeley knows that this claim is surprising, so he remarks that although people think that sensible objects like mountains and houses have an 'absolute', that is, perception-independent, existence, reflection on the points just made show that this is a contradiction. 'For what', he asks, 'are the aforementioned objects but the things we perceive by sense, and what do we perceive besides our own ideas or sensations; and is it not plainly repugnant [illogical, contradictory] that any of these or any combination of them should exist unperceived?'

A point that requires immediate emphasis is that this argument, together with Berkeley's correlative denial of the existence of material substance, is not a denial of the existence of the external world and the physical objects it contains, such as tables and chairs, mountains and trees. Nor does Berkeley hold that the world exists only because it is thought of by any one or more finite minds, such as yours or mine. In one sense of the term 'realist', indeed, Berkeley is a realist, in holding that the existence of the physical world is independent of finite minds, individually or collectively. What he argues instead is that its existence is not independent of mind as such.

The source of the belief that things can exist apart from perception of them is the doctrine of 'abstract ideas', which Berkeley attacks in his Introduction to the *Principles*. Abstraction consists in separating things which can be separated only in thought, not in reality, for example the colour and the extension of a surface; or which involves noting a feature common to many different things, and attending only to that feature and not to its particular instances – in this way we arrive at the 'abstract idea' of, say, Redness, apart from any particular red object. Abstraction is a falsifying move; what prompts the 'common opinion' about houses and mountains is that we abstract existence from perception, and so come to believe that things can exist unperceived. But because things are ideas, and because ideas exist only if perceived by minds, the notion of 'absolute existence outside mind' is a contradiction.

So, says Berkeley, to say that things exist is to say that they are perceived, and therefore 'so long as they are not perceived by me, or do not exist in my mind or that of any created spirit, they must either have no existence at all, or else subsist in the mind of some eternal spirit.' And from this the conclusion follows that 'there is not any other substance than *spirit*, or that which perceives.'

The argument in sum is therefore this: the things we encounter in episodes of perceptual experience – apples, stones, trees – are collections of 'ideas'. Ideas are the immediate objects of awareness. To exist they must be perceived; they cannot exist 'without (independently of) mind'. Therefore mind is the substance of the world.

Berkeley is a rigorous empiricist; we are not entitled to assert, believe or regard as meaningful anything not justified by experience. To deny that there is a 'seems–is' distinction is just another way of asserting that sensible objects (things in the world) are collections of sensible qualities, and hence of ideas. This shows that the concept of matter is redundant, Berkeley claims, because everything required to explain the world and experience of it is available in recognizing that minds and ideas are all there can be. But Berkeley adds to this a set of positive anti-materialist considerations.

An important argument for materialism is that use of a concept of matter explains much in science. Berkeley summarizes the view thus: 'there have been a great many things explained by matter and motion:

take away these, and you destroy the whole corpuscular philosophy, and undermine those mechanical principles which have been applied with such success to account for the phenomena. In short, whatever advances have been made . . . in the study of nature, do all proceed on the supposition that corporeal substance or matter doth really exist.' Berkeley's reply is that science's explanatory power and practical utility neither entail the truth of, nor depend upon, the materialist hypothesis, for these can equally if not better (because more economically) be explained in instrumentalist terms. Instrumentalism is the view that scientific theories are tools, and as such are candidates for assessment not as true or false, but rather as more or less useful. One does not ask whether a knife or a fork is true, but whether it is useful; and not merely useful, in the case of scientific theories, but (as required by Occam's Razor) as simply and economically useful as possible.

Berkeley expressed his early version of instrumentalism as a 'doctrine of signs', in which the regularity and order among our ideas reflect the steady will of God, which is so reliable that we can represent the connections thus observed as laws. Science is thus a convenient summary, for practical purposes, of what at the metaphysical level of explanation would be described in terms of the activity of 'infinite spirit'.

For Locke the concept of primary qualities was important because experience of them puts us most closely in touch with independent reality. Berkeley rejected his view on the ground that 'nothing can be like an idea but an idea': an idea cannot be 'like' a mountain or a tree; one idea can only be like another idea (two ideas of a tree, for example). Materialists hold that primary qualities are 'resemblances' of 'things existing outside the mind', but since primary qualities are ideas, and only ideas can resemble ideas, it follows that 'neither they nor their archetypes can be in an unperceiving substance'.

Some of Berkeley's critics think he failed to separate the question of material substance from that of the primary–secondary quality distinction, since one can reject materialism while retaining the distinction. But this in fact is what Berkeley does, for he does not deny that there is a distinction between primary and secondary qualities – he recognizes that the former are available to more than one sense at a time, the latter available to one sense only; that the former are measurable, the latter not (or not so straightforwardly); and so on – but he points out that in the *crucial* respect of their relation to mind, they are on a par in being both *sensible* and hence mind-dependent.

Berkeley took his arguments to amount to a new and powerful argument for the existence of an 'infinite mind' – a deity. The best statement of his argument occurs in the second of the *Three Dialogues*. From the proposition 'that sensible things cannot exist otherwise than in a mind or spirit' Berkeley concludes 'not that they have no real existence, but that seeing they depend not on my thought, and have an existence distinct from being perceived by me, *there must be some other mind wherein they exist*.' This conclusion is a weaker one than that there is a single infinite mind which perceives everything always; it establishes no more than that there is 'some other mind' – who might for all we know be the next-door neighbour. But in the very next sentence Berkeley adds, 'As sure therefore as the sensible world really exists, so sure is there an infinite omnipresent spirit who contains and supports it.' This is quite a leap. He tries to provide the missing step by saying, 'I perceive numberless ideas; and by an act of my will can form a great variety of them, and raise them up in my imagination: though it must be confessed, these creatures of the fancy are not altogether so distinct, so strong, vivid, permanent, as those perceived by my senses, which latter are called *real things*. From all which I conclude, *there is a mind which affects me every moment with all the sensible impressions I perceive*. And from the variety, order and manner of these, I conclude the Author of them to be *wise, powerful, and good beyond comprehension*.' This 'Author' Berkeley a few lines later describes as the deity of revealed religion. The missing step is, accordingly, provided by a familiar argument from theology, the 'argument from design', while ignoring the problems of both moral and natural evil and the world's many imperfections.

It was another philosopher who sought to argue that the existence of these imperfections shows that the world is in fact 'the best possible world there could be', since a perfect world would not be the best world for us. That philosopher is Leibniz.

LEIBNIZ (1646–1716)

Gottfried Wilhelm Leibniz was recognized in his own day, and is regarded still, as a genius. His contributions to mathematics, logic and philosophy are technical in the way that twentieth-century Analytic philosophy is technical. It might be regretted that he was born when he was – in the middle of the seventeenth century, when the conflicts between Protestant and Catholic Christianity had exhausted themselves on the battlefields of Europe after more than a century – because he peace-mindedly felt a need to try to reconcile Christian with Christian and humankind with the deity, devoting time and great mental powers to this unavailing ambition that might have been more fruitfully employed on other things.

Leibniz was born in Leipzig in 1646 into a highly educated family of Lutheran lawyers and academics. His father was a professor of philosophy at Leipzig University, his maternal grandfather was the university's Professor of Law. He was educated at home until matriculating at the university in 1661, aged fifteen. He studied philosophy and mathematics, like everyone else at the time taking the Aristotle-based Scholastic philosophy curriculum.

A summer spent in Jena while an undergraduate brought him into contact with the mathematician Erhard Weigel, who made him interested in the concept of proof as applied to both logic and philosophy. For his habilitation thesis in philosophy he wrote a highly original logical essay, *On the Art of Combinations*, in which he set out the idea of a logical language, a 'universal characteristic', in which all problems could be stated clearly and solved.

Leibniz moved to Altdorf University for his doctorate in law, and was offered a position in its law department, but by that time he had secured a post as secretary to Baron Johann von Boineburg, a Protestant convert to Catholicism who encouraged Leibniz's interest in achieving reconciliation between Catholics and Protestants. Accordingly Leibniz wrote a series of monographs on the various topics of dispute between the confessions. At the same time he maintained his wide and varied interests in science, law and literature (he wrote poetry in Latin), and added to them a scheme for a calculating machine.

Boineburg introduced Leibniz to the Elector of Mainz, in whose service he went to Paris as a diplomat. In this capacity he lived there for four years, coming to know leaders in the world of science and philosophy, among them Nicolas Malebranche, Antoine Arnauld and Christiaan Huygens. The last became his mentor, teaching him more mathematics and physics, and giving him unpublished manuscripts by Descartes and Pascal to read. Leibniz said that it was when reading some of Pascal's work that the ideas for differential calculus and infinite series came to him.

In 1673 Leibniz went to London to present his idea for a calculating machine to the Royal Society. There he met Robert Boyle, Robert Hooke and John Pell. The last told him that his ideas about infinite series had been anticipated by the French cleric-scientist Gabriel Mouton – Leibniz checked, and found that this was right – and Hooke showed him that his calculating machine had flaws. He returned to Paris chastened but determined.

The controversy over who was first to invent calculus, whether Newton or Leibniz, started immediately and has continued since. The truth appears to be that they each devised a version of it independently, though Newton invented his version earlier than Leibniz did, and both delayed publication, though Newton delayed longer than Leibniz. The dispute grew bitter, and cast its shadow over the later part of Leibniz's life because the powerful and influential Royal Society, in somewhat biased fashion it has to be said, decided in favour of Newton and as good as accused Leibniz of plagiarism.

Leibniz's other contributions to mathematics included a binary arithmetic, methods of solving linear equations, treatises on dynamics, and logic as a 'universal algebra'. One positive outcome of the dispute with Newton was that Leibniz had a long and interesting correspondence with Samuel Clarke, a follower of Newton, on space, time, gravitation, free will and other subjects. Leibniz's relativistic conceptions of space and time, for one example, have advantages over Newton's absolutist conceptions of both.

Leibniz became librarian to the court at Hanover, whose duke was heir to the throne of Great Britain. He would therefore have accompanied the Duke to England in 1714 when the latter succeeded Queen Anne, but his reputation in London was bad as a result of the Newton controversy, and he did not do so. He died two years later, leaving behind him an enormous body of unpublished work, an extensive correspondence in German, French and Latin with scholars and scientists across Europe, and – not least among his legacies – the Academy of Berlin, whose founding he had promoted.

Apart from his monographs on matters of religious doctrine, Leibniz wrote only two books: *New Essays on Human Understanding* (completed 1704, first published in 1765) and *Theodicy* (1710). His philosophical work otherwise appears as essays in journals, letters and unpublished manuscripts. Among the most important of the unpublished works were the *Discourse on Metaphysics*, a relatively early work, and the later *Monadology*. His thinking evolved over time, and the complicated editorial task of dating his many unpublished writings has made understanding his development more difficult.

He said of himself (in a letter to a friend written in 1714, two years before his death) that he had learned much from the Aristotelian, Scholastic and Platonic traditions, and had been stimulated by the discovery as a teenager of the 'moderns' (the philosophers and scientists of the seventeenth century) which led to his work in mathematics and mechanics. As with his reconciliatory efforts in religion, he wished to find the truth in all these different perspectives and thereby 'to uncover and unite the truth buried and scattered' among them all.

Among the moderns who influenced him were Descartes and Locke, who prompted his thinking about physical nature, and Hobbes and Spinoza, whose atheism and materialism troubled him, not least in connection with the question of free will and the relation of God to the world. He said his reasoning was based on what he described as 'two great principles': the Principle of Non-Contradiction ('not both A and not-A') and the Principle of 'Sufficient Reason', which can be expressed either as 'there is a reason for everything' or 'every effect has a cause'. The first is a principle of logic, the second is a principle of metaphysics. His work displays commitment to several other principles, however: another logical principle, 'the identity of indiscernibles', a semantic principle stating that all truth is 'analytic', a metaphysical principle stating that nature is a continuum, and a theological principle claiming that everything God does is for the best.

The principle of 'the identity of indiscernibles' says that 'there cannot be two things possessing exactly the same properties yet differing only in number'; that is, if two things have exactly the same properties, they are not two things but one and the same thing. The significance of the principle becomes more apparent when restated thus: no two or more distinct things exactly resemble each other. Note that this is not the same thing as 'the indiscernibility of identicals', which is trivially true: when putatively two things are in fact identical – there are not two things, but just one thing – then the putatively two things cannot, obviously, be told apart. Combining the two principles gives 'Leibniz's Law': x and y are identical if and only if for every property F, x has F if and only if y has F.

The principle of analyticity says that in all true affirmative propositions the concept referred to by the predicate term is already contained in the concept of the thing referred to by the subject term. In later philosophy such propositions were dubbed 'analytic' because their truth-value can be determined solely by analysing the meanings of the subject and predicate terms; an example is 'all bachelors are unmarried men,' or (more obviously) any tautology, such as 'all tall men are tall.' Leibniz's claim about this immediately looks questionable, for it implies that all apparently empirical propositions are not what they seem. Such assertions as 'Paris is the capital of France' or 'rain sometimes falls in Canada,' described in later philosophy as 'synthetic' propositions because they synthesize or join together unrelated concepts in the subject and predicate, would seem to have to turn out to be analysable in such a way that we find that the concept of being the capital of France is already 'contained' in the concept of Paris, or that 'falling in Canada' is somehow already 'contained' in the concept of 'rain'. But in fact Leibniz had a different and deeper account to give of why he made this claim, explained below.

Leibniz's own statement of the principle of continuity is that 'nature never makes leaps'; all change happens continuously through a series of intermediary steps from the starting state to the end state. And his 'principle of the best' says that everything God does is for the best, so childhood cancer, and whole populations being wiped out in earthquakes, is for the best in the light of some greater ultimate plan. This is how Leibniz can claim that this highly imperfect and suffering-filled world can be 'the best of all possible worlds'. Summarily put, the argument is that God is wholly good, so nothing that happens can be without a good eventual purpose; and therefore if there is much that seems bad in the world, it is because bad things are ultimately good for us, and a perfect world would not be the best possible world because it would provide no opportunity for us, with our free will, to choose to act in ways that earn either the reward or the punishment of the deity.

With these theoretical commitments, all but the last of them of great philosophical interest, Leibniz elaborated a striking metaphysical view, intended to answer what he took to be the fundamental philosophical question: What exists? What is there? 'I consider the notion of substance to be one of the keys to the true philosophy,' he wrote, and proceeded to argue throughout his life – though with changes to the detail of the view – that reality ultimately consists in simple substances, individual entities which, coining a term derived from the Greek prefix *mono-* meaning 'one', he called *monads*. Some of the natural philosophers – scientists – of the seventeenth century had coined the term 'corpuscle' meaning 'little body' to denote the tiny components of physical things; by choosing not to call them 'atoms' they were not committing themselves to the ultimacy or indivisibility of these particles. But Leibniz conceived of monads as indeed being foundational to reality as it appears to us.

The theory begins with Leibniz's concept of 'substance'. A substance is a thing that has a 'complete individual concept', that is, is such that the concept of it contains within itself all the things that can be said about it (predicated of it). This is what he meant by claiming that all true propositions are analytic: the predicate concept in every true affirmative proposition is contained in the concept of the subject. The concept of that substance completely 'individuates' that substance, that is, marks it out uniquely from the infinity of other substances. Since everything that can be said of a substance includes all its past, present and future properties, the only mind that can grasp the concept of it is God's mind. The idea of a completely individuating concept is the same as that of the substance's essence, for it is what makes it the unique thing it is.

There is an interesting corollary of this idea, which is that if you consider what God knows of any individual soul, then because that soul will contain the 'marks and traces' of everything that is or will be true of it, together with traces of everything else that has happened everywhere in the universe, God will be able to read off, from viewing that one individual soul, everything there is to say about the universe in its entirety and in all its history.

Leibniz concludes from the principles he set out, together with this doctrine, that no two substances can be completely indistinguishable but distinct (this is the principle of the identity of indiscernibles at work); that substances are indivisible and forever separate as existents; and that each substance is a complete world in itself and 'mirrors' all the other substances from its own unique perspective on them. It is accordingly a mind-like entity, 'simple' in the logical sense of being 'non-complex', and the most fundamental thing there is. These simple substances are the monads.

Monads are not in space; the properties that uniquely distinguish each one from all the others do not include spatial location. The properties that individuate them are 'perceptions', mental states, including the perceptions each has of all the others. These are not conscious perceptions; only 'rational souls' have conscious perceptions, which Leibniz calls 'apperceptions'. Monads can come into existence or leave it only by an act of explicit creation or annihilation by God. And monads are what everything consists of, which means that they are the constituents of bodies; so even a lump of stone is made up of monads, and indeed an infinity of monads. The answer to the question of how non-spatial entities can constitute spatial or spatial-seeming ones turns on the nature of their mutual perceptions; this is an unclear aspect of Leibniz's doctrine, but if it is really a form of idealism in which a spatial material world is a projection from the mental activity and relationships of monads, it could avoid the obvious objection. In his *Principles of Nature and Grace* Leibniz said that everything in nature is 'full of life', meaning thereby that everything is made of monads.

At this juncture a complication enters, which is that it appears that Leibniz came to think that monads contain monads within themselves, that each indeed is an infinity of monads; if so, this controverts the idea that each is a simple substance and an ultimate constituent of the order of being. His account of how the phenomenal world – the world that appears to us – is constituted by things which conform to his elaborate metaphysical picture of substances is confusingly at odds with itself in the different manuscripts and letters in which he set out his views. The clearest version of it is the relatively early one, in the *Discourse on Metaphysics*, in which the universe and all its parts are seen as a continuous 'emanation' from God, who in his omniscience can see every angle and aspect of how the universe can appear. So the monads, as emanations of the deity, are as it were particular instances of these perspectives, each one its own unique viewpoint on everything else.

Leibniz's version of the traditional arguments for God's existence has his stamp on them. He accepts the ontological argument, saying not only that the concept of a perfect being must necessarily be the concept of an existing being, but also that because this being is perfect, it can contain nothing negative within it that contradicts any of its perfections. He uses the 'principle of sufficient reason' to say that contingent things cannot have a ground of existence which is itself contingent, for that would be insufficient for their existence; and therefore they can exist only because there is a necessary being to serve as the sufficient ground for their existence – this being God.

From this deterministic picture of the universe, in which God knows everything even about the future, it is difficult to see how Leibniz could think that human beings have free will. And if they do not, where is there a role for ideas of sin and moral obligation? Yet he both wants and needs humans to have free will, because without that notion it would be impossible to justify God's arrangement of things in the world, most especially the presence of suffering and evil. For the apparent evil in the world to be good, at least part of the reason has to be that it is formative for humans, who can earn their place in bliss by their response to it.

Leibniz's attempt to make room for free will is neither clear nor, as far as it goes, convincing. He says that humans are ignorant of the future, and that is to all intents and purposes – and maybe even logically – the same thing as freedom. This limitation on human capacities goes further than that, of course, for we cannot know even a fraction of all the predicates that apply to anything in the present or past either. Therefore, he implies, ignorance is tantamount to freedom.

He tries a different tack when he says that intelligent beings are not bound by the 'subordinate' laws of the universe – the kind that we describe in talking about how the physical world, as it appears to us, works – and that therefore they can act 'as it were by a private miracle'. This move is not quite without a ground in the context of his views, for if everything is an emanation from the deity – which in different words and from a different approach is what Berkeley thought, and indeed what much theology thinks – then there is a way one could argue that the deity's great miracle is devolved or delegated in tiny ways to some of what emanates from it; though this reintroduces, with added force, the problem that all defenders of theistic viewpoints have to face: making the deity the ultimate author of evil.

So copious was Leibniz's output, so general his genius and so unfinished and still in development were his philosophical views that it is hard to give a neat summary of them. He is like twentieth-century Analytic philosophers in the detail and technicality of his work; unlike them he sought to build a system out of the technical details; he would have needed more time to see if they could be worked out consistently.

HUME (1711–1776)

David Hume wrote of himself, in an autobiographical note he described as a 'funeral oration', as follows: 'I was a man of mild dispositions, of command of temper, of an open, social and cheerful humour, capable of attachment, but little susceptible of enmity, and of great moderation in all my passions. Even my love of literary fame, my ruling passion, never soured my temper, notwithstanding all my frequent disappointments.' This self-portrait is what one would expect from someone who said he wished he had been encouraged to read Cicero rather than the scriptures when young; and it is a self-portrait confirmed as accurate by everything said of him by others.

It is also the self-portrait of the most important philosopher to write in English before the twentieth century. He has been regarded as the chief of the three British empiricists, finishing what Locke and Berkeley before him had attempted in their different ways. Indeed some thought he had 'finished off' by a *reductio ad absurdum* what empiricism attempted as an epistemology, by showing – so they think – that it collapses into scepticism. This, as the following shows, is arguably not what he meant.

Hume was born in Edinburgh, Scotland, to an old but no longer wealthy family, and brought up on the family estate at Ninewells near the border with England. His mother early recognized his genius, so when his elder brother went to study at Edinburgh University she sent him too. He was then aged eleven. He was destined for a career in law, but he found early that he was uninterested in anything other than 'philosophy and general learning'. He left the university aged fifteen without a degree, and devoted himself to private study. The result was threefold. At about the age of eighteen he believed himself to have discovered an important philosophical idea. At the same time he was losing the religious faith that his family – among them an uncle who was a preacher in the Church of Scotland – professed; and he became an atheist. And because his studies were so intense and consequential, he had a nervous breakdown.

Hume's family thought that a change of scene and occupation would benefit him, so they sent him to Bristol in England to work as a clerk in a sugar merchant's office. That remedy failed, so he went to France to recuperate, and remained there for three years. He chose to live at La

Flèche, the site of the famous Jesuit college which had educated Descartes just over a century earlier. He read, debated with Jesuits and wrote his major philosophical work, *A Treatise of Human Nature*.

Hume returned to Britain in 1737 to arrange publication of his book. He had to remove some controversial sections on religious matters – these eventually appeared posthumously in his *Dialogues Concerning Natural Religion* – before the first two volumes could be printed. They appeared anonymously in 1739, the third volume following in 1741. Hume described the book as 'falling stillborn from the press' because no one took any notice of it. In fact some notice was indeed taken; even with the excision of the more controversial passages, those who read it immediately recognized that he was a religious sceptic, and there was 'murmuring among the zealots' as a result.

The disappointment over the reception of his book – for, as we see, where there was not neglect there was disapprobation – was severe. He went to the lengths of anonymously writing a review of it himself. He had hoped the book would secure him an academic post; when he applied for a chair of philosophy at Edinburgh University he was rejected. A job had become a pressing necessity, so he took a post as tutor to a nobleman's son, only to find that the youth was insane. He then became secretary to his cousin General St Clair, accompanying him on diplomatic missions in Italy and Austria.

During these years he rewrote the *Treatise* as two separate volumes, the first covering the epistemological and psychological themes of Books I and II of the *Treatise*, and the second recasting the ethical discussion in Book III. The resulting books are known respectively as *An Enquiry Concerning Human Understanding* (published 1748) and *An Enquiry Concerning the Principles of Morals* (1751). He called this latter 'incomparably the best' of all his books. A collection of essays followed, and the first part of his *History of England*, the resources and leisure for which were provided by a position he had at last secured, as librarian of the Faculty of Advocates in Edinburgh. His *History* appeared in six volumes between 1754 and 1762.

In this latter year he was asked to serve as private secretary to the British Ambassador in Paris, and soon graduated to being secretary to the embassy, and then the chargé d'affaires, deputizing for the Ambassador. He was immensely popular in Parisian circles, earning the sobriquet '*le bon* David' in its salons, as much appreciated for his enjoyment of good food and wine as he was celebrated for his intellectual qualities and conversation. When he returned to Edinburgh he was able to build himself a house in the fashionable and handsome New Town, and there to enjoy the company of both the scholarly and the 'young and careless'. He died of cancer in 1776, facing his demise with equanimity and good cheer, much to the anxious amazement of James Boswell, who hurried to his deathbed to see how the 'great infidel' would face death without the comforts of religion.

Hume had prepared his *Dialogues Concerning Natural Religion* for the press beforehand, and it appeared not long afterwards. He also wrote a notice, 'The Advertisement', for his publisher saying that his *Treatise* was 'juvenile work' and that the two *Enquiries* contained an accurate and complete account of his philosophical views. This judgment has not commanded the assent of subsequent philosophers, for whom the detail, interest and depth of the *Treatise* outstrip the *Enquiries*. When Hume published these latter he wrote to a friend, '*Addo dum minuo* [I add by taking away].' But he had taken away much of the granularity of argument which, in the *Treatise*, constitutes what is valuable in it. For this reason the *Treatise* is regarded as his most important work.

In Books I and II of the *Treatise* and its more accessible version, the first *Enquiry*, Hume begins by addressing the same problems as had exercised Locke and Berkeley, but with important differences. Locke had aimed to give a general theory of knowledge: knowledge is about relations of ideas, and contingent or empirical knowledge is effectively probabilistic. Berkeley had offered a metaphysical answer to the epistemological problem: the nature of reality explains how we know, for the substance of reality is mind, and experience consists in having ideas. Hume saw that their views turned crucially on their respective theories of the nature of mind. He accordingly set himself to state what we would now call a 'philosophical psychology', which he described as a theory of human nature.

His aim in doing this went further than the aims set by Locke and Berkeley. They had wished to explain knowledge and how we get it; Hume's aim was to explain how a discussion of these same questions tells us something of great importance about the principles of ethics, which is the topic of Book III of the *Treatise* and the second *Enquiry*.

Hume's advancement of the debate beyond the problem of knowledge itself was made possible by the historical setting in which he lived, namely, the Enlightenment. For the entire period between late antiquity and early modern times – which began in the period between the six-teenth and eighteenth centuries, the latter being the century of the Enlightenment's major flowering – there had been little discussion of ethics outside Christian moral theology, and scarcely any discussion of the underlying principles of ethics. Moral discussion was restricted to interpretation of scripture and Church teaching, and any divergence from orthodox doctrine on these matters was for a long time heavily punished. But the beginning of modern times saw a return to the kind of debate about ethical principles that had flourished in antiquity. The chief reason was the loss of religious authority over what it was permis-sible to think and discuss, which meant that the moral sceptic's question, 'Why should I act in this rather than that way?' could again be addressed.

The answer for the Christian moralist is 'Because God says so', and the answer carries the implication of sanctions: reward for obedience, punishment for disobedience. But neither the fact that someone says, 'Do this,' nor the offer of reward or threat of punishment to back up the command, is a reason for obeying it. It might be *prudent* to obey, if the person issuing the order is powerful enough to carry out the threat. But the mere fact of a command, or of promises or threats, is not a logi-cally compelling reason to obey. So whatever is the basis of morality, it cannot be someone's will, even that of a deity.

This is what prompted Hume's question about 'the general foun-dation of Morals, whether they be derived from Reason, or from Sentiment; whether we attain the knowledge of them by a chain of argument and induction, or by an immediate feeling and finer internal sense; whether, like all sound judgement of truth and falsehood, they should be the same to every rational intelligent being; or whether, like the perception of beauty and deformity, they be founded entirely on the particular fabric and constitution of the human species.' His answer, based on his investigation of the nature of mind, experience and know-ledge, is that the 'general foundation of Morals' lies in *sentiment*. The linked points that raised opposition to him were his denial that it is either reason or the will of a deity that provides the foundation of morality. More on this below.

Hume's key claim in the theory that underlies his conclusion about morality is that an investigation of 'the operations of the understand-ing' – that is, of how the mind works – shows that our fundamental beliefs about the world, about ourselves and about morality rest not on reason but on the way our human nature is constituted. Hence the title of his major work, *A Treatise of Human Nature*. His argument for this view is as follows.

First, Hume describes his method as 'anatomising human nature in a regular manner, drawing no conclusions but what are authorised by experience'. So he is engaging in an empirical examination of the way our minds and sentiments work. He saw himself as doing for 'moral philosophy' what Newton had done for 'natural philosophy'; Newton had stated a principle, the principle of gravitation, which explains much about the way the universe works. Hume offers a principle – the principle of the 'association of ideas' – which is the corresponding explanatory principle for the workings of human nature, because in his view it explains experience, belief, causation, induction, our concept of the self and the limits of reason.

Starting absolutely from scratch, with austere reliance only on what we experience in consciousness, and making no assumptions about an external world or anything else, we can note, says Hume, that all our perceptions are of two kinds: *impressions* and *ideas*. They differ only in their degree of vivacity or liveliness: impressions are more vivid than ideas; the latter are faint copies of impressions. There are simple and complex impressions, and simple and complex ideas. Simple ideas are direct copies of simple impressions, but complex ideas can be built by the power of imagination out of many different simple impressions and other ideas: Hume says he can imagine a city 'with streets of gold and walls of rubies. Though I never saw any such.'

Note the important claim that ideas are *copies* of impressions; one never has an idea that was not first an impression. Obviously, an 'impression' (something *pressed on*) is what we normally think of as caused by the external world pressing on our sense organs, or by the pressure of an inner feeling in consciousness; but because we do not yet have a ground for thinking that there is an external world, we cannot speak this way: we must limit ourselves just to the experiences them-selves. So we note that ideas are fainter copies of impressions which precede them; and we can say that we are not entitled to think any idea is valid unless it arises from a preceding impression. This is the empiri-cist constraint.

A second vital point for Hume is that every simple impression is *atomic*; there are no logical or necessary connections between impres-sions; they are independent and self-standing. Yet the simple ideas which arise from these impressions combine together in orderly ways as

if there were 'some bond of union among them, some associating quality, by which one idea naturally introduces another'. This associating
quality 'is a gentle force, which commonly prevails ... nature in a
manner pointing out to every one those simple ideas, which are most
proper to be united in a complex one'.

There are three kinds of associating relation between ideas:
resemblance – if ideas are similar, they will connect; *contiguity in place
and time* – if ideas often occur together, the mind will run from one to
the other naturally; and *cause and effect*. Of the three, this last is by
far the most important. Association also explains belief: to believe
something – call the idea of it 'x' – is for x to be before one's mind with
more 'force and vivacity' than if one did not believe it, as when one is
just thinking about it neutrally. A standard way for this to happen,
Hume says, is when a present impression associated with x, or from
which x derives, imparts some of its force and vivacity to the idea of x.

The more that ideas are associated together, the more our minds
form habits of running from one to the other. This explains our belief
in there being a *necessary connection* between causes and their effects;
we think that the cause 'makes' the effect occur, but if we look for an
originating impression of the idea of 'causal necessity' we do not find
one in the conjunction between the cause event and the effect event.
Instead we find it in the *habit* we have formed of going from the idea
of the cause to the idea of the effect. We feel an impulse to move from
the idea of the cause to that of the effect, and we project this felt neces-
sitation on to the world. It is therefore the way our minds are built that
makes us think as we do about causality. And this applies also to our
belief that there is a world existing independently of our experience:
we simply cannot help believing it. And it applies to our belief in the
reliability of inductive inference, which in large part rests on the belief
that the future will resemble the past. We are just built to think these
ways. There are no philosophical proofs of these points; we cannot
establish them by reason.

It is consistent with this view that Hume's contribution to the debate
started by Locke about the self and self-identity is to say that the idea of
the 'self' is a mere convenience; there is in fact no such thing other than
the word we use to denote what we imagine to be a single enduring
entity. His reason is that there is no originating impression one can find
by 'looking within' for the 'self'; all one will find on introspection is a
bundle of impressions and ideas that happen to be occurring together at

that moment, and which is continually changing. We think of these mutable bundles as a persisting self because the associations between the ideas constituting them lead us to interpret them in that way, just as the constitution of our minds leads us to believe, without option, in an external world and causality. Hume's theories of belief and habits of mind based on the theory of the association of ideas yields the same result here as with the other topics.

Hume concluded that once we understand the way our minds function, and how this solves the traditional epistemological, metaphysical and ethical questions of philosophy, we will agree with him on an important point. This is that our minds engage in two general kinds of activity: comparing ideas, and inferring matters of fact. Relations between ideas are grasped either by intuition, as when one sees that $1 + 1 = 2$, or by 'demonstration', as when we work out a mathematical proof. So questions about 'relations of ideas' are primarily confined to the arenas of mathematics or logic. 'Matters of fact' are discovered by empirical observation and causal reasoning, and relate to how things are in the world. This distinction between 'relations of ideas' and 'matters of fact' led Hume to make a famous remark: 'When we run over libraries, persuaded of these principles, what havoc must we make? If we take in our hand any volume: of divinity or school metaphysics, for instance; let us ask, *Does it contain any abstract reasoning concerning quantity or number?* No. *Does it contain any experimental reasoning concerning matter of fact and existence?* No. Commit it then to the flames, for it can contain nothing but sophistry and illusion.' This view was a powerful influence on the Positivists and Analytic philosophy in general in the twentieth century.

It follows from the claim that there are no philosophical proofs of our fundamental beliefs about causality and the independent existence of the world that this applies to moral judgments also. Here Hume's conclusion is that there are no objective moral facts 'out there' that we perceive and respond to; instead we project our sentiments on to the world. This species of view is known as subjectivism or, in its eighteenth-century version, 'sentimentalism'. It says that what we regard as good and bad are, respectively, what we approve and what we dislike.

Hume's moral theory occupies a position in the debate about the basis of morality which, as noted, emerged from the weakening of religious control over moral thinking. In the absence of any ground for morality in supposed commands issued by a deity, Thomas Hobbes, and on similar grounds Bernard Mandeville (in his *The Fable of the Bees*, 1714), had argued that self-interest is what governs people's actions, and that good behaviour rests on a calculation about the personal benefit that would accrue from it (and likewise the harm to self that might result from bad behaviour). There were two responses to this. One is the 'rationalist' view, then often associated with religion, saying that reason shows us how we must act. The other is that the springs of morality lie in human feelings of benevolence and sympathy; this is sentimentalism, and the view that Hume adopted.

Hume's chief objection to rationalist morality is that having a reason is not by itself enough to motivate action. Only emotion can do this. There is a reason for me to learn another language, but unless I desire or feel a need to do so I will not do it. Reason's function is not to prompt but to guide, once prompting has happened; it can tell me how to achieve a goal once I am motivated to achieve it. 'Reason is, and ought only to be, the slave of the passions and can never pretend to any other office than to serve and obey them,' Hume wrote. The question that therefore must be asked is whether 'we attain the knowledge of [moral principles] by a chain of argument and induction, or by an immediate feeling and inner finer sense; whether, like all sound judgement of truth and falsehood, they should be the same to every rational intelligent being, or whether, like the perception of beauty and deformity, they be founded entirely on the fabric of the human species'.

Hume agreed with the view that people have an innate moral sense which determines what counts as good and bad. Two of the proponents of such a view were the third Earl of Shaftesbury and Francis Hutcheson, both of whom Hume quotes in his *Enquiry*, saying of the latter that 'he has taught us, by the most convincing arguments, that morality is nothing in the abstract nature of things, but is entirely relative to the sentiment or mental taste of each particular being; in the same manner as the distinctions of sweet and bitter, hot and cold, arise from the particular feeling of each sense or organ.' Endorsing this view summarizes Hume's own conviction, that 'Moral perceptions, therefore, ought not to be classed with the operations of the understanding, but with the tastes or sentiments.'

Hume's classic statement of this moral subjectivist theory occurs in the *Treatise* as follows: 'Take any action allowed to be vicious: wilful murder, for instance. Examine it in all its lights, and see if you can find that matter of fact, or real existence, which you would call *vice* . . . You can never find it, till you turn your reflection to your own breast, and find a sentiment of disapprobation, which arises in you, toward this action. Here is a matter of fact: but it is the object of feeling, not reason.' The key notion here is that of a 'matter of fact, or real existence', by which Hume means something objectively in the world, which therefore exists independently of human sentiments. Put in these terms, Hume's claim is that morality is not something objectively in the world, existing independently of anyone's private choices and preferences, but is a product of these latter. The claim that there are no objective moral facts is, says Hume, a chief reason for rejecting rationalism. This supplements his other argument that, even if there were indeed objective moral facts, the mere recognition of them would never motivate anyone to act one way rather than another because action can be prompted only by emotion. He put this point in a way that has since produced much philosophical debate, saying that you cannot derive a prescription from a description – that is, you cannot derive a statement telling you what you ought to do from a statement describing some aspect of the world (as it is sometimes put: you cannot get an 'ought' conclusion from an 'is' premise).

One objection typically urged against subjectivism is that it makes moral judgment an arbitrary matter, dependent upon the whim of the individual, whose subjective responses might vary widely from those of others. But Hume thought that human nature is generally the same everywhere for everyone, and that it is fundamentally benevolent. This optimistic view means that there will be wide agreement in moral responses, just as there is in judgments of beauty. Of course he acknowledged that differences of opinion arise in both the ethical and the aesthetic spheres, but he explained them by claiming that one or some of the parties to the disagreement must either be insufficiently well informed, or confused, or deficient in their moral sense. Comparing moral sense to skill in literary criticism, Hume argued that we can refine our abilities as judges, and grow more competent – provided that we avoid what he called 'the illusions of religious superstition and philosophical enthusiasm'.

For Hume, our moral judgments are principally directed at the virtues and vices of the human character. In his view there are two kinds of virtues, the natural and the 'artificial', the latter in the sense of being dependent on social conventions. Artificial virtues consist in conformity to socially adopted norms, and include justice, chastity and the observance of various kinds of duty, for example adhering to laws and agreements. Whereas the artificial virtues depend on the conventions that specify their content, the natural virtues are found widely diffused among human beings because, as their label implies, they are part of the innate human endowment. They include friendship, faithfulness, generosity, courage, mercy, fairness, patience, good humour, perseverance, prudence and kindness; and Hume saw them as also including the sociable virtues of good nature, cleanliness, decorum and being 'agreeable and handsome' enough as to 'render a person lovely or loveable'.

These last 'virtues' invite criticism, on the grounds that they do not depend on an individual's will. One cannot choose to be or not to be handsome, and it might even lie outside one's power to be charming, witty and generally good company. How then, asks the critic, can these be virtues? Nevertheless it is clear what Hume intended: he was thinking of fellowship and the pleasures of society as counting among the chief goods for mankind, and saw it as a virtue if an individual possessed – and perhaps cultivated – the required characteristics. One might not be able to will oneself into being handsome, Hume might say, but one can endeavour to be, and succeed in being, presentable and clean.

Hume significantly remarked, in a letter to Francis Hutcheson, that his favourite author on morality was Cicero. In the same letter he recalled being made to study, when a boy, a Protestant tract called *The Whole Duty of Man*, a staple for schoolchildren of his day; and he told Hutcheson that even then he rejected its outlook. The contrast between the Ciceronian and Christian views taught him that virtues are what bring pleasure to their possessors and to others, or are genuinely useful in the promotion of good fellowship, whereas 'celibacy, fasting, penance, mortification, self denial, humility, silence, solitude, and the whole train of monkish virtues' are, he said, horrible: 'they stupefy the understanding and harden the heart, obscure the fancy and sour the temper.'

From this and his list of virtues one readily grasps Hume's conception of the good life. It was an outlook whose development began early; in a letter written at the age of twenty-three he said, '[I] read many books of morality, such as Cicero, Seneca and Plutarch, and being smit with their beautiful representations of virtue and philosophy,

I undertook the improvement of my temper and will, along with my reason and understanding. I was continually fortifying myself with reflections against death, and poverty, and shame, and all the other calamities of life.' The Stoicism which forms part of this early view did not survive whole into Hume's mature work; its self-denying, self-disciplining aspects yielded to a more cheerful allegiance to the sociable virtues. And Hume practised what he preached, well meriting that sobriquet '*le bon* David'.

In common with other thinkers of the Enlightenment Hume was adamant that philosophy – here in the generalized sense of enquiry and reflection – belonged to the world at large, and not to the academy or the scholar's study alone. The 'great defect of the last age', he wrote, thinking of the age of the Scholastic philosophers, which the Renaissance had brought to an end, was that it separated 'the learned from the conversable world'; the latter had lost much as a result, while the learned 'had been as great a loser by being shut up in colleges and cells'. The result had been that philosophy had become 'as chimerical in its conclusions as she was unintelligible in her style and manner of delivery'. The reason for this was that the scholars had lost touch with the world; they 'never consulted experience in any of their reasonings, [nor] searched for that experience, where alone it is found, in common life and conversation'. But Hume rejoiced that in his own day men of letters and men of the world were conversing together again – among other things reprising debate about the good life, as had once been done under the shade of the olive trees in ancient Athens.

ROUSSEAU (1712–1778)

Those who think that the personal lives of thinkers are irrelevant to an assessment of their work can cite in their support the example of Jean-Jacques Rousseau. This is because there are respects in which Rousseau's behaviour was at times dramatically inconsistent with his professed views. For example, in *Emile, or On Education* he advances a theory of education which displays much sympathy with a child's viewpoint, beginning with criticism of the practice of wrapping babies tightly in swaddling clothes instead of letting them move freely, and criticizing even more severely the practice of mothers delegating their babies to wet-nurses. Yet the moment each of his own five children was born he left it on the doorstep of the Foundling Hospital in Paris. Again, he was eloquent in arguing for natural and open human relationships, yet behaved with paranoid suspicion of people who tried to help him – a frequent circumstance, given that his life was often a troubled one.

Rousseau was born in Geneva and always felt proud of being a Genevan citizen. His mother died mere days after his birth, and when he was aged ten his father, a watchmaker, left him and his brother to be cared for by an uncle. He subsequently worked as a servant and a secretary in various parts of France and Italy, and for a time enjoyed the patronage of a Savoyard noblewoman, Françoise-Louise de Warens, who helped him to get an education and, when he was aged twenty, took him as her lover. He learned musical performance and composition while in her household; later he had some success as a composer.

Madame de Warens arranged for Rousseau to serve on the staff of the French Ambassador to Venice, but he disliked the work and went instead to Paris. Not long before going there he had unsuccessfully submitted an innovative scheme of musical notation to its Académie des Sciences. On arriving in Paris his career began in earnest. He met Thérèse Levasseur, thereafter his lifelong companion and mother of the children he gave up for adoption. And he met Denis Diderot, chief editor of the Enlightenment's great endeavour the *Encyclopédie*. They became friends, engaging in eager daily conversations. Diderot introduced him to the intellectual world of Paris, and Rousseau wrote several articles on music for the *Encyclopédie*. This led to further commissions for that work, among them the article which launched Rousseau's reputation, the entry on political economy.

His reputation was most fully made, however, by the prize essay he wrote for the Académie de Dijon, on the question whether the arts and sciences had contributed to the moral improvement of mankind. Rousseau's answer, contrary to the founding premise of the *Encyclopédie* and the Enlightenment it championed, was 'No'. An admiring King Louis XV offered him a pension as a reward for the essay; Rousseau turned it down.

In 1754 Rousseau returned to Geneva and began to write the series of works on which his subsequent fame rests. The first was the *Discourse on Inequality*, a development of his Dijon essay. In it, following the lead of Hobbes and Locke, he premises the idea of a state of nature and argues that property is the source of social and economic inequality: 'The first person who, having enclosed a plot of land, took it into his head to say this is mine and found people simple enough to believe him, was the true founder of civil society.' His theory of human nature turns on the idea that 'natural man' is benignly interested in his own welfare, is naturally compassionate and requires only 'food, a woman and sleep' to be happy. Although he did not coin the phrase 'the noble savage', it captures his view of the 'uncorrupted morals' of people in the state of nature, whom he regarded as occupying the high point in human development between the brutish nature of animals and the decadent nature of 'civilized' humanity.

The book that made Rousseau celebrated and admired throughout Europe was his novel *Julie, ou La Nouvelle Héloïse*, presented as a series of letters between two lovers living in the exquisite natural beauty of the Alpine landscape. It was published in 1761. As the subtitle suggests, its model was the correspondence between the medieval lovers Abelard and Héloïse. It was a tremendous bestseller, and prompted a storm of emotion among its readers, who wrote of weeping and sobbing, sighing and suffering seizures, especially over the profoundly poignant death of the heroine Julie at the end. It gave the eighteenth century's cult of 'sensibility' a major boost, and did the same for the budding tourism industry of the Alpine region.

In 1762 Rousseau published *The Social Contract* and *Emile, or On Education*. The first opens with the famous line, 'Man is born free, and everywhere he is in chains.' The second contains a section entitled 'The Profession of a Savoyard Vicar', which sets out a Unitarian defence of religious belief, contrary to the Trinitarian theologies of both the Catholic and major Protestant confessions. (Unitarianism holds that God is a single person and that Jesus was not God but man; Catholic and most Protestant theologies hold that God is 'three persons in one': Father, Son and Holy Ghost.) This would by itself have been enough to get him into trouble, but he added the view that all religions are equally meritorious, and that there is no such thing as original sin or divine revelation.

The idea of what is 'natural' to human nature underlay his theory of education. He argued in *Emile* that the stages of education for a child should mirror the stages of human history, beginning with the unfettered natural state in early childhood, and proceeding with gradual entry into the economic and social relations of life.

These two books provoked much controversy. They represented a turning away from the materialism and empiricism of such Enlightenment thinkers as Diderot, d'Alembert and d'Holbach, who therefore took issue with Rousseau; he and Diderot ceased to be friends. Theologians, and the temporal authorities who supported the theologians, were even more incensed. His books were banned in consequence, and so was he; neither the French nor Swiss authorities would allow him residence in their countries. Voltaire offered to shelter him, and so did Frederick the Great of Prussia, who on the basis of *Julie* and *Emile* said of him, 'I think poor Rousseau has missed his vocation; he should have been a hermit, a desert father, celebrated for his austerities and flagellations.' And he added, 'I conclude that the morals of [Rousseau] are as pure as his mind is illogical.'

Instead Rousseau accepted an invitation from David Hume to go to England. To begin with he was courted as a celebrity there, but when opinion turned against him, and his propensity to paranoia had been inflamed by a prank played on him by Horace Walpole, a public quarrel broke out, and he and Thérèse left England precipitately.

In his later years Rousseau dedicated himself to botany, and to writing self-justifications and defences, including his famous *Confessions*, the first autobiography of its kind. He died following a stroke in the summer of 1778, aged sixty-six, leaving incomplete his last work, *Daydreams of a Solitary Walker*, in which he said that even though he felt like an outcast from society, he had nevertheless found 'serenity, tranquillity, peace, even happiness'.

Rousseau's chief contribution to philosophy is his political theory. The principal text in which it is set out is *The Social Contract*, though the discourses *On the Origins of Inequality* and *On Political Economy*, among others, amplify and clarify its doctrines.

In *The Social Contract* Rousseau sets himself to offer a resolution to a problem that he had described at the end of the *Discourse on Inequality*. There he said that the result of humanity's emergence from the state of nature is an unavoidable but inequality-fostering dependence of people on each other because they are no longer able to meet their own needs. This threatens instability and conflict, which drives people to establish an authority to keep the peace between them. But this authority merely institutionalizes and reinforces the inequality that mutual dependency has prompted, giving it the force of law. Such an arrangement would favour those with wealth and power, exposing the poor and powerless thereby to exploitation. In the *Social Contract* Rousseau sought to outline a way that the benefits of social life might be enjoyed consistently with individual freedom for all. The key concept in his argument to this end is 'the general will'.

What Rousseau meant by 'the general will' is unclear, and is open to being understood in very different ways. The two most common interpretations are, first, that the general will is 'the will of the people' as this is understood in the democratic sense of a consensus of everyone agreeing together. The second is a more abstract notion, something like a transcendently conceived common purpose or interest that exists apart from the actual preferences of any given individual. Both interpretations can be backed by what Rousseau writes, though his text seems to favour the second: 'There is often a great deal of difference between the will of all and the general will. The latter looks only to the common interest, the former considers private interest and is only a sum of private wills. But take away from these same wills the pluses and minuses that cancel each other out, and the remaining sum of the differences is the general will.'

Both interpretations of 'the general will' are consistent with the further view that it is an idealization and, as such, an ideal that no state actually embodies – which has the consequence, if this is what Rousseau meant, that no state has true political legitimacy.

Whether or not this is an implication, Rousseau conceives of 'the general will' as always being directed at the good of each and of all together, which means that it can never be in conflict with the good of any individual. It is this that offers a means of reconciling the existence of the state with freedom as a social and political value. The legitimate state is one that embodies the general will, therefore to be free is to be obedient to the general will. Rousseau talks of the demand to obey the general will as being 'forced to be free'. The appearance of paradox in this idea is reduced when one notes that he contrasts the kind of freedom experienced in the state of nature – 'natural freedom' – with the kind one enjoys in a legitimate state – 'civil freedom'. The former is complete licence to do as I wish, but that means that I am vulnerable to being the prey of others' licence to do me harm. By contrast, in 'civil freedom' I am protected by laws that express the general will, and I am therefore secure in my life and property.

An idea that anticipates Kant's views is Rousseau's claim that in civil society people have 'moral freedom' because they subject themselves to moral laws that they have imposed on themselves. The introduction of this idea adds yet another kind of freedom to the repertoire of freedoms

Rousseau identifies; but one possibility is that the idea of civil freedom as obedience to the general will is close to the idea of moral autonomy in the sense that one's participation in willing the general will in effect makes one a legislator of the laws – including moral laws – under which one lives.

Perhaps it is relevant to adduce the perspective on the question of freedom provided by the discourse of the 'Savoyard Vicar' in Rousseau's *Emile*. The vicar in that tale, having been defrocked as a result of a sexual scandal, and finding himself in a bleak state of personal crisis afterwards, undertakes a Descartes-like review of all his beliefs to see if he knows anything with certainty. One thing he finds himself to be certain of is that he is a free-willed being, not subject to the physical laws of causality but at complete liberty to choose and act as he wills. If we take this conception of freedom to be what Rousseau meant in the *Social Contract* where freedom consists in obeying the general will, then the implication is that the general will is something that, whether consciously or not, the individual indeed wills. As with the idea of 'moral freedom' the act of obeying the general will is therefore an act of autonomy.

Rousseau disliked both the ideas of what might now be called 'representative democracy' with an elected legislature, and the more Hobbesian idea of a sovereign individual or body elected or appointed by the people. He thought that such arrangements involved an alienation of one's self-rule, and thus a form of slavery. His view invites the problem that most societies are too numerous to be able to govern themselves by assembly in the equivalent of the Greek *agora*, so it seems impracticable. Some commentators suggest Rousseau meant to distinguish between the *sovereign* in a state and the *government* of the state, where the latter is the body that carries out the will of the former. So, the people is sovereign, and the administrators of their will do not have power over them, but obey them.

Rousseau was however a pessimist about politics; with some justification he surmised that governments would soon enough come to exercise power over the people rather than being subject to them. That justification is provided by history, including the history of the representative democracies that have come into existence since his time.

In his views of religion, as expressed both in *Emile* and in the *Social Contract*, Rousseau enraged his contemporaries, but an aspect of them was the need for toleration, and the promotion of a 'civic religion' which, by promoting belief in a deity and an afterlife in which reward and punishment are due, would help ensure that people behave well. He had a conventional view of women; they are helpmeets to men, and must be submissive to them. Men do not need women, he says in *Emile*, but they desire them, whereas women both desire and need men. He adds that women are cleverer and more practical than men; their inferior status seems to be justified by their being physically weaker than men.

As this last thought prompts one to think, the opinion of Rousseau held by Frederick the Great of Prussia seems, if on the generous side, about right.

KANT (1724–1804)

Here is a claim that few who are knowledgeable about philosophy would dispute: that the three greatest figures in the history of Western philosophy are Plato, Aristotle and Kant. Other figures have high importance in the story, not least because of the influence they exerted on those who came after them; but there can be little disagreement with the claim that these three names stand above the rest. What marks them out is their intellectual power, their penetration into the deepest parts of difficult questions, and the scope of their contributions. Each created new concepts and vocabularies for exploring the fundamental questions of metaphysics, epistemology and ethics, to say nothing of psychology and social and political theory. Each of them thereby changed and enriched the way humankind thinks.

If Immanuel Kant had died at the age of fifty it is possible we would never have heard of him. In the image of the Chinese saying, 'The orchid fears the singing of the tailor-bird, but the chrysanthemum survives the frosts of autumn,' he is a chrysanthemum, a late blossomer. (Orchids bloom in spring, and by the time the tailor-bird's song heralds the onset of summer on China's northern plains, their time is over; but the chrysanthemum endures.) Indeed most things came late to Kant; he did not have a salaried academic post until the age of forty-six. It was in the years after this, when he was at last able to give up lecturing for fees dependent on the students he could attract – which meant lecturing on a wide range of subjects interesting enough to get customers – that he could focus on writing his great works: the *Critique of Pure Reason*

(1781), the *Prolegomena to Any Future Metaphysics* (1783), the *Groundwork of the Metaphysics of Morals* (1785), the *Critique of Practical Reason* (1788) and the *Critique of Judgment* (1790).

For a short period after the first *Critique* was published no one seemed to take notice of it, because it is a challenging work, and effort was required for its significance and implications to be understood. It seemed that the complexity of his views, his convoluted – indeed, poor – literary style and the new terminology he invented to convey his ideas would be a permanent barrier to appreciation of his work. But then the *Critique of Pure Reason* was understood: and Kant became famous. There have been philosophical celebrities from time to time (think Bertrand Russell and Jean-Paul Sartre for more recent examples), but Kant was a phenomenon among them. The number of visitors to his house became such a nuisance that he limited himself to appearing at his study door for a few moments each day to greet them with a wave before retiring into privacy again, like royalty. One day a visitor, a certain Professor Reuss, having been denied admittance by the servant, forced his way into Kant's study exclaiming, 'I have travelled one hundred and sixty miles to see and speak with Professor Kant!' – nearly a week's hard journey in those days. Soon Kant's ideas were being taught in most German universities, and most philosophy professors in them were Kantians.

Kant's reputation travelled beyond the borders of Germany – the poet Coleridge went to Germany on purpose to learn about 'the Critical philosophy' – but comprehension of his views took longer. It was not until G. H. Lewes' *Biographical History of Philosophy* (1846) that an intelligent appreciation of Kant appeared in English. In fact Kant's first translator into English was a Scottish teenager called John Meikeljohn, a prodigy at languages but nowhere near equipped to render the *Critique* into something intelligible. His practically unintelligible version was published in 1855. When at last a good translation was effected by Norman Kemp-Smith in 1929 – for a long time afterwards it was the standard English text – it was (relatively speaking) so clear that German students used it rather than reading the original.

Kant was born in Königsberg in East Prussia in 1724. His family was of Scottish ancestry, an interesting point given Kant's remark that what 'first interrupted my dogmatic slumber' was reading Hume's *Enquiry Concerning Human Understanding*. His father was a saddler, and both his parents were members of the Pietists, an inward-looking Protestant sect. He was educated at the Collegium Fridericianum before entering the University of Königsberg, where he read philosophy, physics, mathematics and theology. He supported himself with private tutoring while a student and for many years afterwards, among other things lecturing to military officers on the science of fortification. He also became a *Privatdozent* at the university – an unsalaried teacher dependent on the fees that individual students paid if they took the courses he offered. He was at times so poor that he had to sell his books to pay his rent.

Kant was polymathic, not only lecturing on a wide array of subjects from mathematics to astronomy via physics, geography, psychology, anthropology, natural law and philosophy, but contributing to them: in astronomy he anticipated the discovery of the planet Uranus, as Sir John Herschel acknowledged, and he figures in the Kant–Laplace theory of the origins of the universe, based on an application of Newton's principles.

As the remark about Kant's ancestry implies, Königsberg was a city with extensive trading relationships through the Baltic and beyond. It was a city of many nationalities, among them a resident British community. Two of Kant's closest friends were English businessmen, J. Green and R. Motherby. They represented a cosmopolitan tradition in Königsberg that stretched back several centuries, as evidenced by the fact that English theatre companies were touring there and elsewhere in Prussia, Poland and the Baltic states in Shakespeare's day.

Kant knew English, French and the classical tongues, and read widely in them all. He was famously a bachelor of regular habits, starting his walk so precisely at 4 p.m. every day that his fellow-citizens said he was a more accurate timekeeper than the cathedral clock. Only once did he break his routine before being compelled to do so by old age; it was when he received his copy of Rousseau's *Emile* and could not put it down. There was just one picture hanging on a wall in his house: a portrait of Rousseau. His other intellectual heroes were the ancient authors Horace and Virgil and the moderns Milton, Pope and Hume.

In the time of his celebrity he was offered professorships at other universities, but he did not wish to leave Königsberg. Indeed he never left it. He said that because the world came to Königsberg he could travel without leaving home. In the last few years of his life, after the strenuous intellectual labours of the period in which he wrote his major philosophical works, he became mentally and physically frail. He was so thin that he found it painful to sit because no flesh insulated his bones from the chair. He was nearly eighty years of age when he died, attended to the last by his faithful servant Martin Lampe.*

The argument of the *Critique of Pure Reason* is fundamental to Kant's mature philosophical outlook, and to understand it one must recognize, first, that the word 'metaphysics' as used by Kant refers to what we now call 'philosophy' (in his day 'philosophy' mainly meant what we now call 'science'), and second, that central to philosophy as then conceived was epistemology, the question of how and what we know. More accurately: the central concern of philosophy as Kant saw it – and indeed as it saw itself in the tradition of Descartes, Leibniz, Locke, Berkeley and Hume, these being the philosophers Kant explicitly cites – was epistemology linked to the question of what exists, given that knowledge is 'knowledge of or about' something, so it is important to be clear about the nature of the 'something' which is the object of knowledge. In today's parlance, questions about what exists (either in general or in some domain) are labelled 'metaphysical' or 'ontological', and therefore Kant's eighteenth-century use of the term 'metaphysics' might mislead an unwary reader into thinking it is about 'what exists', thereby not recognizing that his fundamental question was, instead, 'what, and how, and how much, do we know?' We would accordingly now describe the subject matter of the *Critique of Pure Reason* as 'epistemology with some metaphysics attached'.

Keeping this in mind, we can identify Kant's aim. Recall the conflict of opinion between empiricists and rationalists in epistemology, the former arguing that the origin of knowledge lies in sensory experience, the latter arguing that reason is the only sure path to knowledge. In the technical terminology of philosophy, knowledge derived from experience is called *a posteriori* knowledge, implying 'after experience', while knowledge derived from reason is called *a priori* knowledge, literally meaning 'before experience' but understood as meaning 'independently of experience'. From Plato onwards the rationalist ambition to arrive at certain

---

* There is a touching essay about Kant's decline and death by Thomas De Quincey entitled 'The Last Days of Kant', drawn from the memoir by Kant's friend Ehregott Wasianski and his long-standing servant Martin Lampe. De Quincey's essay was published in 1827, showing how famous Kant was; De Quincey begins, 'I take it for granted that every person of education will acknowledge some interest in the personal history of Immanuel Kant. A great man, though in an unpopular path, must always be an object of liberal curiosity. To suppose a reader thoroughly indifferent to Kant, is to suppose him thoroughly unintellectual.'

knowledge by *a priori* methods of reasoning, that is, by excogitation and inference, had been opposed by the empiricist claim that genuine knowledge of the world can be secured only by *a posteriori* methods of observation and experiment.

Mathematics was cited by rationalists as a paradigm of *a priori* knowledge, while empiricists in the two centuries before Kant could point to the scientific advances made possible by *a posteriori* investigation. As noted in connection with Locke, it was a typical rationalist move to hold that the basis of knowledge lies in innate ideas or principles, while empiricists argued (as Locke himself did) that the mind is a blank slate on which experience writes.* Kant was struck by Hume's claim that we believe in the existence of a necessary connection between a cause and its effect not because we empirically observe such a thing, nor because we can derive by *a priori* reasoning that there has to be such a thing, but *because of the way our minds work*. Hume argued that we form mental habits of connecting ideas together in such a way that the impression or idea of x makes the mind pass to the idea of y so regularly, with such a feeling of inevitability, that we project that feeling of inevitability on to the relationship between the ideas of x and y, giving rise in us to the further idea of a necessary connection between them – and by projection therefore a necessary connection between regularly conjoined pairs of events in the world. What struck Kant was Hume's notion of 'the way our minds work' as explaining the idea of causality – and not just causality and the related matter of inductive inference, but also our belief that a world exists independently of our experience, and that each of us is an enduring self.

This idea of 'the way our minds work' was the insight that prompted Kant to develop a theory of knowledge that reconciles the rationalist and empiricist approaches. In essence his view is that our minds handle the incoming data of sensory experience in such a way as to organize and interpret that data to make the world seem as it does. It does this by imposing an apparatus of *a priori* concepts upon the data, the resulting marriage of data and concepts thus constituting the world of experience. To take a homely example: think of making cookies. Flour and water are mixed then rolled out into a flat formless shape, on to

---

* Locke himself began by invoking the metaphor of a blank slate, but had to modify it to acknowledge that we have innate capacities for processing experience – comparing, remembering, inferring, and the like.

which pastry-cutters are pressed to make such various figures as circles and stars. Analogously, the faculty of mind which processes incoming sensory data – the data of vision, hearing and the rest – acts like a set of pastry-cutters, imposing order and structure on the raw basic data. The faculty of mind that has this organizing function is called by Kant 'the understanding', and he describes it as consisting in a set of highly general concepts which it applies to the incoming data of sense and, by organizing it, thereby creating experience. He used the word 'intuition' in its original meaning of 'sense-experience' to denote the incoming sense-data. It is the marriage between the *concepts* of the understanding and the *intuitions* delivered by the senses which generates experience. The experience thus generated is 'experience of the world *as it seems to us*' – the *phenomenal* ('apparent') world. The concepts of the understanding are the *a priori* aspect of knowledge, the incoming intuitions are the *a posteriori* element. They are essential to each other; without both, there is no experience, and therefore no world appearing to us. He wrote, 'Concepts without intuitions are empty, intuitions without concepts are blind.'*

This theory was developed by Kant to answer the question, 'Is metaphysics (that is, philosophy in our modern sense) possible?' – that is, Can we solve the fundamental problems of philosophy, and if so, how? These problems are: How do we know? How can we overcome sceptical challenges to knowledge? Is there a world existing independently of our experience of it? How can we justify claims about causality, the reliability of induction, the existence of a self? These questions concern the detailed problems we must solve if we are to reach any conclusions about the most general topics Kant thought we had to understand if we are ever to know how we can justify claims about what is right and good in the moral sense, these topics being the existence of God, freedom of the will and the nature of the soul.

Kant's answer is to say that we can indeed answer the questions about causality, scepticism and the like, because the way the world appears to us is the result of the way we experience it; it is in significant part a construct of our minds. He is therefore saying that both the empiricists and rationalists are right: the empiricists are right to insist that there cannot be knowledge without sensory experience

---

* The exact quotation is 'Thoughts without content are empty, intuitions without concepts are blind.'

('intuition'), but they are wrong to say that the mind is a blank slate, for the rationalists are right to insist that there are *a priori* concepts supplied by our minds – though the rationalists are wrong to say that *a priori* concepts are sufficient by themselves for knowledge of the world. So, knowledge is possible only because of the combination of the two: our minds are not blank slates, but are equipped *a priori* with ways of organizing and interpreting the incoming data of sense, and the indissoluble marriage between these two factors – intuitions and concepts – is what gives rise to our experience of the 'world as it appears to us' – the *phenomenal* world.

As the conception of a phenomenal world implies, however, we do not and indeed cannot know how the world is *in itself*. How the world is in itself, independently of being experienced by us, is unknowable because inaccessible: we cannot circumvent our way of having experience so that we can (as it were) peer behind our experience to see what the *unexperienced* world is like. The world as it is in itself Kant calls *noumenal* reality, and he says that all that can be said about it is that it is not like phenomenal reality. And here is a big problem: God, free will and the soul lie on the noumenal side of the question. Does his conclusion mean that we cannot know or say anything about these subjects?

If there are such things as God, free will and the soul, they *transcend* – in the sense of 'go beyond' – the boundaries of what the senses can tell us. We must therefore ask, Where and what are these boundaries? What are the limits of reason's reach and competence? An enquiry into the place and nature of these boundaries or limits is called by Kant a 'transcendental enquiry', and it is very important to note that he thereby meant not an enquiry into what lies *beyond* the bounds, but instead an enquiry into the boundaries *themselves* – that is, into the *boundary conditions* of what makes experience and knowledge possible in the first place.

The conclusion of Kant's enquiry into these boundaries, as already indicated though in other words, is that claims to knowledge of what lies within them are legitimate, but claims to knowledge of what lies beyond them are not. Philosophical enquiry can yield results regarding the general features of the phenomenal world, the world we experience; for example, it can justify the claim that every event has a cause. But it cannot give us knowledge of what lies outside experience. Talk of God, freedom and the soul has therefore to be understood in a quite different way. And enquiry into the grounds of morality must proceed on its own terms too, its relation to notions of God and the rest likewise requiring to be understood differently.

The first *Critique* has two main parts. In the first part Kant lays out a scheme of how experience arises. Sensory intuition comes before the faculty of understanding already ordered in spatial and temporal form by the way our sensory modalities (vision, hearing and the rest) operate. The faculty of understanding then 'brings the intuitions under concepts', that is, interprets them according to the most fundamental and general concepts we have – concepts such as causality, substance, quality and quantity. One of the most intriguing aspects of this scheme is that Kant's answer to the sceptical question 'How can you justify the claim that these concepts are what we use to create our experience?' is to give an argument – known as the 'transcendental deduction' – which shows that unless we did this we would not be able to have experience at all.

The first part of the first *Critique* thus aims to show how experience arises from the marriage of intuition and conceptualization, and thereby where the bounds of the legitimate use of our minds lie. The second part, called the 'Dialectic of Pure Reason', examines what happens when reason tries to go beyond the legitimate bounds of thought. Here Kant shows why we cannot prove the existence of God or an immortal soul, or of free will. Instead he argues that to make sense of ourselves and especially our moral concerns, we have to *assume* that something answers to these concepts: but to try to claim knowledge of them is not possible.

As with Hume before him, Kant's main philosophical concern was to identify the foundations of morality, and for this the first *Critique* is, despite its importance for metaphysics and the theory of knowledge, just a starting point. In a series of following works, the two most important being the *Critique of Practical Reason* and the *Groundwork of the Metaphysics of Morals*, Kant sets out his austere views about the 'supreme principle of morality'.

If there is to be such a thing as morality, he argued, its laws must apply to a realm of free-willed action, and not to the deterministic empirical realm governed by natural causal laws. This means that the task in moral philosophy is to show how reason by itself ('pure' reason, unmixed with empirical factors) governs and directs the will. The will, in turn, when truly autonomous – when it obeys only laws it makes for itself – thereby expresses the highest good there can be, which is freedom. 'The *summum bonum*', Kant wrote, 'is freedom in accordance with a will which is not necessitated to action.' Free-willed beings are the most valuable things in the world; they are 'ends in themselves' which should never be treated instrumentally as means to other ends.

In Kant's view, moral value resides in the good will of an agent who acts not out of inclination or the desire to achieve some particular end, but out of a sense of duty; specifically, a duty to obey a moral law which reason recognizes as the right one for the circumstances. The law in question will not take the form of a 'hypothetical imperative' advising that if the agent wishes to achieve a certain aim he should do so-and-so. Such imperatives, for example '*if* you wish to protect your health *then* you must give up smoking,' are such that if you do not desire the end (as specified in the 'if' part) you do not have to obey the command (as specified in the 'then' part). Rather, a genuinely moral law will take the form of a 'categorical imperative' bluntly asserting 'do so-and-so.' It is absolute and unconditional, no 'ifs' involved.

Kant arrives at this view by distinguishing between action-guiding principles which are subjective, in the sense that they apply only to the agent himself, and those that are objective, in the sense that they apply to all rational beings. Subjective principles are called 'maxims', objective principles are called 'laws'. If there existed perfectly rational beings, without appetites and passions to interfere with their reasoning, they would invariably act in accordance with objective laws. Animals never act in accordance with such laws, because they do not possess reason but only appetites and instincts, so their behaviour is wholly governed by the laws of nature. The big difference between rational and non-rational beings is summarized by Kant in the *Groundwork* thus: 'Everything in nature works in accordance with laws. Only a rational being has the power to act *in accordance with his idea* of laws – that is, in accordance with principles – and only so has he a *will*.' Human beings are, figuratively speaking, halfway between the animals and the angels, in the sense that they have both reason and the full complement of animal appetites and instincts. They are therefore in the unique position of being able to act in conformity with objective principles identified by reason, but they do not always do so. So they alone are in need of concepts of duty and obligation, and therefore of imperatives unconditionally stating what they ought to do.

The general form of the categorical imperative is 'I ought never to act in any way other than according to a maxim which I can at the same time will should become a universal law,' that is, which I regard as applicable universally, to everyone and not just me. The most famous formulation of the categorical imperative is: 'Act in such a way that you always treat humanity, whether in your own person or in the person of any other, never simply as a means, but always at the same time as an end.' Kant thinks of the moral community of persons as a 'kingdom of ends', a mutual association of free beings, in which each individual seeks to realize freely chosen goals compatibly with the freedom of everyone else to do likewise.

In stating these views Kant had to traverse some very hard terrain. He argued that the supreme principle of morality is the principle of autonomy, and that the 'determining ground of the moral will' is the purely formal concept of *lawfulness* as such, which is a concept of pure reason. Kant claims that the very possibility of morality depends on there being free-willed beings who obey laws of reason they apply to themselves. He therefore had to give an argument to show that there is freedom, and he had to explain how laws can be valid just in virtue of their formal properties and not in virtue of what they enjoin.

The ethical outlook advocated by Kant is a 'deontology', a rule-based or duty-based ethics. This kind of view is sharply contrasted to any form of 'consequentialist' ethics, which evaluates the moral worth of an action by its consequences or outcomes. In deontology an action is moral only insofar as it obeys the rule governing the case, irrespective of outcomes.

Kant did not agree with those, whether among the ancients or among the moderns, who thought that morality is accessible only to an educated elite. Moral principles apply to everyone, and therefore everyone must be capable of understanding the obligations and ideals which govern their moral lives. He believed that in fact all ordinary folk have a basically correct grasp of morality, even if a detailed and technical philosophical treatise is required to spell out both its details and its justification fully. He took his own task to be that of explaining and analysing what is 'inherent in the structure of every man's reason', which includes the supreme principle of morality itself, namely autonomy or freedom, together with the categorical nature of true moral laws. He was criticized by contemporaries for not having introduced anything original in this respect, to which he replied, 'Who would wish to introduce a new principle of morality and, as it were, be its inventor, as if the world had hitherto been ignorant of what duty is or had been thoroughly wrong about it?'

Commentators and biographers alike make much of Kant's Pietist upbringing as a source of his stern morality of duty. The Pietists were numerous and highly influential in eighteenth-century Königsberg where Kant was born and lived all his life. His parents were strictly observing members of the movement, his school, the Collegium Frideri-cianum, was committedly Pietist, and the city's university was a centre of Pietist theology. Pietists believed in original sin and its concomitant, the human tendency to evil, but this had a further concomitant in the form of a doctrine of salvation through spiritual rebirth, good works and the unremitting pursuit of moral perfection. Kant deeply disliked the obligatory pieties of Pietism, and by extension religion in general, but he carried from his experience of it the idea of inner dutifulness and discipline.

The most potent influence on Kant was not Pietism but something opposed to it both temperamentally and in principle: the Enlighten-ment itself. He saw himself as a votary of the Enlightenment, even a custodian of its values. For much of his teaching career he lectured on subjects which all the proponents of Enlightenment sought to make more generally known – physics and astronomy included – and he championed the idea of progress in the condition of mankind through the application of science and its methods. For this, as noted, he argued that the necessary condition is freedom: freedom from external con-straints on debate and the diffusion of knowledge, and freedom internally from the timidity and uncertainty which inhibits independ-ent thought. The enemies of progress are those who impose censorship or conformity, whether of a political or religious kind. Such abuses of power, Kant wrote in 'What is Enlightenment?', 'trample on the holy rights of mankind'. Elsewhere he added, 'Religion through its sanctity, and law-giving through its majesty, might seek to exempt themselves from [criticism], but they then awaken rightful suspicion, and cannot claim the sincere respect which reason accords only to that which has been able to sustain the test of free and open examination.'

Nevertheless, Kant did not think it possible to justify morality to the generality of mankind without invoking metaphysical concepts of a deity and the immortality of the soul. These notions, together with that of the freedom of the will, constitute a trinity of concepts which, although they cannot be proved to be valid, are *useful* for making sense of the practice of morality as a whole – for if, he said, we *assume* that there is a deity and that we survive our earthly existence, and moreover that we are fully accountable, as a result of having free will, for everything we have done in life, then we can think of ourselves as being liable for reward or punishment in a posthumous dispensation. And this is what, in his view, gives people their sense of why they should be moral.

In Kant's terminology, the concepts of God, immortality and freedom of the will are '*postulates* [useful assumptions] of pure practical reason'. His argument for them is that the moral law requires us to attain the highest possible good, and that we do this by conforming our will wholly to the moral law. But success in this amounts to 'holiness', a state not attainable in the empirical world, where the senses will always offer temptations to disobey the moral law. If holiness is possible and is required by the moral law, yet is not attainable in this world, it follows that we must help ourselves to the idea of the possibility of another life, a non-physical one, in which the supreme moral goal of holiness can be reached. 'Thus,' said Kant, 'the highest good is practically possible only on the supposition of the immortality of the soul.'

Similarly, said Kant, it is necessary to postulate the existence of God to make sense of the idea that virtue will be rewarded. Man is not the cause of nature and he is therefore not able to will that nature should reward those who deserve reward. But the idea of moral law requires that such reward should be possible. Therefore we have to postulate that there is a being capable of ensuring that we get the rewards we deserve.

Although these are not proofs of immortality or of deity, said Kant, but merely 'postulates' or assumptions, nevertheless they can be 'rationally believed'. It takes very little to see why most commentators on Kant do not agree that this is so. We might for example ask, Why cannot we think it an obligation to try to attain the highest good without assuming that it has to be attainable? We might think that it is attainable only by a few; or that we might more or less closely approximate it without actually attaining it. So much for the need for immortality. As for the need to reward virtue: there are those who hold that virtue is its own reward, and those who think that virtue is still worth pursuing even if there are no guarantees of reward – so once again morality does not need the concept of a deity. On the contrary, the idea that striving for the good, and living according to a best conception of virtue, without the inducement either of guaranteed success and guaranteed rewards, seems to be a finer thing than Kant offers.

Some find it odd that Kant believed that religion is harmful to morality, and yet that the concepts of deity and immortality are required to give morality point. His meaning is that religion as the organized worship of a deity, and submission to what a church says is its will, is harmful to morality; but the idea that one has an immortal soul which is answerable for everything one does to a supreme judge is, in effect, a useful fiction for rounding off what one might say to justify morality to any sceptic who asks 'Why should I be moral?' Unfortunately for this idea it preserves the kernel of the *argumentum ad baculum* – the appeal to force or threat – and fails on that account too.

Kant was not a personally religious man, and his 'postulates' for making external sense of morality share the notional, deistic character that (for example) Voltaire's views had. The significant fact is that the content of Kant's moral theory is humanistic, in arguing, first, that morality's most fundamental presupposition is the autonomy of the will, meaning that the will obeys laws it imposes on itself and not those prescribed by an outside source such as a deity or sovereign; and secondly that the law such a will thus obeys must be shown to be valid on purely logical grounds. In this respect Kant's theory is a paradigm of Enlightenment thinking.

THE EIGHTEENTH-CENTURY ENLIGHTENMENT

'Enlightenment', Kant wrote in his 1784 essay 'What is Enlightenment?', 'is man's emergence from his self-imposed immaturity. Immaturity is the inability to use one's understanding without guidance from another. This immaturity is self-imposed when its cause lies not in lack of understanding, but in lack of resolve and courage to use it without guidance from another. *Sapere aude!* [dare to know] – "Have courage to use your own understanding!" – that is the motto of enlightenment.'

Neither Kant nor his contemporaries thought that they lived in an enlightened age. By 'enlightenment' they meant the lessening of darkness, the *beginning* of the spread of light. The human mind was starting to shrug off the rule of arbitrary authority in the spheres of thought and belief. Intellectual immaturity is characterized by a need for direction from others; intellectual maturity is characterized by independence. 'Nothing is required for enlightenment except freedom,' Kant wrote, 'and the freedom in question is the least harmful of all, namely, the freedom to use reason publicly in all matters.'

What Kant and his fellow-leaders of the Enlightenment were combating was the denial of that freedom of mind. 'On all sides I hear: "Do not argue!"' Kant continued. 'The officer says, "Do not argue, drill!" The tax man says, "Do not argue, pay!" The pastor says, "Do not argue, believe!"' Whereas the officer and the tax man serve authorities who dislike anyone's questioning the political and social status quo, the pastor is a different matter: he represents authority which dislikes any kind of questioning, and certainly not the kind that is sceptical about received wisdom.

The project that did most to carry the flag for enlightenment in the eighteenth century was the *Encyclopédie, ou Dictionnaire raisonné des sciences, des arts et des métiers*, edited by Denis Diderot and Jean le Rond d'Alembert. It declared war on the authority of past pieties on the grounds that these had always been a barrier to intellectual advance. In taking this stance the Encyclopedists were following the lead of Voltaire, whose battle cry of *écrasez l'infâme* ('crush the infamous') had persistently attacked authority with weapons of logic and satire.

Diderot's call to arms in the *Encyclopédie* is in the same spirit: 'Have courage to free yourselves,' he exhorted his age. 'Examine the history of all peoples in all times and you will see that we humans have always been subject to one of three codes: that of nature, that of society, and that of religion – and that we have been obliged to transgress all three in succession, because they could never be in harmony.'

In his novel *Les Bijoux indiscrets* Diderot recounts a dream. In it there is a building without foundations, whose pillars soar upwards into a fog. A crowd of misshapen and crippled old men move about among the pillars. The building is the Palace of Hypotheses, and the old men are makers of theological and metaphysical systems. But an energetic little child appears, and as he draws near the building he grows into a giant. The child's name is Experiment, and when he arrives at the building he gives it a mighty blow, and it shatters to the ground.

The dream encapsulates one important aspect of the eighteenth-century Enlightenment's source: the rise of science in the seventeenth century. That century began, in scientific respects, with Galileo seeing

the moons of Jupiter through a telescope, an observation adding powerful support to the Copernican view of the universe. Galileo was put
under house arrest by the Vatican for saying that the earth moves, contrary to the definitive pronouncement in scripture that God had 'laid
the foundations of the earth, that it should not be removed for ever'
(Psalm 104:5). The century ended with Newton. It contained a spectacular army of geniuses in philosophy and science, whose work laid
the simultaneous foundations of science and the modern world, chief
among them Hooke, Boyle, Wren, Huygens, Wallis, Descartes, Rooke,
Kepler, Napier, Leeuwenhoek, Fermat, Pascal, Leibniz, Hobbes, Spinoza and Locke.

The key to the scientific advances of the seventeenth century was
the use of observation and reason, experiment and quantification. The
key to the eighteenth-century Enlightenment is that it set about applying this same empirical approach to wider regions of thought: to
politics, society, education, law and the idea of human rights. When it
became clear that empirical enquiry can uncover the secrets of nature,
other doctrines – for two prime examples, that of the divine right
of kings and the doctrines of theology – began to lose intellectual
respectability.

Kant, as we saw, wrote, 'If it is now asked, "Do we presently live in
an enlightened age?" the answer is, "No, but we do live in an age of
enlightenment."' Although he began by describing the immaturity of
the intellect as the state in which it needs guidance from another, he
also attacked the various hegemonies which keep the human mind
shackled to that need. In order to mature, the intellect needs liberty,
'the freedom to use reason publicly in all matters'.

Key *Encyclopédie* entries argued that religion had signally failed to
provide a satisfactory basis either for morality or for a just society. This
followed the lead given by Voltaire. But although Voltaire had circum-
spectly claimed that criticizing superstition was not the same as
criticizing faith, and that criticizing the Church was not the same thing
as criticizing religion, it was faith and religion which felt the blows.

In common with many who took the same view, whether or not they
publicly acknowledged doing so, Voltaire claimed to be a deist, that is,
one who does not believe in any revealed religion, but nevertheless holds
that there had to have been, at some point, an agency which created the
universe. Most deists took it that this being has no personal interest in the
affairs of mankind, and does not intervene in what happens in the world,

leaving it to the operation of natural laws alone. Diderot had no time for deism, seeing it as a mere fudge; it had, he wrote, cut off a dozen heads of the Hydra of religion, but from the remaining one all the rest would grow again. 'In vain, oh slave of superstition,' says Nature to Mankind in his *Supplement to Bougainville's Voyage*, 'have you sought your happiness beyond the limits of the world I gave you. Have courage to free yourself from the yoke of religion.' In saying that humankind has always been subject to the authority of any one or two of nature, society or religion, Diderot argued that there has never been 'a real man, a real citizen, a real believer'.

Perhaps one of the most swingeing assaults on religion occurs in Baron d'Holbach's *Natural Politics*, which he concludes with the remark that religion, by teaching people to fear invisible despots, thereby teaches them to fear earthly ones, and consequently prevents them from seeking independence and choosing the direction and character of their lives for themselves. As this suggests – and this is crucially important for understanding the Enlightenment – the repudiation of the hegemony of religion over thought is, although central, not the sole concern, but just the starting point for what really counts: the project, to be undertaken by each individual, of relying on reason and applying the lessons of science as the chief guides to building better lives and societies. The Enlightenment project was accordingly conceived by its votaries as a creative one, a reforming one, premised on the promise of freedom – most especially intellectual freedom – to deliver a new and improved world.

Peter Gay was careful to point out, in his *The Enlightenment: An Interpretation*, that the Enlightenment has always had its simplistic admirers and its vehement detractors, among the latter those who blame it for those aspects of modernism which exemplify 'superficial rationalism, foolish optimism, and irresponsible Utopianism', including the excesses of the French Revolution and the failed experiments, terribly costly in human terms, of the twentieth century's various upheavals. The reminder is a salutary one. But as Gay and before him Ernst Cassirer remarked, even though such strictures have merit, the Enlightenment has to be understood as an intellectual movement based on a set of aspirations for the improvement of mankind's lot.

'The *philosophes*' experience', Gay writes, speaking of the thinkers of the Enlightenment collectively by the French label they applied to themselves, was a dialectical struggle for autonomy, an attempt to assimilate the two pasts they had inherited – Christian and pagan – to pit them against one another and thus to secure their independence . . . theirs was a paganism directed against their Christian inheritance and dependent upon the paganism of classical antiquity, but it was also a *modern* paganism, emancipated from classical thought as much as from Christian dogma. The ancients taught the *philosophes* the uses of criticism, but it was the modern philosophers who taught them the possibilities of power.

In these remarks, as in those of Kant and the other thinkers quoted, a key notion is that of 'autonomy', by which is meant self-government, independence of thought, and possession of the right and the responsibility to make choices about one's own life – not least moral choices. Autonomy is self-direction in the light of reason and the lessons of nature; its opposite, *heteronomy*, means direction or government by someone or something outside oneself. Heteronomy means subjection of one's own will to the will and choices of an external authority, typically a deity or some other abstraction. Of course, the conditions of social life mean that an individual is subject to many constraints made necessary by the fact of living in community with others. But the autonomy in question is autonomy first and foremost of thought and moral responsibility, and it is the progress towards increasing autonomy, in this sense, that Kant and his contemporaries saw as 'enlightenment'.

If the aim of enlightenment is to think for oneself and choose for oneself – this autonomy conceived as essential to the life worth living – then it is essential that one should be equipped to think fruitfully and to choose wisely. That requires information; and not just information, but information organized into knowledge; and not just knowledge, but knowledge interpreted into understanding. This is why the monument of the Enlightenment is the *Encyclopédie* of Diderot and d'Alembert. Its stated aim was 'to collect all the knowledge scattered over the face of the earth, to present its general outlines and structure to the men with whom we live, and to transmit this to those who will come after us, so that the work of the past centuries may be useful to the following centuries, that our children, by becoming more educated, may at the same time become more virtuous and happier, and that we may not die without having deserved well of the human race'.

The most significant part of this statement is Diderot's assertion that education is the route to the good life. A central theme of the

Encyclopédie, as shown by such of its articles as 'System' and 'Hypothesis', is that empirical methods and logic are keys to knowledge, and that these are not only inconsistent with appeals to the authority of scripture or revelation, but actually controvert them. In the *Preliminary Discourse* d'Alembert begins his account of the organization of knowledge by defending empiricism, and then accepts the implications of this commitment: that the fundamental concepts of morality and justice have to be derived from facts about mankind's experience, not from supposed metaphysical or theological foundations.

The *Encyclopédie* was published between 1751 and 1772 in seventeen volumes of text and eleven of illustrations. The writing of its 72,000 articles was distributed among 140 authors, among them some of the most eminent minds of eighteenth-century France – in addition to its editors they included Voltaire, Rousseau, Marmontel, d'Holbach and Turgot, to name a very few. They shared Diderot's aim not just of collecting and, in clear and accessible prose, diffusing the best of accumulated knowledge, but of deploying this formidable mass as a machine of war to propagate 'Light'. The *Encyclopédie* therefore faced considerable opposition, not least from the censors, whose objections and interference caused many delays in publication. The first seven volumes appeared annually between 1751 and 1757, the last ten appeared in 1766. Six years later the last of the volumes of illustrations was published, completing the original plan. By that time reprints of some of the articles were already in existence, and works inspired either by agreement or by opposition had begun to appear. The *Encyclopédie* had become an institution, and remains a monument to what the most optimistic intellects of the time aspired to.

Although the *Encyclopédie* was a concrete expression of the Enlightenment spirit, for all its significance it represents just one thread in a larger and longer story. Part of that story concerns the contemporary opposition to the Enlightenment project, chiefly from the defenders of the religious and political status quo threatened by its message. A larger part of the story concerns the Enlightenment's historical critics – those who see it as responsible for the excesses of the French Revolution, those who see it as meriting the reaction represented by Romanticism, those who see it as the ultimate source for both Stalinism and Fascism in more recent times, those even more recently who see it as ultimately responsible for 'liberal' values where this is understood pejoratively in the American sense as destructive of 'family values' – and all those who see it as embodying the antithesis of all that matters most richly to the human spirit in its encounters with the mystical, the ineffable and the numinous.

The earliest opponents of the Enlightenment fall into two broad classes: those who would now be described as political or ideological conservatives – ranging from clerics contemporary with the *philosophes* to somewhat later thinkers like Edmund Burke and Joseph de Maistre – and those we now label Romantics, who championed nature, imagination and the emotions, against what they saw as the reductive and mechanistic worldview of Enlightenment rationalism.*

Burke and others who shared his conservative political orientation identified the Enlightenment attack on tradition, and especially tradition as a source of moral and political authority, as the direct cause of all that was worst about the French Revolution. In fact their objection embraced a longer impulse of thought, stemming at least from Locke, which argued that the source of authority in society is not tradition or a monarch ruling by divine right, but the *people*, whose consent is required for all things affecting the common weal, and who have rights, some of them inalienable in that no form of government is entitled to abrogate them. The *philosophes* of the Enlightenment adopted this view as a matter of course, and it has been (despite Burke, because later conservatives adopted it too) the source of the Western evolution of liberal democracy. But in Burke's day 'democracy' was a word of malediction, and 'the people' was an unruly and anarchic entity not to be trusted. From Burke's perspective the philosophes were *sans culottes* before the fact, and all their principles were despicable accordingly.

Romantics interpreted the Enlightenment's championship of science as amounting to the claim that scientific development is synonymous with progress itself, which if so would mean that history and human experience can properly be understood only in mechanistic, even deterministic terms. As a way of recoiling from this degree of empiricism and mechanism, the Romantics asserted instead the primacy of emotion over reason, and accordingly celebrated the subjective, the personal, the visionary and the irrational. They gave a privileged place to moods and passions as sources of insight and as arbiters of truth, and they exalted

---

* One must always keep in mind the difference between rationalism as advocacy of the use of reason, and rationalism as the philosophical doctrine that the best forms of knowledge are *a priori*.

such experiences as the individual's response to natural beauty. By contrast, Enlightenment attitudes are taken to be natural concomitants of the neo-classical preference for order, balance and harmony in music, architecture, art and poetry, a view which gets much support from the applied aesthetics of the eighteenth century.

It scarcely needs saying that we would not now willingly be without either the neo-classicism of the eighteenth century or the Romantic music and poetry of the nineteenth century, so the point here is not to take sides between the best of both styles, nor to choose which did most harm – having agreed that both have their worst sides and consequences too: as with the harsh and mechanical reductivism of the one, and the irresponsible thinking of the other which led to such catastrophes of political and social Romanticism as nationalism, racism and eventually Fascism. If there is one salient difference, it is that the amorphous embrace of Romanticism gave unreflective house-room to many of the shibboleths that the Enlightenment worked hard to abolish, given their negative effects on human flourishing – for a chief example, superstition; and in this respect a preference might be justified as follows: the good life for human individuals certainly requires the best of both traditions, but arguably it least requires the worst aspects of Romanticism, if these come down to yielding authority to such things as race, the Hero, the Genius, the 'Führer principle', tradition, nature, untutored emotions, visions, supernatural beings, and so on.

On the Enlightenment view, reason is the armament of ideas; it is the weapon employed in the conflict between viewpoints. This suggests that reason is an absolute which, responsibly used, can settle disputes and serve as a guide to truth. But reason understood in this uncompromising way has always invited opposition. One main opponent is religion, which claims that revelation, in any form from mystical experience to dictation of scripture by a deity, conveys from outside the world of ordinary experience truths undiscoverable by human enquiry within it. Another opponent is relativism, the view that different truths, different views, different ways of thinking, even those that compete with or contradict each other, are all equally valid, and that there is no authoritative standpoint from which they can be adjudicated. In this sharp contrast the Enlightenment's weight lay emphatically on the side of the argument which says that reason, despite its imperfections and fallibilities, provides a standard to which competing standpoints have to submit themselves. Its votaries accordingly reject any outlook which says that there are authorities alongside or even more powerful than reason, such as race, tradition, nature or gods. The rationalists' defence of reason does not have to be, and of course had better not be, unqualified, not least given the fact that answers to questions about what human beings are (or: what human nature is) are more ironic and conditional than we sometimes realize, and therefore less entitled to confidence. But this was something that promoters of Enlightenment in the eighteenth century themselves understood very well. Consider Voltaire's satire on the excessive adherence to rationalist optimism as exhibited by Dr Pangloss in *Candide*, a work which gives the lie to anyone who thinks that the *philosophes* were unselfcritical or unreflective about the extent of human rationality. And the leading philosophers (not *philosophes*) of the period – Hume and Kant – were likewise careful not to overrate reason, while yet using it to describe its own limits.

Consider a later critical reaction to the Enlightenment, which serves as an example of how its optimistic outlook came to be seen as self-destructive. In *Dialectic of Enlightenment* (1944), which allegedly began as a New York kitchen conversation between Max Horkheimer and Theodor Adorno during the darkest days of the Second World War, the idea is mooted that the Enlightenment's principles and themes have metamorphosed into their opposites. Individual freedom was sought by the *philosophes*, but became a form of enslavement to economic powers for those who came after them. Science was seen as the rational alternative to religion, but 'scientism' – itself taking the form of a salvation myth, in which science will answer all questions and solve all problems – simply came to replace religion and to exert as malign an influence.

Horkheimer and Adorno set great store by their criticism of scientific rationality, because they believed that they were witnessing the moment at which its promise had turned fully toxic. Adopted as the philosophical method of Enlightenment, scientific rationality promised not only to bring progress in all fields, but simultaneously to undermine the dogmas of religion and with them the hegemony of priesthoods. It could do this, the original *philosophes* believed, because of its objective character and its obvious pragmatic success. In its promise both of progress and of liberation from ancient superstitions, scientific rationality was supposed to serve the interests of freedom and tolerance. But scientific rationality has a dynamic of its own, Horkheimer and Adorno argued, which gradually made it militate even against the values responsible for its own rise. In so doing it turned from being a weapon *against* repression into a weapon *of* repression. Believing its own dreams of progress, intoxicated by the successes of rational method, triumphant in its increasing mastery of nature, the humanistic dream of the *philosophes* eventually turned into a nightmare, and the shibboleths it attempted to destroy all reappeared in new disguises – chief among them, so Horkheimer and Adorno held, Fascism.

This analysis was immensely influential in the Frankfurt School, and occasioned a vigorous debate after the Second World War. But defenders of Enlightenment values reject this thesis. They cite the implausibility of equating scientific mastery over nature – for the Enlightenment, a mastery intended to liberate mankind – with political mastery over the majority of mankind exercised by those who, as a result of the material progress made possible by the Enlightenment, came to control the levers of economic and political power in succeeding centuries. In the crisis of the 1940s the oppressive power Horkheimer and Adorno had foremost in mind was Nazism, which they thus saw as the self-fulfillingly paradoxical outcome of the Enlightenment: as they put it, 'instrumental rationality' had transmuted itself into 'bureaucratic politics'. But this, say Enlightenment defenders, is implausible. Nazi ideology drew its strength precisely from the peasantry and petite bourgeoisie who felt most threatened by capital's advance to power, so it is not the latter which has to be seen as the source of the new oppression, but the former, viewed as latter-day representatives of the groupings who had most to lose from Enlightenment and therefore reacted against it – thus, the reactionaries. The embracers of Nazism would, had they inhabited the eighteenth century, have defended the traditions of absolute government, whether in heaven or Versailles, against the 'instrumental rationality' which in the eighteenth century expressed itself as a set of secularizing and democratizing impulses. So, say the defenders of Enlightenment, Horkheimer and Adorno accordingly get matters the wrong way round. Nor is it clear that the alternative form of tyranny available for study in that same era, namely Stalinism, would admit of any better a genealogy to the Enlightenment – and for similar reasons.

The most famous aspect of *Dialectic of Enlightenment* is its authors' attack on what they saw as the repressive nature of the 'culture industry'. They took mass culture to be another long-term outcome of the Enlightenment's instrumental rationalism, and rejected it accordingly; but here too their view invited disagreement. Mass culture is by no means incapable of producing things of value, whether in art or knowledge; and the technologies designed to serve the interests of mass culture are equally capable of producing art as refined as any elitist could require.

The rise of science in the sixteenth and seventeenth centuries, and the eighteenth-century Enlightenment's battle for freedom of the human mind and person from various tyrannies, are products of philosophy's history, showing how revolutionary is the power of ideas.

Philosophy in the Nineteenth Century

A history of philosophy in the nineteenth century, and that more general enterprise, a history of ideas in the nineteenth century, differ in this significant respect: that the latter would include accounts of economics and political economy, jurisprudence, Charles Darwin, controversies over evolution and religion, developments in natural science, the beginnings of systematic sociology, philology, anthropology and archaeology, historiography, biblical criticism, and more. It was a century in which the liberating effect of the eighteenth-century Enlightenment on intellectual activity was felt in full. Much of this ebullition of thought and the rise of new fields of enquiry was the result of aspects of philosophy becoming independent and more empirical; indeed some of the century's thinkers agreed with Auguste Comte, a founder of sociology, that these new fields were successors to philosophical speculation, and that philosophy itself was coming to an end.

But philosophy was far from over, and the work of the principal figures in this period – Bentham, Hegel, John Stuart Mill, Schopenhauer, Marx, Nietzsche, the British idealists, the American pragmatists – was not only intrinsically of great interest and value, but shaped developments in the most philosophically rich period since the classical epoch: the twentieth century.

In the nineteenth century the word 'philosophy' acquired its more specific sense to mean what we mean by it today – enquiry into questions of metaphysics, epistemology, ethics and the rest – and at the same time the word 'science' came to mean what we mean by it today – physics, chemistry, biology and the rest. Even in the first decades of the nineteenth century the word 'philosophy' still denoted science, and indeed the word 'scientist' was coined as late as 1833 (by William Whewell; he first used it in print in 1843). This is why William Hazlitt is described on his tomb as a 'metaphysician', the word 'metaphysician' then denoting what we now call a 'philosopher'.

In the nineteenth century one can begin to discern the beginnings of a separation of the philosophical tradition into two strands. On the one hand there are Bentham, Mill and the American pragmatists, continuing in the manner of Locke and Hume in focusing on specific questions in epistemology, ethics, law and politics. There are also Hegel, Schopenhauer and the British idealists, who offer inclusive frameworks with metaphysical interests at the forefront. Both these groupings still remain identifiably part of the same story in the range of their concerns. A difference enters with Nietzsche. He represents a turn in philosophical interests which in the second half of the twentieth century generalized yet further among 'Continental' thinkers in sociological, historical and literary-critical directions. The principal separation between the two strands occurs as a result of the work of Husserl and Heidegger, and especially the latter, in the first half of the twentieth century: this is more fully explained in Part IV below.

BENTHAM (1748–1832)

In an essay published in 1825 William Hazlitt wrote of Jeremy Bentham, who was then still alive, that 'His name is little known in England, better in Europe, best of all in the plains of Chili and the mines of Mexico. He has offered constitutions for the New World, and legislated for future times. The people of Westminster, where he lives, hardly dream of such a person; but the Siberian savage has received cold comfort from his lunar aspect.'

The chief reason why Bentham was then a prophet in many lands other than his own was that the part of his voluminous writings which were published in his lifetime appealed only to experts in law, government, social and political reform, ethics and economics, and he therefore had a small readership at home; but one of the most immediately influential of his works was first published in translation – in French, then in Russian, Spanish, German and other languages, only appearing in English a decade after his death.

Another reason for his neglect in England was that he was a radical in politics, and a republican, which put him in opposition to the Establishment of the day, with the result that he received neither public recognition nor public honour. Yet he introduced into English the words 'utilitarian', 'codify' and 'international'; he was the first to propose an international court of arbitration for peace and the laying down of principles of international law; and many hospitals, prisons and other institutions are constructed on the 'Panopticon' principle that he and his brother Samuel devised. His influence on the course of practical affairs has been great, not just in his own country but in many parts of the world.

Bentham studied at Oxford, and then became a barrister. He did not practise law for long, deciding to devote himself instead to legal and social reform. This was because he had been inspired by his discovery of the principle of utility in the philosophies of David Hume, Claude Helvétius (1715–71) and Cesare Bonesana-Beccaria (1738–94). In Hume he found the idea that utility is the criterion of virtue. In Helvétius he found the idea that utility can guide conduct by connecting it to the ideas of pleasure and pain, which Bentham took to be the only motivators of action, as Epicurus long before had argued. In Beccaria's treatise on crime and punishment he found the phrase *la massima felicità divisa nel maggior numero* – the greatest happiness of the greatest number. He believed that a range of social problems could be remedied by the application of this fundamental principle, and dedicated himself to the task of putting this principle into effect.

Bentham argued that what he came to call 'utilitarianism' imposes an obligation on legislators as well as individuals to 'minister to general happiness', an obligation which, he said, is 'paramount to and inclusive of every other'. He used the term 'utility' to denote '[whatever] tends to produce benefit, advantage, good or happiness', these all being synonymous in his usage.

Utilitarianism, whether of Bentham's or later more elaborate kinds, is a *consequentialist* theory of morality, understanding moral value in terms only of the outcome of actions, leaving aside any questions about the intentions of agents or the quality of their personal characters. Other theories of morality focus on these two latter, but the distinctive feature of utilitarian theories is that they measure moral value wholly by outcomes. Bentham and John Stuart Mill, who are jointly known as the 'classical utilitarians' though the latter made advances over Bentham's view, agreed in regarding happiness as the greatest good, and each person's happiness as being equal in value to anyone else's. This means that working to produce the greatest happiness for the greatest number is done impartially; anyone's reason for promoting the good is the same as anyone else's reason for doing so.

It is clear that there is a tension at the heart of this view. Bentham regarded pleasure and pain as 'sovereign masters' which, as he put it, 'govern us in all we do, in all we say, in all we think'. This view is known as 'hedonism', and it is in essence an egoistic or self-regarding view. How is this fact about each of us consistent with the demand to promote the greatest happiness of the greatest number, when my own 'sovereign masters' might drive me to act in ways that give me advantages at the expense of the general happiness?

Bentham tried different ways to overcome this difficulty. One was to say that we promote our own happiness by promoting as much happiness as possible for others. Another, more plausibly, was to moderate the hedonistic view, and to accept that we sometimes act out of benevolence towards others. Some theorists have indeed sought to make 'enlightened self-interest' the rule of action, but two obstacles lie in the way of accepting this: first, the empirical fact that we sometimes do indeed act in others' interests at a cost to our own, and second, the bad taste left in the mouth by the idea that, in the end, all we do is ultimately self-serving.

Although Bentham was influenced by Hume he rejected the latter's moral psychology. Hume thought that actions tell us about a person's character, and he held that character is the morally interesting matter. For someone interested in applications of morality to actual social affairs, as Bentham was, character is too subjective to be useful. Only individuals themselves can know what they intend or desire, yet the reasons they have for their actions can often be opaque even to themselves. How can this help us judge right and wrong? Bentham sought a more practical basis.

Bentham's patron was the first Marquis of Lansdowne, a leading Whig politician who introduced Bentham to a Genevan exile called Etienne Dumont, who was a tutor to Lansdowne's sons. Dumont was responsible for Bentham's fame in Europe, for he translated a number of Bentham's manuscripts into French and published them in three volumes as *Traités de législation civile et pénale* (1802), the first two volumes of which were translated back into English much later as *The Theory of Legislation* (1840).

Lansdowne also encouraged Bentham to address the question of how 'perpetual peace' might be achieved in the international order, together with how relations between states can be made subject to law. In the process of drafting the essays that came to form his book *Principles of International Law* Bentham coined, as noted, the word 'international', and there put forward his idea of a court for settling international disputes.

The revolutionary situation in France especially engaged Bentham's interest. Even before the Revolution itself he began to write a series of pamphlets, with Dumont's help, proposing political solutions and judicial reform for France. They were published in French and disseminated among leading figures in Paris. In the period after the fall of the Bastille the proposals were discussed by France's National Assembly. His support for the Revolution resulted in his being given honorary French citizenship in 1792.

Bentham had no parallel influence in England. He wrote about poor law reform, policing, economics and taxation, and above all about law reform, the latter giving him an opportunity to vent his critical attitude to what he saw as the muddled nature of common law and the arbitrary nature of 'judge-made law'.

He accepted the view that law is by its nature negative, in the sense that its whole essence lies in imposing restrictions and limits, thereby reducing individual liberty. His idea of liberty was, like that of Hobbes, what is now called 'negative liberty', that is, absence of restraint. This view has a straightforward consequence when conjoined with Bentham's version of utilitarianism. It is pleasant to be free and painful to be restricted; since pleasure and pain are the criteria of value, it follows that liberty is a good. But Bentham would have no truck with the idea that liberty is a 'natural right', an idea on which he poured unreserved scorn, calling all talk of natural rights 'nonsense on stilts'. This is because he rejected the idea of a social contract which had brought people out of a 'state of nature' in which they had enjoyed primitive rights and freedoms, some of which they forfeited in exchange for the benefits of community. He thought that people had always lived in society, and that laws are the commands of whoever or whatever holds authority in it. This anticipated the 'Legal Positivism' of the theorist John Austin later in the nineteenth century, the view that law is expressly the product of the will of a sovereign. This view entails that whether or not a law is good or bad, moral or otherwise, it is nevertheless law if so enacted. This idea further entails that all rights are created by legislation, and that liberties are conferred either explicitly by law or implicitly by the law's silence.

A more attractive feature of Bentham's legal views concerns the question of evidence. He viewed the law of evidence and its admissibility as extremely muddled; it was full of distinctions, exceptions and a host of obscure technicalities that had accumulated through the process of judge-made decisions. Bentham saw the legal profession's adherence to this unsatisfactory state of affairs as malignly self-interested because it prolonged hearings and added much to lawyers' purses. Previous legal theorists had attempted to impose order on the chaos, and to justify some of the more bizarre doctrines that underlay evidential practice. Bentham took a more robust approach; he sought to sweep aside all 'rules of evidence' and to replace them with a natural approach on utilitarian grounds, an approach premised on ordinary daily experience and common sense.

Bentham corresponded with President Madison in the United States on the subject of codification of laws, and with each of the state legislatures in America. His views bore indirect fruit in another direction; one example is the partial codification of civil procedure in the state of New York (the Field Code) as a result of the indefatigable labours of David D. Field II, who had been influenced by Bentham while on European travels undertaken to research legal codes. A similar service to Benthamite ideas was performed by David Hoffman, the legal scholar, who introduced utilitarian theory into law studies at the University of Maryland in the 1820s.

Bentham was widely read in South America, his writings provoking controversy in Chile and Colombia; in the latter Simón Bolívar, as President, succumbed to pressure by the Catholic Church and banned Bentham's books. Bolívar's successor as President, Francisco Santander, revoked the ban and restored them to the university curriculum. In Greece, after it had liberated itself from Ottoman rule, Bentham's views influenced the drafters of the new constitution, chiefly as a result of the writings of Anastasios Polyzoides, a disciple of his.

All of Bentham's schemes for the improvement of society and its institutions, from penal reform to his views on political economy and the law, faced formidable barriers in Britain because of tradition and vested interests. He came to realize that the only hope for them lay in fundamental political reform. He was encouraged in this by James Mill, who in 1808 became his lieutenant and coadjutor. Bentham had written about political reform earlier in his career, but had put his manuscripts aside; now with Mill's encouragement he revised and extended them.

He had come to think not only that substantive reform was impossible without political reform, but that the only alternative to political reform was revolution; and he preferred the former.

In his view the key to the problem lay in the 'influence' exercised over political institutions by individuals and claques in the Establishment from the King downwards, acting through an unrepresentative Parliament which was in the pockets of wealthy patrons. To combat this, Parliamentary representation needed to be reformed. He therefore set about arguing in favour of an extension of the franchise, annual elections by secret ballot, basic qualifications for those who stand for Parliament, a system of fines to enforce regular attendance by MPs, accurate reporting of Parliamentary debates, and abolition of royal patronage in offices and honours. He associated himself with James Mill's published condemnation of the exclusion of women from the franchise, though he said the franchise should be extended to them only once all adult males had it.

Reform of the system of representation was by itself not yet quite enough; he further argued that there was waste and corruption in government, that public expenditure needed to be reduced and the efficacy of the civil service improved, chiefly by better selection and training of civil servants.

When his proposals on Parliamentary reform were published in 1817, and his attacks on waste and incompetence in public administration were published in 1824, he was confirmed as the country's leading voice of political radicalism. This by itself would have been enough to marginalize him in Establishment terms, but he exacerbated his marginalization by his attitude to religion, which he saw as a barrier to progress. He wrote scathingly about the Church's hold over education, and shocked many of his contemporaries with his *Not Paul, But Jesus* (1823) in which he described Jesus as a political revolutionary and St Paul as a liar.

Characteristically, though, Bentham was in favour of religious liberty, and in particular defended nonconformists against the disabilities they suffered as a result of their refusal to subscribe to the Thirty-Nine Articles of the Church of England. This kept them out of the universities, public schools, Parliament and any civil or military office. As a result nonconformists had founded their own schools, mostly superior in curriculum and teaching methods. When therefore proposals were put forward for a secular school in London and then a university – University College

London, today one of the world's great institutions of higher education – Bentham was enthusiastically in favour. At his request his skeleton, surmounted by a wax model of his head and wearing his clothes and hat, sits in a glass box in the entrance hall of the university's main building, watching the students go by.

Bentham's influence in his home country grew when the son of his associate James Mill, namely John Stuart Mill, reintroduced his countrymen to Bentham's thought, first by editing and publishing the five volumes of Bentham's *Rationale of Judicial Evidence* (1838–43) and then by developing the utilitarian doctrine he had inherited from him. With growing influence came growing criticism. Almost all critics commented unfavourably on Bentham's view of human nature, a rather impoverished, mechanistic picture in which he neglected wholly that side of human beings where imagination, love and sentiment play their typically dominating part. In Hazlitt's opinion Bentham's neglect of these factors rendered his philosophy 'fit neither for man nor beast'. This view of Bentham was shared by Karl Marx, who called Bentham an 'arch-philistine', and regarded utilitarianism as irredeemably superficial and bourgeois.

Particular criticism was levelled at Bentham's claim, in support of utilitarianism, that pleasures could be quantified in a 'felicific calculus' giving an objective measure of what act should be performed in a given set of circumstances. His view was condemned as 'pig philosophy' because a pig would come out higher than Socrates on this scale of felicity, so long as it had plenty of mud to wallow in and plenty of garbage to eat.

Above all – and predictably – Bentham was vilified by the clerical lobby, who were delighted by the exposé written by one John Colls, an Anglican clergyman who, before becoming such, had briefly served as secretary to Bentham, and who wrote an attack called *Utilitarianism Unmasked* (1844) portraying Bentham as a dangerous, bigoted and malign subversive.

Among philosophers the consensus is that Bentham erred in seeking to reduce all human motivation to the desire for pleasure and avoidance of pain just as such, for even if it is right to hold that happiness is the *summum bonum*, the roads to it are many and varied, and without an account of these – and the conflicts between them – as they arise in human nature a theory premised on the idea is in danger of being too crude.

HEGEL (1770–1831)

Georg Wilhelm Friedrich Hegel's thought plays a major role in nineteenth- and twentieth-century philosophy, not least through its influence on Marx and Marxism and on Heidegger and other thinkers, but also both directly on the British idealists and indirectly through the reaction to them of the founders of Analytic philosophy.

For some scholars Hegel ranks as equivalent to Kant in stature. Certainly one major similarity between them is the difficulty and range of their work, for they were both thinkers on a large, ambitious and innovative scale. For some other scholars he is seen as even more significant than Kant because of the impact his thought has had on major strands of philosophy, politics and practical world affairs since his day. For yet other scholars he barely registers: many of those who teach and write about philosophy in the Anglophone Analytic tradition pay little attention to his work; some have scarcely read a word he wrote, and never feel the need to do so.

Hegel was born at Stuttgart in 1770. His father was a civil servant in the government of the Duke of Baden-Württemberg, his mother was the daughter of a lawyer in the duchy's high court. She died when Hegel was aged thirteen. His brother Georg Ludwig was an army officer, who died on active service during Napoleon's Russian campaign of 1812.

Hegel was educated at a Protestant seminary attached to Tübingen University. While there he became friends with Friedrich Schelling and Friedrich Hölderlin. All three were enthusiasts for Hellenic culture and the French Revolution, and by the same token opponents of the stifling atmosphere of the seminary and what they saw as the reactionary nature of politics in the German-speaking states. Although Schelling had already embarked on his philosophical ambitions while a student, Hegel did not follow suit until later, after Schelling became a professor at Jena University and invited him to teach there as a *Privatdozent*. Until then Hegel had been earning his living as a private tutor.

While at Jena, Hegel embarked on what became the most celebrated of his works, *The Phenomenology of Spirit* (1807), the manuscript of which he finished as the sounds of Napoleon's victory at the battle of Jena rolled over the city. He was still not securely employed, having to accept the editorship of a magazine for a short while before becoming headmaster of a school, a post he held for nearly ten years. School-teaching was a prompt to his idea for an encyclopaedic work in three parts respectively covering logic, the natural world and 'Geist' (mind or spirit). While at the school he wrote the first part of this ambitious undertaking, *The Science of Logic*.

In 1816 Hegel at last received a salaried university position, at Heidelberg, where he wrote the *Encyclopaedia of the Philosophical Sciences in Outline* (1817). The following year he moved to the University of Berlin, his fame growing and his lectures attracting students from all over the German world and beyond. He published the *Philosophy of Right* in 1821, and in 1829 became Rector of Berlin University. He died two years later in a cholera epidemic. A legend repeated in various forms is that his dying utterance was a lament that his philosophy had not been understood. One version, doubtless untrue, has him whispering to a disciple, 'No one has understood me except you . . . and even you haven't got it right,' expiring before the anxious student could get a clarification.

From the outset Hegel saw philosophy as part of a movement of political and social reform. He believed that it is necessary as a response to divisions in society, in particular by serving as a means of restoring harmony between ideas and practice, as he and his friends Hölderlin and Schelling believed had been the case in classical Greece. In the earliest of his publications, a defence of Schelling's philosophy against Fichte, Hegel wrote, 'Division is the source of the need for philosophy.' He and his friends were dismayed by what they saw as the lack of integration in German culture, and they were at one in believing that the only thing German culture could be proud of was Kant. Even so, they were critical of Kant's philosophy; Hölderlin said that Kant was like Moses in that he had led his people out of exile, but his people still needed guidance into the Promised Land.

Between them the three friends produced a document, conceived probably by Hölderlin though for a long time thought to be an early work by Hegel (because its manuscript version is in his handwriting), called 'The Oldest System-Programme of German Idealism'. The project it outlines begins with the Kantian idea of the individual as a radically free moral being, where freedom is subjection to laws that individuals impose on themselves. But the document goes beyond Kant in saying that the fact that reason can devise and self-apply such law is a sign that it is not limited in the way Kant described; instead, reason should be seen as capable of transcending the boundary of empirical experience and giving an answer to the question 'What must the world be like for a moral being?'

That answer is cast in terms of a metaphysics of 'Ideas'. It seemed clear to the document's authors that science would benefit from being released from the constraint of what they described as merely 'plodding' experimental procedure. But more importantly still, the concept of 'Ideas' showed how to give a wholly new theory of the state. This was to be done by demonstrating that in fact there is no 'Idea' of the state: 'There is no *Idea* of the state, any more than there is an Idea of a machine, because the state is something mechanical. Only what is an object of freedom can be an "Idea". So we must go beyond the state! For every state will only treat people as cogs in its machine.' And the task of philosophy in this programme is to provide a basis for a new kind of society in which all are equal and free because their minds are liberated, educated and autonomous: there will be 'an absolute freedom of all minds that carry the intellectual world within themselves and seek neither God nor immortality outside'.

These revolutionary beginnings to Hegel's thinking did not last long. By the time he wrote *The Phenomenology of Spirit* he had come to think that the period of history in which he lived was the culmination of a process of cultural transformation, and that therefore philosophy's task was not as he had at first conceived it, but something different, namely, to make everyone aware of what he saw as the following fact: that the *dialectical journey of Geist had reached fulfilment.* These last seven words encapsulate the nub of Hegel's philosophy: the explanation of them is as follows.

The word 'Geist' means 'mind' or 'spirit', and for Hegel it meant a universal mind or agency in which all individual human minds participate. The notorious difficulties over how exactly to translate 'Geist' usually – and wisely – prompt some translators and most philosophical commentators to use the word 'Geist' itself: think of it as meaning a 'world-mind' or 'world-spirit' in which our individual finite minds have a share. As Hegel's later work *The Philosophy of History* was written to show, he sees history as the story of the development or unfolding of Geist, its coming to greater and greater self-realization and self-fulfilment over time.

One way of clarifying Hegel's point is to note that history has indeed witnessed a development of mind in the sense of an increasing degree of understanding, awareness and insight achieved by humanity as knowledge has progressed from the superstitious ignorance of our cave-dwelling ancestors (as they are caricatured) to the degree of sophistication that science has made possible, accompanied by a more extensive knowledge of history and society than our ancestors had. Hegel thought that Geist had reached the summit in these respects; he saw his own time as marking the culmination of its fulfilment, and even (rather startlingly) that the Prussian state – the authoritarian monarchical Prussian state, of which he was a subject – was the embodiment of that fulfilment.

The word 'phenomenology' in the title *The Phenomenology of Spirit* means 'a study of appearances'. The word 'phenomenon' means 'appearance', and does not mean the thing itself that is appearing, or seeming to appear, to us. So the sun appears to us as a fiercely bright object in the sky above us that we could cover with a coin; if you close your eyes after catching a glimpse of the sun there will be a persistent after-image behind your eyelids – that too is a phenomenon, but in this case the real thing is not immediately 'behind' the appearance any longer, for this after-image phenomenon is caused by the continuing excitation of the visual pathway in the eyes and brain. So *Phenomenology of Spirit* means the way Geist *appears* at different stages in its unfolding or development to self-fulfilment in history.

More precisely still, Hegel's view is that this unfolding is an unfolding of *self-awareness* or self-understanding of Geist, and the greater the degree of this self-understanding, the more free Geist is, until it reaches the state of absolute freedom. It attains this state because it is simultaneously the state of absolute knowledge: the two are the same thing. This knowledge of reality as it is in itself – which he called 'knowledge of the Absolute' – is achieved as we develop from mere sensory knowledge through increasing degrees of self-consciousness. Hegel made a particular point of the fact that as self-consciousness requires consciousness of others, it is felt most strongly through desire for what is not itself – for another consciousness, and for possession of things in its environment: desire, in other words, for changing and appropriating the world or aspects of it. This was an idea that greatly interested Marx, for whom the point of philosophy was not merely to understand the world but to change it.

The need that a self-consciousness has for a relationship with another self-consciousness arises from the fact that this is how *self*-consciousness is achieved: through recognition and acknowledgement of another consciousness. One of the most celebrated parts of the *Phenomenology of Spirit* is Hegel's discussion of the relationship between master and slave, and the preceding claim that the first and most natural expression of mutual recognition between two self-consciousnesses is not amity but conflict – even indeed combat to the death. But, he says, combatants soon recognize that destruction of the relationship is inevitable if one does not give way, so an accommodation is reached that ends the conflict, an accommodation that typically takes an asymmetrical form in which the victor has ascendancy over the vanquished: a master–slave relationship.

But this relationship is unstable. The slave acknowledges the master's existence, but this is not satisfying to the master, for whom the slave is a mere thing. The minimal and exploitative recognition by the master of the slave makes the latter seek satisfaction in shaping parts of the material world into objects: the plants he grows, the table he makes out of wood. This would give him a sense of self, and of self-worth. But alas, the objects he makes are not his, but are appropriated by the master: he is *alienated* from the fruits of his work. This key idea inspired Marx to develop his theory of the alienation of labour: the slave's (the worker's) products are not only taken away from him, denying his self-affirmation as their maker, but become a major aspect of what oppresses him.

Hegel saw Stoicism in ancient philosophy as an attempted route out of alienation, by means of finding inner strength and consolation in the solitude of one's own mind, making it a matter of indifference whether one is a slave (like Epictetus) or an emperor (like Marcus Aurelius). But this detachment from reality is ultimately barren, says Hegel, and leads eventually to 'the unhappy consciousness' or 'alienated soul', in which master and slave are discordantly united within a single consciousness. This consciousness yearns to be independent of material things yet it is ineluctably part of the world, the physical condition of which – with all its pleasures and penalties – is inescapable. Accordingly the torn consciousness suffers. Hegel's target is Christianity, or any religion that does what Christianity does, namely, that turns human nature against itself. He sees the alienation of the soul as the inevitable result of postulating a god that exists apart from human beings and outside the world. The idea of this god is a projection of one side of human nature, the more spiritual side, alienating this aspect from the rest of itself, thereby creating the discordance in question.

The goal of Geist's evolving self-awareness is absolute knowledge,

knowledge of reality as it is in itself. Possession of this knowledge is complete freedom. The term Hegel used to describe his philosophical outlook is 'absolute idealism', denoting his conviction that ultimate reality as it is in itself is mental. In less developed states of consciousness mind does not realize that it constitutes reality; it thinks reality is independent of itself, and that our perception and reason are instruments for discovering the nature of that independent reality. The failure of these instruments to grasp the nature of reality *as it is in itself* is what led Kant to say that they can operate only in relation to the world as it appears to us, given that the way it appears to us is in large part the result of how the mind configures it. But when mind arrives at the point where it realizes that *all* reality is its own construction, it ceases to yearn after further knowledge, for there is nothing beyond the self-knowing mind itself. Absolute knowledge accordingly is 'mind knowing itself as mind'.

Note the implication of this. Mind, Geist, has achieved the final goal of its journey to self-awareness because he, Hegel, has understood the nature of reality. World history as the development of Geist has reached its consummation; Hegel's account of reality is the record of that fact. One might in short say that in Hegel the universe has found its point.

This returns us, of necessity, to the question of what Geist is. Since Hegel uses the term 'absolute idealism' to distinguish his view from 'subjective idealism' in which reality is described as somehow dependent on individual finite minds or on a collectivity of such minds, it might be natural to think of Geist as a universal mind, a cosmic consciousness. It might even be natural to think of it as a god, but if so it cannot be God as usually conceived because it would be a god which or who, until Hegel came along, was not fully aware of itself and the nature of reality. Moreover it mattered to Hegel that the individual mind should be understood socially, and the suggestion in his theory therefore seems to be that the universal mind is either constituted by or is shared by all individual minds together. The ideal he postulated in his earliest thought, the ideal of harmony in society, turns on the idea that individuals at their best and most rational, once all selfishness is set aside, would act in accord with each other because they are all partners, so to speak, in the cosmic consciousness.

The method Hegel employed is *dialectics*. In Plato dialectic was the process by which, in a question-and-answer discussion, an approach is made towards truth, the opposing arguments helping each other – pushing each other – to evolve in the direction of that goal. In Hegel, dialectic is the process in which any oppositions can, through the clash between them, produce something new, which in its turn could be opposed by something in another clash, producing yet a further new outcome. Hegel saw his use of the method as going far beyond Plato's, which was confined to particular problems or concepts. In Hegel the entire history of the world – as the history of the development of Geist's increasing self-awareness – is to be understood in terms of the constant evolution of new syntheses out of clashes of opposites.

A given state of affairs can be thought of as the *thesis* to which an opposite, an *antithesis*, poses itself. From the confrontation between them emerges a new state of affairs, the *synthesis*. The synthesis becomes a new thesis to which another antithesis opposes itself, thus producing a further synthesis. This again becomes the thesis to which an antithesis opposes itself . . . and so on and on. The final self-understanding of Geist is the final synthesis of the historical dialectical chain that brought it to that point.

Dialectic is both the process by which history unfolds and the method of philosophical argument and enquiry employed by Hegel. The method is set out in his *Logic*. A point to note is that his view explicitly controverts the idea in standard logic that when a thesis is opposed by an antithesis the result is contradiction, a dead-end from which nothing further can follow (given that, as standard logic has it, anything whatever follows from a contradiction). Instead, the particular contents of the thesis and the antithesis respectively determine what arises from the interplay of their opposition. In the *Logic* he illustrates this at the very beginning by considering the opposites *Being* and *Nothingness*, the relationship between them generating, as synthesis, *Becoming*. As applied to history, the dialectical process is one in which conflicts – within a society, or between states – cause disintegration which is overcome by reconciliation and new arrangements, which in their turn become the theses to new antitheses requiring solution in new syntheses – and so on again.*

This last remark draws attention to Hegel's *Philosophy of History*,

---

* I need hardly point out that this account of dialectic, and indeed of Hegel's views in general as here reported, is abstracted from the obscurity of one of the most impenetrable collections of philosophical texts in the entire canon; they make the fragments of Heraclitus look like *Janet and John* books.

in which he traces what he sees as the dialectically progressive course of history from its beginnings (as he views the matter) in the East, in Asia, to its culmination in the Europe of his own day, particularly in Prussia. 'The history of the world', he wrote, 'is nothing other than the progress of the consciousness of freedom.' This remark could stand as another encapsulation of his whole philosophy. An unavoidable impression has to be recorded here: that Hegel's view of history seems like a Procrustean bed on which the facts are stretched or shrunk to make them fit. This impression is immediately given by his claim that China and India are 'outside history' because they seemed to him to give no evidence of the workings of Geist's dialectical development. He chose Persia as the starting point for 'true history' because it was the first great empire to cease to exist. Persia's desire for empire was the thesis, the Greek city states' desire for independence was the antithesis, the moment of contestation was the Greek victory over the Persian navy at the battle of Salamis in 480 BCE – and the synthesis was the formative rise of classical Greek civilization that followed, and especially of its philosophy.

But Greek society itself depended on slavery, so the principle of freedom was very imperfect in its arrangements, Hegel thought, even though it represented an advance over Persian despotism. Moreover the Greeks relied on auguries and oracles in their decision-making, another mark that Geist was still at a relatively rudimentary stage. But the acceptance by Socrates of the Delphic injunction to 'Know thyself!' marked a turning point; he introduced the principle of independent thought against the custom-dominated culture of the Greeks, and this Hegel saw as one of history's crucial moments.

Hegel's psychological generalizations play a significant role in his view: people of the East completely lack freedom, they have no will of their own and no individual conscience, but are in abject submission to a ruler. The Greeks had a higher but still relatively undeveloped degree of self-awareness, which Socrates subverted by his opposition of a yet higher standard of the same, which is why they condemned him to death because he had so disturbed their outlook. Hegel traces this evolution, not always smooth and linear, onwards through Rome and the different forms of pre-Reformation Christianity, until the beginnings of Geist's approach to perfect self-awareness become discernible in the German world, at the Reformation.

Hegel did not see the Reformation as solely of religious significance. The Reformation idea that each individual must be responsible for his or her own choices opens minds to more general questions about morality, politics and nature, and this led to the Enlightenment's project of applying reason to all aspects of life and society, with the concomitant development of ideas about rights to freedom of the person, thereby challenging old barriers to individual advancement and promoting greater equality and opportunity in society. But this is not to imply that anarchy would be a yet higher stage of development; it is not 'subjective freedom' which is the point, at least until the world is organized in completely rational ways, because law and morality are still required. In a completely rational order, individuals will always choose to behave in conformity with their highest conceptions of law and morality in harmony with all others. The Prussia of Hegel's day was not quite at that point but, he appeared to think, was close.

The political philosophy implied in these remarks is set out in Hegel's *Philosophy of Right*. It is worth noting that he wrote the *Philosophy of History* at a moment when Prussia, after undergoing a series of liberal reforms, had begun to return to a more authoritarian regime under its king, Frederick William III. Hegel's concept of individual freedom was not, as the foregoing indicates, a libertarian one; rather it is that one is free if one does one's duty, because doing so liberates one from the tyranny of mere impulses and desires. Being a member of a society whose values I am infused by – values that the society has adopted in its own best interests – means that acting against the duty I owe to that society is in effect to act against myself. That is what Hegel meant by saying that to choose freely is to choose rationally.

For Hegel the best socio-political arrangement is a constitutional monarchy – somewhat (if not exactly) like the Prussia of his day. He was not a liberal; he did not think the populace should have a vote, he upheld the principle of monarchy, and his view of freedom of expression was a limited one. It seems easy to agree with Karl Popper's strictures on Hegel's political philosophy when one considers his claim that 'the state is the manifestation of the Divine Idea on earth' and that we must therefore 'worship' it. Defenders of Hegel point out that these remarks are reported by his students in their lecture notes, and that by 'the state' he meant society as a whole. Moreover his championing of freedom – even if this meant an idealized conformity with a rational sense of duty – and his correlative championing of the rule of law temper the appearance of what would look unpleasingly like support for authoritarianism. Still, he was clearly neither a liberal nor a democrat.

Hegel's legacy is more important than the details of his thought. Very soon after his death his disciples fell out among themselves, forming two camps: the 'Old' or 'Right Hegelians' who emphasized the politically conservative aspects of his views, and the 'Young' or 'Left Hegelians' who saw the radical implications of his views as a call to bring about freedom, a reconciliation of the individual and society, and a world governed by reason. They took it that Hegel had shown this to be an inevitability, because it is the destination of an historically necessary process. But they also thought that he had failed to follow through on the implications of his ideas, and they were determined to do so themselves.

Whereas the Right Hegelians ceased to be influential within just a few decades of Hegel's death, matters were quite otherwise with the Left Hegelians. Their first target was religion, which they saw as a major obstacle to human progress. They took their start from Hegel's concept of the 'unhappy consciousness' and described religion as a form of alienation: humanity creates the idea of God, projects all that is best about human beings on to this fiction while depreciating human nature in contrast, treats the being it has invented as the world's creator and bows down before it. The Young Hegelians who argued this line most tellingly were David Friedrich Strauss (1808–74) and Ludwig Feuerbach (1804–72). Strauss' *Life of Jesus* treated the Gospels as any other historical source would be treated, thereby launching a new, critical and secular approach to the study of religion and its documents and tenets. Feuerbach in *The Essence of Christianity* examined religious psychology and anthropology, focusing on the projection of positive human traits on to an invented being with all that follows from doing so.

Both Strauss and Feuerbach were translated into English by George Eliot (Marian Evans), the English essayist and novelist, which gave their views a wide reach even before Hegel's own philosophy was much known outside Germany. But even as Hegel's ideas were beginning to be known, so the Young Hegelians were 'standing them on their head'. Feuerbach argued for a materialist inversion of Hegel's idealism: reality is not created by thought, instead thought arises from matter (in the form of human beings). Mind is of the essence of humanity, not something separate from and higher than humanity, as Hegel believed – a view which, Feuerbach argued, is itself a form of alienation. He therefore further argued that philosophy and theology need to be replaced by a science of humankind, focusing on real people in real life. This revised, materialist version of aspects of Hegel's thought was an inspiration for Karl Marx. The 'sociological turn' one might see in Feuerbach's view had important parallels elsewhere in nineteenth-century thought – of course in Marx, but also in Auguste Comte's 'Positivism' and the movement it temporarily inspired. G. H. Lewes, George Eliot's consort and author of *A Biographical History of Philosophy*, was a Comtean who, in rather Hegelian fashion, thought that the history of philosophy had come to an end with Comte, and would thereafter be replaced by sociology.

SCHOPENHAUER (1788–1860)

Among those who acknowledged Arthur Schopenhauer's influence were Richard Wagner, Friedrich Nietzsche, Gustav Mahler, George Santayana, Ludwig Wittgenstein, Erwin Schrödinger, Albert Einstein, Thomas Mann, Jorge Luis Borges and many more. Unlike Hegel, Schopenhauer was a gifted and lucid writer, and his thought applies to life as it is lived rather than to world-historical generalizations about politics. His foremost influence was Kant, but another influence was Indian philosophy. He lived a solitary and ascetic life in adulthood, reading in the many languages he had at his command, and taking his greatest pleasure from music, which he regarded both as the highest of all the arts and as a universal language that alone promises liberation from humanity's suffering.

Arthur Schopenhauer was born in Danzig (now Gdańsk) in 1788. His father Heinrich Floris Schopenhauer was a wealthy merchant of Dutch descent, his mother was a well-known novelist. As an ardent disciple of Voltaire and a passionate Anglophile, Heinrich Schopenhauer wished his first child to be born in England. When Johanna Schopenhauer fell pregnant the family duly moved there, but Johanna was too homesick to stay, so husband and wife returned to Danzig, and there Arthur Schopenhauer was born. As compensation, Heinrich Schopenhauer furnished his house completely in the English style.

Heinrich had enlarged ideas about education, which included

sending Arthur to study in Paris for two years while a schoolboy, and for some months in London. Arthur's command of languages – English, French, Italian, Spanish and Latin – in part explains the high quality of his German prose.

When Schopenhauer was seventeen his father died, a major blow to him. His sister and mother moved to Weimar, the cultural capital of the German world, where Johanna Schopenhauer began her celebrated salon attended by Goethe, the brothers Grimm, Friedrich and August Schlegel, Christoph Wieland the poet, Heinrich Meyer and others. Schopenhauer studied at Göttingen University, then attended lectures in Berlin where he heard the Kantian philosopher Johann Gottlieb Fichte and the theologian Friedrich Schleiermacher.

The relationship between mother and son became an increasingly difficult one. Schopenhauer's closeness to his father made him deprecate his mother's indifference to his father's death. In fairness to her, it must be recorded that it was always understood that she had not married Heinrich Schopenhauer for love, and had never claimed otherwise. She had been eighteen, he nearly forty, when they married. The tension between mother and son came to a head when Schopenhauer offered his doctoral dissertation to his mother's publishers, F. A. Brockhaus. Johanna Schopenhauer's novels were not of great quality, but they were popular and sold well, so to please her Brockhaus accepted the dissertation; it was his *Fourfold Root of the Principle of Sufficient Reason*. Johanna said no one would read it; Schopenhauer retorted that his works would still be read long after her 'trashy novels', as he called them, were forgotten. He was right.

The *Fourfold Root* and personal acquaintance with Goethe prompted the latter, who was much impressed by him, to invite Schopenhauer to collaborate on investigations into colour, a subject to which Goethe had made scientific contributions of note. Schopenhauer later said that this work was one of the inspirations for the development of his philosophical views. While travelling in Italy in 1818 he had with him a letter of introduction to Lord Byron from Goethe, but he made no use of it, being – he said – too shy to do so.

In 1818 Schopenhauer published his principal philosophical work, *The World as Will and Representation*, and in 1820 he became a lecturer at Berlin University. He had developed a profound antipathy towards Hegel's philosophy, and in the hope of drawing students away from it scheduled his lectures at the same hour as Hegel's.* Whereas hundreds flocked to hear Hegel, only five students came to Schopenhauer's class. In disgust he abandoned university teaching and left Berlin, eventually settling in Frankfurt, where he thereafter lived alone with a succession of dogs, devoting himself to writing. He was not always solitary; in 1819 a serving-girl in his lodgings fell pregnant by him, but the child died when just a few months old.

By his own acknowledgement Schopenhauer owed most to Kant's philosophy in the development of his own. He accepted from Kant the idea that the world as it appears to us, the phenomenal world, consists in representations in our experience, its structure and character being the product of the way we experience and conceptualize it. And he accepted also the distinction between the phenomenal and noumenal worlds, the latter being reality as it is in itself. Where Schopenhauer parts company from Kant is in the question of our access to noumenal reality. Kant said that we have no access to it, and that all that can be said of it is that it has nothing of the character of phenomenal reality. It follows that the concepts by which phenomenal reality is constituted, such as causality, do not apply to noumenal reality. This was the chief obstacle to reception of Kant's view, for if causal power cannot be attributed to the noumenon, what explains the occurrence of intuitions – the sensory input on which the understanding operates to produce experience and thus the phenomenal world?

In Schopenhauer's view, the noumenon is indeed accessible: we experience it as *will*. Will is the noumenal reality underlying all appearances, and therefore the whole of nature. We experience will directly, intimately, within ourselves; it predates conscious knowledge, and is completely separate from it. To say that will manifests itself independently of knowledge is to say that it does so independently of the application of concepts. Accordingly, knowledge is secondary. As the

---

* Schopenhauer *really* disliked Hegel. He wrote, 'Hegel, installed from above, by the powers that be, as the certified Great Philosopher, was a flat-headed, insipid, nauseating, illiterate charlatan, who reached the pinnacle of audacity in scribbling together and dishing up the craziest mystifying nonsense. This nonsense has been noisily proclaimed as immortal wisdom by mercenary followers and readily accepted as such by all fools, who thus joined into as perfect a chorus of admiration as had ever been heard before. The extensive field of spiritual influence with which Hegel was furnished by those in power has enabled him to achieve the intellectual corruption of a whole generation.'

substratum of everything, as the single, fundamental, primary reality, everything else being appearance, will is the source of all existence and action.

Schopenhauer viewed will as a blind force, and its relentless expression of itself, manifesting in human experience as desire, craving, yearning and inevitable dissatisfaction, causes suffering. To be released from suffering one must be released from the power of will – in other words, from thraldom to desire. Here one immediately recognizes the parallel with Buddhist thought. Schopenhauer tells us that he found with delight that Buddhism chimed with the views he had himself developed; *The World as Will and Representation* was published at about the same time as he first became acquainted with Buddhist teachings. He had however already come to know and greatly admire the Upanishads, a copy of which always lay open on his work-table, and some of which he read every night of his life before sleeping. In the Upanishads the idea of *moksha* (liberation) from *samsara* (suffering – and, in the Upanishads, rebirth) is achieved or at any rate advanced by understanding the unity of *Atman* (the self) and *Brahman* (underlying universal reality: see Indian Philosophy in Part V below).

Among the guests at Johanna Schopenhauer's salon in 1814 was a scholar of Indian antiquities, Friedrich Majer, who was engaged in writing a book about Hinduism (it was published in 1818). Schopenhauer had made notes about Indian culture in anthropology lectures he had attended at Göttingen University in 1811; now, as a result of encounters with Majer and another Indologist called Klopstock, he borrowed a translation of the Upanishads from the Weimar library. At the time he was writing his *Fourfold Root*, and soon thereafter began work on *The World as Will and Representation*. It is probable therefore that the idea of desire as a source of suffering connected well with his idea of will as noumenal reality, the metaphysics of the noumenon immediately providing a route to an ethical outlook premised on suffering's universality, and the demand for a response to this fact from us.

A relief from suffering, though a temporary one, is provided by aesthetic experience. Rapt contemplation of art and especially of music takes us out of ourselves, collapsing the distinction between the self and its representations and immersing each in the other. Music is the most potent route to this transcendence of suffering; Schopenhauer regarded it as the purest of the arts, universal and timeless.

Schopenhauer's view that to exist is to suffer provides the ground of his ethics. This ground is *compassion*, not only for other people but for all animals and nature. Compassion is 'the immediate participation, independent of all ulterior motives, primarily in the suffering of another and thus in the prevention or elimination of it'. If an act is performed for any other motive it 'cannot have real moral worth'. The point for Schopenhauer is that other systems of morality ultimately come down to a form of egoism. In religion the motive is to please the deity and thus to receive a reward or escape a punishment. Although Kant was right to distinguish between treating people as ends and treating them as means, and to assert that it is morally illegitimate to treat anyone as a means, said Schopenhauer, it is still an egoistic morality because it treats the agent and the patient of the moral act as two separate beings. Compassion, on the other hand, involves identification of the one who feels compassion and the one who suffers. He included all animals in the moral universe because they too are manifestations of the under-lying reality of will, and likewise suffer. He believed that any human being who is unkind to animals of other species cannot be a good person.

In *The World as Will and Representation* Schopenhauer devoted two chapters to the subject of sex, the first serious philosophical discussion it had ever received. His account is quoted with approval by Charles Darwin in *The Descent of Man*. Schopenhauer's view of the powerful and disruptive nature of sexual desire influenced Freud also. He assigned sex a central place as an example of the relentless driving power of will, as one would expect; yet at the same time took a liberal and relaxed view of homosexuality.

In his many essays other applications and extensions of his philoso-phy are to be found, demonstrating the variety of his views on life and society. He was a liberal in politics, agreed with Plato on eugenics and expressed the view that though women are 'more sober in judgment' and more compassionate than men, they are nevertheless best suited to the roles of nurses and teachers of children because they are themselves 'childish, frivolous and short-sighted'. When he came to know the sculp-tor Elisabet Ney towards the end of his life he changed his mind to a far less patronizing view, saying, 'If a woman succeeds in withdrawing from the mass . . . she grows ceaselessly, and more than a man.'

By the end of the nineteenth century Schopenhauer was the most famous philosopher in Europe, and his influence extended into the intellectual life of the twentieth century outside philosophy as such.

Pictures of Schopenhauer show a grim-looking old man with puffs of white hair sticking up like rabbit's ears from the back of his otherwise bald head. They belie the humour, insight and compassion which – despite some unappealing views such as those on women and his inability to suffer fools gladly – are everywhere evident in his writing.

POSITIVISM

The label 'Positivism' has been attached to a number of nineteenth- and twentieth-century outlooks, so it is worth clarifying its various uses. The most famous version is the 'Logical Positivism' of the twentieth century, which is described later in these pages. In the nineteenth century the concept is associated with legal theory, and with the thought of Auguste Comte (1798–1857).

In legal theory Positivism means the view that the answer to the question 'What is a valid law?' is that it was enacted by a properly constituted authority or derived from recognized precedent, which explicitly means that the validity of law has nothing to do with whether it is intrinsically 'moral' or 'just' – that is, has nothing to do with its merits. Even a thoroughly bad law – there are plenty of them – is valid if the proper authorities enacted it. There has been a highly influential school of Legal Positivists in England, from Bentham through John Austin (1790–1859) to Herbert Hart (1907–92).

Much closer in meaning is the Positivism of Comte. Indeed he invented the name 'Positivism'. For him as for the Logical Positivists of the Vienna Circle later, Positivism is the view that the only knowledge worth the name comes from empirical scientific sources, from systematically and logically organized experience of natural phenomena. A corollary is the rejection of metaphysics and theology as sources of knowledge. The difference between Comtean Positivism and that of the Vienna Circle is that the former was a view about politics and social theory, whereas the Vienna Circle Positivists were interested in philosophy of science and epistemology.

Comte did not claim that Positivism was original to him; he believed that Galileo, Bacon, Descartes and Newton – indeed, anyone who had made a genuine contribution to knowledge – were the founders of Positivism even if they had not used the word. Comte thought that humanity's attempts to explain the world had developed through three historical phases: an early theological phase relying on supernatural explanations, a metaphysical phase in which the first speculative efforts at naturalistic explanation were made in terms of unknown forces and principles, and finally the positive stage, in which scientific understanding has been achieved of the scientific laws that govern the world.

Along with Hegel, Marx and others, Comte believed that the laws governing the behaviour of individuals and societies were just as scientific as those discovered in natural science. He drew an analogy with medical science, then increasingly revealing the formerly hidden causes of disease. His early work attracted the attention and agreement of John Stuart Mill, G. H. Lewes (who ended his *Biographical History of Philosophy* with a paean to Comte), George Eliot, T. H. Huxley and others. He and his views became famous, and eventually his fame went to his head; he decided that because Positivism should replace religion, and because religion's attractions and its hold over people depended on ritual, worship, hymn-singing, church-going, saints, martyrs and the like, Positivism needed to compete on direct terms. Accordingly he set up a secular religion, the Religion of Humanity, complete with a catechism, a calendar of saints, priests, rituals, prayers, sacraments and places of worship. He borrowed all the lineaments of his Religion of Humanity from the Catholicism of his native France, except for God and Christ. The serious adherents of his earlier scientific attitudes to matters of society and public policy fell away, and the endeavour collapsed in ridicule. Something of the intention was perceptive and had value; the execution failed the intention.

MILL (1806–1873)

In his *Autobiography* John Stuart Mill records the rigorous education he was given by his father James Mill, Jeremy Bentham's collaborator. Mill began his study of Greek at age three, of Latin at age eight, and by the age of ten was teaching his younger siblings mathematics, history and the classics. History was his principal love, but he read science and composed poetry (this latter at his father's insistence – his first poetical work, written at the age of twelve, was a continuation of the *Iliad*).

Mill's father was the author of the monumental and influential *History of British India*. Mill senior had never visited India, knew no Indian languages and was critical of – indeed, hostile to – almost everything Indian, yet his book was used by the British in India as a handbook for the conduct of the Raj.

Like Bentham, the senior Mill was a man for whom theory was superior to reality; the relentless education he gave his precociously gifted son illustrates that fact. Inevitably, the younger Mill suffered a nervous breakdown; at the age of twenty he found himself sunk in 'dry, heavy dejection', and the purpose he had set himself in life, which was to promote social justice, lost its savour. He was rescued from this misery and attendant suicidal thoughts by reading the poetry of Wordsworth. It taught him to value what had been wholly absent from his father's instruction: the 'internal culture of the individual' as an important part of the process by which the great end of happiness, the 'test of all rules of conduct', is to be achieved.

Achieving happiness is to be done, Mill said, not by seeking happiness – 'Ask yourself whether you are happy, and you cease to be so' – but by seeking the happiness of others, helping to improve man-kind, or pursuing artistic or other goals that are worthwhile in themselves. Happiness will attend these activities; it will be 'inhaled with the air one breathes'. This insight underlay Mill's liberalism and his version of utilitarian ethics.

Mill was born in London in 1806, and grew up in the rarefied air of the great schemes for social, legal and political reform of Bentham and his father. As a nonconformist in religion (though personally an agnostic) he was unable to attend either Oxford or Cambridge because he would not subscribe to the articles of the Church of England. He attended lectures at University College London, founded by his father and Bentham among others, but did not take a degree. Instead he joined the British East India Company, which he served in increasingly senior positions for nearly thirty years. He did not agree with the 1858 change of administration of India, when the Crown took direct control from the Company, and therefore refused a seat on the Council of India.

In 1851 Mill married the woman who had been the object of his affections for many years but who had until then been married to some-one else. This was Harriet Taylor, who shared in the research and writing of some of his work. She died in 1858. Mill became a Member of Parliament in 1865, and was the first MP to advocate votes for women. The book he wrote in collaboration with Harriet Taylor, *The Subjection of Women*, arguing for equality of the sexes, was published in 1869.

Mill's *System of Logic* (1843) was a contribution to discussion of scientific method, a significant point given the historical stage at which science then found itself, and which had attracted the attention of other thinkers, among them John Herschel and William Whewell. Along with the essays that Mill was then publishing on a wide range of subjects in the *Westminster Review*, his book on logic and scientific method helped to establish his reputation. But the work for which Mill is principally remembered is found in two relatively short and accessible books, *On Liberty* (1859) and *Utilitarianism* (1863).

The central question of *On Liberty* is, What should be the limit of the power that a society can legitimately exercise over individuals? Mill held that individuals are not accountable to society for things that concern only themselves, and correlatively that society cannot interfere with individuals except when their actions are likely to harm others. Together these commitments entail that individuals should be free unless a good reason exists why they should not be.

It is natural to think that the concept of liberty has its life principally in opposition to ideas about tyranny and lack of individual rights. Mill argued that liberty also has to be defended against social coercion to conform, not least in morals. People should be free to live as they choose, he argued, provided they do not harm others, for this allows the widest possible exploration of ways for human beings to live flourishingly.

Mill is regarded as a 'classical liberal' because of this view, and in line with it he supported the abolition of slavery. But it has to be noted that he thought that authoritarian government over populations in 'backward states of society' is legitimate. He also invites difficulties by saying that we can harm others not just by what we do but also by what we fail to do. This leaves it open to society to coerce people to do things like go to school, pay taxes and refrain from smoking tobacco in public places.

An admirable feature of *On Liberty* is its defence of freedom of expression, which Mill regarded as fundamental to civil society and progress. Censorship could result in important truths not being known, he argued, and unless there is open debate ideas can ossify into mere dogma.

Mill is one of the chief advocates of a form of utilitarianism in ethics, the view that actions are made right or wrong by their consequences. Kant had argued for a deontological view: right and wrong are matters of an agent's intentions, and whether the behaviour they produce conforms to universalizable moral rules independently of their consequences. Consequentialists argue by contrast that no act is intrinsically right or wrong, and that the only measure of moral value is outcome. As consequentialists, utilitarians argue that the measure of an action's moral worth is the degree to which it promotes a positive result, the aim of any action that seeks to be of moral worth being 'the greatest good for the greatest number'. This is the Principle of Utility.

Mill shared with his predecessor utilitarians the view that what is good is happiness, and that happiness consists in pleasure and the absence of pain. This hedonistic (pleasure-based) view is not however egoistic, but other-regarding; Mill argued that the decision whether or not an action is likely to maximize happiness for the greatest number should be made as if from the point of view of a benevolent and disinterested observer.

Bentham's idea of a 'felicific calculus' had been criticized because it makes a pig come out higher than Socrates on the scale of felicity it measures, if the pig has enough garbage and mud to enjoy. Mill combated this criticism by arguing that there are 'higher' and 'lower' pleasures, and that the person best fitted to judge which is which is the person who knows both. A person who knows only the lower pleasures knows only one side of the question; and a person who knows the higher pleasures, and who has a conscience and refined feelings as a result, would not take pleasure in things that are base.

This elitist view does not quite square with what is commonly thought about human psychology, given that some of the 'higher pleasures' – reading Aeschylus in the original Greek, going to the opera – can seem hard work to some, while the desire to slump on to a sofa before a television set with an alcoholic beverage in hand is felt often enough even by the most epicene of epicures.

Mill was a classic or 'act' utilitarian, in holding that the consequences of each individual action constitute the measure of its moral worth. This view is not entirely consistent with two other important views he held, namely, that no individual is more special than any other individual when it comes to measuring the consequences of actions, and that a fundamental principle of liberty is that everyone's rights should be upheld. A crude utilitarian view would appear to justify neglecting the rights and interests of those in the minority on any question – if you could save six people by killing another five, a crude utilitarian view is that you should do so. In response, some utilitarians have abandoned 'act utilitarianism' for a 'rule utilitarian' view, this being that we should live according to rules which are likely in general to produce the greatest happiness for the greatest number, even if on some occasions a particular act does not do so. Mill's insistence on the rights of minorities and the equal value of all sits more naturally with rule utilitarianism than with his own version.

Mill's godson Bertrand Russell said of him that he merited the high reputation he had in his own day because of his intellectual virtues, his personal moral probity and his elevated view of the aim of life. It is hard to disagree. He certainly merits the reputation he still enjoys because of his defence of individual liberty and his championing of the cause of women.

MARX (1818–1883)

Karl Marx was the descendant of a line of rabbis who had served the Jewish community of Trier in Prussia's Lower Rhine province since the beginning of the eighteenth century. His father Heinrich Marx was the first in this succession to break with tradition, becoming a lawyer and vineyard owner, and taking the even more revolutionary step of converting to Lutheranism: his forename 'Heinrich' replaced his baptismal name 'Heschel'. Marx's mother Henriette Pressburg was the daughter of a wealthy Dutch family, also Jewish, related to the Philips family whose name became famous for its electronic products in the following century. When Marx was later living in impoverished exile in London, his Philips relations were generous with financial help. Henriette followed her husband in converting to Lutheranism.

Marx's father was interested in philosophy and political reform. He had his nine children educated privately in their early years, then sent the sons among them to the Friedrich-Wilhelm Gymnasium whose headmaster, another liberal and Enlightenment-inspired thinker, was a friend. The school attracted hostile attention from the authorities for promoting liberal views among its students; while Marx was there the school was raided and a number of staff dismissed. These antecedents accord well with Marx's eventual direction of travel. But at the time he went to Bonn University at the age of seventeen he was not yet quite the radical he became.

Excused military duty because of a proneness to chest infections,

Marx took to student life at Bonn in typical fashion, skipping classes, fighting a duel and being arrested for drunkenness. His father made him transfer to Berlin University with the admonition to take his studies more seriously. Marx had wished to study philosophy and literature, but his father insisted on law. At the time of his transfer to Berlin Marx had an added reason to become more serious; he had proposed to Jenny von Westphalen, daughter of an aristocrat to whom he later dedicated his doctoral dissertation.

Hegelian ideas lay at the centre of discussion at Berlin University, as they did in most intellectual circles of the Europe of the day. Marx joined a group of radicals who came to be known as the 'Young Hegelians', centred on Bruno Bauer and Ludwig Feuerbach. The Young Hegelians were not uncritical epigones of Hegel; it was his dialectical methodology rather than his metaphysical views they adopted. At this juncture Marx's literary interests were still alive; he wrote a novel, a play and a number of amorous verses addressed to Jenny von Westphalen. But his attention was increasingly focused on philosophy. With Bauer he worked on an edition of Hegel's *Philosophy of Religion*, and in his doctoral dissertation he argued for philosophy's 'sovereign authority' (a quotation he took from Hume) over enquiry in general and especially theology. Although the dissertation's main dedicatee is Jenny von Westphalen's father, it has another: 'the most eminent saint and martyr in the philosophic calendar', namely Prometheus – he who stole fire from the gods and gave it to humankind – whose words Marx quotes with relish in the Preface: 'In simple words, I hate the pack of gods.'*

Marx's hopes of a career as an academic were thwarted by increasing hostility to the radicalism of the Young Hegelians. Instead he became a journalist, moving to Cologne to work for the *Rheinische Zeitung*. His political sentiments and his views about economics were sharpened by the experience, partly by his examination of actual conditions in society and partly by the newspaper's treatment at the hands of the authorities, who soon banned it. Marx moved to Paris to join an even more radical journal, the *Deutsch-Französische Jahrbücher*, for which Mikhail Bakunin had also been recruited. Marx contributed two of his most significant early publications to the only issue to be published. He met Friedrich Engels in Paris, and the two immediately

---

* Marx's dissertation is entitled *The Difference between the Democritean and Epicurean Philosophies of Nature*.

began what was to prove a lifelong collaboration. Engels' *Condition of the Working Class in England* persuaded Marx that the proletariat could be the vehicle of the revolution required to bring about social and economic justice, by hastening the dialectical process which must, on his view of historical inevitability, bring about that state of affairs.

In the writings Marx produced in Paris and Brussels between the years 1843 and 1848, including the *Economic and Philosophical Manuscripts* and the *Theses on Feuerbach*, his close study of economics, political economy and history fuelled the development of ideas that eventuated in his great work, *Capital*. Students of Marx agree in nominating the book he wrote with Engels, *The German Ideology*, as marking his break with the Young Hegelians and with philosophical idealism, asserting instead a concept of historical process as driven wholly by material conditions of life. This book was a prelude to the most famous of the joint Marx–Engels writings, *The Communist Manifesto*, published in early 1848, a few months before the outbreak of a series of revolutions in Europe.

Marx had inherited money from his father's estate, and now he used it to give direct aid to the revolutionary cause and to found a newspaper in support of it. He was expelled from Belgium on suspicion of buying arms for insurrectionaries; back in Paris his newspaper was soon suppressed. In the summer of 1849 he and Jenny left France for England, and settled in London. He spent the rest of his life there, supported mainly by Engels but nevertheless living in great poverty. At first he continued with the promotion of revolutionary activities in the Communist League and among exiled German socialists in London. For a number of years he was the London correspondent of the *New York Daily Tribune*, a newspaper with a working-class appeal in the United States. The work was intermittent and poorly paid, but it gave Marx a wider readership.

Political activity, such as playing a leading role in the International Workingmen's Association (the 'First International'), consumed large amounts of Marx's time and energy, not least because, with the diminishing of revolutionary activity across Europe, activists turned to infighting over questions of strategy and direction. Marx opposed Bakunin's attempt to move the International in the direction of anarchism, and won. By then, however, the success of his *A Contribution to the Critique of Political Economy* (1859), which anticipates the more detailed *Capital* then still in manuscript, had persuaded Marx to devote his main energies to the latter. Among other considerations, he regarded the failure of revolution in Europe as necessitating an examination of capitalism itself.

Poor health, poverty, disappointment in practical politics and relentless work were Marx's lot since his university days. One admires the comradeship provided by Jenny von Westphalen in that life, in which she bore seven children, only three of whom survived. Whatever one's view of Marx's momentous legacy, one has to agree with two points: his was an epic life, and it proves how philosophy can – as he himself said it must – change the world.

Marx's principal efforts were apportioned between practical political activism and the theory that provided the justification for it. A sketch of the activism is given in the foregoing. The theoretical side of his work divides between technical examination of questions in economics and a variety of topics that have more general philosophical interest. The three volumes of *Capital* are almost wholly devoted to the former. They contain extensive discussions of commodity production, requiring the existence of markets and the division of labour, the distinction between use-value and exchange-value and the labour theory of value that underlies it, the nature of capitalism, the argument that surplus value is the source of profit, and related topics. Critics identify flaws in Marx's technical case, but aspects of what he says – the tension between worker and capitalist, the former seeking higher wages and the latter higher profits, and the unstable nature of economic cycles – continue to be persuasive.

The more directly philosophical ideas in Marx have been equally influential. Some of the more salient are as follows.

There are critics of liberalism on both the right and left of the political spectrum. Liberalism is the political philosophy that values individual freedom, equality, the rule of law, democracy, religious liberty and respect for rights such as privacy, freedom of expression, freedom of the press and the right of assembly. Criticisms of it from the political right are what one would expect from a viewpoint that seeks greater control over and uniformity among populaces, subordinating individual preferences to the demands of conventional morality, loyalty and patriotism, a regimented state, perhaps military values, and the like: think of a Fascist state in recent history for an example. In this respect a Fascist state does not differ much from an authoritarian Communist one – it is as if the opposite wings of politics bend so far at their extremes as to circle round and become indistinguishable in their practical effects, differing only in rhetoric.

Marx offers a critique of liberalism from a left perspective. In his essay 'On the Jewish Question' he criticizes Bruno Bauer's argument that religion is an obstacle to human emancipation. Bauer had as his principal target the lifting of proscriptions against Jews, not because he was an anti-Semite but because he thought all religion should be proscribed; he was writing as a robust atheist and militant secularist. Marx's response was to distinguish between political and human emancipation. The former consists in according people rights to protect them from the depredations of other people and institutions, the latter consists in promoting communion and fellowship, so that people do not need to be protected from each other.

Of course Marx welcomed liberalism as an advance over more repressive forms of society marked by religious discrimination and conflict, but he believed that it was itself a barrier to true emancipation, in that it placed protective walls between people rather than promoting their coming together. In a perfected state of society those walls will not be necessary, he said, because harmony will prevail, and people will make common cause with each other. This attractive idea is implausible. The thought that human nature might be so far perfected as not to require measures to protect the weak from the strong, as not to require active promotion of fairness, as not to require methods of resolving frictions when the diversity of human interests and desires conflict, is utopian: one sees why some might prefer to take their chances in a liberal dispensation.

One of Marx's best-known remarks is that religion is the 'opium of the people'. It occurs in the Introduction to his 'Contribution to the Critique of Hegel's Philosophy of Right', where he argues that 'criticism of religion is the prerequisite of all criticism,' and that man and society are the creators of religion, which is therefore an 'inverted consciousness of the world'. Humanity suffers under oppressive social and economic arrangements, and religious feeling is 'the expression of real suffering and a protest against real suffering. Religion is the sigh of the oppressed creature, the heart of a heartless world, and the soul of soulless conditions. It is the *opium* of the people.' It is, he says, the task of philosophy to unmask religion by unmasking the sources of suffering: 'The abolition of religion as the *illusory* happiness of the people is the demand for their *real* happiness.'

To achieve this, the material basis of history has to be understood to see how true community between people has so far been obstructed by the political and economic oppression of the masses. Understanding this will encourage people to break free by revolting against that oppression.

These views arose in the context of Marx's reflections on Feuerbach's claim, striking and controversial when he made it though he was not the first to say this, that God and religion are human inventions. Another of Marx's much quoted statements also occurs in his thinking about Feuerbach: 'philosophers have only interpreted the world; the point is to change it.' The *Theses on Feuerbach* succinctly state Marx's critique of both materialist and idealist philosophy before him. Although he was himself a materialist in his metaphysical views, Marx charged preceding materialism with failing to recognize how human thought and action contribute to the nature of the reality they perceive. Idealists had seen that humans do this, but wrongly concluded that reality itself is therefore ideal. Their mistake was not to see that human activity is material activity, which affects the real physical world: digging tunnels to mine its ore, cutting down its trees, diverting the course of its rivers. This picture of the relationship of humanity to nature is *historical materialism*; a relationship of work, of labour, of muscle and sweat.

A conception of history underlies so much of Marx's thought that, although there is no single text in which he sets it out, it is possible to put it together from various of his writings, most notably from his early collaboration with Engels, *The German Ideology* (1845), and the canonical *Critique of Political Economy* (1859). Both make much the same point about the material conditions of human existence just noted, but conjoin with it the idea that as conditions of production change over time, so do human relationships. As people become more conscious of how their lives are shaped by the economic circumstances in which they live, so they will become more capable, said Marx, of freeing themselves from the oppression of those circumstances.

The historical process is a dialectical one, in which contradictions between the material interests of different sections of society – peasant and landowner in feudalism, worker and capitalist in capitalism – express themselves as conflicts, in a dynamic representable as a Hegelian movement of thesis and antithesis producing a synthesis which in turn is the thesis to a new antithesis, and so forth – in a sequence of 'negating the negations' as Engels put it – until this deterministic evolution results in a pure state of communism where the state 'withers away' because human good fellowship will make laws and government unnecessary.

Such at any rate is a standard view, influenced by later interpreters of Marx, chief among them Lenin. Experts on Marx differ as to whether he really had a philosophy of history, and if so what it was. Some say that when he writes about particular historical occurrences he does not place them into a fixed pattern of historical unfolding; an example cited is the essay 'The Eighteenth Brumaire of Louis Napoleon' on the revolutionary events in France between 1848 and 1851. Yet the opening remarks of that essay suggest otherwise: 'Men make their own history, but they do not make it as they please; they do not make it under self-selected circumstances, but under circumstances existing already, given and transmitted from the past. The tradition of all dead generations weighs like a nightmare on the brains of the living.'

However, the attribution to him of the idea that the historical process is deterministic – that society must necessarily arrive at a communist endpoint – can only with difficulty be made consistent with the idea that the working class must engage in revolution to bring it about; for if one tries to say that this is merely encouragement to hasten the processes of history, one is thereby contradicting the view of those processes as necessary. Perhaps, on the other hand, Marx did not think that historical materialism is a deterministic process; but then the account of the process by which feudalism was supplanted by capitalism, and his view that certain societies were not yet ready for revolution because they had not reached the level of industrialization required for an urban proletariat, seem to oblige a reading of him in the opposite direction.

Although Marx's analysis of labour is central to his economic and political theory, it has a powerful philosophical dimension also. In his *Economic and Philosophical Manuscripts* of 1844 he sets out his view of *alienation*. He argues that workers in a capitalist system suffer alienation in four ways: they are alienated from the things they produce, from the satisfaction of work because their work is harsh and disagreeable, from the exercise of their natural powers, and from other people, their relationship with whom becomes one of exchange rather than mutuality. Everything about the capitalist system is, he argues, connected with alienation – rent, wages, profits and the rest. His preferred alternative is not fully sketched, but turns on the idea of labour which is satisfying to the labourer and which genuinely satisfies his or her own needs and the needs of others.

An underlying assumption of all Marx's work is that economic systems up to and including capitalism are unjust and oppressive, and that communism, properly realized, would be a good state of affairs, because it would be premised upon the mutuality of human beings – fellowship, sharing and true freedom. The question whether there are kinds of society that could be just and humanly good without requiring that we wait to see if utopian hopes for human nature can come true remains as the more immediate question requiring answer.

NIETZSCHE (1844–1900)

Around the name 'Friedrich Nietzsche' plays a romance of genius and madness, of profound insight and philosophical revolution. His writings have the vatic character of the Old Testament prophets – deliberately so: his longest book, *Thus Spake Zarathustra*, is cast in the form of a revelation brought down from the mountains by a seer. It does not impugn the originality and power of Nietzsche's thought to say that he was a dramatist of ideas as much as a philosopher. Indeed in utterance, in appearance and in biography he is the paradigm of thinker as light-ning flash, deliberately shocking those who encounter him, either into outrage or into a different way of thinking.

Nietzsche was born near Leipzig in Saxony, the son of a Lutheran pastor who died of a brain disease in his mid-thirties, when Nietzsche was aged five. He had a brother who died in infancy, and a sister, Elisa-beth, two years younger, who came to play a significant role in his posthumous reputation.

Because his father had been a state employee (pastors were on the public payroll) Nietzsche was given a scholarship to the prestigious Schulpforta school at Naumburg. There he studied classical and modern languages and music, fell in love with the then little-known poetry of Friedrich Hölderlin and first came to hear of Richard Wagner. At Bonn University he studied theology and philology, at first thinking of becom-ing a pastor. To the great disappointment of his mother and sister he lost his faith as a result of reading David Strauss' *Life of Jesus* and Ludwig Feuerbach's *The Essence of Christianity*. Instead he devoted himself to classical philology as a student of Professor Friedrich Ritschl at Leipzig University, and there acquired a passion for philosophy as a result of reading Schopenhauer's *World as Will and Representation*.

In 1867 Nietzsche volunteered for a year's service with a Prussian artillery division. He was a good horseback rider, which in the eyes of his superiors was the chief qualification for being an officer. This might have been his fate had he not had an accident while leaping on to his horse one day, serious enough to invalid him for many months. He therefore returned to his studies, and soon afterwards met Richard Wagner and his wife Cosima, who were to exert a great influence on him.

Nietzsche's teacher Professor Ritschl held him in high esteem, and helped him secure the chair of classical philology at Basle University in 1869 at the amazingly young age of twenty-four, even before he had been awarded a doctorate. At Ritschl's instigation the University of Leipzig gave Nietzsche an honorary doctorate to somewhat regularize matters. Nietzsche's inaugural lecture was on Homer, though the dissertation he had been writing but never finished was an examination of the sources used by Diogenes Laertius for his *Lives of the Philosophers*. Richard and Cosima Wagner lived not far away at Lucerne and he became a regular visitor at their house, there meeting Franz Liszt among others.

At Basle Nietzsche became acquainted with the great historian of the Renaissance, Jacob Burckhardt, and with two others who exercised an influence on his thinking, the theologian Franz Overbeck, who remained a lifelong friend, and a Russian philosopher called Afrikan Spir.

During the Franco-Prussian war of 1870–71 Nietzsche served as a medical orderly in the Prussian army, falling ill in the harsh conditions of the war zone and perhaps contracting syphilis at a brothel frequented by troops. This is hypothesized as the source of the ill-health that was his chronic lot thereafter, and his madness in the last decade of his life, 'General Paralysis of the Insane' being a consequence of syphilitic infection.

In 1872 Nietzsche published *The Birth of Tragedy*, his first book. It was very poorly regarded by the academic community because it failed to observe the standard protocols for a work of scholarship – which Nietzsche did not intend it to be, in any case: he was a speculative and polemical philosopher, and this book set out his stall in that respect. He tried to transfer to the philosophy faculty, but without success. During the early part of the 1870s he wrote the essays published in book form as *Untimely Meditations*, including one on Wagner, though by 1876 his admiration for Wagner had begun to cool because he was surprised and disappointed by what he saw as the false glamour of the Bayreuth Festival and Wagner's self-promotion.

In 1879, too ill to maintain his teaching duties at Basle, Nietzsche retired. He had just published a book of aphorisms entitled *Human, All Too Human*, and now took himself to Italy and the south of France in the wintertime, and to Sils Maria in the Alps in the summers, devoting himself to writing. Between 1879 and 1888 he produced a series of major works, *Daybreak* (1881), *The Gay Science* (1882), *Thus Spake Zarathustra* (1883), *Beyond Good and Evil* (1886), *The Genealogy of Morals* (1887), *Twilight of the Idols*, *The Case of Wagner*, *Ecce Homo*, *The Antichrist* and *Nietzsche contra Wagner* (all 1888), together with draft materials for a book he proposed to call *The Will to Power*. In these years he was assisted by a secretary, Peter Gast (pseudonym of Johann Heinrich Köselitz), who was partly subsidized by Nietzsche's friend Paul Rée.

Rée and Nietzsche both fell in love with same woman, the vivid and gifted Lou Andreas-Salomé, writer and later psychoanalyst, and friend of Freud and Rilke among others. Nietzsche proposed marriage to her a number of times, but his relationship with both her and Rée ended in bitterness as a result of her preference for the latter. It was a painful experience for Nietzsche, who blamed not only Andreas-Salomé and Rée but his sister Elisabeth, who had interfered because of her profound disapproval of Andreas-Salomé, whom she regarded as the type of modern woman that her conventional, indeed reactionary, attitudes could not tolerate. Nietzsche and Elisabeth had a difficult relationship at the best of times, but after this debacle he said that he felt a 'genuine hatred' for her.

Elisabeth later came to have a malign influence on Nietzsche's reputation, in framing him as a sort of Nazi *avant la lettre* after his madness and death. She had married a zealous proto-Nazi called Bernhard Förster who had taken a group of blond blue-eyed Aryans to South America to breed a master race, a plan foiled by the almost immediate deaths of all of them from tropical diseases. Förster himself committed suicide in despair. Elisabeth, adopting the name 'Frau Förster-Nietzsche', edited and published her brother's works to give them the anti-Semitic, nationalistic, Nazi-anticipating twist she desired. But Nietzsche was emphatically against anti-Semitism and nationalism, and his doctrines were not political but ethical, in ways described below.

Partly as a result of falling out with his publisher Ernest Schmeitzner (over Schmeitzner's anti-Semitism, as it happened) and partly because his books sold hardly a copy, Nietzsche began publishing at his own expense. He printed forty copies of the final volume of *Zarathustra* and gave them away to friends and acquaintances. All through the final decade of his life, a richly productive one, he kept thinking and writing at a furious rate.

Nietzsche's poor health had seen little improvement during this time, and he had become dependent on opium to combat his insomnia. By late 1888 he was concerning his friends because of the wild letters he sent them, and his claims to be descended from Polish nobility, whose aristocratic virtues had descended to him despite, he said, the interference of four generations of German mothers. In early January 1889 he suffered a total collapse of his mental health, and never recovered. He lived under the care of his mother and sister, incapacitated by madness and also, in the very final years, by a series of paralysing strokes, until his death in 1900. It is said that what finally tipped him into insanity was seeing a horse being mercilessly beaten by its driver; he rushed to protect the animal, throwing his arms about its neck and sobbing.

Nietzsche's chief philosophical concern was ethics, and very much as it was understood by the philosophers of antiquity, namely, as an answer to the questions, What sort of person should I be? How should I live? What values should shape and guide my choices, my aims, my life? These questions are different from questions that are more narrowly about morals as such: What makes an action right or wrong? What are the principles of morality?

It might come as a surprise to some to see that ethics and morals, although of course intimately connected, are distinguishable in this way. Ethics is a more inclusive matter than morality; it concerns character whereas morality concerns actions. Our actions will mainly of course flow from our character, but the targets of enquiry in ethics (seeking answers to What sort of person shall I be?) and in debates about morality (What is the right thing to do in this case?) are obviously not the same.

Nietzsche thought that the values of Western civilization were wrong. He thought they had been distorted by the Judaeo-Christian legacy of moral thinking. His criticism was levelled not only at Christianity itself, but at those philosophers who accepted much of the moral outlook of Christianity while arguing for an independent justification for it that did not require a theistic grounding.

Accordingly his announcement in *The Gay Science* that 'God is dead' was not just an atheistic assertion, but a declaration that every-thing built on the foundations of theism had collapsed. If the entire culture and civilization founded on Christianity no longer has any basis, then a 'revaluation of all values' is necessary. The confusion and anxiety of life among the ruins of the demolished order are exacerbated by real-izing that the order not only had no foundation, but was actually harmful: its morality undermined, indeed perverted, what humanity could be.

Putting this right is not an easy matter, Nietzsche said; but it has to be done. The first step is to understand what has happened. This is outlined in *The Genealogy of Morals*. It was once the case that what was 'good' was determined according to the self-evaluation of the noble, high-minded and powerful members of society, and what was 'bad' was associated with their opposites, the 'low-minded, the vulgar, and the plebeian'. But this order was upended by 'a slave revolt' prompted by resentment, and the 'good–bad' contrast predicated on the aristo-cratic view was replaced by a new contrast, between 'good' and 'evil'. Pride becomes a sin, the good are those who are humble, meek and suffering – precisely the lot of those who had suffered enslavement or exile. It is good to be compassionate, and to have pity; self-denial and sacrifice are virtues – Nietzsche calls them 'unegoistic' virtues, so dif-ferent from the assertion of the ego which is a noble virtue.

In *The Antichrist* he indicates the value system that he opposes to the 'slave morality' introduced by the Judaeo-Christian tradition, by asking, 'What is good? Everything that heightens the feeling of power in man, the will to power, power itself. What is bad? Everything that is born from weakness. What is happiness? The feeling that power is growing, that resistance is overcome. Not contentedness but more power; not peace but war; not virtue but fitness.'

Nietzsche's sister Elisabeth Förster-Nietzsche was able to make good use of such passages, which if misread yield a sinister interpretation indeed.* But put in juxtaposition to Schopenhauer's views, one sees what he meant. Schopenhauer thought that the will to exist, which for him is the *noumenon*, the underlying reality, is doomed always to frus-tration, and is therefore the cause of the suffering that is ubiquitous in the world. Nietzsche insists instead that the *will to overcome* this

---

* Cardinal Richelieu once said, 'Give me six lines written by the hand of the most honest man, and I will find something in them to have him hanged.'

frustration, to fight and conquer it so that one can live, create and succeed, is the ethical way. To strive and to desire, to wish to grow and expand, are worthy things; to be one who strives and thereby overcomes the barriers to growth and expansion is to be an *Übermensch* – 'Superman' in the sense of 'superior man' – and thus truly moral.

What this involves, said Nietzsche, is the affirmation of life, to be a 'Yes-sayer'. The idea is to live as if one were going to live one's life over and over again for ever – the idea of 'eternal recurrence', contemplating which makes us determined to live as affirmatively, positively and nobly as possible. But that is not to choose to live under any illusions: one has to be honest about what embracing life involves, for it involves suffering and loss, pain and grief too. It therefore also requires courage. These ideas occur variously in *The Gay Science* and *Ecce Homo*.

But there is a salve to the pain that we have to accept in embracing life and living it truthfully and courageously, and the salve – as Schopenhauer had argued also – is art: 'We possess art', Nietzsche says, 'lest we perish of the truth.' Art helps us to know 'how to make things beautiful', as either creators or enjoyers; as the latter we can be 'poets of our lives' and give ourselves satisfaction and style, treating our own lives as a creative work and giving it aesthetic value as part of its ethical character. And this requires that we be autonomous individuals, free spirits, rejecting the restrictions that society and conventional morality seek to impose.

Nietzsche did not present his views systematically, but through polemics and the use of tropes such as the contrast between the attitudes to life and art represented respectively by Apollo and Dionysus. In his early book *The Birth of Tragedy* – which he later came to think badly written and confused – he argued that both the order and rationality of the Apollonian and the instinctive, sometimes ecstatic and often chaotic nature of the Dionysian are essential for drama – indeed, that the tension between them is the source of all art. Whereas Aeschylus and Sophocles represent the high point of that fruitful tension, Euripides and Socrates emphasized the Apollonian over the Dionysian, rationality over feeling, and thus brought the great age of Greek culture to an end.

Some commentators see nihilism at the centre of Nietzsche's philosophy. In light of the 'affirmation' and 'eternal recurrence' themes it is clear that he was not himself a nihilist: rather, he attacked both nihilism and pessimism as outcomes of the loss of faith in traditional theism-based morality when nothing is put in its place. 'The higher species is lacking, i.e., those whose inexhaustible fertility and power keep up the faith in man,' he wrote, 'the lower species ("herd", "mass", "society") unlearns modesty and blows up its needs into cosmic and metaphysical values. In this way the whole of existence is vulgarized: insofar as the mass is dominant it bullies the exceptions, so they lose their faith in themselves and become nihilists.' His recognition of the problem that results from repudiating traditional values wholesale is precisely what makes thinkers like Heidegger see him as a nihilist, but that misses his point: he does not 'devalue all values' but 'revalues' them.

The ideas for which Nietzsche is best known – the immoralist, the Superman, the contrast between master and slave moralities, going 'beyond good and evil', 'the revaluation of all values', 'philosophizing with a hammer' (recalling Zarathustra's 'Smash, smash the old law-tables!') – have been studied and sometimes appropriated and adapted by thinkers in both Analytic and Continental philosophy in the century after his time. As often happens with fertile and original thinkers, Nietzsche's richly interesting views are open to anyone from any tradition of thought as a target for study and reflection; they repay both.

IDEALISM

In the second half of the nineteenth century a number of idealist philosophies were proposed, chiefly in Britain but also in the United States. The principal figures were T. H. Green, F. H. Bradley, J. M. E. McTaggart, James Ward, Bernard Bosanquet and the American Josiah Royce. These thinkers were not of one mind, though some (not all) agreed in thinking that reality fundamentally consists of One Mind; but their motivations for espousing forms of idealism were similar. Partly they were reacting to what they saw as the thin and disagreeable gruel of empiricism and utilitarianism in the two centuries preceding their own time. Partly they were reacting to the impact on the plausibility of religion of German biblical scholarship, geology, Darwinian biology and increased general literacy. And partly it was because they were under the influence of Hegel, for even when any of these thinkers explicitly repudiated the label 'Hegelian', as F. H. Bradley did, there is no doubt that Hegel's presence in their thought was large. For example, Bradley's ethical views were set out in an expressly dialectical series of essays which had to be read, he said, in the order they were printed for his view to be properly understood.

The motivations just listed were connected. T. H. Green (1836–82) led the fightback. One of Green's students at Oxford wrote that the dominance of 'scientific analysis' made everything seem dry and without inspiration: 'We were frightened; we saw everything passing into the tyranny of rational abstract mechanism . . . of individualistic Sensationalism . . . of agnostic mechanism,' and the turn to forms of idealism that had a significant religious dimension, providing a new perspective on thinking about deity and the moral life that seemed to rescue both from the reductive and debunking implications of science, was therefore eagerly embraced by some. Green himself wrote an influential study of Hume in which he characterized Hume's philosophy, with its psychological atomism, as sceptical and therefore destructive of the possibility of knowledge and social morality.

Prompted in part by Green's hostility to the empiricism that had dominated British philosophy since Locke, the interest prompted by publication of J. H. Stirling's *The Secret of Hegel* in 1865 led to renewed attention to idealism. In the Preface to the collection of papers *Essays in Philosophical Criticism* edited by Andrew Seth (later know as Seth Pringle-Pattison) and R. B. Haldane in 1883, Edward Caird wrote, 'The writers of this volume agree in believing that the line of investigation which philosophy must follow, or in which it may be expected to make most important contributions to the intellectual life of man, is that which was opened up by Kant, and for the successful prosecution of which no one has done so much as Hegel.'

Idealism is the metaphysical view that the fundamental nature of reality is mental, that is, is *mind* or *consciousness*. In Berkeley (see pp. 226–32 above) the world exists as ideas in the mind of God; or – to put it in terms he himself used – 'eternal spirit' is the *substance* of the world and keeps it in existence by an act of continual creation, namely, by conceiving it (thinking of it).* Because of the motivations that prompted the idealistic turn in late nineteenth-century philosophy, nothing quite as straightforward as Berkeley's theistic idealism sufficed.

---

* Note that Kant is not an idealist in this metaphysical sense; the label 'transcendental idealism' applied to his views has the quite different meaning that the phenomena constituting the world as it appears to us are the result of the way our minds organize the data of sensory experience; he did not hold that mind is the basis of reality as it is in itself. His view is epistemological, not metaphysical.

Perhaps the closest to it is offered by Green, whose idea of the under-lying nature of reality might, not so inaccurately, be caricatured as an Hegelianized and internalized version of Berkeley.

Green postulated the idea of an 'eternal consciousness' and described it under the headings of two connected unfoldings – or one unfolding describable in two ways: the unfolding of the evolution of an individual will, and the unfolding of the increasing presence or actualization of God in the world. He described the 'eternal consciousness' as 'the law of nature or the will of God or its idea'. Green meant that the 'eternal consciousness' is immanent (indwelling) in humanity, and fully exists only when people themselves properly understand that it is within them, and accordingly help to actualize it in themselves. To say that 'the divine exists the more fully that individuals actualize it within' is almost to say that God exists if people believe in him; though a charac-terization of Green's point closer to his intention would be to say that the evolution of human self-awareness consists in God making himself gradually more manifest in the world. The Hegelian inspiration of this idea is obvious.

Individuals must however further understand, Green argued, that each of them contains only a spark of the eternal consciousness, and that the full realization of the divine in the world requires cooperation and communality. The 'self' of an individual exists as part of a society of selves, and individual self-realization is a contribution to the self-realization of all.

Green developed a complete moral and political theory from the idea of the essentially social character of human beings thus implied. It turns on the idea that we have free will, which is at its freest when it acts to achieve the best and most satisfying state for itself. But this is allied to recognizing that working with one's fellows requires the idea of a common good which a voluntary acceptance of shared laws and customs helps to foster. The relation between the individual and society is reciprocal: individuals together form society and simultaneously are formed by it. Accordingly the state, at both national and local levels, is important, because it provides the circumstances in which individuals can act for the best. But the state should not be too interventive; rather, its role should be to uphold the rights and duties that best conduce to individual self-actualization.

Green has a significant place in nineteenth-century idealism because of his criticism of Hume and his adoption of a philosophical approach that, as it seemed to contemporaries, could reinvigorate moral and political thought on a less reductive basis than the then prevailing empiricism. But he was not the chief flag-bearer of the new idealism; this role was played by F. H. Bradley (1846–1924).

Bradley's first work was in ethics and logic, but his main claim to the considerable fame he enjoyed in his own lifetime was his metaphysical view as set out in *Appearance and Reality* (1893) and the essays written in expansion and defence of its doctrines afterwards. The ideas in this book were extremely influential, though chiefly in a negative sense: for they prompted the reaction from G. E. Moore and Bertrand Russell that resulted in the emergence of twentieth-century Analytic philosophy.

Bradley argued that our ordinary way of thinking and talking about the world – and indeed the more sophisticated discourses of philosophers and scientists – contains internal contradictions which become apparent only when we try to make systematic sense of our experience. Revealing these contradictions obliges us to reject two commonplace assumptions: that there are many independently existing things in the world, and that they exist independently of our or anyone's knowing anything about them. The first assumption is pluralism, the second is realism. Rejecting pluralism and realism together entails thinking of reality as a single complete whole, which he called 'the Absolute' – reality as it is in itself and as the all-inclusive totality of being. The term is a direct borrowing from Hegel's *das Absolute* – and, analogously with Hegel's identification of *das Absolute* as spirit, *Geist*, Bradley further argued that the Absolute consists of experience or sentience.

Bradley's argument for rejecting pluralism and realism turns on his account of *relations*. Relations come in two kinds, external and internal. Examples of external relations are 'on' and 'to the left of'. A cup placed *on* a table makes no difference to the cup or the table; a chair standing *to the left of* the table makes no difference to the chair or the table. Take the cup off the table, it is still a cup; move the chair to the other side of the table, it is still a chair. External relations do not affect the nature of their 'relata' (the things thus related to each other). But *internal* relations are *essential* to their relata and *make* them what they are. 'Brother of' is an example; you cannot be the brother of someone unless you are male and have at least one sibling. 'Being married to' makes its relata both spouses; you cannot be a spouse unless you stand in the relation of 'being married to' someone. Get divorced and you are no longer a spouse. External relations are contingent; internal relations are necessary, are essential to their relata having the nature they must have in order to stand in that relation to each other.

Bradley's argument is that there are no external relations; and if that seems to imply that everything is internally related to everything else, one quickly sees that there cannot even be internal relations. This is because there are not *many* things in reality (and that means no relations, not even internal ones), but only one thing, namely, *everything*: the Absolute. The argument to the first point, that there are no relations, is known as 'Bradley's Regress' and it is most simply described as follows. If A is related to B by relation R, then A must be related to R by some relation R_1. But then A must be related to the relation R_1 by some relation R_2 . . . and so on in regress.

Bradley takes a lump of sugar as an example of a 'thing' which has the properties of whiteness, hardness and sweetness. Iterating the argument of Berkeley, he asks what is the supposed underlying 'thing' in which these qualities inhere? Is there a lump of sugar without any properties, and, independently of it, the properties of whiteness, sweetness and hardness which somehow belong to it? Or is it just a bundle of these properties? But if the latter, what ties the properties together into the bundle? A relation? But what is that relation? He sees these questions as being translatable into the problem of what we are doing when we predicate a property of a thing – when we predicate 'whiteness' of (that is, ascribe it to) the lump of sugar. If the whiteness *is* the sugar – because it is one of the constituent qualities which, bonded with the others, constitutes the sugar – then you are saying nothing at all; and if you are saying that whiteness is not the same thing as the sugar, then to say 'the sugar is white' is to say of the sugar something it is not. Note that he is treating the 'is' as the 'is of identity', which means that when you say 'S is P' you are asserting that S and P are the same thing.

The idea that in external relations the relata are independent of and unaffected by the relations in which they stand seemed incoherent to Bradley. If the relation R is separate from the relata A and B, then – as above – there has to be a relation to relate the relata to R . . . and therefore regress. So much for external relations. He then shows that the idea of internal relations is equally incoherent. If these are 'grounded' in the nature of their relata then there must be some aspect of the relata which grounds them. For example, for there to be a relation of 'brother of', the person standing in this relation to someone else must be male and must share at least one parent with the other person; but then these 'parts' of the relatum – the maleness, the shared genetic inheritance – stand in a relation to each other too, and each of them to the relation of being a 'brother of'. And if so, on both counts regresses again ensue.*

The incoherence of the concept of relations, as Bradley sees it, is his reason for rejecting pluralism. If there is not a plurality of independent things, then *holism* is true: there is just one thing; and this one thing is therefore everything. Bradley's reason for thinking that this one thing is experience or sentience could be reconstructed (he does not give an argument as such) by saying that if it were not experience or sentience, then it would not be one thing, because there is experience (he and you and I have it) and if reality is not itself experience then there would be more than one thing – experience, and what is experienced, which by hypothesis is itself not experience. But if there is only one thing and there is experience, then experience must be that one thing. He argues that the appearance of diversity and plurality is an artefact of our finite and partial thought, which imposes distinctions and differences. But these, and the contradictions we soon notice when we try to think about them rationally, are reconciled and included in the whole: all contradictions are holistically overcome and resolved in the Absolute.

In his ethical thought Bradley addresses the question Why should I be moral? Note that this question appears to presuppose that there is morality, and asks why one should conform one's life and actions to it. His answer to the question is that to be moral is to achieve self-realization, and self-realization is explored in the dialectically arranged essays in his *Ethical Studies* (1876), each of which takes up a suggestion from another ethical doctrine only to reject it as such, while neverthe-less retaining some aspect of it which is helpful. On the way there are highly interesting discussions, particularly in the essays 'Pleasure for Pleasure's Sake' and 'My Station and its Duties', but the terminus of the discussion is an unsatisfactory one, for it is that the ideal self – the 'good self' – is unattainable because it depends for its existence on the evil it must overcome to be what it strives to be; and since this is so, ultimate goodness is unachievable, because evil has to exist.

Of the names mentioned above as among the leaders of idealist thought, one has bequeathed a problem which still bedevils philosophers. This is the proof offered by J. M. E. McTaggart (1866–1925) that time is unreal.

---

* This reconstructs Bradley's argument somewhat: in *Appearance and Reality* itself this argument is not clear.

McTaggart's first works were extensive studies of Hegel. He published three books and a significant short monograph on Hegel's philosophy before setting out in substantial form his own version of idealism in his chief work, *The Nature of Existence* (first volume 1921, second volume published posthumously 1927). He was also an admirer of Bradley, and much influenced by him. Despite these acknowledged influences, the views he developed were distinctively his own.

The interest some folk take in the oddities of philosophers would be much tickled by McTaggart. He had an odd appearance – a large head and a shuffling sideways walk – and he rode a tricycle around Cambridge and was scrupulous about greeting cats whenever he saw them. (By contrast, Bradley in Oxford shot at cats with his revolver if they ventured into the grounds of his college.) McTaggart was very shy, as was Bertrand Russell when young; the latter reports that when McTaggart first called on him at his rooms in Trinity College, Russell was too shy to ask him in and McTaggart was too shy to enter, and so there was a long stand-off with McTaggart hovering at the door.

The monograph that McTaggart published in 1893 – more a pamphlet than a book – entitled *The Further Determination of the Absolute*, argued that reality is spiritual and timeless, and consists in a community of mutually loving spirits. This idea remained his fundamental conception of reality throughout his work. Contrary to Bradley's view, it is a pluralistic and relational version of the Absolute rather than a monistic and holistic one.

McTaggart had already stated in his *Studies in the Hegelian Dialectic* (1896) a commitment to the idea that there is no such thing as time, but the arguments he there offered are not the same as those set out in his enduringly famous paper 'On the Unreality of Time' in the journal *Mind* in 1908. His argument is as follows.

There are two ways of talking about time; one consists in an ordering of events as *earlier than* and *later than*, and the other turns on nominating *the present* and ordering events as *past* or as *future* relative to the present. He called the latter ordering, *past–present–future*, the 'A-series', and the former ordering, *earlier than/later than*, the 'B-series'. He then argued that if time is real we need both series, though it might be said that the A-series is more fundamental than the B-series. The reason is that the place that events hold in the B-series is fixed: two events X and Y are such that if X happened *earlier than* Y then it is forever the case that it did so. But there is no time without change; and change involves events unfolding from the past through the present into the future. So there is only change if the A-series exists.

But the A-series involves a contradiction. This is because it will be true of everything that happens that it is all three of past, present and future from some given standpoint for each. If something *is* happening now, it *was* in the future before now and it *will be* in the past when it is over – but in the past it was *now* and the current now was *will be* from that point of view – and *now* will be *past* when the event has passed into the future. So for any event X we can say that all three descriptions 'X is past,' 'X is present' and 'X is future' apply, and which of these three is 'now' applicable is relative to a choice of when 'now' is. No two of these descriptions can simultaneously apply without contradiction; but because it is arbitrary how the ordering is made as to which is past, which is present and which is future, we cannot say which description is preferable let alone correct.

Put another way: if you try to argue that X is past, present and future *at different times*, then you have to use the A-series concepts to select a point from which X can be said to be past or present or future; but to use the A-series descriptions to position *that* point – call it Point 1 – in the time-series both begs the question (is circular) and generates a regress: as one can see, to justify choosing Point 1 you need to invoke the series to choose a Point 2 in order to fix Point 1, but then to justify invoking a Point 2 from which to fix Point 1, you need to invoke the series to fix a Point 3 . . . and so endlessly on.

So the A-series is contradictory; and if there cannot be change without the A-series, there is no change; and if there is no change, time does not exist. From the point of view of the way the world (misleadingly, as all idealists think) appears to us in experience, descriptions of events in B-series terms as earlier and later have a certain usefulness, as indeed does use of the A-series concepts, if we are given an arbitrary specification of 'now'; but the B-series does not allow for change and is therefore less fundamental than the A-series. The latter is essential to the nature of time if it exists, which is why its contradictory nature is fatal to the idea of time itself.

However, the usefulness of the B-series for our dealings with the way the world (misleadingly) appears to us requires that we explain how this can be. McTaggart does so by offering what he calls the 'C-series', which is the B-series understood without reference to time – that is, without reference to the idea of change. The C-series puts events into an earlier/later ordering that is fixed, linear, asymmetrical and transitive, which is what the B-series is, except that our normal use of the B-series concepts carries the implication, which the C-series dispenses with, that things that were 'earlier than' *became* or *changed* into being 'later than' – that is, it quietly assumes the A-series.

C-series perspectives on (apparent) events are thoughts or experiences, and McTaggart suggests (in *The Nature of Existence*) that they are perspectives particular to individual minds – the minds which, mutually related by love, constitute reality; which suggests that although C-series experiences are individual to each mind, nevertheless they somehow coordinate.

Philosophers still struggle with McTaggart's argument for the unreality of time. Even those who wish to find a way of proving time to be real accept that the A-series/B-series distinction has to be the starting point for discussing the matter.

One might briefly mention 'the last idealist', the remarkable T. L. S. (Timothy) Sprigge (1932–2007), whose views, although chiefly influenced by Spinoza, Bradley, William James and Santayana, were somewhat like McTaggart's in that he believed that reality is fundamentality a community of minds which in their interrelationships constitute the Absolute: reality is 'a single divine consciousness within which an inconceivably vast number of streams of finite experience interact and interweave'. His metaphysics made a genuine difference to how he lived his life: if reality is the totality of experience, the experience of everything – animals, and nature itself – is of great value. His book *The Vindication of Absolute Idealism* (1984) stands as so far the last monument to a tradition of philosophy that was otherwise swept away by the Analytic movement which was in part a reaction to it, though it was also a continuation, empowered and enhanced by developments in logic and science, of the empiricist tradition that idealism sought to supplant.

PRAGMATISM

In the last decades of the nineteenth century, contemporary with the British idealists, a group of philosophers in the United States – Charles Sanders Peirce (1839–1914) and William James (1842–1910) prominent among them – evolved a philosophical outlook to which they gave the name 'Pragmatism'. A somewhat later adherent of this outlook, John Dewey (1859–1952), continued the line of thought they proposed, and was influential in the period between the First and Second World Wars. The movement thereafter went into abeyance for a time before some of its themes resurfaced in the work of several American philosophers in the later twentieth century.

Peirce recorded how he and some friends started a 'Metaphysical Club' in the 1870s in Cambridge, Massachusetts, to discuss philosophy. It met either in his study or in that of William James, and its other members included Chauncey Wright, Oliver Wendell Holmes Jr and Nicholas St John Green, to whom Peirce gives the credit for being 'the grandfather of pragmatism' because he insisted that the group take seriously the definition of 'belief', given by the psychologist-philosopher Alexander Bain, as 'that upon which a man is prepared to act'. Peirce wrote, 'From this definition, pragmatism is scarce more than a corollary.' Alexander Bain (1818–1903) was a Scottish philosopher and psychologist who was one of the first to apply scientific methods in psychology (and was a major influence on William James in this respect). Bain held that it is natural for people to believe, and that doubt is an uncomfortable condition from which enquiry liberates them by leading to what he described as the 'serene, satisfying and happy tone of mind' which is believing. Peirce adopted this view because it fitted well with his opinion that enquiry is a process aimed at correcting and adapting behaviour so that it is more effective in the world. Problems arise when our conduct is inadequate for achieving a goal; the solution to the problem is finding a rule of action that overcomes the problem and advances us towards the goal. And that is the aim of enquiry: the acquisition of stable and enduring beliefs. Such beliefs we call 'true', Peirce said, and we give the name 'reality' to what they are about.

Peirce acknowledged that people employ different methods to try to arrive at stable beliefs – chief among them appeals to authority and *a priori* reasoning. But he insisted that the methods of science are the best way to settle differences of opinion about what to believe, because all who use such methods will 'converge' on the most stable beliefs in the long run. 'The opinion which is fated to be ultimately agreed by all who investigate is what we mean by truth,' he wrote, 'and the object represented in this opinion is the real.'

One of the most influential of Peirce's writings is a paper entitled 'How to Make our Ideas Clear'. In it he enunciates the 'pragmatic maxim', as follows: 'Consider what effects, which might conceivably have practical bearings, we conceive the object of our conception to have. Then, our conception of these effects is the whole of our conception of the object.' For example: our idea of 'hardness' – of something being 'hard' – is just our idea of what this means in practice, such as how difficult it is to break, scratch or pierce a hard thing. To define 'hardness' in this way is similar to what is called an 'operational definition', or relatedly to saying what a thing *is* by saying what it *does*. When we consider the meaning of the word 'hard' and distinguish its meaning from other words, says Peirce, we see that 'there is no distinction of meaning so fine as to consist in anything but a possible difference of practice.'

Note that this is a theory about meaning, not truth, for obviously both true and false beliefs are meaningful. But it guides us towards the appropriate conception of truth; truth is attained when the application of scientific method has eliminated beliefs of no practical worth, and settled on those that prove their utility.

Peirce had to acknowledge that beliefs widely held at one time might come to be revised, and therefore he accepted a *fallibilist* epistemology, although his doing so was chiefly directed against those 'foundationalists' who argued that there are firm starting points for knowledge – innate ideas, as some rationalists argued, or the 'givens' (*data*) of sensory experience, as empiricists argued. This poses a problem for his view, because it implies that to fix the sense of 'truth' and 'reality' something else has to be at work in addition to convergence among enquirers. William James attempted to deal with this problem, but his doing so resulted in a rather different viewpoint.

Instead of focusing on convergence, James focused on a belief's effectiveness. Truth, he said, is *what works*: 'The "true" is only the expedient in our way of thinking, just as the "right" is only the expedient in our way of behaving.' The choice of terminology in the case of 'what is (morally) right' seems rather shocking, but the idea that we call expedient beliefs 'true' is a natural enough view for a pragmatist to take. The objection to it is, however, obvious: there are useful falsehoods, and there are truths that have no practical utility, so the fact that believing something turns out to be useful is no guarantee of its truth.

James thought that he had solved a problem left unsolved by those who assert the truism that, in some sense, truth is 'agreement' between our ideas and reality. He asked, What is this 'agreement', and what is this 'reality'? The nature of the relation of 'agreement', 'correspondence' or 'match' between what is in our heads and what is out there in the world (or in some other realm, for example the realm of abstract objects such as numbers) has always been extremely difficult to specify. If you deny that the mind is merely a mirror that somehow reflects reality, but instead interacts with reality for practical purposes, then you see how 'truth' can be regarded as jointly constituted by that relationship. How we carve up reality, and what we believe about it, has a great deal to do with our needs and interests, and of course with the perceptual and cognitive faculties that have evolved in their service. There is a distinct Kantian flavour to this view.

James' motivations for adopting pragmatism have much to do with the intellectual climate of the second half of the nineteenth century. Following the rise of science and the work of Darwin, there were tensions between the worldview implied by science and the traditional worldviews of religion and the moralities associated with them. He described those who insisted upon the scientific approach as 'tough-minded' and the others as 'tender-minded'. He accepted the deliverances of science, but wanted there to be room in its worldview for religion too. He saw pragmatism as the answer, because while conforming to the demands of a tough-minded stance it offers a defence of tender-minded views also, by noting that they are useful and beneficial to believe. This was challenged by Bertrand Russell, who argued that it committed James to holding that the proposition 'Santa Claus exists' is true.

Dewey developed Peirce's view of enquiry as the quest for 'settled belief' by describing it as beginning in an unsettled 'situation' and aiming to transform that situation into a coherent one. The unclarity in which enquiry begins is not solely a matter of the enquirer lacking appropriate beliefs, but rather is a function of both the enquirer's inadequate beliefs and the objectively unsettled nature of the situation in which she holds them. They thus jointly prompt the need for the situation to be rendered determinate. This implies that 'situations' are objective states of which the enquirer and her beliefs are part; it relates to the further idea, shared by all the pragmatists, that experience – perception, thought and enquiry – is a whole in which we are not merely passive recipients of sense-impressions, but actively inferring and conceptualizing a world, and justifying our beliefs about it by reference to how they hang together – a 'coherence' view of justification.

Dewey pointed out that we start from the perspective of participants in the world, in the midst of things we are already interacting and dealing with, even before we start to philosophize; we do not start from a 'blank slate' position.

It follows from the pragmatist view of beliefs as, in essence, tools that scepticism is not an option – and therefore not a valid starting point for enquiry, as Descartes had proposed. The fallibilism implicit in pragmatism does not constitute a form of scepticism, because, as Peirce argued, accepting the fallibility of beliefs is not the same as saying that they are false, and is consistent with optimism that all enquiry will converge on at least many of them, thus validating them. In any case a posture of doubt itself requires justification, and because it is unproductive by itself it motivates the effort to remove it in quest of the stable and useful beliefs we need.

Commentators on pragmatism connect it with behaviourism in psychology and instrumentalism in the philosophy of science – this latter being the view that scientific theories are ways of organizing our thought about phenomena and predicting their behaviour, and that the concepts in them do not refer to actually existing entities and processes. Interpreting Dewey in this way is prompted by his identifying, as 'the philosophical fallacy', the idea that the terms of our theories about the world and the mind are referential, rather than devices invented for the purpose of problem-solving. The pragmatists took it that this enabled them to steer a path between idealism and realism in metaphysics, a path truer to the dictates of scientific method – while at the same time, as James desired, respecting the validity of other, more 'tender-minded' regions of belief.

There are significant differences between the pragmatists, however. Peirce thought that the application of scientific method would result in views that are impersonal and objective – a tough-minded outlook for tough-minded enquirers. The features of beliefs that satisfy this approach are the observational outcomes of applying them. James' interest in making room for tender-minded concerns meant that the satisfaction in question is not only observational but emotional. The book that gave pragmatism a wider currency in its day, James' *Pragmatism: A New Name for Some Old Ways of Thinking*, made pragmatism serve a personal, subjective agenda, to Peirce's disappointment; for where Peirce was interested in making philosophy more scientific, James made it more psychological.

Dewey's interest was different again. His focus was on society and social ethics, and he saw beliefs as instruments made by human beings so that they can navigate the social reality they inhabit. Arguably he took James' 'cash value' account of truth a step further, saying that what validates a belief as true is the agreement in society to regard it as such, based on society's approval of it. But this was not something to be left to chance; education is the royal road to ensuring that society will always monitor itself regarding which beliefs it would be best to live by.

There is an inconsistency in this view: valuing education as 'what produces a society whose approval validates the beliefs it lives by' implies that there is some other yardstick for identifying the beliefs that merit approval and which education can help us live our lives by. Dewey extolled the idea of a *rational* community, and education as the process which produces it; but the idea of rationality is empty if whatever the community happens to like in the way of beliefs constitutes their truth. Adjudicating between competitor beliefs requires something other than the happenstance of preferences.

A number of American philosophers have self-identified as pragmatists in recent philosophy, among them Richard Rorty, Hilary Putnam, Robert Brandom and Cornel West. The differences between them make application of the label to all of them slightly puzzling, unless Putnam's characterization of pragmatism as the combination of the following views will apply to them all: that scepticism requires as much justification as belief, that no beliefs are immune to the possibility of revision if new evidence comes along, and that considerations about the practical application of our beliefs constrain what we can say and think. 'Neo-pragmatism' might be a somewhat different thing: it is sometimes identified as the postmodernist view that truth is always relative to social context. Although one can see how this version can claim inheritance from Dewey, it would be resisted by Peirce.

PART IV

Philosophy in the Twentieth Century

Someone observing the history of *nineteenth*-century philosophy as it unfolded against the background of developments in natural science, mathematics and logic, the social effect of the Darwinian debate about evolution, and the systematic and scholarly approaches – especially in Germany – to textual criticism and the social sciences might have been able to guess at what would prompt a dividing of the ways in approaches to philosophy's task in the *twentieth* century. That division consists in two strands: one fairly well-defined strand called 'Analytic philosophy', and another, more diffuse and various strand or set of strands misleadingly, but now conventionally, called 'Continental philosophy'.

The first strand, 'Analytic philosophy', is dominant in the mainly Anglophone world. It is not a school or a body of doctrine, but instead is recognizable in its widely shared methods and interests, and by continuity with the mainly empiricist tradition in the history of philosophy. It has been influenced by innovations in logic and science and, using or informed by them, focuses on a set of considerations about truth, meaning, knowledge, the nature of mind and the concepts employed in thinking about value. The motivating idea for this strand is that through a detailed analysis of these matters the traditional concerns of metaphysics, epistemology and ethics will be illuminated (or, at least for some traditional philosophical problems – as in their different ways Logical Positivists and Ludwig Wittgenstein and his followers thought – shown to be spurious).

The 'founders' of Analytic philosophy – meaning the early twentieth-century thinkers whose work gave this style of philosophy its first distinctive impulse – are Bertrand Russell and G. E. Moore. The former's work in particular had a large part in bringing formal logic into the centre of Analytic philosophy's methods and concerns. Other major names include Rudolf Carnap, Ludwig Wittgenstein, W. V. Quine,

Elizabeth Anscombe, Richard Hare, P. F. Strawson, Michael Dummett, Donald Davidson and Hilary Putnam.

Most histories of Analytic philosophy also give a prominent place to the German logician Gottlob Frege as one of those who should be identified as a founding figure. This is because his work influenced Russell, and because Wittgenstein – who for a while in the twentieth century attracted an enormous following – claimed to have been influenced by him. In fact Frege became generally known in philosophy only after the Second World War, and it is chiefly through the monumental studies of his work by Michael Dummett in the last third of the twentieth century that he was given the recognition, and the status, that has led some to accord him that founding position. What is true is that his innovations in logic were of great significance in their own right, and the few who knew and appreciated them included Russell, who could not have developed his own innovations in logical formalism without the work of Frege, Giuseppe Peano and other logicians of the nineteenth century.

The rise of Analytic philosophy coincided with the largest and most rapid expansion since medieval times in the numbers of people teaching and writing about philosophy at academic institutions. The century accordingly produced dozens of outstanding philosophers whose work has attracted the attention and applause of their colleagues. Books and professional journals, conferences and lectures, flourishing philosophy departments in universities, together make for a rich and fertile field of activity. The short list of 'big names' could be well supplemented by a long list of notable individuals who merit mention, and who would not be absent from an encyclopaedia.

The other strand of twentieth-century philosophy, given the somewhat misleading label 'Continental philosophy' because some of its foremost earlier figures wrote in German and French, continued and expanded the endeavour of understanding experience and the nature of reality in the tradition of Hegel, and applied philosophical reflection more broadly to matters of life and society somewhat after the manner of Nietzsche. The major names here include Edmund Husserl, Martin Heidegger, Jean-Paul Sartre, Jacques Derrida, Gilles Deleuze and, in connection with the spread of the philosophical remit into sociology and beyond, Michel Foucault and Jürgen Habermas. But 'Continental philosophy' has many adherents and contributors in the Anglophone philosophical community also, thus belying the geographical implication of its name; and it is as informatively associated with trends and movements as with 'big name' thinkers: phenomenology, postmodernism, deconstruction, existentialism, Frankfurt School critical theory, psychoanalytic theory, and more.

As with Analytic philosophy, Continental philosophy has seen a large expansion of personnel, and not only in the university setting. Although there are philosophy departments in universities all round the world which are principally or exclusively 'Continental' in their focus, those interested in or in some way influenced by Continental philosophers are found not only in philosophy departments, but in the literature, sociology, law and other departments of universities too. This is a function of the broad attraction of both the thinkers and the themes involved.

In what follows I treat Analytic and Continental philosophy separately, in each giving an overview of some leading thinkers and some major themes.

Analytic Philosophy

Analytic philosophy is not a body of doctrine, it is a style of philosophizing, directed at a recognizable set of core concerns. It is not really a new style, except in one particular, which is its employment of tools drawn from the new logic that Frege, Russell and others developed on either side of the turn of the twentieth century. Otherwise the careful argumentation and clarification practised by most of the great philosophers throughout history are familiarly in play. In seeking clarity and precision, in clarifying concepts and their relations to each other, in using new logical tools, and in being attentive to ideas from science that can illuminate philosophical problems, Analytic philosophers emphasize detail over 'big picture' accounts of what they study. The core concerns – as mentioned above: truth, meaning, knowledge, the nature of mind, the concepts of ethics – are of course not new to philosophy but have been central to it throughout its history; what is new is what the emphasis on detail, and the improved tools of logic, have enabled philosophers to achieve in dealing with them.

The best explanation one can give of Analytic philosophy is to show an example of it at work. What was described as 'a paradigm of philosophy' by the Cambridge philosopher Frank Ramsey, who died tragically young in 1930, is a theory advanced by the chief founder of Analytic philosophy, Bertrand Russell. The theory is that if you analyse the underlying structure of things we say, using logic to make that structure completely explicit, you will be able to solve a number of important philosophical problems. To explain this idea requires some context, as follows.

Recall that John Locke, in the third book (entitled 'Of Words') of his *Essay Concerning Human Understanding*, had advanced the view that the meaning of a word is an idea in the mind of the person who uses it.

That seems superficially plausible; but a very little thought shows that it cannot be right. Ideas are private, words public; words have to have the same meaning for most users of them, but how can anyone be sure that the idea in one person's mind matches the idea in someone else's mind when both use the same word? Locke's theory implies that in communication what happens is that an idea is encoded into speech or writing, transmitted by sound waves or marks on paper, then decoded by a hearer or reader. What are these coding and decoding relationships? The same problem arises as before: what guarantee is there that the coding manuals of transmitter and receiver match? What guarantees that what is intended by the transmitter is understood by the receiver in the same way? And again: what kind of thing is the idea 'meant' by a general term like, say, 'dog' – is it a mental image of a particular dog of a particular breed with a definite size and colour, or is it an image of a mixture of all breeds, sizes and colours? If the former, how does it represent all dogs? If the latter – well, how could there be such an image at all?

In light of the difficulties with Locke's suggestion, a better-seeming and indeed very old view recommended itself: that the meaning of a word is what it denotes. This proposal might also seem plausible. If you wish to teach someone the meaning of the word 'handkerchief', a good way is to show him a square of cotton of the kind used to wipe one's brow or blow one's nose. This view is called the 'denotative theory of meaning'. Unfortunately, only some words in the language – nouns – *denote* things; other words – verbs – convey information about activities or happenings; yet others – adjectives and adverbs – describe the properties of things or the manner of happenings; and yet other words neither denote nor describe, but merely have functions in sentences, such as 'and', 'or', 'the', and the like. (These small words have a big name: they are called 'syncategorematic' words.) Moreover, many nouns denote things which are not in space and time, but are fictional, like unicorns and gods, or are abstract, such as the number nine and the property of whiteness. Of course, a *realist* about universals would say that 'whiteness' denotes an existing thing, but as several times shown in earlier pages, that view is at least controversial. But what of 'unicorn' and the like? What is denoted by this word? These questions accordingly raise difficulties for the denotative theory.

The difficulties are well illustrated by the consideration that if a word must denote to be meaningful, it follows that a meaningful word denotes something. So the word 'unicorns', which is meaningful, must denote unicorns; and since we do not think unicorns exist in space and time, as physical entities in the zoological realm, we are pushed towards thinking that they must have some kind of non-physical existence. One suggestion is that they do not exist but *subsist*, a kind of semi-existence, an uncomfortable and ill-defined metaphysical category which appears merely ad hoc to shore up the denotative theory of meaning. It has the absurd consequence that if I say 'my millionth-and-first brother' I immediately have a million subsisting brothers in addition to my one real flesh-and-blood brother.

Bertrand Russell was persuaded by the idea that meaning is denotation, and at first thought that this meant we have to swallow the idea of subsisting entities. But then his 'vivid sense of reality', as he described it, revolted against this idea, and he came up with a solution to the problem of how to retain the denotative theory of meaning without the florid ontology (catalogue of what exists) it seems to require. This was to say that there are only two words in the language that are genuinely denoting expressions, and that all other apparently denoting terms are really disguised 'descriptions'. The two genuinely denoting words are the demonstrative pronouns 'this' and 'that', which are guaranteed to denote something every time they are used, as when one points at an object and says 'that thing there'. But when we employ the word 'unicorn' we are using it as shorthand for 'something that has the property of being a unicorn', and since there is nothing of which one can say 'this (or that) has the property of being a unicorn', nothing is denoted.

Consider how this analysis works in connection with a problem like this: suppose someone says, 'the present King of France is wise,' when there is no king of France at present. Is this true or false? One's inclination is to say that it is false. So does this make 'the present King of France is unwise' true? Again one's inclination is to say, No, it's false. So both claims, that the present King of France is wise *and* that he is unwise, are false. How can that be? If one of the claims is false, must it not be the case that the opposite claim is true? But when we reflect for a moment, we see that the reason for their both being false is that there is no king of France; there is nothing to which the description 'the present King of France' applies.

Russell took this insight to show that whereas the surface forms of language can be misleading as to what is really being said, what *is* really being said can be shown by making explicit its underlying 'logical form'. Doing so shows that the phrase 'the present King of France' *looks* like a denoting expression, but is in fact shorthand for 'the something that has the property of being King of France'. So the sentence is really two sentences, saying (1) 'there is something that has the property of being King of France' and (2) 'that something is wise.' Now you can see that there are two ways for this claim to be false: either if (1) is false, or if (1) is true but (2) is false.

Russell further remarked that when the definite article 'the' is used, it implies uniqueness, that is, that there is one and only one thing with the property in question: '*the* present King of France'. So we should really analyse 'the present King of France is wise' into *three* sentences: (1) there is something which is the present King of France, (2) there is only one such thing, and (3) that thing is wise. In collaboration with his colleague A. N. Whitehead, Russell had devised a notation for formal logic and regarded it as providing a completely perspicuous way of rendering the *underlying structure* of statements like 'the present King of France is wise.' He thought of this notation as the 'perfect language' for making everything clear. Analysis of 'the present King of France is wise' in this notation yields this string of symbols:

$$\exists xFx \;\&\; [[(y)Fy \rightarrow y = x] \;\&\; Gx]]$$

pronounced: 'There is something, x, which has the property F (F = "being the present King of France"); *and*, anything else whatever, call it y, which has the property F, is identical with x (this takes care of "the", uniqueness); *and*, x has the property G (G = "being wise").'

Russell had a second very important motivation for this 'Theory of Descriptions', as this famous theory is called. It has already been hinted at in the foregoing. It concerns the fact that classical logic is based on there being two and only two truth-values, namely *true* and *false*, such that if a claim or proposition is not true, it is false; and if it is false, it is not true. This is known as *bivalence* ('two values'). It seems obvious that truth and falsity exhaust all possibilities between them, but this is not so; there are more ways in which a proposition can fail to be true than just by being false – for example, by being meaningless; or by not having a truth-value at all; or perhaps because there are more than two truth-values, say three, or four – indeed there are now logical systems with many truth-values. The idea that a proposition can have a third truth-value 'neither true nor false' is suggested by the following. Suppose I say, 'the man in the street is whistling.' You look out of the window; there is a man, and he is whistling. 'True,' you say. Suppose when you look out of the window you see a man but he is not whistling. 'False,' you say. But what if, when you look out of the window, you see no man there? Is the proposition 'the man in the street is whistling' true or false when there is no man there? 'It is neither,' you might say – and you thereby commit yourself to a third truth-value, 'neither true nor false'. Sometimes the expression 'truth-value gap' is employed to describe this third option.

Why not treat 'the present King of France is wise' as being 'neither true nor false' on the same grounds? Russell, and he is far from alone, refused to take this route. Abandoning bivalence creates difficulties: for an important example, it involves giving up the 'Law of Double Negation', in which to say 'not not-p' is the same as saying 'p' because two 'nots' cancel out; and this is only the case if the truth-values of 'not-p' and 'p' are direct and exclusive alternatives. And where the Law of Double Negation does not hold, neither does the 'Law of Excluded Middle', which says that 'everything is either A or it is not-A,' no third possibility permitted. Giving up this latter law entails that there are things which are neither A nor not-A. On the face of it, that seems flatly illogical.

One should note, however, that the Law of Excluded Middle does not apply in quantum physics; as Hamlet observed to Horatio, the world is an odder place than we think. The same applies in 'intuitionistic' mathematics and logic where the 'truth-values' are not *true* and *false* but *provable* and *not provable*. Consider: whereas to say 'it is not *not*' is to say 'it *is*' because two 'nots' cancel each other out, saying 'it is not provable that *it is not provable*' is not the same as saying '*it is provable*.' So in intuitionistic logic and mathematics the laws of Double Negation and Excluded Middle do not hold.

But there are other reasons for holding on to bivalence. Without it there are risks of indeterminacy and ambiguity. For example, suppose you argue – as a number of philosophers do – that knowing the meaning of a sentence consists in knowing its 'truth-conditions', that is, what makes it true or false. This implies that every meaningful sentence must be regarded as determinately either true or false, whether or not we know which. If sentences could also be 'neither true nor false' – if we allow that there can be 'truth-value gaps' – then the explanation one gives of what meaning consists in becomes greatly more complicated. Some of these points are explained more fully below.

This excursus into Russell's Theory of Descriptions, and some of the philosophical and logical implications of it, illustrates Analytic philosophy at work. Around all the points just sketched there is detailed debate which explores and refines these and other points about reference, descriptions, meaning, truth, bivalence, 'logical form', and more. A common feature of all these investigations is the method of examining concepts by analysing them, investigating what they involve and what they imply, what they really mean when scrutinized and how they connect to other concepts. Some readers will be relieved to learn that Analytic philosophy is not written in logical symbols, as might seem to be the case from the foregoing; and they will note that careful argument, and methodical examination of concepts and theories, is in fact not much different from what Plato, Locke, Hume and others have always done. The new part is what is borrowed from advances in logic.

It is worth mentioning at the outset that the word 'analysis' itself denotes a number of different techniques. It can mean breaking something down into its constituents; that is 'decomposition', as when one takes a watch apart to inspect the mechanism. It can mean showing that something can be explained in terms of something else which is more basic than it; that is 'reduction', as when one shows that thoughts in the mind are electro-chemical activities of neurons in the brain. It can involve looking for the 'essence' or defining properties of something. It can involve putting a concept into an illuminating relationship with other concepts, as when one sees that understanding the concept of 'necessity' is fruitfully enhanced by understanding its relations with 'possibility' and 'actuality'. It can involve interpreting or translating a concept into other, clearer concepts. It can involve tracing the history of the development of a concept. Standardly, the techniques of Analytic philosophy are a combination of some, most or all of these procedures. The *aim* is clarification and understanding: the *ambition* is that the knottiest problems of philosophy might thereby be solved (or, as some thinkers hope in relation to some traditional problems, 'dissolved', that is, shown not to be problems at all).

RUSSELL (1872–1970)

Bertrand Russell had a long life, and he devoted himself to far more than just logic and philosophy, twice standing for Parliament (in support of votes for women) and, both in the First World War and in the last two decades of his life, campaigning for peace and disarmament.

He wrote both technical and 'popular' books, founded and for a time ran a school, was a columnist for an American newspaper for several years, and won the Nobel Prize for literature. His was an amazingly active and vigorous life, lived in championship of liberally progressive causes always, and made sparkling by the wit, clarity and incisiveness of his mind.

It was also, and therefore, a life of controversy. Trinity College at Cambridge took away his job to punish him for his opposition to the First World War, and his anti-war activities resulted in prison terms both then and again in the last decade of his life, on this latter occasion for his opposition to nuclear weapons. Earlier in his life he campaigned for sensible views about divorce and sex education; later in life he campaigned against the Vietnam War. Indeed the older he grew the more radical he became. Early in life he was (and cheerfully described himself as having been) a prig, an outlook inherited from the austerely moralistic grandmother who brought him up – Countess Russell, widow of the former Prime Minister Earl Russell. Experience liberated his attitudes. He married several times, and one of his more controversial books, *Marriage and Morals*, both lost him a job in New York as the result of a campaign by outraged moralists – nearly leaving him destitute – and fifteen years later won him the Nobel Prize. When he was awarded the Order of Merit, which is the highest possible distinction in the British honours system, King George VI said to him at the award ceremony, 'You have sometimes behaved in a manner that would not do if generally adopted,' to which Russell replied that what one does depends upon what one is; consider, he said, the difference between a postman and a mischievous small boy ringing every doorbell in a street. The King did not know what to reply.

The founding impulse Russell gave to Analytic philosophy was aided by his younger contemporary at Cambridge, G. E. Moore. Indeed Russell, always generous in his praise of others, said Moore gave him the first push towards abandoning the Hegelian idealism he had espoused as a student. But the ground for his doing this was already fertile. When he first arrived at Cambridge, Russell was a disciple of his secular godfather John Stuart Mill, though he disagreed with Mill's account of mathematics. His first philosophical book, published ten years later, was study of Leibniz; in it he wrote, 'That all sound philosophy should begin with an analysis of propositions, is a truth too evident, perhaps, to demand a proof.' But in between, under the influence of the philosophy dons at Cambridge, he became a neo-Hegelian. McTaggart persuaded him to an unfavourable view of empiricism, and G. F. Stout persuaded him to believe in the Absolute. He decided that understanding the nature of the Absolute could and should be achieved from the perspective of science, and he decided to undertake a highly ambitious project to write something similar to Hegel's 'encyclopaedia of the sciences', but using the advanced scientific knowledge available in the 1890s (he made this plan while residing in Berlin in 1895).

The concept was Hegelian, but despite Bradley's strictures against piecemeal investigations which, he argued, always lead to contradictions, Russell made use of Kant's technique of 'transcendental arguments'* to examine particular aspects of experience and reality, aiming by this means eventually to construct a single comprehensive account of the Absolute. He started with geometry and then arithmetic, and soon found the project running into difficulties. This is because the theory of relations necessary to support an absolute idealist thesis is unsustainable; one cannot make sense of there being differences between spatial points, or between numbers, unless one accepts that there are asymmetrical and external relations.

Russell had been trying to write a paper, perhaps a book, speakingly called 'An Analysis of Mathematical Reasoning' – parts of it survived into his first major philosophical work, *The Principles of Mathematics* (1903) – in which he was trying to overcome the contradiction-prompting implications of the doctrine of internal relations.† When he saw that this could not be done he turned the argument on its head, and used the contradictions as a *reductio* of the doctrine instead. A significant prompt for his doing this was his encounter with G. E. Moore (1873–1958).

Moore arrived at Cambridge two years after Russell, almost wholly ignorant of philosophy and quietly aiming for a life as a schoolmaster 'teaching classics to sixth-formers', as he put it himself. At Cambridge he heard McTaggart and others lecture, and decided to devote the second half of his degree to philosophy. He was taught by McTaggart,

---

* A transcendental argument is one that takes something X accepted as being the case, and examines what must also be the case as a condition for X to be the case. It is an argument that works backwards, so to speak, to the necessary conditions of X. A trivial example would be: you are reading these words, so we can know that it is true that you were born and have survived so far, since you could not be reading these words otherwise.

† See the discussion in Part III above of Bradley's doctrine of relations, pp. 323–5.

whom he admired, and as a result he also became a neo-Hegelian. But only for a while; he soon yielded to a sense of amazement at some of the things asserted in philosophy, and in particular came to think that McTaggart's claims about the unreality of time were not just absurd but 'perfectly monstrous'. He said that although most philosophers claim to be motivated by a sense of wonder at the universe, his own inspiration was quite different: it was a sense of wonder that such silly things could be said by philosophers.

The net result of discussions between Russell and Moore was that they rejected neo-Hegelianism's key doctrines of monism and idealism in preference for pluralism and realism. During this process they became committed to the idea that the right method in philosophy is the analysis of judgments or propositions which, in Moore's view, exist independently of acts of judging them, and which consist of complexes of concepts.

Moore's thinking in the period between the mid-1890s and the beginning of the twentieth century led him to write his chief philosophical work, the *Principia Ethica*. In the same period Russell was working on ideas that eventually led to the immense project, which he wrote in collaboration with A. N. Whitehead, of the *Principia Mathematica*. As suggested by the starting point of his grand scheme for an absolute idealist 'encyclopaedia of all sciences', mathematics lay at the centre of his philosophical interests. It was one of his reasons for writing about Leibniz, whose metaphysics was significantly influenced by his mathematical and logical ideas. Leibniz had imagined a *characteristica universalis*, a perfectly clear and ordered language, in which mathematics, science and metaphysics can be expressed without ambiguity, and in which problems could be solved by 'calculation', thus overcoming disagreement. This idea was to inspire Russell's belief that logic can be just such a language; it shaped an aspiration on the part of many of those influenced by Russell and Frege that the logical analysis of language would be the royal road to solving the fundamental problems of philosophy.

In the second half of the 1890s Russell produced a series of intensive studies: his Fellowship dissertation *On the Foundations of Geometry* (1897); 'An Analysis of Mathematical Reasoning' (some time between 1897 and 1899); an unpublished manuscript entitled 'Fundamental Ideas and Axioms of Mathematics' (1899); an unpublished draft of the *Principles of Mathematics* (1899–1900); his book on Leibniz (1900);

and then *The Principles of Mathematics* itself (1903). (He had also written a book about Marxism in Germany, *German Social Democracy*, published in 1896.) When work was under way thereafter for *Principia Mathematica* it generated important philosophical spin-offs, including the paper 'On Denoting' (*Mind*, 1905), containing the celebrated Theory of Descriptions described above, and the germs of ideas Russell later developed about space, time and matter as 'logical constructions'.

The development of Russell's ideas in the years leading to *The Principles of Mathematics* had convinced him that pure mathematics (arithmetic, analysis and geometry) rests on logic: 'all pure mathematics deals exclusively with concepts definable in terms of a very small number of fundamental logical concepts [and] all its propositions are deducible from a very small number of fundamental logical principles.' This idea – that mathematics is reducible to logic – is known as 'logicism' and the inspiration for it was the powerful new developments in logic in the nineteenth century. A major such development was Frege's revolutionary work, including his treatment of quantification – explained below – and of ideas prompted in association with it, which Frege applied to his own attempt to derive arithmetic from logic. Russell learned of Frege's work from Giuseppe Peano at an international congress of mathematics held in Paris in 1900, and adapted some aspects of it to his own logicist project.

Logicism was motivated by the desire to solve two large puzzles about mathematics, one epistemological, the other metaphysical. The epistemological puzzle is: What justifies us in claiming to know mathematical truths such as $1 + 1 = 2$? The metaphysical puzzle is, What are the entities or objects referred to in mathematics? The puzzles connect: we would be justified in claiming to know that $1 + 1 = 2$ only if we know what '1' and '2' are, together with how we understand '+' and '='. These puzzles had not been put to rest by Kant's treatment of mathematical truths as 'synthetic' *a priori*, based on the 'forms of sensibility' which organize 'intuition' (sense-experience) spatially and temporally, thereby underwriting geometry and arithmetic respectively. The first suggestion that mathematics is analytic as opposed to synthetic is attributed to Richard Dedekind (1831–1916), who like Frege was influenced by the trend towards 'arithmetization' in certain branches of mathematics, premising the idea that the foundations of arithmetic and analysis (a part of mathematics developed from calculus) are purely conceptual. Frege continued to believe that geometry was synthetic *a*

priori, but held that arithmetic has a completely different basis. Dedekind likewise had argued that geometric intuitions should have no
place in thinking about 'a scientific basis for arithmetic'. When Frege
developed his *Begriffsschrift* – 'concept-script' – it was with the aim of
basing arithmetic on 'general logical laws and definitions', establishing
that the truths of arithmetic are analytic.

Russell himself had a long-standing desire to see mathematics placed
on unassailable foundations. When he was a boy his elder brother
Frank taught him geometry, and when he questioned the starting points
for it – the definitions and axioms – his brother said he just had to
accept them otherwise they could not go on. Russell was delighted by
the beauty of Euclid, indeed by the whole realm of mathematics, but
was troubled by the fact that it rested on foundations that had to be
taken on trust. The prospect of showing that mathematics rests on
logic was a deeply attractive one therefore.

It was 'on the last day of the nineteenth century' – 31 December
1900* – that Russell completed the first draft of his *Principles of Mathematics*. Just five months later he discovered a paradox which threatened
the whole enterprise, and which, when he communicated it to Frege in a
letter the following year, caused Frege to abandon logicism in despair.
Frege wrote back to Russell, 'Your discovery of the contradiction has
surprised me beyond words and . . . left me thunderstruck, because it
has rocked the ground on which I meant to build arithmetic . . . It is all
the more serious because it seems to undermine . . . the only possible
foundations of arithmetic as such.' Frege not long afterwards gave up
his efforts, but Russell continued, struggling to find ways round the
problem – eventually unsuccessfully also.

The tale of Russell's project and the devastating paradox is, in summary terms, this. First note the intuitive idea of a collection, or set or
class, of things – a collection of tea cups on a tray, a collection of cows
in a herd. Frege and after him Russell sought to define number in terms
of classes. Take a class whose members are a knife and fork, another
class whose members are a husband and wife, another class whose
members are a cow and a bull – they are all classes of couples or pairs.

---

* People everywhere mistakenly thought the twentieth century ended on 31 December
1999. Because there was no year 0, the first year of the Common Era being 1 CE, it follows that the last year of any century ends in 0; thus the last year of the nineteenth
century is 1900, and the last year of the twentieth century is 2000. The twenty-first century began on 1 January 2001.

This provides a way of defining the number 2: '2' is the class of all classes of couples. Likewise the number 3 is the class of all classes of triples (the class containing all the classes like this: a class containing a knife, fork and spoon, another class containing a mother, her husband and son; another class containing a cow, another cow and a bull; and so on). This can be repeated for all numbers. A little more precisely: 'the number of a class is the class of all those classes that are similar to it,' where 'similar' is a technical term in set theory stating that a one-to-one relationship obtains between the members of the classes in question.

Despite appearances, this is not the paradox in question, though it looks circular, for the concepts of pairs, triples, quadruples and so forth do not contain the concept of number: a waiter who cannot count can nevertheless know to put the triple of knife, fork and spoon at each place in a table setting.

Now, however, paradox looms. To prepare for it, consider this related paradox: there is a barber in a village who shaves the men – all the men, and only these men – who do not shave themselves. Does he shave himself, or not? If he does, he doesn't; and if he doesn't, he does. For obvious reasons this is called 'the Barber Paradox'. Russell's Paradox is this: consider the fact that some classes are members of themselves, and some are not. The class of all classes is, obviously, a member of itself, for it is a class; but the class of men is, equally obviously, not itself a man. Now: what of the class of all those classes which are not members of themselves? If it is a member of itself, then it is not a member of itself; and if it is not a member of itself, then it is a member of itself.

The fact that the concept of classes can yield a contradiction is fatal for any system built upon its use. Although the details of how this created problems for Frege's and Russell's endeavours are complex, this sketch is enough to indicate why it wrecked Frege's hopes, and why it obliged Russell to seek various ad hoc and in the end unsatisfactory ways round it, chiefly by means of a 'Theory of Types' which sought to order classes into a hierarchy such that (speaking very schematically) only classes of a lower type can be members of classes of a higher type.

Without a means of circumventing the paradox Russell could not have proceeded with his logicist programme. The devices he proposed – the Theory of Types and two controversial axioms – eventually allowed him and his collaborator A. N. Whitehead to complete the enormous

Principia Mathematica, published in three volumes respectively in 1910, 1912 and 1913. The expense of printing the volumes, with their hundreds of pages of logical symbols, was so great that Russell and Whitehead had to supplement the cost out of their own pockets. The huge manuscript was wheeled to the offices of the Cambridge University Press in a perambulator.

Principia Mathematica has been described as one of the three most important works of logic ever, the other two being Aristotle's *Organon* and Frege's *Grundgesetze der Arithmetik*.* One reason offered is that the notation developed by Whitehead and Russell made logic greatly more effective and accessible as a tool, and revealed far more of its possibilities and uses. This opened the way to significant further developments in logic and philosophy, some of them developed by Russell himself. Other opinions about *Principia Mathematica*, while recognizing its philosophical fruitfulness, have not been so complimentary. The brilliant Austrian logician Kurt Gödel wrote of it, 'It is to be regretted that this first comprehensive and thorough-going presentation of a mathematical logic and the derivation of mathematics from it [is] so greatly lacking in formal precision in the foundations that it presents in this respect a considerable step backwards as compared with Frege. What is missing, above all, is a precise statement of the syntax of the formalism.' Although true, this judgment is harsh; without the advances made by *Principia Mathematica* itself it would have been less easy to see what is required for a fully precise formal account of the foundations.

Among the significant outcomes of this work was Russell's own philosophical endeavours in the long remainder of his life. Released from his labours on the big book he turned his attention to a question which was central to almost everything he did in philosophy thereafter: the question of how science is derived from experience. Note that this is not the same as the question of how, or whether, science is *justified* by experience; it is not an effort to refute scepticism about the possibility of scientific knowledge. Instead Russell wished to explain the foundations of knowledge in empirical experience, just as Locke, Hume and Mill in their different ways had tried to do. And for him the paradigm of knowledge was science. He remained consistent in pursuing

---

* That is the judgment of the author of the related entry in the *Stanford Encyclopedia of Philosophy*.

this aim throughout, though his strategies for doing so changed a number of times, and his later views involved significant compromises.

At the outset Russell's endeavour took the form of showing how the fundamental concepts of physics – which in 1912, when his *Problems of Philosophy* was published, were taken to be space, time, causality and matter – are exhaustively 'verified' by observation and experiment. By the time of his last attempt at this task, in *Human Knowledge* (1948), physics had dispensed with causality and matter, space-time had replaced space and time, and Russell had come to accept what he had once emphatically rejected as Kant's 'Ptolemaic counter-revolution' against scientific objectivity (by putting the human mind back at the centre of the phenomenal universe), namely, that there are ineliminable *a priori* aspects to any account of how science arises from experience.

This late shift in his thinking was a significant one for Russell, because it meant abandoning his early pure form of empiricist commitment to the idea that sense-experience is the foundation of knowledge. He had distinguished 'knowledge by description' from 'knowledge by acquaintance', the former being derived from the latter, and the latter consisting in 'direct cognitive contact' with something: 'we have *acquaintance* with anything of which we are directly aware, without the intermediary of any process of inference or any knowledge of truths.' Knowledge by description, in contrast, is knowledge that is indirect, its justification resting on being ultimately inferred from acquaintance. For example, my knowledge that Everest is the highest mountain is indirect, but ultimately rests on the fact that there is knowledge by acquaintance (not necessarily mine) of what provides the ground for it.

The technique Russell applied in the earlier phases of this programme was 'logical construction'. He coined the term 'sense-datum' to denote a sense-impression – the immediate object of awareness in experience – and proposed that physical objects be regarded as logical constructions out of actual and possible sense-data. Think of perceiving a table: we visually experience shaped patches of colour which we regard as the table-top and some of the legs, say; and we anticipate that if we gave ourselves the experience of doing such things as looking underneath and going round to the other side, we would have further sense-data of a similar kind. The totality of the sense-data we do and could have constitutes the table; the table is a logical construction out of them.

This view, which in developments of it came to be known as 'phenomenalism' – phenomenalists included Rudolf Carnap and other Logical Positivists of the Vienna Circle, and A. J. Ayer – is very similar to Berkeley's idealism, but is distinguished from it in a crucial way. The existence of an object currently unperceived by me, or by any other finite being, is explained by Berkeley as consisting in its being perceived by a ubiquitous and omnipresent 'infinite spirit', or God. That is why the table in my room exists even when neither I nor anyone else is there to perceive it; the infinite spirit is perceiving it. For phenomenalists the currently unperceived existence of the table consists in the 'bare truth' (this being a truth not explained or supported by anything else) of a 'counterfactual conditional' statement that says, 'If I were in my room now, I would see the table.' A conditional statement is an 'if-then' statement; a *counterfactual* conditional is one whose 'if' part states something that is not the case (is contrary to the facts). Note that the verbs in a counterfactual conditional are in the subjunctive mood: 'if I *were* . . . then I *would*,' thus showing that what is meant is 'if I were (but I am not) . . . then I would . . .'

The reliance on 'barely true' counterfactual conditionals is one of the main flaws with this approach. What makes such conditionals true? It is an unhelpful fact about conditionals in general, for these purposes, that they are anyway always true if the 'if' part of them is false; this is a result purely of the logic of conditionality. (See the Appendix on logic below for the truth table of $p \rightarrow q$, 'if p then q'.) How can an epistemological theory turn on this? Yet without accepting the bare truth of counterfactuals it is impossible to 'construct' physical objects out of sense-experience of them, because the experience of them is always partial and limited, so that the number of actual and possible sense-data putatively constituting the object is such that one could never exhaustively 'reduce' the object to experiences.

The point can be put another way: to say that an object is a construction out of actual and possible sense-data is to say that statements about physical objects can be translated into statements about actual and possible sense-experiences. But such translation can never be effected without remainder; there are always statements about objects which outrun statements about actual or possible experience. They include statements about other people's sense-experiences, and statements in which reference is made to all places and times at which sense-data constituting the object are or could be experienced.

These points relate to a problem Russell refused to address, because he took the same dismissive attitude to it as Locke had done, namely, the problem of sceptical challenges to experience as a basis for knowledge. Other sense-datum theorists, such as A. J. Ayer, took this problem seriously, and discovered that it defeats the phenomenalist project. For if phenomenalism were right there would have to be, said Ayer, 'a deductive step from descriptions of physical reality to descriptions of possible, if not actual, appearances. And conversely, the occurrence of the sense-data must be a sufficient condition for the existence of the physical object; there must be a deductive step from descriptions of actual, or . . . possible, appearances to descriptions of physical reality.' But as Ayer then adds, 'The decisive objection to phenomenalism is that neither of these requirements can be satisfied.'

In the Preface to *Human Knowledge* Russell observes that the terms 'belief', 'truth', 'knowledge' and 'perception' all have imprecise common uses which will require progressive clarification. The concepts of them have to be analysed as a preparation for the synthesizing task of showing how the objects of belief and perception are 'logically constructed' from experience. This was his methodology throughout. But at last, after various attempts to work out an account of how experience underlies science, from *Our Knowledge of the External World* (1914), through *The Analysis of Mind* (1921), *The Analysis of Matter* (1927) and acceptance of a view called 'Neutral Monism', first put forward by William James, that mind and matter are expressions of a more fundamental single stuff, he came to the conclusion in *Human Knowledge* (1948) that one can only get from experience to science by aid of certain *a priori* principles. Either we know something *a priori*, he there wrote, 'or science is moonshine.' But science is not moonshine. So we know something *a priori*. These *a priori* principles are what he called 'postulates' and they embody beliefs about causality, the relative enduringness of physical things and the validity of inductive generalizations. He described them as 'instinctive' beliefs, as Hume had similarly done. But in being known *a priori* while applying to how things actually are in the world, they are synthetic *a priori* in Kant's sense, though Russell did not claim that they are 'transcendentally necessary'; indeed the epistemology of *Human Knowledge* is fallibilist and tentative, a far cry from the search for certain foundations that had prompted his work in logic and mathematics, and which he had said – in the opening sentence of his *Problems of Philosophy* – was what philosophy sought to discover.

Perhaps the most important phase in the journey just described, from the point of view of its connection with both the early philosophy of Wittgenstein (see below) and the development of phenomenalism, was the 'logical atomist' phase of Russell's thinking. He sometimes said 'logic is the essence of philosophy' to express his view that the surface forms of language are misleading and that it is therefore necessary to analyse its underlying structure using the perspicuous language of logic. This analysis is demonstrated in the Theory of Descriptions. Applying the same structural analysis to the world over which language ranges, and showing the connections between the respective structures of world and language, offered Russell the account he sought. In his 'Lectures on Logical Atomism', written while in prison in 1918, he argued as follows. The world consists of a plurality of things each possessed of qualities and standing in relations to other things. A description of the world would require to be more than just a list of objects, but an explanation of their qualities and relations too. Things with their qualities and relations are constituents of facts, and facts are expressed by propositions. Propositions which express 'basic facts', that is, which simply assert that something has a certain quality or stands in a certain relation to some other thing, Russell called 'atomic propositions'. When atomic propositions are combined together by means of the logical words 'and', 'or' and 'if . . . then . . .' they constitute complex or 'molecular' propositions. These are exceedingly important because the possibility of inference depends on them. Finally there are 'general propositions' such as 'all men are mortal,' and they require acceptance of some general principles in addition to the empirical evidence provided by acquaintance with the objects and properties referred to in atomic propositions.

The 'atoms' of the world arrived at by analysis are particular sense-data, 'little patches of colour or sounds, momentary things', and they are also properties like 'whiteness' and relations like 'after' or 'next to'. One reason for calling them 'atoms' is that, in this context, they are things which are both basic or fundamental, and logically independent of each other. Analysing complex symbols (propositions) into the 'simple symbols' out of which they are built – the atomic propositions – enables us to make a direct connection between the terms in them and these atoms of experience. In a 'logically perfect language' (the logic of

Principia Mathematica) the ultimate components of the atomic propositions will correspond one to one with the atomic constituents of facts. In the ideal, each atomic object will have its own individual simple symbol corresponding to it.

The atoms of the world are simples – things that are not further analysable – and they are very short-lived; they are fleeting sense-data, so the complexes they constitute, the facts, are 'logical fictions' constructed out of them. We are *acquainted* with the atoms; everything else we know by *description*.

The 'Lectures on Logical Atomism' sketch a programme rather than offering a detailed metaphysics and epistemology, but even so they suggest difficulties, among them the following. The theory ambitiously tries to provide an empiricist account of meaning comprising views about knowledge, perception and mind, and does so by assuming that there is a uniquely correct way of representing the underlying structure of language in logic. That is at least questionable. Russell includes among objects of direct acquaintance not just simple objects but their qualities and relations, treating these as simples (as unanalysable) also. He cites colour-patches as examples of such atoms, but colours cannot be atomic because they are not logically independent of each other. Quite quickly he had to row back on the idea that the simples at the bottom of the logical structure are sense-data – atoms of experience – saying that they can only be known inferentially as the limit of analysis. But then the ambition to connect physics – which is a body of descriptive knowledge – to a ground in experience which supplies a direct connection between simple symbols and simple entities is derailed.

Wittgenstein's *Tractatus Logico-Philosophicus* puts forward a version of this view in a much more rigorous, systematic and pared-down way; see below. Some of the ideas that Russell and Wittgenstein developed in their own ways had been discussed by them when Wittgenstein was Russell's pupil in Cambridge before the First World War.

Russell never thought of himself as a moral philosopher, though he was certainly a moralist – not of a puritanical kind; quite the contrary – but in fact he made genuine contributions to moral theory, anticipating emotivism (the idea that ethical judgments are disguised expressions of how the judger feels about the matter in question) and 'error theory' (the view, associated mainly with J. L. Mackie, that because ethical judgments are not objective, they are false). In light of the fact that Russell had emphatic views about what is right and wrong – the First World War was wrong, nuclear weapons are bad, smacking children is wrong, hypocrisy is bad, kindness and compassion are right, peace is good – there is no straightforward link between his theory and practice.

Russell's popular writings on matters of society and morality were among the influences that helped to liberate at least the Western world from some of the excesses of Victorian moralism, and his popular writings on philosophy brought many to the subject. He became a sage, asked in his old age what message he would like to leave the world, and he rose to the challenge in his old-fashioned tones, saying in effect that he hoped rationality and peace would eventually overcome the follies to which humankind is prone. King George and some others might have had reservations about Russell's private life, but taken in the round there is no denying that he was a great man.

FREGE (1848–1925)

Russell was introduced to Gottlob Frege's work by the logician Giuseppe Peano, but by his own admission did not properly understand all of it, largely because of the unintuitive notation that Frege devised to set out his new and powerful extension of logic. Among the earliest to appreciate the significance of this work, apart from Peano, Russell and a few others, were the logicians Alonzo Church and Kurt Gödel. The beginnings of Frege's philosophical reputation might be traced to Russell's allusion to him in his Lowell Lectures at Harvard in 1914 (published as *Our Knowledge of the External World*), in which he said that Frege had given 'the first complete example' of the 'logical-analytic method in philosophy'. In the *Monist* for 1915 excerpts from the first volume of Frege's *Grundgesetze der Arithmetik* were published in a translation by Johann Stachelroth and Philip Jourdain, who quote Russell's remark in explaining Frege's project in their introductory comments.

But Frege came more fully into the cognizance of the philosophical community when, in 1952, Peter Geach and Max Black published translations of some of his work.* They wrote, 'One aim of this volume

* Michael Dummett in the *London Review of Books* for 18 September 1980 says, 'When Geach and Black's volume of translations first came out in 1952, there existed hardly anything of Frege's in English save his *Foundations of Arithmetic* . . . [their] volume, with its selection of articles and excerpts from the other books, therefore did an immense

357

is to make available to English readers Frege's more important logical essays, which have long been buried in various German periodicals (mostly now defunct) ... Professor Ryle and Lord Russell have been most helpful by lending works of Frege that were otherwise almost unobtainable.' As these remarks show, Frege's ideas were largely inaccessible unless one were a mathematically knowledgeable reader of German and could get hold of rare journals and books. Their volume was followed by the extensive treatment of Frege's ideas by William and Martha Kneale in their *Development of Logic* (1962), which in its turn predated by a decade publication of the major work by Michael Dummett, *Frege: Philosophy of Language* (1973), the first of a magisterial series of books by him about, and influenced by, Frege, which confirmed Frege's place as a seminal figure in Analytic philosophy.

Indeed, in his own history of Analytic philosophy, which he idiosyncratically and controversially defined as the view that 'a philosophical account of thought can only be attained through a philosophical account of language,' Dummett attributes its origin to Frege's *Grundgesetze*, saying that it offers the first clear example of the 'linguistic turn' which is Analytic philosophy's essence. Some of the distinctive themes in Analytic philosophy do indeed come from Frege's need to provide far sharper tools than ordinary language provides for carrying out his plan to show that arithmetic and logic are the same thing. He described his 'concept-script' (*Begriffsschrift*) as bearing the same relation to ordinary language as 'the microscope bears to the eye'. But in the process of creating this new logical language, philosophically important considerations about ordinary language and concepts were themselves magnified into salience.

Frege was born in the Hanseatic town of Wismar on the Baltic coast of Germany, son of the founder and headmaster of a girls' school. He was brought up as a Lutheran and educated at a local gymnasium before attending the universities of Jena and Göttingen. After his habilitation he became a *Privatdozent* at Jena, over the next five years lecturing on various aspects of the undergraduate curriculum in mathematics. The little book in which he set out his *Begriffsschrift* was published in 1879, whereupon he was appointed *Professor extraordinarius* (associate professor), which meant a salary and security. The

---

service by making a representative sample of Frege's writings available to the philosophical public.'

Begriffsschrift was a revolutionary advance in logic, but its difficult notation prevented it from being appreciated as such, or even indeed much understood.

In 1884 Frege published *Die Grundlagen der Arithmetik*, a prospectus in relatively informal terms for the technical work he later carried out in the *Grundgesetze der Arithmetik* (in two volumes, 1893 and 1903). The *Grundlagen* is however the work that both contains and prompted his most important philosophical contributions, as demonstrated by three papers that much later proved highly influential, 'Function and Concept' (1891) and 'On Sense and Reference' and 'On Concept and Object' (both 1892).

As the dates of publication of the *Grundgesetze* volumes show, the second appeared shortly after Russell communicated to Frege the devastating discovery of the paradox. In the exchange of letters between them, about ten on each side, Russell set out a number of the points he went on to develop, and Frege, after the initial shock, tried out his own solution to the problem. Because the second volume of the *Grundgesetze* was just about to appear Frege added a postscript explaining Russell's discovery and suggesting a way of shoring up his project despite it. He persisted in trying to find a solution until 1906, when, it seems, he lost heart altogether, and abandoned the endeavour which had been his life's work. But in the process he had made contributions to logic and philosophy of the very first value.

It is regrettable to report that in old age Frege, always politically conservative, came to express outright Fascist and anti-Semitic views, along with others who supported the rise of Nazi ideology in that place and period – among them Martin Heidegger, whom we meet later.

Frege's importance to logic speaks for itself: he revolutionized it by inventing a formal system and associated notation which is in effect the predicate calculus of modern mathematical logic. Russell and Whitehead invented an improved and more intuitive notation for representing quantification and the structure of complexes which Frege had developed, thus making the ideas more accessible.

But in the process of developing his logic and the ideas necessary for applying it to his chief aim, which was to demonstrate the identity of logic and arithmetic (which is the same as saying: to demonstrate that arithmetic can be reduced to logic, which is analytic), Frege also developed a philosophy of language; and this aspect of his achievement is of equal importance. He arrived at a philosophy of language through the necessity of having to explain *reference* – how a term refers to objects or concepts – and this in turn required devising a theory of *sense*, which is – to speak very roughly at this juncture – what one has to know about a term to be able to identify what it refers to.

It is important to note at the outset Frege's rejection of 'psychologism'. Psychologism is the view that concepts are to be explained by reference to the mental processes or states in the minds of those employing them. Among other things this implies that the laws of logic and mathematics are generalizations from the way minds work. Logic was said to describe 'the laws of thought', and psychology is the science of how we think; hence the connection. On some views – Mill's, for example – mathematical concepts such as number were thought to be empirically grounded in the experience of counting.

Against such views Frege emphatically argued that logic concerns an objective realm which has nothing to do with how people think, and therefore cannot be reduced to empirical or psychological considerations. He offers the example of 'self-identity' in proof of this claim. Self-identity is the principle that everything is identical with itself, and it is true by definition of the word 'identical'; we do not have to tour the world inspecting each thing to see if it is self-identical. If psychologism were true, the meaning of 'identical' would be constituted by ideas in the brain of someone thinking about identity; or more correctly, it would be constituted by the ideas in the various brains of various people thinking about identity, perhaps differently from each other, and perhaps over time coming to think about it differently from how they earlier thought of it. But the meaning of 'identical' is not subjective nor liable to fashion, said Frege; it is objective. Another way to put the point is to say that there is a difference between the belief that some proposition p is true, and p's being true. Frege's argument was that the truth of p cannot be reduced to the belief that p is true. This was his chief argument against psychologism.

The debate about psychologism on either side of the turn of the twentieth century, especially among German philosophers, was intense. Frege convinced Edmund Husserl to abandon his earlier psychologistic stance, and it was Husserl's anti-psychologism that prompted the vigorous debate in which defenders of psychologism claimed, among other things, that the laws of logic are normative and based on considerations of value. On this view, the Law of Non-Contradiction, 'not both A and not-A', is a prescriptive law, an 'imperative', instructing one how to think correctly by, in this case, showing what cannot be thought.* Frege argued that laws of logic are not prescriptive but descriptive, describing how things objectively are. Because empiricism and naturalism are forms of psychologism the debate has in effect continued since, anti-psychologism itself being rejected (by, among many others, Moritz Schlick of the Logical Positivists and W. V. Quine) on empiricist and naturalistic grounds.

As noted, in order to show the identity of logic and arithmetic Frege needed to explain *reference* – how a term refers to objects or concepts, which, in line with his anti-psychologism, are to be understood as existing independently of acts of referring to or thinking about them – and therefore he had to develop a philosophy of language. To see the connection between logic and philosophy of language, note first that the aim in the latter is to give an account of how expressions in a language relate to 'the universe of discourse' to which the language applies. Ordinary language relates to the world of tea-cups, people, trees and mountains; arithmetic relates to numbers and functions like addition and subtraction; the language of physics relates to quarks and leptons, forces and fields – and so on. One of the key relationships is the one that makes what we say true or false; roughly speaking, a correspondence (or, in the case of falsity, a lack of one) between what we say and the way things are. Among the simplest kinds of assertions are those that say a certain thing has a certain property – for example, 'the ball is round' – and we take it that the subject-term 'ball' refers to an object of the appropriate type, and the property-introducing predicate term 'round' is the word for that particular shape. To see whether the sentence is true we need to see if the subject and predicate terms are being correctly used so that they each make the appropriate contribution to the whole sentence. The sentence is composed of the subject and predicate terms and the way they are joined – in this case by the 'is' of predication – so the truth-value of the whole sentence is determined by its parts. This is known as 'compositionality', and it shows why it is a central task in the philosophy of language to analyse sentences into their components and to understand the contributions they make to truth and meaning.†

---

* Note that the Law of Non-Contradiction is equivalent to the Law of Excluded Middle, 'everything is either A or not-A'; this can be proved by De Morgan's Theorems. See the Appendix on logic.
† Mention of the 'is' of predication reminds one to keep in mind the distinction between it and the 'is' of identity, thus: the 'is' of predication says that something has a certain

Such analysis also matters to logic, because the inferential connections between sentences also turn on how their parts are related to each other. Here is where logic and the philosophy of language share an interest. Aristotle long before had recognized that valid inferences depend upon how terms occur in sentences; his theory of the syllogism distinguished between subject and predicate terms, and demonstrated how the arrangement of the terms (and whether the sentences in which they occur are universal or particular, negative or affirmative) determines the inferences that can be drawn. But a weakness in his logic is its inability to deal adequately with sentences containing more than one quantifier expression (quantifiers are such expressions as 'all', 'many', 'most', 'some', 'at least one' – and all the natural numbers). This is known as 'multiple generality'. A standard example is 'Everyone loves someone.' This is ambiguous between there being one person loved by everyone, and everyone loving a person who is in most cases different from all individuals loved by others: 'there is someone who is loved by everyone' and 'for every person there is some other person whom he or she loves.' Note how clarifying the original sentence requires a paraphrase to reveal how the parts are contributing to the whole. Representing the sentences in a perspicuous logical symbolism leaves no trace of ambiguity, and does it very simply by ordering the quantifiers 'all' and 'at least one' suitably:

$(\exists x)(y)(Lyx)$ pronounced 'there is an x such that for all y, y stands in the relation L to x' (there is someone whom everyone loves)

and

$(y)(\exists x)(Lyx)$ pronounced 'for all y there is an x such that y stands in the relation L to x' (everyone has a someone he or she loves).

Frege noticed, however, that the reference of terms occurring in sentences do not do everything required to explain those sentences' meanings and the inferential relationships they can enter into. He noticed this because of two connected puzzles prompted by referring

---

property, as in 'the ball is round,' whereas the 'is' of identity, as in 'x is x,' 'Jane Austen is the author of *Pride and Prejudice*,' says that the things referred to on either side of 'is' are one and the same thing. To say of two or more things that they are identical is, in colloquial speech, ambiguous between 'are one and the same thing' and 'look exactly alike, are exactly similar'; it is the first that is meant by talk of 'the "is" of identity'.

terms. One concerns identity statements, and the other concerns contexts in which referring terms fail to contribute compositionally to the
truth-value of the sentences in which they occur.

Consider the identity statements '1 + 1 = 2', 'Jane Austen is the author
of *Pride and Prejudice*,' 'the morning star, Phosphorus, is identical to
the evening star, Hesperus.' Logically speaking these all have the same
form, 'x = x,' though they appear as 'a = b' where 'a' and 'b' are different
referring expressions, and the meaning of 'Jane Austen is Jane Austen'
is very different from 'Jane Austen is the author of *Pride and Prejudice*.'
For one (big) thing, the latter is more informative than the former.
Whereas you can determine the truth of 'x = x' just by looking at it, you
cannot determine the truth of 'the morning star is the evening star'
without doing some astronomy.

Frege dealt with the problem by distinguishing between the *reference* of a term – its denoting something – and the *sense* of the term,
which very informally might be thought of as its 'meaning' but is better
described as what one knows when one knows how to locate the referent (the thing denoted) by the term. So 'the morning star is the evening
star' is a true identity statement in virtue of the fact that the expressions 'morning star' and 'evening star' both refer to the same thing, but
they differ in sense; which is why, when what had been thought to
be the two stars Phosphorus and Hesperus, the first lingering visibly
in the morning and the second shining brightly in the early evening,
were discovered to be the same heavenly body (in fact, the planet
Venus), this was an exciting discovery despite being an instance of the
unexciting 'x = x'.

The second puzzle also arises from a consideration of identity, this
time in relation to the fact that if 'a' and 'b' refer to the same thing – are
'co-referential' – then in the sentence 'a is round' you can substitute 'b'
for 'a', yielding 'b is round,' the truth-value of the original sentence not
being changed by the substitution. This is known as the principle of the
intersubstitutivity of co-referential terms *salva veritate* ('preserving the
truth-value'). Any language in which this principle applies is called an
'extensional' or truth-functional language.

But consider this: suppose that Tom does not know that Cicero is also
called Tully (his name was Marcus Tullius Cicero), but he does correctly believe that Cicero wrote *De Amicitia*, 'On Friendship'. By the
principle of intersubstitutivity of co-referential terms, the truth-values
of 'Tom believes that Cicero wrote *De Amicitia*' and 'Tom believes that

Tully wrote *De Amicitia*' should be the same. But because Tom does not know that Tully is another name for Cicero he will not believe that Tully wrote *De Amicitia*, so we cannot substitute 'Tully' for 'Cicero' and preserve the truth-value. Here the principle of intersubstitutivity fails.

Expressions like 'believes that', 'knows that', 'hopes that', 'intends that' are reports of *propositional attitudes*, that is, psychological attitudes towards the proposition that follows the 'that' in each case: 'Tom believes that p,' 'Tom hopes that p,' and so on, where 'p' is any proposition. Evidently, when a referring expression occurs inside a propositional attitude context, it does not refer in its normal straightforward way; and that explains the failure of the intersubstitutivity principle. Languages or contexts in which the principle does not hold are called 'intensional' languages or contexts. Propositional attitude contexts are intensional.

Note however that the principle of intersubstitutivity fails only if we treat referring expressions as functioning in the same way inside propositional attitude contexts as outside them. Using the sense–reference distinction, Frege proposed that this is not the case; that referring terms which occur inside such contexts refer not to their referents, but to their senses. Because the senses of terms are, in effect, 'ways of thinking' about their referents, what is being referred to by 'Cicero' in the propositional attitude report is not the man who bears that name, but the way of thinking that allows us to refer to that man. Because the senses of 'Cicero' and 'Tully' are different – they are different ways of 'presenting' the man Cicero – the terms 'Cicero' and 'Tully' inside the propositional attitude context are not co-referring; they refer to different senses. Propositional attitude verbs like 'believes', 'hopes' and the rest effect a 'reference-shift'. Accordingly the principle of intersubstitutivity is not violated; it remains good for all cases where two or more terms refer to the same thing – whether the thing in question is an object or a sense.

These views have proved fertile in the philosophy of language, not least in prompting disagreement and defences. Consider the fact that it seems very natural to say that in 'Cicero wrote *De Amicitia*' and 'Tom believes that Cicero wrote *De Amicitia*' it is the same person, Cicero, being talked about (being referred to) in both cases. In ordinary conversation one would not think that in the first case it is the man we are talking about, but in the second it is a 'mode of presentation' associated with his name. Moreover, taking the reference of the name to be the same across contexts seems indispensable when we say, 'Cicero wrote *De Amicitia*, and Tom believes that he also wrote *De Senectute*.' This is a case of anaphora, where understanding who 'he' refers to requires expressly understanding that it refers to the same thing that 'Cicero' refers to. This is how pronouns work; their job is to preserve reference. Frege's view requires a theory of anaphora more complex than the intuitive one.

Fregeans have their responses to these and other criticisms; the richness and technicality of the debate that has sprung from Frege's work are a testament to its significance. It is another illustration of the fact that, even though the goal of an endeavour might not be reached, the journey undertaken towards it can be very fruitful.

MOORE (1873–1958)

G. E. Moore's association with Russell has already been mentioned. As a student and later a Prize Fellow at Cambridge he was also friendly with Lytton Strachey, John Maynard Keynes and Leonard Woolf, through whom he had a significant influence on other members of the Blooms-bury Group as a result of his chief work, *Principia Ethica*. He concluded in that work that the two intrinsically most valuable things worth pursuing for their own sakes are beauty and friendship, a view calculated to resonate with the literary and artistic sensibilities of the group's members.*

Moore's decision to exchange philosophy for classics as an under-graduate was inspired by McTaggart, then a young and energetic don. McTaggart became his tutor, under whose guidance Moore adopted an idealist philosophy. His Prize Fellowship essay on the metaphysical basis of ethics acknowledged his debt to Bradley, and at the same time subjected Kant's ethics to a sustained critique. In particular Moore criticized Kant for failing to distinguish between the psychological activity of making judgments and the question of the objective truth or otherwise of those judgments. This parallels Frege's rejection of psychologism, and is one of the two aspects of Moore's early views that survived his abandonment of idealism.

---

* One is tempted to surmise that the Bloomsbury Group's members economized by having beautiful friends.

The other aspect was his identification of what he argued was a fallacy in ethical thinking, namely, defining 'the good' in terms of pleasure or desirability, that is, something that can be empirically identified as providing the concept of goodness with its content. Because the usual candidates for defining goodness are natural properties such as pleasure or happiness, Moore called this the 'Naturalistic Fallacy'. He asserted instead that goodness (or 'the good') is indefinable. Any attempt to explain or define 'goodness' is like attempting to explain or define 'yellow': one cannot define the colour yellow in words or in terms of something other than itself, one can only show an example of yellowness to someone wishing to know what 'yellow' means.

This point was more fully developed in *Principia Ethica*. There Moore's argument for the Naturalistic Fallacy is the 'Open Question Argument'. If someone identifies the good as pleasure, you can say 'this is pleasant, but it remains an open question whether it is good.' For any natural property put forward as the analysis of 'good', one can acknowledge the presence of that natural property yet still ask whether what is claimed to be good is indeed good.

These ideas have proved controversial. First, the 'Naturalistic Fallacy' is not well named. It is not a fallacy – it might be wrong to identify the good with some natural property or state, but it is not a contradiction or logical mistake to do so – and it is not restricted to naturalistic candidates for explaining the good because, as Moore himself points out, it is an equal mistake to identify the good with something transcendent or metaphysical, like the commandment of a deity; thus, 'x is good because God commands it' is an instance of the 'fallacy' on Moore's view.

Moreover it is not obvious that identifying a moral property with a natural one does indeed leave open the question 'But is it good?' For if a theory asserts (and, in the better cases, justifies the assertion) that the good is pleasure or happiness, then asking 'But is it good?' misses the point of the theory, or begs the question against it.

Moore's commitment to the Naturalistic Fallacy obliged him to address the question of how we can know or recognize the good when we meet it. His answer, forced by his view that the good is indefinable, is that we simply 'intuit' it; we have a faculty of moral intuition which enables us to recognize the good when we encounter it.

On the face of it this is implausible. What is this faculty and how does it work? Is it different in different people, as the pervasive evidence of moral disagreement would suggest? The claim that a 'faculty of moral intuition' exists leaves no room for consideration of what can justify a moral judgment or, conversely, be invoked to criticize it, leaving moral disagreements undecidable. The worst result would be a species of relativistic anarchy, in which different people 'intuit' the moral value or disvalue of things in their own idiosyncratically different and even contrary ways.

One result of Moore's view in this connection is what came to be called 'non-cognitivism' in ethics, that is, the view that when people make moral judgments they are not stating something true or false, but manifesting an attitude or an emotional response, for there is nothing 'out there' in the world, a moral fact or property, which one is talking about; instead moral utterances are expressions of psychological states such as approval or disapproval, which means that utterances of them are statements of preferences and desires, not judgments of right and wrong or good and bad.

These aspects of Moore's views on ethics are certainly not standard fare, but when it comes to the question of how we are to determine the right thing to do he reverts to a very standard consequentialist utilitarian view, that the right thing to do is what will produce the most good. And since 'act utilitarianism' imposes the difficult if not insuperable burden on us of trying to decide, on each occasion of acting, what will produce the best outcome, he plumps for a form of 'rule utilitarianism' which says that one should follow the rules whose observance tends to produce the best outcomes.

Moore also advanced views in metaphysics and epistemology. In his paper 'The Refutation of Idealism' (1903) he characterized idealism as the thesis that *esse est percipi*, 'to be is to be perceived (or experienced).' He takes the idealists' chief argument to be that denying that *esse est percipi* is a contradiction, and correlatively that because the 'is' (*est*) is the 'is' of identity, existence and experience are the same thing: 'yellow and the sensation of yellow are absolutely identical.' If you can show that they are not 'absolutely identical' you will thereby refute idealism; and this Moore aimed to do.

One argument he offers is that if 'yellow' and 'the sensation of yellow' are identical, 'there would be no reason to insist' that they are; and insisting that they are indicates that in fact they are not. Frege's sense–reference distinction might have come in aid here, as one way of explaining why Moore's argument does not work. Another is to examine the motivation for asserting the identity statement, which is – as Berkeley argued – that claims that there are two yellow things – a yellow (or yellowness-sensation-prompting) something 'out there' and a yellow sensation 'in here', the former lying inaccessibly behind the latter yet postulated as its cause, is to duplicate entities in defiance of Occam's Razor; and moreover it is to claim as the cause of a mental entity (the sensation) something that is not a mental entity (an object in a material world) in defiance of the principle that only like things can cause like things – mental causes for mental effects, material causes for material effects. Moore ignores these kinds of argument for the *esse est percipi* claim and focuses only on an exhaustive analysis of the terms *esse* and *percipi* themselves – to the detriment of his own case.*

His second argument turns on distinguishing acts of conscious awareness from their objects, which by itself would refute *esse est percipi* if shown to be unavoidable. The key to his argument is that in a conscious awareness of greenness and in a conscious awareness of blueness there is something common to both, which is conscious awareness, and therefore this is not the same as what those acts of awareness are awareness of. This question-beggingly assumes an 'act–object' analysis of thought and experience; an idealist might argue instead for an 'adverbial' analysis, in which thinking and experiencing occur in modes, such as 'experiencing greenly' and 'experiencing bluely' where there is just the thinking and experiencing but with a particular greeny or bluey character of its own each time.

The upshot of these arguments for Moore was, for a while, a commitment to 'direct realism', the view that we are acquainted with things 'outside the circle of our own ideas and sensations' without the intervention of any representing medium such as ideas or sensations. There is a parallel here with his intuitionism regarding the good, and for obvious reasons it is no more plausible. He had to abandon it when he realized that it raised a problem about falsehood: how could we ever be wrong if we are in unmediated perceptual relationship with the objects of thought and experience? For a long time he tried out a version of a sense-datum theory in which sense-data are literally identical with the surfaces of objects, thus trying to preserve at least something from the

---

* These remarks are not of course intended to constitute agreement with Berkeley, whose views require a somewhat more searching refutation: see Grayling, *Berkeley: The Central Arguments* (1986).

direct realist view. He felt this to be necessary because as soon as one makes sense-data an intervening *tertium quid* between the world and one's mind, one has opened the door to scepticism.

Moore's solution in the end was to accept that sense-data cannot be identical with the surface of objects, but to block scepticism by a robust appeal to common sense: he claimed to *know* with complete *certainty* many things, such as that he had a body, that his body had always been in contact with or not far from the earth, that the earth had existed for a long time, and other such common-sense beliefs. He said we can know that what the 'ordinary meaning' of common-sense propositions says is 'certainly and wholly true', and that it is simply perverse of philosophers to question them. For example, the ordinary meaning of the assertion that the earth has existed for many years says something indubitable, but philosophers attack it by saying 'well, it all depends what you mean by "earth" and "exists" and "many years".'

In his paper 'Proof of an External World' (1939) Moore defined 'external objects' as things that do not depend upon being experienced to exist, and then said that he could prove the existence of two such things. He did it by holding up his hands and saying, 'Here is one hand, and here is another.' As a refutation of scepticism this is of course wholly inadequate, but Moore claimed that he was trying not to *disprove* scepticism but to *prove* the existence of external objects. This, however, might seem like a sleight of (yes) hand, because it ignores the point made by Descartes, that any claim to know (rather than just believe) something must exclude the possibility of being wrong – and sceptical arguments demonstrate the ways in which we might be wrong even in claiming to know that 'here is a hand' or 'I have two hands.'

To read Moore is to see one example of Analytic philosophy at work, consisting in painstaking, minute, piecemeal examination of particular concepts. His practice is rather at odds with his strictures about the perversity of philosophers asking 'what do you mean by "exists"?' and the like. His technique was aimed at showing that careful attention to concepts will dispose of philosophical problems; this idea, transposed into the view that careful attention to *standard uses of language* will dispose of philosophical problems – indeed, on one view, of philosophy itself – recommended itself to the later Wittgenstein and the 'ordinary language philosophers' of Oxford in the 1950s. In Moore's case the unhurried oakum-picking technique produced, it has to be said, rather feeble results; in the hands of other leading Analytic philosophers then and later the method of painstaking, minute, piecemeal examination of concepts and theories has produced results of great interest.

WITTGENSTEIN (1889–1951): THE EARLY PHILOSOPHY

Because of his unusual personality and unorthodox ways, and the vatic, aphoristic style of his philosophical method and writings, Ludwig Wittgenstein attracted enthusiastic disciples, many of whom regarded him as the greatest philosopher of the twentieth century. He is certainly a compelling figure, some of whose contributions have a permanent place in the thought of his time, while others have been influential beyond philosophy in spheres as diverse as theology and literary theory.

Wittgenstein was born in Vienna, the youngest child in the family of a wealthy industrialist, Carl Wittgenstein, whose home was a centre of Viennese cultural life. Brahms and Mahler were among the visitors, Ravel and Richard Strauss wrote concertos for Wittgenstein's brother Paul after the latter lost an arm in the First World War. His mother Leopoldine was a Roman Catholic – the family's ancestors on both sides were converts from Judaism in the nineteenth century – and Wittgenstein retained an interest in religion, albeit an unorthodox one, all his life.

Carl Wittgenstein had his children educated at home, not very successfully, to a curriculum he devised himself. Eventually when Wittgenstein was aged fourteen he was sent to school. Unable to gain entry to a gymnasium he attended a *Realschule* in Linz, where a fellow-pupil was Adolf Hitler. Although they were the same age, Wittgenstein was in a class two years senior to Hitler. He disliked the school and was unhappy there, in consequence failing to flourish; when he left three years later he did not have the qualifications for university entry.

This was a blow to Wittgenstein because he had conceived a desire to study physics under the famous Ludwig Boltzmann at Vienna University. His father sent him to a technical college in Berlin instead, to study engineering. Although he had an aptitude for this, having constructed a sewing-machine as a boy, he was unhappy there too, and left after just three terms. But he had developed an interest in aerodynamics, in part prompted by a remark that Boltzmann had made, that what was then the very new science of aeronautics needed 'heroes and geniuses', heroes to risk their necks in the flimsy heavier-than-air flying machines and geniuses to work out how to make them fly. Accordingly Wittgenstein took himself to Manchester in England to pursue his new interest.

While working on the design of a propeller Wittgenstein found himself becoming interested in the question of the foundations of mathematics. He asked around for advice on what to read on the subject, and was recommended Russell's *Principles of Mathematics*. This book had a revolutionary effect on him. He had little philosophical background before this – though Schopenhauer, enjoying a great vogue at the end of the nineteenth century, was much discussed in the Wittgenstein household, where he had admirers, so Wittgenstein had heard about his views.

Excited by the ideas in Russell's book Wittgenstein wrote an essay on the foundations of mathematics and sent it to Frege. The latter kindly invited him to visit, and proceeded – so Wittgenstein himself reported – to 'wipe the floor' with him, telling him that he needed to make a serious study of the subject first, and advising him to go and do so with Russell in Cambridge. This he did, and spent five terms there. One of Wittgenstein's friends, David Pinsent, wrote that 'it is obvious that Wittgenstein is one of Russell's disciples and owes enormously to him.' For his part Russell wrote to his mistress Lady Ottoline Morrell that Wittgenstein was 'the ablest person I have come across since Moore'.

In the year before the outbreak of the First World War Wittgenstein spent a summer in Norway, devoting himself to the study of logic. He was visited by Moore there, who took notes of some of Wittgenstein's ideas. Moore thought that Wittgenstein was a genius because 'he was the only person who frowned in my lectures.' The influence of these lectures on Wittgenstein was probably greater than either realized, given the nature of the latter's later philosophy.

During the war Wittgenstein served in the Austrian army, first on the eastern front as a mechanic in an artillery unit, then later, towards the war's end and after being commissioned as an officer, as an artillery observer. While in officer training camp he became friendly with the Viennese architect Paul Engelmann, and discussed religion with him. He read Tolstoy's recension of the Gospels, *The Gospels in Brief*, and was moved by them; later, when he read the Gospels themselves, he thought them inferior to Tolstoy's version.

At the end of the war Wittgenstein was captured and interned at

Monte Cassino, the manuscript of his *Tractatus Logico-Philosophicus* in his knapsack. He managed to get letters to Russell and even, through the influence of John Maynard Keynes, a copy of the *Tractatus* manuscript. He was released in late 1919 and set about trying to get his book published. After much effort a publisher was found who agreed to bring out the book if Russell would write a foreword to it. When Wittgenstein saw the foreword he was angry; he said Russell had misunderstood him and misrepresented his views, despite the fact that the two had met in Holland shortly after Wittgenstein was released from prison camp, and had gone through the manuscript line by line.

The *Tractatus* was the only book Wittgenstein published in his lifetime. He thought that it solved all the problems of philosophy, and therefore abandoned the subject and became a schoolteacher. This proved unsuccessful, so he turned to gardening, and contemplated becoming a monk. He was interested in architecture, and helped to design a house for one of his sisters. Eventually he was persuaded by some members of the Vienna Circle to meet with them to discuss his book; when he did so, it became apparent that he had not solved all the problems of philosophy, so he decided to return to the fray. He went back to Cambridge in 1929 and submitted the *Tractatus* for a PhD. This was the only degree he ever got. It was examined by Russell and Moore; the latter, who objected to the new-fangled PhD degree, wrote in his examiner's report, 'This is a work of genius but it otherwise satisfies the requirements for the PhD.'

Russell arranged for Wittgenstein to have a five-year Fellowship at Cambridge, during which time Wittgenstein gave seminars. Students took notes, and the result was a pair of volumes, the 'Blue Book' and the 'Brown Book', which circulated in samizdat copies causing a stir in the philosophical community. When the Fellowship came to an end Wittgenstein decided to emigrate to Russia, but after a visit there changed his mind. In 1939 Moore retired from the chair of philosophy at Cambridge and Wittgenstein was elected in his place. During the Second World War he volunteered as a hospital porter, returning to Cambridge to teach at the war's end. (He was not interned, having taken British citizenship.) He did not like life as a don, never dining at High Table and avoiding his colleagues, so in 1947 he gave up his professorship and went to Ireland, there continuing to work on the notes that were eventually published as his *Philosophical Investigations*. In 1949 he visited America to see his friend and former pupil Norman Malcolm, on his return discovering that he had cancer. He spent his last two years living with various friends in Cambridge, dying there in 1951.

As might be guessed from this sketch, Wittgenstein was an unsettled individual, a haunted one – some surmise that it was because of his homosexuality, a persecuted condition in those days, about which he might have suffered guilt. He was also an unsettling one, exercising a powerful hold over students who fell under his spell. His reputation, begun by the admiration of Russell and Moore in his early Cambridge days, confirmed by the difficult and vatic *Tractatus*, was amplified to the proportions of a cult by his devoted students and epigones, who imitated his way of speaking and gesturing, and treated philosophy as if it were wholly a matter of understanding, agreeing with and expounding Wittgenstein's views. The spell lasted for a generation after his death, sustained by a series of books made out of his voluminous notes, and by a number of influential followers who carried on interpreting his views and applying his methods.

Wittgenstein's aim in the *Tractatus* was very much of its time. It was to show that the problems of philosophy can be solved by understanding how language works, and that we do this latter by understanding what Frege and Russell had sought to identify as 'the logic of our language'. This thought was indeed the key to all his philosophy, both early and late, even though his later philosophy was based on a completely different view of how language works.

The problems of philosophy to be solved by understanding 'the logic of language' are the traditional ones of knowledge, mind, existence, reality, truth and value. The solution to them, in Wittgenstein's view, is achieved not by tackling the problems themselves, but by showing that they are actually non-problems arising from misunderstanding of language; a correct account of how language works therefore lays an axe to the root of the problems.

The fundamental idea in the *Tractatus*, acquired from Russell, is that language has an underlying structure, inspection of which shows what can be meaningfully said. For Wittgenstein what can be *said* is the same as what can be *thought*, so once one has shown what can meaningfully be said, one has shown the limits of thought. Beyond these limits language and thought are meaningless. It is in this outer zone, he argued, that traditional philosophical problems arise, as the result of trying to say the unsayable and think the unthinkable. At the beginning of the *Tractatus* he accordingly writes, 'What can be said at all can be said clearly, and what we cannot talk about, we must consign to silence'; likewise the very last sentence of the *Tractatus* is the famous remark, 'Whereof we cannot speak, thereof we must be silent.' In a letter to Russell explaining these remarks Wittgenstein wrote, 'The main point [of the *Tractatus*] is the theory of what can be expressed by propositions – i.e. by language – (and, which comes to the same thing, what can be thought), and what cannot be expressed by propositions, but only shown; which, I believe, is the cardinal problem of philosophy.'

Wittgenstein had an explicit agenda in arguing for this view. If the proper task of philosophy is 'to say nothing except what can be said, i.e. the propositions of natural science – i.e. something that has nothing to do with philosophy – and then, whenever someone wanted to say something metaphysical, to demonstrate to him that he had failed to give a meaning to certain signs in his propositions', does this rule out ethics, aesthetics, religion and the 'problems of life' as nonsensical? No: Wittgenstein wished to establish that it is only the attempt to say anything about them which is so. 'There are, indeed, things which cannot be put into words,' he says. 'They make themselves manifest. They are what is mystical.' Here 'showing' rather than 'saying' is all that is possible. Indeed Wittgenstein alludes to the 'more important unwritten second half of the *Tractatus*', meaning that the *Tractatus* shows from within the limits of language what is important. In another letter he wrote, 'For the Ethical is delimited from within, as it were, by my book ... All of what *many* are *babbling* today, I have defined in my book by remaining silent about it.'

The natural sciences, including psychology, and the social sciences, including philology, archaeology, anthropology and history, were closing in on all three of ethics, aesthetics and religion in reductive and debunking ways, explaining them in naturalistic and empirical terms. Religious experiences were hallucinations or delusions, said the psychologists; the Bible was the work of many people over large stretches of time, full of inconsistency and error, said the textual critics and historians; different cultures thought about ethical questions in very different ways, said the anthropologists. The thesis of the *Tractatus* protects ethics and religion from these encroachments of science by placing them outside the realm of what can be talked about.

The argument is as follows. Both language and the world have structure. Language consists of propositions, which are compounds of 'elementary propositions', which in turn are combinations of 'names'. Names are the ultimate constituents of language. Correspondingly, the world consists of the totality of facts, which are compounded out of 'states of affairs', which in turn are combinations of 'objects'. The 'names' and 'objects', and the 'elementary propositions' and 'states of affairs', are *logically* specified levels of structure; what they correspond to in reality is a question for a quite different enquiry to establish. This logically specified structure is purely abstract; it stands for whatever there is at the more elemental levels of the related complexes which are language and world.

Each level of structure in the world is matched by a level of structure in language. Names denote objects, the combinations of names constituting elementary propositions correspond to states of affairs, and each of these in their turn combine to form, respectively, propositions and facts. The arrangement of names at the most fundamental level of language structure 'mirrors' or 'pictures' the arrangement of objects at the most fundamental level of the world's structure. This is the basis of the 'picture theory of meaning' central to the *Tractatus*.

The elementary propositions are logically independent of each other. Therefore we have to say which are true and which false to give a complete account of reality. This says that reality consists of all possible states of affairs, whether actual or not; reality is everything that is and is not the case. Propositions are built out of elementary propositions by the logical connectives 'and', 'or' and the rest (actually, by one primitive connective from which the others can be defined), and therefore the truth-value of propositions is a function of the truth-values of the elementary propositions composing them. This does not apply, of course, in the case of tautologies, which are always true, and contradictions, which are always false. The true propositions of logic and mathematics are tautologies (analytic truths). They do not say anything about the world because their truth-value is consistent with any way the world could be (with the existence or non-existence of *any* states of affairs).

When a string of signs fails to express a proposition it is nonsense. It is not false; it cannot be, because it says nothing capable of being either true or false. The propositions of philosophy belong to this class – including the propositions in which Wittgenstein tells us this. He says, 'My propositions serve as elucidations in the following way: anyone who understands me eventually recognises them as nonsensical, when he has used them – as steps – to climb up beyond them. (He must, so to speak, throw away the ladder after he has climbed up it.)' He borrows the image of the discardable ladder from Schopenhauer.

And of course the propositions of ethics, aesthetics, religion and the 'problems of life' belong to the same class as philosophical propositions; they are not pictures of actual or possible facts, and therefore they are meaningless.

The *Tractatus* sets out these themes in seven numbered propositions, each of which has subordinate propositions appended to it – with the subordinate comments themselves having subordinate comments, and so on – in an elaborate system of decimal notation. The propositions and sub-propositions are highly compressed, but they make out in detail the nature of the structural levels and how they relate. We learn that it is of the essence of objects to be possible constituents of states of affairs, so that if we knew all the objects there are, we would know all the states of affairs there could possibly be. Objects themselves do not undergo change, it is only the combinations they enter into that do so. When they combine, the states of affairs they constitute are determinate. This is why a complete analysis of a proposition will terminate in the specification of a determinate combination of objects, given that there is only one complete analysis of a proposition, and that each of its constituent names denotes an object. Correlatively, the states of affairs that exist thereby settle the question of which states of affairs do not exist.

The 'picture theory of meaning' is based on these considerations. 'A proposition is a picture of reality' and 'A logical picture of facts is a thought,' thoughts being what are expressed by propositions. The totality of propositions is language, and 'the totality of true propositions is science.' Wittgenstein had got his idea for the picture theory from reading a report of a Paris court case about a traffic accident, in which toys were used to portray what had happened. The relationship between the toy cars and their arrangements and the real cars was one of correspondence; the mock-up in the Paris court room was a model of the actual scene. 'Pictorial form is the possibility that things are related to one another in the same way as the elements of a picture ... there must be something identical in a picture and what it depicts, to enable one to be a picture of the other.' He gives an even better analogy later: 'A gramophone record, the musical idea, the written notes, the sound waves, all stand to one another in the same internal relation of depicting that holds between language and the world.'

The restriction of meaningful language to propositions that are actual or possible pictures of facts in the world is what makes talk of subjects other than science meaningless – but not, as noted earlier, therefore unimportant in Wittgenstein's view. Nothing can be said about them, and if efforts are made to say something about them the result will be nonsense. That is the fate of philosophy itself, says Wittgenstein, even on the charitable view that the propositions of philosophy can be viewed as eventually disposable elucidations. Thus did Wittgenstein attempt to achieve his twin aims of solving all of philosophy's problems by showing philosophy itself to be spurious, and protecting what is truly important from the reductive ambitions of science. What he had to say in his own later philosophy about the success of this mission, we will see below.

LOGICAL POSITIVISM

Logical Positivism is a school of thought associated primarily with the Vienna Circle of philosophers in the 1920s and 1930s. The Vienna Circle's influence was great, partly because some of its most prominent members left Europe for the United States or United Kingdom as a result of the 1930s' political pressures, and partly because foreign visitors to its meetings, including W. V. Quine and A. J. Ayer, helped to report its discussions to Anglophone audiences. This is especially so with Ayer, whose bombshell of a bestseller *Language, Truth and Logic* of 1936 set out Positivistic ideas (and made him famous). But the main reason is that through the articles and books by its members, conferences and its journal *Erkenntnis* the Logical Positivists caught a tide at a significant moment: physics in the first three decades of the twentieth century had made giant strides, and the Positivists' question – why has philosophy not made progress as science has? (the same question Kant asked in the eighteenth century) – was answered by themselves: because it was still mired in metaphysics, and had not clarified the question of what demarcates genuinely meaningful questions and answers from spurious ones.

The Logical Positivism of the Vienna Circle is the view that the only forms of genuine knowledge come from empirical science, from systematically and logically organized examination of natural phenomena. A corollary is the rejection of metaphysics and theology as sources of *knowledge*, whatever other uses, if any, they might have. As noted earlier, the difference between Comtean Positivism and that of the Vienna

Circle is that the former was about politics and social theory, whereas the Vienna Circle Positivists were interested in philosophy of science and epistemology.

Logical Positivism is also known by the names 'logical empiricism' and sometimes 'neo-Positivism' (to distinguish it from the Comtean variety). The members of the Vienna Circle were intent on taking empiricism seriously, rejecting anything metaphysical and *a priori* and clarifying the role of conventions and other framework principles of science without appeal to what is not either verifiable by experience or a matter of logic and definition. These commitments lay at the core of their outlook, but in other ways Logical Positivism was far from a settled body of doctrine; the debates of the Vienna Circle's members evolved, and they disagreed with each other over important matters. In the end two divergent strands of the outlook were apparent, one associated with Rudolf Carnap and the Circle's founder, Moritz Schlick, the other associated with Otto Neurath.

Moritz Schlick (1882–1936) was born in Berlin and studied physics under Max Planck there, taking his doctorate in 1904 and for a time thereafter working as an experimental physicist. Planck, like Hermann von Helmholtz before him, was deeply interested in philosophy and had been influenced by the neo-Kantian revival of the late nineteenth century in Germany, to which Helmholtz and other 'philosophical physicists' contributed. Similarly inspired, Schlick moved to Zurich to study philosophy, later teaching in Rostock and Kiel before being appointed Professor of *Naturphilosophie* at Vienna University in 1922. He had made a name for himself with his book *Space and Time in Contemporary Physics* (1917) which, as he said to Einstein in correspondence, was aimed at explaining the latter's comment on the effect of his general relativity theory, that it 'removes the last vestige of physical objectivity from space and time'.

The chair to which Schlick was appointed at Vienna had been created for his predecessor Ernst Mach (1838–1916), in recognition of his contributions to both science and philosophy. Mach's views were decidedly Positivistic, not least in their emphatic rejection of metaphysics and his emphasis on a strictly empirical – and therefore, in his case, instrumentalist – approach to questions about theoretical entities, such as the atom and its components. His Positivism influenced the Vienna Circle.

When Schlick took up his post at Vienna he was invited by the mathematician Hans Hahn to join a study group on the *Principia Mathematica* of Russell and Whitehead. This in turn prompted Schlick's students Friedrich Waismann and Herbert Feigl to encourage him to start an extracurricular discussion group on more general philosophical problems. This was the nucleus of the Vienna Circle, in its early days called the 'Schlick Circle'. Its members were not exclusively philosophers, but included scientists and mathematicians, and it became a very distinguished gathering: in addition to those already mentioned there were the mathematicians Gustav Bergmann and Theodor Radaković, the physicist Philipp Frank, the logician Kurt Gödel, the sociologist and philosopher Otto Neurath and the philosophers Victor Kraft and Rudolf Carnap. Others joined the Circle's discussion from time to time, including Karl Popper (who was however a critic of its outlook), and there were exchanges with a group in Berlin with similar views, the Berlin Society for Scientific Philosophy, which included among its members the philosopher Hans Reichenbach and the mathematician Richard von Mises. Altogether this is a stellar litany of names.

The Circle's discussions continued informally for several years, until its leading members decided that it was time to make a more public statement of its outlook, as a contribution to the promotion of science and scientific philosophy. The occasion for this was the founding of the Ernst Mach Society in 1928, set up by the Austrian Free Thinkers Association as a platform for popular lectures on science and philosophy. Schlick accepted an invitation to be its first President, Hahn became one of its Vice-Presidents, and Carnap and Neurath became members of its secretariat. The following year Carnap, Neurath and Hahn issued a pamphlet, dedicated to Schlick, entitled 'The Scientific World View: The Vienna Circle', its publication timed to coincide with the First Conference for the Epistemology of the Exact Sciences. This was organized in collaboration with the Berlin Society for Scientific Philosophy and took place in Prague as a fringe event of the Fifth Congress of German Physicists and Mathematicians. One senses a certain Teutonic formality at work – the names of these events in German have a marvellous length and brontic quality – but the organization of the Circle's endeavours proved highly effective in disseminating its debates and ideas. In the early 1930s the Circle took over, in collaboration with the Berlin Society, a journal called *Annalen der Philosophie* and renamed it *Erkenntnis* under the editorship of Reichenbach and Carnap. Two book series, one edited by Schlick and Frank and the other by

Neurath, were set going, and conferences were held all over Europe under the joint auspices of the Circle and the Berlin Society in the following years. At the Second Conference for the Epistemology of the Exact Sciences in 1930 Kurt Gödel announced his 'incompleteness theorem', a highly significant result in logical theory which shows that 'logicism' – the attempt to base mathematics on logic, as Frege, Russell and others had hoped – is not possible.

Nazism and the advent of war destroyed this richness of ideas and debate, scattering its participants across the world. But the reputation of the Circle and its debates was already established, which is why Quine, Ayer and others visited Vienna to learn at first hand more about what was being discussed there.

The fundamental commitment of Logical Positivism, despite significant differences over detail and interpretation, is its insistence that meaningful discourse is either analytic (the statements of logic and mathematics) or empirically testable (the statements of empirical science). Everything else is cognitively meaningless. The claims of metaphysics, ethics and theology fall into this latter class, for they are synthetic claims which are not testable by observation or experiment. The best brief statement of the Positivist view was actually given two centuries before the Circle came into existence, by David Hume; at the end of his *Enquiry Concerning Human Understanding* he wrote, 'If we take in our hand any volume: of divinity or school metaphysics, for instance; let us ask, Does it contain any abstract reasoning concerning quantity or number? No. Does it contain any experimental reasoning concerning matter of fact and existence? No. Commit it then to the flames, for it can contain nothing but sophistry and illusion.'

Factual and analytic statements constitute science. Schlick and Carnap both took the view that at base science rests on direct observational reports, which they called 'protocol sentences', and that the observational terms occurring in them are ostensively defined (that is, defined by literally or figuratively pointing at the things being spoken about). Schlick wrote, 'there is no way of understanding any meaning without ultimate reference to ostensive definition, and this means, in an obvious sense, reference to "experience" or possibility of "verification".' The equation of 'experience' with 'possibility of verification' is interesting; having the experience reported by protocol sentences is precisely to realize the possibility of verification – that is, to make verification actual. Carnap put the point by saying that because protocol sentences consist in incorrigible reports of observations, they do not themselves require verification. Schlick agreed, writing that protocol sentences are 'the unshakeable point of contact between knowledge and reality ... we come to know these absolutely fixed points of contact, the confirmations, in their individuality; they are the only synthetic statements that are not hypotheses.'

Otto Neurath pointed out the problem with this account. It assumes that protocol sentences are incorrigible because they directly and neutrally correspond to experience-independent facts. But protocol sentences cannot be incorrigible, Neurath said, because at best it can only be a conventional matter which propositions count as 'basic'; and no statement, not even a putative protocol sentence, is immune to revision or rejection. 'There is no way of taking conclusively established pure protocol sentences as the starting point of the sciences,' he wrote. 'No *tabula rasa* exists. We are like sailors who must rebuild their ship on the open sea.' We begin our enquiries already equipped with a full apparatus of assumptions and theories, and the result of our enquiries is sometimes to make us change some of these – like planks of wood being replaced in a ship at sea – and this further means that the test for truth is not whether a given statement corresponds with reality, but whether it coheres with already accepted and tested statements.

Neurath's view anticipates theories such as the one held by Quine, who argued that observation is not neutral but 'theory-laden', that is, that our observations are conducted in terms of our antecedent theories, which therefore determine what we observe. As actual scientific practice shows, this means that if an observation does not fit with what is expected it is just as likely to be ignored, dismissed as aberrant or attributed to error as it is to make us change our theories to accommodate it. But if theory is carried to observation, then the 'meaning' of observation terms, and the notion of observational confirmation of theory itself, is established in advance – logically speaking – of observation; and observation therefore cannot play the part attributed to it by Schlick and Carnap.

A key concept in the Positivists' outlook is 'verification', the possibility of which is what confers cognitive significance on synthetic statements. Because of its centrality to their position it generated an enormous amount of debate. This debate lies in the background of so much that happened in different areas of Analytic philosophy that it is worth examining it in some detail, as follows.

The idea of verification can be understood in one of two ways. Either it can be regarded as specifying the nature of meaning, or it can be regarded as a criterion of meaningfulness. It does the first in Schlick's claim that 'the meaning of a proposition is its method of verification,' while it does the second in A. J. Ayer's assertion that 'a sentence is factually significant to a given person if and only if he knows how to verify the proposition which it purports to express.' Note that if Schlick's definition of meaningfulness is correct, then Ayer's 'verification principle' is true; but the verification principle can be correct without Schlick's verificationist definition of meaning being correct, for even if it is right that a statement acquires factual significance for a given individual if he knows how to verify it – that is, if he knows what observations would settle its truth or falsity – it does not follow that the method of verifying the proposition constitutes its meaning. Thus, 'the canary is in the cage' is verifiable by the verification principle, but 'the canary is in the cage' does not *mean* 'go into the drawing room and lift the cloth covering the cage.'

The verification principle involves a distinction between sentences and propositions. A sentence is said to be 'factually significant' only if the proposition it purports to express is verifiable. A sentence which does not express a verifiable proposition expresses no proposition at all; it is literally nonsensical, 'without sense'. Consider the following two sentences: 1 'God is in his heaven' and 2 'The canary is in the cage.' Since there are means of verifying whether the canary is in the cage (one can go and look), 2 expresses a proposition, and is therefore meaningful; but there is no way of verifying whether what 1 says is either true or false, so it expresses no proposition, and is therefore meaningless – or, more correctly, 'factually insignificant', for the Positivists allow that 1 might have emotive or aesthetic meaning as expressing a particular non-cognitive attitude to the world.

So far the verification principle has been given in a restricted form, as stating that a sentence is factually insignificant if for a given person there is no means of verifying what the sentence states. But the principle can be generalized: if what a sentence says cannot be verified by anyone, then the sentence is without qualification factually insignificant. In this form the principle itself requires qualification: sentences which are factually insignificant are those for which there is no means of verification *in principle*. If one did not thus qualify the view, a particular sentence might count as meaningless in virtue of the merely contingent fact that no one had so far verified it, but would become meaningful once someone did so.

There are obvious problems with this view. For one thing, the general laws of science are not, even in principle, verifiable, if 'verifying' means furnishing proof of their truth. They can be strongly supported by repeated experiment and accumulated evidence, but they cannot be verified conclusively. Another victim is history: in what way can the truth of assertions about the past be verified by present or future observations? Yet both science and history are bodies of factually significant sentences. Worse still is the consideration that not even an assertion about some currently observed physical object can be conclusively verified, because the number of observations relevant to its verification might be infinite; and while there remains the possibility of a single future observation refuting what one says about the object, that statement is not and cannot be counted as verified.

The verificationists' response is to suggest a liberalization of the principle, so that it admits of cases where all that is possible is evidence relevant to the truth of a statement. A sentence is factually significant, on this view, if empirical procedures are at least a necessary condition of efforts to determine its truth-value.

But this merely causes the problem to reappear in another quarter, concerning the nature of 'relevance'. What is 'relevant' evidence for or against an assertion about empirical matters of fact is to a large extent a matter of policy. What counts as relevant evidence might vary widely according to the conceptual strategy of observers, but only on a relativist view ('your truth is yours and mine is mine, even if they are opposites') would the meaning of terms vary with the relevant verifying context. For example: suppose that in some remote country during a drought it is made to rain. According to the scientists involved, the immediate cause of the rain was silver iodide seeding of clouds from an aeroplane. According to the local community, the rain was brought on by a witch doctor's rain dance. Each school of thought has different views as to what counts as relevant evidence in verifying what each has asserted. Of course this is not an especially good example, because further tests would settle the matter; but it dramatizes the problem.

A better example is offered by the 'Paradox of the Ravens'. The statement 'all ravens are black' is logically equivalent to the statement 'nothing that is not black is a raven' ('all non-black things are non-ravens').* This means that you can confirm 'all ravens are black' by looking at anything that is not black to check that it is not a raven. This makes my white shirt evidence that all ravens are black. But obviously the colour of my shirt has nothing to do with ravens: it is not relevant to settling the truth of 'all ravens are black.' So, what is the criterion of relevance that makes an item of empirical evidence useful for verifying a proposition?

More sophisticated attempts to substantiate the verification principle as a criterion of meaningfulness have turned on the idea that a sentence is verifiable if it entails statements about what can be observed. An objection to this is that the truth of a sentence about some physical state of affairs is consistent with the falsity of any observational report associated with it. Suppose someone says 'Jones is on the other side of the street,' and I look but fail to see Jones – perhaps because he has just gone into a shop or has been obscured by a passing bus. My failing to see Jones – that is, the truth of the statement 'I do not see Jones on the other side of the street' – is consistent with the truth of 'Jones is on the other side of the street.' It would be absurd to take it that the failure of the observation cancels the latter statement's truth. If what a sentence says is true and the observation statement it is supposed to entail is false, we would have a contradiction on our hands; but there is nothing contradictory implicit in the example.

An objection that opponents of verificationism were quick to make is that the principle itself falls into neither of the categories of significant propositions which it is used to demarcate. It is not a tautology, nor is it empirically verifiable. What status, its critics asked, is it supposed to have? One suggestion is that it is a convention, in the sense that it offers a definition of meaningfulness which accords with the conditions that are in practice satisfied by empirically informative propositions. Add the idea that the *a priori* propositions of logic and mathematics have meaning by definition, and a prescriptive element saying that only statements of these two classes should be regarded as having truth-value, and then stipulate that only statements having truth-value can be regarded as literally meaningful – and there you have the verification principle.

---

* This is the 'contrapositive' of 'all ravens are black': $(x)(Rx \to Bx)$ and $(x)(\neg Bx \to \neg R)$ are logically equivalent.

The difficulty with this is twofold. The prescriptive element can be challenged as merely arbitrary legislation; and the descriptive element can be challenged as at most showing that the statements of metaphysics, ethics, aesthetics and theology do not fall into the classes of statements preferred by the Logical Positivists, from which it does not follow that they lack truth-value or fail to be meaningful. At most, the descriptive element affirms what is already recognized, that an account of the meaning and – if the notion is applicable – truth-value of statements, or extremely general statements about the nature of the world or human experience, requires a treatment different from both that which accounts for assertions about observable phenomena and that which characterizes formal languages. This of itself gives no grounds for excluding metaphysics, or any of the other enquiries, in sole favour of what can be of use to natural science.

These objections have been taken to undermine verificationism to such an extent that in its original Logical Positivist form, at least, it is no longer held. But, as mentioned, implications of the debate linger in the philosophy of science, the philosophy of language and metaethical theory, aspects of all of which we shall see below.

Moritz Schlick was murdered on the main staircase of Vienna University in 1936, shot by a student called Johann Nelböck. Different stories are told about this. One is that Schlick was having an affair with Nelböck's fiancée. Another is that he had given Nelböck a failing mark. In either case the murder was prompted by resentment. Much more likely is that Nelböck was a sympathizer of the Nazis and had been encouraged by them to assassinate Schlick, although Schlick – despite being a critic of far-right politics in pre-Anschluss Austria – was not especially influential in political terms. Nelböck was released after just two years in prison, immediately after Hitler's annexation of Austria had taken place.

By this time most of the Vienna Circle's leading figures had fled from the dark shadow of Nazism looming over Europe. The most significant proponent of Positivism's message in this diaspora was Rudolf Carnap. The much discussed outlook of the Positivists had already begun to prompt fertile and influential disagreement, not least from W. V. Quine and Karl Popper, but Carnap continued to develop the Positivist project in significant ways.

CARNAP (1891–1970)

The philosopher who tried to work out in greatest detail, and with the greatest technical sophistication at his command, the programme of Logical Positivism and the idea, central also to Russell's work, of achieving a 'logical construction' of science from experience was Rudolf Carnap. It was in response to Carnap that W. V. Quine developed an influential alternative view which was in important part premised on repudiation of the concept of the analytic–synthetic distinction central to Positivism – this being the distinction between statements of logic and mathematics whose truth or falsity is wholly a matter of the meaning of the terms occurring in them, and empirical statements about how things contingently are in the world.

Carnap was born in Ronsdorf in Germany, and brought up in Barmen, now part of Wuppertal.* At Jena University in the years before the First World War he studied physics and attended Frege's lectures on mathematics and logic, and also studied Kant intensively with Frege's friend and colleague Bruno Bauch, a leading figure in the Kant Society of Germany and editor of its journal *Kant-Studien*. Carnap said he and Bauch spent an entire year discussing Kant's *Critique of Pure Reason* together. In the war itself Carnap served at the front, returning to Jena afterwards to complete his studies. His thesis on space was said by the physicists to be too philosophical, and by the philosophers to be too physical. It was submitted in 1921 and the following year appeared in *Kant-Studien*.

At a philosophy conference in 1923 Hans Reichenbach of the Berlin Society for Scientific Philosophy introduced Carnap to Moritz Schlick, who invited him to visit the Vienna Circle. He did so, and was subsequently offered a post at Vienna University. As shown in the account of Logical Positivism above, he played a leading part in formulating the Circle's doctrines and promoting its activities. In 1928 he published two books, *The Logical Structure of the World* and *Pseudoproblems of Philosophy* (published together in English translation), which are classics of the Positivist outlook and programme.

In 1931 Carnap took the chair in philosophy of science at Charles

---

* Barmen was the site of the famous Barmen Declaration in 1934, promoted by Karl Barth, rejecting Nazism's racially based views of religion, specifically its anti-Semitism.

University in Prague, and was visited there by Quine among others.* The rising threat of Nazism prompted him to leave for America in 1935, taking a job at Chicago University, and later at the Institute for Advanced Study in Princeton and at the University of California.

Carnap worked on logic and semantics, modality (the logic of possibility and necessity), probability and the nature of scientific theories, publishing influential work on all these topics. His influence on Quine and many others, whether directly or by stimulating productive disagreement from them, was great. Quine's own view of the history of twentieth-century philosophy is instructive; writing of Carnap after the latter's death in 1970 Quine said, 'I see him as the dominant figure in philosophy from the 1930s onward, as Russell had been in the decades before. Russell's well-earned glory went on mounting afterward, as the evidence of his historical importance continued to pile up; but the leader of the continuing developments was Carnap. Some philosophers would assign this role rather to Wittgenstein; but many see the scene as I do.'

The language of scientific theories, Carnap argued, consists of sets of both logical and non-logical expressions, the former resting on axioms and rules of inference in the standard way, and the latter resting on a set of postulates that specify their meaning. Rules of correspondence connect the non-logical expressions to a domain, thus providing an empirical interpretation of the theory.

The non-logical expressions themselves divide into those that are observational and those that are theoretical, distinguished by falling under two kinds of laws, respectively empirical laws and theoretical laws. Objects and their properties that can be observed and measured fall under empirical laws. Theoretical laws deal with non-observable objects and properties inferred from empirical observations. The line between them is not always clear, but one can identify focal cases of each. The gas laws, for example, predict an observation: Brownian motion of motes of smoke in a glass jar can be observed as an effect of the behaviour of the molecules constituting the gas. Phenomena of the kind theorized by quantum mechanics, by contrast – for example, the action of gluons in holding quarks together in hadron particles – cannot

---

* Half a century later Quine, by then very old and a grandee of philosophy, revisited Prague at the invitation of its philosophers and was taken by his excited hosts on a car journey to visit the house where Carnap had lived. When the car drew up outside Quine peered out of the window and said, 'This is not the house.' The consternation of the Prague philosophers, as reported to this author who was present on the day, was great.

be observed. As this suggests, the distinction between empirical and theoretical laws is largely predicated on the scale of phenomena under investigation; as the behaviour of macroscopic phenomena invites more and more refined theory about microstructure, so the laws become increasingly theoretical.

This distinction is, however, very problematic. There are good reasons for thinking, as already suggested, that even the most innocuous-seeming observational statements about macroscopic entities – motes of smoke, elephants, planets – are in fact theoretical, or at least heavily theory-laden. After all, how the world seems to us in everyday experience is a construct out of the interpretations our brains make of incoming sensory stimulation, and these interpretations are based on theories about what the incoming data might be conveying about the entities and events, outside our skulls, which we take to be the stimulations' causal origin. This problem might, in turn, be addressed in various ways, for example by accepting that observations are theory-based interpretations, but nevertheless differentiating them from classes of statements whose inferential distance from sensory stimulation requires additional non-stimulation-related features, such as hypotheses whose plausibility turns on how they organize our interpretations of our experience.

But the distinction on which the entire Carnapian structure turns – that between analytic and synthetic statements – was made to seem even more problematic by the attack on it mounted by his student and friend W. V. Quine.

QUINE (1908–2000)

Willard Van Orman Quine, known to his friends and colleagues as 'Van', was born in Akron, Ohio, then the rubber-tyre capital of the world. His father was a successful businessman in that industry. A hidden connection with wheels might have prompted Quine's great love of travel. It was his ambition to visit as many countries as he could, even if it meant just putting a foot over the border so that he could say that he had been there. It was suggested that his autobiography, which is far more about his travels than about his philosophy, should accordingly have been called 'A Moving Van'.

His aptitude for logic began early; he wrote, 'I may have been nine when I began to worry about the absurdity of heaven and eternal life, and about the jeopardy that I was incurring by those evil doubts. Presently I recognised that the jeopardy was illusory if the doubts were right.' At Oberlin College as an undergraduate studying mathematics he heard of Russell and mathematical philosophy, and was enraptured by it. Another significant influence was the behaviourist psychology of J. B. Watson. Both shaped his philosophical outlook.

Because A. N. Whitehead was by that time teaching at Harvard University, his association with Russell prompted Quine to apply for postgraduate study there. He began his studies under Whitehead's (apparently nominal) supervision in the autumn of 1930, and completed his PhD in just two years. Its title was 'The Logic of Sequences: A Generalisation of *Principia Mathematica*'.* He won a Travelling Fellowship in consequence, and went to Vienna, where he attended Schlick's lectures and meetings of the Vienna Circle, meeting Kurt Gödel, A. J. Ayer and Friedrich Waismann there. He hoped to meet 'the great Wittgenstein', as he described him in a letter to his parents, knowing that although Wittgenstein was at Cambridge he might return to Vienna in the summer. In the event he never met Wittgenstein.

Quine went to Warsaw also, meeting the logicians Stanisław Leśniewski, Alfred Tarski and Jan Łukasiewicz, and to Prague, the most significant part of his visit, for here he attended Carnap's lectures and had many hours of discussions with him. 'I eagerly attended Carnap's lectures,' Quine wrote. '[He] was my greatest teacher. I was very much his disciple for six years. In later years his views went on evolving

---

* Decades later a Festschrift was prepared for Quine, and his long-standing friend and colleague Burton Dreben chose to write about Quine's doctoral dissertation. He found something in it he could not understand, and therefore wrote to Quine about it. Quine found that he could not understand it either, and wrote back, 'There is no fathoming the sub-doctoral mind.' A similar story is told of the poet T. S. Eliot who wrote a doctoral thesis at Oxford on F. H. Bradley's philosophy. When it was suggested long afterwards that he publish it, he re-read it and found that he could not understand a word of it. A. J. Ayer claimed that when he was in the grip of a high fever in Sierra Leone during the Second World War (he had been posted there as an intelligence officer) he understood Kant, but on recovering found that he had forgotten what he thought he had understood. These anecdotes show that, sometimes, philosophical insight arises at moments of intense immersion in thinking about a problem, but the insights can be elusive when one is no longer in that frame of mind.

and so did mine, in divergent ways. But even where we disagreed he was still setting the theme; the line of my thought was largely determined by problems that I felt his position presented.'

With the exception of service in the US Navy during the Second World War, Quine's entire career was spent at Harvard University. In a long life – he lived to the age of ninety-two, dying on Christmas Day in the last year of the twentieth century – Quine published over twenty books and scores of papers, contributing to theory of knowledge, logic, philosophy of language and philosophy of science. He was showered with honorary doctorates, awards and medals, and was probably the most publicly honoured philosopher of his century.

The two central commitments of Quine's philosophical outlook are *naturalism* and *extensionalism*. His naturalism consists in regarding natural science as offering the best accounts we have of the nature of reality and of how we find out about it – thus, science provides us with our ontology and our epistemology. Because science is always open to revision in the light of new evidence, he was a *fallibilist* in epistemology. He rejected the idea that there is a philosophical platform outside science from which the assumptions, methods and theories of science can be examined for purposes of justifying or criticizing it.

To accept that science provides our ontology – our view of what exists – is to accept physicalism, the view that what exists is what is describable in physical terms. That of course entails that there are no non-physical entities such as gods or Plato's Forms, and in particular – in the philosophy of mind – that all mental phenomena are or arise causally from physical phenomena only. And correlatively it means that the associated epistemology is a thoroughgoing empiricism. But there is one surprising tweak to Quine's naturalism. He felt obliged to add one category of abstract entities into his ontology, namely *sets*, which are required for mathematics – and since science is impossible without mathematics we are forced, Quine said, to accept that sets exist as well as physical things.

But this is consistent with Quine's other commitment, which is to extensionalism. As noted in connection with Frege's solution to the puzzle about contexts in which co-referring terms cannot be intersubstituted *salva veritate*, an extensional context or language is one where such intersubstitution can happen without trouble, whereas an intensional context (note the spelling: *intensional* with an 's', not *intentional* with a 't')* is one where intersubstitution can change the truth-value of the sentence in which the terms are embedded. 'Cicero wrote *De Amicitia*' is true, and remains so when 'Tully' is substituted for 'Cicero'; but 'Tully' cannot be substituted for 'Cicero' in 'Tom believes that Cicero wrote *De Amicitia*,' because whereas it might be true that Tom believes that Cicero wrote *De Amicitia*, if he does not know that Cicero and Tully are the same person, it will be false that he believes 'that Tully wrote *De Amicitia*'.

Quine held that the only acceptable languages are extensional, and that attempting to explain anything – whether logic, science or language – using such intensional concepts as 'meaning' or 'analyticity', or modal notions such as 'possibly' and 'necessarily', is mistaken. It might not be sufficient for understanding a theory that it be extensional, but it is necessary. The paradigm of an extensional language is predicate logic, and it can be used to ascertain the ontology of any given theory by paraphrasing it into logical terms in a manner similar to Russell's treatment of sentences containing descriptive phrases. Anything x that the theory 'quantifies over' – that is, uses a quantifier to say 'there is at least one x' – is being claimed by that theory to exist. Quine encapsulated this in the slogan, 'To be is to be the value of a variable.' Note that what a theory is prepared to quantify over tells us only what that *theory* says exists; it does not tell us what *in fact* exists. If for other reasons we do not have grounds for accepting the existence of the x in question, then that is a reason for rejecting or adjusting the theory. We use our best available scientific theories to decide what exists.

Additionally, Quine required that for anything to be a legitimate entity, it must have clear 'criteria of identity', that is, it must be possible to distinguish a thing X from some other thing Y if we are to count X into our ontology. He demonstrates this by showing how something without clear identity criteria fares under examination, in this case a

* 'Intention' with a 't' means 'on purpose' in ordinary speech, while in philosophy it means 'directed towards' and concerns the relationship between the thought in a person's mind and what she is thinking about. Thus, when someone is thinking about something X we say that the thought intends X; and we therefore say that all thought has intentional content or 'aboutness' – that is, is always about something. 'Intensional' with an 's' relates to meaning. The difference between intension and extension is the same as that between sense and reference respectively, and is analogous to the grammatical distinction between connotation and denotation.

'possible fat man': 'Take, for instance, the possible fat man in that doorway; and, again, the possible bald man in that doorway. Are they the same possible man, or two possible men? How do we decide? How many possible men are there in that doorway? Are there more possible thin ones than fat ones? . . . is the concept of identity simply inapplicable to unactualized possibles? But what sense can be found in talking of entities which cannot meaningfully be said to be identical with themselves and distinct from one another?' His slogan for this principle is 'No entity without identity'.*

Quine's attack on the analytic–synthetic distinction occurs in a famous paper entitled 'Two Dogmas of Empiricism' (1951), in which, although himself a thoroughgoing empiricist, he addressed the respects in which he thought Positivism had gone wrong. 'One [dogma] is a belief in some fundamental cleavage between truths which are *analytic*, or grounded in meanings independently of matters of fact, and truths which are *synthetic*, or grounded in fact. The other dogma is *reductionism*: the belief that each meaningful statement is equivalent to some logical construct upon terms which refer to immediate experience.'

The rejection of the analytic–synthetic distinction is a consequence of Quine's extensionalism, because the idea of analyticity essentially turns on the intensional notion of *meanings*, and his question is, 'what sort of things are meanings?' Quine identified two kinds of statements standardly described as analytic: those that are logically true, including tautologies, such as 'no unmarried man is married,' and non-tautologous statements, such as 'all bachelors are unmarried.' The former is true in virtue of the logical particles in it – 'no' and 'un-'. The latter, although not as it stands a logical truth, can be shown to be one by demonstrating that the terms in it are synonyms, or by replacing one of the terms with a synonym to reveal its underlying tautological character, for example 'bachelors' with 'unmarried men'. Now, therefore, the question is whether there is a clear notion of 'synonymy' available.

Perhaps such a notion could be provided by means of definition, having it that two terms are synonymous if they can be defined in terms of one another. Might that work? Well, what are definitions based on?

---

* The amusing and pointful 'possible fat man' example occurs in a paper in Quine's *From a Logical Point of View* (1953); the title of this book comes from the refrain of a calypso made famous by Harry Belafonte, 'From a logical point of view Always marry a woman uglier than you.'

Answer: empirical observations by lexicographers of the fact that users of the language treat certain expressions as synonyms, such that one can be used as a definition for the other. But then definition is explained by synonymy, and cannot without circularity be invoked to explain synonymy. (Quine does however allow that definition can *prescribe* synonymy in the case of conventional introductions of new technical notations.)

If definition will not explain synonymy, what about intersubstitutivity *salva veritate*? One can leave aside trivial cases such as the failure of the intersubstitutivity of 'unmarried man' and 'bachelor' in 'bachelor has eight letters,' and note the more interesting fact that heteronymous terms (non-synonymous terms) can be intersubstituted *salva veritate*, as when 'the morning star' replaces 'the evening star' in 'the evening star is Venus.' As this shows, intersubstitutivity is not sufficient for synonymy.

What about the suggestion that analytic statements, if there are any, are necessary? Because 'necessarily, all bachelors are bachelors' is true, then if 'bachelor' and 'unmarried man' are intersubstitutable *salva veritate* we can say 'necessarily, all bachelors are unmarried men' is true, and this in turn allows us to say ' "all bachelors are unmarried men" is analytic' is true. And this says that 'bachelor' and 'unmarried man' are synonymous in the required sense.

Quine rejects this as 'hocus-pocus' on the grounds that talk of 'necessity' already presupposes a notion of analyticity, and that in any case modality is, in his view, deeply suspect. He also rejected Carnap's attempt to show that even if the notion of analyticity is too vague in ordinary language, a precise formal language can be constructed whose semantic rules specify which sentences are analytic, these being the ones true in that language *only* in virtue of those rules. This notion is not of course a notion of analyticity, only of 'analyticity in the constructed language', and therefore does not meet Quine's challenge.

If there is no distinction between analytic and synthetic statements because the notion of the former is incoherent, it follows that all statements are synthetic – even those of logic and mathematics. Quine accepts this conclusion. He has a metaphor to explain it: the idea of a web – the 'web of belief' – whose outer fringes, and only those outer fringes, are directly in contact with the world through the sensory stimulations caused by the world, and where therefore our statements are revisable in the light of that experience. But the deeper we go into the web the less and less effect those impacts have, so that at the centre of the web the statements of logic and mathematics seem to stand fast, as if unrevisable. But if a big enough impact were to hit the web, the shock waves might penetrate even as far as the statements of logic.

This view is a form of 'holism', the idea that the web of belief hangs together as an integrated whole, and sustains itself as a whole. It challenges the other 'dogma' Quine found in empiricism, 'reductionism', the thesis that individual statements in scientific theories are supported or undermined by particular observations relevant to them. Quine's holism resists this by arguing that 'our statements about the external world face the tribunal of sense experience not individually but only as a corporate body . . . scientific statements are not separately vulnerable to adverse observations, because it is only jointly as a theory that they imply their observable consequences.'

It is a consequence of Quine's scepticism about meanings that one cannot say that 'the meaning of a sentence is the proposition it expresses,' which had seemed a natural thing for some to hold. In particular, when we translate between languages, and talk of sentences in the different languages 'meaning the same', what we take ourselves to be saying is that the sentences express the same proposition – we say that 'the same thing is said' by 'snow is white' and 'la neige est blanche.' But, argues Quine, consider a difficulty about translating from another language if you have nothing to help you but the empirical evidence of the native speakers' behaviour and the environment. The translation manual you construct on this basis will be underdetermined by the evidence you gather – if the native speakers say 'gavagai' every time they see a rabbit and point at it, the evidence does not settle for you whether they mean 'rabbit' or 'favourite stew' or 'beast of evil omen'. (Because this example focuses on a single word whose reference cannot be fixed precisely in the translator's language, Quine describes this as the 'inscrutability of reference'.) And Quine takes it that translation of theoretical sentences of the native speakers' language will not be merely underdetermined but *indeterminate*, in that they will always be equally satisfactorily translated by two or more sentences of a translator's own language. 'What the indeterminacy of translation shows', says Quine, 'is that the notion of propositions as sentence meanings is untenable.'

In *Word and Object* (1960) Quine set out his alternative view, called 'linguistic behaviourism', arguing that the translator's task shows that what we mean by the 'meaning' of a sentence is the class of all sensory stimulations that prompt a speaker's assents and dissents to the sentence.

Meaning, accordingly, is 'stimulus meaning'. You achieve a translation (albeit an indeterminate one) when a comparison of your and the native speaker's assents and dissents match in the same stimulus conditions. This applies to meaning in general.

One can see from this survey of Quine's philosophical outlook that it is systematic and governed throughout by the fundamental commitments mentioned – naturalism and the idea that only extensionality provides clarity and determinateness, both of which are lost when intensional concepts of meanings and the modalities are invoked. It is a philosophical outlook much in harmony with a scientific age which, in philosophical terms, began with the developments in logic providing new tools for exploring language, thought and knowledge.

But all of Quine's key theses have been challenged in their turn – as one would expect from how things are in the lively and creative jousting ground that is philosophy. Some of these reactions are canvassed in later pages here. One of a number of significant respects in which this is so is that, contrary to Quine's hostility to them, the modal concepts ('necessarily' and 'possibly') have been given great respectability by Saul Kripke's provision of a semantics for quantified modal logic using the notions of 'possible worlds', defining 'necessarily' as 'true in all possible worlds' and 'possibly' as 'true in at least one possible world'. On this, more later.

POPPER (1902–1994)

Karl Popper was another of Logical Positivism's critics who had attended meetings of the Vienna Circle as a visitor. His reaction to its views resulted in a major contribution to the philosophy of science. He also wrote about politics, making a considerable mark with his controversial two-volumed work *The Open Society and its Enemies* in which he branded Plato, Hegel and Marx as 'historicists' committed to the idea that history is governed by inexorable laws directed towards the attainment of a utopian (more accurately, eutopian) goal. The book attacks totalitarianism and defends the idea of liberal democracy. Written during the Second World War with Nazism and Stalinism as the living models of the political orders Popper opposed, the book found vehement supporters and opponents both, as most discussions of politics do. Critics said that he misrepresented Plato and Hegel, and was 'partisan' in the cause of liberalism – which latter view he would not have denied.

Popper was born in Vienna, then the capital of the Austro-Hungarian Empire, of Jewish parents who had converted to the Lutheran form of Protestantism shortly before his birth. He was accordingly baptized. His father was a wealthy lawyer and book collector, who had an enormous library from which Popper profited. He left school at the age of sixteen and attended lectures at Vienna University, as a guest student, in science and philosophy. He became a Marxist, joined the Austrian Social Democratic Party and at one time worked for the Communist Party in Vienna. A number of his fellow Party members were shot by police during riots in the summer of 1919, part of the upsurge of revolutionary activity in Europe following the end of the First World War. Popper had already begun to be sceptical about what he came to describe as the 'pseudo-science' of Marxist historical materialism, which Party members were expected to accept as gospel, and he eventually converted to a form of social liberalism instead.

Like that of his fellow-Viennese Ludwig Wittgenstein, Popper's education was unorthodox. He worked as a labourer and cabinet-maker for a time, and then trained as a schoolteacher, working with disadvantaged children at a day-care centre while continuing his studies at Vienna's Pedagogical Institute. After earning a doctorate in the psychology of education he became a secondary school teacher in physics and mathematics, in the evenings writing his first book, *The Logic of Scientific Discovery* (1934). The looming threat of Fascism, and the fact that his family's conversion to Lutheranism was no protection against the dangerous anti-Semitism of the time, persuaded Popper to leave Europe. On the strength of his book he secured a post in New Zealand at Dunedin University. After the war he took up a post at the London School of Economics, and taught there until his retirement.

Philosophy appears to have a preservative effect on some; like Russell and Quine, Popper lived into his nineties. He was much honoured, receiving numerous medals and awards internationally, in Britain being knighted and made a Fellow of the Royal Society. His philosophical views generated much debate, arguably serving as the single greatest stimulus to interest in the philosophy of science in the second half of the twentieth century.*

The verificationism of the Positivists was the trigger for development

---

* Popper was generous with his time and encouragement, as his correspondence with the present author attests.

of Popper's own views. On a verificationist view, scientific hypotheses are confirmed by observation and infirmed by the absence of confirming observations. For example: you hypothesize that such-and-such is the case, and you test it by devising an experiment to see if certain outcomes predicted by the hypothesis will be observed. If those observations are indeed made they confirm – so you therefore assume – the hypothesis. This looks plausible. But Popper pointed out that it is in fact a logical fallacy, specifically, the 'fallacy of affirming the consequent'. The first premise in this reasoning is 'if p then q': 'p' is the *antecedent*, 'q' is the *consequent*. The second premise is 'q', that is, an affirmation of the consequent, reporting that an observation of the predicted outcome has occurred. From the conjunction of the two premises 'if p then q' and 'q' it is assumed that 'p' follows, that is, that the hypothesis p has been confirmed:

$$[(p \rightarrow q) \ \& \ q] \text{ therefore } p.$$

To see that this is not a logically valid form of argument one need only substitute sentences into the 'p' and 'q' positions in which 'p' does not follow from 'if p then q, and q', thus: '(p) if it is raining then (q) the streets are wet; (q) the streets *are* wet; therefore (p) it is raining.' Obviously, the fact that the streets are wet is consistent with it *not* raining – for example, there has been a flood, or a burst water pipe, or rain having occurred earlier but no longer occurring now; so that to conclude 'it is raining' is not confirmed by the fact that the streets are wet. It follows from this that if the 'q' in any experiment is observed, it is still possible that 'p' is not the case; any number of apparently confirming observations are consistent with the falsity of 'p'.

We should instead see, Popper argued, that a valid cousin of the 'fallacy of affirming the consequent' is the correct way to describe matters. This is that if an hypothesis predicts certain outcomes, and an experiment does not produce those outcomes, then the hypothesis has been *falsified*: 'if p then q, but not q; therefore, not p.' This is a logically valid form of argument (it is known as *modus tollens*) and it underwrites Popper's alternative to verificationism, namely, *falsificationism*. The governing idea is that whereas any number of apparently confirming observations are consistent with the falsity of 'p' without our knowing it, one *disconfirming* observation is enough to falsify 'p' outright. In Popper's view the mark of a genuine scientific theory is that it will state what will disconfirm it. If a theory is consistent with anything whatever – if nothing is able to falsify it – it is vacuous: 'a theory that explains everything explains nothing.'

In arguing that science proceeds by the deductive technique of seeking to falsify hypotheses, thereby showing that the traditional view of science as inductive is incorrect, Popper suggested that we should construe science as a sequence of 'conjectures and refutations' (this phrase constitutes the title of one of his books). We have a problem, and try to solve it by conjecturing what the solution might be. We test the conjecture; a negative outcome refutes it, a positive outcome 'corroborates' but does not confirm it; it might still be refuted by further evidence.

Falsifiability provides the criterion that demarcates science from non-science. It is important, Popper said, to distinguish the *logic* of scientific discovery from the *psychology* of scientific discovery. All sorts of prompts and cues might suggest conjectures – such as the famous dream of the chemist August Kekulé about a snake swallowing its own tail, which gave him the idea that the benzene molecule is a ring of six carbon atoms, each with a hydrogen atom attached. But the psychological, accidental source of inspiration plays no part in the rigorous testing of hypotheses.

It would be natural to think that the more probable an hypothesis seems, the better justified we are in accepting it if it is in competition with a less probable-seeming one. But Popper argued that improbable hypotheses are scientifically preferable, on the grounds that there is an inverse relationship between an hypothesis' probability and its informational content: the more information it contains, the more ways it might be wrong; and therefore the more valuable it is to science if it resists efforts to falsify it. Because a scientific theory cannot be conclusively established as true, Popper invoked the idea of 'verisimilitude' or 'truth-likeness' to characterize good scientific theories – 'good scientific theories' being those that resist stringent efforts to refute them.

Among critical responses to Popper's views the main one concerns his theory of falsification. A standard move against his view is to say that it does not avoid the charge of being inductively based, because to say that a negative outcome in an experiment falsifies the conjecture it is testing is to say that negative outcomes will occur in any future experimental testing of the conjecture. But Popper has an answer to this objection, which is that 'My proposal is based upon an *asymmetry* between verifiability and falsifiability; an asymmetry which results from the logical form of universal statements. For these are never derivable from singular statements, but can be contradicted by singular statements.'

More general is the problem that falsification cannot be regarded as settling matters against an hypothesis any more than a positive outcome of an experiment can be taken to confirm it. Popper's colleague at the London School of Economics, Imre Lakatos (1922–74), argued that scientific theories are falsified not by negative outcomes even in 'critical tests', but by the eventual overall failure of the research programmes they are part of, such a failure becoming manifest when the research programme is no longer adequate to the various phenomena it addresses. Consider the example Popper himself was fond of citing: the discovery of the planet Neptune. Astronomers had become puzzled by the anomalous nature of Uranus' orbit, and two of them (John Adams and Urbain Le Verrier, independently of each other) hypothesized on Newtonian principles that the anomaly could be accounted for by the gravitational effects exerted by an eighth, hitherto undetected planet. Le Verrier's calculations enabled the astronomer Johann Galle at the Berlin Observatory to see Neptune at precisely the place predictable by Newton's laws. Popper regarded this as a powerful example of corroboration; Lakatos asked, What would have happened if no planet had been observed at the predicted place? Would Newton's theory have been falsified thereby? Given that there could be many reasons why such an observation might fail to be made, the answer is obviously No. A major scientific theory with many moving parts will not be refuted by a single counter-observation, but only by eventual loss of explanatory and predictive power as observational and experimental failures mount.

Such a view is conformable with Quine's holism, and with any idea that scientific theories are accepted or rejected as a whole, not piecemeal. Thomas Kuhn (1922–96) gave expression to such a view in his *Structure of Scientific Revolutions*, which turns on the idea that scientists work within a paradigm, a theoretical framework, which constitutes 'normal science' for them while the framework is accepted; but that the whole framework might come to be replaced by a new and different one – a 'paradigm shift' thus occurring – when anomalies are discovered. Kuhn cites historical examples of paradigm shifts such as the change from the Ptolemaic to the Copernican view of the universe.

Kuhn's view opposes the idea of science as a cumulative project, discoveries being made as older theories are refined or adjusted, as new techniques and instruments are created, and as the body of overall knowledge grows. Instead he says that the concepts and theories of a former paradigm are different in content, even if the same words are used, from those in a later paradigm; the very meanings of expressions change. This aspect of his view was emphasized by Paul Feyerabend (1924–94), implying a strong relativism in which there is no way of comparing, or adjudicating between, competing paradigms – for example, a Sioux rain dance and the seeding of clouds with silver iodide to precipitate rainfall. Feyerabend described different paradigms as 'incommensurable' and argued that not only is it not possible to arbitrate between the Sioux and chemical rain-making procedures, but even such words as 'temperature' and 'mass' have different meanings in different paradigms.

Lakatos sought to make Kuhn's and Popper's views consistent by arguing that the former's 'paradigm' could be recast as 'research programme' and that cumulative falsifications of elements in the 'protective belt' of auxiliary hypotheses of a research programme would lead to it being abandoned when the set of core commitments of the theory can no longer be defended. A virtue of Lakatos' proposal is that in rejecting the abrupt changes and shifts of the Kuhn model it conforms more closely to the apparent cumulative and evolutionary nature of the growth of scientific knowledge. At the same time it needs to address the kind of point Feyerabend raised: does 'electron' mean the same for its discoverer J. J. Thomson as it does in quantum theory? No; but in response one might say that there is continuity, because quantum theory has developed a more powerful and precise grasp of the concept of the electron than was available to Thomson.

WITTGENSTEIN:
THE LATER PHILOSOPHY

After his return to Cambridge in 1929, having some years earlier been persuaded by Moritz Schlick and Friedrich Waismann of the Vienna Circle that he had not, as he claimed to have done in the *Tractatus Logico-Philosophicus*, solved all the problems of philosophy, Wittgenstein wrote copiously. He produced a manuscript on which his application for a Research Fellowship at Trinity College was based, and which evidently he intended to turn into a book; this, together with some other writings Wittgenstein composed in the course of the following two decades, was discussed with Cambridge University Press, but he was never satisfied enough to publish.

Nevertheless his views became known in philosophical circles, partly by word of mouth, partly through discussions with colleagues and visitors, and partly through the circulation of manuscripts, particularly the Blue and Brown Books containing notes from Wittgenstein's lectures in Cambridge in the years 1933-4 and 1934-5 respectively. These notebooks were later published together as *Preliminary Studies for the Philosophical Investigations*, in allusion to one of the principal works that emerged from this period and which appeared after Wittgenstein's death, the *Philosophical Investigations* (1953).

Wittgenstein begins the *Philosophical Investigations* by saying that it ought to be read alongside the *Tractatus* so that a comparison between them can be made, the implication being that this will illustrate the respects in which the views of the earlier work are wrong. In one significant respect there is continuity between the early and late philosophy: in both phases Wittgenstein's claim was that philosophical problems arise because we misunderstand the way language works. What changed was his conception of how language works.

The *Tractatus* had argued that language has a unique underlying logic which a structure-revealing analysis will reveal, displaying the 'picturing' relationship between the propositions of language and the world, resting on the denotative link between 'names' and 'objects' at the bases of the two parallel structures. In the *Philosophical Investigations* the governing idea is that language, instead of having a single underlying essence, consists of many different practices – Wittgenstein called them 'language-games' – within each of which the meaning of expressions consists in the uses made of them in the context (the 'form of life') which is the language-game's setting.

This marks another difference between the *Tractatus* approach and Wittgenstein's late view. In the *Tractatus* he had attempted an austerely systematic account; he now argued that this is the wrong way to proceed. Instead of devising theories to solve philosophical problems we should see our task as a 'therapeutic' one of 'dissolving' those problems by showing that they arise from misuse of language. The metaphor of therapy is applied with perfect seriousness: 'The philosopher's treatment of a question is like the treatment of an illness.' He varies the metaphor: 'What is your aim in philosophy? To show the fly the way out of the fly-bottle.'

A chief source of misunderstanding arises when we take an expression from one context of use and apply it in another where it does not belong. If we look at the proper use of expressions we will resist the temptation – the 'urge' – to misapply them. We begin – as the *Tractatus* had implicitly done – by accepting the beguiling view that we learn the names of objects by associating them with objects. Wittgenstein quotes St Augustine describing how his elders pointed at things and said their names in order to teach him to speak. On this model, says Wittgenstein, we commit ourselves to thinking that 'every word has a meaning. The meaning is correlated with the word. It is the object for which the word stands.' And we then proceed to assume that sentences are combinations of names. That is the *Tractatus* view. It leads us to search for the *essence* of language, as something hidden: the 'logical form' underlying the surface.

But in fact how language works, he now argues, lies open to view. As soon as we look in the right place we see that language is not *one uniform thing* but many different activities. We describe, report, inform, affirm, deny, speculate, give commands, ask questions, tell stories, make jokes, sing, greet, curse, pray, reminisce, play-act, thank, warn, complain and much besides. Each of these activities is a language-game: 'the term "language-game" is meant to bring into prominence the fact that the *speaking* of language is part of an activity, or form of life.' The allusion to 'games' does not imply something unserious; Wittgenstein is trading on the fact that there is no one thing that is common to all games, no single essence or defining property that makes everything that is a game a game, and differentiates all games from non-games.

> Consider . . . the proceedings we call 'games'. I mean board-games, card-games, ball-games, Olympic games, and so on. What is common to them all? – Don't say: 'There *must* be something common, or they would not be called "games"' – but *look and see* whether there is anything common to all. – For if you look at them you will not see something that is common to *all*, but similarities, relationships, and a whole series of them at that . . . I can think of no better expression to characterize these similarities than 'family resemblances'; for the various resemblances between members of a family: build, features, colour of eyes, gait, temperament, etc. etc. overlap and criss-cross in the same way. – And I shall say: 'games' form a family.

In these games expressions have uses, functions, purposes, offices, roles, employment – Wittgenstein uses all these words to talk of what is done with them – and the general idea is that the meaning of expressions consists in the parts they play in the language-games they belong to. This is sometimes described as a 'use theory of meaning', which oversimplifies it, but is not inaccurate, providing one remembers Wittgenstein's insistence that 'knowing the meaning' of an expression is not an inner mental state of 'understanding' but is a *technique*: to know the meaning of an expression is to be master of a technique for following the rules for its use. And the usage-rules not just for that particular expression, but of language as such: to be a speaker is, holistically, to be the speaker of a whole language.

Wittgenstein insists that the rules followed in 'following a rule' must not be understood as constituting a structure coercively determining in advance what their correct application must produce, as for example in arithmetic the rules of multiplication do. What makes a rule a *rule* in language is the collective use that speakers of the language make of it. So although the rules guide and provide a measure of correctness for each individual language-user, they are not like immutable railway tracks, but instead are a product of the forms of language-using life themselves. They record customs, or practices; they are like the signposts that guide one on a footpath. What justifies or provides grounds for them? They do it themselves: 'Giving grounds ... comes to an end ... the end ... is our acting, which lies at the bottom of the language-game.'

We acquire the ability to follow the use of expressions by our training as members of our language community. The training occurs in the 'form of life' shared by teachers and learners alike. The shared form of life is the frame of reference and the ground of the practice of speaking the language. A corollary of this is that language is *essentially public*; there cannot be a language known to and spoken by only one speaker. There can be a *contingently* private language, like the code Samuel Pepys invented to keep secret what he wrote in his diary: but such a code merely disguises a public language. A 'logically private language' could not be learned in the first place; and in any case if being able to speak a language is having mastery of a rule-following technique, then there has to be a distinction between following a rule and only thinking that one is doing so, and the check on usage can be provided only by others in one's linguistic community.

A corollary of the argument in the *Philosophical Investigations* is that examining language to guard against philosophy-generating misunderstandings 'leaves everything as it is', that is, does not change anything about how we view the world or ourselves – other than, of course, to liberate us from the temptation to engage in philosophy and therefore, like the fly, to get ourselves trapped in the fly-bottle.

This might not have been Wittgenstein's final view of the role of philosophy, however. The notes he was working on at the end of his life were edited by Elizabeth Anscombe into a volume entitled *On Certainty*. It is the draft of an argument to the effect that we have to have some indubitable beliefs in order for us to be able to do anything at all. It starts from Moore's 'Here is one hand' argument, and sets out the view that discourses depend upon there being some propositions which are immune to question; they serve as the 'hinges' on which the discourse turns, or (to vary the metaphor) they are the riverbed and banks through which the water of discourse flows. Like the banks of a river they can be eroded away over time, but that has to happen slowly enough for the public meanings of expressions in the discourse to remain relatively stable so that the aims of communication can be fulfilled.

What is interesting about *On Certainty* is that it is an exercise in standard epistemology, a discussion of a central and traditional philosophical problem: how to deal with a sceptical challenge about the possibility of knowledge. It does not treat this as a pseudo-problem that will disappear of its own accord if we pay attention to the ordinary surface forms of language. Perhaps Wittgenstein was at that point moving beyond what he had inspired others to accept, in imitation of his approach: the unlikely idea that, by itself, attention to ordinary language will solve philosophical problems.

As mentioned earlier, Wittgenstein attracted a zealous and admiring following. His disciples were prone to think post-Wittgensteinian philosophy could consist only in reading, accepting and expounding Wittgenstein's views. This was far from healthy, in narrowing the focus of philosophy's concerns and avoiding the critical examination and fruitful disagreement that arises from philosophers trying to think for themselves. The urge to discipleship is a common phenomenon, and far from always a constructive one. However: a more considered assessment of Wittgenstein's place in the history of philosophy emerged two decades or so after his death, and the most valuable aspects of his thought are now better understood.

ORDINARY LANGUAGE PHILOSOPHY

There was never a school or movement of 'ordinary language philoso-phy' as such; the term is a convenience for loosely identifying a group of philosophers whose individual views about how philosophy is best done had much in common, prompted by what they had learned from, and agreed or disagreed with in, the general background of philosophical endeavour of the first half of the twentieth century, which had been shaped chiefly by Russell, the Logical Positivists and Wittgenstein. Just as Cambridge had been the epicentre of philosophy in the first decades of the century, and Vienna between the two world wars, so it happened that Oxford assumed this role in the quarter century after 1945. In that place and in that period the influential figures of Gilbert Ryle, John Austin, Richard Hare and (though he disliked the label 'ordinary lan-guage philosopher') Peter Strawson were among the luminaries in a university town packed to the rafters with much philosophical talent, and to which, therefore, many who later became luminaries of philoso-phy in America, Australia and elsewhere flocked as graduate students. Philosophically, Oxford for several decades after 1945 was as Paris had been to the clerks of medieval times.

Those who merit inclusion under the 'ordinary language philosophy' umbrella would largely share the following commitments about what philosophy is and does. They agreed that it is not science; its problems are dealt with not by observation and experiment, but by careful clari-fication of concepts and by tracing the connections between them. Although they no longer nourished their predecessors' hope that for-mal logic would serve as a perfect language in which to express and thereby solve philosophical problems, they shared their scepticism about metaphysics as the project of constructing grand theories about the nature of reality. And they thought that one good way to begin an investigation of concepts and their interconnections is to examine language – not merely for its own sake, as critics always alleged, but as a good and perhaps necessary starting point.

As an evolution of Analytic philosophy this fairly standard view rep-resents a shift away from the early Analytic philosophers' over-ambitions for logic and, correlatively, the idea that philosophy would itself become part of science. That ambition for logic was an ambition for an 'ideal language' in the sense of Leibniz's *characteristica universalis*, Russell's 'logically perfect language' or Carnap's formal calculus for the 'logical construction of the world'. The aim in formulating an ideal language was to escape the danger of the misleading nature of ordinary language, with its misrepresentations of how we think about the world. The more modest idea in 'ordinary language philosophy' was that this same aim can be achieved not by translating into a formal idiom – which after all had been shown to be impracticable – but by dealing with the misrepresentations in language itself. But it did not go all the way to the view of the later Wittgenstein, that *all* philosophical problems disappear upon observing normal everyday uses of language. At most the idea was that *some* problems would thus disappear, while others would become more tractable if one paid careful attention to distinctions and nuances in use and – if or where this is different – meaning.

Because of this latter point, and its ancestry in the more ambitious commitment to logical regimentation of language for formal analysis, Analytic philosophy in the twentieth century is often described as having taken a 'linguistic turn'. And as these various approaches show, this is true. Examining language and the way it is used is our access to examining how we think, and our thought reveals what we take the world to be, and why we think of it that way. In effect, therefore, you could say that an examination of our language is an examination of our world – of *our* world, the phenomenal reality we live in and talk about, leaving it to a further and different project (science) to formulate ways of thinking about what the world is (so to speak) noumenally: the structure and properties of reality behind and beyond everyday experience.

The two figures who are most paradigmatically 'ordinary language philosophers', apart from Wittgenstein, are Gilbert Ryle and John Austin. The differences between them in both style and interests illustrate the wide range of what can fall under the 'ordinary language philosophy' label.

Gilbert Ryle (1900–1976) passed his whole career – except for military service in the Second World War – at Oxford, where he became the doyen of the philosophical community, a kingmaker whose opinions about individuals could, without much further ado, establish them in academic careers. His influence in this respect was felt as far afield as Australia. He was a genial colleague, a lifelong bachelor and like his younger contemporaries and protégés A. J. Ayer and P. F. Strawson he was a stylist as a philosophical writer, favouring a restrained and understated elegance of expression which, among some later Oxford philosophers, evolved into what critics complain, with some justification, is a practically incomprehensible mannerism of involution and sophistication offered as subtlety.*

Ryle saw philosophy as a form of conceptual geography. At the beginning of his most influential book, *The Concept of Mind* (1949), he says, 'This book offers what may with reservations be described as a theory of mind. But it does not give new information about minds. We possess a wealth of information about minds, information which is neither derived from, nor upset by, the arguments of philosophers. The philosophical arguments which constitute this book are intended not to increase what we know about minds, but to rectify the logical geography of the knowledge which we already possess.' We all use mental concepts with great facility, to help us understand and relate to others in the everyday transactions of life; but whereas it is one thing to know how to apply such concepts, it is another to understand their connections with each other and with non-mental concepts. 'Many people can talk sense with concepts but cannot talk sense about them,' Ryle remarks; 'they know their way about their own parish, but cannot construct or read a map of it.'

The cartographical metaphor is to be taken seriously. 'To determine the logical geography of concepts is to reveal the logic of the propositions in which they are wielded, that is to say, to show with what other propositions they are consistent and inconsistent, what propositions follow from them and from what propositions they follow.' Note that Ryle talks, as Russell and the Positivists had done, of 'reveal[ing] the logic of the propositions in which [the concepts] are wielded'; but he does not mean 'by a paraphrase into the symbolism of logic', but instead by tracing connections. This was Analytic philosophy's new sense of its logical task: it was a move from a more formal to a less formal conception of logic's role.

Ryle's target in *The Concept of Mind* is Descartes' mind–body dualism, the thesis that there is mental substance and physical substance

---

* Critics say that this approach is too often aimed at little more than the hair-splitting of the Scholastics, and its effect has been to make philosophy esoteric again, the preserve of an elect or of initiates, excluding many who might be interested in following and even contributing to debates about truth, meaning, mind, reason, knowledge and the good. They have a point. The technical reaches of philosophy require precision and nuance: achieving these without obscurantism is always welcome.

and they are essentially different. He called Descartes' dualism 'the myth of the ghost in the machine', and argued that it resulted from illegitimately transporting concepts that belong to one realm of discourse to another realm where they do not belong. The acceptance and employment of this myth about mind he called 'the official doctrine' because so many philosophers, psychologists and others unquestioningly assumed its truth.

Ryle gave the name 'category mistake' to the all-too-common misapplication of concepts. One example he offers is this: suppose a child is told he is going to see a march-past by an army division. Its battalions, batteries and squadrons pass by and disappear, whereupon the child asks, 'but where is the division?' As Ryle says, the march-past was 'not a parade of battalions, batteries, squadrons *and* a division; it was a parade of the battalions, batteries and squadrons *of* a division.' Likewise Ryle imagines a foreigner taken to a cricket match and having the batsmen, fielders and bowlers pointed out to him, who then asks, 'But who is left to contribute the famous element of team spirit?' This, then, is the mistake on which the concept of mind, as a substance distinct from body, rests: there are mental powers, capacities and dispositions, but there is not also and separately a thing, *mind*, made of mental stuff, in addition to them.

Moreover the concepts of mind and body do not belong to the same logical category as each other, such that they are equal but opposite metaphysical partners. The concept of body belongs to the category in which other physical concepts such as space, colour, movement and weight apply, and where the subjects of predications of colour, weight etc. are *things*. The concept of mind belongs to the category of what people (and other animals) *do* – such as remember, hope, desire, calculate, think – and of what they are *disposed to do* in given circumstances, such as 'feel pain' when burned, 'desire a drink' when dehydrated, and the like. Ryle argued that the typical mistake of thinking that 'when we refer to something there must be something referred to' prevents us from seeing that when we refer to mental states and processes we are not doing the same as when we refer to physical things. Indeed, he said, talk of mental phenomena is just shorthand for talk about behaviour, a shorthand borrowed from the thing-referring language used for the physical world.

The idea that talk of thoughts, intentions and desires is shorthand for talk about behaviour has come to be called *logical behaviourism*.

Ryle did not repudiate the behaviourist label, though he thought a better name for his view might be 'phenomenology' because it is about what is manifest – what appears, is observable – when we use mentalistic vocabulary that pretends (as he sees it) to refer to entities or events hidden in private mental space. As this shows, 'logical behaviourism' is a thesis about the meanings of concepts and terms, and is different from behaviourist theories in psychology in which psychological states and processes are explored in terms of stimulus, response, learning and reinforcement. But it shares with them, and more closely with 'methodological behaviourism' – the general view that the right method to employ in understanding talk of mental phenomena is to restrict attention to observations of behaviour – the idea that mentalistic language is at very least explicated, and perhaps made redundant, by translation into behaviour-describing terms.

Ryle directs a supporting argument against what he calls 'the intellectualist legend', namely, that the performance of an intelligent action by a person is preceded and directed by a conscious internal act of planning. His argument, known as 'Ryle's Regress', is that this internal act, if it is intelligently directed as we suppose it to be, must therefore itself have been preceded by an internal intelligent act of planning. But if so, then in *its* turn this planning must have been preceded . . . and so on. 'If, for any operation to be intelligently executed, a prior theoretical operation had first to be performed and performed intelligently, it would be a logical impossibility for anyone ever to break into the circle.' This argument has presented a challenge to all subsequent 'cognitivist' theories postulating mental antecedents for rational behaviour such as anticipating, deciding and the formulation of strategies.

There is another point worth noting, in passing. Ryle inconsistently claims, as noted, both that there is an 'official doctrine' about the nature of mind – the doctrine accepted by 'so many philosophers, psychologists and others [who] unquestioningly assume its truth' – and that his doctrine is 'neither derived from, nor upset by, the arguments of philosophers'. The point of his book is to demonstrate that Cartesian mind–body dualism, a philosophical view, which has so misled so many, can be corrected by a philosophical examination of it, thus saving many from being misled by it. Either philosophy is consequential for good or ill, as Ryle demonstrates it is, or it changes nothing, as he claims it does.

J. L. Austin (1911–60) must be distinguished from the nineteenth-century jurisprudent John Austin, and his book *Sense and Sensibilia* must be distinguished from Jane Austen's novel *Sense and Sensibility*. The punning title of Austin's book has been fruitful in moments of tutorial comedy. It was published in the same year, 1962, as his other book, *How to Do Things with Words*, both of them appearing posthumously.

Like Ryle, Austin began as a classicist but soon turned to philosophy. Apart from a distinguished period in military intelligence during the Second World War, and visits to Harvard to give the William James Lectures in 1955 and to Berkeley in California in 1958, his career was passed wholly in Oxford. He published little in his lifetime, the most significant work being a translation of Frege's *Grundlagen der Arithmetik* in 1950. The first of the two books mentioned above was edited from his papers and prepared for publication by his colleague G. J. Warnock, the second by another colleague, J. O. Urmson. The William James Lectures appeared as *How to Do Things with Words*, and the lectures Austin gave annually under the title 'Problems in Philosophy' from 1947 onwards, constantly revised and embellished, were edited into *Sense and Sensibilia*.

In these latter lectures Austin took as his stalking horse A. J. Ayer's second book, *The Foundations of Empirical Knowledge* (1940), which expounds a phenomenalist view of knowledge, and subjected it to a classic 'ordinary language' attack.* As this and the book's title suggest, the principal target of Austin's attention is perception.

Austin had great influence in Oxford through the discussion group he held on Saturday mornings with colleagues. Although always courteous he was a dominating figure; some colleagues were scared of him. The Saturday meetings were informal and collegial in manner, but the unrelenting focus on 'what do you mean by —?' shaped the content of debate, and through it the philosophical outlook prevalent in the Oxford of the day.

An illustration of Austin's style of philosophizing is provided by the way he distinguishes between doing something *by mistake* and doing something *by accident*. Suppose you own a donkey, but one day conceive an intense dislike of it and decide to shoot it. You take your gun to the meadow where it grazes, take aim and fire. Suppose at the very

---

* Ayer, one of this author's teachers at Oxford, was not proud of *The Foundations of Empirical Knowledge* which he wrote in Caterham Barracks while undergoing officer training in the Welsh Guards in 1940. But he felt that Austin had not fully succeeded in demolishing phenomenalism, and in 1967 published an interesting response in the journal *Synthese* entitled 'Has Austin Refuted the Sense-Datum Theory?'

moment you do this, your donkey moves and you therefore hit and kill another donkey that was standing behind it. You have killed the second donkey by accident. But suppose it is evening, your hatred for your donkey is whisky-fuelled: you take aim and fire – at the wrong donkey. You have killed someone else's donkey by mistake.

In *Sense and Sensibilia* Austin defines the thesis he wished to examine as embodied in the claim that 'we never see or otherwise perceive (or "sense"), or anyhow we never *directly* perceive or sense, material objects (or material things), but only sense-data (or our own ideas, impressions, sensa, sense-perceptions, percepts, &c).' And he says that his general response to this doctrine is:

> that it is a typically *scholastic* view, attributable, first, to an obsession with a few particular words, the uses of which are over-simplified, not really understood or carefully studied or correctly described; and second, to an obsession with a few (and nearly always the same) half-studied 'facts'. (I say 'scholastic', but I might just as well have said 'philosophical'; over-simplification, schematization, and constant obsessive repetition of the same small range of jejune 'examples' are not only not peculiar to this case, but far too common to be dismissed as an occasional weakness of philosophers.)

The deconstruction of the phenomenalist case is effected by showing that what it rests upon – the straight stick that looks bent in water, the indistinguishability of a genuine and an hallucinatory experience – is a series of mistakes about such locutions as 'looks like', 'seems', 'appears' and the distinctions between them. Consider the nuances of meaning differentiating the statements '(1) He looks guilty. (2) He appears guilty. (3) He seems guilty.' In the lectures (not in their published version) Austin used the example of encountering a pig: when we do so, we say, 'lo! a pig!' not 'it looks like a pig, smells like a pig, sounds like a pig . . . therefore it is a pig' – that is, we do not judge that we are confronted by a pig on the basis of sense-data we are experiencing. Ayer's response was to agree that we judge straight off that it is a pig, but if asked to *justify* why we so judge, we can and would appeal to the evidence we have – principally, the sensory evidence: what we saw and heard (the sensory impressions of vision and audition). Ayer charged Austin with himself not distinguishing between the psychological and logical order of events. Psychologically the order is 'lo! a pig', logically it is 'I have this and that evidence, and that justifies the assertion that here is a pig.'

And Austin also fails to take seriously the fact that we can have such evidence and yet be wrong: possession of pig-associated sensory data is consistent with the absence of a pig. That is the force of the sceptical challenge that an epistemological theory seeks to meet.

The influence of the ideas in *How to Do Things with Words* has been great, because in these lectures Austin introduced the concept of a *performative* in speech – locutions of the form 'I promise,' 'I do thee wed,' 'I wish it would rain,' 'Close the door!', 'Have you read Tolstoy?' These are not statements of fact, such as 'That animal is a pig,' and therefore they are not candidates for assessment as true or false; yet they are meaningful, and important. The key point is that these utterances constitute the performance of actions: the actions of promising, marrying, commanding and the like. To say 'I promise' is to enter into an undertaking; to say 'I do thee wed' (in the appropriate circumstances) is to marry someone; 'I wish it would rain' expresses a desire; 'Close the door!' is a command; 'Have you read Tolstoy?' is a request for information. They are *speech acts*.

Doing anything with language – whether making statements (Austin called statements *constative utterances*) or promising, commanding, asking and so forth, are all *locutionary acts*. The very act of saying anything is an *illocutionary act* – the act of stating, or asking, or commanding – and relates to what kind of utterance it is: whether it has the force of a statement ('assertoric force'), a question ('interrogatory force') or a command ('imperatival force'), and so on. The *effect achieved by* saying something is the *perlocutionary act*, the act of getting someone to do something if we have issued a command, or the act of informing someone if we have made a true statement – in short, of bringing about a certain effect in an audience. These ideas promoted a fertile discussion, one of the notable outcomes being John Searle's book *Speech Acts* (1969).

Austin sought to overcome the problems that vex the traditional correspondence theory of truth, the theory stating that 'a statement is true if it corresponds with the facts.' The problem with this is: what are the elements of statements and of facts and what is the relation of correspondence said to hold between them? Austin answered by saying that the correspondence relation consists of sets of conventions which govern the way we link what we say to what we are talking about. He specified two kinds of conventions: 'descriptive' ones that correlate words and sentences with types of situations in the world, and 'demonstrative' ones that correlate statements (actual uses of sentences on specific occasions) with currently occurring situations in the world.

An objection by P. F. Strawson (1919–2006) to this proposal is that it confuses two questions: 'How do we use the word "true"?' and 'When are we right to describe a statement as true?' The first question asks for an analysis of the part played by the predicate '. . . is true' in language, and the second asks for the conditions that have to be satis- fied for '. . . is true' to be correctly applied. If Austin's view were right, to say that a given statement is true would be either to say something about the meanings of words used to make the statement, or to say that the conventions are being properly applied – but we are not doing either of those things. Instead we are agreeing with, or confirming, what the statement says.

Austin's view and Strawson's response occurred in a debate between them at an Aristotelian Society conference in 1950. The debate itself is important for its part in the development of views of truth known as 'deflationary theories' or 'minimalist theories', so called because they are aimed at denying that truth is a substantive property of things we say or believe – that is, a substantive property like 'correspondence' or 'coherence' – but instead that talk of truth is talk of not very much. For example: nothing is added to an assertion of a statement 'p' by saying 'it is true that p', so '. . . is true' is redundant (hence this version is a 'redundancy theory'); or, at most, 'is true' just marks agreement, or emphasis (Strawson's view); or it is a shorthand device that saves repetition – someone says, 'Everest is the highest mountain not just in the Himalayas but in the world,' and instead of repeating the whole sentence in order to show that we agree with it, we just say 'that's true.' But the Austin–Strawson debate about truth also exemplifies 'ordinary lan- guage philosophy' grappling with a question which is itself substantive and not merely 'quibbling with words', as some critics put it.

Strawson might have disliked the label 'ordinary language philoso- phy', and indeed the label does not well fit his later work, but what brought him into notice at the beginning of his Oxford career was the skilful attention to linguistic distinctions displayed in these disagree- ments with Austin over truth, and in the paper that made his name, 'On Referring', a critique of Russell's Theory of Descriptions.

'On Referring' appeared in the journal *Mind* in 1950, and its funda- mental argument is that Russell's theory is an effort to solve a problem which would not arise in the first place if we were careful to distinguish *expressions*, such as words and sentences, from *uses* of expressions and from *utterances* of expressions. Imagine the sentence 'the present King of France is wise' being uttered by different people in the reigns of different French kings. It is the same sentence each time, but the *occasions of use* are different each time; different kings would be spoken of, and sometimes the sentence would be used to say something true and sometimes false.

What can be said of whole sentences in this way can be said of phrases occurring in them, such as the description 'the present King of France'. This phrase does not by itself refer to anything, but it can be *used to refer* to a king of France if there is one at present. Behind Russell's theory, one recalls, is the idea that meaning is denotation – and Russell circumvented the problems of this view by saying there are only two 'logically proper names', the demonstratives 'this' and 'that'. Strawson's opposing view is that 'referring' is not something expressions do, it is something that people use them to do. It follows that the meaning of an expression 'cannot be identified with the object it is used, on a particular occasion, to refer to [and] the meaning of a sentence cannot be identified with the assertion it is used, on a particular occasion, to make'. Russell had confused the description with its use: 'The important point', said Strawson, 'is that the question whether the sentence is significant or not is quite independent of the question that can be raised about a particular use of it.'

It was natural for Strawson to generalize the views about language and usage that underlay his critiques of Austin and Russell, and he did so in his first book, *An Introduction to Logical Theory* (1952). The book's aim is to distinguish between the grammar and syntax of ordinary language and the formal structures of logic, arguing that the former are not smoothly represented in or by the latter. This was accordingly a repudiation of the 'logicizing' project of earlier Analytic philosophy. In the course of the book he introduced the idea of 'presupposition' to explain the logical relationship between an assertion such as 'the man in the garden is whistling' and the assertion 'there is a man in the garden' which has to be true for the former sentence to be either true or false. A consequence of this idea is that in the case of presupposition failure – that is, where a presupposed sentence is false – a presupposing sentence falls into a 'truth-value gap'; bivalence does not hold. This aspect of Strawson's views naturally therefore drew criticism.

In 1959 Strawson published one of his two major works, *Individuals*, which had the subtitle – a somewhat provocative one, given the general anti-metaphysical bias of Analytic philosophy – *An Essay in Descriptive Metaphysics*. He justified the subtitle in the Introduction by distinguishing between the descriptive metaphysics of Aristotle and Kant, who examine concepts and categories 'which in their most fundamental character change not at all' and are hence structural features of our thought, and the 'revisionary metaphysics' of such as Descartes, Leibniz and Berkeley, who try to construct a better metaphysical picture of the world. Descriptive metaphysics is therefore conceptual analysis as practised in Analytic philosophy, but with a greater generality, and its chief purpose – as in Ryle's cartography – is mapping the connections between concepts, not least to see which are most fundamental.

Two key ideas in *Individuals* are, first, that what enables us to make identifying reference to things in the world turns on our taking the world to be a single spatio-temporal system, the items in which – the most fundamental ones being particular bodies – we are able to reidentify over time; and secondly, that most of what we refer to in the world we do so under a description, not as a result of direct acquaintance with it – thus, the same view as Russell's 'knowledge by description' and 'knowledge by acquaintance', but with a major difference: that what descriptive knowledge must be traceable back to is not private data of sense, as in Russell, but items in a public world.

The reidentification requirement offers a refutation of scepticism, for if we have to be able to reidentify objects in order for our thought and language to work, which they do only if they range over a unified spatio-temporal realm, then the fact that we succeed in reidentifying particulars shows that sceptical doubts about the perception-independent existence of things are groundless.* Another form of scepticism, about the existence of other minds, is addressed by Strawson's argument that attributing psychological states to oneself – 'I feel a pain' and the like – turns on having learned the relevant language for doing so in a public context so that the meaning of 'pain' is the same when you apply it to yourself and to others; but this means that one cannot doubt the existence of other minds, for otherwise the acquisition of these terms would not be possible.

---

* The present author wrote a doctoral thesis at Oxford under Strawson's supervision which discusses this argument, and modifies it to remove the implicit verification principle on which its original form turned. A part of that thesis is published as *The Refutation of Scepticism* (1985) and its themes are further developed in *Scepticism and the Possibility of Knowledge* (2008).

Yet another original contribution is the solution Strawson offers to the mind–body question. Approaching it through an examination of what we are referring to when we use the pronoun 'I', he argues that its referent is an entity to which, constitutively, two kinds of predicates both essentially belong: physical ones *and* mental ones. This is a form of 'dual aspect' theory of what constitutes a person, but its special interest lies in Strawson's claim that this concept of a person is *primitive*, such that trying to 'separate' a person into physical and mental aspects is, ontologically speaking, a mistake.

Strawson published his second major work, *The Bounds of Sense*, in 1966. It is an investigation of Kant's *Critique of Pure Reason* aimed at separating the valuable from the less valuable parts in it – among the latter, in Strawson's view, Kant's commitment to there being synthetic *a priori* judgments. By this time the supposed hegemony – if there ever was such a thing – of 'ordinary language philosophy' in the sense most closely associated with Ryle and Austin was over, though among those who were still dazzled by the strong light of Wittgenstein there remained a propensity to think that 'philosophy' meant 'reading, discussing and agreeing with Wittgenstein'. This allure was still in force when Strawson wrote, but his work contributed to the maintenance of focus on a wider range of philosophy's problems.

As noted, Strawson rejected the label 'ordinary language philosopher' and his *Individuals* and *Bounds of Sense* well illustrate why. But in two respects the particular interests and techniques most emphasized in this moment in philosophy played their part in other contributions he made. One is that he and his teacher Paul Grice wrote a response to Quine's attack on the analytic–synthetic distinction, arguing that Quine had set far too high a standard for 'clarification' of the concepts required to explain analyticity, thus guaranteeing that it would fail; and that in any case when the concept is explicated in light of the family of concepts it belongs to (meaning, synonymy, logical possibility, and more) it is both a respectable and a useful one.

The second respect is that throughout his life Strawson remained interested in the question of reference and the difference between the grammar and logic of the subject–predicate distinction. It was an interest sparked by his thinking about Russell early in his career, and kept much alive by developments in theories of reference as interest in the philosophy of language burgeoned into Analytic philosophy's chief preoccupation in the last third of the twentieth century. At the same time, his discussions of reference continued to show the sensitivity to nuances of meaning that was the main tool of 'ordinary language philosophy'.

PHILOSOPHY OF LANGUAGE

The outstanding achievement of Analytic philosophy in the last third of the twentieth century is the philosophy of language, which towards the end of the century blended with the philosophy of mind (see below) as the two research projects increasingly recognized the extent of their interdependence. The 'linguistic turn' taken in a variety of ways by Frege, Russell, Wittgenstein, Positivists and 'ordinary language philosophers', all pointed in the direction of the need for a fully systematic treatment of language, and to this, equipped and potentiated by the new techniques of logic, Analytic philosophy turned its full attention in this period.

In medieval times Schoolmen recognized the connection between logic and language, but it was the major developments in logic, especially those made by Frege and their subsequent application by Russell and others, that provided the muscle that made logic itself, and theories of reference and meaning, an arena of genuine progress. It has been pointed out that in all other areas of philosophy – ethics, theory of knowledge, political philosophy, aesthetics – the history of the subject continues to be a resource which enriches contemporary thinking. But in the philosophy of language there is relatively little, other than in the way of some suggestions and insights, that is not original to the twentieth century itself, and to its second half in particular.

Central to the philosophy of language is 'theory of meaning', an expression which denotes two approaches with, in the view of many, significant connections between them. In one approach, a theory of meaning is seen as the effort to provide a general elucidation, analysis or explanation of the concept of meaning. The other approach is a technical project of constructing a formal theory for a specified language, which yields theorems for each sentence of that language that 'gives the meaning' of it.

The first, informal sense of 'a theory of meaning' is the recognizable task of clarifying the concept of meaning, perhaps in terms of what speakers wish or intend to communicate to audiences. The second, formal sense of the phrase is the equally recognizable though different task of constructing a logical calculus 'for a language L' in which each sentence s of L is paired with a 'meaning', call it 'm', of s in a schema 's *means* m in L,' where the word 'means' is replaced by something that provides the sought-for pairing. A moment's reflection on this schema suggests that because 'means' is an intensional notion and a formal representation is preferred precisely because, by its nature, it is extensional (see the discussion of these notions in the Frege and Quine passages above, pp. 357–65 and 388–95), the required schema should be something like 's is X in L if and only if S,' where 'X' is here a dummy or place-holder for whatever needs to be put in its place to yield the required extensionality-consistent alternative to 'means', and where 'S' is whatever, by this equivalence, is the meaning of 's'. The scaffolding '— if and only if —' makes the context extensional (truth-functional).

Many theorists think that the formal approach can clarify what is sought by the informal approach; some think it is the only way to do this. Although such earlier thinkers as Russell and Carnap took it that moving to a formal idiom would explain language or solve problems caused by the vagaries of colloquial usage, most later exponents of a formal approach took the more modest view that seeing how an analogue of meaning can be identified in a formal context will illuminate meaning in natural language.

The idea of a 'theory of meaning' had of course been implicit in much that had happened in the earlier part of the century. Russell's ambition for a 'logically perfect language' holds the idea of natural language meaning itself at deliberate arm's length, as did Carnap's logical constructionism. Positivists had offered a theory of meaning in proposing the verification principle. Quine had argued for a behavioural account of meaning in terms of stimulus conditions, while questioning the intelligibility of intensional construals of the meaning of 'meaning'. Strawson and others had offered piecemeal accounts of aspects of meaning and the component matter of reference; but the key word there is 'piecemeal'. All these efforts had been prompted, in the main, by the desire to solve a problem somewhere else in philosophy. The need had now come to be felt for a systematic account of meaning itself, drawing on what had been learned from these debates.

In the early 1950s there appeared J. L. Austin's translation of Frege's *Grundlagen der Arithmetik*, and, not long afterwards, the *Translations from the Philosophical Writings of Gottlob Frege* by Peter Geach and Max Black. The availability of these works in English gave an impetus to the philosophy of language in subsequent decades. Recall that Frege had taken logic from a position not much distinguishable from where Aristotle left it, and devised a syntax and semantics for propositional and predicate calculus. In the process of working out the applications of this new system to the reduction of arithmetic to logic he evolved ideas that proved important to later philosophy of language, such as the concept of compositionality – the idea that the meaning of expressions is determined by their contribution to the meanings of larger units of language – and the sense–reference distinction.

Another event at the end of that decade abetted the move towards systematic philosophy of language: publication of Quine's *Word and Object* in 1960. It did so by offering a formalization of science in first-order logic enriched by set theory, and by showing how logic illuminates metaphysics by providing a means of identifying the ontological commitments of languages or theories. An equally important effect of it was to stimulate Quine's pupil and colleague Donald Davidson to formulate an approach to theory of meaning which proved to be the most influential of them all.

Donald Davidson (1917–2003) studied classics and literature at Harvard as an undergraduate, but in the course of doing so fell under the influence of A. N. Whitehead and switched to the study of ancient philosophy for a Master's degree. After war service in the US Navy he returned both to Harvard and to his interest in ancient philosophy, writing his doctorate on Plato. But by the time he completed his dissertation he had come to know Quine, and his interests shifted again, this time to contemporary work in the Analytic tradition. He held posts at Stanford, Chicago and Berkeley, but travelled widely to lecture and participate in conferences as his ideas, and the ever-growing interest in philosophy of language generally, exerted their grip on the world of Analytic philosophy.

The key idea in Davidson's approach is that a theory of truth is the right form for a theory of meaning. It seeks to show how the meaning of a sentence is a function of the meanings of its constituent words, and correlatively shows what a speaker knows in 'knowing the meaning' of expressions in her language. A rough formulation of such a theory would list a set of rules showing how to link words and phrases with their meanings, and how to connect the words and phrases together into structures whose meanings are constituted by those connections. Meaning is *compositional*, and the theory must explain how this works. Davidson shared with Quine a commitment to the principle that meanings are not 'meant entities' – that is, objects, states of affairs, concepts or even just 'meanings'. It is easy to see why: if a sentence is composed of expressions that 'mean' *meant entities* then the sentence 'Plato is thinking of the Forms' requires each element of the sentence to 'mean' (respectively) a human being, a mental activity, an abstraction – and in each case a *particular* instance of the thing 'meant' – and further, the expressions that 'mean' them must so combine as to 'mean' *that Plato is thinking of the Forms*. A chief objection to this is that the ontology of meant entities is an implausible mess (recall, for one reason, Quine's 'no entity without identity') since it would contain abstractions, possibilia, universals, concepts, fictional entities, and more. Another and connected reason is that being a competent language user is something that happens naturally – small children learn how to speak on the basis of observing the linguistic behaviour of others; we interpret others' speech in the light of context and general knowledge, not on the basis of linking expressions in the language with a variety of concrete and abstract 'meant entities'.

Accordingly Davidson proposes that we replace talk of 'means that' with something more perspicuous. Consider the case of using English to explain the meaning of expressions in French. We might say, 'The French sentence "la neige est blanche" means "snow is white," ' or, to be more informative, 'The French sentence "la neige est blanche" means that snow is white.' This is more informative because the words after 'means' tell us what is being said by 'la neige est blanche,' not just pairing it with an expression in an uninformative way – as would happen if we told someone who knows neither French nor Mandarin Chinese that 'The French sentence "la neige est blanche" means "xue shi baide." '

In 'The French sentence "la neige est blanche" means that snow is white' the overall English sentence is in the *metalanguage* and the embedded French expression is in the *object language*. Note that a language can be its own metalanguage: we can say 'The English sentence "snow is white" means that snow is white.' This might not at first seem very informative: but it suggests the next step in the theory.

We have not got rid of the unhelpful 'means' idiom yet; and here is the nub of Davidson's proposal. Let us use the extensional '— if and only if —' structure (which is standardly abbreviated to 'iff' to keep things shorter). The idea is that what flanks 'iff' is, on its left, an assertion about a sentence in the object language (call that sentence 's'), and, on its right, a sentence in the metalanguage (call it 'p') that tells us

under what conditions the assertion about 's' can be made. The assertion about 's' is that it has a certain property, let's call it 'T'. So the
schema is: 's is T iff p.' What is the key property 'T' that does the
required trick of making the overall metalanguage sentence tell us what
we want to know about 's'? Davidson argues that the best candidate for
'T' is *true*: 'The sentence "la neige est blanche" is true in French if and
only if snow is white.'

Davidson wrote, 'An acceptable theory of truth must entail, for
every sentence s of the object language, a sentence of the form: s is true
if and only if p, where "p" is replaced by any sentence that is true if and
only if s is. Given this information, the theory is tested by the evidence
that T-sentences are simply true; we have given up the idea that we
must also tell whether what replaces "p" translates s.' So, talk of 'means
that' has been replaced by the relation of 'material equivalence' – which
means: equality of truth-value – in stating the condition under which
the object language sentence in the schema is true.

The problem with this is that 'the sentence "snow is white" is true in
English if and only if grass is green' is also true – and unhelpful. Indeed
the T-schema is such that any materially equivalent (having the same
truth-value) pairs of sentences can be substituted for 's' and 'p'. Davidson's reply is that anyone who knows an adequate truth-theory for a
language will thereby know that the language's lexical items (words and
phrases) have meanings assigned to them, that there are principles governing their composition into sentences, and what both of these entail as
regards the interpretative correlations of sentences in the 's' and 'p' positions. Moreover, the theory is meant to support an empirical account of
meaning, so that the interpretative correlations are not accidental; the
empirical conditions of use will so constrain matters that something
stronger than mere 'material equivalence' will be at work.

The truth-theory borrowed by Davidson for his purposes is one
developed by the logician Alfred Tarski (1901–83) for formal languages.
Tarski assumed the prior availability of a concept of meaning in order
to establish the concept of truth for a formal language L being constructed; 's is true in L iff p' trades on 's' and 'p' being taken as
synonymous across the two languages (metalanguage and object language). Davidson's idea was to turn this on its head and use truth to
explain meaning, instead of using meaning to explain truth as Tarski
had in effect done. However, the concession Davidson made, that something stronger than mere 'material equivalence' has to be involved for

the theory to work, is a significant one. Indeed it looks as though quite a lot of the work that a theory of meaning should do has been done already in connection with the 'assignments of meanings to lexical units', the compositionality principles, and the interpretative correlations between object language and metalanguage substituends for 's' and 'p'. Nevertheless his basic idea, that meanings are truth-conditions, sparked a debate that proved fruitful, not least on the part of those who disagreed with him.

For the empirical aspect of his theory Davidson extended the idea of 'radical translation' in Quine's work into a theory of 'radical interpretation'. The 'field linguist' imagined by Quine observes the utterances and the circumstances of utterance of native speakers, and (indeterminately) matches them to utterances in his own language under the same stimulus-conditions. Davidson has the radical interpreter do something different, which is to relate the native speakers' utterances to the objective conditions in the extra-linguistic environment that would make the utterances true. She assumes that the speakers are rational, generally seek to speak the truth and have generally true beliefs about the world (this is known as the 'Principle of Charity'). On this basis she seeks to give a coherent rendering of what a speaker has said. This does not amount to a unique translation; the data are consistent with competing renderings; so interpretation is still indeterminate.

From much the same considerations Quine had concluded that indeterminacy of meaning means there are no meanings. Davidson more conservatively argues that even though meaning is indeterminate, it is still meaning. The patterns of speakers' behaviours permit the view that meaning lies where interpretations of speaker behaviour converge. The point generalizes: we are all interpreters of each other's speech, even as same-language users; and accordingly we employ something like the same techniques of interpretation in our linguistic transactions with each other in the same language community.

Davidson made important contributions in the philosophy of mind and action also, in each case providing the framework, as with his philosophy of language, for an entire debate. Some of his earliest work was in the philosophy of action, where he argued, against what had become a Wittgensteinian orthodoxy, that explaining someone's reasons for acting a certain way is a form of causal explanation. In the philosophy of mind, and for reasons related to his views about action, Davidson proposed a controversial theory he called 'anomalous monism', consisting of the following three theses: 'mental events cause physical events; all causal relations are governed by natural laws; there are no natural laws governing the causal connections between mental and physical events.' This set of statements appears inconsistent – hence the adjective 'anomalous'. At the same time Davidson is not a mind–brain dualist, hence the 'monism'. In explaining this view Davidson introduced the idea of 'supervenience' to describe how mental phenomena might be 'in some sense dependent' on physical phenomena despite not being reducible to them, and despite there being no psycho-physical laws governing the relationship. The notion of supervenience is notoriously unclear, despite sterling efforts in subsequent discussion to make it less so.

Davidson's truth-conditional approach to meaning was rejected by Michael Dummett, whose arguments for a different approach generated an equally extensive debate because it illustrated just how closely metaphysical questions are connected to questions about how we understand language.

Michael Dummett (1925–2011) was elected, immediately after his undergraduate studies ended in 1950, to a Fellowship at All Souls College, Oxford, one of the world's few non-teaching academic institutions whose members are able to devote themselves solely to their research or other interests. In the first two decades of his Fellowship his country was experiencing an upsurge of racism associated with immigration from countries that had been part of its Empire, and he and his wife became active in anti-racist campaigning. His copious published output mainly began with the first of a series of major works, *Frege: Philosophy of Language* (1973). Further works on Frege, the philosophy of mathematics, philosophy of language and metaphysics and the history of philosophy followed over the next three decades.

At the time Dummett completed his undergraduate studies Wittgenstein's influence was at its height and Dummett regarded himself as a follower. One feature of Wittgenstein's philosophy that retained its hold on him was the idea that 'meaning is use' – more precisely, that knowing the meaning of a word is knowing how to use it. Dummett's contribution to the philosophy of language is, in essence, his endeavour to spell out this view in detail.

Dummett's study of Frege led him to disagree with the view that the meaning of a language's sentences is given by specifying their truth-conditions, on the grounds that this involves an implicit commitment to *realism* concerning the domain of that language. In this context, realism is the thesis that the entities in the given domain exist independently of our knowledge, experience or talk. A realist in mathematics is one who believes that mathematical entities – numbers, or sets – exist independently of our knowledge of them. A realist about the world over which our perceptual experience (our seeing, hearing etc.) ranges is one who believes that rivers, trees and mountains exist independently of our knowledge or experience of them. Realism about any domain allows us to hold that what is said about the domain is either true or false, whether or not we know which, because the way things are in the domain settles its truth-value determinately. But this view, for all the seeming plausibility of both its features – that the domain exists independently of our knowledge, and that it therefore makes every sentence about it determinately either true or false – creates a serious problem for the question of how we understand language.

This is because realism places the truth-conditions of many of our sentences beyond any capacity we have to access them. How do we learn the meaning of sentences if their meaning consists in truth-conditions that transcend our ability to know whether or not they obtain? On Dummett's view, a theory of meaning has to tell us what speakers know when they know – that is: understand – the meaning of their sentences, and, in telling us what they know, the theory must show how that knowledge equips speakers to derive every aspect of the use of sentences from whatever conditions govern their sense. If truth is taken as the basic concept in a theory of meaning then the theory must explain how knowledge of truth-conditions connects with the *practicalities* of language-use. There are two requirements on any acceptable such theory, Dummett says: one is that we must be able to tell what counts as a speaker's manifestation of his knowledge of the meanings of his language's sentences, and the other is that because language is a tool of communication, the sense of its expressions must be public, and therefore what speakers know about meaning must not only be publicly observable in their linguistic behaviour, but also be learnable in public contexts.

A truth-based theory of meaning fails to satisfy both these requirements if truth is realistically understood. A truth-based theory would be unproblematic if knowledge of truth-conditions consists in being able to recognize whether or not they obtain, because this constitutes a practical mastery of a procedure for establishing a sentence's truth-value. 'Understanding a sentence' thus comes down to having a recognitional capacity; grasping the sense of a sentence determines, and is determined by, the uses to which it can be put. Here the connection between *knowing the meaning* and *use* is clear.

But if truth-value is taken to be a possibly recognition-transcendent property of sentences, the link with use is broken and we have no way of saying how a speaker's knowledge of truth-conditions could be displayed. And if we cannot say this, then we cannot say how sense and use determine each other.

This is not to say that truth is irrelevant to the theory of meaning; it is, rather, to say that a different concept of truth is required – one that does not make truth a realistic or recognition-transcendent property of what we say. It is therefore one that has to be associated with the procedures we employ in establishing truth-value: an *anti-realist* conception of truth – something like *verification*. This thought was, of course, immediately controversial.

Dummett suggested that there is a prototype for an anti-realist conception of truth in the intuitionistic account of the meaning of mathematical statements. There the fundamental idea is that understanding mathematical statements rests on being able to recognize proofs of them. To assert a mathematical statement is to claim that there is a proof of it; to understand mathematical expressions is to know how they contribute to determining what counts as a proof of any statement in which they occur. The alternatives to the standard bivalent truth-values 'true' and 'false' are accordingly 'provable' and 'not provable'. Accepting this involves accepting that the Law of Excluded Middle is not generally valid for mathematical statements, for the Law of Double Negation (which states that 'p' and 'not not-p' are equivalent) does not hold: 'it is not provable that it is not provable that p' is not equivalent to 'p is provable.'

In the case of ordinary language, *verifiable* does the work of *provable*, not on the basis that understanding a statement requires actually verifying it, but on the basis that one would be able to recognize a verification of it when one is offered. In the case of ordinary language the capacity to recognize what would verify a statement must be accompanied by a capacity to recognize what would constitute a falsification of it also, because it is unlike intuitionistic mathematics in not having a uniform way to form negation. For both verification and falsification the accounts must be offered systematically in terms of what speakers are able to do.

An immediate objection to Dummett's proposals is that they are revisionary. Ordinary thought and talk is based on assumptions of bivalence and realism, even if (for abstract entities like sets, or for fictional characters like Harry Potter) speakers treat the implicit realist commitments, when pressed, on an 'as if' basis. Our ordinary practice is to accept classical forms of inference, so a theory that demands the substitution of an alternative logic will not be straightforwardly descriptive of our linguistic practice. Usually, if pressed to choose between a revisionist theory and one that conforms with existing assumptions, the conservative option seems preferable. Dummett is robust in response; he remarks that we have no grounds to assume in advance that ordinary language is perfectly in order; Frege had himself remarked that many features of ordinary language make it hard to devise a coherent semantics for it – examples being vagueness, ambiguity and the presence of empty singular terms (singular terms that refer to nothing). Davidson had employed a Tarski-style truth-theory, but Tarski himself said that the way natural languages work generates inconsistencies – 'What I am now saying is false' is a good English sentence, obeying all syntactic and grammatical rules; yet it is self-contradictory. So perhaps a revisionary theory is exactly what is needed.

But the biggest problem appears to be the metaphysics implied by a verificationist view of truth. It entails abandoning realism for the domain to which the language applies, and although that might be easier to argue in the case of mathematics, it is not so easy in the case of the ordinary spatio-temporal world we occupy. Here the idea that there are no facts of the matter, existing independently of our knowledge, which make what we say true or false even if we do not know which, is deeply counter-intuitive. If I say something about the interior of an exoplanet observed orbiting a star elsewhere in our galaxy – for example, that its core consists mostly of molten iron – it seems reasonable to suppose that I am either right or wrong, which entails that it either is or is not the case that the exoplanet's core is as claimed. Dummett's alternative theory seems to imply that every part of the universe which lies beyond our capacities to investigate it is somehow indeterminate, like Schrödinger's cat in the quantum physics example, which is either *neither* dead nor alive or *both* dead and alive until it 'becomes' one or the other when someone opens the box it is in, and observes it (thus 'collapsing the wave function' and getting rid of the indeterminacy).

But this objection is misplaced. Dummett's point is that understanding a sentence consists in knowing a pair of things about it: what would verify it, and what would falsify it. It is a theory about what we have to know in order to understand the sentences of our language, namely, verification procedures. It is not a theory about the nature of what exists. This is why it could be argued that it is a mistake to see the theory as having *metaphysical* implications, because it is really about the *epistemological* connections between what we say and the domain we are talking about. The traditional metaphysical debate had been between materialism and idealism, both of them theses about the nature of reality. The debate between realism and anti-realism in the philosophy of language is about what kind of concept of truth we are to employ in order to explain meaning. So it might well be said that it is misleading to invoke the term 'realism' to encapsulate the idea of what is at stake in a concept of verification-transcendent truth – however natural it seems to do so – given how this usage so readily elides with 'realism' as a metaphysical commitment.

Although much of the debate about meaning theory revolved around ideas sparked by Davidson and Dummett, there were other proposals of significance also. One is the communication-intention theory put forward by Paul Grice (1913–88). Instead of analysing the structure of language, Grice focused attention on what effect a speaker intends to produce in listeners or readers who recognize his intentions. The meaning of his utterance is, roughly speaking, the content of the intention. This is 'utterer's meaning'. There is also 'timeless meaning', derived from utterers' meanings, which is the meaning of a given form of words that speakers can, so to speak, store in their repertoire of utterances and use to say what they intend to convey. One could explain this idea as follows: the practices of speakers confer 'a meaning' on a form of words by their similar intentions to produce similar effects in their hearers, such that, when the form of words has become established as serving that purpose, any of them can employ it to express what they wish to say, and be recognized by others as having that wish. 'Timeless meaning' is in effect *sentence meaning*, which a sentence acquires when there is a practice among speakers to use it to convey the intention it is recognized as being used to convey.

Grice also introduced the idea of *conversational implicature*, which is what an audience recognizes as being implied by the *way* that a speaker says something. For example, suppose I ask a colleague whether a certain student is good at philosophy, and she replies, 'He has nice handwriting.' I might reasonably infer from this that the student is not a budding Plato. Grice observed that language is a cooperative proceeding, in which speakers and hearers both contribute to communicative success. If a speaker says, 'Could you close the window?' the hearer is more likely to close the window than to say, 'Yes,' and continue sitting still, even though this reply is literally correct – he *could* do it, he has legs and hands and is near the window, etc. – but his merely saying 'Yes' does not meet the point of the speaker's utterance in the circumstances. Grice described a set of principles governing implicature and communication. One, the 'Cooperative Principle', is that in taking her turn in a conversation a speaker is to give the right amount of information, neither too much nor too little, which she believes is both true and relevant in the circumstances. Her hearer is to assume that this is the case, and he is to observe the same constraints in response.

A major strand alongside theories of meaning was the development of theories of *reference*. Frege had assumed that the reference of a proper name like 'Aristotle' is fixed by speakers linking a description or set of descriptions with the name, such as 'pupil of Plato and teacher of Alexander the Great', the descriptions enabling speakers to locate the name's referent. Russell agreed for the general case of descriptive knowledge, adding the idea that in episodes of acquaintance with some item, one can refer to it by using the demonstrative pronoun 'this'. These ideas were modified by later thinkers, among them Searle and Strawson, who suggested that linguistic communities fix the references of names by means of clusters of descriptions, any subset of which is enough to identify the bearer of the name. This enabled such a community to discover that, for example, a description traditionally associated with some individual in fact does not apply, without thereby losing the connection between the name and the individual named. For example, suppose the discovery of an ancient papyrus conclusively establishes that Aristotle did not teach Alexander. That fact would not mean that 'Aristotle' no longer names Aristotle, for if it did it would not be information *about Aristotle* that 'Aristotle did not teach Alexander.'

Alternatively put, this idea says that no single description standardly taken to apply to Aristotle denotes a property *essential* to Aristotle. This aligns with an interesting tweak given by Keith Donnellan (1931–2015) to the question of the role of descriptions in reference. He noted that we can sometimes successfully refer to someone by using a description that does not in fact apply – as when we draw attention to someone by saying 'the woman drinking champagne' when she is in fact drinking sparkling water. Donnellan argued that we must therefore distinguish *referential* uses of descriptions from *attributive* uses, these latter uses being those in which it matters that the description applies. For example, suppose someone called Smith is savagely murdered. We might not know who committed the crime, but we can say, 'The murderer of Smith is insane.' This applies the description 'the murderer of Smith' attributively; what we are saying refers expressly to that individual. Now suppose that Jones has been wrongly convicted of murdering Smith, so that he is described as 'the murderer of Smith' and we again say, 'the murderer of Smith is insane.' Even though the description does not truly or properly apply to him, it is enough to pick him out in discussions about him.

Donnellan took it that this distinction showed that both Russell and Strawson had gone wrong about descriptions in the debate between them. Russell took it that to say, 'the F is G' is to say 'there is one and only one thing that is F,' which would only be right in attributive cases (and only if the context made sense of asserting uniqueness; as when one spouse says to the other, 'The baby is crying' in an apartment block full of crying babies). So, Russell failed to take account of referential cases. Strawson, on the contrary, had treated all descriptions as if they were referential, claiming that if a speaker says, 'the F is G' and there is no F, then the speaker has failed to refer to anything. So Strawson had failed to take account of attributive cases.

This led Donnellan, and after him but independently Saul Kripke (b. 1940) and Hilary Putnam (1926–2016), to argue that it is often the case that the referents of proper names – and certain other expressions such as 'natural kind' terms like 'gold' and 'water' – are not fixed via descriptions, but instead are directly linked to their referents, perhaps by a 'causal chain' or a history of usage passed from speaker to speaker. Consider the case of discovering that Aristotle did not teach Alexander; previous theorists had assumed that this did not decouple the name from its referent because other descriptions continue to serve as the information required to identify him. But what if someone said, 'Aristotle not only did not teach Alexander but also did not study with Plato, or write the *Metaphysics* or any of those other works, or ever live in Athens . . .' and it was genuinely *Aristotle* of whom these surprising facts came to light. If some subset of the standard descriptions of

Aristotle is *necessary* to his being Aristotle, this would mean that it is not Aristotle we are talking about, but someone else. But which subset is that? And why? Any one of the descriptions might individually be denied of Aristotle; if it cannot be all, when do we start losing Aristotle as we axe the descriptions one by one? And in any case, if any one of the descriptions might individually be denied of Aristotle it follows that none of them is essential – which implies that collectively they are not essential.

In Kripke's view, names are 'rigid designators', that is, terms that refer to the same individual in every possible world in which the individual exists. This makes sense of the idea that one, some or all of the descriptions traditionally associated with Aristotle might not apply, thus: there is a world in which Aristotle did not teach Alexander; there is a world in which he neither studied with Plato nor taught Alexander; there is a world in which nothing we normally associate with Aristotle applies to him. Possible worlds are indeed distinguished from one another by specifying that the properties associated with a given item in one or some worlds are not the same as those associated with it in other worlds.

Rigid designators are to be distinguished from non-rigid designators such as 'the author of *Hamlet*', because this description might in fact apply to Bacon or Marlowe or Beaumont instead of to Shakespeare. As we would say, there is a world in which *Hamlet* was written by Bacon, not Shakespeare, so 'the author of *Hamlet*' refers to different individuals in different worlds.

An interesting consequence follows for identity statements from Kripke's notion of rigid designation. It was an empirical discovery that the morning star, Phosphorus, and the evening star, Hesperus, are one and the same planet, Venus. All five referring terms refer to the same thing in every possible world in which it exists. Now: empirical discoveries are stated in synthetic *a posteriori* propositions. Yet the identity statement 'the morning star is the evening star,' though discovered to be true *a posteriori* and clearly not analytic, is – as an instance of 'x = x' – *necessarily* true. Here therefore is a case of a necessary truth being discovered *a posteriori*.

This view of reference is significant also, as noted, for natural-kind terms – terms that refer to naturally occurring things like gold, water, tigers and lilies, as opposed to artificial things like bicycles, hats, professors and aeroplanes. Kripke held that natural-kind terms are rigid designators. 'Gold' always ('in every world') refers to the element whose atomic number is 79. Whether or not it is yellow and malleable, it is gold if it has 79 protons in the nucleus. Water is water only if it has the molecular structure H_2O; it does not matter whether it is colourless, odourless and tasteless or whether it is brackish and black; if its molecular structure is two atoms of hydrogen covalently bonded with an atom of oxygen, it is water.

The big question is: if reference does not (to put matters roughly) go via descriptions, how does a name connect with its referent? One suggestion, already made, is that reference works by a causal chain, historically linking present uses of a term to the occasion on which the referent of the term was fixed. So the name 'Tom' refers to Tom because he was given that name by his parents, perhaps in a naming ceremony, and it has continued to pick him out ever since. So long as later speakers intend to refer to the same entity by means of the name as earlier speakers did, the causal chain is of the right kind. Different ways of making this more plausible have been offered; Donnellan talked of an 'historical explanation theory', which helps with more difficult cases such as 'Pegasus' and 'unicorn' where – given that there are neither winged nor horned horses – there was not a naming occasion, only stories and legends.

A criticism of the causal theory of reference is that we have plausible intuitions to the effect that a speaker's non-accidental success in using names is associated with his having relevant knowledge of facts about the referent that assist him in identifying it. Kripke conceded this by saying that descriptions might help in fixing the reference to begin with, but that is not the same as saying that the descriptions are the 'meaning' of the name. Instead he argued that a rigid designator designates what it does in virtue of an essential property of the referent – consider 'gold': the word rigidly designates the element whose essential property is having 79 protons in the nucleus, whether or not any given user of the word knows any particle physics. As this implies, the essence of a thing or a kind of thing is not what identifies it for a user of its name, nor can it constitute the 'meaning' of the name.*

---

* Something like a causal theory of reference was held by John Stuart Mill, who spoke of names having 'denotation but no connotation'. His way of putting matters is not felicitous, for in many languages names do have connotations – even in English: 'Irene' means 'Peace', 'Agatha' means 'Good', and so on – but of course the connotations are not the 'meaning' of the name.

The book in which Kripke first set out his views on these matters, *Naming and Necessity* (1972 and 1980), is a modern classic of philosophy. As a prodigy in youth he had provided a semantics for quantified modal logic; later he wrote about Wittgenstein – controversially: his version of Wittgenstein was dubbed 'Kripkenstein' – and contributed important work in the philosophy of mind. Among the major figures in twentieth-century Analytic philosophy he is a paradigm of what this style of philosophy most admires: great technical power, incisiveness, creativity and a legacy of having made a real difference by moving the debate onwards.

As one would expect, the philosophical literature on language is voluminous and rapidly evolving. Little stands still in such a vigorous debate. Two examples from many will demonstrate this, both resulting from revisits to Wittgenstein's ideas.

Recall Wittgenstein's claim about following a rule, which was that 'no course of action could be determined by a rule, because every course of action can be made out to accord with the rule.' If right, this raises a serious problem for any theory claiming that meaning is to be explained in terms of rules governing the use of words and sentences. Kripke offered a 'sceptical solution' to this dilemma which accepts that there is no objective constraint on the uses that speakers make of expressions in their language, and that instead what counts as correctly following a rule is, simply, the confirming judgment of fellow-language users that the rule is being followed. Because Kripke says that his account of Wittgenstein's point, and the sceptical solution to the problem it implies, might not be what Wittgenstein himself actually proposed, the argument is attributed to a fictional thinker called 'Kripkenstein', and it is always discussed under this name.

The other example also concerns the idea that meaning consists in use, and it is in large part a response to dissatisfaction with truth-based theories of meaning such as Davidson's, and any claim that words denote or represent things or states of affairs – the simplest version of which is that the meaning of a term is what it denotes. It is also a response to criticism of meaning-is-use theories turning on the fact that many things have uses – knives and forks, for example – without having meaning, and indeed many words have uses, often important ones (such as 'the', 'and', 'of'), but no meaning. This updated use theory – or cluster of theories – is variously known as conceptual (or inferential) role semantics, and the key idea is that the meanings of expressions lie in their relationships with other expressions, especially in what is implied by, and can be inferred from, their use. The first to suggest such a view was Wilfrid Sellars (1912–89); his follower Robert Brandom is among those developing it.*

If there had been a hope that philosophy of language might provide a way of solving the big traditional problems of philosophy, it had not, by the end of the twentieth century, fulfilled it. Indeed it might be said that it had not even come near to achieving a 'theory of meaning' that commanded much agreement. Discussion of reference fared better than discussion of meaning. As the century entered its last decades the interest in language began to diverge in two directions: one was the increasingly close connection with philosophy of mind, the other was the closer focus of interest on particular aspects of language and language-use, such as indexical expressions (those that link an utterance to a specified speaker, time and place), vagueness, anaphora, context, pragmatics, fictional discourse and other more specialized concerns. In some of these areas philosophers benefited from working with ideas, and colleagues, in linguistics. The writings of Davidson, Dummett, Kripke and others continued to be explored and to generate new insights in the creative reaction to them on the part of those coming fresh to the study of their ideas; philosophy is never static.

PHILOSOPHY OF MIND

Philosophy of mind was not a separate and self-standing pursuit in the first half of the twentieth century. Introductory books included discussion of the mind–body problem in the chapter on metaphysics, and theories of perception were associated with the problem of scepticism in epistemology. Scientific approaches to psychology had begun to take shape in the second half of the nineteenth century in Germany, Austria and America, and in the first half of the twentieth century, inspired by successes in the natural sciences, especially physics, the desire for an empirical, observational psychology gave behaviourism a significant edge.

---

* Sellars founded what is informally known as the 'Pittsburgh School' of philosophy at the University of Pittsburgh, where his colleagues Robert Brandom and John McDowell were among many both there and elsewhere to be influenced by his thought.

Behaviourism accordingly recommended itself also to philosophers wishing either to reduce mental phenomena to behaviour, or (for most, equivalently) to analyse mentalistic terms into behavioural terms. The Logical Positivists, Quine, Wittgenstein and Ryle all in their various ways appealed to behaviourist strategies for dispensing with talk of the mental. There was no Damascene moment in the two decades after the Second World War that made philosophers give up any form of behaviourism as a resource for understanding the mind, but the demise of behaviourism in psychology was certainly a factor.

The demise of behaviourism, in both psychology and philosophy, was not however the demise of the commitment underlying behaviourism, namely, that mental phenomena ultimately are, or are grounded in, natural phenomena – primarily, brain function. This redirected efforts in philosophy to thinking about how mental phenomena could be understood or interpreted consistently with rejection of both behaviourism and any form of dualism. Increasing sophistication in neurology, physiology and biochemistry gave added impetus to that confidence. The natural first port of call was to hypothesize that mental phenomena in some sense *just are* physical occurrences in the brain and central nervous system, which is to say: that mental events and nervous system events are identical. The first problem was to try to make out how to articulate this idea satisfactorily.

Early identity theories of mind, put forward in the 1950s and 1960s, owed themselves to U. T. Place, Herbert Feigl and J. J. C. Smart. The views of Place and Smart represent something of a halfway house because they thought that *intentional* phenomena* – believing, desiring – are still best understood behaviouristically, whereas *phenomenal* states – pains, hunger pangs – can be associated with physical states of the nervous system. Feigl agreed about phenomenal states, but thought that behaviourism is also insufficient to explain intentional states because an account of them has to include factors that are not *exclusive* to the person (or other organism) in question; other things – other people, or other aspects of the world – frequently have to figure in intentional explanations. How would you explain 'thinking about a tree' if no reference to something other than the thought, namely the

---

* Note once again that this is 'intentional' with a 't' – from *intend* in the literal sense of *be directed towards* (we colloquially use 'intend' to mean 'being resolved to do, or decided about doing, something' but its literal meaning is *directed towards* or *focused on*).

tree itself, is made – especially if you wished to differentiate between 'thinking about a tree' and 'thinking about a river'? Hence it would be a category mistake in Ryle's sense to assimilate intentionalistic explanations to behavioural ones.

Feigl's point about intentional states is an early hint at what came to be called 'anti-individualism'. As described by one of the chief proponents of this view, Tyler Burge in his *Foundations of Mind* (2007), *individualism* in this context is the thesis that an individual's mental states are constitutively independent of any relation to a wider reality, while *anti-individualism* says that many such states are what they are partly by virtue of relations between the individual in those states and a wider reality. Another name for this kind of view is *externalism*, and versions of it apply in meaning theory as well as theories of intentionality. The phrases *broad content* and *narrow content* are often employed to describe the content of mental states on an anti-individualist or externalist view, and on an individualist or internalist view, respectively.

Place argued that the identity in question is not of the 'x = x' variety, but is *compositional* identity: a cloud *is* a collection of water droplets, but a water droplet is not a cloud. In the same way, a mental event is composed out of physical events, and when we know enough about both we will be able to show how the former reduces to the latter.

Feigl and Smart, employing Frege's sense–reference distinction, took the view that the identity between types of phenomenal states and physical states is x = x identity; so, expressions describing the respective states differ in sense but refer to the same thing.

Two of the chief objections to identity theories are, first, that it restricts mental phenomena to brains – what about the possibility that computers or other, not necessarily biological, entities might have mental states? – and secondly, that they say nothing about one of the most puzzling features of mental life, namely, the existence of *qualia* – that is, the felt quality of experiences of pain, pleasure, hunger, desire, depression and the like: the subjective aspect of mental life. This point is central to the vexed debate about consciousness, discussed below.

The first objection says that mental and brain states cannot be identical if mental states could occur in things that are not brains. Identity in the standard sense of x = x is *necessary*, but if mental states are 'multiply realizable', that is, able to be instantiated in different kinds of systems, then the relationship between mental states and brain states is only *contingent*. A response to this is to weaken the identity claim from 'type–type identity' to 'token–token identity': instead of saying, '*types* of mental states, such as feeling pain, are identical to *types* of nervous system states, namely, the firing of C-fibres' (these being the non-myelinated nociceptor fibres in animal bodies that deliver the first sharp sensation of pain), we only claim that '*token* mental states are identical to *token* central nervous system states.' The distinction between type and token is most easily explained thus: 'each individual human being is a token (example, instance) of the animal type (kind, species) *Homo sapiens sapiens*.' Or, 'in "she sells sea-shells on the sea-shore" there are eight tokens of the letter "s".' Token–token identity allows multiple realizability of mental states, while retaining the fundamental commitment of any identity theory to 'this *token* mental state is x = x identical with this *token* other state' (whatever that state is, though in humans it is a state of the body).

Another approach is *functionalism*, which says that mental states are to be identified by the causal roles they play, independently of what wet-ware (brains, say) or dry-ware (computers, say) carries out the causal operations themselves. So, to say what a pain is, or a memory, or a desire, is to say what causal roles are played respectively by pains, memories and desires, independently of what system is doing the work. It is a 'black box' theory, out of consideration for the multiple realizability constraint, and therefore hospitable to widely varying interpretations, including ones that are at direct odds with each other. The basic idea is that mental states are functional states where these latter are nexuses of inputs and outputs, together with relations between inputs and inputs and outputs and outputs. The aim is to avoid restricting mental states only to biological brains, and at the same time to avoid being so permissive as to attribute mental states to almost any functional device (the central-heating control monitor in your house, for example).

An immediate objection to functionalism is that it does not seem to provide a way of locating a place between the too permissive and too restrictive views to satisfy intuitions about mental life. It does not at all address the question of the subjective nature of mental states, which in some cases make no causal difference at all, as one sees from 'inverted spectrum' examples: whenever you see green I see blue, but this difference makes no difference to how we behave in regard to things that seem green to you and blue to me. Moreover I might regret something, but not do anything about the fact that I regret it; what is the causal role in terms of which 'regretting' as an intentional state is to be characterized?

A famous example, offered by John Searle, suggests that functionalism cannot adequately account for such intentional states as understanding. Imagine a person possessed of an exhaustive rule-book for correlating strings of Chinese characters to each other. He is given a string of characters, looks it up in the rule-book to find the string of characters it is there matched with, and hands back this second string. To someone who understands Chinese he is providing intelligent responses to questions or remarks, but he himself has no idea what any of the strings of characters mean. We can suppose that he does not even know they are Chinese characters; to him, Japanese and Korean script might be indistinguishable from Chinese script. On a functionalist account, a mind is just like this person; it carries out a task, but by hypothesis without knowing what it is doing. Searle aimed this example at the claim that the software–hardware relationship in a computer models the mind–brain relationship in animals, minds thus being the software of the brain. But it hits both targets, functionalism and the computer analogy. For Searle the moral is that there cannot be intentionality without consciousness.

Searle's Chinese Room argument prompted a vigorous controversy. One response to it was to say that even though the man in the room does not understand Chinese, the entire system, of which he is just a part, does understand Chinese. Searle replied that if the man made himself the entire system (by learning the rule-book by heart, generating strings of characters, matching them to other strings and issuing the latter) he would still not understand Chinese.

Donald Davidson's 'anomalous monism' constitutes another argument against type–type physicalist identity theories. His view, described earlier, is that although mental events cause physical events, and although all causal relations are governed by natural laws, there are nevertheless no natural laws governing the causal connections between mental and physical events. As we have seen, the inconsistency among these commitments explains the term 'anomalous'.

Davidson's invocation of the idea of supervenience to describe how mental states might 'in some sense be dependent' on physical states, despite the absence of psycho-physical laws, constitutes a form of 'nonreductive physicalism'. Some commentators describe Davidson's view as a token identity theory, although doing so does not sit comfortably either with the notion of supervenience or with its associated rejection of reductionism. The difficulty of locating his view on the spectrum of physicalist theories is a product of the fact, which he emphasizes, that talk of rationality enters essentially into many mental descriptions, but has no role in physical descriptions; every effort to account for the former exclusively in terms of the latter *must* therefore fail to do so adequately. And yet there can be no question of reintroducing any form of substance dualism under the disguise of an 'aspect dualism' or 'property dualism' of the kind that might most naturally characterize anomalous monism.

A significant aspect of Davidson's contribution is his refocusing of the debate away from discussion mainly of sensation and back towards *intentionality* as the mark of the mental, citing the nineteenth-century philosopher-psychologist Franz Brentano's view to this effect: 'Every mental phenomenon', Brentano wrote, 'is characterized by what the Scholastics of the Middle Ages called the intentional (or mental) inexistence of an object, and what we might call, though not wholly unambiguously, reference to a content, direction toward an object (which is not to be understood here as meaning a thing), or immanent objectivity. Every mental phenomenon includes something as object within itself.' This permits identification of mental states by their content; thus, believing and desiring are attitudes understood in terms of what is believed and what is desired respectively.

The attraction of this view for Davidson becomes clear when one recalls his theory of interpretation. Ascribing propositional attitudes is effected by interpreting linguistic behaviour in a context; we 'impose conditions of coherence, rationality and consistency' on the agent's behaviour and its causes, which in effect means that ascertaining the meaning of what an agent says is achieved by applying a theory of mind to what she does. Everything that we wish to know about mind is accordingly revealed by what work mental concepts do in enabling radical interpretation.

Whereas Davidson's version of non-reductive physicalism was attractive to some, its connection with his theory of interpretation proved less so, principally because his claim that it reveals everything that can be said about mind entails that a scientific psychology is not possible. For some this raised the suspicion that anomalous monism might after all just be a version of *epiphenomalism*, the view that mental phenomena are merely by-products or incidental effects of the far more significant physical events in the brain that cause them. This cannot be a criticism of Davidson, though, because epiphenomenalism explicitly denies that mental phenomena exert any causal influence on physical phenomena, whereas it is precisely the anomaly in Davidson's view that mental states indeed cause physical behaviour, but not under the government of any law that contains mental descriptions.

Suspicions of epiphenomenalism raised by unclarities in non-reductive forms of physicalism remind one of the questions it prompts. What is the point of mental phenomena if they are epiphenomenal? They might just be a wasteful accident of evolution. If they have no role to play in causing behaviour, they are no use in interpreting behaviour, linguistic and otherwise; the world might as well be populated by zombies with no minds at all as by creatures whose mental lives are inefficacious by-products of what is really doing the work.

Indeed, the criticism that non-reductive physicalism could too readily collapse into epiphenomenalism makes it look questionable. At very least it makes the theory seem as if it has a latter-day version of the problem Descartes faced. He, one recalls, was unable to explain how a causal connection can obtain between mental and physical phenomena if they are wholly different substances. Any view that says mental phenomena cannot be reduced to physical phenomena, and which is not epiphenomenalist, has to find some account of how they connect. Such an account is, obviously, impossible on the premise that no connecting laws exist. Old problems are not always solved by being dressed in new clothes.

The idea that mental states cause behaviour, and that we explain and predict behaviour by ascribing it to mental states as its inner origin, is such a natural one that it constitutes the ordinary assumed view of most people. We are on the whole rather good at interpreting and predicting others' behaviour, and the ready use of concepts of desire, belief, intention, hunger, lust, hope, misery, joy and other inner states of mind is said to constitute a 'folk psychology' that we pick up as we develop from infancy onwards. It constitutes 'tacit knowledge' – implicit knowledge that we might not even be fully aware we have, rather like our knowledge of grammar. Its success might be taken as an indication that whatever the mentalistic terms refer to, whether neural processes in the brain or something else, 'folk theory' itself has got a lot right about the mind.

This view is robustly rejected by 'eliminative materialism', the theory that folk psychology is radically wrong, and that the states and processes its terms purport to refer to do not exist. Any theory that denies the existence of any class of entities is 'eliminativist' with regard to that class; add 'materialism' and eliminative materialism announces itself as a theory saying that the only things that exist are material (physical) states and processes. Indeed, any theory about the mind which is *materialist* is, just in virtue of that fact, well on the way to being eliminativist already. Quine asked in *Word and Object* whether, if mentalistic terms are taken to denote physical events in the brain, this amounted to a theory of the mental, saying that mental and physical states are identical; or, instead, a recommendation to abandon reference to mental states altogether. And he then argued that since they come to the same thing, why duplicate what we say – let us eliminate talk of the mental.

Eliminative materialism took centre stage with the work of Paul and Patricia Churchland and Stephen Stich. The latter's *From Folk Psychology to Cognitive Science* (1983) and Patricia Churchland's *Neurophilosophy* (1986) are important milestones in this development. Patricia Churchland's argument is that once we have a full understanding of the brain we will fully understand what we now think of as mental states and processes, and will not need the folk-psychological vocabulary to talk about it. Our situation in regard to mind, Patricia Churchland held, is at the same level as Aristotle's understanding of motion; developments in natural science provided a means to explain how motion can occur without appeal to the agenting activity of *anima*, and therefore references to the latter have been eliminated.

What distinguishes the Churchlands' eliminative materialism from earlier attempts at physicalist theories of mind and brain is its explicit identification of brain structures as the entities that do the work. Earlier theories had offered no suggestions as to what the brain structures or states, with which mental states are identical or to which they reduce, *actually* are; they had merely gestured at the 'whatever it is in the brain' that a future science would identify as the right candidate. Developments in neuroscience, the Churchlands said, had now brought philosophy of mind into such intimate connection with itself that it is no longer possible to tell where neuroscience begins and philosophy of mind ends.

But eliminative materialism is not merely a strong identity theory; it is *eliminative*, arguing that *there are no such things* as beliefs, desires, hopes and the rest. Consider the difference between saying that lightning is an electrical discharge, where the nature of a familiar phenomenon is explained by a theory with the right resources for doing so (thus replacing, say, 'lightning is a thunderbolt thrown by Zeus'), and saying that demons do not exist. In the latter case it is not that more adequate resources have come along for explaining 'demon possession' in mental illness; instead, talk of demons has been eliminated from talk of mental illness altogether. Just this will happen, say the eliminativists, as brain science progresses.

The arguments in favour of eliminative materialism are of two kinds: arguments against folk psychology, and arguments for the explanatory potential of neuroscience. Some of them are as follows. A theory of mind should imply a programme of research which will yield explanations of the phenomena at issue. Folk psychology does not do this; instead, it ignores whole tracts of mental life, including dreaming, consciousness, learning, memory, mental illness and those behaviours now known to be the result of brain damage. Moreover, there are parallels with other folk theories about aspects of the world – the weather, physical diseases, animal behaviour – which science has displaced; folk psychology will follow this pattern as knowledge in neuroscience grows. Meanwhile that knowledge – of the brain, neurophysiology, endocrinology and genetics – which has grown enormously in the course of the twentieth century, throws ever more light on mental life, not least as a result of functional MRI scanning (fMRI), which makes it possible to observe, in real time, activation of brain structures in response to various tasks and challenges, greatly enriching knowledge already gained from brain autopsy correlations with psychological deficits.

These are compelling considerations. Yet it remains that folk-psychological explanation is powerful and predictively successful as an everyday theory of mind, and – most importantly – the neurophilosophical approach makes more rather than less mysterious the stubborn facts of introspective experience: we have, or appear to have, direct and privileged access to such mental states as pain, hunger, desire and the qualitatively-rich experience of seeing (in colour – a remarkable fact), hearing, tasting and the like. The eliminative materialist response is to say that our interpretations of what is happening within us might be culturally conditioned by the folk psychology we learn as we grow up; just as people in the past claimed to 'see' the demons being cast out in an exorcism, so we might *think* that we know what some supposedly inner mental state is – and be wrong.

These last points raise the great question of consciousness, and in particular that aspect of consciousness which consists in being self-aware of having experience in a certain way. Talk of consciousness comprises related notions like being sentient, or awake, or aware of things other than oneself, but the key problem for any physicalist theory of mind (or indeed any theory of mind) is how to explain the phenomenon that has come to be called the 'what it is like' aspect of consciousness, following Thomas Nagel's famous 1974 paper entitled 'What is It Like to be a Bat?' On observational grounds we know that bats navigate and find prey by means of echolocation. What we cannot know is what it is like for a bat to 'see' the world through the sound patterns of bounced high-frequency squeaks. There is something it is like for the bat to have such experience; but only the bat can know what it is like.

Nagel argued that the chief challenge for physicalism is to account for the subjective character of such experience. He defines possession of conscious mental states as consisting in there subjectively being 'something it is like to be' the possessor of them, and argues that no reductive theory of mental states captures this because such theories are all compatible with the absence of subjectivity – with, in short, zombiehood. Not only do they not capture it, but they seem in principle to be excluded from doing so, for two reasons. One is that the nature of such experience can be understood only by occupying the experiencer's viewpoint. The other is that however rich the external empirical data available to an observer, it cannot give him access to that viewpoint. We can know facts *about* the bat's echolocation capacities, but we cannot occupy the bat's point of view on what it is like to use them.

This argument was intended by Nagel not to be a refutation of physicalism, but rather to highlight the special difficulty that physicalist theories have to overcome. Another contributor to the debate, Frank Jackson, did however think that these considerations rule out physicalism, and devised the 'Mary's Room' thought experiment to show why. A very clever scientist called Mary lives permanently in a room in which the colours are black and white only. She wears only black and white clothes, has a black and white television, and all the books she gets are likewise only ever black and white. She is a vision scientist, and knows everything there is to know about colour vision – the structure of the eye, the optic nerves, the visual cortex, the part of the electro-magnetic spectrum visible to the human eye, and the nature of the visual system's response to electromagnetic radiation at different frequencies. She knows all this comprehensively, and without herself ever having seen any colour other than black and white. One day she leaves her room, and sees a red rose. When she does so, says Jackson, she *learns something new*: she learns *what it is like to see red*. What she learns is the qualitative character of that kind of experience. This is absent from the comprehensive objective knowledge of colour vision. Therefore, says Jackson, physicalist theories are wrong.

An argument to similar effect is offered by David Chalmers. He postulates a world inhabited only by zombies, understood as beings who are exact duplicates of human beings in every respect other than that their experiences have no qualia, no qualitative, 'subjectively felt' character. This is a conceivable world, and therefore metaphysically possible; and if it is metaphysically possible, physicalism is false – because it describes human beings exactly as if they were the zombies in that world.

Chalmers also distinguishes between the 'hard problem of consciousness' – how to explain qualia – and the easy problems, such as explaining the brain's performance of various cognitive functions such as processing sensory inputs, integrating information and the like. The hard problem is to explain why the performance of these functions is accompanied by the phenomenon of 'what it feels like' to perform them.

The inability of physicalist theories to explain qualia is known as the 'explanatory gap', and some (Chalmers himself, Jackson and Kripke among them) infer an ontological gap from it, namely, that consciousness is not physical. Physicalists respond either by denying that there is an explanatory gap – which by itself closes the ontological gap – or by accepting the explanatory gap but denying that it entails an ontological gap. Daniel Dennett, for a chief example, argues that there is no explanatory gap because, he says, there are no such things as qualia; they are a 'philosophical fiction'. He justifies this by arguing that the brain in fact latches on to just a few significant details at any moment, only thus being able to function because it would become inefficiently overloaded if it sought to handle too many items of information simultaneously. Experiments show that we leave out a lot of information even about a present perceptual environment – for example, the famous 'gorilla and ball-players' experiment, in which most people who watch a video of people passing a ball among themselves, and who are asked to count how many times they do it, completely fail to see a full-sized gorilla figure walk in among the players, beat its chest and walk off screen. Indeed similar such experiments show that the world as we perceive it is a virtual-reality construction.

But critics of Dennett's position argue that this does not show that there is no such thing as consciousness; it is impossible to persuade anyone that the feeling of warmth in her hands as she holds them near a fire, and the feeling of intense pain she feels when she puts them in the fire, are illusions. Just because we cannot explain consciousness on the basis of present knowledge should not be a motivation for denying its existence; nor should the fact that it is irreducibly subjective, and accessible only to one privileged observer, entail that it does not have a physical basis. This view says that the explanatory gap is real, but does not have to entail an ontological gap, and might just be a function of the present inadequate state of neuroscientific knowledge. At the other end of the debate there are those who think that the hard problem is simply too hard ever to be solved: on this view, consciousness cannot understand itself any more than an eyeball can see itself. Not many accept this counsel of despair. One respectable position is that whatever future neuroscience might reveal, the predictive and explanatory utility of folk-psychological concepts still remains, and rather impressively so.

ETHICS

A distinction is standardly drawn between 'normative ethics' – ethical theories or systems offering themselves as guides or, in the case of religious ethics, demands, about how to live – and 'metaethics', which is philosophical analysis of ethical concepts and language, typically without any normative ambitions. Almost all ethical thinking in twentieth-century Analytic philosophy is metaethics, at least until the last few decades when 'applied ethics', addressing dilemmas in medical practice, business, war, scientific research, and more, began to grow in influence alongside the increasingly technical refinement of metaethical debate.

One can be forgiven for thinking that normative ethical questions might have gripped philosophers in light of the immense slaughter and inhumanity of the world wars, the threat of extinction by nuclear weapons, the long grip of totalitarianisms around the world and the seemingly unstoppable violations of individual human rights on every continent. Yet in Analytic philosophy it was as if the sheer horror of so much inhumanity made it necessary to look away to something calmer, cooler and more manageable. Instead of investigating what it is that made such a thing as the Holocaust – industrial murder of millions – morally tolerable to some, at least for a time, Analytic philosophers investigated (for example) the logical connection between an imperative, 'Close the window!', and the ability of someone in the circumstance to obey. (For, if the window is already closed, does that make the imperative in some sense like a statement that is false, and what sense is that?)*

It might be argued in response that there is no point in rushing to moral judgment without having a clear idea about the nature and purport of such judgments, and that is true; and it might also be said that the obvious horrors of the twentieth century should not be allowed to take all the oxygen out of debate, so that other legitimate concerns are neglected. It might further be argued that a return to the civilized examination of how we think about ethical matters, as a contribution to being able to think about them *well*, is precisely the right response to the effort by barbarians to halt debate – indeed, civilization – altogether. This too is right. Still: there is no reason why the two tasks of fighting ethical enormity and clarifying ethical discourse should not both be possible – even, sometimes, together.

Ethics in twentieth-century Analytic philosophy might be said to have started before the twentieth century – in fact, to have started all the way back with Aristotle; for he, Hume and Kant remained and still remain the dominating figures in all ethical debate. Slightly closer in time, the nineteenth-century utilitarians stand at the source of the various forms of act, rule and preference utilitarianism to which many moral philosophers fall back when pushed, at the end of their theorizings, to answer the question, 'So, what helps us to decide how to act in a given case?' Between them these antecedents continued, as they continue, to shape the nature of the discussion, which concerns the intimately interconnected questions of how we understand ethical language, whether or

* The leading Analytic moral philosopher R. M. Hare was imprisoned by the Japanese for three years during the Second World War, and is said to have formulated 'a guide to life in the harshest conditions' which, however, he never published, restricting himself to metaethical investigations until later in his career, when he contributed to debates on abortion, slavery and animal rights.

not there are objective moral facts or properties, how we justify moral claims, and how ethical thought connects with other aspects of the mind, human nature and the human condition – respectively: the semantics, metaphysics, epistemology and psychology of ethical discourse and life.

But for a more proximate beginning, ethics in twentieth-century Analytic philosophy might be said to start with G. E. Moore's *Principia Ethica*, discussed in the section on his philosophical outlook on pp. 365–70 above. His opposition to the 'Naturalistic Fallacy', his intuitionism and his espousal of a form of rule utilitarianism formed the dominant outlook for the first third of the century, even if there were those, like David Ross (1877–1971), who argued that what we intuit in moral life is not what is intrinsically good (friendship and beauty, in Moore's theory), but our *duties*. Ross acknowledged that duties can conflict with each other, and argued that a choice of which to obey has to be made on the merits of the circumstances we find ourselves in. He took it that, with this adjustment, the intuitionistic approach to ethics conforms to what most ordinary people would accept is a correct description of how they think about moral matters.

Logical Positivists agreed about the Naturalistic Fallacy, but disagreed about intuition, which – if it existed – would underwrite a realist view to the effect that ethical judgments involve reference to objective properties or states of affairs whose presence or absence confers truth-value on those judgments. Instead they argued that ethical statements are not statements at all, because they are not verifiable, but instead that they are expressions of attitude. This is *emotivism*, a view held by Russell before the Positivists and by Carnap and others among them, and which was popularized by A. J. Ayer in *Language, Truth and Logic* (1936) and given a more thorough treatment by Charles Stevenson in *Ethics and Language* (1944).

Charles Stevenson (1908–79) was educated at Yale, then at Cambridge – where he attended classes by Moore and Wittgenstein, as a result of which his interests changed from literature to philosophy – and finally at Harvard for his PhD. He taught for a number of years at Yale, which eventually denied him tenure because of his espousal of emotivism, in particular because he argued that some moral disputes cannot be settled on rational grounds, and that we have to resort in such cases to non-rational grounds. The University of Michigan gave him a post instead, where he remained for the rest of his career.

Stevenson saw himself as 'qualifying and supplementing' what Russell, Ayer, Carnap and others had said in favouring a non-cognitivist view of moral language. His chief point was that ethical terms have *emotive meanings*, by which he meant that because of their history of usage they have a 'tendency to express' the attitudes of speakers and to evoke attitudes in hearers. Factual discourse is also expressivist, in that it expresses a speaker's beliefs; people rarely talk *about* their beliefs, as one might in saying, 'I used to believe that Jones insulted Smith,' but instead just express them: 'Jones insulted Smith.' But more than this is happening in an assertion such as 'Jones ought not to have insulted Smith' because it is not just about what happened but – more significantly – conveys the speaker's disapproval of it. Although beliefs are implicit in 'ought' sentences, the attitude they convey is what is relevant to determining what kinds of reasons are relevant to handling cases of moral disagreement and uncertainty that might arise from their use.

But this is not the end of the story. Equally important is that in uttering a moral statement the speaker is not only expressing her attitude but *intending* that her choice of emotive terminology will evoke a similar attitude in her hearer. Stevenson changed the word 'evoke' to 'invite' after discussion with J. O. Urmson, as better capturing the speaker's point in communicating her attitude, for although sometimes speakers will express attitudes simply to vent their feelings, it would be odd to have attitudes of approval and disapproval but not, in most cases, to wish that anything might follow to promote or inhibit what elicits them.

This is the 'autobiographical' model of moral discourse, relating to speakers' own attitudes and their intentions in expressing them. What of non-autobiographical cases such as 'X is good'? In parallel with the autobiographical case, it would seem that the right analysis is that it expresses an imperative or exhortatory injunction, 'Let us approve of X.' Stevenson says, 'It must be remembered that imperatives, in this connection, are useful only for the purpose of analogy, and indeed, only for the purpose of cutting through the supposition that ethical sentences can express nothing but beliefs.' We see this in comparing the connection between 'X is good' and 'Let us approve of X' with the connection between 'X is yellow' and 'Let us believe that X is yellow.' Stevenson says, 'The latter model, unlike the former, is altogether useless, since it cuts through no supposition that needs to be cut through.' The analogy with the autobiographical case therefore highlights the respect in which statements of ethical judgment are *more* than merely expressions of attitude.

In ordinary talk of moral matters people are happy to say 'that's true' (or 'false') in response to statements such as 'Tom is a good man.' On a non-cognitivist view such as Stevenson's – the view that no matter of fact is being described, just the speaker's attitude – how is this to be understood? Stevenson says it is perfectly proper to say of ethical statements that they are true or false when we see that this is for purely *syntactical* reasons – to put 'it is true that' in front of 'p' in 'it is true that p' adds nothing to 'p'. So 'it is true that' and the rest work as described in various 'deflationary' theories of truth – as marking agreement, or applying emphasis, or permitting iteration without having to repeat all the words of the original. They do not imply or require that there be moral facts of the matter as truth-and-falsehood-makers of what we say.

The basic idea that moral statements are expressions of attitude invites criticism on the grounds that it is no better than a 'hurray–boo' theory which does nothing to address why we might sometimes wish to say 'hurray' and sometimes 'boo'. Adding that we want others to join us in our hurrays and boos does not help. Arbitrary facts about our personal biographies might explain our personal inclinations in the matter, but in the absence of any other reasons (let alone good and cogent ones) for saying 'hurray' and 'boo' and wanting others to join in, how does this amount to an ethical theory? Some such reflection led R. M. Hare to toughen the story by arguing that ethical utterances are not mere expressions plus invitations, they are expressions plus *prescriptions*, and the prescriptions are *universalizable*.

R. M. Hare (1919–2002) was White's Professor of Moral Philosophy at Oxford. He studied classics at school and at Oxford, where his undergraduate career was interrupted by service in the Second World War. Like many of his generation his life was greatly affected by the war; he was deployed with an artillery unit in India and Singapore, where he was captured by the Japanese when the latter fell to them. He was their prisoner until the war's end, afterwards being unable to speak of his experiences on the long march up the River Kwai to work as a forced labourer on the Japanese army's Burma–Siam railway line.

Hare returned to Oxford to complete his studies, and became a Fellow and tutor of his college, Balliol, until being appointed to the White's chair of moral philosophy. He taught a number of people who became distinguished in British philosophy in the twentieth century's second half – Bernard Williams, David Pears and Richard Wollheim among them. A supportive and engaged tutor who maintained the Oxford tradition of reading parties with students, Hare is alleged to have discouraged those who were not very good at philosophy by asking, halfway through their reading an essay to him, 'Have you considered a career in the civil service?'

In addition to accepting, with reservations, the force of the emotivist argument, and its corollary that there are no empirical moral facts, Hare was also persuaded by Kant's view that moral discourse is subject to reason, and has a logical structure. Whereas the meaning of factual discourse is *descriptive*, in that its meaning is governed by truth-conditions, the meaning of moral discourse is *prescriptive*, which Hare defines by saying that a prescriptive statement is one that entails at least one imperative: 'do such and such . . . do not do so and so . . .' True to Hume's claim that no statement containing 'ought' can be derived from any number of purely descriptive statements – 'no *is* can entail an *ought*,' meaning that facts can never settle what choices one should make about how to act – Hare accepted that moral reasoning can issue in prescriptive conclusions only if inferred from premises containing one or more prescriptive statements. The action-guiding aspect of moral discourse lies in the choices we make about how to regard the descriptive aspects, as can be seen by this example: suppose you are standing in the path of an oncoming bus. This *fact* is not enough to entail *that you ought to get out of the way*, because you might be standing there by choice, wishing suicidally to be knocked over. Whether to get out of the way or not depends on a prescriptive commitment lodged in the reasons you have for choosing either course of action.

In Hare's view, moral terms such as 'good' and 'ought' commit those who use them to regarding prescriptions as universalizable, that is, as applying to everyone in any relevantly similar situation. The caveat is that the judgments expressing the prescription must themselves contain only universal terms – that is, they must not be indexed to particular agents. This is because the same action performed by different agents may invite different evaluations according to circumstances. Suppose Jones trips up Smith as Smith is running past him. Jones will be doing wrong by tripping up Smith in order to prevent him winning a race, but Jones will be doing right by tripping up Smith as Smith tries to escape with stolen goods.

As always, the question arises: 'How do we judge which choices to make, which prescriptions to universalize?' Hare's answer is a utilitarian one: the ones which in the given circumstances will satisfy the preferences of the majority of those involved.

An aspect of Hare's theory that it shares with other non-cognitivist views is that it regards questions about the objectivity of values as spurious. Hare says he has never met anyone who knows what the question 'Are values objective?' means. When people disagree about values, they are not contradicting one another, they are negating each other's opinions, which is just what claiming that someone else is wrong comes down to. His main argument is this: consider two worlds, in one of which there are objective moral values and in the other of which there are none (for the sake of the example you could imagine that the second world once had them but they have been annihilated). People will continue to talk and behave just the same in both worlds; there is no difference between them. So the idea of 'objective values' does not work; it is empty.

Even someone who agrees with Hare that there are no objective values can think that the two-worlds argument does not work, on the grounds that there is a big difference between what the inhabitants of the different worlds take to explain their value-judgments – why they make them, where they come from – let alone what supports or justifies them, if anything does. Critics also say that his theory leaves out almost everything that makes a moral theory a *substantive* one. A universalizability requirement should itself identify the moral grounds for why the principle it embodies should apply in all relevantly similar cases. Moreover, deciding on what makes relevantly similar cases *relevantly similar* also requires a grasp of what makes them *morally* so.

The view that there are no objective values constitutes the base-note of ethics in Analytic philosophy since the rejection of Moore's intuitionism. The first sentence of J. L. Mackie's *Ethics: Inventing Right and Wrong* (1977) says exactly that: 'There are no objective values.' The title of his book tells us where our non-objective values come from: we invent them. His book was galvanizing because, although the problem of how we think of values and how we justify our value-judgments was of course familiar, his discussion gave a handle to sharper ways of articulating and debating non-cognitivist and cognitivist viewpoints, the debate shifting from questions exclusively about metaphysics – the existence or non-existence of values independently of thought – to questions about whether moral discourse is 'truth-apt', that is, capable of truth-value. Cognitivists say it is, non-cognitivists say it is not. It might be thought that cognitivism and objectivism go hand in hand, but they only do so if the cognitivist is a moral realist also, that is, thinks there are mind-independent moral facts or properties which *make* moral judgments true or false. But a moral anti-realist or subjectivist can be a cognitivist too, in holding that propositions about attitudes or emotional responses are truth-apt; or she can hold an 'error theory', which says that propositions conveying moral judgments are indeed truth-apt, but are all false. This last is Mackie's view.

John Mackie (1917–81) was an Australian from Sydney. His Scottish-born father was a professor at Sydney University and a leading figure in education in New South Wales. His mother was a schoolteacher. After graduating from Sydney University as a prize-winner in philosophy Mackie went to Oxford, graduating just as the 'phoney war' period of the Second World War came to an end. He joined the army and served in the Middle East, afterwards teaching in New Zealand and Australia until returning to the United Kingdom in 1963 as professor at the then newly founded University of York, and afterwards at Oxford.

Mackie's reason for holding an 'error theory' about moral discourse is that it presupposes objective values – it refers to them, talks about them, asserts their presence or absence, assumes them – but because there are none, all such discourse is false. He then proceeds to set out how thinking and theorizing about ethics can be successful without having to presuppose objective values.

What Mackie means by 'objective values' is best exemplified, he says, by Plato's Forms, which give a 'dramatic picture of what objective values have to be'. In addition to existing in the way they do, they are also intrinsically action-directing; merely to be acquainted with them tells one how to act, no further motivation being required. But why should this be so? There could be objective values which are non-necessarily motivating; many people acknowledge that they know the right thing to do, but do not do it.

But the very idea of objective values does not, in any case, withstand investigation. Mackie gives two chief reasons for this. First, there are many and sometimes great differences in moral outlooks, and the differences are often intractable. The best explanation for this is that moral outlooks are associated with a way of life and culture, and cultures differ. It is implausible to think that one culture has correct or privileged access to objective moral values and others do not. He cites the example of cultures which differ in their views about marriage, one monogamous and the other polygamous. It is far more plausible to think that their opposite moral views are the result of cultural-historical factors than that one of them has it right and the other has it wrong about an objective truth of the matter.

Secondly, whatever objective values are supposed to be, they are decidedly 'queer' things, says Mackie. If we think of them metaphysically, we have to imagine them as a sort of property completely different from anything else in the universe. If we consider the matter epistemologically, we have to credit ourselves with a special faculty for detecting and tracking the presence of these queer things, a faculty quite different from those we employ in normal perception of the world. In short, it makes no sense to think that values are 'part of the fabric of the world'.

Critics respond to the first argument – the 'relativity argument' – by saying that moral differences of outlook might not really be as great as at first they appear. In a Western society one might honour and care for one's aged parents by buying them a cottage at the seaside, while in a traditional society one might do this by killing and eating them so that they continue to survive within oneself. The superficial differences are enormous, but express the same underlying principle.

The argument from queerness seems to be no argument at all. There are many things in the world that appear queer on first encounter merely because we are not familiar with them – kangaroos, many extremely weird-looking species of deep-sea fish, occurrences on the event horizon of a black hole, quantum entanglement – so merely being 'queer' relative to what is familiar is no argument that something does not (still less cannot) exist. More to the point is the problem of how, if objective values exist, we detect them. We can leave aside the point that the absence of a faculty for detecting X does not, without further argument, entail that X does not exist, because of course the moral objectivist thinks that we do detect X, and Mackie's question about how we do so is legitimate. We could make it plausible that we do so by citing the example of the entities and properties referred to in mathematics, which we encounter by reason. This thought might redound to Mackie's advantage, however, for in the case of mathematics agreement on axioms and rules will invariably produce agreement about the outcomes of their use. Such convergence is considerably less common in ethics.

Mackie says his view can be described as 'moral scepticism' or 'subjectivism', but this must be understood as a metaethical or 'second-order' position, not a normative or 'first-order' position, where differences and disputes about the good life will remain, but where there are still things that might be said of use to deciding how to achieve such a thing. He is frank in acknowledging that a good life consists in the 'effective pursuit of activities that [an individual] finds worthwhile' either intrinsically or as instrumentally benefiting himself or those he cares about; and this means that 'egoism and self-referential altruism will together characterise, to a large extent, both his actions and his motives.'

Egoism speaks for itself; we are naturally concerned with our own welfare and prospects. 'Self-referential altruism' captures the idea of what Hume described as 'confined generosity', the restriction of our concern to those who are close to us. Accepting these realities means accepting that there will therefore be competition and conflict between individuals and groups. These pragmatic views would, says Mackie, be obvious if it were not for the efforts by both religious and humanist traditions to urge the opposite view, that 'the good life for man is one of universal brotherly love and selfless pursuit of the general happiness,' which Mackie argues is impracticable and in any case implausible even as an ideal. But this can be tempered by the point that 'any possible, and certainly any desirable, human life is social,' and this means that cooperation is a significant value, with all it entails, not least its corollary that extreme individualism is not the answer to the implausibility of universalism.

It was mentioned at the outset that Aristotle, Hume, Kant and utilitarianism loom over ethical debate, but of course the general thrust of the outlooks they each influence is significantly different from the others. One can identify three species of outlook. One is *deontology*, a *rule-based ethics* which seeks to identify our moral duties and says we must obey them no matter what the consequences. Kant was a deontologist. The second is *consequentialism*, a *results-based ethics* which says the right thing to do is what will have the best consequences, however we identify these: 'maximising happiness (or "utility") for the majority' is the nub of the utilitarian version. The third is *virtue ethics*, a *person-centred ethics* which says that the fundamental ethical question is 'What sort of person should I be?' and therefore emphasizes moral character rather than acts or their consequences. The fountainhead of thinking about virtue ethics is Aristotle.

The first two views dominated philosophical ethics in the modern era, that is, from the time that ethical debate resumed in the eighteenth century after more than a millennium during which the dominance of Christianity had silenced discussion of moral principles – the divine-command morality of the scriptures being assumed, or claimed, to settle all matters of right and wrong and how to live. But in a seminal paper published in 1958, 'Modern Moral Philosophy', Elizabeth Anscombe (1919–2001) argued that both deontology and consequentialism assume a foundation for ethics in the concept of *obligation*, which makes no sense in the absence of a lawgiver which or who (such as the deity of religious morality) imposes it. A foundation for ethics must therefore be sought in a quite different place: in the concept of virtue.

Anscombe's paper is now regarded as the starting-gun for a renewed interest in virtue ethics, though in fact it mainly addresses the short-comings of deontology and consequentialism, especially the latter's permissive view that any action is acceptable if its anticipated outcomes benefit a majority. She also attacked the lack of clarity in concepts key to ethical theory, such as *desire, intention, action* and *pleasure*. Her recommendation is that philosophy should go back to Aristotle to think again about the human good, but that before doing so it should engage in a preparatory psychological clarification of these concepts.

Three concepts central to Aristotle's ethics, and therefore central to virtue ethics, are those of (a) virtue itself, which Aristotle called *arete* and which can be translated as 'excellence', especially 'excellence of character'; (b) 'practical wisdom', in Aristotle's Greek *phronesis*; and (c) flourishing or happiness, in Aristotle's Greek *eudaimonia*. Consider each in turn.

Virtues are character traits such as honesty, integrity, courage, prudence, kindness, a sense of justice, self-restraint or continence and the like. From these character traits flow the virtuous behaviour associated with them. A virtuous person keeps promises and honours obligations not because it is a duty to do so or because the consequences are preferable to those that follow from not doing so, but because she is a person of integrity.

Virtues are not all or nothing; some people are more honest than others, some more courageous than others. Being virtuous in one respect does not entail being virtuous in all; a courageous person might not be a kind person, or a continent one. However, in this case there is a danger that courage might in fact turn out to be cruel or rash, so the idea of the *unity of the virtues* becomes an attractive one.

This latter point is connected with the idea of practical wisdom, *phronesis*, which in contemporary terms can be thought of as sober good judgment of the kind you would expect to find in a sensible, reflective, mature person with experience of life. Aristotle indeed thought that experience and maturity are required for virtue, but clearly there can be young people with practical wisdom who accordingly can be courageous, kind, continent and the like.

For Aristotle *eudaimonia* attends the living of a virtuous life. The translations of this term into 'happiness' and 'flourishing' are unsatisfactory because dogs can be happy and forests can flourish, whereas *eudaimonia* is the achievement of a rational life, reason being the highest and most distinctive feature of humanity. Reason plays central roles in the other two species of ethics, of course; for Kant moral laws are rational laws, and for utilitarians judging how to act requires working out and anticipating consequences. In virtue ethics, however, it is not recognizing and obeying a principle or calculating an effect, but possessing practical wisdom, that enters constitutively into the good life. And the good life itself has a character, no doubt different in its details for each individual, but common in what it shares: the quality of *eudaimonia*.

One of the strengths of the virtue-ethics approach is that when one considers what is required for recognizing one's duties and seeing how to act in accordance with them, as deontology requires, or determining what rules to follow in the hope of maximizing utility, as the rule-utilitarian view requires (act utilitarianism only has one rule: 'maximize utility in this case'), it is necessary to apply thought, imagination and the lessons of experience – in short, *phronesis* – to do so. One can therefore cut out the theorizing about duties and consequences and see that cultivation and possession of the virtues which turn on *phronesis* is sufficient of itself. This rebuts the criticism, often directed at virtue ethics, that it focuses solely on the agent herself and not on what she does, thus addressing only the question of what kind of person one should *be* rather than any questions about what one should *do* when faced with a necessity to choose. As the insistence on *phronesis* shows, the account of what one *is* incorporates already an account of what one therefore typically *does*.

Leading figures in the development of virtue ethics included Philippa Foot (1920–2010) and Alasdair MacIntyre (b. 1929). The former once began a lecture by saying, 'In moral philosophy it is useful, I believe, to think about plants.' Her reason is that there is much in common between evaluating whether plants are healthy and flourishing and evaluating whether a human individual is so. The idea of a conceptual structure of evaluations plays its part; the underlying 'grammar' of talking about a healthy human being and a eudaimonic human being have much in common. It is part of human flourishing to be an effective practical reasoner, rather as it is an aspect of being a healthy human that one's knees and stomach are in good working order. Identifying virtues is in part a matter of recognizing what the 'way of going on' as a human being tells us. Think of the example of another species – wolves, say: wolves hunt in packs, and keep themselves going by doing so. A wolf which does not contribute to the hunt but helps to eat the prey is a freeloader, and therefore defective in the required kind of wolfishness. Analogously, part of the way humans 'go on' is by making and keeping contracts. The implication is that breaking contracts is a defective – non-virtuous – thing to do.

MacIntyre in *After Virtue* (1981) gives a communitarian twist to the idea of the virtues, arguing that the latter are constituted by the work they do in constituting communities. He characterizes virtues as dispositions which enable those who possess them to overcome barriers to learning more about themselves and the good, thus contributing to finding what is best both in what we do as human agents, and in life as a whole. But the social dimension of the virtues is integral to them: 'The virtues find their point and purpose . . . in sustaining those relationships necessary if the variety of goods internal to practices are to be achieved . . . goods . . . can only be discovered by entering into those relationships which constitute communities whose central bond is a shared vision of and understanding of goods.'

As a Roman Catholic (who had reconverted from atheism) acknowledging an affiliation with Thomism, it is natural for MacIntyre to attribute the shortcomings of deontology and consequentialism to their aspirations for secular rationality. He remarked that others, like Nietzsche, had rejected the idea of a moral rationality altogether because of that failure; in MacIntyre's view, an Aristotelian conception of 'goods of excellence' can supplement what is lacking in them.

The upsurge of debate about virtue ethics made proponents of deontology and consequentialism consider how its ideas might be addressed, or incorporated, in their own approaches. This now necessitates distinguishing between virtue ethics and 'virtue theory', where the latter incorporates discussion of virtues in all three approaches.

The fastest-growing arena of ethical debate in the second half of the twentieth century has been *applied ethics*. It is the effort to engage practically with ethical dilemmas thrown up by real life – abortion, same-sex marriage, gun control, stem-cell research, designer babies, sexual behaviour, sex and gender identities, discrimination, principles of distribution of scarce resources, religious freedom, physician-assisted suicide and euthanasia, freedom of expression, animal rights, humanitarian aid, laws of war: the list of connoted areas of debate, often heated and divisive, is long. Business ethics and biomedical ethics have been prominent areas in its development. It is an arena where metaethical and normative considerations mesh, often urgently; and one can see how the different approaches to ethical theory each provide resources – for example, reflective business people might ask themselves what kind of corporation they wish to run, that is, what *ethos* or character they wish to have as an entity. They might be faced with a problem whose urgent solution obliges them to consider what would be the outcome of different courses of action, so that they can choose the optimal one. The professional body they subscribe to might prescribe certain duties that members must obey if they wish to continue to be accredited by it. Virtue ethics, consequentialism and deontological considerations are respectively in play – not all such cases might necessarily be *ethical* cases, to be sure, but one can imagine circumstances in which they might be.

POLITICAL PHILOSOPHY

Almost every account one reads of political philosophy in the twentieth-century Analytic tradition – now including this one – begins by reporting the famous remark, made in 1956 by Peter Laslett in the Introduction to a collection of papers he edited, entitled *Philosophy, Politics and Society*, that 'political philosophy is dead.' Writing six years later in the successor volume to that collection, Isaiah Berlin, although rejecting Laslett's view, nevertheless claimed that the twentieth century had produced 'no commanding work of political philosophy'. Yet in the same volume there appeared a reprint of John Rawls' essay 'Justice as Fairness', indicating that proof would soon arrive that Berlin's claim was premature; for in the following decade the century's great classics of Analytic political philosophy appeared:

Rawls' *A Theory of Justice* (1971) and Robert Nozick's *Anarchy, State and Utopia* (1974).

Laslett said that the grand tradition of English political thought from Hobbes to Bosanquet might have been brought to an end by the horrors of the twentieth century, whose wars and atrocities had made politics seem too serious a matter to be left to philosophers. This is an odd view, given that it was turmoil that had prompted Hobbes and Locke (and before them Machiavelli) to write about political ideas. Moreover, the twentieth century's wars and atrocities had prompted Karl Popper to write his *Open Society and its Enemies* (1946), which he described as his contribution to the war effort, but it did not much engage the attention of philosophers. And even as Laslett offered his gloomy pronouncement, so Isaiah Berlin, John Rawls and Michael Oakeshott were writing, and on the continent Hannah Arendt, Louis Althusser, Georg Lukács and members of the Frankfurt School were active but practically invisible to their Anglophone contemporaries.

One reason offered for the temporary marginalization of political *philosophy* in the Analytic tradition was the rise of political *science*. Whereas political philosophy concerns itself with the fundamental concepts of politics – authority, justice, liberty, rights, equality, democracy and totalitarianism, and analysis of particular political orientations such as socialism, Fascism, conservatism, liberalism and Marxism – political science is about government, states, political parties, institutions, citizenship, systems of power, control and policing, and the distribution of economic and social resources. Political philosophy examines principles and justifications, and is speculative, critical and evaluatory; political science examines practices and structures, and it is descriptive and empirical. The thought is that the Positivistic turn in philosophy, with its respect for the methods of science, made some find the empirical task of describing institutions and practices more congenial than the harder and messier task of seeking principles and justifications for them.

But as events proved, political philosophy was not dead; and the contributions made especially by Rawls and Nozick are a permanent contribution to the grand tradition Laslett thought he was mourning.

John Rawls (1921–2002) was born in Baltimore where his father was a lawyer and his mother, Anna Abell Stump Rawls, was an activist for female suffrage. She and her fellow-suffragists had seen the Nineteenth Amendment to the US Constitution, passed in August 1920, six months before Rawls' birth, granting all American women the right to vote. As president of her local chapter of the League of Women Voters she remained active in the campaign to get an Equal Rights Amendment granting women equality with men in all social and economic respects. At this time of writing nearly a century later, the ERA has still not been passed. Her interests undoubtedly had an effect on Rawls' interests; there would seem no more natural a progression from her activism to the subject of Rawls' theorizing, which was motivated by a desire to formulate a genuinely practical political theory.

In childhood Rawls lost two of his four brothers to illnesses from which he had suffered and which, he claimed, they had caught from him. After graduating from Princeton in 1943 he joined the army and served in the Pacific as an infantryman, suffering significant trauma and losing his religious faith because of his experiences there. After the war he returned to Princeton for his PhD, and then had a spell at Oxford on a Fulbright Scholarship, attending discussions with Isaiah Berlin, Herbert Hart and Stuart Hampshire. After a short time on the faculty at Cornell University he went to Harvard and remained there for the rest of his career.

Rawls opposed American military involvement in Vietnam. He was a reserved individual with a stutter, who disliked public exposure, and therefore he did not become an overt campaigner; but his thinking about politics was motivated by a strong desire to find ways in which political conflict can be avoided or managed, in which reconciliation can be achieved when it occurs, and in which the best *reasonably* possible political order can be devised.

These last remarks indicate Rawls' aims in offering a contribution to debate about a central concern for liberal democratic thinking: the apparent inconsistency between liberty and equality. Equality can be achieved only if liberty is restricted; liberty results in inequalities because the differences between people in starting point, talent, energy and luck quickly produce them. Isaiah Berlin, in line with his general view of 'value pluralism', held that liberty and equality are irredeemably in conflict. Rawls was more optimistic, believing that a fair society could accommodate citizens who were both individually free and in germane respects equal. His conception of 'reflective equilibrium' has a role here; it is what is arrived at when deliberation about principles and values brings them into a more coherent relationship with each other.

The first question Rawls addressed was one of method: how is one to approach the task of formulating a conception of justice that will be recognized as reasonable by any reflective citizen? His answer is to generalize the idea of a 'social contract' as put forward by Locke, Rousseau and Kant, by asking what kind of socio-political arrangement people would choose to accept if, as it were before being born, they could do so. Imagine them behind a 'veil of ignorance' regarding what they will be, knowing nothing about their future – what social class they will occupy, how intelligent, gifted or healthy they will be, what kind of society it is, nor what they might come to have in the way of their own values, beliefs and aims. They will know only that 'circumstances of justice' apply and that the situation will be one of moderate scarcity of resources, so that the inhabitants' beliefs about what is morally and politically right will determine the distribution of those resources.

However, the denizens of the 'original position' behind their veil of ignorance will not be entirely bereft of help in choosing what kind of society it should be, for they will have a 'thin theory of the good' that tells them they would rather have more than less of a certain range of 'primary social goods', these being 'things which it is supposed a rational man wants whatever else he wants', namely, 'rights and liberties, opportunities and powers, income and wealth [and] a sense of one's own worth'. Rawls argues that people behind the veil of ignorance would apply what is known as a 'maximin' strategy for choosing what kind of society it should be, this being a strategy in game theory that makes the *most* of the *least* that can be reliably anticipated in a given situation. On this basis, he says, people in the original position would choose to see the following two principles of justice in operation: first, that each member of society should have an equal right to the greatest degree of basic liberty compatible with everyone else's basic liberty, and second, that inequalities in society should be so arranged that they provide the greatest benefit possible to the least advantaged, and should not prevent offices and positions from being open to everyone under conditions of 'fair equality of opportunity'. The first principle has priority over the second, and 'fair equality of opportunity' has priority over ensuring that the least advantaged have the best deal possible for them in their circumstances.

Rawls' governing idea, that justice is *fairness*, postulates a society whose institutions and structures have a 'basic structure' that ensures a distribution of social goods and burdens to which reflective citizens will consent and in which they will cooperate. It is an assumption of his view that the society is reasonably well favoured – that is, is not wracked by war or suffering from drought and famine. He also assumes that arbitrary advantages – being born with talents or into a rich family – do not merit a larger share of the distribution; the distribution has to be equal unless everyone would benefit from an unequal distribution.

A society would not be just if it ignored future generations and consumed all its resources so that nothing is left for those who come afterwards. Accordingly, in the 'original position' a choice would be made to agree to a 'just savings' principle, settling what each generation must conserve for the use of future generations.

The idea of the 'original position' allows Rawls to work through a set of steps that its occupants would take as they learned increasingly more about the society they are to occupy, graduating from the most general principles to more specific ways of ensuring the maximum compatibility of liberty and equality, and in particular whether the society they envisage would be enduring. The aim is to arrive at a *stable* conception of justice that will command assent because it is 'perspicuous to our reason [and] congruent with our good'. So a comparison would be offered between the principles identified and utilitarian principles aimed either at maximizing benefit for the largest number – which would at least mean ignoring a requirement to do the best one can for the worst off – or achieving the highest average utility for all – which would keep in play a degree of consideration for the least advantaged, but would not achieve the best possible distribution of goods and burdens. Rawls claims that citizens would prefer the 'veil of ignorance' principles to utilitarian ones because the maximin rule they rest on is more productive of fairness than are other systems of distribution.

Rawls' work generated an enormous response of both elaboration and criticism; political philosophy since 1971 might be said to be shaped almost exclusively by it. Every step in his argument lies at the centre of a debate: the idea of the 'original position', the treatment of the vexed question of differences in natural abilities and starting points as barriers to equality, the individual principles of justice themselves, and more. To focus on just one – but very important – target of the criticisms, consider the point about the 'thin conception of the good' with which Rawls had to equip the denizens of the original position. The veil of ignorance is designed to constrain the reasoning of the denizens to impartial considerations, which would not be possible if they knew about (say) their race, sex or religious affiliation in advance. The conception they have of the good has to be 'thin' because if it were 'thickened' by being some particular theory of the good – Christian, Muslim or humanist, say – then the outcome would be biased in that direction, not automatically commanding the assent and respect of all. But what is the guarantee that the thin conception will achieve this latter desideratum? Recall that it consists in the view that having more rather than less of a certain range of 'primary social goods' is desirable, these being 'things which it is supposed a rational man wants whatever else he wants', namely, 'rights and liberties, opportunities and powers, income and wealth [and] a sense of one's own worth'. Is that what (every) rational man (man?) wants? These are goods on which a high value is placed in the outlook of *liberal individualism*, certainly, but to credit the denizens of the original position with this conception of the good is to beg the question against the kind of society they would wish to live in; they are being given precisely the values that would guarantee that choice.

This criticism adds to others aimed at the concept of an original position. A powerful one is that occupants of the original position are envisaged not merely as equal, but in effect as identical; they are all in exactly the same boat, with the same information or lack of it, the same thin theory of the good, and the same reasoning powers. As one critic (Brian Barry) put it, 'faced with identical information and reasoning in an identical fashion, they arrive at identical conclusions. We might as well talk of computers having the same programme and fed the same input reaching an agreement.' How can a form of social contract emerge from a situation in which there is nothing to bargain about? The driving consideration would be to protect oneself as much as possible in case one finds oneself at the bottom of the heap in the coming society. Indeed this suggests the reason for the asymmetry in Rawls' view that whereas arbitrary advantages provide no justification for proportionate but therefore unequal shares in any distribution, arbitrary *disadvantages* do; and this, though morally unimpeachable, is not by itself obviously a principle of justice – though it might be one of fairness.

Robert Nozick's *Anarchy, State and Utopia* (1974) stands at a point on a political spectrum rather far from the point at which Rawls stands. Whereas Rawls' *A Theory of Justice* places him firmly in the liberal tradition, Nozick describes the viewpoint of his book as libertarian, a viewpoint on the further right of politics which Nozick himself acknowledges is 'apparently callous' (without justifying the 'apparently'). He says that he arrived at this view, having travelled to it from a more liberal standpoint, as a result of considering the arguments for it: this at least is a hopeful claim, seeming to rebut Hume's view that it is emotion only, and never reason, that can motivate our choices. But there is a special interest in Nozick's remark to this effect, given that in his student days he was a member of the Socialist Party, and in a later work, *The Examined Life* (1989), he indicated areas where the argument of *Anarchy* 'went wrong' and took an 'unduly narrow view' because it left out questions of 'social solidarity and humane concern for others'. These temperings of the view can be borne in mind, though Nozick self-identified as a libertarian to the end.

Robert Nozick (1938–2002) was born in New York to Russian Jewish immigrant parents. He attended schools near his home in Brooklyn, and Columbia University for his undergraduate studies. He took his PhD at Princeton and spent a year at Oxford afterwards on a Fulbright Scholarship. By his own account it was at Princeton that he first encountered arguments in defence of capitalism, in the writings of Friedrich Hayek and Milton Friedman, and in conversation with economist Murray Rothbard. He began by rejecting the arguments, later coming to think, as he said in a *Forbes* magazine interview in 1975, 'Well, yes, the arguments are right, capitalism is the best system, but only bad people would think so. Then, at some point, my mind and heart were in unison.' A feature of this remark, and what it portends, prompts a question. Capitalism and libertarianism are not necessarily linked; there are forms of capitalism which seek to temper the wind to the shorn lamb with welfare provisions and redistributionist state intervention ('welfare capitalism'); there are forms that mix state and private participation in the economy. Why go all the way from accepting arguments for capitalism to libertarianism, which is a particular view about the relationship between the state and the individual?

One of Nozick's main motives for setting out his libertarian views was to combat the ideas of Rawls, by then his colleague at Harvard. The burden of his argument is set out with clarity and succinctness in the preface to *Anarchy, State and Utopia*. It is that 'Individuals have rights, and there are things no person or group may do to them (without violating their rights).' The rights are so strong that they force consideration of the limits of state power relative to individuals. Nozick accordingly focuses on the question of the legitimacy of the state. His conclusion is also clearly and succinctly stated in the preface; it is that 'a minimal state, limited to the narrow functions of protection against force, theft, fraud, enforcement of contracts, and so on, is justified; that any more extensive state will violate persons' rights not to be forced to do certain things and is unjustified; and that the minimal state is inspiring as well as right.' This echoes the classic nineteenth-century 'night watchman' theory of the state, and he wittily summed up one aspect of it by saying that no government has the right to 'forbid capitalistic acts between consenting adults'.

Two implications of these points, Nozick says, are that 'the state may not use its coercive apparatus for the purpose of getting some citizens to aid others, or in order to prohibit activities to people for their *own* good or protection.' The libertarian aspect of the view lies in these implications. Presumably the idea of taxing individuals enough to provide welfare is an example of the state coercing its citizens to aid others; certainly laws prohibiting recreational drugs and requiring the wearing of motorbike helmets are examples of the state legislating for people's good on their behalf.

The 'strong rights' Nozick claims individuals have are those of the state of nature, much as envisaged by Locke. They predate any social contract or the existence of any institutions, and are inviolable, so that the advent of a contract or of institutions cannot abrogate or even limit them. He acknowledges that he offers no grounds for saying what he does about these rights, although his argument against the idea that individuals can bear some costs in the interest of an overall social good might go some way to providing a justification; for he there says that there is no social entity ('society') with interests which would be served by individuals bearing costs; there are only those individuals. To ask an individual to bear a cost on behalf of society is nothing more than to use that individual to benefit other individuals; invocations of 'society' are a fig leaf for that. 'There is no justified sacrifice of some of us for others.'

Individuals are separate persons seeking their own good in their own way, says Nozick, and he sees their separateness as part of the reason for the inviolability of their fundamental rights. They are, in Kant's terminology, 'ends in themselves', and it is presumably also because Nozick is sympathetic to a view he cites from earlier political theorists, about people 'having property in themselves and their labour'.

The minimalist state Nozick envisages is very like a business corporation, not least in that it does not finance itself by imposing taxes. This prompts the interesting thought that a state might finance itself by selling its services to its citizens. And this indeed is one way of interpreting Nozick's 'invisible hand' suggestion about how the state comes into existence in the first place. People in the state of nature will band together to protect themselves from depredations, and there will eventually emerge a dominant protection agency – the state – from this self-organizing process. This however poses a problem that Nozick has to meet from, as it were, the other side of his case: the anarchist challenge. Why should there be any form of state at all? Anarchists claim that a state uses its monopoly of coercive power to punish those who challenge its monopoly. When the state uses its coercive power to oblige some to help others, as it does for example through taxation, it thereby violates their fundamental rights. Nozick's response is to say that the justification for the state's existence, which is the protection it gives its citizens against depredations, of itself draws the limits of its powers. One might say that his 'Utopia' – which he claims is inspirational as well as legitimate – in ensuring peace by protecting those inviolable rights, *ipso facto* implies protection from the violation of them by itself.

One standard criticism of minimalist theories of the state is that they make no provision for redistributive justice. Nozick attacks the implicit idea that there is an agency that collects and then equitably hands out shares of social and economic goods. Instead he proposes what he calls 'justice in holdings'. Consider Locke's idea of coming to own something, not owned by anyone else, by mixing one's labour with it. This is a just acquisition. Coming to own something by a just transfer – buying something from someone who legitimately owns that thing and who sells it voluntarily – is another form. A third form is by rectification of past injustices in either acquisition or transfer, as with having stolen works of art or other property restored to their rightful owners, as with victims of Nazism. Coming to own something by any of these three means gives one entitlement to it. If everyone has what he is entitled to, the distribution of holdings in the state is just. Nozick uses the example of a basketball player who becomes vastly richer than anyone else because everyone else frequently and voluntarily pays small sums to see him play. Imagine that, at the start of his career, everyone has exactly the same amount of money. Presumably that is a just arrangement. Over the course of his career the basketball player becomes vastly richer, quite legitimately. Has the distribution become unjust? Clearly not, Nozick says.

What Nozick leaves out of this picture is the case of acquisition of holdings by inheritance; is that just or unjust? There is the question of what difference is made by differentials in holdings – the advantages they provide in health care, education and opportunities. And might not natural advantages such as intelligence, good looks, athletic skill, be regarded as a kind of holdings violating any idea of entitlement and what follows from it?

Nozick's defence of a libertarian view gave much comfort to political conservatives, and it is what he is best known for. But he also made major contributions in theory of knowledge and ethics, principally set out in his other major book, *Philosophical Explanations* (1981).

FEMINIST PHILOSOPHY

Political philosophy is the arena where, apart from theory of knowledge, feminist thinking has had most impact. There is no single school of thought in political feminism, which ranges widely across all possibilities from Marxism through liberalism to libertarianism. Outside Analytic philosophy there are poststructuralist and psychoanalytic strands of feminist theory, sharing with the Anglophone debate the same fundamental commitment, namely, challenging the silencing of women's voices, the neglect of feminist perspectives, and the social, political and economic subordination of women themselves. Differences of view about the nature of the social and political subordination and how to end it constitute the main substance of the discussion in feminist political theory.

It might be thought that because concepts of justice and equality are central targets of enquiry in political philosophy there is no need for a particular feminist approach. An immediate point is that because almost all debate about these concepts has been conducted by men in the setting of a male-dominated world, there is a serious question about whether their understanding of these concepts, and in particular what it is like to live in circumstances in which they do not apply, can fully accommodate women's perspectives on them. Male discussions assume that their male perspective is gender-neutral, and that the field of application of such concepts is the public domain. Neither assumption allows for the possibility that there are considerations immediately excluded by them.

Consider the following. In discussions of equality, how often do they begin by noting that gender-*inequality* is built into the very fabric of the social and economic order by the way that the world of work is structured? A putatively gender-neutral advertisement for a job assumes that applicants will be able to work from 9 a.m. to 5 p.m. Monday to Friday for forty-eight weeks of the year. That immediately imposes discriminatory difficulties and costs on any woman with children of school age or less. The assumption that lies behind the way the working week is structured is a traditional masculist one that work and public life are the domain of men, while the private domestic sphere is the domain of women. When women work under these arrangements, what is available is too often part-time and low-paid; the discriminatory effects ramify.

In discussions of justice, the starting assumption is that the chief point to consider is how distributions of social and economic goods should be made. One feminist approach is to ask whether, in connection with the concerns that discussions of justice address, the concept of *justice* is the right one to use; perhaps notions of *need* and *care* are more fundamental. For example: the demand that the contributions made to individual and social welfare by women (or anyone) in the domestic sphere should be justly rewarded has never been met, on the grounds that if domestic labour and childcare were properly costed, 'the economy' would not be able to bear the burden. The status of domestic labour is commensurate with the refusal even to countenance the idea of wages for it, unless it is *other* people's houses and children that are being cared for.

This shows that the *family* is one of the key zones of concern about equality and justice, and although Rawls recognized this, he did so from the external, public perspective in which a family is a social unit, rather than an internal private point of view in which a family is itself a social structure with complexity. In liberal theory, problems women face regarding equality, liberty and opportunity are masked by its concern for a vision of private family life which, as Alison Jaggar points out, 'encompasses and protects the personal intimacies of the home, the family, marriage, motherhood, procreation, and child rearing' in ways that militate against the rights and needs of women.

Moreover, treating the family as a repository for those aspects of life – personal bodily and emotional needs; too messy and difficult to regiment, unlike train timetables and troop movements – which are unsuited to a view of what is 'really important' (namely, the public domain's requirement for reason, dispassion, judgment, the management of general interests) contributes to the devaluing of what happens in the family setting, and therefore promotes a commensurate relegation of women's status. Almost everything about the distinction drawn between the public and private spheres instantiates powerful traditional views about masculine and feminine roles, to the detriment of the autonomy and equality of opportunity of women. While the governing conception of society is predicated on this structure, talk of equality and justice will continue to be strongly skewed by it.

These remarks merely hint at the importance and extent of one aspect of feminist philosophy, which ranges more widely than the political. One significant example is the question of gender bias in theorizing about the nature of knowledge. An important line of thinking in this regard invokes the idea of 'situated knowledge', that is, knowledge whose acquisition and justification are shaped by the circumstances of the knowing subject. It is readily appreciated how a marginalized position in the endeavour to acquire and apply knowledge disadvantages a subject in relation to those accorded a more privileged place in that endeavour; this has been and remains the circumstance of women – in the past denied an education, denied access to laboratories and medical schools, denied entry to knowledge-based professions, denied entry to forums where ideas are broached and discussed: the list is long.

On the face of it this might seem to justify including consideration of feminist perspectives *wholly* under the rubric of 'feminist political philosophy', because so many of the deficits suffered by women in relation to getting and using knowledge are the result of social, political and economic subordinations. These subordinations consist in women not only being excluded from education, but being treated as having inferior intellects and as handicapped by the dominance of their emotions and bodily enslavement to hormones, pregnancy and physical weakness generally – a long-standing male view therefore having it that women are formed only to serve the interests of men and children, and are interested chiefly in domestic matters or social trivia such as fashion and gossip.

These denigratory views have been the standard ground for refusing women the opportunity not only to share the epistemic endeavours of men, but to identify and articulate the ways in which masculist approaches to epistemology leave out of account perspectives that feminist approaches bring. For example, how the world is experienced depends upon a knowing subject's embodied encounter with it; how one interacts with other people morally and in interpreting their intentional states is shaped by who and what one is; therefore the experiences, style of thought and emotional responses brought by a subject to the matter of acquiring and evaluating information have to be taken as relevant. On the basis of what is describable as the *gendered* nature of traits, behaviour, language, identity and experience, it is plausible to think that subjectivities differ in ways sufficiently significant for it to be a matter of importance how the task of epistemology should be understood in light of them, paralleling the importance of enriching political and moral theory with feminist perspectives. No theory of knowledge can leave aside these considerations, any more than a political philosophy can proceed as if all denizens of a political society share the same broadly masculine needs and interests.

Feminist philosophy arose contemporaneously with the increasing influence of social and political feminism in the second half of the twentieth century, and is set to be a major component of all future thinking. What compels the interest in feminist epistemology and value theory is the achievement of feminist political theory in tackling the fundamental barrier to both. This is one of the most significant developments in philosophy in the later part of the twentieth century. The auguries suggest that feminist perspectives will have a position of fundamental importance in the history of twenty-first-century philosophy when it comes to be written.

No history of twentieth-century Analytic philosophy can fail to mention at least some of the names of other significant figures, in addition to those discussed in the main text above; a more copious student of the period and the tradition would and should investigate them. The following is a very incomplete list and in no particular order.

Two who made significant contributions in philosophy of language, philosophical logic and ethics are Simon Blackburn and John McDowell. In those fields also, David Wiggins; in the philosophy of language, philosophical logic and theory of knowledge, Timothy Williamson and Christopher Peacocke. In moral philosophy and the history of philosophy, Bernard Williams. In moral, legal and political philosophy, Ronald Dworkin. In political philosophy, Gerald 'Jerry' Cohen. In the philosophy of language, philosophy of mind and epistemology, Wilfrid Sellars. In the philosophy of language and philosophical logic, Crispin Wright.

In moral and political philosophy, Thomas 'Tim' Scanlon. In philosophy of language and mind, Robert Brandom. In philosophy of language, mathematics, epistemology, ethics and aesthetics, David Lewis. In philosophy of mind, Jerry Fodor. Martha Nussbaum in social, moral and legal philosophy. Peter Singer in ethics. Derek Parfit in moral philosophy and aspects of metaphysics. In central areas of Analytic philosophy but later as a critic of it, Richard Rorty. One could easily make a longer list. Future short lists might be different from this one; but with this one at the time of writing, few would disagree.

Continental Philosophy

The label 'Continental philosophy' – inaccurate, as mentioned at the beginning of this part, but established by usage – is an umbrella term for a collection of widely different pursuits: phenomenology, existentialism, hermeneutics, critical theory, psychoanalysis, structuralism, poststructuralism, deconstruction, Marxism, conceptual archaeology and approaches to science, mind, life and feminist issues using the resources of various of the preceding movements of thought.

The major figures of Continental philosophy in the first half of the twentieth century, Husserl, Heidegger, Merleau-Ponty and Sartre, engage in what Analytic philosophers would regard as recognizable philosophy. The methodology employed is continuous with that of Kant and Hegel, the latter providing by far the most significant presence as background. This marks the chief point of divergence from Analytic philosophy, whose adoption of approaches and interests prompted by logic and a respectful attitude to science led to the targeting of a set of topics which, increasingly over time, parted company with those of interest to Continental philosophers, a situation that grew more starkly obvious in the century's second half.

In this latter period the work of some of those whose names stand out – Gadamer, Deleuze, Derrida, Ricoeur, Foucault, but not Habermas – becomes less recognizable as philosophy from the Analytic standpoint, and these writers diverge as widely from one another in their concerns as they do from Analytic philosophers. The question whether what some of these writers do is 'philosophy' or not – some say not, some say it is an expansion of what philosophy is – may be neither here nor there, though for the writer of a history of philosophy it raises questions about who to include and who to exclude given that the work in hand is specifically a history of *philosophy*. How I answer this appears below. It is however true that some of these figures *practise a method* rather than *expound and justify a view*, this latter being a standard procedure in Analytic philosophy – though of course there are views embedded in the methods practised, for no human proceeding is without its assumptions and (even if indirect) aims.

The main reason that so little attention is paid to Continental philosophy by Analytic philosophers has to be frankly acknowledged. It is that the latter are impatient with (at best; at worst, contemptuous of) – and here I will illustrate the point – what they see as the ab/uses and con/fusions of language which, in its unexplained neologizing, its deliberate ambiguity and its overloading, attenuating or deflating of meanings (the use of the virgule is a common device, as above; a form of 'phallus/y'?) seems impressionistic and slippery, the unclarity a mask for unclarity of thought, or worse, a pretence of profundity. Some Continental writers will argue that the problem *is* language and these tricks are intended to display the fact. There is an argument to be had here, out in the open: if conceptual frameworks are misleading because of concealed agendas, or biasing roots or assumptions – concealed even to those who seek to criticize them, perhaps – this is a fact of great importance which requires clarification and correction. If all that is available as remedy is teasing and play, punning and feinting, we would be in a poor case. If the claim is that language (and therefore the thought we seek to transmit by its means) is irreducibly and irremediably misleading, imprecise, clogged beyond recall with the corpses of past beliefs and assumptions, then an announcement to that effect might seem to be a one-time affair – though this is something of a Cretan point: if the claim is true, we have reason not to accept it!*

The quarrel between the Analytic and Continental philosophical traditions is itself a topic for philosophical as well as sociological and historical reflection. Examples of speciation in nature show that as divides grow wider so all ways back come to be blocked. In one way that does not matter; let a hundred flowers bloom. In another it is unfortunate given that, as we shall see, there is matter of great philosophical interest and importance in some of what goes under the name of Continental philosophy.

Because of the diversity of topics under this label, and because it

---

* The allusion is to the Cretan Paradox or Paradox of the Liar: a Cretan says, 'All Cretans are liars,' which if true is false.

is not easy in all cases to give a clear and concise account of their principal points, I shall as with the section on Analytic philosophy proceed by attending sometimes to thinkers and sometimes to themes.

HUSSERL (1859–1938)

Edmund Husserl is the originator of 'phenomenology', the study of the fundamental nature of subjective consciousness and experience, and a major influence on the next three philosophers discussed here.

Born in Prossnitz in Moravia, then part of the Austro-Hungarian Empire, to a middle-class Jewish family, Husserl early displayed a talent for mathematics, and went to the University of Leipzig to study it along with physics and astronomy. Although he attended Wilhelm Wundt's lectures there, the more significant influence on him was his friendship with the future first President of Czechoslovakia, Thomas Masaryk, a keen student of philosophy who encouraged Husserl to read the British empiricists. Masaryk also persuaded him to convert to Protestant Christianity. After moving to the University of Berlin Husserl was taught by the mathematician Karl Weierstrass, who awoke his interest in the foundations of mathematics and introduced him to the work of Bernard Bolzano (1781–1848) whose *Theory of Science* (1837) planted a number of ideas that bore fruit in Husserl's own thinking later.

For his doctorate Husserl went to Vienna, writing on calculus but attending the lectures of Franz Brentano on psychology. At Halle University the subject of his habilitation thesis indicated the change Brentano had wrought; it was 'On the Concept of Number: Psychological Analyses'. The mathematician who invented set theory, Georg Cantor, was one of his examiners. Husserl was given a post as lecturer in philosophy at Halle in 1887, and four years later published his first book, a development of his thesis: *Philosophy of Arithmetic: Psychological and Logical Investigations*.

Gottlob Frege's review of this book appears to have been a turning point for Husserl. Frege criticized him for treating words, concepts and objects all as 'ideas' but with different definitions of 'idea' in different contexts; treating 'objects' sometimes as subjective and sometimes not; claiming that abstract concepts have a psychological origin; and claiming that two thoughts can remain numerically distinct when all the properties that differentiated them have been stripped away. Whether or not this is what made Husserl become as firmly anti-psychologistic as Frege himself thereafter, that is anyway what happened.

In 1901, shortly after the first volume of his *Logical Investigations* had appeared, Husserl moved to a post at what was then the world's leading centre of mathematical research, the University of Göttingen. He had Felix Klein and David Hilbert as colleagues, and Ernst Zermelo, Paul Bernays and Hermann Weyl among his students. The last of these, inspired by Husserl, sought to incorporate phenomenological themes into his work on physics. Over the next three decades, first at Göttingen and then at Freiburg, Husserl's ideas took their distinctive evolving path, especially from 1905 onwards when he became convinced that phenomenology has to be a form of transcendental idealism in the Kantian sense. Because his views developed over time the following sketch focuses on the concepts most associated with them.*

In ordinary experience and in our naturalistic, scientific investigations of the world, we are conscious of things and states-of-affairs outside us and indeed within us – an itch, a pain, a hunger pang. This is the 'natural attitude'. Phenomenology does not investigate these matters. It investigates *consciousness* itself. To focus just on the nature of consciousness requires a 'reduction', a withdrawing of attention from anything other than consciousness itself so that only it is under examination. One does this by the *epoche* or suspension of attention to everything that is not consciousness itself, by 'bracketing' all considerations of the representational content of consciousness or what it is related to. 'Bracketing' is not a denial of the reality of things, but a way of holding them in abeyance so that they do not distract attention from the invariant features of consciousness, which is what the phenomenological reduction is seeking to make visible. This marks a sharp distinction between psychology as an empirical science from phenomenology as a 'pure' science in the Kantian sense, that is, which addresses only the nature and conditions of consciousness as such, shrived of any considerations of what it represents or connects with.

In perception our gaze is directed outwards, on to things. In reflection we gaze inwards, at the experience itself: 'we grasp the subjective lived-experience in which [things] become "conscious" to us.' Husserl employs Brentano's notion of 'intentionality' to describe the character of that

---

* An encapsulation by Husserl himself is found in his article on phenomenology for the *Encyclopaedia Britannica* (1927), originally to have been written in collaboration with Heidegger.

'lived-experience' or consciousness. We focus on the intentional character of consciousness – not on what acts of consciousness intend beyond themselves – by means of the reduction and *epoche*. But this is not the final step. To get at the fundamental structure of consciousness itself another reduction, the 'eidetic' (*eidos* means essence) reduction, is required. This reveals the *a priori* basis of pure lived-experience, its essence, the invariant and necessary conditions that constitute consciousness as such. A technique aimed at achieving this is 'imaginary variation', permutating possible variations of the experience to uncover what has to stay the same throughout the variations. Inspection of the intentional character of consciousness shows that the activity or *noesis* of consciousness is directed upon the content of the activity, the *noema* – again: this is not anything other than the consciousness itself; the normal and putatively external objects of intending have been bracketed. Imaginary variation might accordingly be construed as noesis acting on the noema.

What the phenomenological method reveals, according to Husserl, is that whereas from the 'natural attitude' the world seems to be given and pre-existent, when we reverse our gaze and look at our experience itself we see that the world is present 'for us', that is, is related to the subjectivity of consciousness. It helps to recall Kant's thesis that the way the world appears to us is a function of the way we experience it; in his view our sensory modalities and our *a priori* apparatus of concepts shape and organize the raw data of experience into a world. For Husserl the question to be answered is, How is it possible that a world conceived as independent has its origin 'in us'?*

Problems for the project soon enough became apparent. How is intersubjectivity possible if the fundamental conditions of 'lived-experience' are so deep in subjectivity? What about the unconscious? What about the experience of embodiment, which is hard to explain away even in the best efforts at reduction? Late in his career Husserl became convinced that consciousness cannot be understood solipsistically but has an essentially communal dimension. So he turned his attention to the 'life-world', the world as we live in it prior to analysing and theorizing either about it or about our experience. The life-world

---

* Kant has an answer: not in the scepticism-begging idea of a causal origin of intuition in the noumenal realm – for the category of causality does not apply to noumenal reality – but in the transcendental deduction of the categories and the 'Refutation of Idealism', which show that we must treat the world as existing independently of experience, otherwise we could not have experience.

is the social, political, historical environment in which people interact and communicate with each other.

Abstract though his earlier enquiries appear, Husserl thought that phenomenology would reveal the ultimate underlying nature of what empirical psychology seeks to investigate, and therefore he always had a practical purpose in view. He saw the project of phenomenology as a new science, and hoped that his students would join him in establishing it; none did, including his student and assistant Heidegger, whose defection (as Husserl saw it) from the task was a disappointment to him. Towards the end of his life – as someone of Jewish origin in the Germany of the 1930s Husserl felt the following point poignantly – he became convinced that not understanding the basis of consciousness, but instead predicating all efforts at understanding humanity and the life-world on the basis of the natural attitude alone, was precipitating the world into crisis. He had lost a son in the First World War, now in Freiburg he had to move house because his Jewishness did not permit him to remain in the suburb he had been living in. Few came to his funeral; Heidegger, a member of the Nazi Party, did not attend the funeral, saying later that it was because he had the flu.

Phenomenology remained a major influence in Continental thought, though not in the original form of Husserl's 'transcendental phenomenology', but rather in the form of 'existential phenomenology' associated with Heidegger, Merleau-Ponty and Sartre, towards which Husserl was moving in his last years as the problems of the life-world pressed more heavily.

HEIDEGGER (1889–1976)

Martin Heidegger was born in Messkirch in Baden-Württemberg in Germany, into a Catholic family of small means. The local priest helped him to attend school in Freiburg and Constance. At St Conrad's Seminary in Constance Heidegger had as his spiritual adviser a future Archbishop of Freiburg, Conrad Gröber. Gröber gave him a copy of Franz Brentano's *On the Manifold Meaning of Being According to Aristotle* (1862), which Heidegger said he did not understand at the time, but which later triggered the interest in metaphysics that led to his writing *Being and Time*.

Before turning to philosophy, however, Heidegger had a brief moment as a Jesuit seminarian, and then went to study theology at Freiburg University, changing to philosophy after two years, in 1911. In 1915 he took a post as a philosophy lecturer at that university, soon afterwards marrying one of his students, Elfride Petri. They had two weddings, one Catholic for him and one Protestant for her. They had two sons and their marriage was lifelong, though Heidegger had a well-publicized affair with Hannah Arendt when she was his student at Marburg University after he moved there in 1923. He had a much longer affair – over several decades – with another student, Elisabeth Blochmann, who had a distinguished career as an educational theorist. Blochmann was a friend of Heidegger's wife, and it appears from correspondence that Heidegger and his wife conducted an open marriage in which she too had affairs.*

In the years before Heidegger went to Marburg he was close to Husserl, acting as his assistant. They discussed phenomenology intensively, and Husserl thought that Heidegger would be his colleague in developing a new science of consciousness. In 1919 Heidegger broke with Catholicism, but not with Christianity, and soon thereafter began a detailed study of Aristotle's metaphysics and the Scholastic commentators. In his Marburg lectures he distanced himself from Husserl's views, but dedicated *Being and Time* to him nonetheless.

Husserl retired from the chair of philosophy at Freiburg in 1928 and Heidegger returned to replace him. Five years later Heidegger joined the National Socialist (Nazi) Party and became Freiburg's Rector. He resigned the rectorship after one year, but during it carried out some of the Nazi educational reforms with what has been described as 'enthusiasm'. He remained a member of the Party until 1945, refusing requests by former students to apologize or to condemn the Nazis' atrocities. He

---

* An aside is appropriate here. Private lives are generally no one else's business, but Heidegger's personal and political life, as with Sartre's later, attracts attention because some – choosing Sainte-Beuve's side against Proust on the question of whether we understand writers better if we know their biographies – take it to be of more than merely journalistic interest. On the other hand, as Luce Irigaray pointed out, not only can biographical knowledge distort one's view of a thinker's work, but especially in the case of women it can be used to devalue or discredit that work. A suggestion as to how such understanding might, on the other hand again, help to breach the high barriers that sexism imposes against women is offered by the difference that biographical information makes to the reception of work by women as variously situated as Harriet Taylor and Frida Kahlo. The question is an open but important one.

was banned from teaching between 1945 and 1951, but in the latter year was granted emeritus status.

During the 1930s a change occurred in Heidegger's thinking, 'the Turn', *die Kehre*, marked by an interest in aesthetics, especially poetry and most especially the poetry of Hölderlin, and also in Nietzsche. He came to view the doctrine of *Being and Time* differently, and in part-response, part-development, wrote his second major work, *Contributions to Philosophy*, in the late 1930s. He did not publish it; it appeared in German in 1988, twelve years after his death, and in English translation twenty-three years after his death, in 1999.

When he was at Freiburg University as a theology student Heidegger had Professor Carl Braig as a teacher. Braig was the author of a book entitled *On Being: An Outline of Ontology*. Heidegger's first encounter with Husserl's thought came shortly afterwards, in the form of Husserl's two-volume *Logical Investigations*. Both factors prompted his turn from theology to philosophy. There were other straws in the wind: Henri Bergson was lecturing and writing about time in France, and when Heidegger came to know Husserl personally they discussed the latter's increasing interest in the consciousness of time. The significance of the connection between time and being was apparent to Heidegger early.

But these influences made him think that the key question concerns the fundamental nature of being itself. In the *Metaphysics* Aristotle had catalogued the various meanings of being: as 'the true', as potentiality and actuality, as substance, as property, as purely mental existence, as essentiality, as pertaining to dependent entities, as relating to the categories – but Aristotle said that he wished to know *the* meaning of being, its essence, being *as* being: 'We speak of being in many senses,' Aristotle wrote in the *Metaphysics*, 'but always with a view to one dominant sense . . . it is proper for one science to study being insofar as it is being.' Heidegger's question was exactly the same. He wrote, 'The following question concerned me in quite a vague manner: if being [*Seiende*] is predicated with manifold significance, then what is its leading, fundamental signification? What does Being [*Sein*] mean?' He regarded the topic of being as having been neglected by philosophy on the grounds that it was either indefinable or too general, but that without an investigation of it we would never understand the conditions that make it possible in the most general sense for anything to *be*.

Heidegger's starting point is the idea that an answer to the question

'What does Being mean?' has to be given by considering the *way* the question poses itself, and also *to what* – more suggestively still: *to whom* – it appears as a question. What or who is 'the Being of the question'? Although it might appear that the question of what Being is should be entirely general, and should tell us about the being of anything anywhere, one particular being is consistently present every time the question is asked, namely, 'the being who poses the question'. Investigating this being might lead the way to an understanding of Being in general. But the investigation is not to be conducted in the familiar terms of psychology, anthropology or (for example) Cartesian philosophy, but instead must be conducted phenomenologically, starting with an indeterminate pre-theoretical awareness of being-in-the-world, thus hyphenated to show that the being in question is not something separate from the world, over against it or in a subject–object relationship with it, but as *in* and *of* it.

The Being of this being is called by Heidegger *Dasein*, literally 'there-being' or 'existing'; a Dasein is a being-there, a concept that is primitive and *sui generis*. Heidegger warns against identifying a Dasein with 'a human being' in the ordinary sense of the latter term, but, in pursuit of clarification, one might think of Dasein as 'a (human) being viewed from the metaphysical point of view of his essential awareness of existing and moreover as aware of existing in the world'.

Dasein possesses *logos*, not to be understood in the usual way as reason or language, but as an ability or capacity to collect and remember the manifestations of Being which constitute the world. When we use a spade, for example, the network of meanings of which the spade is part – what purposes it can be used for, why it is needed for those purposes, why those purposes themselves exist, and so on – together with all other such manifestations of Being, constitute 'the world'. Dasein is thus a collecting-point where beings come out of concealment and make themselves present. These two notions, of *coming out of concealment* and being *present*, are key to Heidegger's metaphysics.

Heidegger took Parmenides' idea of *aletheia*, literally 'disclosure' and therefore 'truth', as the 'unconcealment' or 'self-showing' by which beings manifest themselves. He took this to entail that the primary sense of 'being' from Aristotle onwards is therefore 'presence' – the unconcealment shows what is *present* both in the sense of 'not absent' and in the sense of 'at this moment' – hence the connection with time. Indeed the connection with time is fundamental; for Dasein is 'stretched' between birth and death, having been 'thrown into the world' at a point in history, faced with a range of possibilities from which he has to choose in such a way as to exist 'authentically', though it is not a possibility but an inevitability – the inevitability of death – that is especially relevant to achieving authenticity, because it emphasizes Dasein's individuality and opens him to dread or anxiety, *Angst*. The authentic manner of Dasein's dealing with the world – 'having to do with something, producing something, attending to something and looking after it, making use of something, giving something up and letting it go, undertaking, accomplishing, evincing, interrogating, considering, discussing, determining' – is the 'care' (*Sorge*) or concern with things and with others, which is the 'structure of Dasein itself', a relationship Heidegger also calls 'handiness' and 'equipmentality'.

The anchoring concepts of *Being and Time* are *Sein* and *aletheia*, 'being' and 'disclosure' or 'unconcealment'. The discussion of the fundamental nature of Being is confined to the very first part of the treatise, most of the rest being a discussion of Dasein in 'existentialist' terms. 'Disclosure' is effected by anxiety and care – note that anxiety is not *fear*, which is always fear of something particular, but rather is an indefinite and general *mood* of dread or anguish, that alters the way the world seems to Dasein. Disclosure is like a clearing in the forest, which opens to Dasein its self-understanding of the structure of care, this being threefold: *thrownness* – we are thrown into the world without any answers available to the question, 'Why am I here, why am I here now?'; *projection* – the process of looking at the things around us to find possibilities for escaping our dread; and finally *fallenness* – the condition produced by Dasein's tendency to fail itself, to distract itself from authenticity. But only by achieving authenticity can the anguish of existence be overcome.

Given that *Being and Time* is a work that starts by announcing itself as an examination of the fundamental concept of ontology, its focus on Dasein and the quest for authenticity seemed to some critics, Husserl not least among them, to be a distraction; in his terms it amounted to a reduction of phenomenology to anthropology. For Husserl the way Dasein relates to the world is through consciousness, but in adding moods as a way of making the world present to Dasein, not as the object of its attention but as the horizon of its existence, Heidegger insisted that the world is not something over against Dasein treated as a knowing subject, but is part of Dasein's own existence. It is, however,

'Being-towards-death' that is the fundamental key to authenticity: when Dasein accepts its own finitude in the inevitability of death, it opens up – discloses – Dasein's own Being to itself, and completes it by making sense of it as a whole.

Being and Time was never finished. Heidegger published the first parts somewhat in a hurry, under pressure to secure the chair in philosophy at Marburg University, but he did not complete it because over the following years the emphasis of his interests shifted, partly to aesthetics and Nietzsche as mentioned above, but also towards writing an historical enquiry into 'Dasein's understanding of Being'. Later still, after the Second World War when he was again allowed to teach following the denazification period, he turned his attention yet further afield, among other things to the subject of technology, examining what it is and what relationship 'human existence' (the phrase he uses here, not Dasein) can have with it.

Because of Heidegger's membership of the Nazi Party his life and his work have been surrounded by controversy, with there being no simple divide between defenders and apologists on one side and critics on the other, but a scrimmage, consisting of those who defend everything and admire, those who reject the philosophy because of the Nazism, those who reject the philosophy on its own terms and attack him for the Nazism, those who defend the Nazism but criticize the philosophy, those who attack the Nazism but defend the philosophy – and so on.

In 1966 a friend of Heidegger brought journalists from *Der Spiegel* magazine to his house to interview him. He had been persuaded, with much effort over a long period, that he must address his Nazi past. He agreed on condition that the interview would not be published until he had died. If that seemed to promise revelation or confession, the journalists were disappointed. He was tense and nervous in the interview, and remained evasive. Not only that, but he seemed to add a new betrayal to the old: when asked by the journalists whether philosophy influences reality, including political reality, he first hid behind the claim that 'a new kind of thinking is required which is not yet clear,' but has something to do with addressing the advent of technologies that old systems of politics will not be able to manage; and then, when pressed, he retreated into saying, No, philosophy cannot influence reality or politics. This is in direct contradiction to what he had said in the speech made at the grand theatrical event of his inauguration as Rector of Freiburg University, complete with robed processions, many dignitaries and swastika flags. The young journalists from *Der Spiegel* said, 'We, politicians, semi-politicians, citizens, journalists, et cetera, constantly have to make some decision or other ... We expect help from the philosopher, even if, of course, only indirect help, in round-about ways. And now we hear: I cannot help you.' Heidegger replied, 'I cannot.'

To the dismay of those who, like Heidegger himself, wish always to separate the thinker from the thought, his *Black Notebooks*, published in 2014, pose a serious problem, for they appear to reveal his anti-Semitism's connection with his philosophy in implying that Jews are 'anti-Dasein' who manipulate Dasein in the course of their conspiracies. The exponents of literary theory would make short work of connecting the idea of anti-Dasein, 'not-Being-there', with the intentions of the Final Solution.

MERLEAU-PONTY (1908–1961)

Maurice Merleau-Ponty was born in the port town of Rochefort-sur-Mer on the Atlantic coast of France. His father, a captain of artillery, died when he was five years old. His family moved to Paris where he received an education at two prestigious institutions, the Lycée Louis-le-Grand and then the Ecole Normale Supérieure where his fellow-students included Jean-Paul Sartre, Claude Lévi-Strauss, Raymond Aron and Simone Weil. Simone de Beauvoir, a student at the Sorbonne, was a frequent visitor among them. Merleau-Ponty's diploma dissertation on Plotinus was passed in 1929, the year in which he attended Husserl's 'Paris Lectures', which introduced audiences at the Sorbonne to Husserl's views and formed the basis of the book *Cartesian Meditations*. This was an important experience; Husserl remained an influence throughout Merleau-Ponty's work thereafter.

After compulsory military service Merleau-Ponty was awarded a research grant for a study of perception, earning his living as a school-teacher and then as a tutor at the Ecole Normale Supérieure. At the outbreak of war in 1939 he joined the infantry, but was demobilized soon after France's defeat. Back in Paris he and Sartre became involved in the vaguely anarchist Socialisme et Liberté underground group of intellectual resistants. It was the beginning of a working relationship that saw their collaboration on the post-war journal *Les Temps Modernes*, until Merleau-Ponty's disillusionment with Communism caused them to part company in 1950. A partial reconciliation occurred in 1956.

Merleau-Ponty was awarded his doctorate for a thesis on 'The Structure of Behaviour' (1942); his most important book, *The Phenomenology of Perception*, appeared in 1945. After a period as a lecturer on education and child psychology at the Sorbonne he was appointed Professor of Philosophy at the Collège de France in 1952, the youngest ever such appointee. He died of a heart attack in 1961, aged just fifty-three, while preparing a lecture on Descartes.

For Merleau-Ponty the 'body-subject', an *essentially embodied* consciousness, replaces the Cartesian ego as the standpoint from which to overcome the fallacies of what he calls 'Objective Thought', a view that treats the world in a fragmented way as a collection of things standing in external causal relations to each other. This conception of the world generates conflicting approaches to reality: in one, consciousness is just one of the many things that exist, and the other things that exist do so independently of consciousness; in the other, consciousness constitutes the world, and therefore exists outside it. The first view he calls 'empiricism', the second 'idealism'. Both are mistaken, he says; and the fact that we alternate between these inconsistent viewpoints is what generates scepticism and prevents us from gaining a proper understanding of intentionality. In place of both he argues for a holistic conception, an integration of the world and consciousness as indissolubly interdependent.

'Flesh is at the heart of the world' is a much quoted dictum of Merleau-Ponty's; it encapsulates his idea that body is a form of consciousness, and is the place where perception and action coexist so intimately that perceiving already carries within itself a sense of what action that perception invites. What we perceive is in significant part conditioned by what we can do about it; to perceive is to see a range of possibilities of action. Because action is a bodily function, and action and perception are essentially linked, it follows that the subject of experience is essentially embodied. This is further shown by the way emotion expresses itself bodily, and by the fact that feeling a certain way about something colours how one perceives it – for example, seeing the face of a loved one prompts one to act in a certain way towards him.

An interesting component of Merleau-Ponty's view is that because it sees thought as bodily expression (*private* thought is *imagined* bodily expression, he says), we can see dance, mime, painting, music and speech as expressions of thought, as forms of *thinking*. The meaning of expressions is conferred upon them by the contexts in which they are used, the contexts consisting in shared forms of life. Merleau-Ponty's educational work on child pedagogy at the Sorbonne contributed an interest in language-learning to his theory of expression, and in particular to the arena where language both acquires sense and in doing so marks the birth of a thought. This is 'speaking language', *le langage parlant*, the primary mode of expression, to be distinguished from 'spoken language', *le langage parlé*, secondary expression, the repository of culture and the established relations of signs and significations. His chief interest lay with the former.

The notion of a context plays a part in dealing with a problem that arises from rejecting 'empiricism', which has a relatively straightforward account to offer of truth, namely, that truth is a match between what we think and how things are. This is not available to Merleau-Ponty, who therefore needs to explain how we can be right and wrong. He does it by inventing the notion of 'maximum grip', the idea that there is a context in which one's grip on the material on which we act is optimal, such that if it is not optimal – if we have a sense that we are off the mark in how we are viewing it – we feel a tension. What others call 'being right' or 'grasping the truth' is accordingly 'having maximum grip' on whatever is at issue, while 'being wrong' is a failure of grip.

Presupposed to this account is acceptance of the idea that the world as perceived is the result of an interaction between consciousness and things in the world. One's body is a thing in the world too, and as much an object of perception as the thing that perceives. Merleau-Ponty has to show, accordingly, that the mutual and indissoluble interdependence of world and consciousness *precedes* the embodied subject's own awareness of the perception–action nexus. However, the consciousness that precedes perception is itself part of experience, as the general background to particular episodes of perceiving and acting. Like the general effect of gravity on all we do, this background presence of consciousness exerts a kind of 'pull' that we feel in various ways, a significant one being a *social* pull towards the presence of others. This thought is important for Merleau-Ponty's view, given that it might otherwise seem solipsistic, not least because it is clear that one's experience of oneself has to be different from, and more immediate than, one's experience of others, unless one has an immediate sense of them as experiencers also.

Another key point for Merleau-Ponty is that time is constituted in experience both as a sense of the *absence* in the present moment of the past and the future, and as a continuous perception of the actualization of possibilities – this latter is the sense of time passing or flowing. In the former respect, time provides the horizons that structure experience; there is always an implicit sense of the past and future lying just over the horizons that bound the present, thereby giving shape to present experience. In the latter respect, perception as the awareness of possibilities feels itself moving forward in time because one of a range of possibilities becomes actual, generating the next range of possibilities – and so onward.

In later developments of his thought, as published posthumously as *The Visible and the Invisible*, Merleau-Ponty revisits the question of how body and world are intertwined ontologically but with a sufficient gap for communication, introducing the notion of the 'chiasm' or crossing, of which a paradigm example is the body as both the thing sensed and the thing doing the sensing, as when a person touches her own face. The sensible–sentient relation is not a strict identity; if it were, there could not be an exchange between them. The 'visible' is flesh; its crossings are with the 'invisible' disclosed in art, literature, music and emotion, namely, ideas in a 'universe of ideas'. But it would be wrong to think of this as an opposition of two orders, for 'every relation' is, he writes in his latest notes, a simultaneous 'holding and being held', a view continuous with the founding intuition of his view in *The Phenomenology of Perception*.

Merleau-Ponty is included in the roster of 'existentialists' but the lack of exciting topoi in his work such as death, anxiety and radical freedom, together with the lack of interest in his work by those in the generation after his own – Derrida, Deleuze and others, though Derrida wrote to criticize his focus on flesh as emphasizing immediacy and contiguity over distance, rupture and untouchability – deferred response to his work until later. The posthumous publication of his writings revived interest in him.

SARTRE (1905–1980)

Jean-Paul Sartre lived a very public life, and serves as a paradigm of the *engagé* intellectual. His talents were wide ranging: he wrote novels, plays, biography and criticism as well as philosophy, but through all of them his philosophical and political commitments – the latter evolving over time – are never far away. From the strictly philosophical point of view his major work is *Being and Nothingness* (1943), and significant also is *Existentialism is a Humanism* (1946). His own nomination for his most important work is the *Critique of Dialectical Reason* (1960), in which he sought to provide a refreshed basis for Marxism as 'the philosophy of our time', but freed from associations with what he saw as its degraded Soviet version.

Sartre was born and educated in Paris, forming some of his most important relationships while a student at the Ecole Normale Supérieure where he met Maurice Merleau-Ponty and Raymond Aron. He also at this time met Simone de Beauvoir, who was studying at the Sorbonne. While at the Ecole he gained a reputation as a practical joker, one of his pranks – announcing to the press that the wealthy aviator Charles Lindbergh was to receive an honorary degree there – caused such a fiasco that the Ecole's director had to resign. French men were obliged to undertake a form of national service, so Sartre had a spell in the army as a meteorologist before embarking on a career as a schoolteacher, which is what most of his contemporaries did while working on doctoral dissertations.

When the Second World War broke out Sartre rejoined the army, was captured and imprisoned for nine months by the Germans. The experience was transformative. Simone de Beauvoir records that when he returned to Paris he had acquired a new seriousness. The underground resistance group he helped to form, Socialisme et Liberté, contemplated its options, including the assassination of collaborators, but for want of support it collapsed. Disappointed, Sartre decided to concentrate on writing.* The war years produced *Being and Nothingness* and his plays *The Flies* and *No Exit*, and a number of magazine articles.

Soon after the liberation of Paris in 1944 Sartre, with Simone de Beauvoir, Raymond Aron and Maurice Merleau-Ponty, founded *Les Temps Modernes*, named after the film of the same name by Charlie Chaplin. Its first number contained a statement of aims by Sartre,

---

* This version of events has been disputed; it has even been suggested that Sartre and de Beauvoir were in effect collaborators. The fate of reputations will always swing in posthumous helplessness between admirers, hostiles, revisionists, people seeking book contracts – and the merciless exposures effected by time.

defining the idea of *littérature engagée*. Many notable writers were introduced to the world in its pages, including Jean Genet and Samuel Beckett. The Cold War and the vexed question of Stalin took their toll; Aron was the first to leave because of the magazine's support for Communism – he moved to *Le Figaro* as its editor – and Merleau-Ponty left later. Another of its victims was the friendship between Sartre and Albert Camus. The former deeply disapproved of the latter's attitude to the Algerian war – born in Algeria, Camus saw the force of considerations on both sides of that ugly episode; perhaps too much so – and therefore Sartre recruited a hostile reviewer for Camus' *The Rebel*. When Camus remonstrated, Sartre replied in a way that made a rupture inevitable.

Korea, Cuba, Russia, Algeria, the anti-colonialist movements in the rest of Africa and elsewhere, opposition to American hegemony, Vietnam and politics in general, not least in the turbulent period of the late 1960s in France, attracted Sartre's energies in the three decades after 1945. He was arrested for causing a civil disturbance during the Paris riots in the summer of 1968, but was released on the orders of General de Gaulle, who remarked, 'One does not arrest Voltaire.' Sartre refused the Légion d'Honneur in 1945, refused election to the Académie Française in 1949, and refused the Nobel Prize for Literature in 1964, saying that he did not want recognition by institutions associated with political dispensations he opposed. In 1976, however, he accepted an honorary doctorate from the University of Jerusalem. After his death one of the members of the Swedish Academy is said to have claimed that, some years after rejecting the Nobel Prize, Sartre or a representative of his asked whether he could nonetheless have the prize money.

At his funeral in 1980 huge crowds, said to be 50,000 strong, followed his coffin to Montparnasse. Legend has it that one young person told his parents he had gone to the demonstration against Sartre's death. That, like the name of the cemetery itself, is appropriate as a mark of his end.

Whatever else people know about Sartre, they know about his lifelong relationship with Simone de Beauvoir. The two ceased to be lovers in the physical sense quite early in their relationship, and each had many other lovers, in de Beauvoir's case of both sexes. Their lovers included their students and colleagues, whom they shared or bequeathed to one another, the only durable bond being the one between themselves. Because sexism, unconscious or otherwise, has so long permeated everything, de

Beauvoir's stature as a writer and thinker, which is very great, remained a footnote to Sartre's throughout their lives and for a time afterwards. Future history might order them differently.

What attracted Sartre to phenomenology was its promise to overcome the opposition between realism and idealism, in its simultaneous affirmation of both the presence of the world and the pre-eminence of consciousness. Sartre spent a year at the Institut Français in Berlin in 1933, making a close study of Husserl's writings while there; later, in the early years of the war, he studied Heidegger. His 'Phenomenological Ontology' (the subtitle of *Being and Nothingness*) begins from these starting points, but diverges from them. He shares their way of distinguishing between ontology and metaphysics, the former understood as a descriptive project specifically related to consciousness, the latter as an attempt to provide an ultimate synoptic explanatory framework for life and the world. Heidegger had rejected the idea of such a project; Sartre more moderately says that it poses unanswerable questions.

Sartre begins by distinguishing two fundamental categories of being: the in-itself (*en-soi*) and the for-itself (*pour-soi*). In crude terms, the in-itself is non-conscious being, the for-itself is conscious being. Later he adds a third category, the for-others (*pour-autrui*). Each human being is both an in-itself and a for-itself, combined. A person's in-itself aspect is passive, existing inertly and lumpenly; it just is what it is. Her for-itself aspect is dynamic, fluid and metamorphic. It depends on the in-itself – that is, cannot exist without it – but is continually making an effort to transcend it or 'nihilate' it, thus creating a 'situation'. Individuals are always in a 'situation'. Situations are indeterminate, their indeterminacy a function of the differing proportions of the mixture of in-itself and for-itself. Sartre says this shows that we are always trying to be more than we are, or something other than we are. He gives the example of a waiter in a restaurant, who strives to be *a waiter*, a being-in-itself; but he cannot be a waiter as a plate can be a plate, because as a man he is a being-for-itself who is working *as* a waiter while wanting to *be* a waiter. So he is in a condition of 'bad faith', trying to be what he cannot be.

What explains the waiter's dilemma is that the in-itself occupies the role of substance or thinghood; whereas the for-itself is not substantial, not a thing, but as it were an 'acting against' things. The in-itself is facticity, the for-itself is possibility; the relationship between them is like the relationship of past to future or actuality to possibility, hence the 'nihilating' endeavour of the for-itself, just as the future nihilates the past. The experience of time is the experience of the for-itself striving for its possibilities against the inertness of the in-itself's lumpenness as 'what is'.

The category of for-others becomes relevant on the appearance of another subject. A Robinson Crusoe figure could not deduce the existence of an Other from the two categories of in-itself and for-itself; the only way to know of the for-others is to meet with one. Sartre uses the example of being discovered in an embarrassing situation: the shame one feels is a 'phenomenological reduction' of being aware that the Other is a for-itself, a subject of experience. The Other thus objectifies us – we are an object for it: we exist in the Other's consciousness – which is how we come to know ourselves in the first place; but because the primary way in which individuals relate is, in Sartre's view, through conflict, it is also the case that 'hell is other people' (this is the culminating line of his play *No Exit*). The reason is that before encountering the Other we are free and self-constituting, looking outwards from the pre-reflective self at the world. When Others enter the picture they become a suction-pipe draining one into it; for we are made to see ourselves as the Other sees us, objectifyingly, an alienating situation because it renders us into an in-itself for the Other. We see this when we realize that such emotions as shame and pride arise only in response to 'the look' ('the gaze', *le regard*) of an Other. The look does not require the actual presence of an Other; its notional presence is enough.

Of course the relationship between oneself and the Other is mutual and reciprocal – just as the Other objectifies and alienates me, I objectify and alienate him. 'While I attempt to free myself from the hold of the Other, the Other is trying to free himself from mine; while I seek to enslave the Other, the Other seeks to enslave me.' The allusion to Hegel's 'master–slave dialectic' is apparent here. It is an inevitable source of 'bad faith', *mauvaise foi*, because the possible forms of relationship all raise problems. Sartre describes as 'masochism' the effort to annex the Other's freedom by subjugating oneself to her as nothing but an object for her, while 'sadism' is the effort to transcend her attempted objectification of oneself by refusing to let her do it. Love is the endeavour to achieve a wholeness of being as 'for-itself-in-itself' through the merging of the two consciousnesses, mine and the Other's, into one. But since this would obliterate the otherness that is the foundation of a for-itself's consciousness of its existence, and because, further, the obliteration is mutual, the result is contradiction and conflict. But given that there is no escaping relationship with others, the only way we manage to live with the situation is by bad faith.

Central to Sartre's view is commitment to the connected pair of ideas that 'existence precedes essence' and that we are radically, indeed agonizingly, free. The first idea is that individuals are self-creating; they do not arrive in the world, or at the point of self-awareness, with an antecedent purpose or plan waiting for them, but have to make what they become through their choices and actions. In *Existentialism is a Humanism* Sartre writes, 'man first of all exists, encounters himself, surges up in the world – and defines himself afterwards.' The corollary is that each individual is *responsible* for his self-creation: 'Man is condemned to be free; because once thrown into the world he is responsible for everything he does.' Knowledge of that freedom and the responsibility it entails causes *anguish*.

The question arises whether it is possible to achieve authenticity, the chief if not indeed sole value of Sartrean ethics. In light of our condemnation to the alienated and anguished conditions described, his answer does not seem to describe something attainable. It is this: we achieve authenticity if we abandon our desire to become an 'in-itself-for-itself' and thus liberate ourselves from the identification of our ego as being-in-itself – that is, as a thing. Instead we must allow a spontaneous pre-self-aware 'selfness' to emerge to replace 'me' as an ego. If I cease from being in relationships of 'appropriation' and self-identification with my ego, and instead focus on my aims and goals in an outward-directed way, I cease living in bad faith.

There is a widespread view that Sartre's *Existentialism is a Humanism* is a summary of his outlook as it stood in the mid-1940s – the origin of the text was a lecture given in Paris in 1945 – in large part because its brevity and accessibility made it the one strictly philosophical work of Sartre's which, in translation, reached a wide audience. It drew considerable fire from other philosophers, and Sartre himself rejected aspects of it later. It is, however, a *locus classicus* for the themes of freedom, its anguish and the responsibility imposed by freedom to be self-creating. These themes were an inspiration for the generations of young people who came into a sense of their own freedom and responsibility in the 1950s and 1960s, even if they knew of them only as slogans detached from their source in the ontology and phenomenology of *Being and Nothingness*.

At that time it was common for Albert Camus (1913–60) to be bracketed with Sartre as an 'existentialist' although he repudiated the label, and insisted instead on describing his view as 'absurdist'. He argued that humankind's absurd condition consists in the gratuitous nature of the relationship between humanity and the world; the fact that neither has any intrinsic meaning is 'the only bond between them', as he puts it. It invites one of three responses: literal suicide, intellectual suicide in the form of accepting some form of religious solace, or courageous acceptance and embrace of the absurdity of things. His essay 'The Myth of Sisyphus' is, apart from his novels, the chief statement of this view. It concludes by saying of Sisyphus, condemned for eternity to a futile task – never succeeding in getting a boulder to the top of a hill – that in view of the fact that 'the struggle itself' confers meaning, 'one must imagine Sisyphus happy.' Camus' novels exemplify and expand on aspects of this central theme, and gave it a powerful hold on the imagination of his time.

In just the way that Camus' reputation as a contributor to philosophy has become overshadowed by the connection with Sartre, so – and arguably, even less excusably – has that of Simone de Beauvoir (1908–86). Her reputation as a feminist and novelist is of course outstanding; but her specifically philosophical contribution has been subordinated to her achievements in those fields. One can mention the following in illustration. Sartre had learned from Hegel the idea that consciousness is made 'for-itself' by relationship with another, and through the conception of 'the look' he had developed the idea into his theory of alienation and the futile effort to achieve a transcendence, by means of love, of what is in effect the master–slave bond. De Beauvoir makes use of these ideas in terms that concretize and illuminate the actual situation of relationships between men and women. She does so by characterizing the prevailing ideology as one in which *man* is the Subject and *woman* is the Other and the slave, whose role is to recognize man's endeavours and thereby validate and serve them. She describes romantic love as a woman's effort to capture a man's subjectivity by 'fascinating' his 'gaze', even while she allows him to legislate what her own interests and aims can be. De Beauvoir concludes, as Sartre did, that the attempt to forge a relationship must fail, given the conditions which Otherness imposes. In her case, however, what she writes must have a revelatory character for any reader because it cleaves so closely to reality; in Sartre the argument is stated in wholly abstract terms.

Add to these thoughts de Beauvoir's application, at the opening of volume 2 of her most famous book, *The Second Sex*, of the point that existence precedes essence in her declaration that one is not born a woman but becomes one, with all that this implies – and one sees that her deployment of these themes puts her in the first rank of existentialist thinkers. In combination with the emphasis on the social possibilities of ethics outlined in her *Ethics of Ambiguity* (1948 – this title is a weak translation of *Pour une morale de l'ambiguïté*) her influence on Sartre's own shift towards more universal concerns in his activism in the 1950s becomes clearer likewise.

A significant work of Sartre's last years was his biography – though it is far from an orthodox one – of Gustave Flaubert, *The Family Idiot* (1971–2). Though incomplete, it brings together the earlier existentialist and later Marxist themes in Sartre's work, embellished by the considerable powers of psychological observation that inform his plays and novels. The result is described by one well-equipped reviewer as 'admirable but mad', appropriating a remark that Sartre himself had once applied to someone else. In the biography Sartre draws a surprising comparison between Flaubert's unhappy childhood and his own blissfully happy one. The reviewer writes mischievously of the Sartres, 'How selfish and irredeemably unfair of this bourgeois family to have inflicted untarnished contentment on the future Marxist, Existentialist and creator of Roquentin. The Flaubert family, on the other hand, was more properly bourgeois and supplied the correct degrees of trauma and unhappiness which Sartre was deprived of.' It is a joke which raises an interesting question.

GADAMER (1900–2002)

Phenomenology and existentialism dominated Continental philosophy in the first half of the twentieth century. The second half saw diversification of interests, one of the first being Hans-Georg Gadamer's theory of hermeneutics.

Gadamer was born to strictly observant Protestant parents in the small town of Marburg in the valley of the River Lahn in Hesse,

Germany. He was an only child; his mother died when he was aged four, leaving him to the tutelage of his uncompromising father. He was brought up in Breslau in the Prussian region of Silesia, where his father had taken a post as a professor of chemistry. Soon after beginning his university studies in Breslau Gadamer returned to study in Marburg where his father had been appointed to the professorship of pharmacy. It was a consequential move because, soon after completion of his doctoral dissertation on Plato, Gadamer became an assistant to the newly arrived Heidegger. The latter formed a poor opinion of his assistant's abilities, so Gadamer turned from philosophy to philology.

Gadamer's work for his habilitation thesis, again on Plato, restored Heidegger's good opinion of him, and a close if not always easy relationship ensued, with Gadamer holding teaching posts at Marburg, Kiel and Leipzig universities over the next two decades before succeeding Karl Jaspers in the chair of philosophy at Heidelberg.

Living in Germany during the Nazi period was not easy for anyone not aligned with the regime, and not easy for anyone at all in the last year of the war. Somehow Gadamer managed to survive without becoming too compromised, beyond joining the National Socialist Teachers League in August 1933 – 1933 was the year of the Nazi takeover – and signing the 'Loyalty Oath of German Professors to Adolf Hitler and the National Socialist State'. His first job, at Kiel University, was as the replacement for a Jewish lecturer who had been thrown out. Along with others Gadamer saw that keeping a job under the Nazis meant having to toe a line, so he voluntarily attended a camp at which Nazi doctrine and gymnastics were provided to help shape the right sort of citizen for the new Germany. While he was at the camp it was visited by Hitler, who seemed to Gadamer to be 'simple, indeed awkward, like a boy playing the soldier'. At the war's end Gadamer was one of those on whom the occupying powers relied to help with reconstruction of the devastated country and society.

The work that established Gadamer's reputation came relatively late in his life: he was aged sixty when *Truth and Method* (1960), the book in which he sets out his theory of hermeneutics, was published. He describes its aim in the Introduction as legitimating the truth communicated by modes of experience that cannot be verified by the methods of natural science. What kind of knowledge and truth is it that hermeneutics – the endeavour of interpretation and understanding proper to the 'human sciences' and art – can attain? The answer is: the knowledge of truth that resides in understanding. He writes, 'The current interest in the hermeneutic phenomenon rests, I think, on the fact that only a deeper investigation of the phenomenon of understanding can provide this legitimation' – a conviction he says is strengthened by 'the importance that contemporary philosophy attaches to the history of philosophy', explained by the fact that the truths in the texts of the great thinkers can be known only by a hermeneutical method, and not by the methods consecrated by natural science.

And the same thing is true of art. Nothing systematic and quantitative can replace the experience of art, which grasps truths that art conveys in its own unique way: 'The experience of art', he writes, 'is the most insistent admonition to scientific consciousness to acknowledge its own limits.' Likewise history: here too Gadamer resisted efforts by those such as Wilhelm Dilthey to solve the problem that humans are historical beings trying to understand history by a methodology unsuited, as he saw it, to the task. Dilthey had written, 'The first condition for the possibility of historical science lies in the fact that I am myself a historical being – that the one who studies history is the same as the one who makes it.' To avoid relativism a rigorous approach is needed to help the historian, as interpreter, transcend the limits of her cultural and historical embedding. Gadamer, and Habermas after him for similar reasons, reject this approach. But Gadamer also rejects Heidegger's view that ontology has priority in the hermeneutical endeavour. Instead he argues that hermeneutics has to bring ontology and history together to show that it is through language and the lived context of interpretation that Being is fully disclosed.

Hermeneutics is the endeavour to 'recover meaning' from texts and the past, and began as a technique applied in biblical studies and classical philology in the rapidly advancing scholarship of the eighteenth and nineteenth centuries, an Enlightenment quest in pursuit of objective truth and understanding – or as objective as possible. For scholars the question of hermeneutical method was therefore important. Dilthey broadened its application to the human sciences in general, and argued that it involved going 'from outside in' – from the outside of other people to their inner consciousness by means of the external signs they offer: speech, writing, behaviour, artistic productions, deeds.

Heidegger had a different view. Consistently with the ambition to get beyond the surface of things, and therefore to go deeper than theories and methods of hermeneutics to what underlies them in the structure of understanding itself, he rejected the established idea of the 'hermeneutic circle' – the idea that in any meaning structure the parts and the whole are mutually and interdependently interpretative – and argued that the possibility of understanding anything involves having 'to have already understood it' in the sense that the very basis of our being able to understand anything at all requires us to be in the world *with* that thing. At the ontological level, therefore, the possibility of understanding is 'already' there, and hermeneutics is the process of making the structure of this aspect of the ontological foundation explicit.

Gadamer sought to take further the idea that human beings are, in the most basic aspects of their nature, constitutively given to understanding, and to determine the capacities and limitations of that endowment. He takes art as especially revealing of the nature of truth, for it demonstrates that truth is an *event*, something that happens as we are drawn into a realization that art presents us with something beyond ourselves. It is not a matter of applying criteria, laying a measure against the work of art and judging its worth from an objective standpoint. The idea that truth is 'something that happens' is key; his concern is to show 'not what we do or what we ought to do, but what happens to us over and above our wanting and doing' in the process of interpreting.

The account is not subjectivist; Gadamer rejected the subjectivist standpoint of earlier hermeneutical theory. Rather, it turns on the idea that in encountering truth we are taken out of ourselves into something larger, as happens when we *play* – think of playing tennis or chess – when we are caught up in the act of playing, a situation in which the game takes over the player's consciousness and as it were plays itself through him. It is not the subject playing, but the play which absorbs the subject. This does not mean that the player becomes an unaware pawn in the game's playing of itself; it means, rather, that the subject is effortlessly involved – very like the idea of the Zen mode of playing tennis where self-consciousness does not obtrude to render the activity unspontaneous and forced. The game unfolds of itself, but the player is nevertheless an agent in it, one of the factors in it, yet experiencing a new freedom that attends giving up the effort to control.

In playing the game the player *presents* herself as a participant, with a view not to winning but purely to being in the game and to furthering the task of the game itself. This explains the genesis of art: when the self-presentation of the player ceases to be solely for the sake of playing itself, and offers itself as a presentation to others, it transforms into a possibility for truth – not as an intention either of the player or of the spectator, but because that is the 'mode of being of the work of art itself'. For art speaks: in the encounter with art one hears something that claims and makes a difference to one; the experience is not merely theoretical – not *merely* recognizing a truth – but something practical and existential, making a difference to one's life. Art speaks to us saying, 'Thou must alter thy life!'

Behind every thought, Gadamer says, lies a whole body of assumptions and background beliefs, which he calls 'prejudice' – not in a negative but in a neutral sense, for some of our assumptions and beliefs might be worth keeping, while others might merit rejection. It is not possible to do without prejudices in this sense – assumptions, inherited beliefs – and they are a source of knowledge, so Gadamer rejects the Enlightenment 'prejudice against prejudice', and assigns to understanding the task of disclosing and evaluating prejudices, and the authority and tradition that constitute them. Tradition is what makes our own situation intelligible – understanding is an essentially historical process, and without openness to the manifestation of tradition in ourselves and the works of art and literature we encounter, the work of understanding could not be achieved.

There are two other tenets crucial to Gadamer's overall view. One is the concept of the 'horizon' or limit of knowledge, understood not in a negative sense but rather as something like the frame around a picture that enables one to see the picture properly. When one's own horizon 'fuses' with that of another, or (say) of a text, one sees 'beyond what is close at hand – not in order to look away from it but to see it better, within a larger whole and in truer proportion'. The other tenet is that human nature is fundamentally linguistic. Language is 'a medium where I and world meet, or rather, manifest our original belonging together'.

Some critics took Gadamer to be impugning science; others that he was opposing the kind of scientism that a Positivist outlook can unwittingly prompt. One of the former critics was Jürgen Habermas, who understood Gadamer to be saying that truth is directly opposed to method (in the sense of scientific method). He also faulted Gadamer for failing to take account of the power of ideology in his discussion of tradition and authority, which require, said Habermas, critique not acceptance. Gadamer replied that this was to fall prey to the modernist fallacy that subjects can free themselves from the past, whereas it is instead the case that such legacies cannot be rejected wholesale but have to provide the starting point for the process of understanding.

Even from so condensed an account of Gadamer's principal themes one can see how they entered into his wide-ranging practical contributions to debates about education, European ideals, the humanities and the promotion of mutual understanding between different cultures. As a result his ideas have been influential in fields outside academia – in medicine, architecture, law and environmental concerns. He lived to the age of 102 and was still at work when he died.

RICOEUR (1913–2005)

Hermeneutics found a second champion in Paul Ricoeur, a younger contemporary of Gadamer.

Ricoeur was orphaned very young; his mother died shortly after his birth, and his father was killed in the second battle of Champagne in September 1915. His family were Huguenots, and the grandparents who brought him up were assiduous in their study of the scriptures, which encouraged bookish and studious habits in him. He attended the Lycée Emile-Zola at Rennes and studied as an undergraduate at its university before going to the Sorbonne, where he wrote a dissertation in theology.

The advent of war resulted in a further lengthy period of study – in prison camp, after being drafted into the army and captured. The 'Offizier Lager' (Oflag II-D) in which he spent the next five years organized itself into such a rigorous centre of study that the French Vichy government gave it degree-awarding status. There he made a close study of Karl Jaspers, the psychiatrist and religious thinker, and translated Husserl's *Ideas I*. The translation formed part of his doctoral submission after the war. His teaching career began in the theology faculty of the University of Strasbourg (the only French university with a Protestant theology department) where he remained until 1956, in which year he was appointed to the chair in philosophy at the Sorbonne.

Ricoeur's three most important books were published during the Sorbonne years; *Fallible Man* and *The Symbolism of Evil* both appeared in 1960, followed by *Freud and Philosophy* in 1965. In this latter year he made the mistake of accepting a position as Dean at the new university of Nanterre, at the time called 'Paris X Nanterre', located in the city's western suburbs. It became one of the most riotous campuses in the *événements* of 1968, Ricoeur himself coming under attack and being labelled an 'old clown' by the students. He had taken a post there full of optimism for a fresh new approach to university education, and was disenchanted by the unexpected effect of reforms that had been intended to vent Paris' university system of its stuffy traditionalism and overcrowding. In consequence he resigned and went to teach at the Catholic University of Louvain in Belgium, and then at the University of Chicago's Divinity School. He returned to retirement in France in 1985.

With a background such as this Ricoeur would seem to belong to the same category of thinker as Søren Kierkegaard, Jaspers and Emmanuel Levinas, that is, thinkers who find their solutions in some form of theological or theistic commitment. On the grounds that such a commitment is no solution to the problems of philosophy, I do not include religious thinkers among philosophers, at least without qualification. For if there is an omnipotent, omniscient and eternal being then anything whatever is possible; 'all bets are off' as the saying has it; and therefore there is no point even in thinking about the problems given that the solution, even if incomprehensible, is already available without the necessity for further thought. But Ricoeur, despite his extensive writings on religion and faith, did not postulate a deity as a philosophical answer to anything, but offered a profound ethical metaphysics which does not depend on a privileged revelation or doctrinal basis.

Ricoeur's chief contribution was his combining of phenomenology and hermeneutics in such a way as to fulfil what he saw as the main aim of the latter, namely, to 'overcome distances', for example between the present and the culture of the past. 'By overcoming this distance, by making himself contemporary with the text, the interpreter can appropriate its meaning to himself: foreign, he makes it familiar, that is, he makes it his own. It is the growth of his own understanding of himself that he pursues through his understanding of others. Every hermeneutics is thus, explicitly or implicitly, self-understanding by means of understanding others.'

Indeed Ricoeur saw all philosophy as hermeneutics, which show that existence both expresses itself and arrives at meaning by the continual activity of interpreting the signs through which culture manifests itself. Selfhood, or more accurately the discovery of the self, is attained by the process of coming to appropriate these meanings and reflecting upon them. This provides the route to an answer to a question he saw at the root of philosophy: 'Who am I?' Reflection shows that we have a 'double nature', lying on either side of a line that divides what is voluntary and involuntary within us. But the discovery of the self can never be complete, because the 'I' who asks 'Who am I?' is both the seeker and the thing sought. The only way this dialectical circularity can be managed is by the hermeneutical approach.

What such an approach makes us see is that as embodied beings whose selfhood cannot be grasped by a Cartesian act of introspection, we have to recognize ourselves as linguistic, social and bodily unities. But not static unities; we live a narrative in time, and the way we experience time is part of what makes the reflectiveness required for self-discovering possible. This insight prompted Ricoeur to develop a theory of time, distinguishing 'phenomenological time' (the passage of time from past through the present towards the future experienced linearly) and 'cosmological time', the more abstract general conception of the 'river of time' itself. 'Human time' is the integration of both. The two conceptions of time presuppose each other, and in their integrated aspect as human time require to be understood in narrative terms, with the story in which we are characters being both 'written' and 'read' by ourselves, the latter constituting the basis of self-identity.

But self-identity is a fragile construct; it has to be constructed from the 'reading' we give of the narrative we write for ourselves, but it also depends on what others think about us, how they treat us and how we relate to them. Selfhood can be lost, and because the ethical aim of life is to achieve a sense of merited self-worth, such loss is moral failure. Given that achieving this aim depends on the nature of relationships, there has to be a reciprocity of benevolence between oneself and others, and the attitude of 'solicitude' that underlies reciprocity is fundamental, connecting self and others through sympathy. Ricoeur's treatise on ethics, originally given as the Gifford Lectures in 1985–6, is entitled *Oneself as Another* (1990).

For Ricoeur the highest values lie in friendship and justice, because both protect selfhood, and when selfhood is lost or harmed they provide means for its repair and restoration – indeed, for 'redemption'; those studious hours over the scriptures in his grandparents' home had left their trace in this attractive and humane approach to the question of living.

DELEUZE (1925–1995)

Until beginning his collaboration with the radical psychiatrist Félix Guattari in the late 1960s Gilles Deleuze was an historian of philosophy, though a very unusual one. He was also unusual in standing apart from the main thrust of Continental philosophy to that point, shaped as it was by phenomenology and the influences of Hegel and Heidegger; for he was an empiricist (of a sort) who looked to a philosophical tradition containing members mostly invisible to others writing philosophy in French and German in the twentieth century: Spinoza, Leibniz, Hume (these were the ones invisible to Continentals), Kant and Nietzsche. Although influenced by Kant he treated him with affection as 'an enemy'. Just as formatively for his thought, he despised Hegel. He saw a deep connection between the philosophers he chose to write about, which he described as 'a secret link constituted by the critique of negativity, the cultivation of joy, the hatred of interiority, the exteriority of forces and relations, the denunciation of power'.

Deleuze was born and lived all his life in Paris, save for a brief but lucky year in Normandy following the German invasion of France in 1940. It was a lucky time because he had a teacher there who inspired him to read, and thereby brought his intellectual interests to life. The subsequent war years, during which he was educated at the Lycée Henri-IV and the Sorbonne, were not unalloyed: Deleuze's brother Georges was arrested for resistance activities, and died while on his way to prison in Germany.

In the normal way of French academics Deleuze began by teaching at various schools, including Louis-le-Grand, before becoming a teacher at the University of Paris. In the early 1960s, at the time of publishing one of the more influential of his historical studies, *Nietzsche and Philosophy* (1962), he met and became friendly with Michel Foucault. The even more significant meeting with Guattari happened at the same time as the student and worker uprisings of 1968, and it marked the point at which he began to philosophize in his own voice, instead of through studies of others. He colourfully if not very tastefully described his historical studies in his 'Letter to a Critic' as follows: '[I saw] the history of philosophy as a sort of buggery or (it comes to the same thing) immaculate conception. I saw myself as taking an author from behind and giving him a child that would be his own offspring, yet monstrous . . . monstrous because it resulted from all sorts of shifting, slipping, dislocations, and hidden emissions that I really enjoyed.'

Among the influential books Deleuze wrote with Guattari were the two-volume *Anti-Oedipus* (1972) and *A Thousand Plateaus* (1980). The events of 1968 made him an activist; he campaigned on prison conditions (with Foucault) and gay rights, and wrote about the cinema and art. Guattari died in 1992, the last of their collaborations, *What is Philosophy?*, appearing in 1991.

Deleuze suffered from lung problems all his life, and in 1969 had to have a lung removed. Breathing became increasingly difficult over the following years, making the simplest tasks onerous, eventually unbearably so. From the early 1990s onwards he found it difficult even to write. In 1995 he committed suicide by casting himself from a window in his apartment.

Two principles lie at the centre of Deleuze's philosophical outlook. One is that 'all identities are effects of difference,' the other is that 'genuine thinking is a violent confrontation with reality, an involuntary rupture of established categories.' His early engagement with philosophy's history was motivated by the view that 'history of philosophy' exists as a kind of official barrier – 'how can you think without having read Plato, Descartes, Kant and Heidegger, and so-and-so's book about them? A formidable school of intimidation' – which consecrates experts and expertise, whereas engagement with the philosophical tradition should be a creative enterprise, generating new concepts. This connects with Deleuze's claim to be an empiricist, though not in the standard sense: 'I have always felt that I am an empiricist,' he wrote, because he believed that 'the abstract does not explain but must itself be explained; and the aim is not to rediscover the eternal or the universal, but to find the conditions under which something new is produced.' He particularly stresses this latter point: the *creative* role of empiricism. Alternatively put, his empiricism is a rejection of anything 'transcendental' and a correlative commitment to everything being immanent. The implication is a challenge to claims about the privileged role of *a priori* reason and the metaphysical duality of being.

Deleuze's favourite philosopher is Spinoza, whom he describes as 'the prince of philosophers ... the Christ of philosophers ... the absolute philosopher'; even the greatest among other philosophers 'are hardly more than apostles who distance themselves from or draw near to this mystery'. The reason, in his view, is that Spinoza exactly combines the two principles just described – empiricism, in the sense of rejection of the transcendent, and immanence; a single 'plane' on which all things exist because everything is a mode of the single substance that Spinoza called *deus sive natura*. Moreover, the point of Spinoza's *Ethics* is, as its title tells us, *ethics*: the entire argument of the book aims at dispelling the illusions that prevent us from attaining freedom and joy – freedom from illusion and unavailing striving against necessity, and joy in the rejection of the 'sad passions'.

A key concept for Deleuze is 'immanence'. It means what is empirically real, and it is understood as entailing that everything real exists on the same plane of being – there is no deeper, higher, different transcendental plane which is other than what is empirical, or which constitutes its essence. Everything there is has to be understood in terms of its relations to other things. A fundamental such relation is *identity*. In thinking of the concepts of identity and difference we normally start with identity, Deleuze points out, distinguishing between *numerical* and *qualitative* identity, the first meaning 'x = x' and the second meaning that two things 'x' and 'y' look so similar that one cannot tell them apart, as with 'identical twins'. But we should instead see *difference* as the more fundamental concept, because everything that is given – things, their properties, their relations to other things – is given *as different* from other things, and moreover as 'self-differing' because being is a process, namely, the process of becoming. Accordingly – to employ terms not Deleuze's own – both individuality and plurality are effects or outcomes of difference.

Making difference more fundamental than identity raises questions about repetition. Pondering Nietzsche's 'eternal recurrence' Deleuze observes that the 'return' is not a recapitulation, an exact simulacrum, of a former life and circumstances, but it is the *return* itself which returns – the returning is what is repeated, but each time to something different because 'difference inhabits repetition,' and the time of the return is not the past but the future: 'the subject of the eternal return is not the same but the different, not the similar but the dissimilar.'

One of Deleuze's most striking remarks (among many such) is what he says about the aim of ethical striving, which is 'to become worthy of what happens to us', for then we will 'become the offspring of one's own events, and thereby be reborn'.

Again as with others mentioned in these pages, Deleuze's philosophical creativity ranged widely, and he saw his writings about cinema, art

and novelists not as critical works but as philosophy. They were opportunities for philosophical creativity, the same motive that had prompted
his historical studies; philosophy is in his view an essentially constructive
endeavour. His writings on the history of philosophy are accessible; his
chief work, *Difference and Repetition* (1968), is difficult, and the collaborative writings with Guattari are even more so, to the point of
impenetrability. The claim that they are deliberately obscure, with un-
announced shifts in the sense attached to key terms, is met by the
counter-claim that Deleuze wished to keep his readers on their toes, forcing them to think. In this he succeeds.

DERRIDA (1930–2004)

Sartre was an intellectual celebrity, and known the world over; he travelled, appeared on television and was interviewed often. But life was
slower then, there were fewer television channels and long-distance travel
was considerably more effortful. By the time Jacques Derrida arrived on
the scene all the means for amplifying presence in the world as an intellectual celebrity – yet more television, frequent and easy transatlantic
travel, the increased opportunities for semesters at American universities –
had become vastly greater, and at least one aspect of Derrida's reputation
has to do with this fact. The other is that he was an iconoclast, and wrote
in a way that, to say the least, permits multiple interpretations. For this
reason, to explain Derrida requires observing the truth – if he would
accept such a term – of his principle, that nothing exists outside a context. One might say that, in his case, context is all.

Derrida was born in Algiers to a Sephardic Jewish family. The Vichy
government's anti-Semitic policies denied him a place at the local lycée,
requiring him and other Jewish children to attend a separate school. He
devoted himself to football instead for an entire year, and had ambitions to become a professional player. The lacuna might have had some
influence on his failure to pass the entrance examination for the Ecole
Normale Supérieure at first attempt. He succeeded at the second
attempt. The dissertation he wrote there was on Husserl. He later said
that Husserl and Heidegger were the two great influences on his
thought, and that without them he would not have been able to speak.

After schoolteaching for several years Derrida secured a post at the
Sorbonne and worked as assistant to Paul Ricoeur, before being offered

a post in 1964 at the Ecole Normale Supérieure which he occupied for twenty years. His reputation was established soon afterwards, in 1967, when the three books that made his name were published: *Of Grammatology*, *Writing and Difference* and *Speech and Phenomena*. By the end of his life he had published over forty books, and spent much time in his last decades in the United States. He became an enormously controversial and divisive figure, as exemplified by the furore at Cambridge University in 1992 over the question of an honorary doctorate for him. Many leading Analytic philosophers regarded him as a fraud, or at best as someone whose imperial robes were made visible only by the less exigent lights of literature departments.

By Derrida's own principles it ought to be impossible to say exactly what his views are. But at risk of achieving the impossible, here follows an attempt.

Derrida's *deconstructionism* turns on the claim that there is no such thing as a 'subject matter', a topic or point of a discourse, a singularity that brings one's understanding to a focus. To think that there is something that can be grasped in a discourse is to continue to be imprisoned by a 'metaphysics of presence'. There is neither subject matter nor 'truth', there are only perspectives and their deferral, this latter being the continual escape of meaning from the effort to pin it down, the escape of a text or utterance from efforts to attach it securely to a definite sense. When we try to understand, all that we encounter is ruptures and deviances; the effort to understand merely exposes misunderstandings.

Western philosophy's principal way of thinking is, says Derrida, 'logocentric' in that it privileges language as the expression of reality, and hence stands as a mediator between consciousness and reality. He inherits from Heidegger an opposition to the 'metaphysics of presence' which promotes appearances above the conditions that make appearances possible. And it proceeds by way of positing binaries – positive and negative, good and evil, simple and complex – and again favours one side of the divide. The result is that philosophy neglects a great deal, not least the fact that the supposed binaries are in any case not real opposites, but themselves part of a hierarchy of subordinations. Deconstruction seeks to take account of all aspects, with the aim of 'displacing' the system constituted by these commitments.

A key idea in *Of Grammatology* is that the continual deferral of meaning introduces a gap between what a producer of signs wishes to convey by their means and what the signs succeed in conveying. He coins the term *différance* with an 'a' where the second 'e' usually is, as the name for that gap (Derrida says it is not a concept, or even a word). It is also in itself, when spoken, an illustration of the point; for its pronunciation is (in French) indistinguishable from that of the regular term *différence*, illustrating the difference between signification in speech and writing. It also suggests the idea of where alternative and suppressed readings might be found – in the margins of a text, in footnotes, in the space between the intention and the result, in what is not said or what is in fact excluded by a given speech or text.

As Derrida's ideas developed, and as responses to them, both critical and appropriative, increased in number and frequency, they changed. He responded to criticisms of the obscurity of his writings by asserting and defending it as deliberate and necessary; in a late interview in *Le Monde* in August 2004 he said that his approach embodied 'an intransigent, even incorruptible, *ethos* of writing and thinking ... without concession even to philosophy, and not letting public opinion, the media, or the phantasm of an intimidating readership frighten or force us into simplifying or repressing. Hence the strict taste for refinement, paradox, and aporia.'

Commentators on Derrida attribute to him a shift of interest towards politics and ethics in the last decades of his life. He wrote about biblical texts, Kierkegaard and Levinas, and like a number of his contemporaries turned his attention to literary criticism, architecture, psychoanalysis, debates about feminism and gays, and – inevitably, for it is the great cultural and art form of the twentieth century – film.

Despite Derrida's own refusal to be pinned to a central commitment, instead claiming to be enacting a process which, in light of the eternal deferral of meanings, is the only option open to thought, one can see very definite influences, and recognizing them tells us much. Heidegger had written of a 'destructive retrieve' which opens texts to differing and usually suppressed possibilities of interpretation. Claude Lévi-Strauss' account of the Nambikwara tribe in Brazil – especially of its chief, who saw in the prospect of learning to write a chance to entrench his authority over his tribe – afforded a number of lessons about speech and writing and the implications for distortions of power that one way of appropriating them might cause.

But the most interesting reference might be to Maurice Blanchot (1907–2003), who wrote in his 'Literature and the Right to Death' (1948) of the deep strangeness of the authorial experience, and the idea that 'literature begins at the moment when literature becomes a question.' Blanchot quoted from Mallarmé's *'Crisis in Poetry'*, 'I say: a flower! and outside the oblivion to which my voice relegates any shape, insofar as it is something other than the *calyx*, there arises musically, as the very idea and delicate, the one absent from every bouquet,' and discusses the poet's sense of the 'double condition of the word' and 'the two aspects of language which he distinguishes so absolutely. In order to characterize each, he lights on the same term, which is "silence". The crude word is pure silence: "It would, perhaps, be enough for anyone who wants to exchange human speech, silently to take or put in someone else's hand a coin." Silent, therefore, because meaningless, crude language is an absence of words, a pure exchange where nothing is exchanged, where there is nothing real except the movement of exchange, which is nothing.'

Therefore despite – again despite – the refusal to acknowledge a theory that can stand still long enough for evaluation by the canons of a philosophical approach that Derrida is at pains to deconstruct, it is hard to see how to avoid the charge that if he is right, forty books about it would be thirty-nine (perhaps even forty) too many.

CONTINENTAL THOUGHT:
UN SALON DES REFUSÉS

Like the Ganges' many mouths, Continental philosophy's varieties of thought proliferated so diversely in the second half of the twentieth century that an account of them is in danger of mutating into a general history of ideas. Because this is not such a book, but instead is specifically a history of philosophy, the question presses as to who and what to include and exclude. Almost every thumbnail of every notable writer of non-fiction in German and French in the twentieth century describes him or her as a 'philosopher' along with his or her several other avocations – cultural critic, literary critic, social theorist, psychiatrist, novelist, and so on – which begins to make the term too broad to be helpful, unless (and perhaps why not?) the term is to be revised to embrace more in its extension.

Fortunately for the present author, answering the question about who to include (and therefore exclude) is not an entirely arbitrary matter. In the Introduction above I point out that 'the history of philosophy' is identified by what today's philosophers select from the general history of ideas as the antecedents and precursors of their concerns. The debates they select are the case law of those concerns, the thinkers they study are those whom they have good reason to choose as guides. The philosophical tradition itself, accordingly, tells us much about who and what it identifies as significant for the enquiries we label as metaphysics, epistemology, ethics and their associated pursuits. But of course this is a judgment made at a point in time; and therefore some thinkers and writers might be over-valued, and others ignored, whom later generations will see differently.

The foregoing account of Continental philosophy has focused on a number of significant individuals whose inclusion is obvious, and some whose inclusion is less so. For example, it will not be clear to everyone that Derrida is a philosopher *au pied de la lettre*, while others will say that if he merits separate treatment, so even more does Habermas, and Foucault – if not most of those mentioned in the paragraphs below. The writers and thinkers mentioned in the paragraphs below have not been given such treatment, thus constituting a sort of *salon des refusés*, and an explanation for this is merited. In the process they get a place in these pages after all – and doubtless some would enjoy the exemplification of their rejection of binaries in being included by being excluded. The future might find one or more of them of much greater importance than those separately treated above. And indeed, it might turn out that people not mentioned here at all will come to be regarded in future as the really great philosophers of the twentieth century. In any case, my choice of who to include and exclude will doubtless be controversial. As a general criterion I have been guided by two considerations. The first is that if a view is informed by, and/or designed to terminate in, a religious conclusion, the appropriate place for discussion of it is in religious studies; this explains what I say about Levinas and Jaspers below. The second is that if those who chiefly engage with a given set of views are identifiably in the field of debate to which the views themselves most obviously contribute – cultural studies, sociology, history of ideas – then the appropriate place for discussion of it is in those fields; this explains what I say about Foucault and Habermas below. In all these cases there are philosophical sources, dimensions and significances in these writers, as there are in most thoughtful engagement with matters of intellectual importance, but where a line has to be drawn these considerations are persuasive in showing where it lies.

The writers now to be mentioned fall into the following two groups. The first group consists of individuals who were primarily philosophers, the second group consists of individuals who were primarily political, social and cultural theorists.

The first group, ordered by date of birth, consists of Henri Bergson (1859–1941), Karl Jaspers (1883–1969), Gaston Bachelard (1884–1962), Jean Wahl (1888–1974), Alexandre Kojève (1902–68), Emmanuel Levinas (1906–95). The following thumbnails do none of them justice, but not, one hopes, too much injustice either.

Bergson was an excellent prose stylist, and his arguments in favour of free will, based on the intuited experience of time and duration, made him very famous in his own day, not least because he seemed to many to offer successful resistance to the deterministic implications of science. He received the Nobel Prize in Literature and many other honours. His reputation was damaged by his effort to put Einstein right about time in a head-to-head debate in April 1922. (A few months later Einstein was awarded the Nobel Prize in Physics, not for his theory of general relativity, which the Swedish Academy said had been called in question by Bergson – and such was Bergson's reputation that it weighed with the Academy – but for his work on the photoelectric effect.) In old age, though wishing to convert to Catholicism, Bergson remained a Jew as a statement of opposition to the Nazis. His lack of philosophical influence is doubtless connected with his valuing of intuition and non-rationalism over science. Like Nicolas Malebranche two centuries before him, the enormous celebrity he enjoyed in his own day seems to have drained his reservoir of reputation, leaving none to be enjoyed posthumously. Such things happen.

Jaspers began as a medical doctor and psychiatrist, making valuable contributions in the latter role, not least in the conception of biographical approaches to therapy. He formulated a richly worked-out version of an existentialist philosophy, with quasi-religious overtones informed by his views about the need for 'transcendence' as the answer to existential angst. The conclusion of his thought is, in effect, that believing in God is soothing. This latter explains the influence he has among theologians.

Alexandre Kojève gave a famous set of lectures on Hegel in 1930s Paris, which had great influence on the development of French thought thereafter. The lectures were attended by – among many others – Raymond Queneau, Georges Bataille, Maurice Merleau-Ponty,

Jean-Paul Sartre, Jacques Lacan and Raymond Aron. In the years following the Second World War Kojève became a leading statesman in France and was one of the founding fathers of the European Economic Community.

Jean Wahl did much to promote interest in the religious existentialism of Søren Kierkegaard, and was an effective ringmaster of the academic and institutional side of philosophical activity, keeping French thought alive in the 'University in Exile' in the United States during the Second World War, and serving as the editor of the journal *Revue de Métaphysique et de Morale*.

Gaston Bachelard was an historian of science, and his disagreement with Bergson's philosophy probably played a role in the latter's relative posthumous invisibility. He anticipated Thomas Kuhn's notion of 'paradigm shifts' in science in his rejection of Auguste Comte's view that the history of science consists in a smooth upward approach to its culmination in Comtean Positivism.

Emmanuel Levinas is an attractive figure whose ethical concerns exerted a life-transforming influence on some. Whether it is more correct to describe him as primarily a religious thinker, and chiefly concerned to expound a normative doctrine, is enough of a question to explain his inclusion among these thumbnails. He has had a great influence on theologians.

Jürgen Habermas (b. 1929) is the member of this *salon* over whose inclusion in it most thought was given. He is a figure of great stature, whose contributions as a public intellectual, and whose defence of Enlightenment values as a scholar, are equalled only by the advances made in his work on communication and the public sphere. If lines of demarcation mean anything at all – and perhaps they should not – then this work belongs to sociology, though of a philosophical kind. Habermas is one of the few thinkers who speaks to both sides of the widening divide between Continental and (broadly) Anglophone thought, although in the latter tradition he is almost exclusively read by sociologists and political theorists.

The second group, somewhat approximately ordered here by affiliation and area of activity, is even more heterogeneous, but its members might reasonably be described as having primary interests in sociology, politics, social and critical theory, and the history of ideas.

The outstanding members or associates of the Frankfurt School of critical theory – Max Horkheimer (1895–1973), Herbert Marcuse

(1898–1979), Erich Fromm (1900–1980), Theodor Adorno (1903–69) – are very clearly political sociologists and proponents of critical theory, as are those in a wider circle of Marxist thinkers and other theorists whose names stand out in defiance of their troubled century: Georg Lukács (1885–1971), Ernst Bloch (1885–1977), Henri Lefebvre (1901–91), Raymond Aron (1905–83) and Louis Althusser (1918–90).

Hannah Arendt (1906–75) resolutely refused the description of 'philosopher', though it is highly merited by her insights into human nature and political extremity. She is an exemplar of intellect that is both penetrating and courageous. Her chief concern was to argue for the importance of political engagement as a civic responsibility, in order to defeat totalitarianism and the peculiar horror of *banal* evil – the evil done by ordinary people in seemingly ordinary, undramatic ways – by keeping alive the resistance of hope against the kind of 'dark times' she had witnessed in the Nazi era and so penetratingly studied afterwards. It is a matter of striking poignancy that she had been Heidegger's lover before he became a Nazi, and after the Second World War forgave him.

Michel Foucault (1926–84) made his sociology and history of ideas indispensable to any understanding of modernity. The point of genuine philosophical importance repeatedly made by his work is that power – whatever form this power takes: institutional, political, personal, in diffuse, covert, unobvious and non-institutional forms as well as recognizable and structured ones – determines what is to count as knowledge, madness, crime or acceptable sexual expression; and this alerts us to the perennial need to resist, to be suspicious and alert. The point might not be original to Foucault, but the extent of his generalization of it is.

Foucault argued that accepted ideas about human nature and history distort our effort to arrive at good theories in medicine, psychology and criminology, not least because they turn on a model – that of the natural sciences – which requires them to be rigorous and quantitative. He argued, in opposition to this idea of correct methodology, that a different conception of human nature is required, an alternative to the one created by the *pouvoir-savoir*, 'power-knowledge', of dominant ways of thinking, however mediated.

Reflection on the preoccupations of Foucault and other philosophically inspired and philosophically minded sociologists, historians of ideas and critical theorists mentioned here directs our attention to something that a great deal of Continental thought is fundamentally about, namely, resisting what it sees, or fears, in science: reductivism, determinism, objectivity, neutrality, rationality and monopoly of truth and epistemic power. These anti-science (or anti-scientistic) thinkers insist instead on the irreducibility and centrality, however described or theorized, of *human being*. The 'postmodern' impulse is captured in Jean-François Lyotard's *The Postmodern Condition: A Report on Knowledge* (1979), with its twin claims that the 'grand narratives' of modernism (about progress, science, rationality) have lost their credibility, and that therefore authority in all its forms, including cultural and epistemological authority, should be challenged. Much Continental thought of the second half of the twentieth century is an answer to that call.

One cannot close the catalogue of the *salon* without listing the names of the cultural critic Walter Benjamin (1892–1940), the psychoanalyst Jacques Lacan (1901–81), the mystic Simone Weil (1909–43) and the psychoanalyst and feminist Luce Irigaray (b. 1930), all of whom have likewise made a difference to the wider landscapes of recent and contemporary thought. Mere mention of them shows how the landscape of *thought* is a far larger thing than the strict confines of academic philosophy suggest, an instance of a more general fact: that the Venn diagram of the classes of intellectuals and scholars shows at best only a partial overlap. It has always been so.

There are two reasons for the proliferation of names just noted here and in connection with the twentieth century's Analytic tradition. One is that there are more people, more universities, more travel and communication, more ways of keeping records, more publications of every type – more everything of relevance to increasing the numbers of people studying, writing, thinking and teaching – than at any time in history. Like the physical universe itself, the universes of discourse are ever expanding. A day in the life of modern times is like a decade – sometimes, a century – in the past.

The second reason is that time has not yet winnowed the pressing crowds of those who write and speak, offering up their views and claiming our attention. If the historian of recent philosophical – or more broadly intellectual – history could leap ahead a couple of centuries, to see what the work of time has wrought, her choices would be easy: there would be the Aristotles and Kants, looming high like mountain peaks above a scurry of foothills. That prompts one to say: look around and ask, Who are they, in this century just gone and today, who will be the great ones visible from the future? Have we even heard their names yet? At the back of one's mind echo the words of Shelley's 'Ozymandias':

> I met a traveller from an antique land
> Who said: 'Two vast and trunkless legs of stone
> Stand in the desert . . . Near them on the sand,
> Half sunk, a shattered visage lies, whose frown
> And wrinkled lip and sneer of cold command
> Tell that its sculptor well those passions read
> Which yet survive, stamped on these lifeless things,
> The hand that mocked them and the heart that fed.
> And on the pedestal these words appear:
> "My name is Ozymandias, King of Kings:
> Look on my works, ye mighty, and despair!"
> Nothing beside remains. Round the decay
> Of that colossal wreck, boundless and bare,
> The lone and level sands stretch far away.'

PART V

Indian, Chinese, Arabic–Persian and African Philosophy

As mentioned in the main Introduction, although this book is chiefly devoted to the story of Western philosophy, it is both relevant and desirable that it should take note of the great traditions of philosophy in India, China and the Islamic world, and the emerging debate about 'African philosophy'. I am an observer rather than an expert in these fields; expertise in at least aspects of them would be the minimum qualification one should have for writing about them, yet I can only claim this for myself, with due modesty, in the case of Western philosophy. However, a lively interest in these traditions, not least from the point of view of being fascinated by the comparisons and differences between them and Western philosophy, is a requisite for the serious student of ideas, even if access to those in other traditions has always to be achieved via translation.

A full account of the philosophical traditions of India, China and the Islamic world would require tracing their developments over time. In the surveys offered here attention is focused on the originating ideas and subsequent core doctrines. I strongly recommend that the section on Indian philosophy be read only after Parts I–IV above have been read; and that the section on Arabic–Persian philosophy be read only after at very least Part I has been read.

In the interests of dispassion I have to say the following. It would seem that there is a recipe for being a great civilization-dominating figure such as the Buddha, Confucius, Socrates, Jesus and Muhammad. It is this: *Write nothing. Have devoted disciples. Be lucky.* Note that this recipe does not include: *Be original. Be profound.* None of these figures were either of these things, though in the Be Lucky department they had followers who were both, and who made from the remembered fragments of their sayings, and the legends that embroidered memory of their persons, whole systems of thought and practice which they themselves might not have recognized or even perhaps approved.

If these seem to be disparaging things to say, as a kind of *lèse-majesté* against the greatest and most iconic of names, note this. Each of these figures was, in his own time, one among many who were doing what he was doing: teaching or preaching, gathering followers, variously borrowing from and disagreeing with others and with earlier teachings. In the case of some it was decades, in the case of others centuries, before the teachings attributed to them were written down. In each case the followers of their followers soon began to disagree and split from each other, the schisms and quarrels forming different versions of the legacies thus surviving.

Take Siddhartha Gautama – he who came to be known as the Buddha – as an example. Legend makes him the son of a king who led a life so sheltered and opulent that when he first encountered a sick man, an old man and a corpse in the world outside the palace walls he was shocked, and therefore abandoned his station and family and set off as a mendicant wanderer in search of release from the sufferings of life. He tried deep meditation at the feet of the yogis, he tried severe self-mortification after the fashion of the ascetics, seeking by these means to secure release from the endless cycles of pain that constitute existence. Neither worked. But one day, seated in thought under a Bodhi tree, he found enlightenment: he became the *Buddha*, 'the enlightened', and was released; and spent the rest of his life teaching disciples.

This fabulized and abbreviated account makes Gautama seem as if he were unique, as if he appeared from nowhere with a great and transforming revelation to offer the world. But what of the yogis and ascetics with whom he first studied? In fact he arose out of a period in the history of India that was tumultuous in the tens of thousands of seekers and mendicants, of yogis and ascetics, of teachers and preachers, who congregated in huge crowds in great public debating halls and in parks in the cities of the Ganges, where they argued among themselves, lectured the public and taught their followers. It was common currency that acts of charity would help towards a more fortunate reincarnation in a next life, and therefore these swarms of mendicants were able to rely on being fed and clothed by the communities through which they passed. Nothing was more helpful to fostering the abundance of philosophy and religion in the India of that time than the coupled ideas of reincarnation and karma.

The teachings of the Buddha began to be written down three to four centuries after his death. The two oldest sources of what he is believed to have taught are the *Suttapitaka* (the 'Basket of Discourses') and the *Vinayapitaka* (the 'Basket of the Disciplinary Code'). They were gathered from memorized oral transmission of the teachings, an approximate canon of which had been formed by about a century after his death. The oral nature of this first record introduced formulaic and repetitive expressions required for memorization, and variations in the eventual texts made from them are in part attributable to the vagaries of memory. But there were certainly also misunderstandings, interpolations and reinterpretations of the material passed down too, adding to the variability of the written versions.

Moreover, whatever language the Buddha spoke in his native land among the Sakya people, who lived in what is now the border area between India and Nepal on the northern slopes of the Ganges basin, it was not Pali, Sanskrit or one of the Pakritic dialects, and the transmission of Buddhist teachings through these languages, and later through other south Asian languages and Tibetan, Chinese and Japanese, introduced many differing additions and changes to create what Buddhism is now.

Nevertheless there is a recognizable core to Buddhist doctrine, centring on the Four Noble Truths and the Eightfold Path. A striking fact about Buddhism, as with the rival outlook that arose at the same time in history, namely Jainism, is that it is not a religion but a philosophy. It involves no deity or deities, and relies on no messages from transcendent sources about the purpose of life and how to live it. Later versions of Buddhism in Tibet, China and Japan gathered a great penumbra of superstitions and beliefs in gods and non-human beings – a typical development for the human imagination – but this constitutes a corrupted version of the original, as the austere scholars of the Theravada school of Sri Lanka will readily tell one, as they look with disdain at the excesses of the Mahayana schools and their encrustations of the 'true doctrine' with what these scholars think is nonsense.

Matters are no different as regards Confucius. He too was one of many 'literati' who sought to advise princes and teach a way of life; he had the good fortune to inspire a follower who lived a century after his time, Mencius, whose admiration prompted even later scholars to collect sayings attributed to Confucius and write them down. About two and a half centuries after Confucius' death the first Emperor of unified China, Qin Shi Huangdi (r. 221–210 BCE), made a bonfire of the books of all previous philosophers – and, as it happened, any available living authors of them too – in order to efface the past and to establish the Legalist philosophy of his own day, which supported his rule. Fortunately he was unable to destroy all copies of previous classics such as the *Book of Songs*, the *Spring and Autumn Annals*, the *Analects* of Confucius, the *Yijing* (in an earlier Anglicization known as 'I Ching') and Mencius' book, the *Mengzi*. When the next dynasty came to power, known as the 'Former Han', Confucius' reputation blossomed; many of the ancient classics were attributed to his authorship or editorship, and preferment in the bureaucracy of the Empire turned on success in examinations on the classics attributed to him. The Confucian character of China was shaped by the many and long periods when the teachings attributed to Confucius were the subject of these imperial examinations; they ceased to be so only in the first decade of the twentieth century.

The pattern of post-mortem collections of sayings and teachings, the earliest written down decades after the event, and a canon being established only centuries after the event, is repeated in the case of Jesus and Muhammad. The stand-out figure is Socrates, personally known to Plato, Xenophon and others who wrote about him – but even here too, with the exception of some lampoons by Aristophanes, nothing was written about him or recorded of him until after his death. Subsequent philosophers developed different aspects of Socrates' legacy – Aristotle the trope of the considered life, the Cynics his disdain for convention, the Stoics his fortitude and adherence to principle – but in the case of the Buddha, Jesus and Muhammad the divergences and schisms among their followers in the centuries after their deaths descended into conflict and violence. This too, alas, is a typical feature of things human.

Socrates is however like all the others in having been one among a large number of people – in his case the sophists – who were doing much the same thing as he was: teaching, influencing, attracting pupils. Jesus was likewise one of a large number of enthusiasts and preachers, and his form of execution – reserved by the Roman authorities for political insurrectionaries – suggests that he was not viewed as being much different from the many others who were disturbing the peace at the time. Gautama competed for the attention of his contemporaries with the Jains, with other atheist philosophers and with the theistic devotees of the India of his day. Why did Confucius rather than Mozi come to have followers long after his own time who elaborated teachings in his name, thus making him the venerated sage of China? Why did St Paul choose to make a religion out of the deceased Jesus rather than some other zealous preacher of the day? You might reply: the intrinsic merits of the teaching. Perhaps so. But undoubtedly there was a large measure of luck in it. And it makes one ask, prompted by Thomas Gray's *Elegy Written in a Country Churchyard*, how many village Hampdens and mute inglorious Miltons in their thousands thought and taught, but have been long forgotten? Refocus the question and ask, Why is it that romantic novels sell in far greater numbers than literary ones? Were there teachers and thinkers of profound insight whose teachings were too difficult to understand or to follow, leaving the legacy of the more popular ones to flourish in history? A survey of the history of philosophy suggests an answer: in it are to be seen the thinkers who may well have more to offer the thoughtful than the popularized teachings associated with those 'big names'.

One thing we certainly learn from these considerations is that 'Buddha', 'Confucius' and the rest are the names of images or icons rather than of people – or better, perhaps, the ideas of notional people to whom can be attributed for convenience the inspiration for a philosophy or (in the case of Jesus and Muhammad, who are therefore not considered in this book) a religion.

Picking out a few individuals for elevation to iconic status in this way is a kind of shorthand for the entire period in which they and increasingly many others were raising questions about values, society, ideas of the good, and enquiry into fundamental questions about the world and humankind. No doubt others had done the same in the millennia before them, but at this period – between the eighth and third centuries BCE especially – there was a marked efflorescence of debate, both in numbers of people involved and in written records of what emerged from their discussions. For this reason the period has been labelled 'the Axial Age' (*axiology* is the study of values, from Greek *axia* meaning 'worth', 'value') – a name coined by Karl Jaspers on the basis of views advanced by scholars in the nineteenth century who were struck by the emergence of philosophy in India and China contemporaneously with its appearance in the Greek world. Jaspers included Zoroastrianism in Persia and Judaism in the Middle East among the movements constituting the age, and might have added many more which have since vanished into historical curiosities, such as the mystery cults, Hermeticism and then-contemporary versions of the mythopoeic religions of Egypt and Mesopotamia. It would seem that philosophy – what we recognize specifically as philosophy – stood out against the increasingly busy background of speculation in all these forms, and it is a striking fact that the great iconic figures at the heart of the period – Buddha, Confucius, Socrates – are all philosophers, not prophets or religious leaders, still less gods (though Buddha has since acquired divine status in the minds of worshippers in some schools of Buddhism).

Finally: there is an emerging field of study in African philosophy which is also discussed in these pages. The term 'African philosophy' is controversial because the different histories and cultures of the different parts of that great continent do not easily lend themselves to generalization, and there are as yet no identifiable bodies of doctrine, schools of thought or major figures to latch on to as an entry point. With one exception: in southern Africa the prominence of the concept of *Ubuntu* – humanity, with emphasis on the essential nature of our shared humanness and connectedness: 'I am because we are' – brings into focus an ethical tradition, both implicit and explicit, which was ignored by colonizers and their accompanying missionaries and yet has depths which put some other outlooks to shame. *Ubuntu* aligns with the best and richest aspects of what one means by 'humanism' in the contemporary sense of this term (a subject for treatment elsewhere). I discuss *Ubuntu* in its due place below.

Indian Philosophy

What a pity it is that the richness and depth of thinking in the Indian philosophical traditions should be all but sealed off from Western philosophy by the veils of Sanskrit and Pali. The metaphysics, epistemology, logic and ethics of the Indian schools also lie behind the veil of a misapprehension about their nature, namely, that they are exclusively religions or theologies rather than philosophies. In fact most of the schools are non-theist. The misapprehension arises from the fact that one instructive way of explaining the aim of all Indian philosophy is to say that it is soteriological – a 'soteriology' is a doctrine of salvation – in that it seeks to bring to an end the suffering that is existence by understanding the true nature of reality. Accordingly all the schools offer a complete package of metaphysics, epistemology and ethics as a system, and the fact that their practical aim is escape from suffering offers to many an invitation to apply a lazy extension of the term 'religion' to them.

The schools of Indian philosophy are known as *darshanas* – 'darshana' literally means 'sight' and by extension 'view' in the sense of viewpoint or standpoint. They divide broadly into two groups, those that are *astika*, 'orthodox', and those that are *nastika*, 'heterodox'. The distinction turns on whether or not the darshana accepts as fundamental the authority of the *Vedas*, the ancient writings of India, 'Veda' meaning 'knowledge' or 'wisdom'. The darshanas that do not accept the authority of the Vedas are Buddhism, Jainism and the Carvaka school, and that is why they are described as heterodox.

The Vedas consist of four collections or *Samhitas*, the *Rgveda*, *Yajurveda*, *Samaveda* and *Atharvaveda*. The Rgveda is the Veda of the hymns of wisdom; the next two share much the same content as the Rgveda but are especially applied to use in sacrificial rites and as liturgical hymns respectively, while the Atharvaveda stands apart as a collection of formulae for counteracting evil and disease. The Rgveda is regarded as the earliest, dating to around 1100 BCE but emerging from a long oral tradition beforehand.

The history of the period between 1500 and 500 BCE in north-western India is known as the 'Vedic period', when the Vedas took shape and with them, in the later part of this period, instruction manuals called *Brahmanas* for carrying out the Vedic rites and commentaries on the inner meaning of the texts and rituals, called *Aranyakas*. Discussion of a philosophical kind is found in some of these latter. But the chief philosophical texts connected with the Vedas are the *Upanishads*. 'Upanishad' literally means 'to sit attentively close' (that is, to a master or teacher), and they are known as *Vedanta* because they are regarded as the final parts or closing sections of the Vedas, encapsulating the Vedas' high meaning or purpose.

The Vedic literature is regarded as *Sruti*, 'what is heard', meaning 'revealed' either directly by supreme reality itself, or through apprehension by *Rishis*, 'sages', of the ancient past in the course of their meditations. Sruti is contrasted with *Smrti*, 'remembered', which describes all other literature. Various of the Sruti texts themselves say that they were 'crafted' by the skill of Rishis in the same way as a carpenter builds a chariot.

Of the hundred or so Upanishads, ten are regarded as most important, and among them the *Brhadaranyaka* (the 'Great Forest Teaching') holds a significant place. It was composed about 700 BCE and is attributed to the sage Yajnavalkya. It begins, 'Om. Dawn is the head of the sacrificial horse. The sun is the eye of the sacrificial horse, the wind is his breath, the fire that is in all men is his open mouth, the year is his body.' That gives a misleading impression of what follows, for the exchanges and discussions constituting the main body of the text are a striking source of concepts about the self (*Atman*), and its oneness with ultimate reality (*Brahman*), which appear in more express detail in the darshanas of the philosophical tradition.* The manner in which the theses are presented admits of widely varying interpretations, but the richness of suggestion is great. The Sanskrit scholar who did

---

* Among the cleverest and most interesting participants in the *Brhadaranyaka* are the female philosopher Gargi Vachaknavi and Maitreyi wife of Yajnavalkya. There are, however, aspects of what this Upanishad says that are repugnant: in Book VI, Chapter 4, men are told to strike women 'with a stick or the hand' if they refuse to have sex with them.

much to bring the Upanishadic tradition to serious Western attention, Paul Deussen (1845–1919), wrote of it that it throws 'if not the most scientific, yet still the most intimate and immediate light upon the last secret of existence', a view shared by Schopenhauer, who kept a copy of the Upanishads at his bedside and said of them, 'In the whole world there is no study so beneficial and so elevating. It has been the solace of my life and it will be the solace of my death.'

Before looking at some of the darshanas in more detail, it is useful to have a brief survey of them all. The six orthodox schools are Samkhya, Yoga, Nyaya, Vaisheshika, Purva Mimamsa (sometimes just 'Mimamsa') and Vedanta (sometimes 'Uttara Mimamsa'). The three main heterodox schools (there were other, minor schools) are, as already mentioned, Carvaka, Buddhism and Jainism.

Samkhya is the oldest of the orthodox schools, and was originated by the author of the Samkhya Sutras, the sage Kapila (seventh or sixth century BCE). It asserts a dualism of matter (*prakriti*) and consciousness (*purusha*, which also means spirit or self), and it regards both as equally real. It is pluralistic in holding that purusha is many.

Yoga is associated with the Samkhya school as the practical application of its teaching. The writings of one Patanjali, dated some time before the fifth century CE, set out the techniques of posture, breathing and meditation that later schools of yoga developed. The yoga sutras attributed to Patanjali, though very much later than those by Kapila, accept the Samkhya ontology and epistemology, but add a commitment to a form of deism lacking in the non-theistic Samkhya doctrine.

The Nyaya school's teachings on epistemology and logic were written down by Aksapada Gautama in the sixth century BCE in the *Nyayasutras*. In advancing a form of direct realism it emphasized the importance of critical evaluation of the sources of knowledge (*pramanas*), which it identified as sense-perception, inference and the testimony of experts.

The Vaisheshika school is a variant of and development from the Nyaya school. Its founder is said to be Kanada Kashyapa who lived somewhere between the sixth and second centuries BCE. The school proposed a naturalistic and atomistic metaphysics, arguing that everything is composed from indestructible, indivisible and eternal atoms (*paramanu*). Its theories of relations and causation are highly sophisticated. The Nyaya and Vaishesheika schools are often treated as a single school.

Purva Mimamsa is the closest thing among the darshanas to a religion in the standard meaning of this term. It is ritualistic and requires of its adherents an unquestioning faith in the Vedas and observance of the sacrifices they prescribe, most particularly the fire sacrifices, believing that unless these are performed the universe will suffer ill-effects. Another name for Purva Mimamsa is therefore 'Karma Mimamsa', because of the focus on action, *karma*. However it is not straightforwardly theistic; its earlier adherents did not attribute importance to deities, but later developments of the outlook imported theistic elements. The founder of the school, Jaimini, lived in the fourth century BCE. He argued that verbal testimony, the Word or *Shabda* of the Vedas, is the only authoritative source of knowledge. The school regarded the Vedas as *apaurusheya*, 'self-revealed', 'unwritten', and held that this established their authority.

Vedanta or Uttara Mimamsa is the school whose metaphysics is similar enough to that of Buddhism to make it seem somewhat familiar to Western eyes. 'Vedanta' means 'end of the Vedas' and accordingly takes much of its inspiration from the Upanishads. It teaches that the world is an illusion, *Maya*; one of the strands of Vedanta owing to the sage Adi Shankaracharya, said to have lived in the eighth century BCE, teaches the doctrine of *Advaita*, non-dualism, laying stress on the Upanishadic theme that the individual soul, Atman, and the ultimate reality, 'Brahman', are one and the same. Vedanta lays stress on the ideas of reincarnation (*punarjanma*), and the effect of accumulated karma on the prospects of reincarnation and ultimate liberation from it.

The earliest of the heterodox (nastika) schools is Carvaka, also known as Lokayata (or it could be that a school of that name was so close in doctrine to Carvaka that the two merged). It dates from the eighth century BCE. It is non-theistic, materialist in metaphysics and empiricist in epistemology, regarding direct perception as the principal source of knowledge.

Buddhism was founded by Siddhartha Gautama, who lived somewhere between the early sixth century and the late fourth century BCE, and probably in the latter. It is a non-theistic philosophy teaching a means of liberation from suffering, as the other schools do, but with a radically different metaphysics, denying the reality of Atman and Brahman altogether. Later versions of Buddhism accreted supernaturalistic trappings over time, as almost all systems do when they become a popular outlook and system for dealing with life ('popular' here meaning 'of the people'). Buddhism is familiar the world over, attracting both adherents and interest, although no longer much of a presence in its country of origin. Legends of the Buddha (making him a prince who had lived a sheltered life until one day he left his palace and saw the suffering of the world) grew over the centuries; what remains basic to the various Buddhist schools is the doctrine of the Four Noble Truths and the Eightfold Path to liberation from existence by attainment of *nirvana* (extinction). The Four Noble Truths are that life is suffering, that suffering arises from desire and ignorance, that suffering can be escaped, and that one can achieve liberation by living an ethical life and by meditation. The Eightfold Path is Right Vision (understanding), Right Emotion, Right Speech, Right Action, Right Livelihood (work that does not harm others), Right Effort, Right Mindfulness and Right Meditation.

Jainism was said to have existed for a long time before being given a fresh impetus by the sage Mahavira in the sixth century BCE. Jains regard him as the twenty-fourth *Tirthankara*, or discoverer of a ford across the sea of endless births and deaths (*samsara*). Tirthankaras are those who reach a true understanding of the nature of the self, and are able therefore to cross *samsara*, leaving behind them guidance to others who can follow and thus attain liberation (*moksha*). It is non-theistic, and teaches asceticism and *ahimsa* (non-harm).

The astika schools are the tributaries that flow into Hinduism, a set of related outlooks and practices which, in the course of their evolution, became theistic during the period of the emerging 'Hindu synthesis' between 500 BCE and 300 CE. It was in this period that the authority of the Vedas was proclaimed, together with the integration of the Smrti writings, notable among them the *Mahabharata* and the *Ramayana*, and especially the section of the former known as the *Bhagavad Gita*, which has such a high status in Hinduism that it is sometimes regarded as Sruti rather than Smrti, 'heard' rather than 'remembered'.

Of the nastika schools, Buddhism in its various and evolved forms, and Jainism in one of its two principal traditional forms, continue to exist. Carvaka has long been extinct.

All the schools share much in outlook – some or all of the themes of suffering, liberation by extinction following upon grasp of the true nature of reality and/or the accumulation of sufficient good karma, the illusory nature of things in common experience, asceticism and meditation as potentiators of the liberating process; these recur across the schools, and bear upon the central ethical concern they share: the goal of an escape from suffering. The differences are chiefly of fine technical detail in the epistemological and metaphysical underpinnings of these themes.

A more detailed look at some of the darshanas gives a better indication of their philosophical sophistication. Consider the dualism of Samkhya. This is not a 'mind—matter' dualism in the sense of the Western tradition, but a dualism of consciousness and everything that is not consciousness, respectively purusha and prakriti. Moreover purusha is *pure* consciousness, something more fundamental than what might ordinarily be meant by 'mind'.

Samkhya holds that prakriti – everything other than consciousness – consists of three qualities or properties (*gunas*) in combination, respectively *sattva*, 'essence', the concept of which suggests illumination, clarity, harmony, goodness; *rajas*, 'dust', the concept of which suggests activity, passion, movement, change; and *tamas*, 'darkness', the concept of which suggests lethargy, heaviness, despair, chaos. Prakriti is stable, in a state of pure latency or potentiality, when the three gunas are in equilibrium. When there is imbalance between them a sequence of events unfolds, in which prakriti manifests itself in twenty-three independent structures called *tattvas*. The highest is *buddhi*, will or intellect, which although not conscious is so close to purusha that it seems to be so. The other structures – going swiftly through the list – are a sense of individual selfhood which can be called 'egoity'; the animate capacities of sensing, speaking, moving, eating and procreating; the 'subtle elements' of sound, taste, touch, sight and smell; and the 'gross elements' of space, air, fire, water and earth, which in their combinations constitute the ordinary objects of the physical world.

The three reliable sources of information according to Samkhya epistemology are perception, inference and expert testimony, in that order of importance. We know that there is a fire when we see it; we know, with a degree of defeasibility, that there is a fire when we infer its existence from seeing smoke rising in the distance; we know, with a greater degree of defeasibility, that there is a fire that we can neither see nor infer, but which is reported to us by a reliable informant. In perception the sense organs perceive their objects – colours for the eye, sounds for the ear – and these perceptions in their turn are assembled into a representation by the mind (*manas*) to which the ego (*ahamkara*) contributes its perspective and the intellect (*buddhi*) contributes understanding.

This threefold combination is knowledge. As this shows, manas, aham-kara and buddhi are the three constituents of what in English would be given the overall name 'mind'. This tripartite mind is not purusha; but purusha 'witnesses' this activity, thereby contributing consciousness to it. A simile has it that purusha is the lord of the house, the tripartite mind is the door-keeper, and the sense organs are the doors.

The soteriological aspect of Samkhya – that is, the doctrine about liberation from suffering – has a subtlety that arises from the fact that purusha is in ontological terms completely distinct from prakriti, that is, is a different order of reality. The doctrine is not that purusha as True Self needs to be liberated from the bonds of prakriti, because as a different order of reality purusha cannot be in any relation – other than as witness – of anything that is or arises from prakriti. Rather, liber-ation consists in the realization *that one is not bound by or to prakriti*; it consists in recognizing the ontological difference and its entailment that purusha is *already* free and has always been free. A common fea-ture of Indian soteriologies is that they are gnostic: liberation is the attainment of knowledge, the source of suffering is ignorance.

Causation is an important theme in the darshanas. Samkhya teach-ing on this is that effects exist prior to their manifestations, in the form of a latency in their causes. Causation is the making manifest of what was implicit in the cause already. The importance of this for the Sam-khya metaphysics is that it entails that the world, as an emanation of the Absolute (Brahman), was already in the Absolute before its manifest-ation. In terms of prakriti the idea seems to be that causation is the unfolding of the cause itself into the effect. In justification of this view Samkhya says that it does not require the bringing into existence of any-thing that did not exist beforehand, and it explains why effects are always of the same nature as their causes (cows always give birth to cows).

Samkhya is regarded as the least developed or sophisticated of the darshanas because it is the earliest. The philosophies – or, because of the connection between them, the philosophy – of the Nyaya–Vaisheshika school not only are more developed but have features which are recog-nizably similar to major ideas in Western metaphysics.

Nyaya can be translated as 'logic' and much of its debate concerned methods of proof. Vaisheshika is a philosophy of nature, which seeks to identify the variety of things that cognition and language apply to, thus providing them with their objective basis. Earlier commentators and developers of these views connected them; much later commentators and developers – in the later centuries of the first millennium CE – gave them a theistic dimension and associated the combined school with Shiva worship.*

A defining commitment of Nyaya–Vaisheshika is summed up as 'existence is knowability and nameability.' In its classical period the Vaisheshika developed a sophisticated theory of causation involving a set of rigorously defined 'primary existents', *padarthas*, of substance, quality, motion, particular, universal, inherence and nonexistence. The Sanskrit term 'padartha' etymologically means 'referent (*artha*) of a word (*pad*)', and the first three categories, of substance, quality and motion, are regarded as primary. But all the categories have *astitva*, which means 'isness', that is, *being*, required for their knowability and nameability. They are accordingly real and objective. 'Nonexistence' or 'absence', added to the list of categories later, has independent existence likewise, for the absence of something can be known about and talked about.

There are nine substances in the category of substance: earth, water, air, fire, ether, time, space, self and mind. There are twenty-four qualities in the category of quality, a very disparate list including sensory qualities of colour, sound and smell, and abstractions like hatred, merit and nearness. In the category of motion there are five types: throwing upwards, throwing downwards, expanding, contracting and going. Across the categories there are particular associations between qualities and substances: earth is related to smell, water to taste, fire to colour, and so on. The self is associated with knowledge, pleasure, desire, frustration and hatred, among other qualities.

Substances (*dravya*) are either permanent or impermanent. The permanent, because indestructible, substances are the atoms and what they constitute. The atoms are not only ultimate in the ontological sense – there is nothing into which, as the name implies, they can be divided – but they are also ultimately individual or distinct from each other. The expression *antya vishesha* to indicate this is a source of the school's name, 'Vaisheshika'. By their nature atoms combine and separate to form the

---

* Shiva 'the destroyer and transformer' is one of the 'Trimurti' or Hindu trinity, with Brahma and Vishnu. He has many guises and plays many roles, as images of him (with a serpent round his neck, a third eye in his forehead, the Ganges river gushing from his hair, a trident in his hand, and more) show.

substances of intermediate size which are therefore impermanent. Space, time and selves are, however, both completely individual and infinite in size (although each self is constricted when linked to a physical body).

The school distinguished between 'being white' as a quality and 'whiteness' as a universal. This relates to the fundamental substratum–property model of its ontology: the substance, *dharmin*, has the property, *dharma*, inhering in it – 'inherence', *samavaya*, being a special concept in the doctrine. A technical reformulation of ordinary language statements into *dharmadharmin* form provides an ontologically perspicuous account of what is being said, thus: to talk or think of a cow is to talk or think of a universal *cowness* being instantiated at a location X (the substratum) by the relation of inherence – yielding something like 'cowness is inhering here.' It has been pointed out that, in a way even more marked than in German, Sanskrit terms can be compounded and supplemented both to increase abstraction and to nominalize abstractions in such a way that reference to them imputes independent reality to them. One result is that the relation of *inherence* is treated as independently real. This was thought to be required because the unity of inseparable things (for example, a surface and its colour) compounded from a substance and a quality requires that what links them should be as real as they are.

The Vaisheshika doctrine of samavaya – inherence – is fundamental to its realist cosmology. Inherence holds between part and whole, quality and substance, action and substance, generic characters and their individual manifestations, the eternal substance and the ultimate individuality of atoms. From the smallest to the largest scale everything hangs together because of samavaya.

Inherence is one of the three types of cause recognized by the school: inherent, non-inherent and efficient. The inherent cause is what the effect inheres in, as the cloth inheres in the threads from which it is woven. The non-inherent cause is a correlative of either the cause or the effect; for example, the position of the threads is a non-inherent cause of the cloth (the threads could have been woven together in a different arrangement). The efficient cause is the working of the loom that wove the threads into a cloth. The Vaisheshika doctrine differs markedly from the Samkhya view that the effect must exist in its cause, holding that the effect must be a new existence, not contained in the cause but freshly created by it. A cause is defined as 'an invariable precedent of the effect', to avoid treating anything and everything that preceded an effect as part of its cause. To avoid difficulties about how long a period can elapse, or how many intervening factors there can be, between a cause and its effect, a qualification is added that the cause must not be 'too remote' from the effect, remoteness or irrelevance being defined in several ways according to the length and nature of the intervening chain of factors.

In Nyaya–Vaisheshika four forms of cognition, *pramanas*, are regarded as valid: perception, inference, comparison and testimony. In the great debate between the philosophers of this school and the Buddhists, the latter argued that there are only two valid forms of cognition, perception and inference. The leading Buddhist scholar Nagarjuna in the second century CE challenged the Nyaya–Vaisheshika to explain what validates the pramanas themselves. If a knowledge claim is based on perception, what justifies perception itself as a basis for knowledge? The danger of a regress threatens; it is parallel to the problem of induction as a form of reasoning, whose only justification seems to be the inductive ground of its past successes. The Nyaya–Vaisheshika thinkers could reply that the pramanas are self-validating in that they demonstrate their validity when they validate knowledge-claims, just as lamplight illuminates the lamp from which it shines. Nagarjuna replied that this kind of example works only if we think of lamplight as first not being light, which is a contradiction.

The *Nyayasutras* define perception, *pratyaksa*, as a non-verbal, non-deviant connection between sense and object. Over time an evolution in the concept occurred, shifting its focus from the act of perceiving as classical Nyaya–Vaisheshika had it, to the percept itself, a change that was pounced on by Buddhist critics, forcing a late (sixth-century CE) return to insistence on the act instead of its content. Error and illusion are explained as having three sources. One is to believe that a non-existing thing exists. The second is to think that something that exists only in consciousness exists outside consciousness. The third is the case where what is perceived cannot be regarded as unreal, because it is perceived; and yet what one thought was being perceived is not real but is something else, as in illusion or misperception – for example, seeing a bush in the dark and thinking it is a dog.

Nyaya's particular province is, as mentioned, logic. Its classical inferential schema has this form: first there is the statement of a position, followed by the evidence in its favour, then a statement of the general principle involved, then a demonstration that the instant case falls under the principle, and then the conclusion that the statement of position is correct. A classic Nyaya example is as follows. Proposition: there is fire on the hill. Evidence: smoke is rising above the hill. Principle: where there is smoke, there is fire. Subsumption: this particular event of smoke rising above the hill accords with the principle that connects smoke and fire. Conclusion: This proves the proposition, that there is fire on the hill. The metatheory of such inferences employs an interesting anticipation of the use of Venn-like or set-theoretical-like techniques of inclusion and exclusion from classes or kinds: thus, what is proposed must refer to something that falls within the class of things covered by the principle – or if a negative instance is cited, must fall outside it (vary the example to 'there is no fire on the hill' inferred from an absence of smoke) – and the concept of what is referred to by the subject term of the proposition to be proved must likewise fall within the concept of the ground of evidence offered. And so on.

The Nyaya–Vaisheshika is a living philosophical tradition. Navya-Nyaya is a highly developed technical form of it, which from the late thirteenth century CE to the present occupies something like the same relation to its classical antecedents as modern Western philosophy bears to ancient philosophy. Its theories of universals, truth and knowledge, as the rudimentary sketch of them just given only hints, are of the first interest and refinement, and make an illuminating and enriching comparison with the same themes in Western philosophy.

The astika schools of philosophy share a common point of departure, whether in dualist or monist forms, from the Upanishadic conception of the relation between Atman (self, soul) and Brahman (the Absolute, reality as a whole, the universal self). In the classical Upanishadic view Atman and Brahman are two sides, subjective and objective, of the same reality; they are – as the Advaita 'non-dualist' form of Vedanta teaches – one and the same. This is the meaning of the *mahavakya*, 'great saying', of the Upanishads: *tat tvam asi*, 'That thou art,' interpreted to entail 'I am that,' and hence 'Atman is Brahman.' The articulation of this conception of the ultimate nature of reality, together with the working out in detail of the metaphysical and epistemological aspects of a view that would identify the correct route to the soteriological outcome – namely, how to achieve liberation from suffering by overcoming the ignorance that is its fundamental cause – is what the astika schools aim to achieve.

Buddhism's claim is that this is a mistake. In sharp contrast to the astika programmes Buddhism asserts that there is no Atman, no Brahman, no absolute reality; there is not only no self, but no permanence of any kind. The postulation of the existence of, and attempt to explicate the nature of, a permanent self is not only the wrong target, it is the very source of suffering itself. The rigorously critical argumentation of the Buddhist thinkers is aimed at achieving a reduction of phenomenal thinking and its objects to a liberating grasp of *dharma-dhatu*, 'how things really are'.

The Buddhist schools argued among themselves with great sophistication. A way of illustrating this is by reference to a distinction drawn in the *Abhidharma* texts, dating from the third century BCE onwards, and consisting of commentaries upon and developments of the suttas or teachings of the Buddha. The distinction is between primary or substantial existence and secondary, conceptual or derived existence. The Madhyamaka school argued that everything is a secondary existent; when a search is made for primary existents, nothing is found. If an attempt is made to reduce secondary existents to the primary existents which are their putative basis, the reduction leads to emptiness: nothing has inherent existence. Transposed to the idiom of truth, this amounts to saying that 'the ultimate truth is that there are no ultimate truths.' But emptiness, *sunyata*, is itself the outcome of causes and conditions, not in the sense that there were, once upon a time, primary existents which have since ceased to be, leaving just the secondary existents behind, but in the sense that the things we take to be real in our experience of them are mere conventionalities with no substance. To understand that they are empty, meaningless, insubstantial, a mere flow of nothings, is to see them as not worth the desire or craving we have for them. So long as we think them substantial, we are ignorant of their true nature, and that is why suffering arises.

The Yogacara school thought that the Madhyamaka doctrine was unsustainable, on the ground that nothing can be a secondary existent without there being a primary existent for it to be secondary to. They therefore had to postulate a primary existent, and nominated the non-dual stream of consciousness for the role: 'mind only' or *cittamatra*. As the name implies, Yogacara adherents had a particular interest in meditation, which explains the motivation for identifying the primary existent with what lies at the deepest phenomenological level of untrammelled consciousness in meditation. Nevertheless, the Yogacara's doctrine of the Three Aspects specifying the nature of cittamatra shows that the terminus of the argument – emptiness, though differently described – is the same as in the Madhyamaka doctrine. The first aspect is the realm of subject–object duality (as those who are unenlightened think of the world, demonstrated by the language they use). The second aspect is the 'dependent' aspect, the flow of experience which the unenlightened incorrectly polarize into subject and object, whereas the flow of experience is all there is. The third 'perfected' aspect is the truth about things, which is grasped in meditation: emptiness, but redefined as 'non-duality'.

In the Dinnaga–Dharmakirti school only two modes of cognition are recognized, perception and inference. They constitute 'right cognition', defined as 'knowledge not contradicted by experience'. Dinnaga's argument for there being only two modes of cognition is that ordinary experience gives us just two aspects: the particular, which is what we perceive, and the universal, which is what we infer. Universals are not real, and the perception of a particular occurs only momentarily, that moment consisting in 'unconstructed' perception, whereas what immediately follows is 'constructed' by the interpretative attribution of qualities and properties – namely, universals. The constructed perception can, however, lead to right action, and therefore, in virtue of not being contradicted by experience, counts as knowledge. Given that this view could be described as turning on a distinction between 'knowledge by acquaintance' and 'knowledge by description' one can see the clear similarity to views such as Russell's in later Western epistemology: see p. 352 above.

Dinnaga held that there are four kinds of perception: sense-perception, mental perception, yogic (extra-sensory) perception and reflexive perception or self-awareness. Other Buddhist scholars were critical of the inclusion of this last as a form of perception, which they took to imply a form of 'awareness of being aware', implying a self – a higher self? – which in a doctrine teaching the unreality of self is a complication.

Influential ideas were developed by the Dinnaga–Dharmakirti school in logic as well as epistemology, Dinnaga's *hetucakra*, 'the wheel of reasons', showing all the possible combinations of a reason with its positive and negative instances, and specifying which of them constitute a valid inference. Of the nine such combinations, only two are valid: in both cases when the reason, *hetu*, is present in the subject and in the positive example, and absent from the negative example. For example: in judging that there is a fire on that hill over there because one sees smoke rising above it, one has a positive example of fire and smoke being connected (e.g. the fire in one's kitchen) and a negative example where there is never a connection of fire and smoke (e.g. in the waters of a lake).

The path to liberation for Jains – their name derives from *jina*, 'victory', implying conquest of suffering by passing over the cycle of rebirths to the liberation of non-existence – consists of doing no harm (*ahimsa*), detachment (*aparigraha*), asceticism and acceptance of the fact that reality is infinitely complex and many-sided (*anekantavada*), so that it is never possible to give a single definitive description of anything. This means that anything we think or say can at best only be partly true, and is ever only 'from a certain point of view' (*syadvada*). Every point of view has some truth in it; so 'from a certain point of view X is' and 'from a certain point of view X is not' are both possible simultaneously. The Jain doctrine of substance accordingly allows that it both decays and is stable. To assert that it must definitely be one or the other is 'one-sided', *ekanta*, or even 'extremist'. The parallel with scepticism is striking. It was suggested (see p. 120 above) that Pyrrho of Elis visited India and learned his outlook from its 'naked philosophers', the gymnosophists; these could very likely have been Jains, whose most assiduous devotees indeed went about naked.

The only sources of knowledge about the Carvaka–Lokayata school are the hostile comments and criticism of its adversaries. They report that the school was empiricist, materialist and hedonistic. It was radically empiricist in epistemology, holding that sense-perception is the only valid form of cognition; it was radically materialist in metaphysics, denying the existence of souls, gods or an afterlife; and it was said to be hedonistic in ethics, extolling the virtues of pleasure. 'Lokayata' means 'of the people', and perhaps initially referred to the materialistic and this-worldly assumptions and lifestyle of unlettered ordinary people. But it came to mean 'sceptical' because the restriction to sense-experience as the only valid means to knowledge implies that inference is inherently doubtful and conditional, an implication accepted by the school.

'Carvaka' is the name of the suppositious founder of the school, although an earlier founder and supposed author of a lost sutra (known only in fragments) is one Barhaspatya. The *Barhaspatya-sutra* is quoted as saying that perception tells us nothing about reincarnation, or whether or not rituals and sacrifices do any good, or whether other worlds such

as hells and heavens exist, or whether actions produce good or ill consequences in this or supposed other lives. Accordingly there is no reason to
believe any of it. Instead perception tells us that natural things are their
own causes, their properties residing in and arising from their physical
constitution. Consciousness is a product of physical processes in the
body. Since physical existence is reality, pleasure and the avoidance of
pain are what is good. 'Delicious food, young women, fine clothes, per-
fumes and garlands' are said (by way of criticism in the *Sarvasiddhanta
Samgraha*) to be the Carvaka school's idea of heaven, while *moksha*, the
liberation of extinction, occurs naturally and inevitably with death.

The view of life actually or functionally held by most people in
today's developed societies is precisely that of the Carvaka school.

These sketches of ideas in some of the Indian philosophical schools
are intended to indicate that if one had the linguistic competence to
make a detailed study of them, doing so would provide great insight
into problems that are as fundamental to Western philosophy as to
them. It has been surmised that there was communication between
Indian and Greek thinkers – the great Persian Empire abutted both
their worlds, to east and west respectively, for many centuries, and it is
implausible to think that there was no contact or exchange of ideas.
Greek and Sanskrit are descendants of a single earlier language, Indo-
European or Simple Aryan, and languages carry hints of their users'
worldviews in their vocabularies and structures; ideas of substance and
property, causality, knowledge, mind and consciousness, the question
whether what we encounter in everyday experience reveals or misleads
as to the true nature of reality – these lie at the heart of philosophy, and
both Indian and Western traditions of thought address them in remark-
ably similar ways.

Chinese Philosophy

Confucianism, Mohism, Daoism and Legalism are the principal schools of philosophical thought in China. From the first century CE Buddhism became an influence also, being dominant during the Sui (581–618) and Tang (618–960) dynasties. But apart from this and certain other, briefer periods, Confucianism was the leading outlook. In the Han dynasty (206 BCE–220 CE) examinations for Imperial civil service entry were based on the Confucian texts; after the Tang had been replaced by the Song dynasty (960–1279), civil service examinations based on the Confucian texts were reintroduced, and the practice lasted for the thousand years from then until 1905 (bar an intermission during the Mongolian invader dynasty of the Yuan, 1279–1368).

Classification of the philosophical schools in the pre-Han period owes itself to Sima Qian (145–86 BCE) in his *Records of the Grand Historian* (known in Chinese as the *Shiji*).* This remarkable man had inherited the role of Court Historian from his father, but had fallen foul of a political intrigue and been castrated and imprisoned, with the expectation that he would, as all scholar-gentlemen who had suffered these indignities were supposed to, commit suicide on being released. But he refused to do this so that he could continue with his great work of history. His book is the first major work of Chinese historiography, and – discounting for its Confucian moral slant – a valuable resource. Subsequent scholarship, not least on the texts of the schools themselves, has introduced many correctives to Sima Qian's picture, but that

---

* In giving Chinese names and titles of works (typically the name of a thinker is used as the title of his book also) I use the Pinyin form of rendering Chinese into Roman letters. This has now replaced the Wade-Giles system, slightly confusingly: for example, the classic work *Daodejing* was known in its Wade-Giles rendering as *Tao Te Ching*.

picture did much to establish the traditional classification of Chinese thought, and in particular the status of Confucius, for the rest of China's history.

Confucius himself, *Kong Fuzi* (Master Kong), is traditionally said to have been born in the state of Lu in 551 BCE and to have died in 479 BCE, which places the latter event just nine years before the birth of Socrates, and within a year or two of either the birth or the death of Siddhartha Gautama, the Buddha (depending on whether you accept Buddha's later or earlier life dates). Lu was a vassal state of the Zhou kingdom (*c*.1046–256 BCE) roughly in the area of today's Shandong Province in eastern China. Lu figures significantly in China's history as the home state not only of Confucius but also of Mozi (470–391 BCE), the founder of Mohism, and as the subject of the *Spring and Autumn Annals*, a chronicle of the state's history covering the period 722–481 BCE. According to Mencius (Mengzi, 372–289 BCE), the second most important philosopher in the Confucian school, the *Annals* was written by Confucius himself, so it is placed among the *Five Classics* attributed to him, the other four being the *Classic of Poetry* (*Shijing*, sometimes called *The Book of Songs* or *Book of Odes*), the *Book of Documents* (*Shujing*), the *Book of Rites* (*Liji*) and the *Book of Changes* (*Yijing*).

At the time of Confucius' birth the Zhou kingdom was in decline, and had been so for more than a century. The many small tributary states it once controlled had begun to form into a number of larger states, vying among themselves for hegemony. The continual warfare this involved gave the epoch from the fifth to the third centuries BCE the name the 'Warring States Period'. In the *Analects* (*Lunyu*), the text of Confucian teachings said to have been compiled by his disciples and followers (but almost certainly edited together much later, in the first or second century BCE), Confucius is described as looking back with regret to the early history of the Zhou kingdom, regarded as a golden age.

Confucius probably held a civil service post as a young man, but he was anxious to contribute his ideas to any ruler who would listen, and he therefore travelled through the fragmented Zhou world seeking a hearing. There were many such as he, known as *Ru* or 'literati', all trying the same thing. He was unsuccessful; but in the course of his efforts he accumulated a following of disciples. For several centuries the *Analects* were regarded merely as commentaries on the Five Classics, and the relatively minor status it therefore had may explain why something like three-quarters of the Confucian sayings quoted by Mencius do not appear in the *Analects*, their source in other or variant compilations having since been lost. Much later, in the Song dynasty when Confucius' reputation was restored to the high levels it had enjoyed in the Han dynasty, the *Analects* was given the status of a supremely authoritative text, and was enrolled among the *Four Books*, the other three being the *Great Learning* (*Daxue*), the *Doctrine of the Mean* (*Zhongyong*) and the *Mencius* (*Mengzi*). The *Daxue* is a chapter from the *Book of Rites* with a commentary by a Confucian scholar called Zengzi. The *Zhongyong* is also a chapter from the *Rites*, said to have been contributed by Confucius' grandson Zisi. The *Mengzi* is the book written by Mencius, setting out Confucian doctrines and his own developments of them, in the form of long conversations with various kings and rulers. The Four Books and Five Classics are the corpus on which the Confucian tradition – and therefore the culture of China for much of the history of the last two thousand years – is based.

Confucius' argument was that if those in government behave ethically – which means: with propriety and benevolence – they will create the good society. A life disciplined by the correct observance of rituals and formalities would ensure this. A key to the achievement of social harmony and right order is how such relationships as those between ruler and ruled, father and son, are observed. A passage in the *Analects* relates an anecdote in which Confucius is told of a village with an inhabitant known as the 'True Person' because he reported his father to the authorities for stealing a sheep. Confucius replied, 'In my village the "true people" are the fathers who cover for their sons and sons who cover for their fathers.' This might strike modern Western sensibility as questionable – loyalty trumping honesty – but on a generous interpretation (and, as it happens, one that is conformable with everything else Confucius says) the point he is making is that if all relationships were correctly conducted, there would be no wrongdoing to lie about.

The theory is top-down: if rulers rule well, fathers will be good parents, sons will be well brought up and dutiful – and therefore society will be harmonious and flourishing. The direction of ethical flow is *from* those in positions of authority, who set the standards and examples of good behaviour, *to* those who depend on them. Accordingly, the people who are to set the standards have to observe the very highest standards themselves.

The two fundamental concepts in Confucian ethics are those of *ren*, benevolence or humanity, and *li*, which literally means 'rites' but denotes proper behaviour generally. In origin *ren* means 'manly', rather like the root meaning of the Sanskrit word *vir*, 'hero', and the Latin word *vir* to mean 'man' in the masculine sense, 'manly' – from the latter comes *virtue*, once accordingly restricted to the male of the species.

Ren has a variety of senses. Its principal sense is humaneness or benevolence, and therefore includes kindness, consideration, compassion and a concern for humanity in general. But its proper exercise requires a knowledge of human character, an ability to distinguish good people from bad (*zhiren* is 'knowledge of men'). Accordingly the *Analects* reports Confucius' reply to a disciple who asked, 'To repay ill-will with goodwill; what do you think of that?' Confucius asked, 'Then what will you repay goodwill with? Repay ill-will with uprightness, and goodwill with goodwill.'

The idea of reciprocity, *shu*, at work here underlies the Confucian Golden Rule: 'do not do to others what you would not wish them to do to you.' It is a familiar point that this is the negative version of the rule that says, 'Do to others as you would have them do to you.' George Bernard Shaw's comment regarding this latter – 'don't do to others what you would like them to do to you, because they may not like it' – shows why the negative formulation is better. It requires the exercise of moral imagination, putting oneself in another's place and seeing things from that perspective: 'Zeng said, The way of the Master is to do one's utmost and to put oneself in the other's place.'

Other terms also apply to those who are *ren*. There is the *sheng* or *sheng-ren*, 'sage' or 'wise man' – this term occurs even more frequently in Mencius. There is the *junzi* or 'superior man', 'exemplary man'; there is *xian*, 'admirable man', 'man of excellence'; and these are contrasted with the *xiao ren*, literally 'small man', the opposite of the *junzi*.

A generic term *de* denotes 'virtue' but not in the sense of 'the virtues' as commonly understood; perhaps something more like *virtù* in Machiavelli's sense (see p. 189 above). 'The virtues' have their own names. Loyalty is *zhong*; filial piety – proper respect for and deference to one's ancestors and parents, a very important Confucian virtue – is *xiao*; good faith is *xin*; courage is *yong*; politeness, courtesy, respectfulness is *rang*.

A term that occurs frequently in Chinese philosophy, as in the *Analects*, is *Tian*, 'heaven' (literally 'the sky'). It is a mistake to interpret this in a religious sense. Rather like *logos* in the philosophy of the Stoics, it captures a very complex concept combining all, most or some of the following ideas: an overarching independent order of the way things properly are; what should be complied with in order to do things properly or rightly; natural law; fate, destiny; what is not within personal control; necessity. Perhaps the most direct way for a Western sensibility to grasp *Tian* would be to describe it as 'the universe' *behaving as if* it were a purposive entity. But *Tian* is not a deity nor any kind of conscious agency. As the sky it figures as a place; at the beginning of the classic novel by Cao Xueqin, *The Dream of Red Mansions* (or *Dream of the Red Chamber*; in the definitive English translation by David Hawkes it is entitled *The Story of the Stone*), a goddess called Nu-wa is repairing the sky with melted rocks, one of which is left at the foot of the Great Fable Mountains. Two monks find it and it asks them to take it to see the world. It turns into a boy (this being Jia Baoyu, the novel's central character) and the novel tells the story of his family, friendships and loves. In this eighteenth-century Qing dynasty work the sky and the immortals are as fairyland and wizards would be in Western stories, or as Middle Earth and Hobbits. They are not part of the ontology of the *Analects* or other schools of Chinese philosophy.

Much is said in the *Analects* about study or learning, *xue*, to achieve the status of *ren* and to acquire understanding of people and society, *zhi*. A learned man of understanding will know how to follow the Way, *dao*.

Dao (often written *Tao*) is a key term in Chinese thought in general, with its own nuances and rich sets of associations for different schools. In Confucian thought it is often expressed in terms of 'the Way of the gentleman', 'the Way of one's father', 'the Way of Wen and Wu' (these being two legendary founding kings of the Zhou period, father and son, who respectively chose civil and military means of rule). But the general idea of the Confucian Way is that of correct, appropriate, humane, benevolent, mutually courteous, loyal conduct of government in general and relationships in particular.

To become a superior person who follows the Way of *ren* one needs to learn the four subjects taught by Confucius: culture, good conduct, loyalty and honesty. The word for culture, *wen*, literally means 'ornament' or 'decoration', but as applied to people it denotes the intellectual and personal graces that make for a *junzi*, a 'superior man'. King Wen of 'Wen and Wu' was known as the Cultured King. A cultured person respects and observes the rites, *li*, the practice of which ensures that everything is done with respect, courtesy, reverence and discipline. The importance of *li* for Confucius is that if due process is followed in the business of both government and ordinary life, everything will be orderly and clear, because relationships will be maintained in the proper way. One whole book of the *Analects* is dedicated to a discussion of rites, mastery of which (alongside music, writing, mathematics, archery and charioteering) was regarded as a necessary accomplishment for a gentleman.

For Confucius the family is the foundation of society; it is where filial piety and brotherly respect are learned, and with them a caring and considerate attitude to humanity in general – *ren* itself. To exercise *ren* is a practical matter, a pragmatic matter, and the implication is that it can be learned, rather as in Aristotle the virtues can be practised in order to become habits.

For the Confucian tradition a question arose about the relative importance of the two fundamental concepts of *ren* and *li*. Which is the most important? This came to be called the *nei–wai* debate, *nei* meaning 'inner' and *wai* meaning 'outer'. Confucius himself, appropriately, argued for balance: 'When basic disposition overwhelms refinement, the person is boorish. When refinement overwhelms basic disposition, the person is officious. The exemplary person balances his basic disposition and his refinement.' At the same time, other texts in the *Analects* can be read as privileging *ren* over *li*, or *li* over *ren*, allowing the Confucian tradition its scope for debate.

The Confucian outlook as expressed in the *Analects* is idealistic and optimistic, not least in its view of human nature or at least the possibility of appropriate cultivation of human nature. Mencius, the second master of the Confucian tradition, whom legend says was taught by Confucius' grandson Zisi (483–402 BCE – the dates themselves do not allow this; Mencius was born in 372 BCE), took the view that human nature is fundamentally good. It follows that the prospects for the ideal Confucian state and society are good too. The third master of the tradition, Xunzi – his name was Xun Kuang (c.310–c.235 BCE; he is standardly known by the name of his book the *Xunzi*) – disagreed; his more realistic attitude resulted in the most carefully worked-out position for a Confucian approach to social ethics.

Mencius' view about human nature places him on the side of the inner, *nei*, in the *nei–wai* debate. What matters most, he said, is *xin* – the heart and mind or 'heart-mind' – from which comes all that can lead people to be *ren*. Mencius explained wrongdoing as the result of external forces; in hard times people commit crimes or become violent because they are struggling for survival. It is not a natural disposition for people to be like this, but suffering is 'what sinks and drowns their hearts'. As proof of innate goodness Mencius cites such phenomena as the distress anyone feels when they see that a child is in danger of falling into a well; they do not feel distress because they wish to please the child's parents or to get social approval; the sentiment arises in their *xin*.

In good Confucian fashion Mencius identified the cardinal virtues as benevolence, *ren*; righteousness, *yi*; wisdom, *zhi*; and propriety, *li*. Each is associated with an emotional attitude that expresses or enacts it: benevolence arises from compassion, righteousness from disdain for what is bad or wrong, wisdom from feelings of approval and disapproval, and propriety from the respect or reverence we feel for something or someone. The idea that virtues are expressed via their connection with emotions agrees with the argument in Hume and others that emotions are the source of motivation; an assumption in Mencius' account is that virtues both arise from and are exercised through a correlative motivational state of feeling, and these feelings are natural endowments of human psychology.

Mencius held that two of the four virtues, benevolence and righteousness, are primary. A ruler who possesses both virtues will be aware of the effect of his policies on his people, and will act always to benefit them. His sense of honour will make him disdain doing wrong, or acting corruptly, in small ways just as much as in large ways. With a benevolent and righteous ruler, the state will flourish and the people will be happy. The reason why they will be happy is not just the obvious one that they will have peace and prosperity, but also that in such circumstances their natural goodness will be able to express itself most fully, thus icing the cake: in a good society the people are at their best, making the society yet better. It is a virtuous upward spiral. Perhaps it says more about the *nei* disposition of Mencius himself, and to his credit therefore, that he thought this to be achievable. The next Confucian master, Xunzi, thought very differently.

Xunzi lived during the later part of the Warring States Period, by which time Confucianism itself, Daoism, Legalism and other schools had grown both in numbers of adherents and in energy of debate, constituting what is known as the 'Hundred Schools of Thought', the golden age of Chinese philosophy. There were not literally a hundred schools – the Chinese idiom uses large round numbers (a hundred, a thousand, ten thousand) to denote significant pluralities. It meant that Xunzi knew the arguments of other philosophers and schools, and he engaged with them in the book that bears his name, the *Xunzi*.

Xunzi took the view that human beings are by nature inclined to be bad, and that being good takes conscious effort. People are, he said, basically greedy; they seek personal profit; they see others as rivals, and therefore envy and hostility arise, and this causes crime, violence and betrayal. People are born with sense organs, which makes them seek dissolute pleasures. Therefore education is required, and models of upright behaviour. Only then do courtesy, refinement and loyalty develop. He wrote, 'Thus, a warped piece of wood requires the press-frame, steam to soften it, and force applied to straighten it. A blunt piece of metal must be whetted on the grindstone to make it sharp.'

An interesting idea in Confucianism, and one stressed by Xunzi, is the 'rectification of names' (*zheng ming*). The idea is that because the names of things are conventional and depend for their usefulness on agreement about their application, problems arise when agreement is lost. Therefore, said Xunzi, the ruler should establish the meanings of names by decree, so that they are standard for everyone everywhere – and orders will be obeyed appropriately. 'Names share no intrinsic reality,' he wrote. 'One agrees to use a certain name and issues an order that it shall be applied to a certain reality, and if the agreement is abided by and becomes a matter of custom, then it may be said to be a real name.' This looks like a simplistic idea but it is not. In circumstances of large distances and slow travel, and given that pronunciation and ter-minology can differ from one valley to the next in any pre-broadcast part of the world, difficulties of communication present problems for government. The 'rectification of names' idea is a plea for an official common language that everyone can understand clearly, not just for effi-cient administration – although in this respect its value is obvious – but for promoting shared values and standards, a medium for transmission of cultural norms.

Another way of achieving social cohesion is to standardize the *li*, the rituals, and to promote their use. Here too the idea concerns the promotion of norms and standards, because the performance of the *li* enacts the order and relationships of society, in a disciplined and serious way that brings society together in witness of what it expects of itself. Xunzi talks of the *li* as comparable to the flavours and spices of cuisine and the nourishment they give to the body politic. All societies have communal observances, ceremonies and celebrations – Fourth of July, the Queen's Birthday parade, Thanksgiving, Christmas, Eid, Diwali – and the intention they serve is to promote a sense of identity, loyalty to a shared purpose and remembrance of the founding events for both. In the way that a military parade is arranged one sees, among other things, orders of rank and precedence; the event itself displays hierarchy and the order of command – in writing of the *li* Xunzi says that among other things they manifest the 'differentiations', that is, the place that different groups occupy in society. One of the great virtues Confucianism impressed on Chinese political sensibility is *order*: disorder has acquired a superstitious dread in the course of China's history because every change of dynasty resulted from it, and much is explained in recent and contemporary China by seeing what happens there through this lens.*

The founder of Mohism is Mozi, a contemporary of Socrates. Much later, in the Ming and Qing dynasties, Mozi was portrayed by some Chinese scholars as an opponent of Confucianism, and moreover not a very effective one. Others, and especially those engaged in more recent scholarship on Chinese thought, recognize the independent interest of Mohist philosophy, and the contributions of the Mohist school to mathematics and logic.

The text setting out Mozi's thought, the *Mozi*, sets out its principal doctrines in three versions, which some scholars see as representing the approach of three different factions within the school, while other scholars – more plausibly – see the versions as the result of editing the text from variant traditions descending from Mozi and the debates of his followers. How the variant readings are understood, not least as regards which are earlier and which later, influences detailed understanding of the principles themselves. But running through the principles are two notable commitments: first, concern for others, brotherly love, *ai*; and second, a strong utilitarian theme of weighing benefits (*li*) and disbenefits (*hai*).

The first principle is 'elevate the worthy individual' and 'follow the

---

* As an illustration of how philosophy makes a difference to practice, this point is one of the keys to understanding China. See A. C. Grayling and Xu Youyu (jointly writing under the pseudonym 'Li Xiao Jun'), *The Long March to the Fourth of June* (1989) on the history of the Communist Party of China between Mao Zedong's 'Long March' of 1934–5 and the murderous events in Tiananmen Square on 4 June 1989.

standard [yi] he sets.' A society can be seen to be flourishing when it is populous, wealthy and orderly. To achieve this it must be governed by men who are committed to yi. A clear 'chain of command' structure in government helps to ensure that such men will be in government.*

'Impartial concern', jianai, or equal treatment and consideration for all by the government, protects social safety and harmony. The term jianai means 'to value others as you value yourself'. (It is sometimes translated as 'universal love' – ai means love – and jianai might better be translated as 'equal' or 'disinterested' love.) Mozi associates with this a further principle, 'seek peace', in the sense of opposing militarism and not resorting to military aggression; the connection is that if you would not yourself wish to fight in a war, do not send others to suffer and die in one. The disbenefits of war far outweigh the benefits; and aggression by states against one another is motivated by greed for wealth or power, which is unworthy – not yi. 'When we enquire into the causes of harms, what do we find? Do they come from loving others and trying to benefit them? Certainly not! They come, rather, from hating others and trying to injure them. Such actions are motivated by partiality, selfishness, and this gives rise to all the great harms in the world.'

'Moderation in expenses' (including specifically 'moderation in funerals' – not just their cost but the three-year mourning period for parents, during which the mourner did not work) is supported by a clear-minded weighing of li and hai, benefits and disbenefits. Although that length of mourning is probably psychologically right – two years is about the least time it takes to get fully over the loss of a loved one, whether through death or the ending of a significant relationship – Mozi thought that the conventional manner of marking respect and filial devotion by such an excessive observance was the result of 'confusing what is habitual with what is proper, and what is customary with what is right'. This is not the only respect in which one recognizes a congruence between Mohist thought and the New Testament criticism of the 'whited sepulchres' of Pharisaism.

Noting and conforming to the impartiality of Tian, which is the same for all, and as in effect 'nature' or the natural right order of things, which exists for the benefit of all, will ensure that individuals and society alike will be yi.

---

* It is specifically 'men' who are meant: there was no chance in any period of China's history until the recent past that women were even considered for such roles.

Mozi's concern for the welfare of all – 'loving others and trying to benefit them' – is the chief motive of his outlook. Although the word *ai* means 'love' it might in this context be better translated as 'benevolent concern' (remembering the etymology of *benevolent* as 'well-wishing', 'desiring the good of others'). When this is mutual among individuals, and the principle on which government operates, the result will be a good, flourishing society. When it is absent it is the source of harm. 'All the disorder in the world', Mozi says, 'arises from a lack of benevolent concern' between members of a family, between rulers and the ruled, between one state and another.

There is a tension implicit in these thoughts, however, one that is familiar in all ethical reflection: the tendency of people to care more for kin than for strangers, which works against the idea of universality of concern. In Christian moral theology just the same problem arose about friendship in light of the injunction for *agape*, impartial love of mankind; Augustine, who had greatly loved a friend of his young adulthood, wrestled with the dilemma that doing so is inconsistent with *agape*. Mozi addresses the problem by asking whether, if you had to entrust the care of your children to someone else, you would choose an impartial person or a partial one. 'On a question like this,' he says, 'there are no fools in the world; though one may not be impartial oneself, one would assuredly entrust one's family to an impartial man.'

The sense of familiarity one feels in contemplating Mozi's thought – the idea of fraternal love or concern, the adjuration to promote collective good – is heightened further by his description of what the alternative is: an anarchic situation in which different standards apply and people seek only to get the best for themselves – something like a Hobbesian state of nature. Shared values and standards prevent this, says Mozi, so if one 'elevates the worthy man' and everyone adopts his standard (*fa*), good order will prevail. But this means that the ruler has to be a model of rightness and benevolence, and the rest have to conform. In Hobbes the sovereign power is not required to be a standard of virtue; in Mozi he is.

Moreover Mozi specifies how to determine the nature of the standard which the ruler must set. There are three ways. One way is that one can look at the past to see examples of great rulers who were virtuous and benevolent, and whose states flourished as a result. The second way is that one can use empirical tests, for the ruler's behaviour will be evident in the effects on society, and the 'eyes and ears of the multitude' will register what these are. And the third way is that one can apply the test of benefits over disbenefits – *li* and *hai* – a utilitarian principle of decision that can be applied to every action and situation.

Mozi's followers developed a school of logic and metaphysics which came to be called the 'School of Names'. It is best known for a debate over the proposition 'a white horse is not a horse.' The puzzle about this turns on niceties of ancient Chinese language and the understanding of the negative *fei*, 'not' or 'is not', in the formula *bai ma fei ma* (*bai* means 'white', *ma* means 'horse'; so the whole means 'white horse not horse'). The argument in the 'White Horse Dialogue' of a book by the Mohist logician Gongsun Long is that 'horse' describes a shape and 'white' a colour, and a colour-name cannot be used to describe a shape, and therefore (claims the argument's proponent) one can assert *bai ma fei ma*. The scholar of Chinese philosophy A. C. Graham suggests that the appearance of paradox arises from a failure to distinguish between the 'is' in *fei*, 'is not', as the 'is' of inclusion (x is part of y) and 'is' of identity (x is y, x is the same thing as y). This suggests a plausible interpretation which saves the claim from being a mere fallacy, category mistake or muddle: this is to view the expression as shorthand for 'the concept *white horse* does not exhaust the concept *horse*,' that is, not all horses are white.

Mohist ethics offers an attractive and sympathetic outlook; so too, though in a rather different way, does Daoism (or Taoism, the older Anglicization of the term which unhelpfully represented the 'd' sound by a 't'). Perhaps many readers will recognize the saying, 'The world is won by those who let it go. When you try and try, the world is beyond winning.' Zen Buddhism (called Chan Buddhism in China) has a similar attitude to practices – the Zen method of playing a game is not to focus on what you are doing, because that inhibits and interrupts you, but instead to go (as the saying has it) with the flow. This idea might well have been derived from Daoism, the philosophy of the Way, *dao*. In fact there are several movements, groups and doctrines that can loosely be gathered under the label 'Daoism', the one thing they have in common being the concept that there is a way or path that will lead to some desired destination, whether it is becoming *ren*, achieving tranquillity, escaping the pointless demands of society, or whatever is identified as the right goal. But there is a text regarded as significant for this outlook, the *Daodejing* (old Anglicization, *Tao Te Ching*), sometimes also named for its supposed author, Laozi.

Either Laozi is a legendary figure, as indeed the name suggests – it just means 'Old Master' – or he was a person who lived in the sixth century BCE, possibly by name Lao Dan, in some traditions a teacher of Confucius. Promoters of Daoism held that their doctrines had been handed down from the remotest antiquity, even perhaps by the fabulous Yellow Emperor, Huangdi, whom legend places in the third millennium BCE and who is regarded as the founder of Chinese civilization. In the *Records of the Grand Historian* Sima Qian says that Confucius was overawed by Laozi and called him a 'dragon', thus likening him to the grandest and most lauded of China's mythological creatures. The notion, which dates to the pre-Han period itself, that Confucianism and Daoism were opposed in outlook is promoted by the later Daoist classic, the *Zhuangzi*, which says in the course of promoting the Daoist view that wisdom consists in a relaxed, skilful, sensitive kind of flexibility, and that Confucius lacked this quality.

Scholarship shows that the *Daodejing* was not written by a single person. It provides the kernel of a set of ideas called *daode*, and Sima Qian gave the label *Daojia* to those who put these ideas into practice, *jia* meaning 'family' or (figuratively) 'tribe'. There were in fact several Daojia, now classified as 'Huang-Lao', 'philosophical Daoism' and 'religious Daoism'. But they all draw on the central concepts of Daoism, *dao* meaning 'Path', *de* power, potency, virtue, *wuwei* do-nothing, and others. The *Daodejing* itself (*jing* means 'classic') is in two parts: the classic of *Dao* and the classic of *De*.

The concept of *dao* is extremely complex, rich and multiple. The very first sentence of the *Daodejing* says, 'The *dao* that can be explained is not the eternal *dao*.' This looks like a door shut on understanding. Matters are worse: use of 'the' before the final occurrence of 'dao' suggests that there is one eternal Dao. Some interpret it this way. Others argue that the original Chinese – *dao ke dao fei chang dao*, literally 'Dao possible to say not ever-enduring Dao' – leaves it open that there are many Ways. Nor can Dao even be named: the *Daodejing*'s second sentence is, 'The name that can be named is not the name' – meaning, 'The (a) name (of Dao) that can be named is not (its, their) name.' Dao is *wanwu*, 'ten thousand things' – suggesting the Dao is reality that transcends anything that can be comprehended; it is inexhaustible, indifferent, ungraspable. Or it is the origin or source of all things, inaccessible to understanding. It is what sustains everything, the fountain of existence and its continuation. These metaphysical renderings are suppositious, given the ineffability of Dao. Later commentators have added their personal take on what could or should be meant, some giving it a religious connotation, associating it with divination, cosmology and meditation.

De was translated above as 'virtue', goodness or morality, while in renderings of the *Daodejing* it is often given as 'potency', a sort of life-force towards self-realization. On this view to follow the Way is to apply, direct or unleash one's life-potential. 'Following the Way' mostly echoes the early understandings of Dao as a teaching or path. The Chinese character for Dao has two components, one associated with walking or going on a journey, and the other with following. But the essence of the *Daodejing*'s view of the journey that ought to be followed is that it is a deeper and prior thing than the 'ways' or virtues taught by other schools: 'When the great Dao declined, the doctrines of humaneness and uprightness arose. When the ideas of knowledge and wisdom came along, hypocrisy arose. When relationships are out of harmony, ideas of filial piety and love for children arise. When the country is disordered, praise will arise for good ministers. Abandon these ideas, and there will be wisdom, and uprightness, there will be filial piety, and love.' The injunction implicit here is to adopt the way of *wuwei*. It carries the implication that in a time before society and social organization, people behaved naturally and spontaneously, and therefore with effortless goodness. With society comes the need to make an effort to be humane, to be honest, to be filial.*

Wuwei means 'non-action'. It does not mean that one should literally do nothing at all in order to be in conformity with the Way; a more accurate rendering, as just suggested, is 'effortlessness', 'non-striving'. This is consistent with the quite definite idea of *wuwei* in the *Zhuangzi* where it relates to non-attachment and the achievement of serenity. Later Legalist philosophers recommend *wuwei* to rulers – what politicians sometimes regard as 'masterly inaction' – letting things play out of their own accord, without interference. Daoist masters use various analogies to explain *wuwei*, likening it to water which flows round things without troubling itself. 'The wise man acts without effort, teaches without many words, produces without possessing, creates but is indifferent to the outcome, lays claim to nothing, and therefore has nothing to lose.' One can learn how to live the principle of *wuwei* by

---

* The Daoists' state of nature is therefore the opposite of Hobbes' and more like Locke's: there are easy models for the Daoist conception in the lives of those animals that live untroubled by predators at the top of a food chain.

observing nature, its spontaneity and rhythms. 'Nature says little. A whirlwind does not last the whole morning. A rainstorm does not last the whole day. Who makes them? Nature. If nature cannot make them last long, how can man?' The idea of 'nature' and 'naturalness' is *ziren*, *zi* meaning 'self' and *ren* meaning 'thus', 'as it is'. The idea is that what one is and does comes from within, arises from the inner nature of things (including oneself).

The other great classic of Daoism is the *Zhuangzi*, named for its author of the same name (his dates, 399–295 BCE, give him a very long life; he was born in the year that Socrates died). It is more playful and teasing than the *Daodejing*, more critical, more sceptical, full of anecdotes drawn from animal and insect life, and it asks questions and poses problems but leaves them suggestively unresolved. The tales are entertaining and instructive, and some have become well known outside the context of the *Zhuangzi* and Daoist philosophy itself. There is for example the story of the man who dreamed he was a butterfly, flitting happily about; and then he woke, and wondered whether he was a man who had dreamed he was a butterfly, or a butterfly dreaming that he is a man.

Some commentators regard the *Zhuangzi* as more sophisticated than the *Daodejing*, and it is certainly less concerned with following the Way for this-worldly purposes, instead focusing on the inward journey, the personal experience of being on the Way. It is not however clear what the exact relationship is – still less, the respective dates of composition – between the *Zhuangzi* and *Daodejing*, so these comparisons might be misleading; the difference might not be one of development but one of tone and intent or emphasis.

The *Zhuangzi* teaches that one should distance oneself from politics and practical life, and instead should align oneself with the Way and follow its lead spontaneously, without striving and desiring. Thinking about things analytically or overmuch is the wrong thing to do. *Wandering along the Way*: that is the ideal. Later, in the first centuries CE, a form of Daoism known as 'Highest Clarity Daoism' became popular among the elite, despite the anti-rationalist and anarchic tendencies of the *Zhuangzi*'s version of Daoism. It is likely that familiarity with Daoism of this form made it much easier for Buddhism to be accepted in China at about this same period.

The warring states of the Warring States Period were forcibly unified by a determined and ferocious individual who, on becoming ruler of a unified China, called himself Qin Shi Huangdi (259–210 BCE), thus coining the term *huangdi* to denote 'emperor'. He is accordingly known as the First Emperor of China. His dynasty was very short – it lasted from 221 to 206 BCE merely – but it changed the course of China's history. He had begun his career as ruler of the state of Qin, and from there conquered his neighbours. The famous Terracotta Army guards his tomb outside Xian.

In addition to unifying China and having his amazing tomb constructed, Qin Shi has another claim to fame, or in this case infamy: in 212 BCE he burned thousands of books and buried alive 460 Confucian scholars. So says Sima Qian, at any rate, and whether or not Qin Shi's behaviour was quite so murderous, the loss of many of the texts of pre-Qin China is confirmed by such evidence as the absence of any other sources for quotations in surviving texts (for example, Mencius' quotations of Confucius), and the fact that the imperial library of the Qin was burned down in the violence that attended the Han takeover of the dynasty in 206 BCE. This library was said to contain two copies, for palace use only, of every book otherwise burned by Qin Shi. If so, the combination of the two book-burnings, one intentional and one accidental, must be accounted a great tragedy.

In light of the teachings of Confucianism and Mohism, Qin Shi must appear as a complete contradiction to the tenor of Chinese political and ethical thought. And so he is; but he did not appear from an intellectual vacuum. Instead, the theoretical background to his draconian approach to government was provided by Legalist philosophy, summarized by Han Fei (c.280–233 BCE) in the book known by his name, the *Han Feizi*. This outlook rejected the idea that a ruler's priorities should be shaped by principles of benevolence, and in doing so rejected the idea that the aim of effective government is the welfare of the people. Instead it argued that a ruler's priorities are his own tenure of power, and keeping order in the country. The similarity of this claim to Machiavelli's views, see pp. 189–90 above, is striking. The word for 'law', as for 'standard' as noted earlier, is *fa*, and the idea is that order is kept by imposing punishment through the operation of laws. Han Fei himself imported the idea from Daoism that the ruler should (seem to) 'do nothing' from behind the wall of the law, hidden and remote.

A number of the Legalist thinkers were in government. Li Si (c.280–208 BCE) was Qin Shi Huangdi's Prime Minister. Their writings were pragmatic and focused wholly on the business of government. Three concepts were fundamental to their outlook: law and punishment, the technique of statecraft, and the nature of power and its retention. 'To govern by law [*fa*] is to praise the right and blame the wrong,' Han Fei wrote. The conflation of 'standard' and 'law' came naturally to the Legalists, given that any meaning other than the idea of a 'standard' as in (say) weights and measures was irrelevant. The Legalist philosopher Shang Yang (390–338 BCE), the minister of the state of Qin who helped Qin Shi achieve his conquest of the rest of China, believed that severe punishments, far more severe than would be merited by crimes on a doctrine of proportionality, was a way to ensure order, for people would be too frightened by the prospect of them ever to step out of line. 'In punishing,' he wrote in the *Book of Lord Shang*, 'light offences should be heavily punished; if light offences are prevented, heavier offences will not appear. Thus will penalties be abolished by penalties, and affairs will succeed.'

As Shang Yang's book further shows, the Legalists were concerned with precise bureaucratic intervention in the running of the state. Regulation of trade and markets, prices – especially of food – and military organization were all examined in detail. Preparation and organization were all; a ruler must not be taken by surprise. It must be remembered that at the time of the Qin the population of China was heading towards thirty million people, enormous for the time, in a country stretching from north of the Bohai Gulf to close to today's border with Vietnam in the south, and as far west as Chengdu in today's Sichuan Province – a very big country too, though the bulk of the population lived along the Yellow and Yangtze rivers, and the capital was at Xianyang, more or less coterminous with the Xian of today, in today's Shaanxi Province. To manage such a large country and population required a dispassionate approach to the business of government, and to maintaining stability. Accordingly, effective control of the hierarchy was seen as key. The ruler must have a tight grip on his ministers, who in their turn must have a tight grip on officials throughout the country, and the officials, in their own turn, must have a tight grip on the people. The example of rulers who had become mere ciphers of their advisers was cited to explain the instability of the Warring States Period, and their weakness was the reason that Qin Shi was able to topple them all. Whereas governments had been based on personal loyalties and family connections in the past, the Legalists insisted on institutional arrangements that would limit the discretion of individuals by the operation of rules governing the institutions' functioning. Ministers and officials themselves were to have precise job descriptions, and close monitoring to ensure that they did exactly what was required of them – and no more than was required of them.

What if a ruler is unintelligent and not very capable? It has been suggested that Legalist insistence on institutions, rules and the operation of law was intended to safeguard the state against incompetent rulers. Han Fei believed that the age of sage kings was long over, and that it was pointless hoping that another would come along. He tells the story of a farmer who was ploughing a field in which there stood a tree. A hare racing through the field collided with the tree, broke its neck and died. The farmer so enjoyed eating the hare that he thereafter set aside his plough and sat and waited for another hare to come along and break its neck. The folly of doing the same in hopes of another sage king to appear, said Han Fei, speaks for itself.

This connects with Legalist thinking about power or authority, *shi*, in general. An early Legalist-cum-Daoist philosopher known as Shen Dao (350–275 BCE) is quoted and discussed in both the *Han Feizi* and the *Zhuangzi* on the question of power. He believed that it has sources either in the love of the masses or in the subduing of the masses. He also argued that position carries power just by virtue of being position – so, the ruler's power belongs to him just in virtue of his role. Han Fei made use of this point: 'I discuss the power of position because of mediocre rulers ... if they hold to the law and rest on the power of their position, there will be order, otherwise there will be disorder.' Because naturally good rulers will be rare, the institutional arrangements of power and law need to be maintained so that states can function even under mediocre rulers. Forget trying to rule by virtue, especially if the ruler's level of virtue is modest. Only the exercise of power can ensure that the people will remain orderly.

And this degree of realism runs all through the theory: Legalists agreed with Xunzi that ordinary people are basically inclined to selfishness and wickedness, although their focus was not on discussing the question of human nature but on the practical means of managing its worst aspects. Legalism was indeed downright cynical about *xiao ren*, the common people (the words literally mean 'small man'): Han Fei described them as having children's minds, and said that a sensible ruler does not rely on hoping that his people will seek to do him good, but instead should rely on ensuring that they cannot do him harm.

Other Legalists advised taking measures to *weaken* the people's ability to rise against their ruler; Shang Yang said that the people should be kept fully occupied in either agriculture or war, which apart from giving them no time to be a nuisance would ensure that the state is strong in other respects.

Han Fei also advised that whereas the *fa*, laws, should be publicized as widely as possible, the government's strategy, *shu*, should be kept a close secret. Strategy and plans work effectively only if opposition to them can be avoided or minimized, and the people are politically weak if they do not know what the government has in mind. The people are instruments of the ruler's power; they serve to increase his wealth and influence, and care must be taken to ensure that they do not gain an advantage that lessens their serviceability. This extends to ensuring that not too much wealth is accumulated in private hands, because wealth is power too.

The one place where Legalism was put fully into effect was the state of Qin. Advocates of its draconian outlook might say that this is why a ruler of Qin eventually came to be the Emperor of the whole of China. When Xunzi visited Qin in the early third century BCE he found the people uneducated and fearful, the officials wooden and impersonal, the society backward-seeming, brutal and dull. And as tends to happen when such views are put into effect, those who advocate them themselves become prey to them when they fall out with the rulers they served: Shang Yang was tied to four chariots and torn in pieces; Li Si was cut in two in public; Han Fei committed suicide in prison to avoid being subjected to a similar horrific execution.

Perhaps these unfortunate philosopher-politicians should have prepared themselves for their fate – or avoided it – by consulting the *Yijing*, the 'Book of Changes', the famous divinatory text thought to date to 1000 BCE or near it. The book came to have its current basic arrangement – there are variations – late in the first millennium BCE. It contains arrangements of lines in hexagrams, with statements attached to each hexagram and each line, not unlike fortune-cookie statements. The philosophically interesting aspect of the *Yijing* is the set of commentaries that came to be appended to it, known as the 'Ten Wings'. Their authorship was attributed to Confucius in the traditional way, as a convenience. The vatic and enigmatic nature of the *Yijing* permits a variety of interpretations of its meanings and theories about its origin and purpose; it is a Rorschach blot in which anyone who looks can see whole cinema shows of significance. Perhaps that is its real value.

An example of how the *Yijing* is treated in modern scholarship is provided by those who say that it is based on systematic observation of nature and its changes, together with empathetic feelings thus generated, and that this underlies Chinese philosophy subsequently. Thought about reality proceeds by way of images, and the diagrams map 'all basic human situations'. Between them the observations of nature and the mapping of human situations provide a comprehensive system covering the origin of the cosmos, the ethics of both human relationships and relationships with the environment, and philosophical considerations about society. This would be a very substantial yield from a terse, repetitive and enigmatic set of remarks appended to blocks of lines – 'Before completion, success' reads one – but of course it arises from the 'Ten Wings' written many centuries later, by commentators for whom the original *Yijing* served as the occasion rather than the substance of their thoughts. A great deal of what is said in the commentaries offers interpretations of what is to be understood by how the yarrow sticks have fallen when cast in asking the *Yijing* a question, so the claim that matter of philosophical substance is to be found there is a tendentious one.

Contrasting the Confucian and Mohist schools with Daoism, all three with Legalism and all four of these with the place of the *Yijing* in Chinese sensibility – and nothing has been said here about the later development of Confucianism into 'Neo-Confucianism' in the Song dynasty (contemporary with the West's high middle ages, tenth to thirteenth century CE) and afterwards under the influence of Daoism and Buddhism – shows what a rich intellectual history China has had. The foregoing might and should serve as a taster to encourage further exploration. But it has to be acknowledged that (as with Indian philosophy) the language barrier, presented in this case by ancient Chinese – even more difficult than Sanskrit, which is difficult enough – inhibits the depth of engagement that would assuredly prove as educative as it is fascinating.

Arabic–Persian Philosophy

It cannot fail to be noticed that discussions of philosophical traditions – Western philosophy, Indian philosophy, Chinese philosophy – refer to them geographically or ethnically, and subdivisions within them – ancient Greek philosophy, medieval philosophy, Analytic philosophy, Continental philosophy – do so by historical period or genre. Alone among labels for distinguishable slices of the history of philosophy there is one that makes an explicit identification with a religion: 'Islamic philosophy'. This is as misleading as it would be to attach the label 'Christian philosophy' to philosophy originating in Europe. For apart from boundary questions about what distinguishes theology from philosophy, and – even more pertinently – what distinguishes religious doctrine from philosophy, there is the fact that some of those who contributed to philosophical debate in the areas conquered by people who had adopted one or another version of Islam – the Middle East, Persia, north Africa, Spain – in the first half-millennium after Islam's foundation, were not Muslims; there were Jews, Christians, Zoroastrians, atheists and others living, thinking and writing in those regions during that time.

Moreover, much of the substance of philosophical thinking in that time and place was an inheritance from philosophy as it developed in the Greek and Roman worlds – indeed, much of the region had been Roman and (Byzantine) Greek for centuries. It matters that the chosen label of identification should recognize these facts. One candidate might be 'Arab–Persian' as the closest approximation to an ethnogeographical marker. But this is far from ideal also, given that some of the most important work in this phase of philosophy's history was done in Spain, and that the actual ethnicity of individual philosophers is irrelevant. Moses Maimonides was a Sephardic Jew, Averroes an Andalusian

Arab, Avicenna was born of Uzbek–Afghan parentage in what had been a far northern corner of the Persian Empire.

Some therefore choose to demarcate this slice of philosophy's history as 'Philosophy in the Islamic World'. Despite the persistence of an association with a religion – it is like calling philosophy in Europe 'Philosophy in the Christian World', which would not be true for nearly half of the history of Western philosophy – it is a less inaccurate option, and its adoption as an historico-geographical label of convenience is acceptable. Equally if not more so is the label I have chosen, 'Arabic–Persian', this time relating to the *languages* in which the philosophy was written. The virtue of this is that it keeps in mind the fact, significant for philosophy in the Western tradition, that it was via Arabic that some of the key texts of antiquity were preserved and recovered.

What follows here is an account of the leading thinkers in the Islamic world in the period between al-Kindi (*c*.801–73 CE) and Ibn Rushd (Averroes, 1126–98 CE). The focus here is on the treatment of questions of strictly philosophical interest, not least in connection with their influence on debates, just alluded to, in the wider philosophical community of their time, through translations from Arabic into Latin and the use of texts such as Averroes' commentaries on Aristotle in the universities of Europe. The work of these thinkers is emphatically an aspect of the wider history of philosophy as such; the theology of Islam is a different subject, though a line of demarcation is often hard to draw, given the insistence of some Muslim historians of the subject that 'the tradition of Islamic philosophy is deeply rooted in the world view of the Qur'ānic revelation and functions within a cosmos in which prophecy or revelation is accepted as a blinding reality that is the source not only of ethics but also of knowledge.'* In these words lies the problem; if the starting point for reflection is acceptance of a religious doctrine, then the reflection that follows is theology, or theodicy, or exegesis, or casuistry, or apologetics, or hermeneutics, but it is not philosophy.

If this seems too sharp a demarcation, consider this: if you accept as an unquestionable basis the existence and continuing interested activity of an omnipotent, benevolent, eternal and supernatural creator,

---

* This is a claim made by Seyyed Hossein Nasr in his Introduction to the *History of Islamic Philosophy*, co-edited with Oliver Leaman.

then you have certain immediate commitments that are not open to discussion – for example: that the world has a beginning in time – and certain tricky problems to solve, for example: the existence of moral and natural evil, which on the face of it would have to be viewed as ultimately the responsibility of the being in question because it caused everything to exist, but which contradicts that being's goodness and benevolence, typically supposed to be total. Or: if the being is One, because Oneness is perfect, complete, self-consistent and self-subsistent, why are there many things? – why would such a being create or emanate pluralities? Or: if reality is a continuous emanation (in Islamic thought, *fayd*) from the divine being by some necessity of its nature, does that entail that free will does not exist in the universe? If the being emanates the universe by its own free will, why does it do so, given the imperfection of plurality and the evil that results? Finding solutions to these problems is a matter for theology and theodicy; a philosophical approach would question the conceptual robustness of the ontology (the existence of a being or beings of the kind at issue) which creates such difficulties in the first place.

In Arabic the words for 'philosophy' and 'philosopher' are respectively *falsafa* and *faylasuf*, adapted from Greek. Philosophy, mathematics, physics, astronomy and medicine were known as 'foreign sciences', having been acquired from Hellenic sources in the regions conquered by the spread of Islam in its first century. But what were these Hellenic sources? If one consults the catalogue of the Baghdad bookseller Ibn al-Nadim who, in 988 CE, produced a survey of the books available in the Islamic world, one can see what had been translated from the classical tongues. There is no Homer or Thucydides, nor Ovid nor Virgil; there is no Aeschylus or Cicero. It is only *part* of the legacy of the classical world that figures in the catalogue, for between the classical world and the arrival of Islam there had been Christianity – Syria was a Nestorian Christian domain, the Greek-speaking Roman Empire in the East, centred on Constantinople, was an Orthodox domain – and the Christians not only had *not* sought to preserve the humanistic culture of classical times, they had taken active steps to expunge it.* What the Christians

---

* Mention has already been made above, pp. 3–4, of the vigorous efforts made by Christianity to expunge preceding classical civilization. A little indicative snippet of information: in fifth-century CE Alexandria there were organized Christian gangs who attacked and beat up 'pagan philosophers', rather like White Supremacist groups in the southern United States who sought out African Americans for beatings and lynchings, an

kept was technical literature – mathematics, medicine, logical treatises, astronomy. There were works by Plato and Aristotle, Euclid, Galen and Ptolemy; but there were none of the poets, none of the plays, no letters and speeches.

It is interesting but futile to speculate what impact the humanistic culture of classical antiquity might have had on Islamic culture had it survived in any quantity. We know the effect its rediscovery had on the European Renaissance. Might something similar have happened? Nevertheless what chiefly stood out, as Ibn al-Nadim's catalogue shows, was *Aristotle*. Aristotle *was* philosophy to almost all the Muslim scholars (al-Farabi, a Platonist, was the exception), and even parts of the Neoplatonist corpus were credited to him.

By the time of the Arab conquest, the chief centres of philosophy in the Christian Hellenic world were Athens – a very pale imitation of its former glory – and, much more importantly, Alexandria, which fell to the Muslim forces of Ibn al-As in September 642. By one of the strange reversals of history Aristotle, whose philosophy had only just managed to survive, centuries before, by the skin of its teeth (see pp. 81–2 above), had become the most admired and studied figure at Alexandria in the period directly before this event, while Plato had gone into relative eclipse. In any case the Neoplatonism that preserved ideas from Plato was by then a syncretistic form of theosophy (a family of views claiming the possibility of direct intuitive encounter with and knowledge of a deity), having absorbed other strands of thought and emphasized the more mystical Plato of the *Timaeus*. So the view that Arab scholars had of the history of Greek philosophy was idiosyncratic.

Another conduit of philosophy into the Islamic world was Persia. The Emperor Justinian closed the Academy in Athens in 529 CE, confiscating its property and expelling the philosophers. They went as refugees to Persia, to the court of Chosroes Anushirvan (Khosrow I, 501–79 CE), King of the Sassanian Empire, who had a reputation for wisdom. Little is known of Athenians' activity there, but a number of Greek philosophical texts were incorporated into the collection of Zoroastrian texts, the *Avesta*, over the following decades of that century, which demonstrates that their presence left a mark. They would

---

expression of racial hatred carried into action in that region in the period between the 1860s (when slavery ended) and 1960s.

not have been introducing anything unfamiliar to Persian scholars, though, because intercourse between the Greek and Persian worlds had persisted for more than a thousand years by that point, so perhaps what they achieved was an increase in interest in the philosophical tradition they represented, enough to recommend some of the texts they brought with them to the *Avesta*'s editors.

Some final preparatory remarks are required, concerning the theological background to the rise of philosophy proper in the Islamic world. A brief timeline prepares this preparation. The prophet Muhammad died in 632 CE, succeeded by his father-in-law Abu Bakr. The latter's appointment by the elders at Medina angered those who expected to see Muhammad's cousin and son-in-law, Ali, become Caliph. Ali eventually became the fourth Caliph, but the damage had been done; the rift that was to split Sunni from Shi'a was permanently opened by this disagreement over the succession. Ali's appointment was opposed by the Umayyad clan, and he was murdered in 661, to be succeeded by his son Hasan, who abdicated that same year, at which point the Umayyads took control. Under them the Empire expanded hugely and rapidly, until it touched the Atlantic shores in the west and the borders of China in the east.

The Umayyads ruled from Damascus for a century before being overthrown by the Abbasids, who established themselves at Baghdad and ruled most of the Islamic world for the next five hundred years, from 750 to 1258. This was the golden age of Islam, promoted by the Abbasids' desire to foster culture and learning. They built a great library in the capital, the Bayt al-Hikmah (the House of Wisdom; *hikmah* means 'wisdom'), as a centre for study and for translation of Greek and Syriac manuscripts into Arabic. The early Abbasid caliphs – Harun al-Rashid (r. 786–809), Abu al-Abbas al-Ma'mun (r. 813–33) who famously had a dream that translations must be made, and al-Mu'tasim (Abū Ishaq Muhammad ibn Harun al-Rashid, r. 833–42) – all sponsored scholars and translators, and included them among their courtiers.

In this environment of learning the theology, *kalam*, encouraged by the ruling house was Mu'tazilite, which promoted reason and evidence as adjuncts to faith. 'Mu'tazili' means 'withdrawer', one who withdraws – that is, one who withholds judgment, who sees two sides of the question, who uses rational and evidential tests in evaluating arguments. While the Mu'tazila theology was ascendant, the Sunni–Shi'a split was not especially serious, and it was possible for thinkers to question orthodoxy, disagree with one another without fear and freely debate difficult points in *kalam*. A significant aspect of the rationalist and evidentialist approach of the Mu'tazilites was that it provided a means of distinguishing between genuine and fake teachings and teachers, and between true and false beliefs – which of course mattered because true beliefs are what get the believer to heaven.

From the early ninth century the Mu'tazilites began to be opposed by three other groups: the fundamentalist Hanbalites (followers of Ahmad ibn Hanbal, 780–855) who demanded an unquestioningly literalist reading of the Qu'ran, the Zahiris (followers of Dawud al-Zahiri, 815–84) and most importantly the Ash'arites, named after Abu al-Hasan al-Ash'ari (874–936). All these groups were more literalist and dogmatic than the Mu'tazilites. The Ash'ari school became, and is still, the most important of the Sunni theological schools (it is sometimes described as the 'Sunni orthodoxy'). The Mu'tazila remained influential among Shi'a, and is today regarded as authoritative by the Zaydi Shi'a school of law. Islamic philosophy has mainly been associated with Shi'a Islam as a result; the Sunni schools, based on the ideal of following the 'tradition of Muhammad and the consensus of the *ummah* [community]', are inhospitable to philosophizing and cleave instead to orthodoxy.

The first recognized Muslim philosopher is al-Kindi (*c.*801–73 – Abu Yusuf Ya'qub ibn Ishaq al-Kindi). He was not the first to engage with Greek philosophical ideas; the Mu'tazila *kalam* had absorbed some influence from that source already, as Ash'arite criticism of Mu'tazilite teaching shows; al-Ash'ari himself blamed Aristotle for some of the Mu'tazilite doctrines. But al-Kindi was interested in more than applying Greek thought to theology. He was eager to learn from the entire range of what was on offer, and wrote scores of treatises – Ibn al-Nadim's bibliography lists 260 titles of works by him – covering every subject from medicine and astrology to mathematics and philosophy. Unfortunately only a few of these manuscripts survive, perhaps because of the hostility to him of Caliph al-Mutawakkil (822–61) who confiscated his books – and who also persecuted the Shi'a, destroyed the shrine of the third Shi'ite Imam Husayn ibn Ali, forced Jews to wear identifying clothing and cut down the sacred cypress of the Zoroastrians to use in building a new palace.

Al-Kindi was born in Kufa, the son of its Emir. He was reputed to be a descendant of the kings of Kinda, one of whom was a companion of Muhammad. He had the patronage of both Caliph al-Ma'mun and Caliph al-Mu'tasim; he dedicated his major work *On First Philosophy* to the latter's son Ahmad, whom he tutored. The caliphs appointed him to oversee the translation projects at the Bayt al-Hikma, which gave him complete access to the collections. Among his achievements is the introduction of the Indian system of numerals (0, 1, 2, 3 . . .) now universally in use.

Al-Kindi was eager to establish that 'the philosophy of the ancients', as it was called, is consistent with Muslim teaching, and is consistent within itself. His main focus was geometry, logic and physics, and here the problem of compatibility was not serious. The next challenge was to justify the claims of reason against unquestioning acceptance of tradition or dogma. He therefore argued that 'For the seeker after truth nothing takes precedence over truth, and there is no disparagement of the truth or of him who speaks it . . . no one is diminished by the truth; rather, the truth ennobles all.' Using the only version of Aristotle's *De Anima* then available, which was a paraphrase, al-Kindi was able to claim that the Greeks believed in the immortality of the soul, and therefore a dualistic ontology in which the perishable body and imperishable soul are distinct existences. This further involved establishing that the soul is substantial, which he did by invoking the Aristotelian notion of essence to argue as follows: 'Since bodies can perish, "being alive" is not an essential property of them. Being alive is, however, an essential property of being a person. Therefore a person is not identical with his body. Living things are substances. Persons are living things. Therefore persons (souls, the essentially "being alive" aspect of us) are substances.' One problem with this is that for Aristotle a substance is a combination of form and matter, which requires a substantial soul to consist of some kind of non-bodily matter. How is it to be understood? Al-Kindi did not offer a solution.

For Muslim theology, *kalam*, the oneness of God is a key commitment, since unity and singularity are properties of perfection, and the greatest degree of reality attaches to the greatest degree of unity. Christian Trinitarian theology was anathema to Islam, so Plotinus' doctrine of the primordial One was highly attractive to al-Kindi, and reinforced his claim that *falsafa* and *kalam* are consistent. If a thing is one, without parts, it is not subject to change and decay, and is therefore eternal.

This incidentally gave al-Kindi ammunition against the Hanbalist fundamentalists, who were committed by their literalism to saying that God does things, as reported in the Qu'ran, like sit on a throne, which entails that he undergoes change and is therefore not eternal. Moreover the plenitude of reality that is constituted by the oneness of God explains creation: God emanates the universe from the plenitude of his reality – it issues from his overflowing abundance of reality like water spilling from an over-full tank.

An emanationist view of reality was also accepted by al-Farabi (*c.* 872–950, Abu Nasr Muhammad ibn Muhammad al-Farabi), who was known as the 'Second Teacher', not after al-Kindi, but instead – in such esteem was al-Farabi held – after Aristotle. Little is known about his biography, but a tradition saying that he was born in central Asia has led to the National University of Kazakhstan being named after him, while another tradition assigns him to Persia. Most of his life was passed in Baghdad, although he travelled in Egypt, Morocco and elsewhere, and died at Damascus.

Al-Farabi took the view that philosophy is superior to theology as a way of arriving at truth. He had spent time with Christians in Baghdad, studying logic with them either as a pupil or as a colleague, and his researches in logic were profound. He made epitomes of the Aristotelian *Organon* and wrote commentaries on it and on the *Rhetoric* and *De Interpretatione*, and also on Porphyry's *Isagoge*.

Investigation of the forms of valid inference carried a significant implication for al-Farabi: it convinced him that logic is universal, and as such underlies all languages and thought. This contradicts the view that, as the Qu'ran had been dictated by God in Arabic, the grammar of Arabic encapsulates the fundamental structure of language and thought. In al-Farabi's view logic is superior to grammar, which seemed to imply that, because of the close association of grammar with theology, this further entailed the superiority of logic (of philosophy in general) over theology. The task of translating Greek philosophical texts and creating a vocabulary for *falsafa* in Arabic had made the opponents of philosophy suspicious that the philosophers were attempting to substitute Greek grammar for Arabic grammar. Al-Farabi made the irenic move of pointing out that the 'art of grammar' was indispensable for helping logicians to describe the principles of logic. But in the *Book of Letters* al-Farabi iterates the inadequacy of Arab grammar to reveal logical structure, and describes ordinary language as merely a popularizing method of expressing philosophical truths in ways that people can understand.

Al-Farabi follows Aristotle in his account of the soul, identifying its chief faculties – in descending hierarchical order – as rational, imaginative, sensitive and nutritive. Like Aristotle he describes the 'common sense' as the sensorium combining and integrating everything apprehended by the five senses into a unified cognition, and locates it in the heart. Imagination is given a special place by al-Farabi because of its association with divination and prophecy. Aristotle had thought of imagining as having images of things when the things themselves are absent, and of the faculty of imagination as the power to rearrange images, as when one takes the head and wings of an eagle and the hindquarters of a horse, and combines them into the mythological creature known as the Hippogriff. To these two functions al-Farabi added a third: the power of imitation, allowing the recreation not just of pictures but of emotions and desires also. This fitted with his view that poetry exists to prompt feelings as well as images, and offered an account of prophecy as the reception in imagination of sensory images and associated feelings in a form communicable to a non-philosophical wider public – images and feelings that encapsulate ideas that would normally be available only to the highest form of intellect, the kind alone capable of being in tune with truth and reality.

Al-Farabi also wrote about politics, and here he was a Platonist rather than an Aristotelian. He followed Plato in thinking that the best ruler would be a philosopher-king, but was realistic enough to consider it unlikely that such would be available on a regular basis; so he addressed instead the question of why and how societies decline from the ideal. He said this happens for one of three reasons: because of ignorance, or because of wickedness, or because of error. Ignorant cities fail to grasp the true nature of humanity and the reason for its existence. Wicked and errant cities once knew, or perhaps still know, what the reason is for humanity's existence, but they fail to act on that knowledge. The wicked ones fail to act on the knowledge because they are wicked, the errant ones because they misapply the knowledge or because their rulers mislead them.

Later philosophers in the Islamic world were unanimous in their admiration of al-Farabi's logical works, and some of them – such as Avicenna – acknowledged his influence on their philosophical outlook more broadly. Maimonides described him as 'a great man' and said that 'all his writings are faultlessly excellent.' Although Avicenna and Averroes were more influential on European thought when their writings became known, it was certain of al-Farabi's works that alerted Europe's philosophers to the treasures that were to be found in Aristotle.

Avicenna (980–1037, Abu Ali al-Husayn ibn Abd Allah ibn al-Hasan ibn Ali ibn Sina) was born in Afshana near Bukhara in what is now Uzbekistan, in a region once part of the Persian Empire. His father was a respected Ismaili scholar from Afghanistan, who worked as a government official. Avicenna relates in his autobiography – he is one of very few Muslim philosophers to have written one – that he had read the Qu'ran by the age of ten, that he learned mathematics from an Indian shopkeeper, and that he learned the rudiments of medical science from an itinerant healer. Later he studied Islamic jurisprudence, *Fiqh*. He began his studies of *falsafa* as a teenager, and said that he read Aristotle's *Metaphysics* forty times before understanding it – and that understanding came only when he read al-Farabi's short treatise on it, which he bought at a market stall for a tiny sum because he was importuned to do so by the bookseller. He was so delighted to have the key, thus serendipitously, to understanding Aristotle that he hastened out the next morning to give alms to the poor, in gratitude.

Avicenna began his career as a physician, having given free medical help to the sick of his home town in order to practise the craft. His first appointment was as a medical attendant to the local Emir. Here he had access to a copious library, and made good use of it. After his father's death he moved from place to place in the region of the Caspian Sea, seeking employment, and sometimes – for they were troubled times in the region – having to hide to escape arrest and imprisonment. He was at last able to settle in Jibal as physician to Ala al-Dawla (r. 1008–41, Muhammad ibn Rustam Dushmanziyar), who had carved out an independent and, as it proved, short-lived dynasty in western Iran. One of the most influential of Avicenna's books was written in Persian for al-Dawla to explain the doctrines of philosophy, simply entitled *Philosophy for Ala al-Dawla*. Avicenna passed the last decade of his life in Jibal, dying at the age of fifty-seven while on the march with al-Dawla's army during one of its many campaigns. When he fell ill his companions advised him to stay home and rest; he replied, 'I prefer a short life with width to a narrow life with length.'

Avicenna wrote that he saw philosophy's task as 'determining the realities of things, so far as it is possible for human beings to do so'. Two tasks invite the philosopher, one theoretical, which aims at finding the truth, and the other practical, which aims at finding the good. Seeking the truth perfects the soul through knowledge as such; seeking the good perfects the soul through knowledge of what must be done. Whereas theoretical knowledge concerns what exists independently of our choices and actions, practical knowledge concerns how we choose and act.

Each of these forms of knowledge has three subdivisions. In theoretical knowledge they are physics, mathematics and metaphysics. In practical knowledge they are managing the city, managing the household and managing oneself. The first two subdivisions of practical knowledge concern the principles by which things are to be shared. The third concerns coming to know the virtues, thus refining the soul, and coming to know the vices so that they can be avoided, thus purifying the soul. Practical knowledge is taught us by the divine sharia, the law derived from the Qu'ran, and the *hadith*, the reported sayings of Muhammad.

Logic is the basis of philosophy, Avicenna held, and it is also the high road to happiness. This is because it enables us to reach what is not known from what is known, by inference and derivation. It gives us rules for right reasoning, so that we reason validly; valid reasoning leads to knowledge, invalid reasoning to falsehood. (Very rarely, Avicenna conceded, God might give us knowledge gratuitously.) Logic is about concepts, and therefore we have to understand the terms in which they are expressed, and also the forms of valid proof involving them.

Physics deals with the three principles of bodily things: matter, form and the intellect. Intellect holds matter and form together and is therefore the cause of the existence of bodies. The heavenly bodies move in a circular motion and are not subject to generation and corruption; but generation and corruption happen to the bodies made out of the four elements – earth, air, fire and water – whose different combinations give rise to the different kinds of sublunary things: minerals, plants and animals. The highest of these latter are humans, whose form is the soul.

Avicenna devoted much attention to the soul, saying that if its function is restricted to nutrition, growth and reproduction it is a plant soul, if movement and sensation are added to these it is an animal soul, and if rationality is added to all five it is a human soul. Rationality has two parts, theoretical and practical; it is cultivation of the theoretical part that makes a human being achieve his proper perfection – a very Aristotelian view.

The enquiry that applies par excellence to theoretical principles is metaphysics. Its subject matter is existence, existence *as such*. That means that it examines what is essential to existence: unity and multiplicity, cause and effect, universality and particularity, potentiality and actuality, possibility and necessity, completeness and incompleteness. Existents are either substances or accidents, distinguished by the fact that the former are existents which are not *in* a substance, whereas the latter are. A thing's existence is either necessary or contingent. To deny that a necessary thing exists is contradictory; to deny that a contingent thing exists is not contradictory. Something can exist necessarily in itself, or necessarily through another thing. This doctrine, utilizing the modal notions of necessity and possibility, provided Avicenna with an important argument, as follows.

One can note that a thing x must have a certain property F in order to be the thing it is; that is, F is *essential* to x. But this is true whether or not x exists. The question whether something x itself exists necessarily is a different matter. Things exist only if they are *caused* to exist. The things that make up the world exist contingently, because they would not exist unless caused to do so by something else. Now, the causal chain that brings things into existence cannot run backwards ad infinitum, so there must be an uncaused, non-contingent – necessary – being as the first cause of everything. Avicenna identifies this being with God. So God is a necessary being; but the fact that he causes everything else to exist (by emanation from the necessary overflowing of the abundance of his reality) means that they are necessary too; theirs is 'necessity through another necessary thing'. The creative activity of the necessary being makes it necessary that everything else exists – and that makes them necessary in themselves too.

What pleased Avicenna about this argument is that there was a potential problem in the view adopted from Aristotle that the highest intellect thinks (only) about the highest things there are – namely, universals and necessary truths. This would mean that God does not think about – or, which would be worse, perhaps cannot think about – particular things. However, if everything is necessary as a result of receiving transmitted necessity from God, then God can think about them. A theological difficulty is solved by this.

It also solves an allied theological difficulty – or the same difficulty in different guise. Particular things and events undergo change, so if God knows about them, then God's knowledge – and therefore God himself – undergoes change. But God, being one and perfect, does not undergo change. To protect the eternal unchangeability of God, God's knowledge has to be restricted to what does not change: universals and essences. But then this makes God not the God of revealed religion, who is interested in individual sin and virtue. By making everything necessary by the transmission of the necessity of God's being to everything that emanates from him, this difficulty too is overcome.

The God of Avicenna is very close to the abstract, non-personal 'thought thinking about itself' God of Aristotle. Avicenna's God is simple, without parts, unchanging; and since it has neither genus nor difference it cannot be characterized or defined, only named. Because it is immaterial it is wholly good, because evil only arises from matter, which Avicenna had already defined as 'the source of privation' or negativity. It is absolute beauty, because there is no greater beauty than absolute intellect. It is the highest pleasure, because it does the highest thing possible – thinking. As the most perfect goodness and beauty and pleasure, it is the most desirable and lovable thing there is. Everything else, in a hierarchy from celestial things down to mundane things, emanates from God continually and eternally, because if at any point this did not happen then that would be something that had not happened before, creating a perturbation in all the perfections. But this, happily, is impossible anyway, given the nature of the being in question. This conception of God prompts two associated thoughts: one is of Spinoza's *deus sive natura*, and the other is that if references to a deity in Avicenna's account were replaced by references to the natural universe, it is hard to see what difference it would make. This recapitulates the thought that if it is conceivable for anything to cause itself, why not say that the universe causes itself? And that the necessities of everything that follows are the necessities of natural physical laws?

Avicenna's thought had a very large impact on both Western and Eastern thinking, and it did so both positively and negatively. The negative impact was felt by al-Ghazali among Muslims, who attacked him therefore; and by Thomas Aquinas and William of Auvergne among Scholastics in the West. They disagreed strongly with his views about the nature of God and God's relationship to the world, and about the eternity of the universe – orthodoxy on both sides of the religious divide required an act of creation in time. Even Avicenna's later supporters – including Averroes and Mulla Sadra – did not think he had understood Aristotle correctly, and disagreed with some of his views. But as this sketch shows, his was a powerful philosophical mind, and its influence – exercised far from the metropolitan centres of learning and power, and achieved in a mainly unsettled life – was remarkable.

Al-Ghazali (1058–1111, Abu Hamid Muhammad ibn Muhammad al-Ghazali) did not like *falsafa*, did not regard himself as a *faylasuf*, did not like to be called a *faylasuf* and wrote a book called *The Incoherence of the Philosophers*. He was a jurist – and made his initial reputation as such – a theologian of the Ash'arite school, and a mystic inspired by Sufism. He is regarded in Sunni Islam as a *Mujaddid*, a 'renewer of the faith', one of those who appears once a century to re-inspire the *ummah*, the community of the faithful. Yet he figures as a major philosopher of the Islamic world, and one of his works was influential among the Schoolmen of Europe.

Born at Tabaran in the region of Khorasan on the borders of central Asia, al-Ghazali studied at Nishapur and Isfahan before being appointed to teach at the prestigious Nizamiyya Madrasa in Baghdad. His high reputation had made him the confidant of sultans and viziers, but the proximity of political and military power, and the corruptions of court life, repelled him. After four years teaching in Baghdad he suddenly left his post and travelled to Damascus and Jerusalem, vowing to be independent of patronage thenceforth. After making his pilgrimage to Mecca he returned to his home town and founded a small private school and a Sufi convent. But five years before his death he once again changed his stance, and returned to teaching at a public institution, the Nizamiyya Madrasa at Nishapur. He told his followers that he did so because people were theologically confused, and because the authorities had begged him to teach the people once again.

Al-Ghazali wrote an autobiography, and in it claims that while teaching in Baghdad he undertook a two-year study of philosophy in order to refute it, spending a third year writing his *Incoherence of the Philosophers* to complete the project. Some commentators suggest that this was to avoid the imputation that he had studied philosophy extensively while younger, because the *Incoherence* is a work of both literary and philosophical stature, and reads as a long-meditated and mature production. Among his other works are an untitled manuscript in which he had copied out many passages of other philosophers, and a book called *The*

Doctrines of the Philosophers, which is an Arabic version, loosely translated and adapted, of Avicenna's Persian-language book *Philosophy for Ala al-Dawla*. It was once thought that this compendium was preparatory work for the *Incoherence* but subsequent scholarship suggests that it is later in composition and has a different aim.

The translation al-Ghazali made of Avicenna's *Philosophy for Ala al-Dawla* was translated into Latin several times in the century and a half after his death, and also into Hebrew. The first Latin translation appeared in the second half of the twelfth century CE, made by Dominicus Gundisalvi (d. 1190) and Iohannes Hispanus (*fl.* 1190), the latter possibly a Mozarab (an Arab Christian) in Toledo. It was the only work by al-Ghazali known to the philosophers of Europe in the twelfth and thirteenth centuries, and because it was a translation and adaptation of the *Philosophy for Ala al-Dawla* it was assumed that al-Ghazali was a disciple of Avicenna, and that the book was a summary of his master's work. This impression was fostered by the fact that most of the Latin translations omitted the prefatory material in which al-Ghazali distances himself from what he is translating.

Because al-Ghazali described his *Incoherence of the Philosophers* as a 'refutation' of philosophical views, it is assumed that he rejected everything associated with Aristotelian thought. In fact matters are more complex. His principal target was the philosophers' claim that logic and reason are superior as a source of knowledge to theology, which is based on revelation and faith. This undermines Islam, al-Ghazali says, and encourages some among the philosophers to neglect their religious duties. His procedure is to take a number of major philosophical doctrines and demonstrate that the philosophers fail to establish them by the standards of their own methods, chiefly because the assumptions from which they start are uncritically accepted. In some cases he shows that truths which he himself accepts could not be established by the philosophers' methods. The counter-arguments he uses are not all original to him; he makes use of the work of Christian anti-Aristotelian critics which had been known in *kalam* debates since the ninth century.

In his discussion of the philosophers' views on causality al-Ghazali anticipates Hume's view regarding why, given that there is no 'necessary connection' at work in causal relationships, we think there is. A problem that characteristically bedevils thinkers with theological constraints to observe is whether there can be such a thing as 'secondary causes' – that is, causes in nature other than the causal agency of a deity. The solution al-Ghazali proposes is that there are no such causes; everything that happens is a product of God's will; but what appears to humans to be a connection between a cause and an effect, this being what putatively distinguishes their linked occurrence from merely fortuitous juxtapositions of events, is the habit of expectation we form as a result of seeing those events so often linked.

Although most of the doctrines al-Ghazali contests were not regarded by him as heretical, there are three that he takes to pose serious challenges to the Islamic faith. They are all to be found in Avicenna's philosophy, namely, the eternity of the universe, the restriction of God's knowledge to universals, and denial of bodily resurrection. Islam teaches the opposite: that the universe was created by God at a point in time, that God knows particulars as well as universals, and that the souls of the dead will one day be reunited with their bodies. Because Avicenna's doctrines are dangerous to the faith, and would lead astray anyone who accepted them, al-Ghazali issues a *fatwah* at the end of the *Incoherence* saying that anyone who teaches these doctrines is a *kafir* (an unbeliever) and an apostate, and should therefore be killed.

It was not only philosophers of Avicenna's stamp but Ismailis whom al-Ghazali attacked as heretics and apostates; in the case of the latter he seems to have misunderstood their views, attributing to them belief in two gods. His writings laid down the limits of tolerance from the perspective of sharia, stipulating a test for whether a doctrine constitutes apostasy and disbelief. This was that there are three fundamental teachings that cannot be challenged: monotheism, the prophecies of Muhammad and the teaching of the Qu'ran on life after death. Anything that impugns these principles is forbidden and must be punished by death. Everything else must be evaluated on its merits, but even if it is erroneous it should be tolerated.

He also proposed a means of reconciling conflicts between the results of valid demonstrative reasoning and revelation, which can – because they are both true – only be *apparent* conflicts. This was to treat Qu'ranic utterances as symbolic if they seem to be challenged by sound argument. For example: such argument demonstrates that the nature of God is such that he does not have hands nor does he sit on a throne. Passages in the Qu'ran that make reference to hands or sitting on a throne are therefore symbolic. But it is forbidden to give a symbolic interpretation to anything in the Qu'ran that is not inconsistent with the results of valid demonstration. Most Muslim theologians and jurists after al-Ghazali accepted these views, though some said that in cases of conflicts between reason and revelation, revelation should always be regarded as superior.

In the Islamic world al-Ghazali's chief work is his *Revival of the Religious Sciences*, treating of the ethics of daily life for the faithful, covering rituals and customs, the things that lead to perdition and those that lead to paradise. He criticizes materialism and extols a life of restraint and good actions, saying that theological and jurisprudential niceties are not nearly as important as the inner purity that virtue brings. He was attracted to the Sufi approach to holiness, and the treatise that some regard as a popular recension of the *Revival*, known in English as *The Alchemy of Happiness*, promotes the ideal of spiritual self-realization and union with the divine. 'The mystics, not the men of words, are those who had real experiences,' he wrote in his autobiography. 'I had already progressed as far as possible in the path of learning. What remained was not to be gained by study, but by immediate experience and walking in the mystic way.'

Al-Ghazali must be credited with a major role in establishing the Sunni Ash'arite ascendancy in Islam, and thereby the boundaries of tolerance and orthodoxy in this most numerous branch of the religion. Although he was far from proscribing the use of reason in logic and mathematics and the citing of empirical evidence in astronomy and physics, the net effect of three things – his attack on *falsafa* (though in fact restricted to metaphysical matters impinging on theology), the teachings of the *Revival*, and his own tendency to mystical enlightenment – was to empower doctrinal rigour and fideism over reflection and critical thought. There was a political dimension to this, turning on the differences between Sunni and Shi'a in other – theological – respects. A consequence, already noted, has been that philosophy has remained an avocation more among the latter, by a considerable margin, than among the former.

Ibn Rushd, known to the West as Averroes (1126–98, Abu al-Walid Muhammad ibn Ahmad ibn Rushd), responded to al-Ghazali's *Incoherence of the Philosophers* with his *The Incoherence of the Incoherence*. This work did not rescue philosophy's reputation among the Sunni, and indeed neither did Averroes' other doctrines. But his commentaries on Aristotle made him a major figure among Europe's Schoolmen, some among whom were for their own reasons as critical of him as his co-religionists.

Averroes was born in Cordoba in Andalusia, the grandson of a famous and influential judge and legal theorist, Abdul-Walid Muhammad (d. 1126), whose son, Abdul-Qasim Ahmad, was also a judge until dismissed when the Almohad dynasty supplanted the Almoravid dynasty in 1146. Averroes followed in the family legal tradition, establishing his reputation as a jurist. But he also attained a great reputation in medicine, his treatise on the subject, the *Generalities*, serving as one of the chief medical textbooks in both Europe and the Islamic world for centuries. It was in response to a request by the Almohad Caliph Abu Yaqub Yusuf to have Aristotle explained to him that Averroes set to work writing commentaries on all of Aristotle's texts (other than the *Politics*), a task that took thirty years. He also wrote on Plato's *Republic* and Porphyry's *Isagoge* among others. His concern was to recover the original Aristotle from the Neoplatonist overlay that earlier philosophers in the Islamic world had imposed, and to understand the philosophy itself. His interpretations were occasionally questionable, but the extent and depth of his engagement with the Aristotelian corpus was the single most significant reason for the recovery of Aristotle among European Schoolmen.

Averroes took from Aristotle the idea that the universe is eternal, which entails that it was not created by God. He also interpreted Aristotle as rejecting the idea of personal immortality. For his part Averroes held that only a single, universal mind exists – the mind of God – which contradicts the idea that there are individual souls with minds and will. These tenets conflicted with both Muslim and Christian doctrine, and when Averroes' commentaries arrived among the Schoolmen in Latin translation they caused uproar. People took sides; there were enthusiasts for Aristotle – they were called Averroists – and opponents. A number of schools and universities banned lectures on Aristotle, and in 1231 Pope Gregory IX set up a commission to investigate his works. By this time Aristotelian texts were beginning to appear in Latin directly from the Greek originals, rather than through the intermediary of Arabic and Syriac. Thomas Aquinas' contributions did not stop at the mere reconciliation of Aristotle with Christian doctrine, in large part by detaching Aristotle from Averroes' interpretations of him, but made Aristotelian thought (as interpreted by him, in the doctrine known as Thomism) the official philosophy of the Church.

Averroes' defence of philosophy begins with the claim that the Qu'ran enjoins the study of it, quoting a number of suras (verses) including no. 3, 'They thought about the creation of heaven and earth,' and no. 59, 'Think; you can see.' It is done best by following the practice of lawyers, he said, which is to draw inferences carefully from facts and accepted premises. Anyone with the capacity for such thinking should do it, and should draw on the work of predecessors, whether or not they share the same religion; not uncritically, but accepting whatever is found to be true. Those who wish to study philosophy should be allowed to, because any harm that comes to them from it is merely accidental, like spilling water on yourself when drinking from a cup. Not everyone will have the capacity for philosophy, however, which is why the Qu'ran speaks of three paths for people to reach the truth: the demonstrative (logic and proof), the dialectical (debate and interpretation) and the rhetorical (ordinary speech). Averroes characterized these as, respectively, the ways of philosophy, theology and the masses.

Because the Qu'ran contains the ultimate truth, knowledge arrived at by demonstrative reasoning cannot be in conflict with it. Apparent conflicts must be just that: apparent only; so if philosophy and scripture disagree, scripture must be interpreted symbolically. This has anyway always been done, said Averroes, because God has mixed hidden with open meanings to encourage study of the scriptures and attentiveness when doing so. This might be taken as another reason for his view that philosophical knowledge is superior. He conceded that if the *ummah* has reached a consensus about the meaning of a certain text, then that is its meaning and other interpretations are forbidden; but where there is no agreed interpretation, discussion of the text should be free. Given that there are very few texts for which a meaning has been agreed, there is much scope for debate. In particular, said Averroes, this means that al-Ghazali is wrong to proscribe such views as that the universe is eternal, that resurrection of the body does not occur and that God's knowledge concerns only universals; all three points are still open for discussion.

The existence of God can be proved by observation of purpose and design in the universe, Averroes said, but he did not agree with the doctrine of emanationism, holding instead that God transcends the universe. In accordance with his intention to reconcile philosophy and religion he argued that the dispute over whether the universe is eternal or was created at a point in time can be solved on Aristotelian principles by saying that the universe is eternal, but form was imposed on it at a point in time.

Those among the Schoolmen who were troubled by Averroes' views understood him as accepting the implication that if talk of God's knowledge and will can at best only be metaphorical, it would follow that God's relationship to the world is such that it excludes the possibility of providence – 'providence' meaning God's acting in the world to direct, change or intervene in the lives of individuals and societies. The scriptures suggest otherwise, but in Averroes as in some of the Schoolmen the doctrine of 'Double Truth' – philosophy and theology each having access to truth in its own way, or (more concessively) seeing the same truth in a different way – solves or avoids the problem. Responding directly to al-Ghazali on the question of creation, Averroes argued that eternal and temporal agents behave very differently. A temporal agent can make a decision and then delay implementing it, but for God there is no difference between one time or another and no gap between intention and action. Why would God create a world at a particular time as opposed to any other time? But in any case, before there was a world there was nothing to distinguish points in time so the dispute is empty.

A distinctive doctrine in Averroes is the 'unicity of the intellect'. He thought that intellect is a single, eternal entity in which individual human beings participate, rather as if many individual laptop computers were all running the same, indeed a single, programme, but with each individual laptop able to access whatever the single programme is using it, individually, to do. Averroes took this doctrine to explain how universal knowledge is possible. He thought the doctrine had been expounded by Aristotle in *De Anima* ('On the Soul'), but Aquinas argued in his own treatise 'On the Unity of the Intellect: Against the Averroists' that this was a misinterpretation. The section in *De Anima* is notoriously obscure, partly because it is brief but also because by Aristotle's own admission the question is an extremely difficult one; but he there appears indeed to argue for the immortality and immateriality of the 'agent intellect' part of the mind.

The chilling effect that al-Ghazali had on *falsafa*'s reputation in the Islamic world resulted, as noted, in its disappearance – or perhaps it might be more correct to say its complete absorption into *kalam*, theology – in Sunni Islam, which by numbers is 90 per cent of Islam today. But after the time of Averroes philosophy did not flourish, even among Shi'a, as it had done in the golden age between the ninth and thirteenth centuries, in the sense of producing great thinkers whose contributions were fully and importantly a part of the general history of philosophy. The reason is a simple one: religious doctrine is not hospitable to philosophical reflection; philosophical reflection has too ready a propensity to challenge, upset or undermine dogmatic certainties. The degree of latitude that al-Ghazali was prepared to extend to *falsafa* looks very generous by subsequent standards, but it was still not enough.

African Philosophy

Europe, India and China have traditions, religions, folklore, poetry, art and collections of maxims embodying the wisdom taught by experience. They also have developed bodies of thought which are distinctively philosophical, in the form of detailed and in almost all cases written debates about metaphysical, epistemological, ethical and political theories and ideas.

Europe, India and China are large geographical areas, and contain numerous different strands of folklore and tradition in their various internal regions. When the labels 'Indian philosophy' and 'Chinese philosophy' are used, they are intended to embrace not all the folklore, tradition and religion in the geographical area connoted, but the developed schools of thought to be found in their history, for example Advaita, Confucianism and Buddhism. To learn of them and perhaps to engage with them one can go to bodies of writings, and to named contributors, together constituting a recognizable and addressable discussion of themes – themes which, to be sure, intermittently intrigue, puzzle and disturb almost everyone at some time or other: among them truth, meaning, existence and value – which in philosophy are subjected to extended, advanced and thorough exploration in intellectually rigorous ways.

Does the term 'African philosophy' function in the same way as 'Indian philosophy' and 'Chinese philosophy' in this sense? Are there developed philosophical schools of thought in Africa that are distinguishable from traditions, religions, folklore, mythology, poetry, art and collections of maxims embodying the wisdom taught by experience?

An answer must begin with a distinction. If Augustine of Hippo, and the Neoplatonists of Alexandria in Egypt, are regarded as 'African philosophers', then the answer is immediately Yes. But if we regard the geographical regions of Egypt and north and north-east Africa as historically and culturally linked to Europe and the Middle East, this appropriation is misleading. If 'African philosophy' is to denote systems of thought about metaphysical, epistemological, ethical and political questions that are particularly *African* and which evolved through debate, then we must seek them in west Africa and sub-Saharan Africa.

In these large expanses of the landmass of Africa there are rich veins of folklore, story-telling, sagacity, tradition, art and religion. Does it constitute philosophy? The same rich material in the other continents of the world is not regarded as doing so. But a strongly held view has arisen in relation to post-colonial Africa that distinctively philosophical thought can be drawn from such material. The idea is that folklore, tales, wise maxims, tradition, art and religion contain and express worldviews, and the claim is then added that a worldview is, just in virtue of being one, a philosophy. Is this right? The material does indeed contain worldviews associated with the peoples and languages of different parts of Africa, from the Yoruba of Nigeria and Benin to the Zulus of KwaZulu-Natal. If one attaches an extended and very loose sense to the label 'philosophy', and thus allows oneself to comprehend any worldview under that label, then the worldview implicit in (for example) Homer, predicated on the interaction of the Olympian deities with humankind, or in indigenous Australian traditions, which are ancient and elaborate, would count as a philosophy. Is this satisfactory?

This is the crucial question for determining whether the worldviews identifiable in African traditions can be placed in the same category as the work of Plato and Kant (as unarguable benchmarks of what 'philosophy' is). At very least one has to say that there is a great difference at issue here, and that, in a book such as this, more definite work is required for the word 'philosophy' to do. If a much looser sense of the word were accepted, this book would need to be an encyclopaedic account of anthropology and ethnography, of folklore, legends, traditions, aphorisms and comparative linguistics, as well as philosophy in the sense associated with Plato and Kant.

It is important that thus insisting on an unequivocal use of terms should not be taken to imply a continuation of the discreditable view, near-universally held by white colonizers of the past, that African cultures are 'inferior'. The invaluable work of Edward Wilmot Blyden in initiating the 'decolonization of the African mind', the political activity of James Beale Horton, a military doctor and later a businessman, the codification of Akan law and constitutional principles by barristers

John Sarbah and Joseph Hayford (the 'King of West Africa'), would by themselves give the lie to such a view. All three of the latter were educated in Britain, but as with many others whose inspiration was drawn from their sense of belonging to their adopted or native lands, and their sense of what Blyden was proud to call 'Negritude', the readiness with which their political and cultural sophistication took the opportunity to express itself is proof against that falsehood.

These thinkers are just four examples of many whose contribution to the political self-awareness of colonized Africa is significant.* In that respect they are comparable to Gandhi in India. To say that their thinking constitutes a distinctive 'African political philosophy', rather than political thinking applied to an African context, is to misdescribe their contribution. It might seem more plausible to claim identifiable African tradition as the sources of the concepts of 'Consciencism' advanced by Kwame Nkrumah of Ghana, and *Ujamaa* or 'familyhood' proposed by Julius Nyerere of Tanzania, both drawing on the way traditional African tribal societies organize themselves. But insofar as they are close cousins of the underlying assumptions about human social interconnectedness in communalism and socialism generally, they are not uniquely African ideas, but in fact universal.

A similar thought applies to 'Africana philosophy', that is, philosophical work done by Africans or people of African descent, whether in Africa or abroad. To describe as 'African philosophy' the work done by the eighteenth-century Anton Amo, born in Ghana but taken to the Netherlands when aged three, would be a misdescription – though the laudatory remarks made about him and his continent of origin by academic colleagues at Wittenberg University in Prussia reflect much glory on both. To describe as 'African philosophy' the work done by a distinguished philosopher of African descent such as Kwame Anthony Appiah, British born but teaching in the United States, would likewise be a misdescription. And it would be the same so to describe the present born-in-Africa author.

In contesting the view that Africa has no written systematic philosophy, the example of the seventeenth-century Ethiopian thinker Zara Yacob and his book *Hatata* is cited. There is reason to question the

---

* Even here one notes the role of distinctions: a great figure like Nelson Mandela would be listed at the head of exemplary political activists rather than with Blyden, still less Locke and Rousseau.

authenticity of this book; its discoverer, the nineteenth-century missionary Padre Giusto d'Urbino, has been suspected of forging it.* But for present purposes let us suppose it authentic.

Yacob argues for a rationalistic approach to discovery of the universal nature of truth and morality, saying that observation of the world and people will reveal God's purpose, which was deliberately to make humans imperfect so that to be 'worthy of reward' they must strive for perfection. Yacob was raised and trained as a Coptic Christian, refused to convert to Catholicism when King Susenyos of Ethiopia, under the influence of Portuguese Jesuits, required that all his people should do so, and instead developed his own version of a theistic morality under the influence of the Psalms of David, which he much admired. He was followed by a disciple, Walda Heywat, who supplemented the *Hatata* with his own writings.

It will be noted that Yacob and Heywat were products of a literate culture which had long been in contact with Christian, Jewish and Muslim belief and thought – in the *Hatata* Yacob cites discussions he had with representatives of all three faiths – and therefore they merit classification with Augustine and the thinkers of Alexandria, and thus as inheritors of the traditions of theology and philosophy developed in the Middle East and Europe. Yacob had been trained in schools whose curriculum included *sewasewa*, scriptural interpretation, which can be a lively prompt to the view that differences in interpretation – and by extension, differences between religions generally – obscure whatever truths underlie them all. That there are such universal truths was, in essence, Yacob's view. He is an African philosopher in the sense that he was born and lived in Africa; but his philosophy arises from the same general context as that of Augustine.

The view that much of what is claimed as 'African philosophy' does not fall under the second term in this phrase is controversial precisely because it withholds one significant kind of status from the intellectual and cultural traditions at issue. Someone of acidulous temperament who takes this view might say, 'In an age when status-conferring terms have become vastly capacious in order to accommodate the self-affirming ambitions of as many people and things as possible, we succumb to the danger of their losing any real usefulness. If "philosophy" means anything anyone thinks or says, rather than something that clears a high

* I was alerted to this possibility by my colleague Dr David Mitchell.

bar as to what it addresses and how it does so, then we have lost a useful term, and will have to retreat to describing philosophy differently – perhaps with the cumbersome title "metaphysical, epistemological, ethical and logical studies" or "MEELS" for short, so that we can leave all other opinions, and any traditional views of any kind, to be celebrated under the dignifying but, in that event, newly uninformative label "philosophy".'*

This kind of view prompts proponents of the concept of 'African philosophy' to say that denials of its existence represent 'an implicit dismissal of Africa', even 'an implied insult'. But to take such a defensive view is to lose the opportunity of addressing a key question: 'Is there something both uniquely African and fundamentally philosophical within African culture or tradition?' Henry Odera Oruka's taxonomy of African cultural and intellectual endeavours which, he argued, meet this condition, comprises: traditional worldviews, wise sayings, political viewpoints, professional academic philosophy, literary philosophy and 'hermeneutic' study of the grammar of African languages to unearth philosophically significant commitments embedded in them. As the foregoing suggests, this does not persuade; and one main reason why can be shown by a comparison: what counts as clearly philosophical in the philosophies of e.g. India and China does not have to meet so exigent a criterion as having to be *uniquely* Indian or *uniquely* Chinese. That is why 'Indian philosophy' means 'philosophy in India, or by Indian philosophers'. The term 'African philosophy' strives for a different meaning, and wants that meaning for purposes of post-colonial identity rather than for truth or understanding per se. The controversy about this is not a matter of philosophers in other parts of the world refusing admittance to their club for reasons that are not intrinsic to the question of the matter and manner of philosophy; leading African philosophers Paulin Hountondji, Kwasi Wiredu and Kwame Anthony Appiah all oppose the ethnophilosophical approach, and the two latter take the same view of 'sage philosophy'.

It is more persuasive to observe that the traditions and outlooks that provide structure to a society and social relationships, and the justifications offered for those traditions, can be said to constitute an *ethical*

---

* Indeed this same remark would apply to those thinkers included in the *salon des refusés* in Part IV above – the sociologists, political theorists, anthropologists, historians of ideas and 'critical theory' exponents, all of whom are sometimes labelled 'philosophers'.

view. In this sense there is much to discover in Africa, for example the rich and deeply attractive concept of *Ubuntu* (see below). As this idea and its implications have increasingly been discussed and written about, so it has come to constitute a substantial philosophical contribution. It is unarguable that African philosophers – philosophers of African ethnicity writing, teaching or both, whether somewhere in Africa or in other parts of the world – might find in the cultural resources of one or another particularly *African* tradition of cosmology, history or traditional wisdom the materials for articulating metaphysical and epistemological theories, and contributing to logical theory also. It does however need *not* to be ethnography masquerading as philosophy.

As suggested, the concept of *Ubuntu* is just such a topic; here is a concept of significant interest to ethical thought in the humanist tradition. It is a definition of human moral existence in terms of mutuality, a recognition of the essential and therefore constitutive, defining, humanity-forming interconnectedness of persons to each other. 'Humanity' – expressly in the sense of 'humanness' and 'humaneness' combined – is exactly what *ubu-ntu* means in Nguni languages such as Zulu, Xhosa and Ndebele: *-ntu* is 'human' and the prefix *ubu-* does the work that the suffix '-ity' does in English, namely, it makes an abstract noun out of a concrete one. It resonates with the ideas of 'Consciencism' and *Ujamaa* already mentioned, and has direct parallels in other Bantu outlooks, for example the Shona idea of *Hunhu*.

The constellation of ideas captured by *Ubuntu* includes kindness, goodness, generosity, friendliness, compassion, caring, humane attitudes and actions, and the recognition of interdependence which confers a freely claimed entitlement and, simultaneously, a willingly accepted obligation to reciprocity. The briefest encapsulation of these humanistic values is the assertion, 'I am, because of you.' Although an old concept, its contemporary salience is owed to advocacy of it by the writer Jordan Kush Ngubane in the 1950s, and its adoption by Archbishop Desmond Tutu in his chairmanship of the Truth and Reconciliation Commission after the end of apartheid in South Africa.*

---

* C. B. N. Gade in 'The Historical Development of the Written Discourses on *Ubuntu*' traces its use back to at least 1846. Ngubane's discussion of the concept occurred in his novels and the magazine *African Drum*. Expressly philosophical discussion of the concept is attributed to S. J. T. Samkange and T. M. Samkange, *Hunhuism or Ubuntuism: A Zimbabwe Indigenous Political Philosophy* (1980).

The virtues of generosity and kindness are not unique to *Ubuntu*, of course; they lie at the heart of all moralities, whether humanistic or religious. The adjuration to fraternal love and concern in Mohism (a secular philosophy) and Christianity (a religion) asks for more than just generosity and kindness – not everyone is lovable, so this is a demanding injunction – but the more realistic because more modest demands are good commonplaces, and doubtless arise from the essentially social nature of human beings, making reciprocity an evolutionarily advantageous attitude. But *Ubuntu*'s insistence on an active meaning of this is a healthy alternative to a negatively phrased version which says 'do no harm,' or even, as a still paler version of the positive, 'maximize utilities.' To merit being described as *Ubuntu* (rather like being called a 'mensch' but even more fulsome) is to *be* the characteristics that the term denotes: and this is exactly what an ethics – from *ethos*, character – aspires to be. It lies between the over-ambitious 'love your neighbour' and the under-ambitious 'do no harm' as a realistically positive ethical principle which contains its own justification within it, namely, that as social animals who need one another we should live as that fact about us dictates. It abolishes the is–ought divide by saying that the 'ought' (the value) is implicit in the 'is' (the fact): the fact of being human *essentially* involves – because human relations are internal, relata-modifying ones – the mutually constituting virtues of humanness.

It is appropriate that as humankind itself came out of Africa, so one of the best ideas about how it can flourish – the idea of *Ubuntu* – should emanate from there too.

Concluding Remarks

Reflection on the great adventure of philosophy shows two things. One is that philosophy rests on two deep and fundamental questions. The first is, What is there? The second is, What matters?

The first is a question about the nature of reality. What exists? What is existence? What kinds of things exist? What is ultimately and finally real? This raises questions about knowledge. How can we know and say anything about reality, about the world and ourselves, and the relationship between ourselves and the world? What is knowledge? What is the best means to get it? This raises questions about concepts we have to understand in understanding knowledge and how to get it: reason, experience, truth and meaning – thus involving logic, perception, thought, theorizing, making sense of language, mind and consciousness.

This shows that the question 'What is there?' is the source of metaphysics, epistemology, logic, the philosophy of language and the philosophy of mind.

The second question, 'What matters?' is about value – about ethics, and politics which as Aristotle saw is continuous with ethics; it is about the good life and the good society, the question of our obligations and responsibilities, our judgments about wrong and harm and how to remedy them, about how to live and what sort of people we should be, both individually and socially. It is about what ultimately and most deeply matters. And it is also about aesthetics, which relates to the quality of lived experience. Taking all these considerations together, this question about value is about humanity, and relationships, society and the meaning of life.

The second thing that is shown by reflection on the great adventure of philosophy is that philosophy is a highly consequential enterprise. It began as reflective and serious enquiry about anything and everything, and as it matured a number of central themes emerged – those just identified as implicated in the two great questions. Efforts to answer them have taken many forms. But progress has been made. In the sixteenth and seventeenth centuries CE philosophers interested in the structure, properties and behaviour of the material universe – people like Copernicus, Galileo, Newton – began to find good ways to ask and answer their questions, and the result was the birth of modern science. In the eighteenth and nineteenth centuries philosophers interested in what we now call psychology, sociology, linguistics, philology and historical research gave birth to the social sciences. In the twentieth century philosophy and logic played a major part in the rise of computing and cognitive science.

We still do not know what ultimately exists. We still wrestle with problems about what is good and right, about how society should be organized, about meaning and value, and especially about the quest for the good and worthwhile life. Many people do not think about these things, preferring instead to take a prepacked set of views from some tradition, typically a religion, from which most of them cherry-pick what is convenient, and ignore what is inconvenient. But philosophy is the refusal to be lazy about the great questions. It patrols the circumference of the little patch of light that is knowledge, looking out into the dark of ignorance to seek the shapes there. Even though most people shy away from accepting the challenge to think (Russell said, 'Most people would rather die than think, and most people do'), they still find themselves often enough confronted by a philosophical question: about right and wrong, about what choice to make in some fundamental respect, about what it all really means. Thus everyone is a philosopher at times; everyone takes part. And that makes us all players in the history of philosophy.

Appendix: A Sketch of Logic

Just as mathematics is the tool of science, so logic is the tool of philosophy. It is useful to have a glimpse of what goes on in logic – and an acquaintance with some of the terms and concepts of logic – in appreciating many of the debates in philosophy. What follows is just such a sketch.

Logic is the study of reasoning and argument. It has three distinct branches. There is formal deductive logic, concerned with the study of valid forms of deductive reasoning. There is inductive logic, concerned with the kind of enquiry and reasoning typical in ordinary life and some of the sciences. And there is informal logic, which is about the many kinds of reasoning employed in debate, in law and politics, indeed in the setting out and defending of theses in any branch of discursive enquiry, and in the fallacies and rhetorical devices typical of such debate. In informal logic both deductive and inductive logical considerations apply, but an important feature is the identification and avoidance of informal fallacies of reasoning, that is, those that do not arise because of the form or structure of the argument itself, independently of its content.

In formal deductive logic the concept of *form*, as the very name implies, is central. Formal deductive logic studies not individual arguments, but *types* of arguments, to see which type is so structured or formed that, if the premises are true, the conclusion is guaranteed to be true also, independently of subject matter. This is what 'valid' means; it is a concept that applies only to the *structure* of arguments, not to their content. An argument is *sound* if in addition to having a valid form it also has true premises, that is, if *both* its content *and* its form stand up. Thus it is that the soundness of arguments is in part a matter of the facts, namely, those asserted in the premises, and partly a matter of how the argument is structured. But to repeat: formal deductive logic is interested only in this latter matter – the form or structure – and its aim is to identify which types of argument are valid in virtue of their form so that *if* true premises are supplied, that form will guarantee a true conclusion.

Inductive arguments, by contrast, if they are good ones, only make their conclusions probable to some degree. That the degree of probability can be very low despite the argument appearing plausible can be shown by an example of the simplest form of induction, 'induction by simple enumeration', in which a wholly general conclusion is inferred from a limited number of particular premises: 'This swan is white, that swan is white, the next swan is white . . . so all swans are white.' Some swans, in fact, are black; some are even black and white.

Inductive inference always goes beyond what the premises say, whereas deductive inferences contain no new information in the conclusion, which is simply a rearrangement of the information in the premises. Consider: 'All men are mortal; Socrates is a man; therefore Socrates is mortal.' All that has happened is that the terms occurring in the argument have been redistributed to yield the conclusion.

But although there might be no new information in the conclusion of a deductive argument, it can nevertheless be psychologically informative. This is shown by the story of the duke and the bishop. A famous bishop was the guest of honour at a country party hosted by a duke. At one point the duke left his guests to order something from his servants, and the bishop entertained the company by telling them that when, long ago, he was a newly ordained priest the first person whose confession he heard was a multiple murderer of an especially vile kind. The duke thereupon returned, clapped the bishop on the shoulder and said, 'The bishop and I are very old acquaintances. In fact, I was the first person whose confession he heard.' The rest of the guests, evidently logicians to a man and woman, hastily left.

The first systematic study of logic was made by Aristotle. With additions and extensions, especially by logicians of the medieval schools, his logic remained an apparently completed science until the nineteenth century. But then, in the hands of the mathematicians Augustus De Morgan, George Boole and especially Gottlob Frege, it was transformed into mathematical or 'symbolic' logic, an instrument of far greater range and power than Aristotelian logic. One of the innovations that made this possible was the development of a notation for expressing more and more complex notions. (The notation now standard is derived from one first devised by Bertrand Russell and Alfred North Whitehead in their *Principia Mathematica*.)

Aristotelian logic rests on three so-called 'laws of thought': the *Law of Identity* which states 'A is A', the *Law of Non-Contradiction* which states 'not both A and not-A', and the *Law of Excluded Middle* which states 'either A or not-A'. (Augustus De Morgan showed that the latter two are merely different ways of saying the same thing.)

An example of the way inferences were explored in the framework of Aristotelian logic is afforded by the 'Square of Opposition'. Taking the letters S and P to stand respectively for Subject and Predicate (in the sentence 'the horse is brown' the subject is 'the horse' and the predicate is 'brown'), one can describe the four standard forms of the proposition as follows:

A: universal affirmative 'All S is P'
E: universal negative 'No S is P'
I: Particular affirmative 'Some S is P'
O: Particular negative 'Some S is not-P'

Arranging them thus:

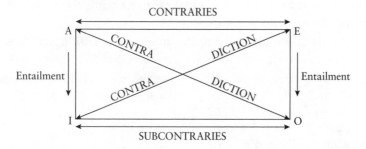

allows one to read off the 'immediate' inferences: A *entails* I, E entails O; A and O are *contradictories*, as are E and I; A and E are *contraries* (they can both be false together, but they cannot both be true together) and I and O are *subcontraries* (they can both be true together, but cannot both be false together). Making up appropriate versions of an English declarative sentence to put in the place of A, E and the others quickly demonstrates what all this means; take the example A: All men are tall, E: No men are tall, I: Some men are tall, O: Some men are not tall.

The main object of study for Aristotle and his tradition of logic was the syllogism, an argument form in which a conclusion is derived from two premises. In his *Prior Analytics* Aristotle defined syllogistic reasoning as a discourse in which 'Certain things having been supposed, something else necessarily follows from them because they are so.' The syllogism 'All men are mortal; Socrates is a man; therefore

Socrates is mortal' is the standard example. This is a 'categorical' syllogism, and it consists of two premises – a major premise 'All men are mortal,' a minor premise 'Socrates is a man,' and the conclusion that can be inferred from them, 'Socrates is mortal.' It will be noted that in this syllogism the major premise is a generalization, whereas the minor premise and conclusion are particular. The Aristotelian tradition classified all the forms of the syllogism according to the quantity (all, some), quality (affirmative, negative) and distribution of the terms in the premises and conclusion, devising mnemonics such as 'Barbara', 'Celarent', 'Darapti', etc. for the 256 thus identified: 'Barbara' is AAA (bArbArA), 'Celarent' is EAE (cElArEnt), 'Darapti' is AAI (dArAptI) and so on. Of these 256 forms only nineteen are valid (and even some of these nineteen are controversial).

The new 'symbolic logic' is a far more powerful and extensive instrument than this traditional syllogistic. Its use of symbols alarms people who do not like the look of anything that smacks of mathematics, but a little attention at the outset shows that far from being alarming, they are extremely useful and clarifying.

In the standard way of notating this logic, lower-case letters from later in the alphabet are used to stand for propositions: p, q, r . . . and a small set of symbols is coined to show the relationships between them: & for 'and', ∨ for 'or', → for 'if . . . then . . .', and ¬ for 'not', thus:

p & q (pronounced 'p and q')
p ∨ q (pronounced 'p or q')
¬p (pronounced 'not p')

The operators '&' and the rest can be very simply and informatively defined by 'truth tables', thus (where 'T' stands for 'true' and 'F' for 'false'):

p	q	p & q
T	T	T
T	F	F
F	T	F
F	F	F

Under 'p' and 'q' are listed the possibilities of truth and falsity combinations – in the first row both are true, in the second row 'p' is true but 'q' is false, and so on down. In the third column is the result for 'p & q'. A 'T' for true occurs only in the row where 'p' and 'q' are independently both true; in all other cases, where one of 'p' and 'q' is false or both are, 'p & q' is false. This gives a picture of the meaning of the logical operator '&' ('and'): '&' propositions are true only when the propositions joined by it are both true.

For '∨' ('or') matters are thus:

p	q	p ∨ q
T	T	T
T	F	T
F	T	T
F	F	F

This shows that 'p ∨ q' is true if at least one of 'p' and 'q' is individually true, and is false only if both are false. This defines the meaning of '∨' in the logical calculus.

With these simple elements, and intuitive use of brackets to keep all clear, forms of arguments can be explored for validity or otherwise. For example: from the premises 'p → q' and 'p' one can always deduce 'q', no matter what truth-values are assigned to 'p' and 'q' individually. Write this argument as:

$$[(p \rightarrow q) \& p] \rightarrow q$$

and one can show that this is a logical truth by making a truth table thus:

p	q	p → q	(p → q) & p	[(p → q) & p] → q
T	T	T	T	T
T	F	F	F	T
F	T	T	F	T
F	F	T	F	T

The fact that 'T' appears in all four rows under the main arrow in the last column shows that the whole string '[(p → q) & p] → q' is T no matter what the individual Ts and Fs are of the components. This is a 'logical truth' or tautology; it follows that any argument of the form:

Premise 1: p → q
Premise 2: p
Conclusion: q

is valid. This form of argument happens to be called *modus ponens*.

One can use truth tables to test for the validity of the following:

Premise 1: p → q
Premise 2: q
Conclusion: p

and

Premise 1: p → q
Premise 2: ¬q
Conclusion:¬p

One will find that the first is a *fallacy*, called the 'fallacy of affirming the consequent' (in 'p → q', 'p' is the 'antecedent' and 'q' the 'consequent', here being 'affirmed' by being used as the second premise), because there is an 'F' in one of the rows under the arrow in '[(p → q) & q] → p', thus:

p	q	p → q	(p → q) & q	[(p → q) & q] → p
T	T	T	T	T
T	F	F	F	T
F	T	T	T	F
F	F	T	F	T

In cases where an 'F' appears in *every* row under the final operator, one has not merely a fallacy but a *logical fallacy*.

The second example is, however, a logically valid form of inference, as its truth table will show; it is known as *modus tollens*.

These are the rudiments of the 'propositional calculus', which deals with arguments involving whole propositions. But the real work begins when one adds a few powerful devices to this calculus, transforming it into the 'predicate calculus' by getting inside propositions. This is important, given that propositions assert that all or many or a few or some or at least one of a certain thing has a certain property; and we wish to understand validity in terms of this finer degree of structure using quantifier ('how many') expressions.

To this end lower-case letters from the end of the alphabet x, y, z are used to stand for individual things, and the quantifier symbols (x) and (∃x) are used to denote respectively 'all things x' and 'at least one thing x' (this latter doing logical duty for all other quantifier expressions short of 'all', for example 'some', 'many', 'the majority', 'a few', 'three', 'four', 'a million', and so forth). Upper-case letters from earlier in the alphabet F, G, H stand for predicate expressions such as '. . . is brown' and '. . . belongs to the Queen'. So the sentence 'the table is brown' would be symbolized as (∃x)(Fx & Gx), pronounced 'there is an x such that x is F and x is G', here standing for 'there is an x such that x is a horse and x is brown.'

Equipped with supplementary rules allowing *general* expressions of the form (x)Fx to be 'instantiated' to give individual expressions of the form Fa (using lower-case letters from the beginning of the alphabet to stand for particular individuals), arguments can be tested for validity as before. Thus *modus ponens*, represented above by [(p → q) & p] → q, might look like this in quantified guise:

(x){[(Fx → Gx) & Fx] → Gx}

The instantiation rules allow us to rewrite this as:

[(Fa → Ga) & Fa] → Ga

which one can plainly see is an instance of *modus ponens*.

Discussion of inductive logic often occurs in connection with discussions of scientific methodology, for the obvious reason that scientific enquiry concerns contingent matters of fact, and the process of formulating a hypothesis or prediction and then testing it empirically can never have the conclusiveness expected in deductive logic, except perhaps when an hypothesis had been shown definitely to be mistaken.

The interesting thing about inductive reasoning is that it is always invalid from the point of view of deductive logic. Its conclusions, as mentioned above, always go beyond what is licensed by the premises. Accordingly much of the debate about induction concerns the sense in which it can be regarded as justified. A sticking point seems to be that the only available justification for induction is itself inductive, namely, that it has worked well in the past. If this is not to be merely circular, then the underlying assumption that the world is a consistent realm in which laws and patterns of occurrence remain stable and reliably repeat themselves has to be accepted as a general premise. Attempts to justify this premise can only themselves be inductive; so if they are made they simply reintroduce the circularity that the assumption is intended to make virtuous rather than vicious.

Inductive inference can take a number of forms. Induction by simple enumeration has been noted; there are also – and more generally better – inductions taking the form of causal inferences, statistical and probabilistic inferences, and arguments by analogy, all of which, when responsibly controlled and their defeasibility accounted for, are of use in practical concerns and scientific investigation. Opinion polls infer from representative samples of the population to overall views, generally with a reasonable degree of reliability; that is one compelling example of how effective controlled induction can be.

An argument in support of induction might proceed by appealing to the concept of rationality: one who does not take seriously the conclusion of an inference such as is involved in thinking 'I'd better take an umbrella because rain looks likely' is behaving irrationally. If it is rational to take the conclusions of inductive inferences seriously, that fact justifies induction.

A celebrated twist to the debate about induction was given by the American philosopher Nelson Goodman. He argued that the problem could be recast as one about how we justify thinking that our description of things in the future depends on our description of them now. For example, we think we will be entitled to describe emeralds we encounter in future as green, because all emeralds so far encountered in history have been green. But consider this: suppose one makes up a new word, 'grue', to mean 'green until now, and blue after a future date X'. Then the word 'grue' applies to emeralds just as legitimately as the word green, because emeralds have been green until now, and the definition of 'grue' requires only that they turn blue in the future. Now, obviously we think that we are better justified in taking 'green' to be the right description for future emeralds than 'grue'. But on what grounds do we think this? After all, the evidential basis for both descriptions is exactly the same – namely, that all past and present emeralds are green.

In addition to inductive logic and formal deductive logic there are other domains of this science in which logical principles and notions are put to work in exploration of allied ideas. So there is 'fuzzy logic', concerned with domains containing vague terms and imprecise concepts; 'intensional logic', concerned with domains where context violates the ordinary workings of logic (for example, by interfering with the reference of certain terms); 'deontic logic' concerned with reasoning, chiefly in ethics, involving ideas of obligation (expressed by such words as 'must' and 'ought'); 'many-valued logic' in which there are more than just the two truth-values 'true' and 'false'; 'paraconsistent logic', which contains, accepts and manages contradictions; 'epistemic logic' in which the operators 'believes that' and 'knows that' occur; and others.

FALLACIES OF INFORMAL LOGIC

'Informal logic', as the name suggests, concerns not the technical matter of forms of reasoning alone, as discussed above, but everything involved in real-life discussion and argument: rhetoric, persuasion, exhortation, disagreement, enquiry, thinking things through, working things out, making decisions, putting forward a case in court or in parliament or in the classroom or in the marketing meeting.

An important – and interesting – consideration in informal reasoning is the detection and avoidance of *fallacies*. For everyday use the identification of fallacies is of great value. There are many of these, and many of these many are standard rhetorical devices that politicians, advertisers, even friends and lovers, use to try to persuade other people and to get their way.

First it is useful to be reminded that an argument can be valid in form but unsound, either because one or more premises are false or because a fallacy has been committed. Consider this syllogism for example: 'Nothing is brighter than the sun; a candle is brighter than nothing; therefore a candle is brighter than the sun.' This is valid but unsound, because a fallacy – the Fallacy of Equivocation – is committed by it. This fallacy involves using a word in two different senses, as happens with 'nothing' in the first and second premises, thus unsoundly allowing the nonsense conclusion to be drawn.

Some of the commonest fallacies, not a few of them employed on purpose to mislead, are as follows.

The Fallacy of False Dilemma works by offering an alternative – 'either we have nuclear weapons or the country will be in danger of attack' which pretends to be exclusive in the sense that no other options are possible, whereas in fact several other options exist.

The Slippery-Slope Fallacy involves saying that if X happens or is allowed, Y and Z and so on will inevitably follow. 'If you give your son a mobile phone he will next want a television in his bedroom and then a car.'

The Straw-Man Fallacy occurs when someone attacks an opponent or a point of view by representing either in his or its weakest, worst or most negative version so that he or it is easy to knock down.

The Fallacy of Begging the Question, more illuminatingly known as Circular Reasoning, involves assuming in the premises what the argument claims to prove as a conclusion, for example, 'God exists because it says so in the Bible, which was inspired by God.' People nowadays typically misuse the expression 'begging the question' to mean 'prompts or invites or urges us to ask the question'. These latter formulations should be used if that is what one means to say; 'begging the question' should be reserved to its proper meaning of 'arguing circularly'.

A number of fallacies turn on the illegitimate use of emotion to get someone to accept a conclusion which does not follow from the offered premises. One is the 'appeal to force': 'believe what I say (do what I tell you) or I will beat you up' (*argumentum ad baculum*; this, though it puts the matter more bluntly than usual, is the essence of divine-command moralities).

A second is the 'appeal to pity': 'I will be upset, hurt, troubled, miserable if you do not believe or do what I say'; 'I'm poor'; 'I'm offended'; 'I'm from a minority'; 'I've been discriminated against' (*argumentum ad misericordiam*). The joke example given for this fallacy is the man who has been convicted of murdering his parents and who asks for the court's leniency on the grounds that he is an orphan. Associated with this is the idea that people who have been victimized or who have suffered are therefore good, or right, or can be excused for bad things they do.

A third is 'prejudicial use of language', which means using emotive or laden terms to 'spin' the view taken of something. Racist and sexist language provide one kind of example, another is the use of euphemism to hide the real purpose of something; so Idi Amin's death squads were called 'public safety units' and the CIA calls assassination of unfriendly foreign leaders 'extreme prejudice'.

There are also the fallacies of appealing to 'what everyone thinks' (*argumentum ad populum*), to what people in an authoritative position think (*argumentum ad verecundiam*), or the claim that no one knows the answer so you can believe more or less what you like (the argument from ignorance or *argumentum ad ignorantiam*). None of these are good grounds for accepting a view or believing anything.

A very common form of fallacy is the *ad hominem* argument, which is an attack on a person rather than on his or her argument. It takes different forms; there can be direct abuse of an individual, insinuations and hints that associate the individual with bad people or happenings, ridicule of the individual and redounding a charge on the individual ('you too', *tu quoque*).

Equally common is the use of biased statistics, introducing red herrings to distract people from the true thrust of an argument, reasoning that if y happened after x then it happened because of x (*post hoc ergo propter hoc*), and generalizing from just one or a very small sample of something. These are all fallacies.

And so finally is attributing a property of part of a whole to the whole itself – which we know to be wrong because we know that a school of whales is not itself a whale. This fallacy, called the Fallacy of Composition, is one applied to groups and nations all the time: 'I met a Frenchman who was impolite, so the French are an impolite nation.'

Although fallacies of informal reasoning are often deliberately employed to win arguments by trickery, thus persuading and coercing people into a way of thinking or a belief, it is also very frequently the case that we each reason badly because we commit one or more such fallacies without realizing it. A course in 'straight and crooked thinking' (to borrow the title of a celebrated book on informal reasoning by Robert Thouless) would be to everyone's benefit – and it does not commit the Fallacy of Composition to say: to the world's benefit as a whole therefore.

Before Common Era

600   500   400   300   200   100

Thales (*fl.* 585 BCE)
Anaximander (*fl.* 570 BCE)
Confucius (551–479 BCE)
Anaximenes (*fl.* 546 BCE)
Xenophanes (*fl.* 540 BCE)
Pythagoras (*fl.* 532 BCE)
Heraclitus (*fl.* 495 BCE)
Anaxagoras (*fl.* 470 BCE)
Parmenides (*fl.* 465 BCE)
Zeno of Elea (*fl.* 450 BCE)
Empedocles (*fl.* 450 BCE)
Leucippus (*fl.* 5th cent. BCE)
Democritus (*fl.* 415 BCE)
Socrates (470–399 BCE)
Plato (*c.*425–347 BCE)
Zhuangzi (399–295 BCE)
Aristotle (384–322 BCE)
Mencius (372–289 BCE)
Xunzi (*c.*310–*c.*235 BCE)
Han Feizi (*c.*280–233 BCE)

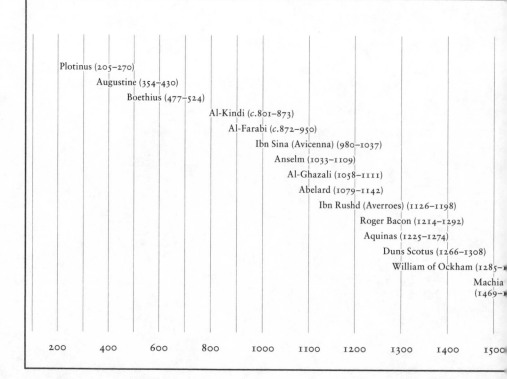

Plotinus (205–270)
Augustine (354–430)
Boethius (477–524)
Al-Kindi (*c.*801–873)
Al-Farabi (*c.*872–950)
Ibn Sina (Avicenna) (980–1037)
Anselm (1033–1109)
Al-Ghazali (1058–1111)
Abelard (1079–1142)
Ibn Rushd (Averroes) (1126–1198)
Roger Bacon (1214–1292)
Aquinas (1225–1274)
Duns Scotus (1266–1308)
William of Ockham (1285–
Machia
(1469–

200   400   600   800   1000   1100   1200   1300   1400   1500

TIMELINE OF PHILOSOPHERS

Bacon (1561–1626)
Hobbes (1588–1679)
Descartes (1596–1650)
Spinoza (1632–1677)
Locke (1632–1704)
Leibniz (1646–1716)
Berkeley (1685–1753)
Hume (1711–1776)
Rousseau (1712–1778)
Kant (1724–1804)
Bentham (1748–1832)
Hegel (1770–1831)
Schopenhauer (1788–1860)
John Stuart Mill (1806–1873)
Marx (1818–1883)
Nietzsche (1844–1900)
Frege (1848–1925)
Husserl (1859–1938)
Russell (1872–1970)
Moore (1873–1958)
Wittgenstein (1889–1951)
Heidegger (1889–1976)
Carnap (1891–1970)
Ryle (1900–1976)
Gadamer (1900–2002)
Popper (1902–1994)
Sartre (1905–1980)
Merleau-Ponty (1908–1961)
Stevenson (1908–1979)
Quine (1908–2000)
Austin (1911–1960)
Ricoeur (1913–2005)
Mackie (1917–1981)
Davidson (1917–2003)
Hare (1919–2002)
Strawson (1919–2006)
Rawls (1921–2002)
Deleuze (1925–1995)
Dummett (1925–2011)
Derrida (1930–2004)
Nozick (1938–2002)
Kripke (1940–)

1600   1700   1800   1900   2000

Bibliography

ANCIENT PHILOSOPHY
General

Algra, K., J. Barnes, J. Mansfeld and M. Schofield (eds.), *The Cambridge History of Hellenistic Philosophy*, Cambridge: Cambridge University Press, 1999

Burnet, J., *Early Greek Philosophy*, 3rd edn, London: A&C Black, 1920. Available online: https://archive.org/details/burnetgreekooburnrich/page/n5

Frede, M., *Essays in Ancient Philosophy*, Minneapolis, MN: University of Minnesota Press, 1987

Gerson, L. P. (ed.), *The Cambridge History of Philosophy in Late Antiquity*, 2 vols., Cambridge, UK and New York City, NY: Cambridge University Press, 2010

Gill, M. L. and P. Pellegrin (eds.), *A Companion to Ancient Philosophy*, Oxford: Wiley-Blackwell, 2009

Guthrie, W. K. C., *A History of Greek Philosophy*, 6 vols., Cambridge: Cambridge University Press, 1962–81

Long, A. A. and D. N. Sedley, *The Hellenistic Philosophers*, 2 vols., Cambridge: Cambridge University Press, 1987

Sedley, D. (ed.), *The Cambridge Companion to Greek and Roman Philosophy*, Cambridge: Cambridge University Press, 2003

Presocratics

Graham, D. W. (ed.), *The Texts of Early Greek Philosophy: The Complete Fragments and Selected Testimonies of the Major Presocratics*, 2 vols., Cambridge: Cambridge University Press, 2010

Barnes, J., *The Presocratic Philosophers*, 2nd edn, London: Routledge & Kegan Paul, 1982

Hussey, E., *The Presocratics*, London: Duckworth, 1995

Kirk, G. S., J. E. Raven and M. Schofield, *The Presocratic Philosophers*, 2nd edn, Cambridge: Cambridge University Press, 1984

Osborne, C., *Presocratic Philosophy: A Very Short Introduction*, Oxford: Oxford University Press, 2004

Socrates

Ahbel-Rappe, S. and R. Kamtekar (eds.), *A Companion to Socrates*, Oxford: Wiley-Blackwell, 2005

Annas, J., *Ancient Philosophy: A Very Short Introduction*, Oxford: Oxford University Press, 2000

Benson, H. H. (ed.), *Essays on the Philosophy of Socrates*, New York City, NY: Oxford University Press, 1992

Rudebusch, G., *Socrates*, Oxford: Wiley-Blackwell, 2009

Taylor, A. E., *Socrates*, Boston: Beacon Press, 1932

Taylor, C. C. W., *Socrates: A Very Short Introduction*, Oxford: Oxford University Press, 2000

Vlastos, G., *The Philosophy of Socrates: A Collection of Critical Essays*, Notre Dame, IN: University of Notre Dame Press, 1980

Vlastos, G., *Socrates: Ironist and Moral Philosopher*, New York City, NY: Cambridge University Press, 1991

Vlastos, G., *Socratic Studies*, Cambridge: Cambridge University Press, 1994

Plato

Jowett, B. (trans.), *The Dialogues of Plato (428/27–348/47 BCE)*. Available online: http://webs.ucm. es/info/diciex/gente/agf/plato/The_Dialogues_of_Plato_vo.1.pdf

Annas, J., *Plato: A Very Short Introduction*, Oxford: Oxford University Press, 2003

Annas, J., *Virtue and Law in Plato and Beyond*, Oxford: Oxford University Press, 2017

Dancy, R. M., *Plato's Introduction of Forms*, Cambridge: Cambridge University Press, 2004

Fine, G. (ed.), *Plato 1: Metaphysics and Epistemology*, Oxford: Oxford University Press, 1999

Irwin, T., *Plato's Ethics*, Oxford: Oxford University Press, 1995

Kraut, R. (ed.), *The Cambridge Companion to Plato*, Cambridge: Cambridge University Press, 1992

Ryle, G., *Plato's Progress*, new edn, Cambridge: Cambridge University Press, 2010

Vlastos, G., *Studies in Greek Philosophy*, vol. II: *Socrates, Plato, and their Tradition*, ed. D. W. Graham, Princeton, NJ: Princeton University Press, 1995

Aristotle

Aristotle, *The Nicomachean Ethics*, rev. edn, ed. H. Tredennick and Jonathan Barnes, trans. J. A. K. Thomson, London: Penguin Classics, 2004

Barnes, J. (ed.), *The Complete Works of Aristotle*. Available online: https://searchworks.stanford. edu/view/5975805

Ackrill, J. L., *Aristotle the Philosopher*, Oxford: Oxford University Press, 1981

Anagnostopoulos, G. (ed.), *A Companion to Aristotle*, Oxford: Wiley-Blackwell, 2009

Barnes, J. (ed.), *The Cambridge Companion to Aristotle*, Cambridge: Cambridge University Press, 1995

Ross, W. D., *Aristotle*, London: Methuen, 1923

Shields, C., *Aristotle*, 2nd edn, London: Routledge, 2014

Epicureans

Bailey, C., *Epicurus: The Extant Remains*, Oxford: Clarendon Press, 1926

Clay, D., *Lucretius and Epicurus*, Ithaca, NY: Cornell University Press, 1983

Rist, J. M., *Epicurus: An Introduction*, Cambridge: Cambridge University Press, 1972

Wilson, C., *Epicureanism: A Very Short Introduction*, Oxford: Oxford University Press, 2015

Wolfsdorf, D., *Pleasure in Ancient Greek Philosophy*, Cambridge: Cambridge University Press, 2013

Stoics

Inwood, B. (ed.), *The Cambridge Companion to the Stoics*, Cambridge: Cambridge University Press, 2003

Long, A. A., *Epictetus: A Stoic and Socratic Guide to Life*, Oxford: Clarendon Press, 2002

Long, A. A., *Stoic Studies*, Cambridge: Cambridge University Press, 1996
Rist, J. M., *Stoic Philosophy*, Cambridge: Cambridge University Press, 1969
Sellars, J. (ed.), *The Routledge Handbook of the Stoic Tradition*, London: Routledge, 2016

Neoplatonism

Plotinus, *The Six Enneads*, trans. S. MacKenna and B. S. Page. Available online: http://pinkmonkey. com/dl/library1/six.pdf
Porphyry, *Life of Plotinus*, trans. S. MacKenna, and *Isagoge*, trans. O. F. Owen. Available online: https:// www.sacred-texts.com/cla/plotenn/enno01.htm; http://www.tertullian.org/fathers/porphyry_isa gogue_02_translation.htm
Gerson, L. P., *Plotinus*, London and New York City, NY: Routledge, 1994
Remes, P. and S. Slaveva-Griffin (eds.), *The Routledge Handbook of Neoplatonism*, London and New York City, NY: Routledge, 2014
Wallis, R. T., *Neoplatonism*, 2nd edn, London: Duckworth, 1995

MEDIEVAL PHILOSOPHY

Abelard, P., *Ethical Writings*, trans. P. V. Spade, Indianapolis: Hackett, 1995
Aquinas, T., *Selected Philosophical Writings*, Oxford: Oxford University Press, 2008.
Augustine, *City of God*, trans. H. Bettenson, London: Pelican Books, 1972
Bacon, R., *Opus Majus*, Oxford: Oxford University Press, 1931
Boethius, *The Consolation of Philosophy*, trans. V. Watts, London: Penguin Classics, 2003
Bosley, R. N. and M. M. Tweedale (eds.), *Basic Issues in Medieval Philosophy: Selected Readings Presenting the Interactive Discourses among the Major Figures*, 2nd edn, Peterborough, ON: Broadview Press, 2006
McGrade, A. S., J. Kilcullen and M. Kempshall (eds. and trans.), *The Cambridge Translations of Medieval Philosophical Texts*, vol. 2: *Ethics and Political Philosophy*, Cambridge: Cambridge University Press, 2000
Pasnau, R. (ed. and trans.), *The Cambridge Translations of Medieval Philosophical Texts*, vol. 3: *Mind and Knowledge*, Cambridge: Cambridge University Press, 2002
Spade, P. V. (ed. and trans.), *Five Texts on the Mediaeval Problem of Universals: Porphyry, Boethius, Abelard, Duns Scotus, Ockham*, Indianapolis: Hackett, 1994
Gracia, J. J. E. and T. B. Noone, *A Companion to Philosophy in the Middle Ages*, Oxford: Wiley-Blackwell, 2005
Grayling, A. C., *The God Argument*, London: Bloomsbury, 2013
Koterski, J. W., *An Introduction to Medieval Philosophy: Basic Concepts*, Chichester: Wiley-Blackwell, 2009
Luscombe, D., *Medieval Thought*, Oxford: Oxford University Press, 1997
Marenbon, J., *Medieval Philosophy: An Historical and Philosophical Introduction*, London: Routledge, 2006

RENAISSANCE PHILOSOPHY

Machiavelli, N., *The Prince*. Available online: https://www.victoria.ac.nz/lals/about/staff/publica tions/paul-nation/Prince-Adapted2.pdf
Machiavelli, N., *The Prince*, ed. Q. Skinner and R. Price, Cambridge: Cambridge University Press, 1988
More, T., *Utopia*. Available online: http://www.gutenberg.org/ebooks/2130

Pico della Mirandola, G., *Oration on the Dignity of Man*. Available online: http://bactra.org/ Mirandola/

Blum, P. R. (ed.), *Philosophers of the Renaissance*, Washington, DC: The Catholic University of America Press, 2010

Copenhaver, B. P. and C. B. Schmitt, *Renaissance Philosophy*, Oxford: Oxford University Press, 1992

Grayling, A. C., *The Age of Genius*, London: Bloomsbury, 2016

Hankins, J. (ed.), *The Cambridge Companion to Renaissance Philosophy*, Cambridge: Cambridge University Press, 2007

Nederman, C. J., *Machiavelli: A Beginner's Guide*, Oxford: Oneworld Publications, 2009

Rice, E. F., *The Renaissance Idea of Wisdom*, Cambridge, MA: Harvard University Press, 1958

Schmitt, C. B. et al. (eds.), *The Cambridge History of Renaissance Philosophy*, Cambridge: Cambridge University Press, 1988

MODERN PHILOSOPHY
Descartes

Descartes, R., *Meditations on First Philosophy*, trans. E. S. Haldane, Cambridge: Cambridge University Press, 1911. Available online: http://selfpace.uconn.edu/class/percep/DescartesMeditations.pdf

Cottingham, J. et al. (trans.), *Philosophical Writings of Descartes*, 3 vols., Cambridge: Cambridge University Press, 1984–91

Cunning, D. (ed.), *The Cambridge Companion to Descartes' Meditations*, Cambridge: Cambridge University Press, 2014

Curley, E. M., *Descartes against the Skeptics*, Cambridge, MA: Harvard University Press, 1978

Gaukroger, S., *Descartes: An Intellectual Biography*, Oxford: Oxford University Press, 1995

Grayling, A. C., *Descartes: The Life of René Descartes and its Place in his Times*, London: The Free Press, 2005

Kenny, A., *Descartes: A Study of his Philosophy*, New York City, NY: Random House, 1968

Spinoza

Spinoza, B., *Ethics Demonstrated in Geometrical Order*, 2004. Available online: https://www.early moderntexts.com/assets/pdfs/spinoza1665.pdf

Spinoza, B., *Political Treatise*, 2008. Available online: https://www.dascolihum.com/uploads/ CH_70_Spinoza_Political_Treatise.pdf

Spinoza, B., *The Collected Works of Spinoza*, 2 vols., trans. E. Curley, Princeton NJ: Princeton University Press, 1985–2016

Allison, H., *Benedict de Spinoza: An Introduction*, New Haven, CT: Yale University Press, 1987

Garrett, D. (ed.), *The Cambridge Companion to Spinoza*, New York City, NY: Cambridge University Press, 1996

Huenemann, C. (ed.), *Interpreting Spinoza: Critical Essays*, Cambridge: Cambridge University Press, 2008

James, S., *Spinoza on Philosophy, Religion, and Politics*, Oxford: Oxford University Press, 2014

Popkin, R. H., *Spinoza*, Oxford: Oneworld Publications, 2004

Locke

Locke, J., *An Essay Concerning Human Understanding*, Book II: *Ideas*, 2004. Available online: https://www.earlymoderntexts.com/assets/pdfs/locke1690book2.pdf

Nidditch, P. H. (ed.), *The Clarendon Edition of the Works of John Locke: An Essay Concerning Human Understanding*, Oxford: Oxford University Press, 1975

Ashcraft, R. (ed.), *Locke's Two Treatises of Government*, London: Routledge, 2012. Available online: http://www.yorku.ca/comninel/courses/3025pdf/Locke.pdf

Lowe, E. J., *Routledge Philosophy Guidebook to Locke on Human Understanding*, London: Routledge, 1995

Mackie, J. L., *Problems from Locke*, Oxford: Clarendon Press, 1976

Tipton, I. C. (ed.), *Locke on Human Understanding: Selected Essays*, Oxford: Oxford University Press, 1977

Yolton, J. W., *John Locke and the Way of Ideas*, Oxford: Oxford University Press, 1956

Berkeley

Berkeley, G., *A Treatise Concerning the Principles of Human Knowledge*, ed. D. R. Wilkins, 2002. Available online: https://www.maths.tcd.ie/~dwilkins/Berkeley/HumanKnowledge/1734/HumKno.pdf

Berkeley, G., *Philosophical Works: Including the Works on Vision*, ed. M. Ayers, London: Dent, 1975

Fogelin, R. J., *Routledge Philosophy Guidebook to Berkeley and the Principles of Human Knowledge*, London: Routledge, 2001

Foster, J. and H. Robinson (eds.), *Essays on Berkeley: A Tercentennial Celebration*, Oxford: Clarendon Press, 1985

Grayling, A. C., *Berkeley: The Central Arguments*, London: Duckworth, 1986

Urmson, J. O., *Berkeley*, Oxford: Oxford University Press, 1982

Leibniz

Leibniz, G. W., *The Principles of Philosophy Known as Monadology*, 2004. Available online: https://www.earlymoderntexts.com/assets/pdfs/leibniz1714b.pdf

Leibniz, G. W., *Discourse on Metaphysics*, 2004. Available online: http://www.earlymoderntexts.com/assets/pdfs/leibniz1686d.pdf

Hooker, M. (ed.), *Leibniz: Critical and Interpretive Essays*, Minneapolis, MN: University of Minnesota Press, 1982

Jolley, N. (ed.), *The Cambridge Companion to Leibniz*, Cambridge: Cambridge University Press, 1995

Mates, B., *The Philosophy of Leibniz: Metaphysics and Language*, Oxford: Oxford University Press, 1986

Mercer, C., *Leibniz's Metaphysics: Its Origins and Development*, Cambridge: Cambridge University Press, 2001

Hume

Hume, D., *A Treatise of Human Nature*, ed. L. A. Selby-Bigge, Oxford: Clarendon Press, 1896. Available online: https://people.rit.edu/wlrgsh/HumeTreatise.pdf

Hume, D., *An Enquiry Concerning Human Understanding*. Available online: https://socialsciences.mcmaster.ca/econ/ugcm/3ll3/hume/enquiry.pdf

Hume, D., *An Enquiry Concerning the Principles of Morals*, ed. H. Lewis, 1912. Available online: https://www.axiospress.com/wp-content/uploads/Hume-An-Enquiry-Concerning-the-Principles-of-Morals.pdf

Millican, P. (ed.), *Reading Hume on Human Understanding: Essays on the First Enquiry*, Oxford: Clarendon Press, 2002

Pears, D., *Hume's System: An Examination of the First Book of his Treatise*, Oxford: Oxford University Press, 1990

Penelhum, T., *Hume*, London: Macmillan, 1975

Stroud, B., *Hume*, London: Routledge & Kegan Paul, 1977

Wright, J. P., *Hume's 'A Treatise of Human Nature': An Introduction*, Cambridge: Cambridge University Press, 2009

Rousseau

Bertram, C., *Rousseau and the Social Contract*, London: Routledge, 2004

O'Hagan, T., *Rousseau*, London: Routledge, 1999

Zaretsky, R. and J. T. Scott, *The Philosophers' Quarrel: Rousseau, Hume, and the Limits of Human Understanding*, New Haven, CT: Yale University Press, 2009

Kant

Kant, I., *Critique of Pure Reason*, ed. and trans. P. Guyer and A. W. Wood, New York City, NY: Cambridge University Press, 1998. Available online: http://strangebeautiful.com/other-texts/kant-first-critique-cambridge.pdf

Kant, I., *Groundwork for the Metaphysics of Morals*, ed. and trans. A. W. Wood, Binghamton, NY: Yale University Press, 2002. Available online: http://www.inp.uw.edu.pl/mdsie/Political_Thought/Kant%20-%20groundwork%20for%20the%20metaphysics%20of%20morals%20with%20essays.pdf

Gardner, S., *Kant and the Critique of Pure Reason*, London: Routledge, 1999

Guyer, P. (ed.), *The Cambridge Companion to Kant and Modern Philosophy*, Cambridge: Cambridge University Press, 1992

Luchte, J., *Kant's 'Critique of Pure Reason': A Reader's Guide*, London: Bloomsbury, 2007

Scruton, R., *Kant: A Very Short Introduction*, Oxford: Oxford University Press, 2001

Strawson, P. F., *The Bounds of Sense*, London: Methuen, 1965

Uleman, J. K., *An Introduction to Kant's Moral Philosophy*, Cambridge: Cambridge University Press, 2010

Eighteenth-Century Enlightenment

Gay, P., *The Enlightenment*, 2 vols., 2nd edn, New York: W. W. Norton, 1995

Horkheimer, M. and T. Adorno, *Dialectic of Enlightenment*, reprint of 1st edn (1944), Stanford, CA: Stanford University Press, 2002

Hegel

Hegel, G. W. F., Preface to *The Difference between Fichte's and Schelling's Systems of Philosophy*, in R. Bubner (ed.), *German Idealist Philosophy*, London: Penguin Books, 1997

Hegel, G. W. F., *Phenomenology of Spirit*, trans. A. V. Miller, Oxford: Oxford University Press, 1977

Hölderlin, F., 'The Oldest System-Programme of German Idealism', trans. T. Cowan, *European Journal of Philosophy* (August 1995) 199–200

Baur, M. (ed.), *G. W. F. Hegel: Key Concepts*, Abingdon: Routledge, 2014

Forster, M. N., *Hegel's Idea of a Phenomenology of Spirit*, Chicago IL: University of Chicago Press, 1998

Houlgate, S. and M. Baur (eds.), *A Companion to Hegel*, Oxford: Wiley-Blackwell, 2011

Moyar, D. and M. Quante (eds.), *Hegel's Phenomenology of Spirit: A Critical Guide*, Cambridge: Cambridge University Press, 2008

Rosen, M., *Hegel's Dialectic and its Criticism*, Cambridge: Cambridge University Press, 1984

Stern, R. (ed.), *G. W. F. Hegel: Critical Assessments*, 4 vols., London: Routledge, 1993
Taylor, C., *Hegel*, Cambridge: Cambridge University Press, 1975
Westphal, K. R. (ed.), *The Blackwell Guide to Hegel's Phenomenology of Spirit*, Oxford: Wiley-Blackwell, 2009

Schopenhauer

Schopenhauer, A., *The Basis of Morality*, ed. and trans. A. B. Bullock, London: Swan Sonnenschein, 1903. Available online: http://www.archive.org/stream/basisofmoralityooschoiala/basisofmorali tyooschoiala_djvu.txt
App, Urs, 'Schopenhauer's Initial Encounter with Indian Thought', *Schopenhauer-Jahrbuch* 87 (2006) 35–76
Gardner, P. L., *Schopenhauer*, London: Penguin, 1971

Marx

Marx, K., *Karl Marx: Selected Writings*, 2nd edn, ed. D. McLellan, Oxford: Oxford University Press, 2000
Online texts: https://www.marxists.org/archive/marx/works/download/pdf/Selected-Works.pdf
Bottomore, T., *Karl Marx*, Oxford: Wiley-Blackwell, 1979
Elster, J., *Making Sense of Marx*, Cambridge: Cambridge University Press, 1985
Singer, P., *Marx: A Very Short Introduction*, Oxford: Oxford University Press, 2000
Wolff, J., *Why Read Marx Today?*, Oxford: Oxford University Press, 2002

Nietzsche

Online texts: http://www.openculture.com/2014/11/download-nietzsches-major-works-as-free-ebooks.html
Came, D. (ed.), *Nietzsche on Art and Life*, Oxford: Oxford University Press, 2014
Cate, C., *Friedrich Nietzsche*, London: Hutchinson, 2002
Gemes, K. and J. Richardson (eds.), *The Oxford Handbook of Nietzsche*, Oxford: Oxford University Press, 2013
Higgins, K. M., *Nietzsche's Zarathustra*, Philadelphia, PA: Temple University Press, 1987
Janaway, C., *Beyond Selflessness: Reading Nietzsche's Genealogy*, Oxford: Clarendon Press, 2007
Leiter, B., *Nietzsche on Morality*, London: Routledge, 2014
May, S., *Nietzsche's Ethics and his War on 'Morality'*, Oxford: Clarendon Press, 1999
Welshon, R., *The Philosophy of Nietzsche*, Montreal: McGill-Queen's University Press, 2004

Idealism

Connelly, J. and S. Panagakou (eds.), *Anglo-American Idealism: Thinkers and Ideas*, New York City, NY: Peter Lang, 2009
Dunham, J., I. Hamilton Grant and S. Watson, *Idealism: The History of a Philosophy*, London: Routledge, 2010
Mander, W. J., *British Idealism: A History*, Oxford: Oxford University Press, 2014
Sprigge, T. L. S., *The Vindication of Absolute Idealism*, Edinburgh: Edinburgh University Press, 1983
Sweet, W. and S. Panagakou (eds.), *The Moral, Social and Political Philosophy of the British Idealists*, Exeter: Imprint Academic, 2009

Pragmatism

Dewey, J., *The Essential Dewey*, 2 vols., ed. L. A. Hickman and T. M. Alexander, Bloomington, IN: Indiana University Press, 1998

Goodman, R. B. (ed.), *Pragmatism: A Contemporary Reader*, London: Psychology Press, 1995

Haack, S. (ed.), *Pragmatism, Old and New: Selected Writings*, Amherst, NY: Prometheus Books, 2006.

James, W., *Pragmatism*, Cambridge, MA: Harvard University Press, 1975

James, W., *The Will to Believe*, London: Longmans, Green, 1896. Available online: https://archive.org/details/willtobelieveoojamegoog/page/n8

Menand, L. (ed.), *Pragmatism: A Reader*, New York City, NY: Random House, 1998

Peirce, C. S., *The Essential Peirce: Selected Philosophical Writings*, 2 vols., ed. N. Houser, C. J. W. Kloesel and The Peirce Edition Project, Bloomington, IN: Indiana University Press, 1992–8

Bacon, M., *Pragmatism: An Introduction*, Oxford: Polity, 2012

Malachowski, A. (ed.), *The Cambridge Companion to Pragmatism*, Cambridge: Cambridge University Press, 2013

PHILOSOPHY IN THE TWENTIETH CENTURY
Analytic Philosophy

Austin, J. L., *How to Do Things with Words*, Oxford: Clarendon Press, 1975

Austin, J. L., *Sense and Sensibilia*, London: Oxford University Press, 1962

Ayer, A. J., *Language, Truth and Logic*, New York City, NY: Dover Publications, 1952

Ayer, A. J., *The Problem of Knowledge*, New York City, NY: Penguin Books, 1957

Beaney, M., *Analytic Philosophy: A Very Short Introduction*, Oxford: Oxford University Press, 2017

Boundas, C. V. (ed.), *Columbia Companion to Twentieth-Century Philosophies*, New York City, NY: Columbia University Press, 2007

Brentano, F., *Psychology from an Empirical Standpoint*, London: Routledge, 1973

Churchland, P. S., *Neurophilosophy: Toward a Unified Science of the Mind-Brain*, Cambridge, MA: The MIT Press, 1989

Davidson, D., *Essays on Actions and Events*, 2nd edn, Oxford: Clarendon Press, 2001

Davidson, D., *Inquiries into Truth and Interpretation*, 2nd edn, Oxford: Clarendon Press, 2001

Dummett, M., *Frege: Philosophy of Language*, New York City, NY: Harper & Row, 1973

Dummett, M., *Truth and Other Enigmas*, London: Duckworth, 1998

Evans, G. and J. McDowell (eds.), *Truth and Meaning*, Oxford: Oxford University Press, 1976

Grayling, A. C., *An Introduction to Philosophical Logic*, 3rd edn, Oxford: Blackwell, 1998 – provides an elementary introduction to many of the themes in Part IV, 'Analytic Philosophy'

Grayling, A. C. (ed.), *Philosophy 1: A Guide through the Subject*, Oxford: Oxford University Press, 1995

Grayling, A. C. (ed.), *Philosophy 2: Further through the Subject*, Oxford: Oxford University Press, 1998

Hare, R. M., *The Language of Morals*, Oxford: Clarendon Press, 1952

Kneale, W. and M., *The Development of Logic*, Oxford: Oxford University Press, 1962

MacIntyre, A., *After Virtue: A Study in Moral Theory*, London: Bloomsbury, 2011

Mackie, J. L., *Ethics: Inventing Right and Wrong*, London: Penguin Books, 1990

Martinich, A. P. and D. Sosa (eds.), *Analytic Philosophy: An Anthology*, Oxford: Blackwell, 2001

Moore, A. W., *The Evolution of Modern Metaphysics*, Cambridge: Cambridge University Press, 2012

Moore, G. E., *Principia Ethica*, Cambridge: Cambridge University Press, 1903

Moran, D. (ed.), *The Routledge Companion to Twentieth Century Philosophy*, London: Routledge, 2008

Nagel, T., *Mortal Questions*, Cambridge: Cambridge University Press, 1979

Nozick, R., *Anarchy, State, and Utopia*, New York City, NY: Basic Books, 1974

Popper, K., *Conjectures and Refutations: The Growth of Scientific Knowledge*, London: Routledge, 2002

Popper, K., *The Logic of Scientific Discovery*, London: Routledge, 2002

Putnam, H., *The Many Faces of Realism*, Chicago, IL: Open Court, 1988

Putnam, H., *Representation and Reality*, Cambridge, MA: The MIT Press, 1991

Quine, W. V. O., *From a Logical Point of View*, 2nd edn, Boston, MA: Harvard University Press, 1961

Quine, W. V. O., *Word and Object*, Cambridge, MA: The MIT Press, 1964

Rawls, J., *A Theory of Justice*, Oxford: Oxford University Press, 1999

Russell, B., *Human Knowledge: Its Scope and Limits*, London: George Allen & Unwin, 1948

Russell, B., *The Problems of Philosophy*, London: Williams & Norgate, 1912

Ryle, G., *The Concept of Mind*, London: Penguin Books, 1990

Searle, J. R., *Speech Acts: An Essay in the Philosophy of Language*, Cambridge: Cambridge University Press, 1969

Sluga, H. and D. Stern (eds.), *The Cambridge Companion to Wittgenstein*, Cambridge: Cambridge University Press, 2010

Stevenson, C. L., *Ethics and Language*, New Haven, CT: Yale University Press, 1958

Strawson, P. F., *The Bounds of Sense*, London: Methuen, 1966

Strawson, P. F., *Individuals: An Essay in Descriptive Metaphysics*, London: Routledge, 1959

Wittgenstein, L., *Philosophical Investigations*, Oxford: Blackwell, 1967

Wittgenstein, L., *Tractatus Logico-Philosophicus*, London: Routledge & Kegan Paul, 1974

Continental Philosophy

Blanchot, M., *The Space of Literature*, trans. A. Smock, Lincoln, NE: University of Nebraska Press, 1982

Boundas, C. V. (ed.), *Columbia Companion to Twentieth-Century Philosophies*, New York City, NY: Columbia University Press, 2007

Camus, A., *The Myth of Sisyphus*, trans. J. O'Brien, London: Penguin Books, 2013

Crowell, S. (ed.), *The Cambridge Companion to Existentialism*, Cambridge: Cambridge University Press, 2012

de Beauvoir, S., *The Second Sex*, London: New English Library, 1970

Deleuze, G., *Difference and Repetition*, London: Bloomsbury, 2014

Deleuze, G., *The Logic of Sense*, trans. M. Lester, London: Continuum, 2004

Deleuze, G. and F. Guattari, *Anti-Oedipus: Capitalism and Schizophrenia*, trans. R. Hurley, M. Seem and H. R. Lane, London: Continuum, 2004

Deleuze, G. and F. Guattari, *A Thousand Plateaus: Capitalism and Schizophrenia*, trans. B. Massumi, London: Continuum, 2004

Deleuze, G. and F. Guattari, *What is Philosophy?*, trans. H. Tomlinson and G. Burchell, New York City, NY: Columbia University Press, 1994

Derrida, J., *Of Grammatology*, trans. G. C. Spivak, Baltimore, MD: Johns Hopkins University Press, 2016

Derrida, J., *Speech and Phenomena: And Other Essays on Husserl's Theory of Signs*, trans. D. B. Allison, Evanston, IL: Northwestern University Press, 1973

Derrida, J., *Writing and Difference*, trans. A. Bass, London: Routledge, 2001

Gadamer, H.-G., *Philosophical Hermeneutics*, trans. J. Weinsheimer and D. G. Marshall, London: Bloomsbury, 2013

Gadamer, H.-G., *Truth and Method*, New York City, NY: Continuum, 2004

Heidegger, M., *Being and Time*, New York City, NY: Harper & Row, 1962

Husserl, E., *Ideas: General Introduction to Pure Phenomenology*, London: Routledge, 2012

Moore, A. W., *The Evolution of Modern Metaphysics*, Cambridge: Cambridge University Press, 2012

Moran, D. (ed.), *The Routledge Companion to Twentieth Century Philosophy*, London: Routledge, 2008

Ricoeur, P., *Fallible Man: Philosophy of the Will*, New York City, NY: Fordham University Press, 1993

Ricoeur, P., *Freud & Philosophy: An Essay on Interpretation*, New Haven, CT: Yale University Press, 1965

Sartre, J.-P., *Being and Nothingness*, New York City, NY: Washington Square Press, 1993

Sartre, J.-P., *Critique of Dialectical Reason*, London: Verso Books, 1976

Sartre, J.-P., *Existentialism is a Humanism*, New Haven, CT: Yale University Press, 2007

Wrathall, M. A. (ed.), *The Cambridge Companion to Heidegger's Being and Time*, Cambridge: Cambridge University Press, 2013

INDIAN PHILOSOPHY

Buddhist Sutras. Available online: http://buddhasutra.com

Paramânanda, Swâmi (trans.), *The Upanishads*, Boston, MA: The Vedânta Centre, 1919. Available online: https://www.vivekananda.net/PDFBooks/The_Upanishads.pdf

The Vedas. Available online: http://www.cakravartin.com/wordpress/wp-content/uploads/2008/08/vedas.pdf

Fosse, L. M. (trans.), *The Bhagavad Gita*. Available online: http://library.umac.mo/ebooks/b17771201.pdf

Chatterjee, S. and D. Datta, *An Introduction to Indian Philosophy*, New Delhi: Rupa, 2007

Dasgupta, S., *A History of Indian Philosophy*, 5 vols., Cambridge: Cambridge University Press, 2009

Deussen, P., *Outlines of Indian Philosophy*, Collingwood, Victoria: Trieste, 2017

Deussen, P., *The Philosophy of the Upanishads*, trans. A. S. Geden, New York City, NY: Cosimo, 2010

Hamilton, S., *Indian Philosophy: A Very Short Introduction*, Oxford: Oxford University Press, 2001

Perrett, R. W., *An Introduction to Indian Philosophy*, Cambridge: Cambridge University Press, 2016

Radhakrishnan, S., *Indian Philosophy*, 2 vols., Oxford: Oxford University Press, 2009

Sharma, C., *A Critical Survey of Indian Philosophy*, London: Rider, 1960

Williams, P., 'Indian Philosophy', in A. C. Grayling (ed.), *Philosophy 2: Further through the Subject*, Oxford: Oxford University Press, 1998

CHINESE PHILOSOPHY

The Analects of Confucius. Available online: http://www.indiana.edu/~p374/Analects_of_Confucius_(Eno-2015).pdf

Chan, W., *The Way of Lao Tzu*, Indianapolis, IN: Bobbs-Merrill, 1963

de Bary, W. T. et al. (eds.), *Sources of Chinese Tradition*, vol. 1, 2nd edn, New York City, NY: Columbia University Press, 1999

Ivanhoe, P. J. and B. W. Van Norden (eds.), *Readings in Classical Chinese Philosophy*, 2nd edn, Indianapolis, IN: Hackett, 2005

Kirkland, R., *The Book of Mozi (Mo-Tzu)*. Available online: https://faculty.franklin.uga.edu/sites/faculty.franklin.uga.edu.kirkland/files/MOTZU.pdf

Lau, D. C. (trans.), *Mencius*, New York City, NY: Penguin Books, 1970

Legge, J. (ed. and trans.), *The Chinese Classics*, vol. II: *The Works of Mencius*, Hong Kong: Hong Kong University Press, 1960. Available online: http://starling.rinet.ru/Texts/Students/Legge,%20James/The%20Works%20of%20Mencius%20(1960).pdf

The Original I Ching (Yi Jing) Oracle. Available online: http://www.downloads.imune.net/medicalbooks/I%20Ching%20-%20Introduction.pdf

Watson, B. (trans.), *Han Feizi: Basic Writings*, New York City, NY: Columbia University Press, 2003. Available online: https://www.jstor.org/stable/10.7312/wats12968

Xunzi. Available online: http://www.iub.edu/~g380/2.9-Xunzi-2010.pdf

Chan, A. K. L. (ed.), *Mencius: Contexts and Interpretations*, Honolulu: University of Hawai'i Press, 2002

Creel, H. G., *What is Taoism? And Other Studies in Chinese Cultural History*, Chicago, IL: University of Chicago Press, 1970

El Amine, L., *Classical Confucian Political Thought: A New Interpretation*, Princeton, NJ: Princeton University Press, 2015

Garfield, J. L. and W. Edelglass (eds.), *The Oxford Handbook of World Philosophy*, Oxford: Oxford University Press, 2011

Graham, A. C., *Disputers of the Tao: Philosophical Argument in Ancient China*, La Salle, IL: Open Court, 1989

Grayling, A. C. and Xu Youyu (jointly writing under the pseudonym 'Li Xiao Jun'), *The Long March to the Fourth of June*, London: Duckworth, 1989

Hsiao, K., *History of Chinese Political Thought*, vol. 1: *From the Beginnings to the Sixth Century, A.D.*, trans. F. W. Mote, Princeton, NJ: Princeton University Press, 2016

Lai, K. L., *An Introduction to Chinese Philosophy*, 2nd edn, Cambridge: Cambridge University Press, 2017

Shun, K., *Mencius and Early Chinese Thought*, Stanford, CA: Stanford University Press, 1997

Slingerland, E., *Effortless Action: Wu-wei as Conceptual Metaphor and Spiritual Ideal in Early China*, Oxford: Oxford University Press, 2003

Van Norden, B. W., *Introduction to Classical Chinese Philosophy*, Indianapolis, IN: Hackett, 2011

ARABIC–PERSIAN PHILOSOPHY

Adamson, P. (ed.), *Interpreting Avicenna: Critical Essays*, Cambridge: Cambridge University Press, 2013

Adamson, P., *Philosophy in the Islamic World: A Very Short Introduction*, Oxford: Oxford University Press, 2015

Adamson, P. and R. C. Taylor (eds.), *The Cambridge Companion to Arabic Philosophy*, Cambridge: Cambridge University Press, 2004

Arnaldez, R., *Averroes: A Rationalist in Islam*, Notre Dame, IN: University of Notre Dame Press, 2000

Fakhry, M., *Averroes: His Life, Works, and Influence*, Oxford: Oneworld Publications, 2001

Fakhry, M., *A History of Islamic Philosophy*, New York City, NY: Columbia University Press, 1983

al-Farabi, *Book of Letters*, Beirut: Dar el-Mashreq, 1969

al-Ghazali, *The Incoherence of the Philosophers*, Provo, UT: Brigham Young University Press, 2000

Griffel, F., *Al-Ghazali's Philosophical Theology*, Oxford: Oxford University Press, 2009

al-Kindi, *The Philosophical Works of Al-Kindi*, ed. P. Adamson and P. E. Pormann, Oxford: Oxford University Press, 2012

McGinnis, J., *Avicenna*, Oxford: Oxford University Press, 2010

Nasr, S. H. and O. Leaman (eds.), *History of Islamic Philosophy*, New York City, NY: Routledge, 2001

Street, T., *Avicenna: Intuitions of the Truth*, Cambridge: The Islamic Texts Society, 2005

Urvoy, D., *Ibn Rushd (Averroes)*, London: Routledge, 1991

AFRICAN PHILOSOPHY

Boundas, C. V. (ed.), *Columbia Companion to Twentieth-Century Philosophies*, New York City, NY: Columbia University Press, 2007

Brown, L. M. (ed.), *African Philosophy: New and Traditional Perspectives*, Oxford: Oxford University Press, 2004

BIBLIOGRAPHY

Eze, E. C. (ed.), *African Philosophy: An Anthology*, Oxford: Blackwell, 1998

Gade, C. B. N., 'The Historical Development of the Written Discourses on *Ubuntu*', *South African Journal of Philosophy* 30 no. 3 (2011) 303–29

Kidane, D. W., *The Ethics of Zär'a Ya'əqob: A Reply to the Historical and Religious Violence in the Seventeenth Century Ethiopia*, Rome: Editrice Pontificia Università Gregoriana, 2012

Mawere, M. and T. R. Mubaya, *African Philosophy and Thought Systems: A Search for a Culture and Philosophy of Belonging*, Bamenda: Langaa, 2016

Ngũgĩ, wa Thiong'o, *Decolonising the Mind: The Politics of Language in African Literature*, Woodbridge: James Currey, 1986

Nichodemus, Y. N., *African Philosophy: An Introduction*, Scotts Valley, CA: CreateSpace, 2013

Odera Oruka, H. (ed.), *Sage Philosophy: Indigenous Thinkers and Modern Debate on African Philosophy*, Leiden: E. J. Brill, 1990

Samkange, S. J. T. and T. M. Samkange, *Hunhuism or Ubuntuism: A Zimbabwe Indigenous Political Philosophy*, London: Graham, 1980

Serequeberhan, T., *African Philosophy: The Essential Readings*, Walton-on-Thames: Paragon House, 1991

Wiredu, K. (ed.), *A Companion to African Philosophy*, Oxford: Wiley-Blackwell, 2004

Index

In Arabic names the definite article (al-), used as a prefix, is ignored in the ordering of entries.

Abbasid caliphs 558
Abdera 47n, 48, 52
Abelard, Peter 148–50
  and Aristotle 149
  A Dialogue between a Philosopher, a Jew and a Christian 150
  and Héloïse 148, 149
  and Kant 150
  logic 149–50
  nominalism 149
  and perception 150
  realism 149
  Scholasticism 149–50
  and semantics 149–50
  Sic et Non 149
  and universals 149
Abhidharma texts 530
abstraction 230, 420, 527
  and Berkeley 162, 230
  and Ockham 165
absurdism 491
Abu Bakr 558
Abu Yaqub Yusuf 571
Acragas, Sicily 10, 39
action, philosophy of 422
Acton, John Dalberg-Acton, 1st Baron 72
ad hominem argument 594–5
Adam 129, 149, 181, 225
Adams, John 399
Adorno, Theodor 510
  Dialectic of Enlightenment (with Horkheimer) 276–7
Advaita 522

Aenesidemus 121–2
Aeschines 58
Aeschylus 4
aesthetics xvii, 583 *see also* art; beauty
  and Gadamer 494, 495–6
  and Heidegger 478
  and Nietzsche 319
  and relief from suffering 300
Aetius 6
African philosophy 518, 575–81
  and Consciencism 577, 580
  and familyhood (*Ujamaa*) 577, 580
  function and appropriateness of term 'African philosophy' 575–9
  political thinking in an African context 577
  and *Ubuntu* 518, 580–81
Agathemerus 7
Agathocles 189
Agrippa, 'Five Tropes' 122
ahamkara (ego) 524, 525
Ahmad, Abdul-Qasim 571
Ahmad, son of al-Mu'tasim 560
Akan law 576
akrasia 64
Alberti, Leon Battista 135
Albertus Magnus 149, 151, 154, 158, 179
alchemy 134, 158, 159, 170, 195
Alcibiades 59
Alembert, Jean le Rond d'
  and *Encyclopédie* 269, 272–3
  and Rousseau 252–3
Alexander of Aphrodisias 6

Alexander the Great 83–4
  and Aristotle 83–4
  death 98
  and Diogenes the Cynic 101
Alexandria
  and Aristotle 557
  as a centre of philosophical debate
    10, 126, 557
  Christian gangs in 556n
Algerian war 487
Ali (fourth Islamic caliph) 558
alienation
  and Feuerbach 297
  Left Hegelians and religion as a form
    of 296
  and Marx 313
  and Sartre 489, 490, 491
  of the soul (Hegel) 291
Althusser, Louis 458, 510
altruism 107
  self-referential 453
Ameinias 31
American pragmatists 279, 280, 333
Ammonius of Alexandria 125
Ammonius Saccas 126–7
Amo, Anton 577
Amsterdam 211
Amyntas III 82
Anacreon 19
analytic–synthetic distinction 348–9,
    380–81, 386
  Quine's attack on 386, 388, 392–4
Analytic philosophy 335, 339–470
  and Aristotle's logic 85 see also
    Aristotle: and logic ('Analytics')
  Carnap see Carnap, Rudolf
  characteristics, influences and
    motivating idea 335
  Davidson 336, 419–23, 437–9
  divergences from Continental
    philosophy 471, 472
  ethics/morality 444–57;
    'autobiographical' moral discourse
    447–8; Hare 448–50; intuitionistic
    approach to 366–7, 446; Mackie
    450–53; moral discourse as
    prescriptive 449–50; moral
    statements as expressions of attitude
    (emotivism) 356, 446–8; and non-
    cognitivism 367, 447–8, 450–51;
    and non-existence of objective

values 450–53; normative morality
    xvii, 444–5; Stevenson 446–8; virtue
    ethics see virtue ethics;
    Wittgenstein's placement outside
    realm of the discussable 374–6
  feminist 466–9
  founders and major figures 335–6,
    469–70
  Frege see Frege, Gottlob
  and Hegel 287
  of language 417–33; Carnap and
    language of scientific theories 387–8;
    communication-intention theory
    427; Cooperative Principle 428;
    and Davidson's theory of truth
    419–22, 432; debate between
    realism and anti-realism 427; and
    Dummett 336, 358, 423–7; and
    extensional/truth-functional
    language 363, 390–91, 418; and
    Frege see Frege, Gottlob:
    philosophy of language; and Kripke
    395, 429–32; and logic 347, 361–5,
    405–6, 417; logical analysis of
    language 347; and meaning see
    meaning; and metaphysics 423;
    move towards systematic discipline
    417, 418, 419; non-cognitive view
    of moral language 367, 447–8;
    'ordinary language philosophy' see
    'ordinary language philosophy'
    (Oxford); and propositional
    attitudes 364; Tarski's truth-theory
    for formal languages 421; and
    theories of reference see reference:
    theories of; Wittgenstein's early logic
    of language 373–7; Wittgenstein's
    language games 401, 402–3
  Logical Positivism see Logical Positivism
  logicism see logicism
  and meaning see meaning
  of mind 433–44; anomalous monism
    (Davidson) 422–3, 437–9; anti-
    individualism 435; and
    behaviourism 434 see also
    behaviourism; and consciousness
    442–4; and Davidson's theory of
    interpretation 438; functionalism
    436–7; identity theories of mind
    434–41; and intentionality see
    intentionality: in Analytic

philosophy; psychologism 360–61;
and qualia 435, 443–4; and Ryle
407–9; and supervenience
(Davidson) 423, 437–8
Moore *see* Moore, G. E.
and physicalism *see* physicalism
political 457–66; feminist 466, 469;
marginalization with rise of political
science 458; Nozick 458, 462–6;
and Popper 395, 396; Rawls 457–62
Popper 395–400
Quine *see* Quine, W. V.
Russell *see* Russell, Bertrand
and verification *see* verification/
verificationism
Wittgenstein *see under* Wittgenstein,
Ludwig
Analytical Thomism 157
anamnesis 69
anarchy 73, 295, 309, 465, 544, 548
relativistic 367
Anaxagoras 43–7
and Anaximenes 43
and Aristotle 45
and Athens 43
birth details 43
cosmology 44–6
and Derveni Papyrus 8n
intellectual reputation 43
nous 45–6
panspermia 45, 46
and Parmenides 44–5
and Pericles 44
and Plato 44
theory of perception 46
Anaximander 10, 14–16
and the *arche* 14, 15–16
map of world 14
'On Nature' (*Peri Phuseos*) 14
and Parmenides 31
Anaximenes 10, 16–18
and Anaxagoras 43
and the *arche* 16–17, 33–4
and condensation 16–17, 33–4
and rarefaction 17
anchorites 182
Andreas-Salomé, Lou 316
Andronicus of Rhodes 82, 97
anomalous monism (Davidson) 422–3,
437–9
Anscombe, Elizabeth 157, 404

and Analytic philosophy 335, 454
'Modern Moral Philosophy' 454
Anselm of Canterbury 132, 145–8
arguments for existence of God 146;
ontological argument 146–8
Monologion 146
Proslogion 146
Scholasticism 146
and truth 146
De Veritate 146
anti-individualism 435
anti-Semitism
of Frege 359
and Heidegger 482
Nazi *see* Nazism
and Popper 396
and twisting of Nietzsche's works 316
Antigonus II Gonatas of Macedon 112
Antiochus of Ascalon 79
Antipater 83
Antiphon 56
Antisthenes 58, 99, 100–101
apatheia (indifference) 61, 101, 108,
112, 113, 114, 120–21
Apellicon 82
Aphrodite 55
Apollo worship 19
Apollodorus of Athens: *Chronicles* 7
aporia (inconclusiveness)
and Derrida 505
and scepticism *see* scepticism
Socratic 62, 66, 71, 77, 80, 115
Appiah, Kwame Anthony 577, 579
Aquinas, Thomas *see* Thomas Aquinas
Arabic–Persian philosophy 133, 554–74
Averroes *see* Averroes (Ibn Rushd)
Avicenna *see* Avicenna (Ibn Sina)
emanationism 556, 561, 565
ethics 570
and existence 565
al-Farabi 561–3
al-Ghazali *see* al-Ghazali
al-Kindi 559–61
logic: Avicenna 564; al-Farabi 561;
al-Kindi 560
and Muslim theology *see* Islam: *kalam*
and the Qur'an 555, 559, 561, 564,
569–70, 571–2
Arabic numerals 21
Arcesilaus 78, 116–18
and Cicero 116, 118

arche (principle of the cosmos)
  Anaximander 14, 15–16
  Anaximenes 16–17, 33–4
  and atomism 50
  and Heraclitus 29–30
  as infinite 15–16
  and material monism 12, 16, 29–30
  vs Parmenides' One 32–4
  and Stoicism 109
  Thales 12–13
Arendt, Hannah 458, 477, 510
arguments for existence of God
  Aristotle 89
  Averroes 572
  cosmological *see* cosmological
    argument
  Descartes 202, 204, 206
  Leibniz 238–9
  Ockham and impossibility of proofs
    164–5
  ontological *see* ontological argument
  as *post facto* justifications for
    faith 148
  teleological 156n
argumentum ad ignorantiam 594
argumentum ad populum 594
argumentum ad verecundiam 594
Argyropoulos, John 172
Arianism 139
Aristippus 58
aristocracy, and Plato 72
Aristophanes 4
  and Cleon 44
  The Clouds 59
  and Socrates 59
Aristotle 80–97
  and Abelard 149
  and Alexander the Great 83–4
  Alexandrian study of 557
  and Anaxagoras 45
  and Anaximenes 17
  De Anima 152, 573
  and Aquinas *see* Thomas Aquinas:
    and Aristotle
  and art: and 'noble use of leisure' 94,
    95, 191; politics as highest art 91;
    techne 84–5, 170
  in Athens 82, 83–4
  and atomism 47, 48, 49–50
  and Averroes *see* Averroes (Ibn
    Rushd): and Aristotle

and beliefs 117
birth details 82
Categories 81, 85, 142
and the Church 133
and citizenship 94
commentaries on: Alexander of
  Aphrodisias 6; Aquinas 152, 153;
  Averroes 133, 153, 555, 571;
  Avicenna 133; Boethius 133, 142; al-
  Farabi 561; Lefèvre 184; Maimonides
  133; and 'political science' 186;
  Renaissance 184; Scotus 162;
  Simplicius 7; Veronese 177
comparative studies of scripture
  and 183
cosmology 95–6
De Interpretatione 142, 561
death 82, 84
and debate between *via antiqua* and
  via moderna 166–7
and Democritus 48
and education 91, 94 *see also*
  Peripatetic school
and Empedocles 42
and empiricism 89
and Epicurus 104–5
epistemology 87–8, 115–16
ethics 81, 91–5, 445; and Aquinas
  182; as continuous with politics 84,
  94–5, 178–9, 583; and doctrine of
  the mean 93–4; and *eudaimonia*
  92–4, 454, 455; Luther's attack on
  Scholastic use 183; and moderation
  83, 93–4; reason and wisdom as
  basis of ethics 61; and the
  Renaissance 178–9, 184; and virtue
  92–3, 453, 454
Ethics 133
and *eudaimonia* (happiness) 92–4,
  454, 455
Eudemian Ethics 81, 91
family background 82
On Generation and Corruption 80
Gryllos 81
On the Heavens 80, 95
and Heidegger 478–9
and Heraclitus 28
and imagination 89, 562
and the infinite 15–16
influence on medieval philosophy 132;
  Roger Bacon 159

On Interpretation 81
and leisure 94, 95, 191
and the life of contemplation 94
and logic ('Analytics') 85, 110, 586,
   587–8; and classes 86–7; and
   classification into 'five words' 86;
   and epistemological matters of
   explanations and causes 87–8; 'laws
   of thought' 587; and the Megarian
   school 96; and Ockham on logic of
   syllogism 165; and propositions
   85–7
lost dialogues 81
marriage to Pythias 82
metaphysics 84, 88, 90; and Being 90,
   478; and change 88; and first cause
   89, 163; and four causes 88, 163;
   and Scotus 162; and the soul 89;
   and substance (*ousia*) 90, 560
Metaphysics 26, 49, 78, 80, 115–16,
   133, 478
Meteorology 80
and Muslim *kalam* 559, 560
Nicomachean Ethics 81, 91–2, 107n,
   153, 156, 184; and Renaissance
   humanism 178, 179, 184
Organon 85, 351; and al-
   Farabi 561
and Parmenides 31, 33
Peripatetic school 26, 65, 81, 83
and philosophy's theoretical/practical
   division 84–5
Physics 15–16, 84, 104–5, 133, 152;
   Ockham's commentary 165;
   Simplicius' commentary 7
and Plato 65, 77, 88; George of
   Trebizond on 172; and Nicholas of
   Cusa 174; Plethon on 172
at Plato's Academy 81, 82
Poetics 81, 84–5
and politics: as continuous with ethics
   84, 94–5, 178–9, 583; dislike of
   monarchy and empire 94; and
   governmental provision for a
   'sufficient life' 186; and harmony
   within the state 94; as highest art
   91; humans as 'political animals'
   94; and 'political science' 186; and
   Renaissance Italian city states
   185–6; small republican polities 83;
   and the state's provision of best life
for man 94; and a well-run
   state 94
Politics 11, 91, 133, 178; and Italian
   city states 185–6; William of
   Moerbeke's Latin translation 185
Posterior Analytics 81, 115–16
and practical wisdom (*phronesis*) 61,
   92–3, 454, 455
Prior Analytics 81
psychology 89–90
and Pythagoreanism 18, 22
and reason 61, 81, 94, 455
rediscovery of work in Middle Ages
   132, 154, 185
Rhetoric 28, 81, 84–5, 169, 170; al-
   Farabi's commentary 561
and scepticism 115–16
and the Schoolmen 570, 571
and Scotus 162
Short Treatises on Nature 81
and Socrates 63, 516
Sophistical Refutations 81, 85
On the Soul 81
and souls 89
and space 162
style 81
and substance 90, 560
summarizing Presocratic thinkers 5
syllogism theory 165, 362, 587
systemization of knowledge 80–81
and *techne* 84–5, 170
Technon Sunagoge 81
and Thales 11, 12
and 'Third Man' problem 76
and time 162
Topics 81, 85
translations: Arabic 133; Boethius
   133; Latin 133, 154, 160
and understanding 87–8
and universals 143
and Xenophanes 26, 27
and Zeno of Elea 35, 37, 43
Aristoxenos 20
Arnauld, Antoine 233
Aron, Raymond 482, 486, 509, 510
Arrian 113
art *see also* aesthetics
   and Apollonian–Dionysian
      tension 319
   and Aristotle *see* Aristotle: and art
   and Deleuze 502–3

art – *cont.*
  as expression of thought
    (Merleau-Ponty) 483–4
  and Gadamer 494, 495–6
  and mass culture 277–8
  and Nietzsche 319
  and *otium* (graceful leisure for
    cultivation of arts) 187
  politics as highest art (Aristotle) 91
  and Protagoras 53
  Renaissance 168–9, 181
  and truth 495–6
artificial intelligence xx
asceticism
  and Antisthenes 101
  and the Cynics 101, 102
  hermits/anchorites 27, 102, 182
  in Jainism 523, 532
  and liberation 523–4
Asclepiads (medical guild) 82
al-Ash'ari, Abu al-Hasan 559
Ash'arites 559, 567, 570
Assos 82
Astrolabe, son of Abelard 148
astrolabes 160
astrology 158, 159, 160, 170, 173,
    195, 559
astronomy 5, 9, 258, 266, 269–70, 399
  and Roger Bacon 158, 159, 160
ataraxia (peace of mind) 99
  and Cynicism 99, 102–3
  and Epicurus 107
Atharvaveda 519–20
atheism 211, 516
  Berkeley and 'theological
    scepticism' 227
  and deism 211n, 227
  Hume 240
  Locke 224
  Marx 311
  Nietzsche 317–18
  and Prodicus 55–6
  Spinoza 211, 235
Athenodorus Calvus 112
Athens
  and Anaxagoras 43
  and Antisthenes 100
  Aristotle in 82, 83–4
  as a centre of philosophy 10, 557
  Crates in 102, 108
  defeat by Sparta 66

  defeat by Sulla 82
  democracy of 66
  Diogenes the Cynic in 101
  Epicurus in 103–4
  'the Garden' school of Epicurus
    10, 104
  and Gorgias 55
  in Peloponnesian War 66
  and Pericles 60
  Peripatetic school 26, 65, 81, 83
  and Plato 65–6
  playwrights in 4
  School of see Platonic Academy
  and Socrates 58, 60
  and Stoicism 108, 112
  and Zeno of Citium 108, 112
Atman 300, 520, 522
  and Brahman 529–30
  denied by Buddhists 522, 529–30
atomism/atomists 10, 47–51 see also
    Democritus; Leucippus
  and the *arche* 50
  and Aristotle 47, 48, 49–50
  and change 49–50
  and Epicurus 50, 104–6, 107
  Hume's psychological atomism
    244–6, 321
  and justice 50
  and Lucretius 50–51
  and motion 49–50, 104–5
  and pluralism 50
  Russell's logical atomism 355–6
  and Simplicius 49
  Vaisheshika 521, 526–7
  and Zeno of Elea 50
atuphia (clarity of mind) 102
Augustine of Hippo 132, 137–42
  and *agape* 544
  birth details 137
  and Cicero 137
  The City of God 140–41
  Confessions 137
  death 98
  and doubt of everything except
    doubt 206
  fallor ergo sum idea (if I am deceived,
    I exist) 142
  and free will 139–40
  and a 'just war' 138, 141
  De Libero Arbitrio 139
  and Manicheism 137, 139

Neoplatonist influence on 130, 132
and Plato's *Timaeus* 132–3
and problem of evil 139–40
on time 140–41
De Vera Religione 139
and Wittgenstein 142, 402
Augustus Caesar 112
Aurelius, Marcus *see* Marcus Aurelius
Austin, John (1790–1859) 283, 302
Austin, J(ohn) L(angshaw) (1911–60)
283, 409–13
and Ayer 410, 411–12
and correspondence theory of truth
412–13
How to Do Things with Words 410,
412
and 'ordinary language philosophy'
410–13
and perception 410, 411
phenomenalist deconstruction 411–12
Sense and Sensibilia 409–10, 411–12
and speech acts 412
and Strawson 413
translation of Frege's *Grundlagen der
Arithmetik* 410, 418
Austrian Free Thinkers Association 379
autarkeia (self-sufficiency) 102
authenticity 480–81, 490
autonomy
choosing one's way of life 272,
305, 319
and the Enlightenment 272
and Kant's moral theory 263–4,
265, 268
moral 255
and rejection of conventional morality
(Nietzsche) 319
Averroes (Ibn Rushd) 154, 554–5, 563,
570–73
and Aquinas 153
and Aristotle 571, 573; commentaries
133, 153, 555, 571
and Avicenna 567
Generalities 571
and al-Ghazali 570, 572, 573
and God 571, 572–3
*The Incoherence of the
Incoherence* 570
and medicine 571
and Neoplatonism 153
and Plato's *Republic* 571

and Porphyry's *Isagoge* 571
and the Schoolmen 570–71, 573
and 'unicity of the intellect' 573
Avesta (Zoroastrian texts) 557–8
Avicenna (Ibn Sina) 153, 555, 563–7
and Averroes 567
commentary on Aristotle 133
and al-Farabi 562
and al-Ghazali 566, 569; translation
of *Philosophy for Ala al-Dawla* 568
Scholastic criticism of 566–7
Avignon, papal court 164
Axial Age 517
Ayer, A. J. 354, 377, 406
and Austin 410, 411–12
and emotivism 446
*The Foundations of Empirical
Knowledge* 410
Kant anecdote 389n
Language, Truth and Logic
377, 446
and phenomenalism 353, 354
verification principle 382
and Vienna Circle 377, 389

Bachelard, Gaston 509
Bacon, Francis 159n, 197–200
The Advancement of Learning 198
as an empiricist 196, 198–9
Instauratio Magna 197, 198–9
The New Atlantis 197
rejection of Scholasticism 196
and science: and cooperation 197–8,
199; scientific method 198–9;
system of physics 197
Bacon, Roger 158–61
Aristotle's influence 159
and the Bible 158
calendar reform 158–9
and education 159–60
as an empiricist 158, 159
and grammar 159
and morality 160
and the occult 160–61
and optics 158, 159, 160
Opus Maius 158, 159–60
philosophy of language 159, 160
and rhetoric 159, 160
and *The Secret of Secrets* 159
and Seneca 160
Stoic influence on 160

Baghdad 558, 561
  Bayt al-Hikma 558, 560
  Nizamiyya Madrasa 567
Bain, Alexander 329
Bakunin, Mikhail 308, 309
'barbarians' 3–4
Barber Paradox 350
Barhaspatya-sutra 532–3
Barnes, Jonathan 51
Barry, Brian 462
Basil of Caesarea (St Basil the
  Great) 130
  *Address to Young Men on Greek
  Literature* 182
Basle University 315
Bataille, Georges 508
Bauch, Bruno 386
Bauer, Bruno 308
Bayle, Pierre 123
Bayreuth Festival 315
beauty *see also* aesthetics
  absolute (Avicenna) 566
  as highest pleasure 566
  and intellect 566
  intrinsic value of 365
  love of 69
  natural 275
  as a Platonic Form 74, 76
  and Renaissance art 181
  and Romanticism 275
Beauvoir, Simone de 482, 486, 491–2
  Ethics of Ambiguity 492
  existentialism 492
  as feminist 491–2
  and the Other 491–2
  and Sartre 482, 486, 487–8, 491–2
  The Second Sex 492
Bec, abbey of 145
Beccaria, Cesare Bonesana- 281
Beckett, Samuel 487
Begging the Question Fallacy 594
behaviourism
  demise in psychology and
   philosophy 434
  linguistic 394–5
  logical 408–9
  methodological 409
Being *see also* existence; ontology;
  reality
  Aristotle 90, 478
  'Being-towards-death' 480–81

God as absolute being 156
Heidegger and *Dasein* 478–81, 482
necessary 165, 213, 239, 565, 566
and Nothingness and Becoming in
  Hegel's dialectic 293
and padarthas (Vaisheshika) 526
Plato's realms of Being and Becoming
  68–9, 125
and relation of existence and essence
  (Aquinas) 154–5, 162
and Sartre 488–9
and Scotus 162
beliefs
  and Aristotle 117
  and Carneades' 'persuasive
   impressions' 118–19
  coherence view of justifying 331
  and eliminative materialism 440–41
  expedient 330
  holism and Quine's 'web of belief'
   393–4
  Hume's theory of 245–6
  hypothetical 119
  inherited beliefs as source of
   knowledge 496
  'instinctive' 354
  knowledge and true belief 69, 77
  knowledge differentiated from 69
  Mu'tazilites and true/false beliefs 559
  and perception 117
  Plato on how false belief is
   possible 77
  pragmatism and acquisition of stable
   and enduring beliefs 329
  reason in tension with faith 154
  soothing beliefs in God 508
  superstitious *see* superstition
  suspension of belief 116, 117
  Zeno of Citium on believing 111
Benjamin, Walter 511
Bentham, Jeremy 279, 280–86
  and the Church: Catholic banning of
   his books 284; and education
   285–6
  and Colls 286
  and Dumont 282
  'felicific calculus' 286, 306
  and franchise 285
  and the French Revolution 283
  and the Greek constitution 284
  Hazlitt on 280, 286

and human nature 286
and Hume 282
and Lansdowne 282
and law 283–4
as a Legal Positivist 283, 302
and Madison 284
and Marx 286
and James Mill 284
and John Stuart Mill 286
Not Paul, But Jesus 285
and political reform 284–5
Principles of International Law
    282–3
Rationale of Judicial Evidence 286
and religious freedom 285–6
and South America 284
The Theory of Legislation 282
and University College London
    285–6
utilitarianism 281–2, 283
Bentham, Samuel 281
Bergmann, Gustav 379
Bergson, Henri 508
Berkeley, George ('Bishop Berkeley')
    226–32
attack on abstraction in metaphysics
    162, 230
birth details 226
as an empiricist 226, 228–9, 230
epistemology 227–9, 242
and existence as dependent on deity/
    spirit/mind xxi, 227–31
idealism 227, 321; compared with
    phenomenalism 353; and God as
    infinite mind 227, 232, 353
and ideas 228–9
and identity statements 368
immaterialism 227
instrumentalism 231
and Locke 218, 226, 227–8
as member of Protestant Ascendancy
    226–7
on perception and the perceiver
    227–30
Principles of Human Knowledge 227,
    228, 230
as realist 229–30
refutations of scepticism 227–9
and science 231
Three Dialogues between Hylas and
    Philonous 227, 228, 232

Berlin, Isaiah 457, 458, 459
and negative/positive liberty 210
Berlin
Academy of 234
Society for Scientific Philosophy
    379, 386
University 298–9, 308
Bernays, Paul 474
Bessarion, Basilios, Cardinal 172
Bhagavad Gita 523
biblical criticism/scholarship
    176, 320
and hermeneutics 494
and Strauss' Life of Jesus 296, 314
bivalence 110, 342–3, 344, 414, 426
Black, Max, Translations from the
    Philosophical Writings of Gottlob
    Frege (with Geach) 357–8, 418
Blackburn, Simon 469
Blanchot, Maurice 505–6
Bloch, Ernst 510
Blochmann, Elisabeth 477
Bloomsbury Group 365
Blyden, Edward Wilmot 576
Boccaccio, Giovanni 175
Decameron 175–6
Genealogia Deorum Gentilium 176
Boethius, Anicius Manlius Severinus
    133, 142–5, 154
Aquinas' commentaries on 152
De Arithmetica 184
commentaries on ancient philosophers
    133, 142
Consolation of Philosophy 142,
    144–5
and free will 143–4
and logic 142–3, 145
Opuscula Sacra 143
and Porphyry 142
and universals 143
Boineburg, Johann von, Baron 233
Bolívar, Simón 284
Boltzmann, Ludwig 370–71
Bolzano, Bernard 473
Boole, George 586
Borges, Jorge Luis 297
Bosanquet, Bernard 320
Bosso, Matteo 183
Boswell, James 242
Bovelles, Charles: Liber de Sapiente
    180–81

Boyle, Robert 234, 270
Bracciolini, Poggio 175, 177
  minuscule 178
  De Miseria Humanae Conditionis 179
  and Valla 176
bracketing 474, 475
Bradley, F. H. 320, 323–5
  Appearance and Reality 323
  Eliot's doctoral thesis on 389n
  Ethical Studies 325
  ethics and morality 325
  holism 325
  idealism 320–21, 323–5
  and McTaggart 326
  and Moore 323
  rejection of concept of relations
    323–5
  rejection of pluralism 323, 325
  rejection of realism 323
  and Russell 323
  and self-realization 325
  and Sprigge 328
'Bradley's Regress' 324
Brahman 300, 520, 522, 525
  and Atman 529–30
  denied by Buddhists 522, 529–30
Brahms, Johannes 370
Braig, Carl 478
brain
  and consciousness 204–5
  and epiphenomalism 438–9
  fMRI scanning 441
  and identity theories 434–41
  and mental phenomena xviii, 434
  and the mind–body problem 204–5
  pineal gland 205
  relationship between mental states
    and brain states 435–6
Brandom, Robert 333, 433, 470
Brentano, Franz 473
  and intentionality 438, 474
  *On the Manifold Meaning of Being
    According to Aristotle* 476
Breslau (Wrocław) 493
Brhadaranyaka ('Great Forest
  Teaching') 520–21
British idealists 279, 280
  and Hegel 287
Brockhaus, F. A. 298
Bruni, Leonardo 135
  and citizenship 187

humanism 187
  Laudatio Florentinae Urbis 187
  and the Renaissance 170, 187
  and *vita activa* 187
Bruno, Giordano 96n, 135
  death at the stake 184
Buddha 513–15, 516, 518, 522, 523
buddhi (will/intellect) 524, 525
Buddhism 514–15, 519, 522–3
  in China 534
  denial of Atman and Brahman
    522, 529–30
  Dinnaga–Dharmakirti school 531–2
  Eightfold Path 515, 523
  Four Noble Truths 515, 523
  and liberation from suffering
    300, 522, 523
  Mahayana 515; Madhyamika 530;
    Yogacara 530–31
  and Manicheism 138
  and Schopenhauer 300
  and *sunyata* (emptiness) 530, 531
  Suttapitaka 515
  Theravada 515
  transformation into a religion 130
  Vinayapitaka 515
  Zen 545
Burckhardt, Jacob 315
Burge, Tyler: *Foundations of Mind* 435
Buridan, Jean 166
'Buridan's Ass' 166
Burke, Edmund 274
Burnet, John 24
Byron, Lord 298
Byzantium 4n, 5n, 172

Cabala 130, 170, 173, 174, 195
  Christian Cabalism 174–5
  and Pico 173, 174
Caird, Edward 321
calculus 38, 110, 359, 589–90
  and 'arithmetization' 348
  Carnap's formal calculus for the
    'logical construction of the
    world' 406
  controversy over inventor of 234
  'felicific' (Bentham) 286, 306
  and Husserl 473
  and Leibniz 233, 234
  logical 589; 'for a language L' in
    theory of meaning 417–18

and Newton 234
predicate 359, 419, 590
propositional 110, 419, 590
calendar reform, Bacon 158–9
Callisthenes 83–4
Calvinism 181, 195
Cambridge Platonists 218, 219
Camus, Albert 491
'The Myth of Sisyphus' 491
The Rebel 487
and Sartre 487, 491
Cantor, Georg 38, 473
Cao Xueqin: The Dream of Red
Mansions 538
capitalism 311
and Marx 310, 314
Carnap, Rudolf 335, 386–8, 418
and Bauch 386
birth details 386
and emotivism 446
and language of scientific theories
387–8
logical constructionism 386, 406, 418
and Logical Positivism/the Vienna
Circle 378, 379, 380–81, 385, 386
The Logical Structure of
the World 386
Pseudoproblems of Philosophy 386
and Quine 386, 387, 389–90, 393
Carneades 118–19
Carrara, Francesco da 187
Cartesians 218
Carvaka–Lokayata 519, 522, 523, 532–3
and perception 522, 532–3
Cassirer, Ernst 271
categorical imperatives 264–5
category mistakes 408
Catullus 177
causality
arche as inherently causal 45
and Aristotle: explanations and causes
87–8; final cause 88; first cause 89,
163; four causes 88, 163
and association of ideas (Hume)
244–5
Roger Bacon and the causes of
error 159
causal theories of reference 429, 431
and cosmological argument see
cosmological argument
first cause see first cause

and al-Ghazali 568–9
and God see God: divine causality
and inherence 526, 527
of Love and Strife 41, 42, 45
Neoplatonist ultimate cause 124
and the nous of Anagagoras 45
and reality 124
in Samkhya 525
secondary causes 568–9
in Vaisheshika 526, 527–8
Censorinus: On Birthdays 7
censorship 266
and the Encyclopédie 273
and Mill 305
Ceos 55
Chaerophon 59
Chalcis 82, 84
Chalmers, David 443
change 16–17
and Aquinas 154–6
of arche states 16–17, 33–4
and Aristotle 88
and atomism 49–50
Changes, Book of see Yijing
Charles II 218
Châtelet, Emilie du 218
Chinese philosophy 534–53
Buddhist influence 534
Confucian see Confucianism
Daoist see Daoism
dao's key place in Chinese
thought 538
Legalism see Legalism, Chinese
Mohism see Mohism
and Tian (heaven/sky) 537–8, 543
Chosroes Anushirvan (Khosrow I) 557
Christianity and the Church
Arian controversy 139
and Aristotle 133
assault by Christian zealots on the
past 3, 129, 556–7
and the basis of morality 182–3, 243
and Bentham 284, 285–6
and biblical scholarship see biblical
criticism/scholarship
and the Cabala 174–5
Catholicism see Roman Catholicism
Christian heresies and Greek
philosophy 6
Church Fathers xxi, 132, 182 see also
individuals by name

Christianity and the Church – *cont.*
  and cosmology *see* cosmology: and
    the Church
  and the dignity of man 172–3, 180
  and divine-command morality 454
  Donatist controversy 139
  and Edict of Milan 3, 137
  and education 285–6
  and Enlightenment criticisms/rejection
    of superstition/religion 270,
    271, 272
  eremetic life 102, 182
  Gnostic Christianity 138
  God *see* God
  and Hegel 291, 294–5
  and Hermeticism 173–4
  Holy Spirit as basis of ethical choice
    182–3
  immortality of soul doctrine adopted
    by 182
  intellectual activity under Church
    authority 131
  Jesus *see* Jesus Christ
  and Leibniz 233
  mendicant orders *see* Dominicans;
    Franciscans
  monasticism *see* monasticism
  and Neoplatonism 124, 129, 182
  and Nietzsche *see* Nietzsche,
    Friedrich: and Christianity
  nonconformists 285, 304
  as official religion of Roman Empire
    3, 98, 137, 182
  and original sin *see* original sin and
    Fall of Man
  and paganism *see* paganism: and
    Christianity
  and Plato 133, 183 *see also*
    Neoplatonism/Neoplatonists: and
    Christianity
  'Prosperity Gospel' 130n
  Protestant *see* Protestantism
  Reformation *see* Reformation
  and religion as harmful to morality
    (Kant) 266, 268
  and Renaissance humanism 181–3
  Second Coming expectations 181–2
  separation of Church and state 166
  and silencing of discussion of moral
    principles 454
  superstition used by (Spinoza) 216

Syrian 133
  theology *see* theology
  Thirty-Nine Articles of Church of
    England 285, 304
  Unitarianism 252
  and Voltaire 270
Chrysippus 108, 110
Church, Alonzo 357
Church, Christian *see* Christianity and
  the Church
Church of England, Thirty-Nine Articles
  285, 304
Churchland, Patricia 440
Cicero, Marcus Tullius xvii, 5–6, 119
  and Arcesilaus 116, 118
  on Aristotle's style 81
  and Augustine of Hippo 137
  and Epicureanism 103
  Epistulae ad Familiares 176
  and Erasmus 182
  Hortensius, or On Philosophy 137
  and Hume 249
  and learning how to die 114
  De Officiis 187, 190
  and Plato's Academy 78
  on Plato's style 81
  Renaissance admiration for 182
  on rhetoric 81, 169
  and Salutati 176
  and Stoicism 114
  Topics 142
  Tusculan Disputations 103
  Veronese's commentary on 177
  and *vita activa* 187
circular reasoning 594
Citium, Cyprus 108
citizenship
  and Aristotle 94
  and Bruni 187
  cosmopolitan citizenship of
    the world 102
  and Plato 53, 72
civil liberties 210–11
civil service 285
civil society
  and Locke 225
  and Rousseau 251–2, 254–5
classes
  and Aristotle 86–7
  Russell and paradox of concept of
    349–50

Clazomenae 43
Cleanthes 108
Clement IV, Pope 158
Clement of Alexandria 6
Cleomenes III of Sparta 112
Cleon 44
Clitomachus 118
cognitive apprehensions 116
cognitive science xx, 584
Cohen, Gerald 'Jerry' 469
Cold War 487
Coleridge, Samuel Taylor 257
Colls, John 286
Cologne 151, 161
Colophon 25
Columbus, Christopher 175
Communism
    and Fascism 310–11
    International Workingmen's Association
        ('First International') 309
    and *Les Temps Modernes* 487
    and Marx 309, 312–14 *see also*
        Marxism
    and Merleau-Ponty 482–3
compassion 252, 301, 302, 318, 357,
    540, 580
Composition, Fallacy of 595
computing 584
Comte, Auguste 279
    Positivism 297, 302–3, 377–8
    and Religion of Humanity 303
conatus 215
Confucianism 515–16, 534 *see also*
    Confucius
    Analects (Lunyu) 516, 535–6, 537,
        538, 539
    classics 516, 535
    and Daoism 546
    and education 541
    ethics 536–42; benevolence (*ren*)
        536–7, 538, 539–40; the Confucian
        Way 538–9; Golden Rule 537;
        nei–wai debate 539–40; reciprocity
        (*shu*) 537; and rites (*li*) 537, 538–9,
        540, 541–2; and virtue 537, 540
    and the family 539
    Five Classics 535, 536
    Four Books 536
    and human nature: innate goodness
        (Mencius) 540; *ren* 536–7, 538,
        539–40; Xunzi 541

'Hundred Schools of Thought'
    540–41
and order 542
and Qin 515–16, 549
and 'rectification of names' 541
rites (*li*) 537, 538–9, 540, 541–2
transformation into a religion 130
and Xunzi 539, 540–42
Yijing 516, 535, 552–3
Confucius 513–14, 515–17, 518,
    535–6, 539
    Five Classics attributed to 535, 536
    and Laozi 546
Consciencism 577, 580
consciousness
    and Analytic philosophy 442–4
    and the brain 204–5
    cosmic 292
    and Dennett 443–4
    and Gadamer on play and art 495–6
    Green and an 'eternal
        consciousness' 322
    and Husserl 474–5, 476
    and intentionality 437
    and Locke: and 'ideas' 219–20; and
        personal identity 222
    and materialism xviii
    and Merleau-Ponty 483, 484
    and Moore's refutation of
        idealism 368
    and Neoplatonism 128
    non-dual cittamatra (mind only) as
        primary existent 530–31
    and pain 444, 474
    and phenomenology 474–5, 488 *see
        also* phenomenology
    and physicalism 442–4
    purusha (Samkhya) 521, 524, 525
    and qualia 435, 443–4
    and Sartre: and Hegel 491; on love
        489–90
    self-consciousness *see*
        self-awareness/-consciousness/
        -knowledge
    and Sprigge's view of reality 328
    'the unhappy consciousness' (Hegel)
        291, 296
consequentialism 265, 281, 305, 306,
    367, 453, 454, 456, 457
consonance 21–2, 23–4
Constantine the Great 3, 137, 138

Constantinople
  fall to Ottomans 172
  Guarino in 177
  Hagia Sophia 200
Continental philosophy 168, 335,
    336–7, 471–512
  absurdism 491
  Arendt 510
  associated movements 336–7
  and authenticity 480–81, 490
  Bachelard 509
  de Beauvoir 491–2 see also Beauvoir,
    Simone de
  Bergson 508
  Camus 491 see also Camus, Albert
  Deleuze 500–503 see also Deleuze,
    Gilles
  Derrida 503–6, 507 see also Derrida,
    Jacques
  divergences from Analytic philosophy
    471, 472
  existentialism see existentialism
  Foucault see Foucault, Michel
  Frankfurt School see Frankfurt School
  Gadamer see Gadamer, Hans-Georg
  Habermas 509
  Hegel's influence on 471
  Heidegger 476–82 see also Heidegger,
    Martin
  and hermeneutics 492, 493–7, 498–9
  Husserl 473–6 see also Husserl,
    Edmund
  Jaspers 508
  Kojève 508–9
  Levinas 509
  Merleau-Ponty see Merleau-Ponty,
    Maurice
  and Otherness see Otherness
  phenomenology 337, 474–6, 479,
    480, 488–91, 498–9, 500; Merleau-
    Ponty's The Phenomenology of
    Perception 483, 485
  and postmodernism 337, 511
  Ricoeur 497–9
  Sartre 485–91, 492 see also Sartre,
    Jean-Paul
  Wahl 509
continuity, principle of (Leibniz)
    235, 236
conversational implicature (Grice)
    427–8

Cooperative Principle (Grice) 428
Copernicus, Nicolaus 584
corpuscularians 51
cosmic consciousness 292
cosmological argument
  Aquinas 156
  and Scotus 162–3
cosmology
  arche see arche (principle of the
    cosmos)
  Aristotle 95–6
  and atomism see atomism/atomists
  and the Church 96, 137; possible
    agreements between scriptures and
    Plato's Timaeus 133
  'cosmological time' 499
  and four elements see elements, four
  Manichean 138–9
  Presocratic 12; Anaxagoras 44–6;
    arche see arche (principle of the
    cosmos); atomism 49–50 see also
    atomism/atomists; Democritus
    49–50; Empedocles see Empedocles:
    cosmology; and the four elements
    16, 29–30, 40, 41, 42, 46, 96;
    and harmony of the spheres
    22, 23; Heraclitus 28–30; and
    Love–Strife interaction 41, 42, 45;
    Parmenides 32–4; Pythagorean 22;
    Xenophanes 26
  realist 527
  Vaisheshika 527
Cracow Thomism 157
Crates of Thebes 100, 101, 102–3
  and Zeno of Citium 108
creativity 180
Cretan Paradox 472n
Critias 56
Croesus of Lydia 11–12, 24
Croton 10, 19
Cudworth, Ralph 218
Cynics/Cynicism 10, 99, 100–103
  Cynic virtues 100; Zeno of Citium's
    internalization of 108, 112
  founding by Antishenes 99, 100–101
  and Socrates 61, 516
Cyrus of Persia 24

Dante Alighieri 186
Danzig 297
dao 538, 545, 546, 547

Daodejing (Tao Te Ching) 545,
546–7, 548
Daoism 534, 540, 545–8
and Confucianism 546
Daodejing (Tao Te Ching) 545,
546–7, 548
'Highest Clarity Daoism' 548
and *wuwei* 547–8, 549
Zhuangzi 546, 548, 551
Darwin, Charles 279, 331
Autobiography 198
The Descent of Man 301
and Schopenhauer 301
Darwinism
Darwinian biology 320
evolution debate 335
and pragmatism 331
Davidson, Donald 336, 419–23
and Dummett 423
and philosophy of action 422
and philosophy of mind: and
anomalous monism 422–3, 437–9;
interpretation theory 438; and
supervenience 423, 437–8
and Quine 419–20
truth-conditional approach to
meaning 419–22, 432
and Whitehead 419
de Gaulle, Charles 487
De Morgan, Augustus 165n, 586, 587
Theorems 110n, 361n; Ockham's
anticipation of De Morgan's
Theorems 165n
death
'Being-towards-death' 480–81
Cicero and learning how to die 114
freedom from fear of 114
and the soul 70
deconstruction
and Continental philosophy 337;
Derrida 504
of phenomenalism 411–12
Dedekind, Richard 38, 348, 349
deism 211n, 227, 270–71
in Patanjali sutras 521
Deleuze, Georges 500
Deleuze, Gilles 336, 471, 500–503
Anti-Oedipus (with Guattari) 501
and art 502–3
birth details 500
Difference and Repetition 503

as an empiricist 500, 501
and ethical striving 502
and Foucault 500, 501
and Guattari 500–501, 503
and Hegel 500
and immanence 502
and Kant 500
'Letter to a Critic' 500–501
Nietzsche and Philosophy 500
and Spinoza 501–2
suicide 501
A Thousand Plateaus
(with Guattari) 501
What is Philosophy?
(with Guattari) 501
Delphi, oracle of (Pythian Apollo) 59,
180, 294
democracy
Athenian 66
and Burke 274
and Marsilius 186
and Plato 66, 73
and Popper 395
representative, and Rousseau 255
Democritus 10, 99, 120
and Aristotle 48
atomism 47–51
birth details 48
cosmology 49–50
The Little World System
('Microcosmos') 48
and Simplicius 49
and 'true-born' vs 'bastard'
knowledge 50
Dennett, Daniel 443–4
denotative theory of meaning 340–41, 414
deontology 265, 305–6, 453, 454, 455,
456, 457
Derrida, Jacques 336, 471, 503–6, 507
birth details 503
and Blanchot 505–6
deconstructionism 504
and deferral of meaning 504–5
Of Grammatology 504–5
and Heidegger 168, 503, 505
and Husserl 503
influences on 503, 505–6
and Merleau-Ponty 485
and Ricoeur 503
Speech and Phenomena 504
Writing and Difference 504

Derveni Papyrus 7, 7–8n
Descartes, René 200–206, 270
  and Aquinas 157
  arguments for existence of a god 202,
    204, 206
  birth details 200, 201
  cogito, ergo sum argument 201–3;
    precursors 206
  and deity xxi, 202, 204, 206
  demon hypothesis 203
  Discourse on Method 206
  dualism *see* dualism: Cartesian
  epistemology: and chain of reasoning
    201; influence 206; method of
    doubt 201–4
  as 'father of modern philosophy'
    200
  followers (Cartesians) 218
  influence of Sextus on 123
  at La Flèche 142, 241
  and Leibniz 235
  and mathematics 200
  Meditations on First Philosophy 200,
    204, 206, 207
  and methodology 159n, 200–204
  mind–body problem and dualism
    204–6, 213, 407–8, 439
  and Neoplatonism 204
  and physics 200
  Principles of Philosophy (examination
    by Spinoza) 212
  as a rationalist 196, 201
  rejection of Scholasticism 196
  and Silhon 206
  writings placed on Index of Forbidden
    Books 157
Descriptions, Russell's Theory of
  341–4, 355
desire
  control over 215–16
  and eliminative materialism
    440–41
  release from 215–16, 300
  sexual 301
  and the will to overcome (Nietzsche)
    318–19
determinism 511 *see also* predestination
  and freedom through acceptance of
    the inevitable 113, 213
  and historical materialism 312–13
  and Leibniz 239

  and Spinoza 213, 215
  and Stoicism 110–11, 117
Deussen, Paul 520–21
Deutsch-Französische Jahrbücher 308
Dewey, John
  and education 333
  ethics 333
  pragmatism 329, 331–3
dialectic
  and Arcesilaus 116
  and Bradley 320–21
  dialectical journey of Geist
    289–94
  and Hegel 289–94, 489, 491
  of historical process 292–4, 309,
    312–13
  and Marx 309, 312–13
  and Plato 292–3 *see also* Socratic
    method
  quodlibetical disputation 134, 152
  Socratic *see* Socratic method
  and Zeno of Elea 35
Diderot, Denis 251
  Les Bijoux indiscrets 269
  and deism 271
  and *Encyclopédie* 269, 272–3
  and Rousseau 251, 252–3
  *Supplement to Bougainville's
    Voyage* 271
Didymus the Blind 55
dignity of man 172–4, 179–81
  and Montaigne's rational
    scepticism 181
Dilthey, Wilhelm 494
Dinnaga 531
Diogenes the Cynic 99, 100, 101–2
Diogenes Laertius: *The Lives of the
    Philosophers* 6, 122
  and Anaxagoras 44
  and Anaximander 14, 15, 31
  and Antishenes as founder of
    Cynicism 100–101
  and Crates 103
  and Diogenes the Cynic 101
  and Empedocles 42
  and Epicurus 103, 104
  and Heraclitus 28
  and Nietzsche 315
  and Parmenides 31
  and Pyrrho 120–21
  and Pythagoras 19

and Thales 14
and Zeno of Elea 35–6
Dion of Syracuse 66–7
disclosure (*aletheia*) 479, 480
dissonance 21
Dobson, Susannah 179
Dogmatists 123
Dominicans 151, 152, 153
Domitian 113
Donatism 139
Donnellan, Keith 428–9
Double Negation, Law of 343, 425
doxography 5–6
Dreben, Burton 389n
dualism *see also* matter: interaction/
    relationship of mind and;
    mind–body problem
  al-Kindi on Greek dualistic
    ontology 560
  Cartesian 204–6, 213, 439; and Ryle's
    'ghost in the machine' 407–8
  'dual aspect' theory of a person 416
  Manichean 138
  Samkhya dualism of purusha and
    prakriti 521, 524, 525
Dummett, Michael
  and Analytic philosophy and
    philosophy of language 336, 358,
    423–7; and realism 423–4
  Catholicism 157
  and Davidson 423
  and Frege 336, 357–8n, 423; *Frege:
    Philosophy of Language* 358, 423
  and Wittgenstein 423
Dumont, Etienne 282
Duns Scotus, John 161–3
  and Aquinas 162
  argument for existence of God 162–3
  and Aristotle 162
  commentaries: on Aristotle 162; on
    Lombard's *Sentences* 162
  and Henry of Ghent 162
  and Ockham 163
  and 'prime matter' 163
  and space 162
  and time 162
  and universals 163
duty xvii, 249, 446, 457
  civic 108, 225
  and deontology *see* deontology
  and freedom 295

of a good man (Aquinas) 186–7
and Kant 264, 265–6
of a prince/sovereign 186–7, 190, 209
religious 568
and Stoicism 101, 108
and virtue-ethics 455
Dworkin, Ronald 469

earthquakes 14, 17
East India Company, British 304
eclipses 10, 14
  lunar 46, 47
economic systems
  capitalism *see* capitalism
  Communism *see* Communism
  and Marx 310, 311, 314
Eden 140, 181, 225
Edinburgh 240, 242
  University 240, 241
education
  and Aristotle 91, 94 *see also*
    Peripatetic school
  and Roger Bacon 159–60
  and the Church 285–6
  and Confucianism 541
  and Dewey 333
  and *Encyclopédie* 272–3
  and 'noble use of leisure' (*otium*) 94,
    187 *see also* leisure, 'noble' use of
  nonconformist 285–6, 304
  philosophy as education of the mind 107
  Plato's Socrates on (*Republic*) 71–2
  and Renaissance humanism 177–8
  and Rousseau 250, 252
  as route to the good life 272–3
  Socrates on (in Plato's *Republic*) 71–2
  sophists as educators 52
  'unforgetting' and theory of
    recollection 69
  women's exclusion from 468
egoism 301, 453
Einstein, Albert 297, 508
  General Relativity theory 378
Elea 10
Eleatic school of philosophy 10 *see also*
    Melissus; Parmenides; Zeno of Elea
  and atomism 50, 51
  and reality as single unchanging
    eternal thing 26–7, 32–4, 36, 44
  Xenophanes as 'first of the Eleatics'
    (Plato) 26–7

elements, four 16, 29–30
  and Anaxagoras 46
  and Aristotle's fifth element, the
    quintessence 95–6
  and Empedocles 40, 41, 42, 96
  and Heraclitus 30
  and Stoicism 109
elenchus see Socratic method
Eliot, George (Marian Evans) 296, 303
Eliot, T. S. 389n
Elis, Peloponnese 56, 121
Elisabeth of Bohemia 206
emanationism 138
  of Brahman (Samkhya) 525
  in Islamic thought (*fayd*) 556,
    561, 565
  Leibniz 238, 239
  Neoplatonism and matter as
    emanation of *nous* 128
emotivism 356, 446–8
Empedocles 7, 10, 39–43
  and Aristotle 42
  cosmology: *arche* 41; and the elements
    40, 41, 42, 96; and Love–Strife
    interaction 41, 42, 45; and random
    combinations of elements 41
  death 42
  On Nature 40
  and Parmenides 40, 41
  as a physician 40
  politics 39
  powers claimed by 40
  Purifications 40
  and Pythagoreanism 40, 42
  and reason 41–2
  and Strasbourg Papyrus 7, 8n, 40
Empiric medical school 122–3
empiricism
  and Analytic philosophy 335 *see also*
    Analytic philosophy
  and Aristotle 89
  and Francis Bacon 196, 198–9
  and Roger Bacon 158, 159
  and Berkeley 226, 228–9, 230
  of Carvaka 522, 532
  and Deleuze 500, 501
  empiricial knowledge 196, 222–3,
    242, 410
  empiricist constraint 244
  and *Encyclopédie* 273
  and the Enlightenment 270

and epistemology 240, 260–63, 302,
    522, 532 *see also* Positivism
  as a form of psychologism 361
  Green's hostility to 321
  and Hobbes 207
  and Hume 240
  and idealism 321
  and Locke 218–19
  logical *see* Logical Positivism
  and mind as a blank slate 260,
    262, 381
  and natural science 196
  and Nicholas of Cusa 174
  and *a posteriori* investigation leading
    to scientific advances 260
  and Quine 390, 392
  and rationalism 196–7, 259–62
  and Russell 351–2
  and Spinoza 502
  triad of British empiricists 218, 240
emptiness (*sunyata*) 530, 531
Encyclopédie 251, 269, 270, 272–3
Engelmann, Paul 371
Engels, Friedrich 312
  The Communist Manifesto (with
    Marx) 309
  *Condition of the Working Class in
    England* 309
  Critique of Political Economy (with
    Marx) 312
  The German Ideology (with Marx)
    309, 312
  and Marx 308–9
English Civil War 207, 210, 226
Enlightenment 268–78
  and autonomy 272
  and courage to use own
    understanding 268, 272
  and empiricism 270
  Encyclopédie 251, 269, 270, 272–3
  and Frankfurt School 277
  and Hume 242–3
  and Kant 266, 268–9, 270
  and Locke 211
  and moral philosophy 243
  and Nazism 277
  and Newton 211
  opposition and opponents 271, 273–4
  and power *see* power: and the
    Enlightenment
  and reason 271, 275–6

and religion 270–71, 272
and Romanticism 273, 274–5
and science 271, 274, 277, 278
and Spinoza 211, 217
and Utopianism 271
Epictetus 109, 113
    Poliziano's Latin translation 177
Epicureanism 10, 98, 99, 103–7
    materialism 124
    and pleasure 104, 105, 106, 176
    and the Renaissance 184
Epicurus 103–7, 281
    and Aristotle 104–5
    and atomism 50, 104–6, 107
    birth details 103–4
    and friendship 107
    and happiness 104
    and justice 107
    and perception 105
    Peri Phuseus 103
    and pleasure 104, 105, 106
    Renaissance criticism of 184
    school ('the Garden') 10, 104
    and souls 105–6
    and testing of claims 116–17
    Valla's defence 176
epiphenomalism 438–9
epistemology *see also* knowledge
    and Aristotle 87–8, 115–16
    and Berkeley 227–9, 242
    Carvaka 532
    and chain of reasoning 201
    conferences for the Epistemology of
        the Exact Sciences 379, 380
    Descartes *see* Descartes, René:
        epistemology
    Dinnaga–Dharmakirti school 531
    and empiricism 240, 260–63, 302,
        522, 532 *see also* empiricism;
        Positivism
    epistemological scepticism
        (Berkeley) 227
    and ethics 242–3
    fallibilist 330, 390
    feminist approach to 468–9
    folk psychology and tacit
        knowledge 439
    and foundationalists 330
    and Hume *see* Hume, David:
        epistemology
    inadequacy of impression 111

and Kant *see* Kant, Immanuel:
    epistemology
and Locke 219–23, 242
and mathematics 348
method of doubt 201–4
and Moore 367–8
and the nature of reality 583
Nyaya 521
and physicalism 390
and Plato *see* Plato: and knowledge
and Quine 390
and reason (Kant) 259–63
and Russell 352–5
Samkhya 524–5
Socratic *see* Socratic method
and Spinoza 214
and Stoicism 110–11
summary of meaning of xvi
'unforgetting' and theory of
    recollection 69
unknowability of world in itself
    (Kant) 262, 292, 299
and Wittgenstein 404
epistocracy 72
Equivocation Fallacy 593
Erasmus of Rotterdam 135, 184
    and Cicero 182
Erkenntnis 377, 379
Ernst Mach Society 379
error theory 356, 451
eternity 141, 143–4
'eternal consciousness' (Green) 322
ethics
    altruism 107, 453
    in Analytic tradition *see* Analytic
        philosophy: ethics/morality
    applied 444, 457
    Aquinas *see* Thomas Aquinas: ethics
    Aristotle *see* Aristotle: ethics
    authenticity in Sartrean ethics 490
    Bradley 325
    and Christian dependence on Holy
        Spirit 182–3
    Confucian *see* Confucianism: ethics
    consequentialist *see* consequentialism
    and Cynicism 99, 100–103
    Deleuze and ethical striving 502
    deontology 265, 305–6, 453, 454,
        455, 456, 457
    and Dewey 333
    distinguished from morality xvii

ethics – *cont.*
doctrine of the mean 24, 93–4
and duty *see* duty
and emotions as source of motivation 247, 248, 540
emotivism 356, 446–8
and epistemology 242–3
and error theory 356, 451
and al-Ghazali 570
Heraclitus and ethical significance of knowledge 30
and Hume *see* Hume, David: ethics and morality
Jain *ahimsa* (non-harm) 523, 532
Kant *see* Kant, Immanuel: moral philosophy and ethics
Luther's attack on Scholastic use of Aristotle's ethics 183
metaethics xvii, 444 *see also* Analytic philosophy: ethics/morality
Mohist 542–5, 581
Moore *see* Moore, G. E.: ethics
and Neoplatonism 129
Nietzsche *see* Nietzsche, Friedrich: ethics and morality
normative xvii, 444–5
philosophy rejected as offering insight into 183
politics as continuous with 84, 94–5, 178–9, 583
and practical wisdom (*phronesis*) 61, 92–3, 454, 455
Protestant use of pagan philosophical ethics 183
reason and wisdom as basis of 61, 182, 183
and Renaissance humanism 178–84
Renaissance views of basis of ethical choice for pagans and Christians 182–3
and rhetoric 169
Ricoeur's ethical metaphysics 498, 499
Schopenhauer *see* Schopenhauer, Arthur: ethics
'slave morality' 54n, 318
and Socrates *see* Socrates: ethics
and Spinoza 212–16
Stoicism 109, 111–12, 114
and suffering 300–301, 524

summary of meaning of xvi–xvii
and *Ubuntu* 518, 580–81
utilitarian *see* utilitarianism
and virtue *see* virtue; virtue ethics; virtue theory
and will *see* free will; will
Euclid, Porphyry's commentary on 127
Euclides 96
Eudemus 5, 91
Eudoxus 96
eugenics 71, 301
eulogon 117
Eupalinos of Megara 19
euphemism 594
Euripides
and Anaxagoras 44
rationality emphasized over feeling 319
and Socrates 28, 59
Eusebius
and Ammonius Saccas 126
on Anaximander 14
and Origen 126n
Eve 140, 225
evidence, law of 284
evil
Aquinas on 156
and free will 129, 139–40, 156–7
as lack of good 156
and matter: Avicenna 566; Neoplatonism 128
and original sin 129, 140 *see also* original sin and Fall of Man
problem of: and Augustine 139–40; and Leibniz 239; and Proclus 128–9; and theodicy 139–40, 239, 555, 556
Excluded Middle, Law of 165n, 343, 361n, 425, 587
existence *see also* reality
and Avicenna 565
and Being *see* Being
Berkeley and its relationship to/ dependence on spirit/deity/mind xxi, 227–31
as central concern of philosophy 583 *see also* metaphysics
cogito, ergo sum argument 201–3, 206
cosmological theories of *see* cosmology

emanationist views of *see* emanationism

and essence (Aquinas) 154–5, 162

of God, arguments for *see* arguments for existence of God

independent existence of 'absence' (Vaisheshika) 526

and Leibniz 236–9

and necessary being 165, 213, 239, 565, 566

non-dual flow of consciousness (cittamatra) as primary existent 530–31

and Nyaya–Vaisheshika 526

and perception 227–30, 367–8

phenomenal world experienced through marriage of intuitions and concepts 261–2

and physicalism *see* physicalism

primary–secondary distinction 530

and Scotus 162

unknowability of world in itself (Kant) 262, 292, 299

Existential Thomism 157

existentialism 337, 471, 476

de Beauvoir 492

Heidegger 476

Jaspers 508

Kierkegaard 509

Merleau-Ponty 485

religious 509

Sartre 476, 490–91, 492

and Wahl 509

explanations

Aristotle 87–8

qualia and the explanatory gap 443–4

teleological 88

extensionalism 363, 418

Quine 390–91, 392, 418

externalism 435

Fall of Man *see* original sin and Fall of Man

fallibilism

fallibilist epistemology 330, 390

and pragmatism 330, 332

False Dilemma Fallacy 593

falsificationism 397–9

family

in Confucianism 539

and feminist concerns about equality and justice 467–8

Ujamaa (African concept of familyhood) 577, 580

al-Farabi, Abu Nasr 153, 561–3

and Aristotle 561

Book of Letters 561–2

Fascism 273, 275, 277, 310–11, 359, 396, 458

and Communism 310–11

Nazi *see* Nazism

fatalism 113 *see also* determinism; predestination

Federigo da Montefeltro 177

Feigl, Herbert 379, 434, 435

feminist philosophy 466–9

de Beauvoir 491–2

Fermat, Pierre de 270

Ferrara 171

Feuerbach, Ludwig 296–7

The Essence of Christianity 296, 314

and Marx 308, 309

materialist inversion of Hegel's idealism 296–7

and Young Hegelians 308

Feyerabend, Paul 400

Fichte, Johann Gottlieb 298

Ficino, Marsilio 130, 135, 168–9, 172, 180

and the Academy 172, 177

and Aquinas' *Summa Contra Gentiles* 168

and Pico 173

Platonic Theology 172–3

translations of others' works 172; Hermetic Corpus 172; Iamblichus 172; Plato 172; Plotinus 172; Porphyry 172

Field, David D., II 284

Field Code 284

Le Figaro 487

Filmer, Sir Robert 224

first cause 156, 163, 565

and Aristotle 89, 163

and Scotus' argument for existence of God 162–3

and souls 89

Flaubert, Gustave 492

Florence 171, 172, 173

and Boccaccio 176

Brunelleschi's Duomo 200

Florence – *cont.*
  Bruni on 187
  Machiavelli in 188, 189
  Medici rule 188
  as a military power 187
  Petrarch in 176
  Pico in 173
  Platonic Academy in 172, 175, 177
  Renaissance 185
  republicanism 187, 188
  ruling council (*signoria*) 176, 185
Fodor, Jerry 470
folk psychology 439, 441
  and eliminative materialism 440–42
  and tacit knowledge 439
Foot, Philippa 455–6
foreknowledge, divine 140–41
  and free will 140–41, 143–4
Forms, Platonic *see* Plato: Forms/Ideas
Förster, Bernhard 316
Förster-Nietzsche, Elisabeth 316
Foucault, Michel 168, 336, 471,
    507, 510
  and Deleuze 500, 501
  and Heidegger 168, 169
  and human nature 510
fragments, Presocratic 5, 7
franchise
  and Bentham 285
  and Locke 224
  and James Mill 285
  and Russell 344
  women's 285, 304, 344, 458–9
Franciscans 151–2, 153
  exiles in Bavaria 164
  John XXII and Franciscan rule of
    poverty 164
  and Scotus 161
Frank, Philipp 379
Frankfurt School 458, 509–10
  critical theory 337, 509–10
  and the Enlightenment 277
Frederick the Great 253, 256
Frederick William III of Prussia 295
free will
  and Augustine 139–40
  and Boethius 143–4
  and divine causation 157
  and divine foreknowledge 140–41,
    143–4
  and emanationism 556

and evil 129, 139–40, 156–7
and Kant's transcendental enquiry
    262–5
and Leibniz 236, 239
and Ockham 166
and possibility of morality
    263–4, 265
as a postulate (Kant) 267
and Spinoza 215, 235
freedom/liberty
  as absence of dependence/
    impediments/restraint ('negative
    liberty') 209–10, 283
  through absolute knowledge 291–2
  through acceptance of the inevitable
    113, 213
  and anguish 490
  through asceticism 523–4
  and autonomy *see* autonomy
  Berlin and negative/positive
    liberty 210
  to choose way of life 272,
    305, 319
  civil freedom and the general will
    (Rousseau) 254, 255
  civil liberties 210–11
  through control of desire 215–16
  and creativity 319
  divine freedom 165
  and duty 295 *see also* duty
  Enlightenment combating denial of
    freedom of mind 269
  from fear of death 114
  forced freedom of demands to obey
    the general will (Rousseau) 254
  free use of reason 216–17, 270
  freedom of thought 216–17
  and Hegel 294, 295
  as highest good (Kant) 263–4
  and Hobbes 209–11
  and ignorance 239
  Jain path to 532
  and Kant 263–4
  and licence/anarchy 73
  Marx's distinction between political
    and human emancipation 311
  and Mill 305, 307
  moksha of Indian thought 300,
    523, 533
  moral freedom 254–5
  'natural freedom' 254

and natural rights 209, 224
political liberalism *see* liberalism,
  political
and power 210
and progress 266
through realization that purusha has
  always been free 525
religious 285–6
republican liberty 176, 209–10
and responsibility 490
rights for protection of 210–11
Rousseau's 'Man is born free' 252
and Spinoza *see* Spinoza, Baruch: and
  freedom
in 'state of nature' 224–5
through understanding the nature of
  things 216
of will *see* free will
Frege, Gottlob 85, 336, 339, 357–65,
  418–19
anti-Semitism 359
Begriffsschrift 349, 358–9
birth details 357, 358
and Dummett *see* Dummett, Michael:
  and Frege
family background 358
Grundgesetze der Arithmetik 351,
  357, 358, 359
Grundlagen der Arithmetik 359;
  Austin's translation 410, 418
and Husserl 360, 473
and logic 339, 357, 359–65, 418–19,
  586; and identity statements 360,
  363–4; logicism 160, 348–9, 380,
  419; and multiple generality 362;
  and principle of intersubstitutivity
  of co-referential terms 363–4;
  and reference 361–3, 364, 367
and mathematics reduced to logic
  160, 348–9, 380, 419
and meaning, sense-reference
  distinction 363, 364, 367, 419
philosophy of language 359–60,
  361–5; and semantics 419, 426
and quantification 348, 362
and reference 361–3, 367, 428;
  'reference-shift' 364;
  sense–reference distinction 363,
  364, 367, 419
rejection of psychologism 360–61
and Russell 348–9, 357, 359

translations by Geach and Black
  357–8, 418
and Wittgenstein 371
Freiburg University 474, 477, 478, 481
French Revolution 271, 273, 274, 287
and Bentham 283
and Locke 211, 218, 226
Freud, Sigmund 301
Friedrich-Wilhelm Gymnasium,
  Trier 307
friendship
and Epicurus 107
and pleasure 107
Fromm, Erich 510
Fulbert 148
functionalism 436–7

Gadamer, Hans-Georg 471, 492–7
and art 494, 495–6
birth details 492
family background 492–3
and Habermas 496–7
and Heidegger 493
and hermeneutics 492, 493–7
and the horizon/limit of knowledge 496
and human nature 495, 496
influence 497
and Nazism 493
and ontology 494, 495
and Plato 493
and prejudice 496
during Second World War 493
Truth and Method 493–7
Gade, C. B. N. 580n
Galen of Pergamon 40
  Poliziano's Latin translation 177
Galileo Galilei 96n, 137, 269–70, 584
Galle, Johann 399
Games, ancient Greece 25, 66
Gast, Peter (Johann Heinrich
  Köselitz) 316
Gaunilo of Marmoutiers, Lost Island
  argument 148
Gautama, Aksapada 521
Gautama, Siddhartha *see* Buddha
Gay, Peter: *The Enlightenment* 271–2
Geach, Peter 157
  *Translations from the Philosophical
  Writings of Gottlob Frege* (with
  Black) 357–8, 418
Geist 289–94, 323

gender
  and applied ethics 457
  bias 468
  and feminist philosophy *see* feminist
    philosophy
  gendered nature of traits 469
  inequalities 467, 468 *see also*
    franchise: women's
  and Otherness 491–2
  women *see* women
General Relativity theory 378
Genesis 180
Genet, Jean 487
Geneva 251
George I, Duke of Hanover 234
George VI 345, 357
George of Trebizond 172
al-Ghazali 567–70
  autobiography 567, 570
  and Averroes 570, 572, 573
  and Avicenna 566, 568, 569
  and causality 568–9
  The Doctrines of the Philosophers
    567–8
  The Incoherence of the Philosophers
    567, 568, 569; and Averroes 570
  and Ismailis 569
  Revival of the Religious Sciences 570
  and Sunni Ash'arite ascendancy
    570, 573
Gibbon, Edward 3
'Glorious Revolution' 218, 223–4
Gnosticism 138
God
  as 'absolute being' 156
  actualization of the divine
    (Green) 322
  Aquinas on 156–7
  and Arabic–Persian philosophy
    555–6
  arguments for existence of *see*
    arguments for existence of God
  and Aristotle's first cause 89, 163
  and Averroes 571, 572–3
  and Avicenna 565–6
  'death' of (Nietzsche) 317–18
  divine causality: Aquinas 157;
    Augustine 139–40; and evil
    139–40, 239, 556; and free will 157
  divine consciousness and Sprigge's
    view of reality 328

divine knowledge 237, 566, 569, 572,
  573 *see also* foreknowledge, divine
divine power reflected in man's
  creativity and imagination 180
emanations from God/the Absolute
  see emanationism
foreknowledge of *see* foreknowledge,
  divine
freedom of 165
general revelation of 159
grace of 156
and Green's idea of an 'eternal
  consciousness' 322
and happiness 156
Hobbes' materialistic view of 207
the Holy Spirit 182–3
as a human invention 312
incarnation in Christ 180
and the individuating of substances
  (Leibniz) 237
as infinite or universal mind/spirit
  213, 227, 231, 232, 353, 571
and instrumentalism 231
Islam and the oneness of 560–61
and Kant's transcendental enquiry
  262–3
as love 183
monotheism 569
and morality (Kant) 267, 268
as necessary being: Avicenna 565,
  566; Leibniz 239; Ockham 165;
  Spinoza 213
omnipotence 165, 204, 498, 555–6
omniscience 132, 140–41, 143, 144,
  204, 238, 498
as a postulate (Kant) 267
and principle of the best (Leibniz)
  235, 236
reason, faith, and grasping the ways
  of (Ockham) 164–5
rulers appointed by 185
self-sacrifice of 129
soothing beliefs in 508
soul's Platonic love for 173, 183
Spinoza's equating of nature/the
  universe with 212–14, 235
and theodicy 139–40, 239, 555, 556
time, eternity and 141, 143–4
as wholly good 236
Gödel, Kurt 351, 379, 389
Goethe, Johann Wolfgang von 298

Gomperz, Theodor 51
Gongsun Long: 'White Horse
    Dialogue' 545
Goodman, Nelson 592
goodness
    Aristotle and the highest good/
        supreme end 91–2, 181
    Descartes and a good god 201, 202
    evil as lack of good 156
    and freedom 263–4
    God as wholly good (Leibniz) 236
    happiness as highest good 92,
        181, 286
    innate 540
    Kant and the highest good 263–4, 267
    philosophy's aim of achieving the
        good life 52, 63, 99, 249–50
    Plato and the supreme Good 183
    as a Platonic Form 74, 174, 183
    Plato's lectures on the Good 78
    as that which is in accordance with
        nature 111
Gorgias 55, 100
Gothic script 178
Goths 3–4
Göttingen University 298, 300, 358, 474
government
    Aristotle: and governmental provision
        for a 'sufficient life' 186; and small
        republican polities 83
    'chain of command' (Mohism) 543
    and Chinese Legalism 549–52
    corruption 285
    democratic see democracy
    and epistocracy 72
    Hobbes and absolute authority of
        207–9
    and Locke 218, 224–5
    and Mill 305
    by monarchy see monarchy
    and oligarchy see oligarchy
    Parliamentary representation 285
    and Plato's Republic 72–3; and
        philosopher-kings 66, 71–2, 73
    and the rights of the people 274
    ruler qualities see rulership qualities
    and timocracy 72–3
    utilitarian obligation on legislators
        281
    waste 285
Graham, A. C. 545

grammar 48, 110, 169, 175
    of African languages 579
    Arabic 561
    and Roger Bacon 159
    distinguished from syntax 414
Gray, Thomas: Elegy Written in a
    Country Churchyard 517
Greek philosophy
    Aristotelian see Aristotle
    and Christian heresies 6
    Platonic see Plato; Platonism; Socrates
    post-Aristotelian Greek and Roman
        philosophy see Cynics/Cynicism;
        Epicureanism; Neoplatonism/
        Neoplatonists; scepticism; Stoicism/
        Stoics
    Presocratic see Presocratic philosophy/
        philosophers
Green, J. 258
Green, Nicholas St John 329
Green, T. H. 320, 321, 322–3
Greene, Robert: Honorable Historie
    of Frier Bacon and Frier
    Bungay 161
Gregorian calendar 159n
Gregory Nazianzen 130
Gregory of Nyssa 130
    and the soul 154
Gregory IX, Pope 133, 571
Gregory XIII, Pope 159n
Grice, Paul 416
    communication-intention
        theory 427
    and conversational implicature
        427–8
    Cooperative Principle 428
Grimm brothers 298
Gröber, Conrad 476
Grosseteste, Robert 158
Guarino Veronese/da Verona 177, 178
Guattari, Felix 500–501, 503
Guicciardini, Francesco 135, 190
gunas 524
Gundisalvi, Dominicus 568
Gutenberg, Johannes, printing press
    178, 195
gymnosophists 120, 532

Habermas, Jürgen 336, 494, 509
    and Gadamer 496–7
Hahn, Hans 379

Haldane, R. B. (ed.): *Essays in
Philosophical Criticism* 321
Halley's comet 43
Hampshire, Stuart 459
Han Fei 549, 551, 552
Hanbal, Ahmad ibn 559
Hanbalites 559, 561
happiness 114–15
  ataraxia see *ataraxias* (peace of mind)
  and Epicurus 104
  eudaimonia: Aristotle 92–4, 454, 455;
    Diogenes the Cynic 102
  final happiness and the afterlife 150
  and God 156
  greatest happiness for greatest number
    281–2, 306, 307 see also
    utilitarianism
  as highest good 92, 181, 286
  illusory (Marx) 311
  through living in accordance with
    nature 54, 111
  and Mill 304, 306
  and pleasure 306 see also hedonism
  and power 318
  and the sceptics 118
  and Stoicism 111, 112, 114
  and utilitarianism 281–2, 286, 306,
    307 see also utilitarianism
  and virtue 92–4, 454, 455, 456
Hare, R. M. 336, 405, 445n, 448–50
harmony
  Aristotle and harmony within the
    state 94
  and consonance 21–2, 23–4
  and justice (Plato) 73
  in Plato's ideal aristocracy 72
  and Pythagoreanism 22, 23–4
  of the spheres 22, 23
  and temperament 24
Harpagos 24
Harrington, James 210
Hart, Herbert 302, 459
Harun al-Rashid 558
Hasan ibn Ali 558
Hayford, Joseph 577
Hazlitt, William xv, 279–80
  on Bentham 280, 286
hedonism 282, 306, 532
Hegel, Georg Ludwig 287
Hegel, Georg Wilhelm Friedrich
  279, 280, 287–97, 471

absolute idealism 292, 320
birth details 287
and Christianity 291; and the
  Reformation 294–5
death 288
and Deleuze 500
and dialectical journey of Geist
  289–94
*Encyclopaedia of the Philosophical
  Sciences in Outline* 288
family background 287
and freedom 294, 295
'historicist' branding (Popper) 395
and Hölderlin 287, 288–9
influence 287, 291; on Heidegger 287;
  on idealists 320, 322, 323; on Marx
  287, 290, 291, 297, 308
at Jena University 287
and law 296
Logic 293
and master–slave relationship 291,
  489, 491
The Phenomenology of Spirit 287,
  290, 291
The Philosophy of History 289–90,
  293–4
Philosophy of Religion 308
Philosophy of Right 288
political philosophy 288, 295–6
and Popper 295, 395
psychological generalizations 294
and the Reformation 294–5
and Sartre 491
and Schelling 287, 288–9
and Schopenhauer 298–9
The Science of Logic 288
and Stoicism 291
Hegelians
  neo-Hegelians 346, 347
  Old/Right 296
  Young/Left 296, 308; and Marx
    308, 309
Heidegger, Martin 280, 336, 471,
  476–82
and aesthetics 478
'The Anaximander Fragment' 16n
and Arendt 510
and Aristotle 478–9
and authenticity 480–81
Being and Time 477, 478–81
birth details 476

Black Notebooks 482
and Blochmann 477
and Brentano 476
Contributions to Philosophy 478
Der Spiegel interview 481–2
and Derrida 168, 503, 505
on 'destructive retrieve' 505
existential phenomenology 476
and Foucault 168, 169
and Gadamer 493
and Hegel 287
and Hölderlin 478
and Husserl 476, 477, 478
as a Jesuit seminarian 476–7
and Nazism 359, 476, 477–8,
    481–2, 510
and Nietzsche 478
and ontology 480, 494
personal life 477
and Sartre 488
Heidelberg University 212,
    388, 493
Helen of Troy 55
Hellenism 98, 99
Helmholtz, Hermann von 378
Héloïse d'Argenteuil 148, 149
Helvétius, Claude 281
Henry I 146
Henry VIII 162n
Henry of Ghent 162
Heraclitus 10, 27–31
    and the *arche* 29–30
    and Aristotle 28
    book by 28
    and Derveni Papyrus 8n
    and Epicurus 104
    and ethical significance of
        knowledge 30
    flux 28–9, 115
    on Hesiod 30
    and justice 30
    and *logos* 28
    and material monism 29–30
    and Parmenides 31
    and Plato 28–9, 31
    and pursuit of fame 30
    and Pythagoras 18
    and rule of law 30
    and Socrates 28
    and unity of opposites 29
    wisdom teaching 30

Herennius 126n
Hermeias 126
hermeneutics 492, 493–7
    'hermeneutic circle' 495
    and phenomenology 498–9
Hermeticism 130, 517
    and Christianity 173–4
    Ficino's translation of the Hermetic
        Corpus 172
    and Neoplatonism 173–4
Hermias of Assos 82, 84
Herschel, Sir John 258, 305
Hesiod 104
    Heraclitus on 30
    satirical attacks by Xenophanes 25
    Theogony 12
hesychasts 182
heteronomy 272
Heywat, Walda 578
Hilbert, David 474
Hinduism 523 *see also* Advaita;
        Upanishads; Vedanta; Vedas
    Hindu trinity 526n
    and Majer 300
Hipparchia of Maroneia 102–3
Hipparchus 95
Hippias 56
Hippocrates 123
Hippolytus of Rome: *Refutation of All
        Heresies* 6
Hispanus, Iohannes 568
history, philosophy of xix
    and Hegel's dialectic of Geist
        289–94
    historical materialism 309,
        312–13, 396
    and Marx 309, 312–13
    and Popper on 'historicists' 395
Hitler, Adolf 370, 493
Hobbes, Thomas 207–11
    birth details 207
    De Cive 210
    The Elements of Law 210
    as an empiricist 207
    and 'law' and 'state' of nature
        56, 209
    and Leibniz 235
    Leviathan 207, 208, 210
    and Locke 224
    materialism 207
    as a nominalist 207

Hobbes – *cont.*
  political philosophy 207–10, 458; and
    absolute authority of government
    207–9; and liberty as 'absence of
    impediments to motion' 209–11; vs
    Mozi on sovereign power 544; and
    natural laws 209; and natural rights
    209; and republicanism 207, 210,
    224; self-preservation of subjects as
    constraint on sovereign 209; and
    sovereign power and rights 207–9,
    210, 544
  as a Royalist 207
  self-imposed exile in France 207
  and self-interest 247
  and sensation 207
  Skinner's critique 209–10
  and universals 207
Hoffman, David 284
Holbach, Paul Henry Thiry,
    Baron d'
  Natural Politics 271
  and Rousseau 252–3
Hölderlin, Friedrich
  and Hegel 287, 288–9
  and Heidegger 478
  and Kant 288
  and Nietzsche 314
holism 325, 393–4, 399
Holmes, Oliver Wendell, Jr 329
Holy Roman Empire
  and Italian city states 185
  and medieval university study of
    Roman law 185
  and Ottoman Empire 171
Holy Spirit 182–3
Homer 25, 315
  Poliziano's Latin translation 177
homosexuality 301
  gay rights 501
Hooke, Robert 234, 270
Horace 169, 258
Horkheimer, Max 509–10
  Dialectic of Enlightenment (with
    Adorno) 276–7
Horton, James Beale 576–7
Hountondji, Paulin 579
Huangdi 546
human nature
  and Bentham 286
  in Chinese Legalism 551

  in Confucianism *see* Confucianism:
    and human nature
  corruptibility of 128
  dignity of man 172–4, 179–81
  and education (Rousseau) 252
  fallen 129, 140, 181, 204
  and Foucault 510
  and freedom *see* free will; freedom/
    liberty
  and Gadamer 495, 496
  as halfway between animals and
    angels 264
  and Hegel 291
  Hume and human nature:
    'anatomising human nature' 244–6;
    benevolence of human nature 248;
    A Treatise of Human Nature 241,
    242, 244, 247–8
  innate goodness 540
  and Kant 264
  and language (Gadamer) 496
  man as measure of all things
    (Protagoras) 55
  man as 'stepchild of nature'
    179–80
  and Neoplatonism 128–9
  and the Renaissance 179–81, 184
  and Ricoeur 499
  Rousseau's theory of human nature
    and 'natural man' 252
  and Rousseau's views on women 256
  and self-knowledge *see*
    self-awareness/-consciousness/
    -knowledge
  and the soul *see* soul
  and *Ubuntu* 518, 580–81
  and Xunzi 541
humanism
  and Kant's moral theory 268
  and Pico 173; and *The Oration* 174
  and Plato 183
  Renaissance 135, 175–84; and
    Aristotle 178–9, 184; and Bruni
    187; and Christianity 181–3; and
    education 177–8; and ethics
    178–84; and Florence's Platonic
    Academy 172, 175, 177; and
    human nature 179–81, 184; and
    Petrarch 175, 179, 186, 187; and
    Pico 173, 174; and Plato 183; and
    political theory 178, 186, 187, 188,

189; and use of force 187; and *vita activa* 175, 187
and *Ubuntu* 518, 580–81
Hume, David 240–50
association of ideas 244–5
atheism 240
and Bentham 282
birth details 240
and Cicero 249
death 242
Dialogues Concerning Natural Religion 241, 242
in Edinburgh 242; and Edinburgh University 240, 241
on effects of Scholasticism on philosophy 250
as an empiricist 240
and the Enlightenment 242–3
Enquiry Concerning Human Understanding 241, 242, 380
Enquiry Concerning the Principles of Morals 241, 242, 247
epistemology 242–6; attaining knowledge of moral principles 247
ethics and morality 242–50, 445; and benevolence of human nature 248; and character revealed by actions 282; and emotions as source of motivation 247, 248, 540; and epistemology 242–3; and the good life 249–50; impossibility of deriving a prescription from a description 248, 449; and innate moral sense 247; and natural vs artificial virtues 248–9; objections to rationalist morality 247–8; sentiment as foundation of morality 243–8
Green's study of 321, 322
History of England 241
influence of Sextus on 123
and Kant 258, 260
at La Flèche 240–41
Locke's influence 218
and the mind 243–6; and association of ideas 244–5; and idea of causality 244–5; and idea of the 'self' 245–6; and Kant 260; and theories of belief and habits 245–6
in Paris 241–2
and perceptions 244–5

and philosophy's belonging to world at large 250
and Positivism 380
psychological atomism 244–6, 321
and reason 247, 276
and Rousseau 253
self-portrait in 'funeral oration' 240
and Stoicism 250
subjectivism 246–8
A Treatise of Human Nature 241, 242, 244, 247–8
utility principle 281
humours 24
Hunhu 580
Huns 3–4
Husayn ibn Ali 559
Husserl, Edmund 280, 336, 471, 473–6
abandonment of psychologism 360, 473
birth details 473
and Bolzano 473
Cartesian Meditations 482
Derrida's dissertation on 503
and Frege 360, 473
and Heidegger 476, 477, 478
Ideas 1 translated by Ricoeur 497
Logical Investigations 474, 478
and Masaryk 473
and mathematics 473
and Merleau-Ponty 482
'Paris Lectures' 482
and phenomenology 474–6
Philosophy of Arithmetic 473
and Sartre 488
Hutcheson, Francis 247, 249
Huxley, T. H. 303
Huygens, Christiaan 233, 270
hypotheses 36, 119, 198, 388, 397–9, 591
hypothetical imperatives 264

I Ching see *Yijing*
Iamblichus 20, 127, 128
Ficino's translation 172
On the Pythagorean Life 20
Ibn Rushd see Averroes
Ibn Sina see Avicenna
idealism xviii, 320–28
absolute: Hegel 292, 320; Sprigge 328
Berkeley's theistic idealism see Berkeley, George: idealism

idealism – *cont.*
  and Bradley 320–21, 323–5
  British idealists *see* British idealists
  and empiricism 321
  and *Essays in Philosophical
    Criticism* 321
  and Green 320, 321, 322–3
  Hegelian influence on 320, 322, 323
  and Leibniz 238
  and Marx 312
  materialist inversion of Hegel's 296–7
  and McTaggart 325–8
  metaphysical debate between
    materialism and 427
  and Moore 365, 367–8
  and Neoplatonism 124, 128, 130 *see
    also* Neoplatonism/Neoplatonists
  'The Oldest System-Programme of
    German Idealism' 288–9
  phenomenology as bridge between
    realism and 488
  principle figures in late
    19th century 320
  Russell's scheme for an idealist
    'encyclopaedia of all sciences'
    346, 347
  Sprigge 328
  subjective 292
  theistic 227, 232, 321, 353
  transcendental 321n, 474
ideas
  abstract 230 *see also* abstraction
  Berkeley 228–9
  as copies of impressions (Hume)
    244–5
  equated with things (Berkeley) 228–9
  Hume and the association of 244–5
  innate 219, 260, 330
  James, and truth as 'agreement'
    between reality and 330–31
  Locke *see* Locke, John: and ideas
  matters of fact and relations of ideas
    (Hume) 246
  metaphysics of 'Ideas' in 'The Oldest
    System-Programme of German
    Idealism' 289
  Platonic *see* Plato: Forms/Ideas
  power of 278
  reason as the armament of 275
  sensory 220
  and theory of the state 289

identity
  as Atman in Indian thought *see*
    Atman
  criteria (Quine) 391–2
  and difference (Deleuze) 502
  of indiscernibles 235, 237
  Law of 587
  personal *see also* personhood;
    selfhood: discovery of the self
    (Ricoeur) 498–9; dual aspect theory
    of a person 416; and Frege's
    rejection of psychologism 360–61;
    Hume and idea of the 'self' as a
    mere convenience 245–6; and
    Locke 221–2; and mind–body
    problem *see* mind–body problem;
    and self-realization *see*
    self-realization
  statements 360, 361–2n, 363–4,
    367–8; and rigid designation 430
identity theories of mind 434–41
  and eliminative materialism 440–42
  and pain 435, 436
  token–token identity 436; and
    Davidson 437–8
  type–type identity 436, 437
illocutionary acts 412
imaginary variation 475
imagination 180, 228, 232, 244,
  274, 286
  and Aristotle 89, 562
  and al-Farabi 562
  moral 537
immanence 502
immaterialism 227
immortality
  and morality (Kant) 263, 266,
    267, 268
  as a postulate (Kant) 267
  of the soul *see* soul: immortal
imperatives
  categorical 264–5
  hypothetical 264
impressions
  cognitive (Stoicism) 110–11
  Hume 244–5
  'persuasive' (Carneades) 118–19
  and sceptics 111
Indian philosophy 519–33
  darshanas (schools): heterodox *see*
    Buddhism; Carvaka–Lokayata;

Jainism; orthodox *see* Nyaya; Purva
    Mimamsa; Samkhya; Vaisheshika;
    Vedanta; Yoga
Dinnaga–Dharmakirti school 531–2
gymnosophists 120, 532
illusion and reality 120n, 121, 522
and Pyrrhonism 120, 121, 532
and Schopenhauer 297, 300
self *see* Atman
as soteriological 519, 522, 523, 524,
    525, 532
Upanishads *see* Upanishads
Vedanta *see* Vedanta
Vedas *see* Vedas
indifference see *apatheia*
indifferents 111–12
indiscernibility of identicals 235
individualism 435, 453 *see also*
    anti-individualism
    liberal 462
individuality
    and Scotus 163
    and Spinoza 214–15
induction 585, 586, 591–2
    Anaxagoras 46–7
    Francis Bacon 198–9
    Mill 199
infinity
    of the *arche* 15–16
    and Aristotle 15–16
    God as infinite or universal mind/
        spirit 213, 227, 231, 232,
        353, 571
    infinite series 234
    of 'triangular numbers' 20–21
    and Zeno of Elea 38–9
inherence (samavaya) 526, 527
Innocent III, Pope 179
instrumentalism
    and Berkeley 231
    and God 231
    and pragmatism 332
    and truth 231
intension 390–91
    intensional logic 592
intentionality
    in Analytic philosophy: behaviouristic
        understanding of intentional
        phenomena 434; communication-
        intention theory 427; and
        consciousness 437; externalism and

theories of intentionality 435;
    intentional states 434–5
and Brentano 438, 474
and Husserl 474–5
meanings in ordinary and
    philosophical discourse 391n
International Workingmen's Association
    ('First International') 309
intersubstitutivity of co-referential
    terms, principle of 363–4
intuition 214, 246
    intuitionist logic 343
    intuitionist mathematics 343, 425
    intuitionistic approach to ethics
        366–7, 446
    and Kant 261–2
    Locke's 'intuitive knowledge'
        222–3
    and Logical Positivists 446
    moral: Moore 366–7, 446; Ross 446
    phenomenal world experienced
        through marriage of intuitions and
        concepts 261–2
    and realism 446
    sensory 263
Ionia 9
    conquered by Harpagos 24
    and the Persians 24, 43–4; and
        Cyrus 24
Ionian philosophers 9–10, 11–31, 43–7
    see also Anaxagoras; Anaximander;
        Anaximenes; Heraclitus;
        Pythagoras; Thales; Xenophanes
    and atomism 50
    material monism 12, 16, 29–30
Irigaray, Luce 477n, 511
irrational numbers 22–3
Islam 5, 31n, 133, 559
    golden age of 558
    hadith 564
    Islamic philosophy *see* Arabic–Persian
        philosophy
    kalam (theology): and Aristotle 559,
        560; Ash'ari 559, 567, 570; and
        Averroes 571–2; and Avicenna
        565–7; and al-Ghazali 569–70;
        Hanbalist 559, 561; and al-Kindi
        560–61; Mu'tazila 558–9; and
        oneness of God 560–61;
        relationship to philosophy 560,
        561, 568–70, 571–4; Zahiri 559

Islam – *cont.*
　sharia 564
　Shi'a school 558–9; Zaydi Shi'a
　　school of law 559
　Sunni–Shi'a split 558–9, 570
　Sunni school 558–9, 570; al-Ghazali
　　and Ash'arite ascendancy
　　570, 573
Ismailis 563, 569

Jackson, Frank, Mary's Room thought
　experiment 442–3
Jaimini 522
Jainism 516, 519, 523, 532
　ahimsa (non-harm) 523, 532
　transformation into a religion 130
James II 218
James, William 328–9, 330–31, 332
　'cash value' account of truth 333
　and 'Metaphysical Club' 329
　Neutral Monism 354
　Pragmatism 332
　as a pragmatist 328–9, 330–31, 332
　and Russell 331
Jaspers, Karl 493, 508
　and the Axial Age 517
　and Ricoeur 497
Jena 233, 287–8
　University 287, 358, 386
Jerome 126
Jesuits
　and Heidegger 476–7
　La Flèche college 142, 240–41
　Portuguese 578
　and the Reformation 151
　and Susenyos of Ethiopia 578
Jesus Christ 180, 513–14, 516, 517
　and Paul 517
　sacrificial death of 129, 181
　Second Coming 181–2
John XXII, Pope 164, 186
Jourdain, Philip 357
Judaism, and Neoplatonism 127
just war theory
　Aquinas 138, 141, 187
　Augustine 138, 141
justice
　and the *arche* 50
　and atomism 50
　and compact-keeping 107
　and Epicurus 107

and the family 467–8
feminist approach to 467–8
and Heraclitus 30
'in holdings' (Rawls) 465–6
'impartial concern' (*jianai*) 543
and Plato: and balance/harmony 73;
　and good citizenship 53; in *Republic*
　71; and social contracts 71
and Protagoras 53–4
Pythagorean numerical value assigned
　to 22
and Rawls 460–61, 465–6
and reason 56
and strife 29, 30
Justinian 6, 78, 98, 131, 557

Kabbalah *see* Cabala
Kanada (Kashyapa) 521
Kant-Studien 386
Kant, Immanuel 256–68
　and Abelard 150
　and the arising of experience 263, 475
　and astronomy 258, 266
　Ayer's anecdote on 389n
　and Bauch 386
　birth details 257
　and Carnap 386
　Critique of Judgment 257
　Critique of Practical Reason 257, 263
　Critique of Pure Reason 256, 257,
　　259–63, 386; and Strawson's *The
　　Bounds of Sense* 416
　death 259
　and Deleuze 500
　and the Enlightenment 266,
　　268–9, 270
　epistemology 259–63; and marriage
　　of intuitions and concepts 261;
　　reconciling rationalist and
　　empiricist approaches 260–63; and
　　unknowability of noumenal reality/
　　world in itself 262, 292, 299
　family background 257
　and freedom 263–4; free will and
　　transcendental enquiry 262–5; free
　　will as a postulate 267
　*Groundwork of the Metaphysics of
　　Morals* 257, 263, 264
　Hölderlin on 288
　and human nature 264
　and Hume 258, 260

intellectual heroes 258
and intuition 261–2
at Königsberg University 258
and laws 264, 265–6, 267, 455
and mathematics 348
and Moore 365
moral philosophy and ethics 263–8,
    445; and autonomy 263–4, 265,
    268; and the categorical imperative
    264–5; deontology 265, 305–6,
    453; and duty 264, 265–6; as
    humanistic 268; and immortality of
    the soul 263, 266, 267, 268; moral
    law 264, 265–6, 267, 455; and
    religion as harmful to morality 266,
    268; and Schopenhauer 301;
    universal applicability of moral
    principles 265
and ontological argument 147
and Pietism 257, 266
as polymathic 258
and postulates 267
Prolegomena to Any Future
    Metaphysics 257
and reason: and epistemology 259–
    63; and its limitations 262, 276;
    and morality 263–8; a priori
    reasoning 259–62
and religion 266–8
and Rousseau 258
and Schopenhauer 297, 299, 301
and sensory modalities 263, 475
synthesis between empiricism and
    rationalism 196–7, 260–62
transcendental deduction/arguments
    263, 346, 475n
transcendental enquiry 262–5, 266–8
and 'transcendental idealism' 321n
and 'the way our minds work' 260–63
'What is Enlightenment?' 266, 268
Kant Society of Germany 386
Kant–Laplace theory 258
Kapila 521
karma 514, 522, 523
Karma Mimamsa see Purva Mimamsa
Kashyapa (Kanada) 521
Kekulé, August 398
Kemp-Smith, Norman 257
Kepler, Johannes 270
Keynes, John Maynard 365
    and Wittgenstein 372

Khosrow I (Chosroes Anushirvan) 557
Kiel University 378, 493
al-Kindi, Abu Yusuf Ya'qub ibn Ishaq
    559–60
    On First Philosophy 560
Kircher, Athanasius 174
Klein, Felix 474
Klopstock, Friedrich Gottlieb 300
Kneale, William and Martha:
    Development of Logic 358
knowledge see also epistemology
    of the Absolute (Hegel) 290, 291–2
    absolute knowledge as mind knowing
        itself as mind 292
    by acquaintance 352
    and Arcesilaus 116
    Aristotle's systemization of 80–81
    Avicenna's theoretical and practical
        knowledge 564
    and Francis Bacon: and birth of the
        modern mind 200; on practical
        knowledge and natural history 199
    boundary conditions for (Kant) 262
    and cognitive apprehensions 116
    and correct/true belief 69, 77
    demonstrative (Locke) 222
    by description 352
    differentiated from beliefs 69
    in Dinnaga–Dharmakirti school 531
    divine 237, 566, 569, 572, 573;
        foreknowledge see foreknowledge,
        divine
    empirical 196, 222–3, 242, 410 see
        also empiricism
    and Encyclopédie 272
    Foucault and 'power-knowledge' 510
    and foundationalists 330
    freedom through absolute knowledge
        291–2
    Gadamer and the horizon/limit of 496
    gnostic soteriologies 525
    Heraclitus and ethical significance
        of 30
    and hermeneutics see hermeneutics
    Hobbes and scientia (true
        knowledge) 207
    and hypotheses see hypotheses
    identified with virtue 63–4, 68, 116
    impossibility of 118, 119, 120, 122
        see also scepticism
    inherited beliefs as source of 496

knowledge – *cont.*
  intuitive *see* intuition
  Leibniz, and God's knowledge of the
    soul 237
  Locke's topics of 219
  Logical Positivists' rejection of
    metaphysics and theology as source
    of 377, 380
  and mass culture 277–8
  and mathematics: as the highest
    knowledge 174; as *a priori*
    knowledge 260, 384
  of moral principles 247
  mystical experience as a source of 159
  Ockham and propositional
    knowledge 165
  through perception *see* perception:
    and cognition
  and perfecting of the soul 564
  Pico and the human search for 174
  and Plato *see* Plato: and knowledge
  a posteriori 156, 259, 260, 261, 430
  and pramanas (forms of
    cognition) 528
  a priori: and Kant 259–62; and
    mathematics 260, 384; and
    rationalism 259–60, 274n; and
    science 329, 354, 384; synthetic
    a priori 348–9; and verification
    principle 384
  probabilistic 115, 242
  and quest for essential definitions 62–3
  and rationalism 196 *see also*
    rationalism; and *a priori* knowledge
    259–60
  of right and wrong, and the
    'considered life' 63–4
  in Samkhya 524–5
  and scepticism *see* scepticism
  self-knowledge *see* self-awareness/
    -consciousness/-knowledge
  sense-experience as foundation of 352
  sensitive (Locke) 223
  sensory 165, 259, 290 *see also*
    sense-data; and Carvaka 532;
    sensory intuition 263
  situated 468, 469
  Socratic method to *see* Socratic
    method
  superstition as enemy of 216
  tacit 439

theory of *see* epistemology
'true-born' vs 'bastard' (Democritus) 50
universal knowledge and 'unicity of
  the intellect' (Averroes) 573
unknowability of world in itself
  (Kant) 262, 292, 299
Zeno of Citium on knowing 111, 116
Kojève, Alexandre 508–9
Königsberg 257–8
  University 258
Koran *see* Qur'an
Kraft, Victor 379
Kripke, Saul 395, 429–32
  Naming and Necessity 432
  rigid designation and theory of
    reference 429–31
  'sceptical solution' to problem of
    meaning explained in terms of
    rules 432
  and Wittgenstein 432
Kuhn, Thomas: *Structure of Scientific
  Revolutions* 399–400

Lacan, Jacques 509, 511
Lakatos, Imre 399, 400
Lampe, Martin 259
Lampsacus 44, 104
language, philosophy of
  in Analytic tradition *see* Analytic
    philosophy: of language
  and Roger Bacon 159, 160
  and al-Farabi 561–2
  and grammar *see* grammar
  and intersubstitutivity of co-referential
    terms 363–4
  and Leibniz's *On the Art of
    Combinations* 233
  and Locke 221
  and logocentrism 504
  and meaning *see* meaning
  meaning of, summarized xviii
  'ordinary language philosophy' *see*
    'ordinary language philosophy'
  and prejudicial use of language 594
  and public nature of language 403
  public nature of language
    (Wittgenstein) 403
  and 'rectification of names' 541
  and rhetoric *see* rhetoric
  semantics *see* semantics
  speech acts (Austin) 412

and verification *see* verification/
    verificationism
language games 401, 402–3
language-learning 484
Lansdowne, William Petty, 1st
    Marquess of Lansdowne, and
    2nd Earl of Shelburne 282
Laozi 545–6
    Daodejing (*Tao Te Ching*) 545,
      546–7, 548
Laslett, Peter 457, 458
laws
    Aristotelian 'laws of thought' 587
    and Bentham 283–4
    and Chinese Legalism *see* Legalism,
      Chinese
    codification of 284; Akan law 576
    and Comte 303
    of evidence 284
    and Hegel 296
    Heraclitus and rule of law 30
    and Kant 264, 265–6, 367, 455
    Legal Positivism 283, 302
    of logic *see* Double Negation, Law of;
      Excluded Middle, Law of; identity:
      Law of; Leibniz's Law (identity of
      indiscernibles); Non-Contradiction,
      Law of
    and moral convention vs nature 54
    moral law 254–5, 264, 265–6,
      267, 455
    of nature *see* natural law
    and pain 56
    Roman 185
    sharia 564
    Zaydi Shi'a school of law 559
Le Verrier, Urbain 399
Leaman, Oliver 555n
Leeuwenhoek, Antonie van 270
Lefebvre, Henri 510
Lefèvre, Jacques: *Moralis in Ethicen
    Introductio* 184
Legal Positivism 283, 302
Legalism, Chinese 516, 534, 540,
    549–52
    Book of Lord Shang 550
    Han Feizi 549, 551, 552
    and human nature 551
Leibniz, Gottfried Wilhelm 38, 232–9
    and Academy of Berlin 234
    and analyticity principle 235–6, 237

and apperceptions 238
arguments for existence of God 238–9
On the Art of Combinations 233
birth details 232–3
and Boineburg 233
calculating machine 233, 234
characteristica universalis 347, 405
and Christianity 233
continuity principle 235, 236
and Descartes 235
determinism 239
Discourse on Metaphysics 234–5, 238
dualism and interaction of mind and
    matter 205
and Duke of Hanover (George I) 234
emanationism 238, 239
and existence 236–9
family background 233
and free will 236, 239
and Hobbes 235
influences on 233, 235
and Locke 218, 235
and logic 232, 233, 235; identity of
    indiscernibles 235, 237; as a
    'universal algebra' 234
and mathematics 232, 234;
    differential calculus 233, 234
and metaphysics 235, 236, 238–9
Monadology 235
and monads 236–8
*New Essays Concerning Human
    Understanding* 218, 234
and Newton 234
in Paris 233
and Pascal 233
principle of the best 235, 236
Principles of Nature and Grace 238
and the Royal Society 234
Russell's study of 345, 347
and Spinoza 235
and substance 236–8
Theodicy 234
and Weigel 233
Leibniz's Law (identity of indiscernibles)
    235, 237
Leipzig 233, 314
    University 233, 314, 315, 473, 493
leisure, 'noble' use of (*otium*)
    and Aristotle 94, 95, 191
    and More 191–2
    and Petrarch 187, 191

Lenin, Vladimir 313
Leo XIII, Pope 154
Leoniceno, Niccolò: 'On the Errors of
    Pliny' 175
Lesbos 82–3
Leśniewski, Stanisław 389
Leucippus 10
    atomism 47–51
    birth detail uncertainty 47–8
    The Great World System
        ('Macrocosmos') 48
    On Mind 48
    and Parmenides 48
    and Theophrastus 49
Levasseur, Thérèse 251, 253
Lévi-Strauss, Claude 482, 505
Levinas, Emmanuel 509
Lewes, George Henry 297
    A Biographical History of Philosophy
        xi, 303; and Kant 257
    and Comte 303
Lewis, David 470
Li Si 549
liberal individualism 462
liberalism, political
    criticisms: from political left 311;
        from political right 310–11
    and Locke 218, 226
    and Marx 310–11
    and Mill 304, 305
    and Popper *see* Popper, Karl: and
        liberalism
libertarianism (Nozick) 462–6
liberty *see* freedom/liberty
linguistic behaviourism (Quine) 394–5
linguistic philosophy *see* 'ordinary
    language philosophy'
Liszt, Franz 315
Livy 176
    and Machiavelli's *Discourses* 190
Locke, John 217–26
    atheism 224
    and Berkeley 218, 226, 227–8
    birth details 217
    and 'blank slate' metaphor of mind
        260n
    and civil society 225
    as an empiricist 218–19
    epistemology 219–23, 242
    *Essay Concerning Human
        Understanding* 218, 219–23, 339–40

and evolution of society 107
and the 'Glorious Revolution' 218,
    223–4
and Hobbes 224
and ideas 219–21, 242, 339–40; and
    Berkeley 227–8; innate 219
influence on Enlightenment ideas 211
and language 221
and Leibniz 218, 235
meaning, theory of 339–40
perception, theory of 220–21, 226
and personal identity 221–2
political philosophy 218, 223–6, 458;
    and French and American
    revolutions 211, 218, 226; and just
    acquisitions 465; and liberalism
    218, 226
and power as a trusteeship 225–6
and the Royal Society 218–19
Second Treatise of Government 224
and Shaftesbury 217–18
and the soul 221–2
and state of nature 107, 224–5, 226
Two Treatises of Government 218
Voltaire on 218
locutionary acts 412
logic 585–95 *see also* reason/rationality
    and Abelard 149–50
    Arabic–Persian *see* Arabic–Persian
        philosophy: logic
    Aristotle's science of *see* Aristotle: and
        logic ('Analytics')
    and bivalence 110, 342–3, 344,
        414, 426
    and Boethius 142–3, 145
    and De Morgan 586, 587 *see also* De
        Morgan, Augustus
    deontic 592
    Dinnaga–Dharmakirti school
        531–2
    distinction between logic and
        psychology of scientific discovery
        398
    and *Encyclopédie* 273
    epistemic 593
    formal deductive 585–6
    and Frege *see* Frege, Gottlob: and
        logic
    fuzzy 592
    and identity of indiscernibles 235, 237
    inductive 198–9, 585, 586, 591–2

informal 585; fallacies 593–5
intensional 592
intuitionist 343
Law of Double Negation 343, 425
Law of Excluded Middle 165n, 343, 361n, 425, 587
Law of Identity 587
Law of Non-Contradiction 165n, 235, 360–61, 587
and Leibniz *see* Leibniz, Gottfried Wilhelm: and logic
logical analysis of language 347
'logical fictions' 356
many-valued 592
and mathematics *see* mathematics: logic's relationship to
Megarian school 96, 108, 120
modus ponens 110n, 589, 591
modus tollens 110n, 397, 590
and Mohism 542, 545
notation (of, or derived from, Russell and Whitehead) 342, 586
Nyaya 521, 525, 528–9
and Ockham 165
paraconsistent 592–3
and philosophy of language 361–5, 405–6, 417
and propositions 85–7
and Quine 389
and rationalism 196
reductio ad absurdum 36, 166, 240
and Russell *see* Russell, Bertrand: and logic
and Stoicism 110–11
summary of meaning of xvi
syllogisms *see* syllogisms
symbolic 588–90
as a 'universal algebra' 234
use to attack authority 269
logical behaviourism 408–9
logical constructionism
    Carnap 386, 406, 418
    Russell 348, 352, 386
logical empiricism *see* Logical Positivism
Logical Positivism 302, 377–85
    and Ayer *see* Ayer, A. J.
    and Carnap 378, 379, 380–81, 385, 386
    vs Comtean Positivism 302, 377–8
    divergent strands of outlook 378
    and intuition 446

and Naturalistic Fallacy 446
and Neurath 378, 379, 380, 381
and phenomenalism 353
and Popper 379, 385, 395
and Schlick *see* Schlick, Moritz
and science 302, 378; and protocol sentences 380–81
and verification principle *see* verification/verificationism
and Vienna Circle *see* Vienna Circle
logicism 160, 348, 349
    Frege 160, 348–9, 380, 419
    Russell 160, 348, 349, 380
    undermined by Gödel's incompleteness theorem 380
logos 45
    and Heraclitus 28
    and Plato 77
    and Stoicism 109
Lokayata *see* Carvaka–Lokayata
Lombard, Peter: *The Book of Sentences* 136, 158
    Aquinas' study of 151
    commentaries: Ockham 164; Scotus 162
London School of Economics 396, 399
Longinus, Cassius 126n, 127
Louis/Ludwig IV, Holy Roman Emperor 164, 166, 186
Louis XV 251
love *see also* compassion
    agape 544
    of beauty 69
    benevolent concern (*ai*) 544
    disinterested (*jianai*) 543
    Empedocles and Love–Strife interaction 41, 42–3, 45
    fraternal, in Mohism 581
    God as 183
    Plato's theory of 173, 183
    and Sartre 489–90, 491
Lu, China 535
Lucretius
    and atomism 50–51
    De Rerum Natura 40, 50–51, 103, 176
Lukács, Georg 458, 510
Łukasiewicz, Jan 389
Lull, Raymond (Ramon Llull) 174
Luther, Martin 134–5, 183, 195

Lutheranism
  and Frege 358
  and the Marx family 307
  and the Popper family 396
Lycopolis 125
Lyotard, Jean François: *The Postmodern Condition* 511

Macedon 112
Mach, Ernst 378
Machiavelli, Niccolò 135, 186, 188–90, 458
  Discourses 190–91
  in Florence 188, 189
  and the Medicis 188
  Il Principe 189–90
  virtù 189, 191, 537
MacIntyre, Alasdair 455
  After Virtue 456
Mackie, J. L. 356, 451–3
  error theory 356, 451
  Ethics: Inventing Right and Wrong 450–51
  and non-existence of objective values 450–53
Madhyamika 530
Madison, James, Jr 284
magic 40, 104, 134, 170, 197–8
  and Neoplatonism 128, 130
  and the Reformation 195
  and the Renaissance 170, 173
Mahabharata 523
Mahavira 523
Mahler, Gustav 297, 370
Maimonides, Moses 133, 554
  and al-Farabi 562–3
Maistre, Joseph Marie, Comte de 274
Maitreyi 520n
Majer, Friedrich 300
Malcolm, Norman 372–3
Malebranche, Nicolas 233, 508
  dualism and interaction of mind and matter 205
Mallarmé, Stéphane 506
al-Ma'mun, Abu al-Abbas 558, 560
manas (mind) 524, 525
Mandela, Nelson 577n
Mandeville, Bernard: *The Fable of the Bees* 247
Mani 138

Manicheism 137, 138–9
Mann, Thomas 297
Mantua 177, 188
Marburg 492
  University 477, 481, 493
Marcus Aurelius 99, 109, 112–13
  To Himself/Meditations 113
Marcuse, Herbert 509–10
Marmontel, Jean-François 273
Marsilius of Padua 186
  Defensor Pacis 166, 186
Marx, Heinrich 307
Marx, Henriette, née Pressburg 307
Marx, Karl 279, 307–14
  and alienation 313
  atheism 311
  and Bakunin 309
  and Bauer 308
  and Bentham 286
  at Berlin University 308
  Capital 309–10
  The Communist Manifesto (with Engels) 309
  'Contribution to the Critique of Hegel's Philosophy of Right' 311
  A Contribution to the Critique of Political Economy 309–10
  Critique of Political Economy (with Engels) 312
  with *Deutsche-Französische Jahrbuch* 308
  doctoral dissertation 308n
  Economic and Philosophical Manuscripts 309, 313
  'The Eighteenth Brumaire of Louis Napoleon' 313
  and Engels 308–9
  in England 309
  family background 307
  and Feuerbach 308, 309
  at Friedrich-Wilhelm Gymnasium 307
  The German Ideology (with Engels) 309, 312
  and Hegel 287, 290, 291, 297, 308, 311
  and idealism 312
  'On the Jewish Question' 311
  and materialism 309, 312–13
  with *New York Daily Tribune* 309
  in Paris 308–9
  and his Philips relations 307

philosophy/conception of history 309,
312–13
political activity 309, 310
political philosophy: and capitalism
310, 314; and Communism 309,
312–14; and dialectical process
309, 312–13; and labour 313; and
liberalism 310–11; and
oppressiveness of economic systems
314; and the proletariat 309
Popper's branding as a 'historicist' 395
on religion 311–12
with *Rheinische Zeitung* 308
Theses on Feuerbach 309
and Jenny von Westphalen 308, 310
and Young Hegelians 308, 309
Marxism 510
and Hegel 287
historical materialism 309,
312–13, 396
and Sartre 486
Mary's Room thought experiment
442–3
Masaryk, Thomas 473
mass culture 277–8
materialism
Berkeley's refutation of 230–31
of Carvaka 522, 532
and consciousness xviii
eliminative 440–42
Epicurean 124
and evil in Neoplatonism 128
and al-Ghazali 570
historical 309, 312–13, 396
and Hobbes 207
Ionian material monism 12, 16, 29–30
and Marx 309, 312–13
materialist inversion of Hegel's
idealism 296–7
metaphysical debate between idealism
and 427
Neoplatonist opposition to 124
and science 230–31
Stoic 124
mathematics
as analytic 348–9 *see also* logicism
and Aristotle 84
binary arithmetic 234
calculus *see* calculus
and Descartes 200
and epistemology 348

and Husserl 473
infinite series 233, 234
international congress, Paris 348
intuitionist 343, 425
and Kant 348
as knowledge *see* knowledge: and
mathematics
and Leibniz *see* Leibniz, Gottfried
Wilhelm: and mathematics
logic's relationship to: Roger Bacon's
grounding of logic in mathematics
160; and Frege 359; logic as a
'universal algebra' (Leibniz) 234;
mathematics reduced to logic *see*
logicism
and metaphysics 348
and Mill 360
and Mohism 542
and occultism 174
and Pico 174
Pythagorean 18, 20–23
and rationalism 196
realism in 424
and Russell 160, 347–51
and sets 390, 424
as synthetic 348–9
and Wittgenstein 371
matter *see also* substance
and Avicenna 566
and Berkeley 227–31
created substances as compounds
of matter and form (Aquinas)
154–6, 163
and evil 128, 566
as extended substance 205, 213
interaction/relationship of mind and
see also mind–body problem: and
Berkeley's theory of perception and
the perceiver 227–30; Descartes
204–6; identity theories of mental
and brain states 434–41; Leibniz
205; occasionalism 205; parallelism
205; reduction of all mental
phenomena to matter 205–6; and
Spinoza's view of mind and body as
modes of one substance 214
and monism 205–6
and Neoplatonism: matter as
emanation of *nous* 128; mind
ontologically prior to matter 124,
128; and Plotinus 128

matter – *cont.*
 prakriti (Samkhya) 521, 524, 525
 'prime matter' (Scotus) 163
 qualities *see* qualities of things
maxims 264, 265, 575, 576
 Peirce's 'pragmatic maxim' 329–30
Maya 522
McDowell, John 469
McTaggart, J. E. M. 320
 and Bradley 326
 The Further Determination of the Absolute 326
 and Moore 346–7, 365
 The Nature of Existence 326
 and Russell 326, 346
 Studies in the Hegelian Dialectic 326
 and unreality of time 325–8
mean, doctrine of the 24, 93–4
 Zhongyong 536
meaning
 as compositional (Davidson) 419
 and conversational implicature 427–8
 Derrida and the deferral of 504–5
 Frege's sense–reference distinction 363, 364, 367, 419
 indeterminacy of 422; 'indeterminacy of translation' (Quine) 394
 intuitionist account of meaning of mathematical statements 425
 and language games 401, 402–3
 and linguistic behaviourism (Quine) 394–5
 Logical Positivism and meaningful discourse 380 *see also* Logical Positivism
 Moore and ordinary meaning 369
 and Peirce's 'pragmatic maxim' 329–30
 Quine's scepticism about 394–5
 and Russell's ambition for a 'logically perfect language' 355–6, 405–6, 418
 theory of 417–28; communication-intention theory 427; denotive theory 340–41, 414; Dummett 423–7; and externalism 435; in formal sense 417–18; in informal sense 417; Locke 339–40; picture theory 375–6; 'stimulus meaning' (Quine) 394–5, 418, 422; truth-conditional approach 419–22, 432;

 and truth-theory for formal languages (Tarski) 421; use theory 403, 432–3; and verification *see* verification/verificationism
 'timeless meaning' 427
Medici, Cosimo de', the Elder 171, 178, 185
Medici, Lorenzo de' 173, 175
Medici, Piero de' 188
Medici family 188
meditation 514, 520, 521, 523–4, 530, 531, 547
Megara 96
Megarian school 96, 108, 120
Meikeljohn, John 257
Melanchthon, Philipp 183
Melissus 10, 35
Mencius 515, 535, 536, 537, 539–40
 Mengzi 516
Meno 5
Merleau-Ponty, Maurice 471, 482–5, 486
 birth and family background 482
 and the 'body-subject' 483
 and 'chiasm' between body and world 485
 and consciousness 483, 484
 death 483
 and Derrida 485
 and existentialism 485
 and flesh 'at the heart of the world' 483
 and Husserl 482
 and Kojève 508
 and language-learning 484
 and *Les Temps Modernes* 482–3, 486
 and 'maximum grip' 484
 and perception 484, 485
 phenomenology 476
 The Phenomenology of Perception 483, 485
 and Plotinus 482
 and Sartre 482–3
 and scepticism 483
 and social pull 484
 'The Structure of Behaviour' 483
 and thought as bodily expression 483–4
 and time 485
 The Visible and the Invisible 485

metaethics xvii, 444 *see also* Analytic
philosophy: ethics/morality
metaphysics *see also* ontology
and Aristotle *see* Aristotle:
metaphysics
atomist *see* atomism/atomists
Being *see* Being
Berkeley's attack on abstraction in
162, 230
causality *see* causality
continuity principle 235, 236
'descriptive' 415
existence as concern of 565 *see also*
existence
idealism *see* idealism
and Leibniz 235, 236, 238–9
materialism *see* materialism
and mathematics 348
meaning, summarized xvi
and Moore 367–9
Neoplatonist *see* Neoplatonism/
Neoplatonists
as old term meaning what is now
called 'philosophy' xv, 259, 280
and philosophy of language 423
and philosophy of mind xvii–xviii
of presence 504
and reality *see* reality
rejected by Logical Positivists as a
source of knowledge 377, 380
'revisionary' 415
Ricoeur's ethical metaphysics
498, 499
Samkhya 525
and Sartre 488
Scotus vs Aquinas 162
and the soul *see* soul
and substance *see* substance
sufficient reason principle 235, 238–9
truth *see* truth
universals *see* universals
Vedanta 522
and verificationist view of truth
426–7 *see also* verification/
verificationism
metempsychosis 18, 19, 26, 40, 42
see also reincarnation
methodological behaviourism 409
Metrodorus of Stratonicea 119
Meyer, Heinrich 298
Michael of Cesena 164

Milan 188
Edict of 3, 137
Miletus 9, 11, 44
Mill, James 284
and education of his son,
John Stuart 304
History of British India 303–4
Mill, John Stuart 279, 280, 303–7
Autobiography 303
and Bentham 286
birth details 304
and British East India Company 304
and censorship 305
and Comte 303
as a consequentialist 305–6
education 304
and government 305
and happiness 304, 306
and induction 198–9
liberalism 304, 305
and liberty 305, 307
On Liberty 305
marriage to Harriet Taylor 304
and mathematics 360
nervous breakdown 304
and reference 431n
and Russell 307, 345
The Subjection of Women (with
Taylor) 304
System of Logic 199, 305
utilitarianism 281–2, 286, 304,
305–7
Utilitarianism 305
Westminster Review essays 305
and women's equality 304, 307
and Wordsworth 304
Mill's Methods 199
Milo of Croton 19
Milton, John 210, 258
mind, philosophy of
in Analytic tradition *see* Analytic
philosophy: of mind
Averroes' 'unicity of the intellect' 573
and the brain *see* brain
consciousness *see* consciousness
Descartes, René 204–6, 213, 439
and Epicurus 105–6
essence of mind as thought (Descartes)
205, 213
and folk theory *see* folk psychology
functionalism 436–7

mind, philosophy of – *cont.*
  and God as infinite/universal mind
    213, 227, 231, 232, 353, 571
  human minds as 'modes' of infinite
    mind 213
  and Hume *see* Hume, David: and the
    mind
  idealism *see* idealism
  ideas *see* ideas
  identity theories *see* identity theories
    of mind
  intentionality *see* intentionality
  Kant and 'the way our minds work'
    260–63
  meaning, summarized xvii–xviii
  and metaphysics xvii–xviii
  mind as a blank slate 260, 262, 381
  mind as thinking substance 205, 213
  mind–body problem *see* mind–body
    problem
  in Neoplatonism: matter as emanation
    of *nous* 128; mind as basis of
    reality 124; mind ontologically
    prior to matter 124, 128; the
    unitary mind 124
  and neuroscience xx, 107, 204, 434,
    440, 441
  and physicalism *see* physicalism
  reality as a community of minds
    (Sprigge) 328
  relationship of mind to matter/body/
    brain *see* matter: interaction/
    relationship of mind and; mind–
    body problem
  Samkhya 524–5
  Spinoza and active and passive mental
    states 215
  truth and *phantasia kataleptike*
    110–11
  ultimate reality as mental (Hegel) 292
Mind (journal) 326, 348, 413
mind–body problem
  Descartes 204–6, 213, 439; and Ryle's
    'ghost in the machine' 407–8
  and occasionalism 205
  and parallelism 205
  Spinoza 214
  and Strawson 416
minuscule 178
Mises, Richard von 379
Mitchell, David 578n

Mithridatic War, First 82
modernism 511
Mohism 534, 535, 542–5
  ethics 542–5, 581
  School of Names (logic and
    metaphysics) 542, 545
monads (Leibniz) 236–8
monarchy
  Aristotle's dislike for 94
  constitutional 295
  and Hobbes 207, 224
  Macedonian 82
  'virtuous' 186
monasticism
  Henry VIII's dissolution of the
    monasteries 162n
  preservation of manuscripts
    by monks 4
  and tonsures 145n
Le Monde 505
Monica, mother of Augustine 137
monism 205–6
  anomalous 422–3, 437–9
  Eastern non-dualist thought: Advaita
    of Vedanta 522; Yogacara's non-dual
    flow of consciousness (cittamatra) as
    primary existent 530–31
  Eleatic 26–7, 32–4, 36, 44
  Ionian material monism 12, 16,
    29–30
  neo-Hegelian 347
  Neoplatonic primordial One 126,
    128, 560
  'Neutral' 354
  Parmenides' theory of the One 27,
    32–4, 36, 44
  and Presocratic idea of *arche* see *arche*
    (principle of the cosmos)
  reality as One Mind *see* idealism
Monist 357
monotheism 569
Montaigne, Michel de 123, 135
Moore, G. E. 335, 363–70, 446
  and Bloomsbury Group 365
  and Bradley 323
  epistemology 367–8
  ethics 365–7; and moral intuition
    366–7, 446; and 'Naturalistic
    Fallacy' 366, 446; and non-
    cognitivism 367; utilitarian 367
  and idealism 365, 367–8

and identity statements 367–8
and Kant 365
and McTaggart 346–7, 365
and metaphysics 367–9
and ordinary meaning 369
Principia Ethica 347, 366, 446
'Proof of an External World' 369
and realism 347, 368–9
'The Refutation of Idealism' 367–8
and Russell 345, 346–7
and scepticism 369
and Wittgenstein 371, 372
moral philosophy
  agape in Christian morality 544
  in Analytic tradition *see* Analytic
    philosophy: ethics/morality
  and Roger Bacon 160
  and Bradley 325
  and the categorical imperative
    264–5
  Christianity and the basis of morality
    182–3, 243
  consequentialist theory of morality *see*
    consequentialism
  deontology 265, 305–6, 453, 454,
    455, 456, 457
  dependence of morality on free will
    263–4, 265
  and distinction between ethics and
    morality xvii
  and divine-command morality 454
  and duty *see* duty
  and the Enlightenment 243
  ethics *see* ethics
  and T. H. Green 322
  and Hume *see* Hume, David: ethics
    and morality
  and innate moral sense 247
  and Kant *see* Kant, Immanuel: moral
    philosophy and ethics
  moral autonomy 255
  moral freedom 254–5
  moral intuition *see* intuition: moral
  moral law 254–5, 264, 265–6,
    267, 455
  moral perceptions 247
  moral will 265
  vs 'natural philosophy' xv
  nature vs convention 54–5
  Nietzsche *see* Nietzsche, Friedrich:
    ethics and morality

  rationalist morality and Hume's
    objection 247–8
  and reason (Kant) 263–8
  and religion as harmful to morality
    266, 268
  and Russell *see* Russell, Bertrand: and
    moral theory
  Schopenhauer 300–301
  and self-interest 247, 282
  Socrates and moral excellence 63–4
  superstition as enemy of true
    morality 216
  and *Ubuntu* 518, 580–81
  utilitarian theories *see* utilitarianism
  and virtue *see* virtue; virtue ethics
  and will *see* free will; will
More, Thomas 135
  Utopia 191–2
Morgan, Augustus De *see* De Morgan,
    Augustus
Morrell, Lady Ottoline 371
Motherby, R. 258
motion
  and atomism 49–50, 104–5
  eternal: Anaximenes 16–17;
    Epicurus 105
  paradoxes of 36–7, 38–9
  and Parmenides 32, 33
  and Pythagoreanism 34
  'rotary' (Anaxagoras) 46
  Zeno and the impossibility of 36–7
Mouton, Gabriel 234
Mozi 535, 542–5
Muhammad 513–14, 516, 517, 558
  prophecies of 569
  sayings (*hadith*) 564
Muhammad, Abdul-Walid 571
multiple generality 362
music
  consonant intervals 21–2, 23
  pitch 21–2
  Romantic 275
  and Rousseau 251
  and Schopenhauer 297, 300
  and the soul 20
  of the spheres 22, 23
  and transcendence of suffering
    297, 300
Musonius Rufus, Gaius 113
al-Mu'tasim 558, 560
al-Mutawakkil 559

Mu'tazilites 558–9
mysticism
    alphabet's mystical implications 174
    of Cabala see Cabala
    mystical experience as a source of
        knowledge 159
    Neoplatonism
        and theurgy 128, 129–30
    Neoplatonist influence on 130
    numerology 174
Mytilene 104

al-Nadim, Ibn 556, 557, 559
Nagarjuna 528
Nagel, Thomas 442
Nambikwara tribe 505
Napier, John 270
Naples 151, 153, 154
Napoleon I 287
Nasr, Seyyed Hossein 555n
nationalism
    fascist see Fascism
    and Nietzsche 316
    and Romanticism 275
natural law 56, 209, 224, 258, 264,
        271, 423, 437, 538
natural rights 209, 224, 283
naturalism 361
    'Naturalistic Fallacy' (Moore) 366, 446
    Quine 390
nature
    Francis Bacon on practical knowledge
        and natural history 199
    as a continuum 235, 236
    goodness as that which is in
        accordance with 111
    happiness through living in
        accordance with 54, 111
    Hobbes and 'law' and 'state' of
        56, 209
    human see human nature
    vs law/moral convention 54
    law of see natural law
    man as 'stepchild' of 179–80
    morality and the nature vs convention
        debate 54–5
    'occult sciences' and the control of
        195–6
    and principle of continuity 235, 236
    Romanticism and natural beauty 275
    scientific mastery over 277

Spinoza's equating with God
    212–14, 235
state of: and Bentham 283; in Daoism
    547n; and Hobbes 56, 209; and
    Locke 107, 224–5, 226; and
    'natural freedom' 224–5, 254; and
    Rousseau 107, 252, 254
and Tian 537–8, 543
Nausiphanes 104
Nazism
    and Arendt 510
    and Bergson 508
    and the Enlightenment 277
    and Gadamer 493
    and Heidegger 359, 476, 477–8,
        481–2, 510
    and Popper 395
    and Schlick's murder 385
    and Vienna Circle 380
Nearchus 35–6
Nelböck, Johann 385
Neleus 82
neo-Positivism see Logical Positivism
neo-pragmatism 333
Neoplatonism/Neoplatonists 10, 79,
        123–30
    and Augustine 130, 132
    and Averroes 153
    and Christianity 124, 129, 182
    and consciousness 128
    and Descartes 204
    doctrines 128–30
    emergence of movement 123–4
    ethics 129
    Ficino's Platonic Theology 172–3
    and Hermeticism 173–4
    and human nature 128–9
    and idealism 124, 128, 130
    influence 130; on Aquinas 130, 154
    and Judaism 127
    and the mind see mind, philosophy of:
        in Neoplatonism
    and Orphism 127
    and Platonic Forms 125
    and the primordial One 126, 128, 560
    and Pythagoras 20
    and rational enquiry 127–8
    relationship and divergence from
        Platonism 79, 124, 125–6
    religion derived from 124, 129–30
    and the soul 128–9

as theosophy 557
and theurgy 128, 129–30
Neopythagoreanism 126
Neptune, discovery of 399
Nero 113, 114
Neurath, Otto 378, 379, 380, 381
neurophilosophy (Churchland) 440
neuropsychology xx
neuroscience xx, 107, 204, 434,
    440, 441
New York Daily Tribune 309
Newton, Isaac 38, 218, 270, 584
    and the absolutes of space and time 162
    and calculus 234
    and gravitation 244
    influence on Enlightenment ideas 211
    and Leibniz 234
    Principia 198
Ney, Elisabet 301
Ngubane, Jordan Kush 580
Niccoli, Niccolò de' 178
Nicholas v, Pope 172
Nicholas of Cusa 135, 180
    and mathematics as the highest
        knowledge 174
Nicomachus 91
Nicopolis 113
Nietzsche, Elisabeth (later Elisabeth
    Förster-Nietzsche) 316
Nietzsche, Friedrich 54n, 279, 280,
    314–20
    and Andreas-Salomé 316
    The Antichrist 316, 318
    and art/aesthetics 319
    Beyond Good and Evil 316
    birth details 314
    The Birth of Tragedy 315, 319
    The Case of Wagner 316
    and Christianity: distortion of
        Western values by Judaeo-Christian
        moral thinking 317–18; 'God is
        dead' announcement 317–18;
        personal loss of faith 314
    and creativity 319
    Daybreak 316
    Ecce Homo 316, 319
    ethics and morality 317–20; autonomy
        and rejection of conventional
        morality 319; and 'eternal
        recurrence' 319, 502; need for
        'revaluation of all values' 318, 320;

and 'Superman' 54n, 319; Western
    values distorted by Judaeo-Christian
    moral thinking 317–18; and the will
    to overcome 318–19
family background 314
during Franco-Prussian war 315
and Gast 316
The Gay Science 316, 317–18, 319
The Genealogy of Morals 316, 318
and Heidegger 478
and Hölderlin 314
Human, All Too Human 316
madness at end of life 315, 317
Nietzsche contra Wagner 316
and nihilism 319–20
and Overbeck 315
and pain 319
and power 318–19
Prussian artillery service 315
and Ree 316
reputation twisted by sister
    Elisabeth 316
and Ritschl 314, 315
and Schmeitzner 316
and Schopenhauer 297, 318–19
syphilis conjecture 315
Thus Spake Zarathustra 314, 316–17
Twilight of the Idols 316
at University of Basle 315
Untimely Meditations 315
and the Wagners 314, 315, 316
The Will to Power 316
nihilism 319–20
Nkrumah, Kwame 577
nominalism
    Abelard 149
    Ockham 165
    vs realism 74–5, 166
    and universals 149, 207
non-cognitivism 367, 447–8, 450–51
Non-Contradiction, Law of 165n, 235,
    360–61, 587
nonconformists 285, 304
nonexistence 526
nous 45–6
    in Neoplatonism 128
Nozick, Robert 462–6
    Anarchy, State and Utopia 458, 462–3
    libertarianism 462–6
    and the minimalist state 464–6
    Philosophical Explanations 466

numbers 20–21
  and gender 22
  irrational 22–3
numerals 20–21
numerology 174
Nussbaum, Martha 470
Nyaya 521, 525–9
  epistemology 521
  and logic 521, 525, 528–9
  and Vaisheshika 521, 525–9
Nyayasutras 521, 528
Nyerere, Julius 577

Oakeshott, Michael 458
observation
  and Anaxagoras 46–7
  and Anaximenes 17–18
  and Francis Bacon 198, 199
  and empiricism see empiricism
  and induction 46–7, 198–9
  and protocol sentences 380–81
  and rise of science in 17th century
    198–9, 270
  and Thales 13, 199
  as 'theory-laden' 381, 387–8
Occam's Razor 164, 231
occasionalism 205
occultism 135, 161, 174, 195, 197–8
  and Roger Bacon 160–61
  and mathematics 174
  'occult sciences' 134, 170, 172, 173,
    195; alchemy see alchemy;
    astrology see astrology; Cabala see
    Cabala; Hermeticism see
    Hermeticism; magic see magic; and
    Pico 173, 174; and the Renaissance
    170, 172, 174
Ockham, William of 164–7
  commentary on Aristotle's
    Physics 165
  commentary on Lombard's
    Sentences 164
  excommunication 164
  and free will 166
  and logic 165
  and necessity of faith to grasp
    theological truths 164–5
  as a nominalist 165
  principle of not unnecessarily
    multiplying entities (Occam's
    Razor) 164, 231

and propositional knowledge 165
and Scotus 163
and separation of Church and state 166
via moderna 164
Ockhamists 166–7
Octavian 112
Odera Oruka, Henry 579
Oeconomics (pseudo-Aristotle) 178–9
Oedipus 144
Oenoanda 103
oligarchy 73
  Italian city-state oligarchies 186
ontological argument
  Anselm 146–8
  Augustine's anticipation of 141
  Descartes 204
  Gaunilo of Marmoutiers'
    repudiation 148
  Kant's repudiation 147
  and Leibniz 238
ontology see also Being
  dualistic 560 see also metaphysics;
    soul: immortal
  and Gadamer 494, 495
  and Heidegger 480, 494
  and hermeneutics 494–5
  Islamic 556
  of meant entities (Davidson) 420
  and Quine 390, 391
  Samkhya 521
  and Sartre 488
  and science 390 see also physicalism
  Vaisheshika 527
'ordinary language philosophy' (Oxford)
    405–17
  Austin 410–13
  and Moore 369
  Ryle 405, 406, 407–9
  Strawson 413–17
Origen of Alexandria 126n, 127, 154
Origen the Pagan 126n
original sin and Fall of Man 129,
    140, 181
  and Pietists 266
Orphism 20
  and Neoplatonism 127
  Orphic hymns 7, 8n
Otherness
  de Beauvoir 491–2
  Sartre 489–90
otium see leisure, 'noble' use of

Ottoman Empire 171
and fall of Constantinople 172
Overbeck, Franz 315
ownership 465
Oxford, 'ordinary language philosophy'
see 'ordinary language philosophy'

padarthas 526
paganism
and Christianity: basis of ethical
choice for pagans and Christians
182–3; Christian borrowings from
'pagan' philosophy 182; Christian
gangs in Alexandria 556n; Gay on
272; and Justinian's banning of
'pagan' philosophy 6, 78, 98, 131;
'pagan' books destroyed by
Christian zealots 3, 129, 556–7;
and the Renaissance 181–3
Enlightenment and modern
paganism 272
pain
avoidance of 104, 286, 533
and consciousness 444, 474
and Epicureanism 104, 106
and hedonism 306
and identity theories 435, 436
and laws 56
and the mind–body problem 205
and Nietzsche 319
and pleasure as criteria of value 283
and Strawson 415
and utilitarianism 281, 282, 286, 306
panspermia 45, 46
papacy 161–2n see also Vatican
papal court at Avignon 164
papal power 166, 171; Marsilius and
separation from secular/imperial
power 166, 186
paradoxes
of motion 36–7, 38–9
of Zeno see Zeno of Elea: paradoxes
parallelism 205
Parfit, Derek 470
Paris, son of Priam 55
Paris (city)
Aquinas in 152, 153, 154
Deleuze in 500
Derrida in 503–4
Ecole Normale Supérieure 482, 486,
503–4

Foundling Hospital 251
Hume in 241–2
Husserl's 'Paris Lectures' 482
international congress of mathematics
(1900) 348
Leibniz in 233
Marx in 308–9
Merleau-Ponty in 482–3
Nanterre University 497–8
Rousseau in 251
Sartre in 486
Schopenhauer in 298
Scotus in 161
Socialisme et Liberté underground
group 482, 486
University (Sorbonne) 133, 148, 153,
166, 173, 482, 483, 484, 486, 497,
500, 503
Paris X Nanterre 497–8
Parliamentary representation 285
Parmenides 7, 10, 31–5
and Ameinias 31
and Anaxagoras 44–5
and Anaximander 31
and Aristotle 31, 33
birth details 31
and Derveni Papyrus 8n
and Empedocles 40, 41
and Heidegger 479
and Heraclitus 31
and Leucippus 48
and motion 32, 33
and Plato/Platonism 35, 36, 126
poem of 31–3
and Pythagoreanism 31
and question of What Is 27, 32–4,
36, 44
and the senses as delusive 32, 41,
50, 68
and Socrates 31
theory of the One 27, 32–4,
36, 44
and Xenophanes 26, 31
Pascal, Blaise
influence of Sextus on 123
and Leibniz 233
Patanjali 521
Paul, St 181–2, 183, 517
Peacocke, Christopher 469
Peano, Giuseppe 336, 348, 357
Pears, David 449

Peirce, Charles Sanders 329
  fallibilist epistemology 330
  'How to Make our Ideas Clear'
    329–30
  'Metaphysical Club' 329
  pragmatism 328–30, 332, 333
Pell, John 234
Pella 83
Peloponnesian War 66
perception
  and Abelard 150
  Anaxagoras' theory of 46
  and Austin 410, 411
  and Roger Bacon's study of the eye
    and vision 160
  and beliefs 117
  Berkeley's theory of perceiver and
    227–30
  in Carvaka, as principal source of
    knowledge 522, 532–3
  and cognition: and Buddhism 528;
    and Carvaka 522, 532–3; in
    Nyaya–Vaisheshika 528
  delusive powers of 69 see also sensation:
    scepticism of sense-experience
  Dinnaga–Dharmakirti school 531
  Epicurus and sense-perception 105
  and existence 227–30, 367–8
  and Hume 244–5
  ideas as perceptions 244–5
  impressions as perceptions 244–5
  Leibniz, and 'apperceptions' 238
  Locke's theory of 220–21, 226
  and Merleau-Ponty 484, 485
  moral perceptions 247
  and the perceiver 227–30
  Presocratics' theories of 5
  in Samkhya 524–5
  'veil' of 220, 226
  Zeno of Citium on perceiving 111
Pericles 44, 60
Peripatetic school 26, 65, 81, 83
perlocutionary acts 412
Persia 24, 557–8
  and Anaxagoras 43–4
  Arabic–Persian philosophy see
    Arabic–Persian philosophy
  and battle of Salamis 43
  and Hegel 294
  and the Ionians 24, 43–4
  magi 120

Mani in 138
  Persian Empire 533, 555, 563
personhood 221–2 see also identity,
  personal; selfhood
'persuasive impressions' (Carneades)
  118–19
persuasiveness 118–19
Petrarch (Francesco Petrarca) 169,
  175, 179
  in Florence 176
  and humanism 175, 179, 186, 187
  and otium (graceful leisure for
    cultivation of arts) 187, 191
  De Remediis Utriusque Fortunae 179
  and the state 186, 187
Petri, Elfride 477
phenomenalism 353
  Austin's deconstruction 411–12
  and Ayer 353, 354
  and logical atomism 355–6
Phenomenological Thomism 157
phenomenology
  as bridge between realism and
    idealism 488
  in Continental philosophy see
    Continental philosophy:
    phenomenology
  and hermeneutics 498–9
  Husserl 474–6
  'phenomenological reduction' 489
  'phenomenological time' 499
  and physics 474
  and Ryle's logical behaviourism
    408–9
Philip of Macedon 83
Philo Judaeus 126
Philo of Larissa
  and the Academy 79, 119–20
  and hypothetical belief 119
Philodemus 103
philology 7
philosophy
  African see African philosophy
  aims: achieving the good life 52, 63,
    99, 249–50; determining realities of
    things 563–4; peace of mind
    see ataraxia; understanding the
    world 99
  Analytic see Analytic philosophy
  Arabic see Arabic–Persian philosophy
  Aristotelian see Aristotle

as belonging to world at large 250
Chinese *see* Chinese philosophy
Christian borrowings from 'pagan'
    philosophy 182
as a constructive endeavour
    (Deleuze) 503
Continental *see* Continental
    philosophy
diverging into *via antiqua* and *via
    moderna* 166–7
as education of the mind 107
of the Enlightenment *see*
    Enlightenment
expansion of academic studies in 20th
    century 336
feminist *see* feminist philosophy
and the Golden Age 200
Greek *see* Greek philosophy
of history *see* history, philosophy of
Indian *see* Indian philosophy
insights that prove elusive 389n
of language *see* language, philosophy of
meaning of word xv
as 'metaphysics' xv
moral *see* moral philosophy
natural xv, 158, 244 *see also* science
Neoplatonic *see* Neoplatonism/
    Neoplatonists
Persian *see* Arabic–Persian philosophy
Pittsburgh School of 433n
Platonic *see* Plato; Platonism;
    Socrates
'practical' 84, 179
principle areas of enquiry xv, 583 *see
    also* aesthetics; epistemology; ethics;
    language, philosophy of; logic;
    metaphysics; mind, philosophy of;
    moral philosophy; political
    philosophy
as pursuit of the truth 57
relationship to theology *see* theology:
    relationship to philosophy
Renaissance *see* Renaissance:
    philosophy
Roman *see* Cynics/Cynicism;
    Epicureanism; Neoplatonism/
    Neoplatonists; scepticism; Stoicism/
    Stoics
of science *see* science: philosophy of
science denoted by term 'philosophy'
    xv, 279

separation from 19th century into two
    strands 280
sophist *see* sophists
Stoic *see* Stoicism/Stoics
theoretical–practical divide (Aristotle)
    84–5
as therapy of the soul 107
timeline of philosophers 596–7
physicalism 390
    and Chalmers 443
    and consciousness 442–4
    and epiphenomalism 438–9
    and Nagel 442–3
    non-reductive 437–9
physics
    and Aristotle 84 *see also* Aristotle:
        Physics
    Francis Bacon's system of 197
    and Descartes 200
    Einstein's General Relativity
        theory 378
    and phenomenology 474
    and Russell 352
    and Schlick 378
    of Stoics 109–10
Pico della Mirandola, Giovanni 135,
    173–5
    900 Theses 173
    and dignity/near-divinity of man 180
    and Ficino 173
    and humanism 173, 174
    and Lorenzo de' Medici 173
    and mathematics 174
    and occultism 173, 174
    The Oration on the Dignity of Man
        173–4
    and Platonism 174
Pietism 257, 266
pineal gland 205
Pinsent, David 371
Pittsburgh School 433n
Pius x, Pope 157
Place, U. T. 434
Placita 6
Planck, Max 378
Plantinga, Alvin 148
Plato 65–79
    Academy *see* Platonic Academy
    agrapha dogmata (unwritten doctrine)
        speculation 77–8, 125, 126
    and Alexandria 557

Plato – *cont.*
and Anaxagoras 44
Apology 59, 60n
and aristocracy/meritocracy 72
and Aristotle *see* Aristotle: and Plato
and Athens 65–6
cave allegory 67–8, 69
Charmides 59, 60n
and Christianity 133, 183 *see also*
    Neoplatonism/Neoplatonists: and
    Christianity
and citizenship 53, 72
Cratylus 28
Crito 60n
and democracy 66, 73
dialectic 292–3 *see also* Socratic
    method
and Diogenes the Cynic 100, 101
early *aporetic* dialogues 62, 66
and education 71–2
and eugenics 71
Euthydemus 51
Euthyphro 60n
family background 65
Forms/Ideas 68–9, 74–6, 143; and
    Aristotle 88; Form of the Good 74,
    174, 183; later reduction to a 'One'
    and a 'Dyad' 126; and Mackie on
    objective values 451; and
    Neoplatonism 125; and theory of
    knowledge 77; and 'Third Man'
    problem 76
and Gadamer 493
Gorgias 54, 60n; Bruni's Latin
    translation 170
Greek of 81
and Heraclitus 28–9, 31
and Hippias 56
and humanism 183
influence on medieval philosophy 132
and justice *see* justice: and Plato
and knowledge: and Aristotle 88, 174;
    and correct/true belief 69, 77;
    differentiation of knowledge from
    beliefs 69; Forms and theory of
    knowledge 77; philosophical system
    and the acquiring of knowledge 67,
    68, 174; self-questioning of theory
    of knowledge 76–7; and Socratic
    method *see* Socratic method
Laches 60n, 61–2

Latin translations: Bruni 170;
    Ficino 172
lectures on the Good 78
and *logos* 77
Meno 60n, 61, 68, 77, 115
and Parmenides 35, 36, 126
Parmenides 35, 36, 59, 75, 143
Phaedo 60n, 69–70, 183
Phaedrus 44, 70
and philosopher-kings 66, 71–2, 73
philosophy as 'footnotes to' 67
Physics 77
Popper's branding as a 'historicist' 395
and Protagoras 52, 53–4
Protagoras 53, 54, 60n, 64
and Pythagoras 18
and Pythagoreanism 18
and rationalism 196
realism 75
realms of Being and Becoming
    68–9, 125
relativism 115
and the Renaissance 170
Republic 18, 70–74, 77, 115, 183;
    Allegory of the Cave 67–8, 69;
    and Averroes 571; and More's
    Utopia 191
and rhetoric 170
and Socrates *see also* Socrates: early
    dialogues throwing light on
    Socrates 60n; relationship as pupil
    and teacher 65; 'Socratic question'
    58, 59; works relating to trial and
    death of Socrates 59, 60n
and Socratic *aporia* 62, 66, 71, 77,
    80, 115
and the sophists 51, 52, 56, 57
and the soul 69–71, 183
summarizing Presocratic thinkers 5
and the supreme Good 183
Symposium 69, 183; and 'Platonic
    love' 173; theory of love 183
and Syracuse 66–7
and Thales 11
Theaetetus 11, 53, 76–7, 115
Timaeus 76, 115, 133, 174
'unforgetting' and theory of
    recollection 69
Whitehead on 67
and Xenophanes 26–7
and Zeno of Elea 35, 36

Platonic Academy 65, 78
  abolition under Justinian 6, 78, 98, 131, 557
  and Aenesidemus' *Pyrrhoneoi logoi* 121
  and Aristotle 81, 82
  Assos branch 82
  and Cicero 78
  Florence branch 172, 175, 177
  and Middle Platonism 127
  under Philo's leadership 79, 119–20
  under scepticism's influence 78–9, 98, 116, 120
  under Speusippus' leadership 78, 82, 126
  and Stoicism 108, 110–11, 116
  under Xenocrates' leadership 78, 126
  and Zeno of Citium 108, 116
Platonic love 173, 183
Platonism
  and the Academy *see* Platonic Academy
  and the Church Fathers 182
  development into Neoplatonism 79, 124, 125–6 *see also* Neoplatonism/ Neoplatonists
  Middle 79, 127
  and Parmenides 35, 36, 126
  and Pico 174
  of Plotinus 79, 125 *see also* Plotinus
  Renaissance 170–75
  Tübingen School of Platonic studies 77–8
pleasure
  beauty as highest 566
  and Bentham's 'felicific calculus' 286, 306
  and Epicureanism 104, 105, 106, 176
  and friendship 107
  and hedonism 282, 306, 532
  Mill's view of higher and lower pleasures 306
  and pain as criteria of value 283
  and power 215
  and Renaissance art 181
  utility, pain and 281
Plethon (George Gemistos) 171–2
  De differentiis Aristotelis et Platonis 172
Plotinus 77, 79, 124–5, 127
  birth details 125

Enneads 125, 127
  Ficino's translation 172
  and al-Kindi 560
  and Merleau-Ponty 482
  and Porphyry 125, 127–8
  and the primordial One 126, 560
pluralism
  and atomism 50
  Bradley's rejection of 323, 325
  McTaggart's pluralistic and relational view of the Absolute 326
  and Moore 347
  and Russell 347, 355
  Samkhya 521
Plutarch 83, 116
  and Anaximander 15
  Moralia 6
  translations of: Poliziano 177; Veronese 177
plutocracy 73
pneuma 109–10
political philosophy
  in Analytic tradition *see* Analytic philosophy: political
  and anarchy *see* anarchy
  Aristotle's practical philosophy *see* Aristotle: and politics
  Bentham 284–5
  Confucian order and 542
  democracy *see* democracy
  ethics as continuous with 84, 94–5, 178–9, 583
  and al-Farabi 562
  and franchise *see* franchise
  government *see* government
  T. H. Green 322
  Hegel 288, 295–6
  Heraclitus and rule of law 30
  Hobbes *see* Hobbes, Thomas: political philosophy
  just war theory *see* just war theory
  and justice *see* justice
  liberalism *see* liberalism, political
  Locke *see* Locke, John: political philosophy
  Marx *see* Marx, Karl: political philosophy
  meaning, summarized xviii
  Plato's *Republic* 72–3 *see also* Plato: *Republic*
  and 'political science' 186

political philosophy – *cont.*
  political thinking in an African
    context 577
  'politics' as study of the state (*polis*)
    84 *see also* state
  qualities for rulership *see* rulership
    qualities
  and Renaissance thought 185–92;
    and humanism 178, 186, 187,
    188, 189
  Rousseau *see* Rousseau, Jean-Jacques:
    political theory
  and social contracts *see* social
    contracts
  Spinoza 216–17
  and the state *see* state
  turmoil as catalyst for writing 458
political science 186, 458
Poliziano/Politian (Angelo
    Ambrogini) 175
  and the Academy 177
  Latin translations by 176–7
  as Lorenzo de' Medici's children's
    tutor 177
Polycrates 19
Polyzoides, Anastasios 284
Pontifical University of St Thomas
    Aquinas 157–8
Pope, Alexander 258
Popper, Karl 395–9
  in Austrian Social Democratic
    Party 396
  awards 396
  birth details 395, 396
  education 396
  and falsificationism 397–9
  family background 396
  and Hegel 295, 395
  and 'historicists' 395
  and Lakatos 399, 400
  and liberalism 395, 396; defence of
    liberal democracy 395
  *The Logic of Scientific
    Discovery* 396
  at London School of Economics 396
  and Marxism 396
  The Open Society and its Enemies
    395, 458
  and philosophy of science 395; and
    distinction between logic and
    psychology of scientific discovery

    398; and falsificationism 397–9;
    and verisimilitude of good scientific
    theories 398
  and politics 395, 396
  and verificationism 396–9
  and Vienna Circle 379, 385,
    395
Porphyry 125, 126, 127–8
  and Boethius 142
  commentary on Euclid 127
  and the *Enneads* of Plotinus 125, 127
  Ficino's translation 172
  Isagoge 142, 143, 561; and
    Averroes 571
  Life of Pythagoras 20
  as a Neoplatonic leader 127–8
  and universals 143
Positivism 302–3
  analytic–synthetic distinction 380–81,
    386; Quine's attack on 386, 388,
    392–4
  and Carnap *see* Carnap, Rudolf
  Comtean 297, 302–3; vs Vienna
    Circle's Positivism 302, 377–8
  and Hume 380
  Legal Positivism 283, 302
  Logical *see* Logical Positivism
  of Mach 378
  and verification *see* verification/
    verificationism
  of Vienna Circle *see* Logical Positivism
postmodernism
  and Continental philosophy 337, 511
  and neo-pragmatism 333
power
  divine power reflected in man's
    creativity and imagination 180
  and the Enlightenment 272; economic
    power 277; political power 277
  equated with virtue (Spinoza) 215
  Foucault and 'power-knowledge' 510
  and happiness 318
  and Hobbes: and liberty 210;
    sovereign power 207–9, 210, 544
  of ideas 278
  legislative 225 *see also* government
  and Nietzsche 318–19
  papal power 166, 171; Marsilius and
    separation from secular/imperial
    power 166, 186
  and pleasure 215

Shen Dao and the exercise of 551
trusteeship of 225–6
pragmatism 328–33
American pragmatists 279, 280, 333
Dewey 329, 331–3
exclusion of scepticism as starting
point for enquiry 332
and fallibilism 330, 332
and instrumentalism 332
James 328–9, 330–31, 332
and Mackie 453
'neo-pragmatism' 333
Peirce 328–30, 332, 333
Prague 379, 389
Charles University 386–7
prakriti (matter, Samkhya) 521,
524, 525
pramanas (forms of cognition) 528
predestination 140–41
Presocratic philosophy/philosophers
9–57
arche see arche (principle of the
cosmos)
atomists see atomism/atomists
and cosmology see cosmology:
Presocratic
Cynic see Cynics/Cynicism
Eleatic see Eleatic school of
philosophy
Epicurean see Epicureanism
fragments 5, 7
Ionian see Ionian philosophers
and the nature and source of the
world see arche; cosmology:
Presocratic
Peripatetic school 26, 65, 81, 83
sophists see sophists
and the soul see soul: Presocratic
notions
Stoic see Stoicism/Stoics
testimonia 5, 7
Pressburg, Henriette 307
primary qualities 220, 231
printing press 178, 195
Proclus 6, 127, 128–9
as head of Academy 128
Prodicus 55–6
propositions
'analytic' (Leibniz) 236, 237
and Aristotle 85–7
'atomic' 355–6

'elementary' 374–5
foundational 111
'general' 355
inferred 198
in Nyaya 528–9
Ockham and propositional
knowledge 165
propositional attitudes 364
and Quine's scepticism about meaning
394–5
and Russell 355–6
and Stoicism 110, 111
synthetic 236, 348–9, 354
tautological see tautology
and verification see verification/
verificationism
and Wittgenstein 373–7
'Prosperity Gospel' 130n
Protagoras 10, 52–3
and art 53
and justice 53
and man as the measure of
all things 55
and Plato 52, 53–4
relativism 53
Truth 53
Protestantism
Calvinism 181, 195
conflicts with Catholicism 233
and Husserl 473
Lutheran see Lutheranism
Pietism 257, 266
Reformation see Reformation
rejection of philosophy as means of
ethical insight 183
and use of pagan philosophical
ethics 183
The Whole Duty of Man (tract) 249
protocol sentences 380–81
Proxenus 82
pseudo-Plutarch 52
psychoanalytic theory 337
psychologism 360–61, 473
psychology
Aristotle 89–90
behaviourism's demise in 434
neuropsychology xx
and philosophy xx
scientific approaches to 433
Ptolemy, Claudius 95, 557
public expenditure 285

purusha (consciousness, Samkhya) 521, 524, 525
Purva Mimamsa 521, 522
Putnam, Hilary 333, 336, 429
Pyrrho of Elis 120–21
   and Indian philosophy 120, 121, 532
Pyrrhonism 116, 120–23
   Aenesidemus' *Pyrrhoneoi logoi* 121–2
   and Empiric medical school 122–3
   and Indian philosophy 120, 121, 532
Pythagoras 10, 18–24
   birth details 18–19
   and Neoplatonists 20
   and Plato 18
   and Xenophanes 18, 26
Pythagoras' theorem 21–2
'Pythagorean system' (Copernicus) 200
Pythagoreanism 18, 19–20
   and Empedocles 40, 42
   and harmony 22, 23–4
   and irrational numbers 22–3
   and mathematics 18, 20–23
   and metempsychosis 18, 19, 26, 40, 42
   and motion 34
   and musical pitch 21–2
   Neopythagoreanism 126
   and Parmenides 31
   Pythagoras' theorem 21–2
   and vegetarianism 19, 40
   and Zeno of Elea 37–8
Pythias 82

Qin Shi Huangdi 515–16, 549, 550
qualia 435, 443–4
qualities of things
   and Berkeley 228, 229, 230
   and Bradley 324
   as *gunas* 524
   and Locke 220
   in Nyaya 526
   primary 220, 231
   and Russell 355, 356
   secondary 220, 231
   and unity of opposites 29
   universals *see* universals
quantifiers 362, 391, 590–91
Queneau, Raymond 508
Quincey, Thomas De 259n
Quine, W. V. 335, 385, 388–95
   attack on analytic–synthetic distinction 386, 388, 392–4

birth details 388
and Carnap 386, 387, 389–90, 393
and Davidson 419–20
and Dreben 389n
and empiricism 392
extensionalism 390–91, 392, 418
fallibilist epistemology 390
From a Logical Point of View 392n
holism 393–4, 399
and identity criteria 391–2
and indeterminacy of meaning 422;
   'indeterminacy of translation' 394
influences on 389
linguistic behaviourism 394–5
'The Logic of Sequences: A Generalisation of *Principia Mathematica*' 389
naturalism 390
and reductionism 392, 394
scepticism about meaning 394–5
and sets 390
stimulus conditions/meaning 394–5, 418, 422
and Strawson 416
and 'theory-laden' nature of observation 381
'Two Dogmas of Empiricism' 392
and Vienna Circle 377, 389
and Whitehead 389
Word and Object 394–5, 440;
   furthering move towards systematic philosophy of language 419
quodlibetical disputation 134, 152
Qur'an 555, 559, 561, 564, 569–70, 571–2

racism 423
   racist language 594
   and Romanticism 275
Radaković, Theodor 379
Ramayana 523
Ramsey, Frank 339
rationalism 196–7
   as advocacy of use of reason 274n, 275–6
   and the Cambridge Platonists 218, 219
   and empiricism 196–7, 259–62
   and innate ideas 219
   instrumental 277

and logic 196
and mathematics 196
of Mu'tazilites 558–9
and Plato 196
and *a priori* knowledge 259–60,
274n
rationalist morality and Hume's
objection 247–8
Voltaire's attack on excessive
rationalist optimism 276
rationality *see* reason/rationality
Ravel, Maurice 370
Ravens, Paradox of the 383–4
Rawls, Anna Abell Stump 458–9
Rawls, John 457–62, 467
birth details 458
family background 458–9
and justice 460–61, 465–6
and Nozick 463
and the 'original position' 460,
461, 462
and 'reflective equilibrium' 459
and social contracts 460, 462
A Theory of Justice 458
and utilitarianism 461
realism
and Abelard 149
and Berkeley 229–30
Bradley's rejection of 323
and Chinese Legalism 551
and Dummett 423–4
and intuition 446
in mathematics 424
and Moore 347, 368–9
vs nominalism 74–5, 166
Nyaya 521
phenomenology as bridge between
idealism and 488
and Plato 75
and Russell 347, 355
and the Schoolmen 74–5
about universals 149, 163, 340
Vaisheshika's realist cosmology 527
reality *see also* Being; truth
access to noumenal 262, 292, 299–300
Bradley and 'the Absolute' 323
as Brahman in Indian thought *see*
Brahman
and causality 124
as central concern of philosophy 583
as a community of minds 328

dualistic views of *see* dualism
emanationist views of *see*
emanationism
epistemology and the nature of 583
see also epistemology
as formless, unstable and
indeterminate 121
idealist views of *see* idealism
and illusion in Indian philosophy
120n, 121, 522
and immanence (Deleuze) 502
and Indian soteriology 519, 525
and indistinguishability of things 121
James, and truth as 'agreement'
between ideas and 330–31
knowledge of reality/the Absolute
(Hegel) 290, 291–2
and Leibniz's monads 236–8
and logocentricism 504
and materialism *see* materialism
mind as basis of *see* idealism
monistic/non-dualist views of *see*
monism
and necessary being 165, 213, 239,
565, 566
noumenal: and Kant 262, 292, 299;
and Schopenhauer 299–300, 318;
and will 299–300
and Plato: Allegory of the Cave 67–8,
69; Forms *see* Plato: Forms/Ideas;
philosophical system 67; and
realms of Being and Becoming
68–9, 125
pluralistic views of *see* pluralism
Presocratic question of What Is, and
distinction between appearance and
reality 35, 39; Anaxagoras 44–6,
47; and atomism 48–9, 50; and
Heraclitus' flux 28–9, 115;
Parmenides 27, 32–4, 36, 44
Pyrrho's view 121
and sophist double-sided argument
115
as spiritual and timeless
(McTaggart) 326
ultimate reality as mental
(Hegel) 292
and unknowability of world in itself
(Kant) 262, 292, 299
world of perception as a virtual-
reality construction 444

reason/rationality 259–63
  action in conformity with the
    reasonable (*eulogon*) 117
  Apollonian 319
  a priori reasoning 46–7, 199, 259–62,
    329, 354, 384, 501; and verification
    principle 384
  and Aristotle 61, 81, 94, 455
  as armament of ideas 275
  and Avicenna 564–5
  as basis of ethics 61, 182, 183
  capacity to know God's nature
    through 162
  chain of reasoning (Descartes) 201
  circular reasoning 594
  and deductive logic 585–6
  and Empedocles 41–2
  emphasized over feeling 319
  and the Enlightenment 271, 275–6
  and epistemology (Kant) 259–63
  fallacious reasoning 85
  free use of 216–17, 270
  and Heraclitus 30
  and Hume 247, 276
  incapacity of grasping theological
    truths 164–5
  inductive reasoning *see* induction
  'instrumental rationality' and
    'bureaucratic politics' 277
  and justice 56
  and Kant *see* Kant, Immanuel: and
    reason
  and the life of contemplation
    (Aristotle) 94
  logic *see* logic
  logos see *logos*
  MacIntyre and secular rationality 456
  and morality (Kant) 263–8
  Neoplatonism and rational enquiry
    127–8
  primacy of emotion over reason in
    Romanticism 274
  principle of sufficient reason 235,
    238–9
  probabilistic reasoning 85
  rationalism as advocacy of use of
    274n, 275–6
  vs relativism 275
  vs revelation 162, 275, 568, 569–70
  and rise of science in 17th century
    198–9, 270

  scientific rationality 276–7
  as 'slave of the passions' (Hume) 247
  and the soul *see* soul: and rationality
  in tension with faith 154
  and Thales 13, 199
  will and 'pure' reason (Kant) 263–4
recollection, theory of 69
rectification of names
    (Confucianism) 541
reductio ad absurdum 36, 166, 240
reductionism/reductivism 274, 275, 321,
    374, 377, 442, 511
  'phenomenological reduction' 489
  and Quine 392, 394
Rée, Paul 316
reference
  Quine and the 'inscrutability' of 394
  and reidentification 415
  sense–reference distinction 363, 364,
    367, 419
  theories of 428–31; causal 429, 431;
    Donnellan 428–9; Frege *see* Frege,
    Gottlob: and reference; Kripke
    429–31; Mill 431n; Putnam 429;
    rigid designation 429–31; Russell
    428, 429; Strawson 413–14,
    416–17, 429
'reflective equilibrium' (Rawls) 459
Reformation 183
  and Hegel 294–5
  and release of philosophy from
    theological orthodoxy 195
  and rise of modern thought 195
  trigger/birth 134–5, 195
Reichenbach, Hans 379, 386
reidentification 415
reincarnation 18, 514
  Pythagorean metempsychosis 18, 19,
    26, 40, 42
  and Vedanta 522
  and wheel of rebirth 20
relativism
  and competing paradigms 400
  Plato 115
  Protagoras 53
  vs reason 275
religion
  Buddhist *see* Buddhism
  Christian *see* Christianity and the
    Church; Protestantism; Roman
    Catholicism

'civic' 255–6
Eastern philosophies transformed into
  religions 130
and the Enlightenment 270–71, 272
and God *see* God
as harmful to morality (Kant) 266,
  268
Hindu *see* Hinduism
Marx on 311–12
Muslim *see* Islam
mysticism *see* mysticism
Neoplatonism
  as a religion 124, 129–30
religious duties 568
religious freedom 285–6
theology *see* theology
Wittgenstein's placement outside
  realm of the discussable 374–6
Xenophanes' rejection of 25
Zoroastrian *see* Zoroastrianism
Renaissance
  art 168–9, 181
  dates 134
  humanism *see* humanism: Renaissance
  and Italian city states 185, 186,
    187–8
  'occult sciences' 170, 172, 174
  and paganism 181–3
  philosophy 168–92; Epicureanism
    184; ethics 178–84; humanism *see*
    humanism: Renaissance; Platonism
    170–75; political *see* political
    philosophy: and Renaissance
    thought; Stoicism 184
  and rhetoric 169–70, 178
republicanism
  Aristotle and small republican
    polities 83
  and Hobbes 207, 210, 224
  and Italian city states 185, 187, 188
  republican liberty 176, 209–10
  Roman 176
Reuchlin, Johann 174
revelation
  divine general revelation 159
  Qur'anic 555
  vs reason 162, 275, 568, 569–70
Revue de Métaphysique et de Morale
  509
Rgveda 519, 520
Rheinische Zeitung 308

rhetoric
  and Antiphon 56
  Aristotle's works on 28, 81, 84–5,
    169, 170, 561
  and Roger Bacon 159, 160
  Cicero on 81, 169
  and ethics 169
  and Ficino 169
  and Gorgias 55
  and Plato 170
  and the Renaissance 169–70, 178
  and the sophists 51, 52
  theory of 169
  and *vita activa* 170
  and Zeno of Elea 43
Riccio, Paolo 174
Richelieu, Cardinal 318n
Ricoeur, Paul 471, 497–9
  and Derrida 503
  ethical metaphysics 498, 499
  Fallible Man 497
  family background 497
  Freud and Philosophy 497
  and hermeneutics 497, 498–9
  Husserl's *Ideas I* translation 497
  and Jaspers 497
  Oneself as Another 499
  The Symbolism of Evil 497
  and time 499
Rigveda *see* Rgveda
Rishis 520
Ritschl, Friedrich 314, 315
River Forest Thomism 157
Roman Catholicism
  and Bentham 284
  conflicts with Protestantism 233
  and cosmology 96
  and Descartes 157
  Index of Forbidden Books 157
  Jesuits *see* Jesuits
  monasticism *see* monasticism
  papacy *see* papacy
  Thomistic doctrine *see* Thomism
  and Trent 154
  Vatican *see* Vatican
Roman Empire
  and Augustine on 'just war' 138
  'barbarian' invasions and collapse of 3–4
  Christianity becomes official religion
    of 3, 98, 137, 182
  of East *see* Byzantium

Roman philosophy *see* Cicero; Cynics/
  Cynicism; Epicureanism;
  Neoplatonism/Neoplatonists;
  scepticism; Seneca; Stoicism/Stoics
Romanticism
  and the Enlightenment 273, 274–5
  and nationalism 275
  and primacy of emotion over
    reason 274
  and racism 275
  Romantic music 275
  and superstition 275
Rome
  Aquinas in 152
  Carneades in 118
  as a centre of philosophy 10
  liberated from tyranny of kings 187
  and Pico's *900 Theses* challenge 173
  Plotinus in 125
  republicanism 176
Romulus Augustulus 142
Rooke, Lawrence 270
Rorty, Richard 333, 470
Ross, David 446
Rousseau, Jean-Jacques 250–56
  birth details 250, 251
  and botany 253
  and 'civic religion' 255–6
  and civil society 251–2, 254–5
  Confessions 253
  and d'Alembert 252–3
  Daydreams of a Solitary Walker 253
  death 253
  and d'Holbach 252–3
  and Diderot 251, 252–3
  Discourse on Inequality 251–2, 253
  Discourse on Political Economy 253
  and education 250, 252
  Emile, or On Education 250, 252–3,
    255–6
  and *Encyclopédie* 273
  essay for Académie de Dijon 251
  and evolution of society 107
  and Frederick the Great 253, 256
  and Hume 253
  Julie, ou La Nouvelle Héloïse
    252, 253
  and Kant 258
  and Thérèse Levasseur 251, 253
  and music 251
  in Paris 251

  political theory 253–5; and 'the
    general will' 253–4, 255; and
    inequality 253; and representative
    democracy 255
  and property 251–2
  The Social Contract 252–6
  and state of nature 107, 252, 254
  theory of human nature 252
  Unitarianism 252
  and Voltaire 253
  on women 256
Royal Society, London 197, 218–19
Royce, Josiah 320
rulership qualities
  cold-blooded cruelty condemned by
    Machiavelli 189
  of control, in Chinese Legalism
    550–51
  divine appointment 185
  effortlessness/seeming to 'do nothing'
    547, 549
  generosity 187
  incorruptibility 71
  of the just ruler 187
  Machiavelli on a prince's qualities
    189–90
  of philosopher-kings 66, 71
  ruthlessness when needed 189–90, 191
  virtuous expertise (in epistocracy) 72
  virtus 186–7, 189
  wisdom 71
Russell, Bertrand 257, 335, 339,
    344–57, 418
  'An Analysis of Mathematical
    Reasoning' 347
  The Analysis of Matter 354
  The Analysis of Mind 354
  anti-war activities 344, 345
  awards 345
  and Bradley 323
  'On Denoting' 348, 414
  and empiricism 351–2
  and epistemology 352–5
  On the Foundations of Geometry 347
  and Frege 348–9, 357, 359
  *Fundamental Ideas and Axioms of
    Mathematics* 347
  and George VI 345, 357
  German Social Democracy 348
  History of Western Philosophy xi
  Human Knowledge 352, 354

influence of Cambridge philosophy
dons 345–6
influence on Quine 389
and James 331
'Lectures on Logical Atomism' 355
Leibniz study 345, 347
life of controversy 345
and logic 339, 347; ambition
for a 'logically perfect language'
355–6, 405–6, 418; of Aristotle
85; and bivalence 342–3; logical
analysis of language 347; logical
atomism 355–6; logical
construction 348, 352, 386;
logicism 160, 348, 349, 380;
notation for formal logic 342,
586; and Theory of Descriptions
341–4, 355
Marriage and Morals 345
and mathematics 347–51; logicism
160, 348, 349, 380
and McTaggart 326, 346
and Mill 307, 345
and Moore 345, 346–7
and moral theory 356–7; and
emotivism 356, 446; and *Marriage
and Morals* 345
*Our Knowledge of the External
World* 354, 357
and paradox of concept of classes
349–50
peace and disarmament
campaigning 344
and pluralism 347, 355
Principia Mathematica (with
Whitehead) 67, 347, 350–51
The Principles of Mathematics (1903)
346, 347, 348, 349
Problems of Philosophy 352, 355
and reference 428, 429
and science 346, 347, 351–2
Theory of Descriptions 341–4,
355; Strawson's critique
413–14
Theory of Types 350
and Wittgenstein 371, 372, 374
and women's franchise 344
Russell, Frances Anna Maria,
Countess 345
Russell, Frank 349
Rye House plot 218

Ryle, Gilbert
and category mistakes 408
The Concept of Mind 407–9
and 'myth of the ghost in the machine'
407–8
and 'ordinary language philosophy'
405, 406, 407–9
phenomenology/logical behaviourism
408–9
Plato's Progress 66n
'Ryle's Regress' 409

Sadra, Mulla 567
St Clair, James 241
Sakya people 515
Salamis, battle of 43, 294
Salomé, Lou Andreas- 316
Salutati, Coluccio 175, 176
and Christian vs pagan moral
philosophy 182
and Cicero 176
recovery of lost manuscripts 176
De Tyranno 176
Samaveda 519
Samkhya 521, 524–5
and causation 525
and dualism 521, 524, 525
epistemology 524–5
metaphysics 525
soteriology 525
Samos 18–19, 103, 104
Santander, Francisco 284
Santayana, George 297
and Sprigge 328
Sarbah, John 577
Sartre, Jean-Paul 257, 336, 471, 482,
485–91, 492
and alienation 489, 490, 491
and authenticity 490
and de Beauvoir 482, 486, 487–8, 491–2
Being and Nothingness 486,
488–9, 491
birth details 485, 486
and Camus 487, 491
and consciousness 489–90, 491
Critique of Dialectical Reason 486
death and funeral 487
existentialism 476, 490–91, 492
Existentialism and Humanism
486, 490
The Family Idiot 492

Sartre, Jean-Paul – *cont.*
The Flies 486
and Hegel 491
and Heidegger 488
and Husserl 488
and Kojève 509
and *Les Temps Modernes* 482–3,
486–7
and love 489–90, 491
and Marxism 486
and Merleau-Ponty 482–3
No Exit 486, 489
and the Other 489–90
and phenomenology 488–91
political activity 487
during Second World War 486
Sarvasiddhanta Samgraha 533
satire 25, 26, 59, 269, 276
Savonarola, Girolamo 188
Scanlon, Thomas 'Tim' 470
Scepsis 82
scepticism 115–23
about existence of other minds, and
Strawson 415
and *aporia* 115
and Arcesilaus 78, 116–18
and Aristotle 115–16
Berkeley's examinations and
refutations of 227–9
Cartesian methodological scepticism
201–4
'dignity of man' and Montaigne's
rational scepticism 181
epistemological 227
excluded, as starting point for
enquiry, by pragmatism 332
and happiness 118
and impossibility of knowledge 118,
119, 120, 122
Mackie's 'moral scepticism' 450–53
and Merleau-Ponty 483
Moore's refutations 369
and persuasiveness 118–19
Plato's Academy under influence of
78–9, 98, 116, 120
of Pyrrhonian school 116, 120–23,
532
of Quine about meaning 394–5
reidentification refutation 415
and sense-experience *see* sensation:
scepticism of sense-experience

and Sextus Empiricus 116, 119,
122–3
and suspension of judgment 120
theological (Berkeley) 227
and theological literature 131–2
Schelling, Friedrich 287, 288–9
Schlegel, August 298
Schlegel, Friedrich 298
Schleiermacher, Friedrich 298
Schlick, Moritz 361, 378–9, 380, 381,
382, 386
murder 385
and Quine 389
and Schlick Circle (nucleus of Vienna
Circle) 379
*Space and Time in Contemporary
Physics* 378
and verification 382
and Wittgenstein 400
Schmeitzner, Ernest 316
Scholasticism and the Schoolmen xxi,
74–5, 187, 417, 567
and Abelard 149–50
and Anselm 146
and Aristotle 570, 571
and Averroes 570–71, 573
and Avicenna 566–7
Francis Bacon's rejection of
Scholasticism 196
Descartes' rejection of Scholasticism
196
Hume on effects on philosophy 250
Luther's attack on Scholastic use of
Aristotle's ethics 183
and realist–nominalist debate
74–5
Scholastic Thomism 157
and Scotus 161, 162
Schönborn, Johann Philipp von, Elector
of Mainz 233
Schoolmen *see* Scholasticism and the
Schoolmen
Schopenhauer,
Arthur 279, 280, 297–302
access to noumenal reality 299–300
birth details 297
and Darwin 301
ethics 300–301; and compassion 301;
and suffering 300–301
and eugenics 301
family background 297, 298

Fourfold Root of the Principle of Sufficient Reason 298
and Goethe 298
and Hegel 298–9
and Indian philosophy 297; Buddhism 300; Upanishads 300
influence 297, 301
and Kant 297, 299, 301
and Klopstock 300
and Majer 300
and music 297, 300
and Nietzsche 297, 318–19
in Paris 298
and suffering 297, 300–301
and will as noumenal reality 299–300, 318
and women 301
The World as Will and Representation 298, 300, 301, 314
Schopenhauer, Heinrich Floris 297–8
Schopenhauer, Johanna 297, 298
Schrödinger, Erwin 297
science
and activity of 'infinite spirit' in Berkeley's instrumentalism 231
and Francis Bacon *see* Bacon, Francis: and science
and Berkeley 231
birth of natural sciences xx, 584
birth of social sciences 584
Carnap and language of scientific theories 387–8
cognitive xx, 584
conferences for the Epistemology of the Exact Sciences 379, 380
cooperation in 197–8
denoted by term 'philosophy' xv, 279
distinction between logic and psychology of scientific discovery 398
and empiricism 196 *see also* empiricism
and the Enlightenment 271, 274, 277, 278
freedom, and human progress through 266
idealism as reaction to dominance of 'scientific analysis' 321
and instrumentalism *see* instrumentalism

and Logical Positivism *see* Logical Positivism: and science
and materialism 230–31
and Mill's *System of Logic* 305
as 'natural philosophy' xv, 158, 244
neuroscience xx, 107, 204, 434, 440, 441
and ontology 390 *see also* physicalism
paradigms: paradigm shifts 399–400, 509; relativism and competing paradigms 400
philosophy of xix; instrumentalism *see* instrumentalism; and Popper *see* Popper, Karl: and philosophy of science; and verisimilitude of good scientific theories 398; and Vienna Circle 302, 378
physics *see* physics
political 186, 458
and *a posteriori* investigation 260
of Presocratics, discussed by Theophrastus 5
and *a priori* knowledge/reasoning 329, 354, 384
rise in 17th century 198–9, 200n, 270, 278
and Russell 351–2; scheme for an idealist 'encyclopaedia of all sciences' 346, 347
scientific approaches to psychology 433
scientific mastery over nature 277
scientific method 198–9, 458, 496
scientific rationality 276–7
and truth 214
Wittgenstein and the natural sciences 374
Scotism 166 *see also* Duns Scotus, John
Scotus, John Duns *see* Duns Scotus, John
Searle, John
functionalism and Chinese Room argument 437
Speech Acts 412
secondary qualities 220, 231
Secret of Secrets 159
self-awareness/-consciousness/-knowledge 180–81
and conatus 215
and dialectical journey of Geist 289–94

self-awareness/-consciousness/
-knowledge – *cont.*
  discovery of the self (Ricoeur) 498–9
  and Epictetus 113
  'Know thyself' injunction: Pythian
    Apollo 180, 294; Thales 13
  political self-awareness of colonized
    Africa 577
  in Samkhya 525
  and Sartre 490
  and Socrates 59, 294
  of Tirthankaras in Jainism 523
self-interest 247
  'enlightened' 282
self-mastery 108, 113
self-preservation
  right of 225
  and Spinoza 214–15
  of subjects as constraint on
    sovereign 209
self-realization 322, 325
  discovery of the self (Ricoeur)
    498–9
  and al-Ghazali 570
self-sufficiency (*autarkeia*) 102
selfhood *see also* identity, personal;
    personhood
  ahamkara (ego) 524, 525
  Atman *see* Atman
  denied by Buddhists 522, 529–30
  'egoity' in Samkhya 524
  purusha as True Self 525
  Ricoeur 498–9
  soul *see* soul
  Vaisheshika and the Self 526
Selinus, Sicily 40
Sellars, Wilfred 433, 469
semantics
  and Abelard 149–50
  and Frege 419, 426
  and Kripke 395
  principle that all truth is analytic 235
semiotics
  and Roger Bacon 159
  and Locke 219
Seneca the Younger 109, 113
  and Roger Bacon 160
  Renaissance admiration for 182
  and Stoicism 114
sensation
  and Hobbes 207

  and Locke 220
  scepticism of sense-experience: and
    Arcesilaus 117; and Francis Bacon
    199; and Carneades 118; and
    Descartes 202–3; and Empedocles
    41–2; and Parmenides 32, 41, 50, 68
  sense-experience as foundation of
    knowledge 352
  and the soul 89
  Spinoza's relegation of sensory
    experience to level of opinion 214
sense-data 158, 260–61, 352, 353–4,
    355, 356, 368–9, 411, 412
  and sensory intuition 263
sensory ideas 220
sensory knowledge *see* knowledge:
    sensory
sensory modalities 122, 263, 475
sentimentalism 243–8
Septuagint 127
Serapion of Alexandria 122
Seth, Andrew (later Seth Pringle-
    Pattison), (ed.): *Essays in
    Philosophical Criticism* 321
sets
  existence of 390, 424
  and Quine 390
  realist treatment of 390, 424, 426
sex
  homosexuality 301; gay rights 501
  sexual desire 301
  and will 301
sexism 477n, 487–8
  sexist language 594
Sextus Empiricus 6, 116
  influence through Latin translations
    123
  Against the Mathematicians 122
  Outlines of Pyrrhonism 122
  and scepticism 116, 122–3; and
    persuasiveness 119
Shaftesbury, Anthony Ashley Cooper,
    1st Earl of 217–18
Shaftesbury, Anthony Ashley Cooper,
    3rd Earl of 247
Shakespeare, William 4
  Hamlet 29, 55, 114, 343
  King Lear xv
Shang Yang 550, 552
Shankaracharya, Adi 522
Shaw, George Bernard 537

Shelburne, William Petty, 1st Marquess of Lansdowne and 2nd Earl of 282
Shelley, Percy Bysshe: 'Ozymandias' 512
Shen Dao 551
Shi'a Islam *see* Islam: Shi'a school
Shiva 526
Siena 188
Siger of Brabant 133
Silhon, Jean de: *The Two Truths* 206
Sima Qian 534, 549
   Records of the Grand Historian (Shiji) 534, 546
Simplicius 7
  and Anaxagoras 44
  and Anaximander 15
  and Anaximenes 16–17
  and atomism 49
  and Democritus 49
  and Xenophanes 26
Singer, Peter 470
Sinope 100
Skinner, Quenten 209–10
Slippery-Slope Fallacy 593
Smart, J. J. C. 434, 435
social contracts 71, 224, 283, 460, 462
  Rousseau's *The Social Contract* 252–6
Socialisme et Liberté underground group, Paris 482, 486
Socrates 58–64, 513–14, 516, 518
  and Alcibiades 59
  and Antisthenes 99, 100
  aporia 62, 66, 71, 77, 80, 115
  and Aristophanes 59
  and Aristotle 63, 516
  and Athens 58, 60
  birth details 58
  and the 'considered life' 63–4
  and Critias 56
  Cynics' imitation of 61, 516
  death 58
  ethics 9, 61, 335; and moral excellence 63–4
  and Euripides 28, 59
  and Heraclitus 28
  and knowledge identified with virtue 63–4, 68
  and moral excellence 63–4
  and the oracle at Delphi 59, 294
  and Parmenides 31
  Plato and the 'Socratic question' 58, 59
  and Prodicus 55

  and Protagoras 53
  quest for essential definitions 62–3
  rationality emphasized over feeling 319
  refutation *see* Socratic method
  and the sophists 51, 52
  and the Stoics 516
  and unity of the virtues 64
  wisdom of 59
  and Xenophon 58, 108, 516
Socratic method 58, 61
  and Arcesilaus 117
  and Carneades 118
  in *Laches* 61–2
Songs, Book of (Confucian) 516
sophistry 51–2
sophists 10, 51–7
  as educators 52
  and Plato 51, 52, 56, 57
  and rhetoric 51, 52
  and Socrates 51, 52
soteriology 519, 522, 523, 524, 525, 532 *see also* suffering: release from
soul
  alienated (Hegel) 291
  and Aquinas 155
  and Aristotle 89
  Atman in Indian thought *see* Atman
  and Avicenna 564–5
  and death 70
  and divine love 183
  and Epicurus 105–6
  and al-Farabi 562
  and first cause 89
  and al-Ghazali 569
  immortal 221; Christian adoption of doctrine 182; and Kant 263, 266, 267, 268; and al-Kindi 560
  and Kant's transcendental enquiry 262, 263, 266–7
  Leibniz, and God's knowledge of the soul 237
  and Locke 221–2
  music and the 20
  and Neoplatonism 128–9
  'nutritive' souls 89
  as perceiver (Berkeley) 229
  perfected through seeking truth 564
  and personhood 221
  philosophy as therapy of the soul 107
  Plato and theory of immortal soul 69–71, 183

soul – *cont.*
  Platonic love for God 173, 183
  Platonic non-corporeal theory of 69,
    70, 154
  as a postulate (Kant) 267
  Presocratic notions: Empedocles 42;
    metempsychosis 18, 19, 26, 40, 42;
    and music 20; Thales 13
  and rationality: and Aristotle 89; in
    Plato's division of the soul 70;
    'rational souls' 155, 238; and the
    tripartite mind in Samkhya 524
  and sensation 89
  and tensions between philosophy and
    theology in twelfth century 154
  Tertullian's corporeal version 154
  transmigration/reincarnation of souls
    see metempsychosis; reincarnation
  and *via antiqua–via moderna*
    debate 167
space, absolutes of time and 162
Spain 554
  expulsion of Moors and Jews
    from 175
Sparta 14, 66, 100
speech acts 412
Speusippus 78, 82, 126
Spinoza, Baruch (also Benedict and
    Bento) 211–17
  as atheist 211, 235
  birth details 211
  and Deleuze 501–2
  determinism 213, 215
  and emotions/affects 215–16
  and empiricism 502
  epistemology 214
  Ethics 212–16
  excommunication from synagogue
    211
  exposition of Descartes' *Principles of
    Philosophy* 212
  and freedom 215–17; free will 215,
    235; and politics 216–17
  and individuality 214–15
  influence on Enlightenment ideas
    211, 217
  and Leibniz 235
  and mind–body problem 214
  political philosophy 216–17
  *Short Treatise on God, Man and his
    Well-being* 212

  and Sprigge 328
  Tractatus Politicus 212
  Tractatus Theologico-Politicus 212,
    216–17
Spir, Afrikan 315
Sprigge, Timothy L. S. 328
Spring and Autumn Annals 516, 535
Stachelroth, Johann 357
Stagira 47n, 82
Stalin, Joseph 487
Stalinism 273, 395
state
  absolutist state of Hobbes 207–9
  as an aristocracy (Plato) 72
  and Aristotle 94, 185–6
  and best life for man 94
  citizenship *see* citizenship
  and epistocracy 72
  government *see* government
  Hegel and the Prussian state 290
  idealized as embodiment of 'the
    general will' (Rousseau) 254, 255
  'Ideas' and theory of 289
  and individual rights (Nozick) 463–4
  and Machiavelli 189–91
  minimalist theories of 464–6
  and oligarchy *see* oligarchy
  and Petrarch 186, 187
  and philosopher-kings 66, 71–2,
    73, 562
  'politics' as study of the state
    (*polis*) 84
  provision for a 'sufficient life' 186
  public expenditure 285
  and relation between individual and
    society (Green) 322
  Renaissance and Italian city states
    185, 186, 187–8
  republican *see* republicanism
  ruler qualities *see* rulership qualities
  seeking fame, honour and glory
    186–7
  separation of Church and 166
  support of self-actualization 322
  and timocracy 72–3
  and tyranny *see* tyranny
statistical bias 595
Stevenson, Charles 446–8
  Ethics and Language 446
Stich, Stephen 440
Stillingfleet, Edward 222

Stilpo 120
stimulus conditions/meaning (Quine)
    394–5, 418, 422
Stirling, James Hutchison: *The Secret of
    Hegel* 321
Stobaeus, John 52
    'Selections on Natural Philosophy' 6
Stoicism/Stoics 10, 99–100, 101,
    108–15
    and the Academy 108, 110–11, 116
    and *apatheia* 108, 112, 113
    applauded by Athenian public 112
    arche 109
    and Roger Bacon 160
    and Carneades 118
    and the Church Fathers 182
    and Cicero 114
    and cognitive apprehensions 116
    and determinism 110–11, 117
    epistemology 110–11
    ethics 109, 111–12, 114
    founder of Stoicism *see* Zeno of
        Citium
    and happiness 111, 112, 114
    and Hegel 291
    and Hume 250
    and indifferents 111–12
    logic 110–11
    and *logos* 109
    materialism 124
    physics 109–10
    and pneuma 109–10
    and the Renaissance 184
    and Socrates 516
    truth and *phantasia kataleptike*
        110–11
Stout, G. F. 346
Strabo 81
    Veronese's translation of 177
Strasbourg Papyrus 7, 8n, 40
Strasbourg University 497
Strauss, David Friedrich 296
    Life of Jesus 296, 314
Strauss, Richard 370
Straw-Man Fallacy 593
Strawson, P. F. 336, 405, 406
    and Austin 413
    The Bounds of Sense 416
    *An Essay in Descriptive
        Metaphysics* 415
    and existence of other minds 415

Individuals 414–15, 416
    *An Introduction to Logical
        Theory* 414
    and Kant 416
    and mind–body problem 416
    and Quine 416
    and reference 413–14, 416–17, 429
    'On Referring' 413–14
    and reidentification 415
    and Russell's Theory of Descriptions
        413–14
subjective idealism 292
subjectivism 246–8, 274
substance *see also* matter
    Aristotle (*ousia*) 90, 560
    and Berkeley 227–31
    created substances as compounds of
        matter and form (Aquinas)
        154–6, 163
    Descartes 205
    God and the individuating of
        substances 237
    in Jainism 532
    and Leibniz 236–8
    matter as extended substance
        205, 213
    mind as thinking substance 205, 213
    and monism 205–6
    padartha (Vaisheshika) 526–7
    and qualities of things *see* qualities of
        things
    and Spinoza 213–14; and
        individuality 214–15
    sunyata and lack of 530, 531
suffering
    and ethics 300–301, 524
    and Indian soteriology 519, 522, 523,
        524, 525, 532
    and Marx on religion 311–12
    and Mencius 540
    release from: across nastika schools of
        India 524; through aesthetics 300;
        Buddhism 300, 522, 523; Jainism
        532; Schopenhauer 297, 300–301
    and *samsara* of Indian thought
        300, 523
    and will 318–19
suffrage *see* franchise
Sulla the Dictator 82
sundials 14
Sunni Islam *see* Islam: Sunni school

sunyata (emptiness) 530, 531
superstition 130, 248
    and Francis Bacon 200
    Church's use of (Spinoza) 216
    as enemy of knowledge and
        morality 216
    Enlightenment criticisms of 270, 271
    and Romanticism 275
    and Spinoza 216
Susenyos of Ethiopia 578
suspension of attention (*epoche*)
    474, 475
suspension of belief 116, 117
suspension of judgment (*epoche*) 119,
    120, 121–2
Suttapitaka 515
Sybaris 19
Sydney, Algernon 210
syllogisms 165, 587–8, 593
    Aristotle's syllogism theory 165,
        362, 587
    disjunctive 110n
Synthese 410n
synthetic–analytic distinction *see*
    analytic–synthetic distinction
Syracuse, Sicily 66–7

Tacitus 114
Tao Te Ching see *Daodejing*
Taoism *see* Daoism
Tarski, Alfred 389
    truth-theory for formal
        languages 421
tautology 34, 236, 375, 392, 589
Taylor, Harriet 304
teleological argument 156n
teleological explanations 88
temperament 24
Les Temps Modernes 482–3, 486–7
Tertullian 154
testimonia 5, 7
Thales 9–10, 11–14, 21
    and the *arche* 12–13
    and Aristotle 11, 12
    birth details 11
    death 13–14
    'Know thyself' injunction 13
    observation and reason employed by
        13, 199
    and Plato 11
Themistocles 43

theodicy 139–40, 239, 555, 556
Theodoric 142
Theodosius I 3
theology
    Aquinas 152–4, 156–7 *see also*
        Thomism
    Augustine 139–41
    and the dignity of man 172–3, 180
    diverging into *via antiqua* and *via
        moderna* 166–7
    divine causality *see* God: divine
        causality
    and divine foreknowledge *see*
        foreknowledge, divine
    Ficino's *Platonic Theology* 172–3
    incarnation of Christ 180
    medieval 131–4
    Muslim *see* Islam: *kalam*
    'natural' xxi, 152
    necessity of faith to grasp theological
        truths 164–5
    original sin *see* original sin and Fall
        of Man
    and predestination 140–41
    problem of evil *see* evil: problem of
    rejected by Logical Positivists as a
        source of knowledge 377, 380
    relationship to philosophy: and
        Averroes 571–3; cosmological
        possible agreements between
        scriptures and Plato's *Timaeus* 133;
        'Double Truth' 573; and ethics 183;
        and falling of intellectual activity
        under authority of the Church 131;
        and al-Farabi 561; and fundamental
        difference xxi; and al-Ghazali
        568–70, 573, 574; Hobbes and
        philosophy's self-exclusion from
        theology 207; and interpretations of
        Aristotle 133–4; and al-Kindi 560;
        loosening of theology's grip in
        Reformation 195; main difference
        xxi; philosophy as handmaiden of
        theology 195; and revelation vs
        reason 162, 275, 568, 569–70; in
        Scholastic tradition *see*
        Scholasticism and the Schoolmen;
        Spinoza's argument for separation
        216; tensions in twelfth century
        154; Thomistic combination *see*
        Thomism

sceptical attitudes to theological
literature and the matter of deity
131–2
Scotus 162–3
theological scepticism (Berkeley) 227
Thomistic *see* Thomism
Trinitarian 252, 560
Theophrastus 5, 81
and Anaximenes 16–17
and Leucippus 49
On Sensation 5
Tenets of Natural Philosophy 5
theosophy 557
Thessalonica, Edict of 3, 137
theurgy 128, 129–30
Thomas Aquinas 132, 150–58
and Albertus 151, 179
and Aristotle 97, 133–4, 152, 153,
154, 156, 571 *see also* Thomism;
and ethics 182; and 'political
science' 186
and Averroes 153
and Avicenna 566
canonization 153
and change 154–6
at Cologne 151
commentaries: on Aristotle 152,
153; on Boethius 152; on Old
Testament 151
cosmological argument 156
death 153
defence of mendicant orders 151–2
and Descartes 157
and the Dominicans 151, 153
'ecstasy'/stroke 153
education 151
Errors of the Greeks 152
ethics 182; contempt of glory and
temporal goods 186–7
and evil 156
family background 151
on God 156–7
The Golden Chain 152
and 'the good' as target of all
striving 156
influences on 130, 154
just war theory 138, 141, 187
and Leo XIII's *Aeterni Patris* 154
in Naples 151, 153, 154
Neoplatonist influence on 130, 154
in Paris 152, 153, 154

and Pontifical University of St Thomas
Aquinas 157–8
The Powers of God 152
quodlibetical responses 152
in Rome 152
school combining theological and
philosophical thought of *see*
Thomism
and Scotus 162
and the soul 155
study of Lombard's *Sentences* 151
and substance, matter and form
154–6, 163
Summa Contra Gentiles 152,
162, 168
Summa Theologiae 152–3, 154
'On the Unity of the Intellect' 573
Thomism 133–4, 154–8, 571
Analytical 157
Cracow 157
decreed definitive statement of
Catholic doctrine 154
Existential 157
and the Ockhamists 166
official Catholic status confirmed by
Pius X 157
Phenomenological 157
River Forest 157
Scholastic 157
Thomson, J. J. 400
Thucydides 44
Tian (heaven/sky) 537–8, 543
time
absolutes of space and 162
all times present to God in eternity
141, 143–4
and Aristotle 162
Augustine on 140–41
cosmological 499
human 499
McTaggart and unreality of 325–8
and Merleau-Ponty 485
and Newton 162
and paradoxes of motion 36–7, 38–9
phenomenological 499
and Ricoeur 499
river of 499
and Scotus 162
timocracy 72–3
Timon of Phlius 120, 121
Tirthankaras 523

Tolstoy, Leo: *The Gospels in Brief* 371
transcendental deduction/arguments 263, 346, 475n
transcendental idealism 321n, 474
transmigration of souls *see* metempsychosis; reincarnation
Trent, Council of 154
Trier 307
truth
  as 'agreement' between ideas and reality (James) 330–31
  as 'analytic' (Leibniz) 235
  Anselm's argument that truth has always existed 146
  anti-realist conception of 425, 427
  and art 495–6
  Austin–Strawson debate about 413
  Carneades' view that there can be no criterion of 118
  'cash value' account of 333
  correspondence theory of 412–13
  Davidson's theory of 419–22, 432
  and disclosure (*aletheia*) 479, 480
  'Double Truth' 573
  and expedient beliefs 330
  and hermeneutics *see* hermeneutics
  Hobbes and *scientia* (true knowledge) 207
  and instrumentalism 231
  and intuition 214
  knowledge and true belief 69, 77
  and 'maximum grip' (Merleau-Ponty) 484
  necessity of faith to grasp theological truths 164–5
  perfecting of soul through seeking of 564
  philosophy as pursuit of 57
  as a Platonic Form 74
  and science 214
  speaking the truth 30, 422
  and Stoicism 110–11
  sunyata and non-existence of ultimate truths 530
  tables 353, 588, 589, 590
  Tarski's truth-theory for formal languages 421
  tautological (analytic) propositions of *see* tautology
  verification of *see* verification/ verificationism
  verisimilitude of good scientific theories 398
  way of, vs way of seeming 32
  of What Is *see* reality
truth-conditions 343, 422, 423–5, 449
truth-values 110, 342–3, 363–4, 375, 425, 589
truth-value gaps 343, 414
Turgot, Anne Robert Jacques 273
Turmeda, Anselm (later Abd-Allah at-Tarjumen) 180
Tutu, Desmond 580
Types, Theory of (Russell) 350
tyranny 66, 72, 73, 107, 186, 187, 277

Ubuntu 518, 580–81
Umayyads 558
understanding
  and Aristotle 87–8
  Enlightenment, and courage to use own 268, 272
  freedom through understanding nature of things 216
  Geist's self-understanding and dialectical journey 289–94
  and Heraclitus 30
  and intellectual maturity 269
  Kant on 261, 263
  Leibniz's *New Essays Concerning Human Understanding* 218, 234
  Locke's *Essay Concerning Human Understanding* 218, 219–23, 339–40
  in Samkhya 524
  of the self *see* self-awareness/-consciousness/ -knowledge
  the world, as aim of philosophy 99
  Zeno of Citium on comprehending 111
Unitarianism 252
United States Constitution
  Equal Rights Amendment (ERA) 459
  Nineteenth Amendment 458–9
universals 143
  and Abelard 149
  and Aristotle 143
  and Boethius 143
  Dinnaga–Dharmakirti school 531
  and Hobbes 207
  nominalist views of 149, 207

and Porphyry 143
  realist views of 149, 163, 340
  and Scotus 163
University College London 285–6, 304
Upanishads
  Brhadaranyaka 520–21
  mahavakya ('great saying') 529
  and relation between Atman and
    Brahman 529
  and Schopenhauer 300
  and Vedanta 522
Urbino, Giusto d' 578
Urmson, J. O. 447
utilitarianism 281–2, 445
  act utilitarianism 306, 445
  and Bentham 281–2, 283
  as a consequentialist theory of
    morality 281, 305, 306, 367, 453
    see also consequentialism
  and happiness 281–2, 286, 306, 307
  and Hare on prescriptions 450
  and Hoffman 284
  and Mill 281–2, 286, 304, 305–7
  and Mohist *li* and *hai* 545
  and negative liberty 283
  and pain 281, 282, 286, 306
  and Rawls 461
  rule utilitarianism 307, 367, 445, 446
  and rules of evidence 284
Utopia 191–2
  Enlightenment, and Utopianism 271
  and Nozick 465
Uttara Mimamsa *see* Vedanta

Vachaknavi, Gargi 520n
Vaisheshika 521, 525–9
  atomistic metaphysics 521, 526–7
  and causation 526, 527–8
  inherence (samavaya) 526, 527
  and Nyaya 521, 525–9
  ontology 527
Valéry, Paul xx
Valla, Lorenzo 176, 183
  and biblical criticism 176
Vanini, Giulio Cesare 96n
  death at the stake 184
Vatican 135, 161
  and Galileo 270
Vedanta 520, 521
  and karma 522
  and reincarnation 522

Vedas 519–21
  collections 519–20
  commentaries (*Aranyakas*) 520
  and Purva Mimamsa 522
  as Sruti 520
  and Upanishads *see* Upanishads
  Vedic rites (*Brahmanas*) 520
vegetarianism 19, 40
Venice 185
  constitution 190
  Guicciardini on 190
  Machiavelli on 190–91
Venn diagrams 87n, 511
verification/verificationism 381–5, 418
  Ayer's verification principle 382
  as a criterion of meaningfulness 382
  and Dummett's theory of meaning
    424–5
  metaphysics and verificationist view
    of truth 426–7
  and Paradox of the Ravens 383–4
  and Popper 396–7; and
    falsificationism 397–9
  and protocol sentences 380–81
  and Schlick 382
  as specifying the nature of meaning
    382
  status of verification principle queried
    to undermine verificationism 384
Vienna 370, 380, 389, 396, 405
  University 370, 378–9, 385, 386, 396,
    473 *see also* Vienna Circle
Vienna Circle 353, 372, 377–81, 385
    see also Logical Positivism
  and Ayer 377, 389
  Carnap/Schlick vs Neurath strands of
    outlook 378
  vs Comtean Positivism 302, 377–8
  Erkenntnis journal 377, 379
  influence 377 *see also* Logical
    Positivism
  and the Nazis 380
  nucleus (Schlick Circle) 379
  philosophy of *see* Logical Positivism
  and Popper 379, 385, 395
  and Quine 377, 389
  'The Scientific World View: The
    Vienna Circle' 379
  and Wittgenstein 372, 400
Vietnam War 345, 459, 487
Vinayapitaka 515

Virgil 177, 258
virtù (Machiavelli) 189, 191, 537
virtual reality 444
virtue
  and Antisthenes 100
  and Aristotle 92–3, 453, 454
  and citizenship 53, 72
  in Confucianism 537, 540
  Cynic virtues 100; Zeno of Citium's
    internalization of 108, 112
  equated with power (Spinoza) 215
  as foundation for ethics 454 *see also*
    virtue ethics
  and happiness 92–4, 454,
    455, 456
  identified with knowledge 63–4,
    68, 116
  identifying virtues 456
  and living without shame 102
  MacIntyre and social dimension of
    virtues 456
  natural vs artificial (Hume)
    248–9
  pursued for its own sake (More's
    Utopia) 191
  regaining knowledge of 69
  and Socrates 61, 62, 63, 64, 68
  sound thinking as greatest virtue
    (Heraclitus) 30
  teachability of 100
  theory 456
  'unegoistic' virtues (Nietzsche) 318
  unity of the virtues (Socrates) 64
  utility as criterion of 281 *see also*
    utilitarianism
virtue ethics 453–7
  and Aristotle 92–3, 453, 454
virtue theory 456
virtus 186–7, 189
vis (force) 186, 189
Visconti, Giangaleazzo, Duke of Milan
  176, 187
Visigoths 3–4
Vittorino Rambaldoni/da Feltre 177
Voltaire 218
  attack on excessive rationalist
    optimism 276
  Candide 276
  as a deist 270
  Encyclopédie articles by 273
  and the Encylopedists 269

  and Rousseau 253
  use of logic and satire to attack
    authority 269, 270

Wagner, Cosima 315
Wagner, Richard 297
  and Bayreuth Festival 315
  and Nietzsche 314, 315, 316
Wahl, Jean 509
Waismann, Friedrich 379, 389, 400
Wallis, John 270
Walpole, Horace 253
Ward, James 320
Warens, Françoise-Louise de 251
water
  as *arche* of the cosmos (Thales) 12–13
  and the elements *see* elements, four
Watson, J. B. 389
Weierstrass, Karl 473
Weigel, Erhard 233
Weil, Simone 482, 511
Weimar 298
West, Cornel 333
Westminster Review 305
Westphalen, Jenny von 308, 310
Weyl, Hermann 474
Whewell, William 279, 305
Whitehead, Alfred North
  and Davidson 419
  notation for formal logic (with
    Russell) 342, 586
  on Plato and philosophy 67
  Principia Mathematica (with Russell)
    67, 347, 350–51
  and Quine 389
Wieland, Christoph 298
Wiggins, David 469
will
  autonomy of 263–4, 265, 268
  buddhi 524, 525
  free *see* free will
  heteronomy and subjection of 272
  intentionality *see* intentionality
  moral will 265
  and noumenal reality 299–300
  to overcome (Nietzsche) 318–19
  and 'pure' reason (Kant) 263–4
  release from desire and the power of
    215–16, 300
  Rousseau and 'the general will'
    253–4, 255

and Schopenhauer 299–300, 318
and sex 301
Spinoza and 'conatus' 214–15
and suffering 318–19
weakness of 64
William II (William Rufus) 145–6
William III, Prince of Orange 218, 223–4
William of Auvergne 566
William of Moerbeke 185
Williams, Bernard 449, 469
Williamson, Timothy 469
Wiredu, Kwasi 579
Wittgenstein, Carl 370
Wittgenstein, Leopoldine 370
Wittgenstein, Ludwig 335, 370–77
  and aeronautics 370–71
  Analytic philosophy, early thought 372–7; and the natural sciences 374; picture theory of meaning 375–6; propositions, and philosophy/logic of language 373–7; removal of ethics and religion from realm of the discussable 374–6
  Analytic philosophy, later thought 400–404; epistemology 404; and 'following a rule' 403, 432; language games 401, 402–3; and public nature of language 403; as therapy 401
  and Augustine 142, 402
  birth details 370
  'Blue' and 'Brown' books 372; published as Preliminary Studies for the Philosophical Investigations 401
  at Cambridge 371, 373
  On Certainty 404
  death 373
  and Dummett 423
  education 370, 372
  family background 370
  during First World War 371–2
  and Frege 371
  and Keynes 372
  and Kripke 432
  and mathematics 371
  and Moore 371, 372
  Philosophical Investigations 142, 372, 401–4

Preliminary Studies for the Philosophical Investigations 401
and Russell 371, 372, 374
and Schopenhauer 297
Tractatus Logico-Philosophicus 356, 372, 373–7, 400, 401–2
and Vienna Circle 372, 400
Wittgenstein, Paul 370
Wollheim, Richard 449
women
  in China 543n
  Equal Rights Amendment proposal for US constitution 459
  exclusion from education 468
  feminist philosophy see feminist philosophy
  franchise 285, 304, 344, 458–9
  and John Stuart Mill 304, 307
  Rousseau's views of 256
  and Schopenhauer 301
  and sexism see sexism
  subordination of 468
Woodger, J. H. 80
Woolf, Leonard 365
Wordsworth, William 304
Wren, Christopher 270
Wright, Chauncey 329
Wright, Crispin 469
Wundt, Wilhelm 473
wuwei 547–8, 549
Wycliffe, John 166

Xantippe 59
Xeniades 101
Xenocrates 78, 82, 126
Xenophanes 24–7
  and Aristotle 26, 27
  birth details 25
  and the Games 25
  and Parmenides 26, 31
  and Plato 26–7
  and Pythagoras 18, 26
  rejection of religion and Olympian deities 25
  satirical attacks by 25, 26
  'World is One' idea 26, 27
Xenophon 56
  and Socrates 58, 108, 516
Xerxes 43
Xunzi (Xun Kuang) 539, 540–42

Yacob, Zara: *Hatata* 577–8
Yajnavalkya 520–21
Yajurveda 519
Yijing ('I Ching') 516, 535, 552–3
Yoga 521
Yogacara 530–31

al-Zahiri, Dawud 559
Zahiris 559
Zen Buddhism 545
Zengzi 536
Zeno of Citium 99, 100, 101, 111, 112
  birth details 108
  and Crates 108
  and internalization of Cynic virtues
    108, 112
Zeno of Elea 10, 35–9
  and Aristotle 35, 37, 43

  and atomism 50
  birth details 35
  and infinity 38–9
  and Nearchus 35–6
  as orator 43
  paradoxes 36–9; 'Achilles' 37, 38–9;
    'Arrow' 37; 'Stadium' 36–7,
    38–9
  and Plato 35, 36
  and Pythagoreanism 37–8
  torture and death 36
Zermelo, Ernst 474
Zhou kingdom, China 535, 538
Zhuangzi 546, 548, 551
Zisi 536, 539
Zoroastrianism 138, 173, 517
  Avesta 557–8
  and Hussayn ibn Ali 559